A HISTORY

OF

THE CHURCH

FROM

The Earliest Ages

TO

THE REFORMATION.

BY

THE REV. GEORGE WADDINGTON,

Vicar of Masham, and Prebendary of Chichester.

PUBLISHED UNDER THE SUPERINTENDENCE OF THE SOCIETY FOR THE
DIFFUSION OF USEFUL KNOWLEDGE.

SECOND EDITION, REVISED:

IN THREE VOLUMES.

VOL. I.

6835

LONDON: BALDWIN AND CRADOCK,

PATERNOSTER-ROW.

1835.

LONDON:
Printed by W. Clowes and Sons,
Stamford Street.

PREFACE

TO

THE SECOND EDITION.

I HAVE availed myself of the opportunity now afforded
me to make some considerable additions to the
First Part of this History; and have so enlarged the
First, Second, Third, and Fifth Chapters, as to embrace all that seems most important in the much-
controverted records of the Antenicene Church. My
deepest consideration they had long ago received;
only I thought it then sufficient to present little more
than the general results of my researches, and compressed several particulars which will be found more
amply treated in the present edition. In the Thirteenth Chapter, which is for the most part a retrospect
of the earliest annals of the Church, I have inserted
a short account of the probable character and sources
of the original Liturgies, compiled from a learned
work, not, I think, in existence when that chapter
was published. Several remarks, before interspersed
through the notes, will now be found incorporated in
the text. The general Index has been much enlarged;
and at the end of the Second Volume I have placed
a tabular Appendix of a great number of Councils,
important in their day, which are slightly, or not at

a 2

all noticed in the body of the work. To detail their
proceedings and digest their decrees would alone be
the labour of a life ; but even the scanty selections
which I have made will serve to instruct the reader
in some particulars not elsewhere presented to him,
and at the same time to illustrate the general course
and ever-varying aspect of ecclesiastical history.

I have been sorry to observe that the account
which I have published, and to which I still adhere,
of the original constitution of the Church, has given
offence to some respectable sectarians ; and those
gentlemen will learn, perhaps with surprise, that the
same account has equally disappointed the views of
some learned and zealous divines within the Church.
Thus doubly unfortunate, I can only seek consolation,
under the dissatisfaction of the one party, in the opposite murmurs of the other : secure in the reflection,
that, in our common liability to error, the more moderate generally proves the wiser judgment; and that
extreme opinions seldom long survive the controversies
which have given them birth.

Such errors as I have discovered in the revisal
of the work have been anxiously removed. To the
friendly suggestions that have been made to me by
others, I have applied, with advantage and gratitude,
my most careful consideration. Yet is it a harder
task than some imagine to thread the entangled paths
of ecclesiastical contention. It is not enough to
possess an earnest desire to arrive at just conclusions,

nor to apply to the solution of disputed questions the most unwearied industry, the keenest sagacity, the finest criticism, unless the mind be previously prepared for the office by a process of moral discipline to which few can bring themselves to submit. And however eagerly we may set out in pursuit of truth, we can scarcely hope to overtake it, unless we shall first acquire the mastery over our passions and our prejudices—unless we shall learn to suspect every bias that birth, or education, or profession, or any other accident may have given us—unless we shall wash away from our inmost bosoms the faintest speck of sectarian animosity—unless, in short, we shall put away from us our own particular opinions, or institutions, or interests, and forget them in the subjects that we have undertaken to investigate. He that shall attain this temper, and to a modest respect for the opinions of others shall add a perfect fearlessness in the expression of his own, may still fail indeed through defect of talents or lack of learning; but he will at least escape the reproach of that narrow spirit of party, which degrades history into mere advocacy—which disqualifies the mind for any bold inquiry—which precludes any enlarged views or generous principles, and leads even those who least intend it into perpetual misrepresentation.

To mark the deviations from the precepts of the Gospel, and from the principles which lead to human happiness; to denounce the bigot and the hypocrite

who have filled the world with discord in the name of
the Prince of Peace ; to expose the frauds by which
the mass of mankind has been deceived and degraded,
for the profit of the few who have done the wrong; to
honour and extol the men who have contended with
these iniquities, who have laboured to restore a purer
system, and have practised the law of concord and
charity which they professed;—such is the proper
office of the Historian of the Church of Christ. And
he, who would discharge it worthily, must not only
love mankind and feel a general concern in the interests of all his fellow-creatures; but he must love
his Redeemer likewise, and be filled with the sincere
spirit of that Religion, which, in its natural operation
upon mankind, is the simple revelation of philanthropy.

G. W.

Masham, *April*, 1835.

INTRODUCTION.

An attempt to compress even into three moderate volumes the ecclesiastical history of fifteen centuries requires some previous explanation, lest any should imagine that this undertaking has been entered upon rashly, and without due consideration of its difficulty. This is not the case; I am not blind to the various and even opposite dangers which beset it; and least of all am I insensible to the peculiar and most solemn importance of the subject. But I approach it with deliberation as well as reverence, willing to consecrate to God's service the fruits of an insufficient, but not careless diligence, and also trusting, by His divine aid, to preserve the straight path which leads through truth unto wisdom.

The principles by which I have been guided require no preface; they will readily develop themselves, as they are the simplest in human nature. But, respecting the general plan which has been followed in the conduct of this work, a few words appear to be necessary. In the first place I have abandoned the method of division by centuries, which has too long perplexed ecclesiastical history, and have endeavoured to regulate the partition by the dependence of connected events, and the momentous revolutions which have arisen from it. It is one advantage in this plan, that it has very frequently enabled me to collect under one head, to digest by a single effort, and present, in one uninterrupted view, materials bearing in reality upon the same point, but which, by the more usual method, are separated and distracted. It is impossible to ascertain the proportions or to estimate the real weight of any single subject amidst the events which surround it—it is impossible to draw from it those sober and applicable conclusions which alone distinguish history from romance, unless we bring the corresponding portions into contact, in spite of the interval which time may have thrown between them : for time has scattered his lessons over the records of humanity with a profuse but careless hand, and both the diligence and the judgment of man must be exercised to collect and arrange them, so as to extract from their combined qualities the true odour of wisdom.

It is another advantage in the method which I have adopted, that it affords greater facility to bring into relief and illustrate matters which are really important and have had lasting effects : since it is chiefly by fixing attention and awakening reflection on those great phenomena which have not only stamped a character on the age to which they belong, but have influenced the conduct and happiness of after ages, that history asserts her prerogative above a journal or an index; not permitting thought to be dispersed nor memory wasted upon a minute narration of detached incidents and transient and inconsequential details. And, in this matter, I admit that my judgment has been very freely exercised in proportioning the degree of notice to the permanent weight and magnitude of events.

As regards the treatment of particular branches of this subject, all readers are aware how zealously the *facts* of ecclesiastical history have been disputed, and how frequently those differences have been occasioned or widened by the peculiar *opinions* of the disputants. Respecting the former, it is sufficient to say that the limits of this work obviously prevent the author from pursuing and unfolding all the intricate perplexities of critical controversy. I have, therefore, generally contented myself, in questions of ordinary moment, with following, sometimes even without comment, what has appeared to me to be the more *probable* conclusion, and of signifying it as probable only. Respecting the latter, I have found it the most difficult, as it was certainly among the weightiest of my duties, to trace the opinions which have divided Christians in every age regarding matters of high import both in doctrine and discipline. But it seems needless to say that I have scarcely, in any case, entered into the arguments by which those opinions have been contested. It is no easy task, through hostile misrepresentation, and the more dangerous distortions of friendly enthusiasm, to penetrate their real character, and delineate their true history. For the demonstration of their reasonableness or absurdity I must refer to the voluminous writings consecrated to their explanation.

This history, extending to the beginning of the Reformation, will be divided into five Parts or Periods. The *first* will terminate with the accession of Constantine. It will trace the propagation of Christianity; it will comprehend the persecutions which afflicted, the heresies which disturbed, the abuses which stained the early Church, and describe its final triumph over external hostility. The *second* will carry us through the age of Charlemagne. We shall watch the fall of the Polytheistic system of Greece and Rome; we shall examine with painful interest the controversies which distracted the Church, and which were not suspended even while the scourge from Arabia was hanging over it; and that especially by which the East was finally alienated from Rome. In the West, we shall observe the influx of the Northern barbarians, and the gradual conquest accomplished by our religion over a second form of Paganism. We shall notice the influence of feudal institutions on the character of that Church, the commencement of its temporal authority, and its increasing corruption. Our *third* period will conduct us to the death of Gregory VII. And here I must observe, that, from the eighth century downwards, our attention will, for the most part, be occupied by the Church of Rome, and follow the fluctuations of its history. About 270 years compose this period—the most curious, though by no means the most celebrated, in the papal annals. From the foundations established by Charlemagne, the amazing pretensions of that See gradually grew up; in despite of the crimes and disasters of the tenth century, they made progress during those gloomy ages, and finally received development and consistency from the extraordinary genius of Gregory. Charlemagne left behind him the rudiments of the system, without any foresight of the strange character which it was destined to assume; Gregory grasped the materials which he found lying before him, and put them together with a giant's hand, and bequeathed the mighty spiritual edifice, to be enlarged and defended by his successors. The *fourth* part will describe the conduct of those successors, as far as the death of Boniface VIII., and the removal of the seat of government to Avignon. This is the era of papal extravagance and exultation. It was during this space (of about 220 years) that all the energies of the system were in full action and exhibited the extent of good and evil of which it was capable. It was then especially that the spirit of Monachism burst its ancient boundaries, and threatened to quench the reviving sparks of knowledge, and to repel the advancing tide of reason. The concussion was indeed fearful; the face of religion was again darkened by the blood of her martyrs, and the rage of bigotry was found to be more destructive than the malice of Paganism. The *last* division will follow the decline of papal power, and the general decay of papal principles; and in this more grateful office, it will be my most diligent, perhaps most profitable, task, to examine the various attempts which were made by the Roman Church to reform and regenerate itself, and to observe the perverse infatuation by which they were thwarted; until the motives and habits which attached men to their ancestral superstitions at length gave way, and the banners of reason were openly unfurled in holy allegiance to the Gospel of Christ.

There is a sober disposition to religious moderation and warm but dispassionate piety, with which the book of Ecclesiastical History must ever inspire the minds of those, who approach it without prejudice, and meditate on it calmly and thoughtfully. May some portion of that spirit be communicated to the readers of the following pages! May they learn to distinguish the substance of Christianity from its corruptions—to perceive that the religion is not contaminated by the errors or crimes of its professors and ministers, and that all the evils, which have ever been inflicted upon the world in the name of Christ, have invariably proceeded from its abuse! The vain appendages, which man has superadded to the truth of God, as they are human so are they perishable; some have fallen, and all will gradually fall, by their own weight and weakness.

This reflection will serve, perhaps, to allay certain apprehensions. From the multitude of others, which suggest themselves, I shall select one only. The readers of this work will observe, from the experience of every age of Christianity, that, through the failings and variety of our nature, diversity in religious opinion is inseparable from religious belief; they will observe the fruitlessness of every forcible attempt to repress it; and they will also remark, that it has seldom proved dangerous to the happiness of society, unless when civil authority has interfered to restrain it. The moral effect of this great historical lesson can be one only—uncontentious, unlimited moderation—a temperate zeal to soften the diversities, which we cannot possibly prevent—a fervent disposition to conciliate the passions, where we fail to convince the reason; to exercise that forbearance, which we surely require ourselves; and constantly to bear in mind that, in our common pursuit of the same eternal object, we are alike impeded by the same human and irremediable imperfections.

GEORGE WADDINGTON.

Trinity College, Cambridge.

CONTENTS

OF

VOLUME THE FIRST.

PART I.

FROM THE TIMES OF THE APOSTLES TO THE ACCESSION OF CONSTANTINE.

CHAPTER I.—*The Propagation of Christianity.*

Method of treating the subject. I. Church of *Jerusalem*—Its earliest members —Death of St. James—Succession of Symeon—Destruction of the city by Titus—Secession to Pella—Bishops of the Circumcision—Destruction of the city by Adrian—Ælia Capitolina—Second succession of Bishops—Testimony of Justin Martyr. (II.) Church of *Antioch*—Its foundation and progress— Ignatius — his epistles and martyrdom — Theophilus — Mesopotamia — Pretended correspondence between the Saviour and Abgarus, prince of Edessa. (III.) Church of *Ephesus*—The Seven Churches of Asia—The latest years of St. John—Piety and progress of the Church of Ephesus—Polycrates—his opposition to Rome. (IV.) Church of *Smyrna*—Polycarp—his martyrdom— Sardis—Melito—Hierapolis—Papeas—Apollinaris—Bithynia—Testimony of the Younger Pliny. (V.) Church of *Athens*—Character of the people—Quadratus—Aristides—Athenagoras—Their Apologies—Other Grecian Churches. (VI.) Church of Corinth—Character of the people—Nature of their dissensions—Clemens Romanus—His Epistle—Form of government—Dionysius of Corinth—his seven general Epistles—Remarks. (VII.) Church of *Rome*— The persecution of Nero described by Tacitus—Martyrdom of St. Paul and St. Peter—Probable effect of this persecution—Extent of the superiority of Rome over other Churches—Controversy respecting Easter—Conduct of Victor, Bishop of Rome—of Polycrates of Ephesus—Irenæus—*Gaul*—Church of Lyons—Churches of Spain—Britain—Carthage. (VIII.) Church of *Alexandria*—St. Marc—Its increase and importance—Epistle of Hadrian— Remarks on it—Education of the first Christians—Pantænus—Clemens Alexandrinus—The Catechetical School—Concluding remarks, p. 1.

CHAPTER II.—*On the Numbers, Discipline, Doctrine, and Morality of the Primitive Church.*

(I.) General view of the extent of the Church—Facility of intercourse favourable to Christianity—Other circumstances—Miraculous claims of the Church

the character of their adversaries—Philosophy—Excuses advanced for the persecutors—Their futility—General character of persecuting emperors—Absurd opinions on this subject—Effect of the persecutions—upon the whole favourable—For what reasons, p. 108.

CHAPTER V.—*On the Heresies of the first three Centuries.*

Meaning of the word Heresy—Charges of immorality brought against Heretics —Their treatment by the early Church—Number of early Heresies—Moderation of the primitive Church—Three classes of Heretics. (1.) Two kinds of Philosophy—Gnosticism—Origin and nature of that doctrine—its association with Christianity—Moral practice of the Gnostics—Their martyrs—Various forms of Gnosticism—Basilides—Carpocrates—Valentinus—Cerdo and Marcion—Tatian and Encratites. (2.) The Ebionites—Eusebius's account of them—Conclusions from it—The Heresy of Artemon—revived by Paul of Samosata—his sentence and expulsion—how finally enforced—Heresy of Praxeas—Doctrines of the Church stated by Tertullian—Sabellius—his opinions — Patripassians. (3.) Simon Magus—Montanus—his preaching and success—On the life, pretensions, and doctrines of Manes, and the discipline of his followers—Their unrelenting persecution by the Church—Controversy on the Baptism of Heretics—The Novatians—their schism and opinions—Conclusions respecting the general character of the early Heresies, and the manner of opposing them, p. 136.

PART II.

FROM THE ACCESSION OF CONSTANTINE TO THE DEATH OF CHARLEMAGNE.

CHAPTER VI.—*Constantine the Great.*

Victory of Constantine over Maxentius—his supposed conversion—the miracle of the luminous Cross—evidence for and against it—the latter conclusive—The Edict of Milan—its nature and effects—union of the whole Empire under Constantine—His moral character—sincerity of his conversion—unjustly disputed—Remarks on his policy—Power of the Christians—Alterations introduced into the constitutions of the Church—Its nature at Constantine's accession—Spiritual and temporal power—Union and strength of the early Church—how cemented—View of the Church probably taken by Constantine—he sought its alliance—Three periods of the ecclesiastical life of Constantine—How circumstanced with regard to the state in which Constantine found the Church—He assumes the supremacy—Rights of the Church—its *internal* administration—little altered in theory—permission to bequeath property to the Church—Independent jurisdiction of the Bishops—on what founded—*External*—subject to the Emperor—what particulars included in it—General observations—Constantine usurped nothing from the

Chapter XII.—*On the Schism between the Greek and Latin Churches.*

Chapter XIII.

HISTORY OF THE CHURCH.

PART I.

FROM THE TIMES OF THE APOSTLES TO THE ACCESSION OF CONSTANTINE.

CHAPTER I.

The Propagation of Christianity.

It is our object in this chapter to state what is material in the early history of such of the Churches of Christ, whether founded by the apostles themselves, or their companions, or their immediate successors, as were permitted to attain importance and stability during the first two centuries. For this purpose we have not thought it necessary to describe the circumstances which are detailed in the sacred writings, and are familiar to all our readers. The Churches which seem to claim our principal attention are eight in number, and shall be treated in the following order:—Jerusalem and Antioch, Ephesus and Smyrna, Athens and Corinth, Rome and Alexandria; but our notice will be extended to some others, according to their connexion with these, their consequence, or local situation. It is thus that we shall gain the clearest view of the progress made by infant Christianity, and the limits within which it was restrained.

I. The converts of Jerusalem naturally formed the earliest Church of Christian society, and for a short period probably the most Jerusalem. numerous; but their jealous adhesion to the Mosaic observances, which repelled the communion of the Gentile world, and thus occasioned some internal dissensions, as well as the unceasing hostility of the Jewish people and government, no doubt impeded their subsequent increase. The same causes operated, though not to the same extent, on the Churches established in other parts of Palestine, as in Galilee and Samaria, and even on those of Tyre, Ptolemais, and Cæsarea.   About the year 60

James the
Just. A. D., James, surnamed the Just, brother of the Saviour, who
was the first President, or Bishop, of the Church of Jerusalem,
perished by a violent death*; and when its members † subsequently assembled for the purpose of electing his successor,
their choice fell on Symeon, who is also said to have been a
kinsman of Jesus.   To this circumstance, or at least to his
alleged descent from the house of David, it is ascribed that he
too suffered martyrdom, during the reign of Trajan, in extreme
old age ‡.   Shortly after the death of St. James an insurrection
of the Jews broke out, which was followed by the invasion of
the Roman armies, and was not finally suppressed until the
year 70, when the city was overwhelmed by Titus, and utterly
destroyed.   During the whole progress of this war, as well as
in the events which concluded it, the Holy Land was subjected
to a variety and intensity of suffering, to which no parallel can
be found in the records of any people.

A short time before the Roman invasion, we are informed §
that the Christian Church seceded from a spot which prophecy
had taught to hold devoted, and retired to Pella, beyond the
Jordan.   From this circumstance it becomes at least probable
that the Christians did not sustain their full share of the calamities of their country; but though their proportion to the

---

* Le Clerc, H. E. (vol. i. p.415) ad ann. 62, in which year he places the death
of St. James, and affirms that nothing is known respecting its manner.   The
state of the question is this: Eusebius (lib. ii. cap. 23), on the authority of
Hegesippus, gives a very long and circumstantial narrative of the Bishop's martyrdom; of the circumstances many are clearly fabulous, and all may be suspected;
but the leading fact, that St. James was killed in a tumult of the Jews, it would
not be safe to reject.   His violent end, with some variation in particulars, is confirmed by Josephus, Antiq. b. xx. chap. 9.

† Eusebius (lib. iii. cap. 11) places the election of Symeon (ὡς λόγος κατέχει)
after the destruction of Jerusalem, which he makes immediately subsequent to
St. James's martyrdom; the Jewish rebellion probably was so.

‡ It is again on the authority of Hegesippus that Eusebius (lib.iii. cap. 32) relates these circumstances.   Now Hegesippus was a Jewish convert, who lived under
the Antonines, and composed five books of Ecclesiastical History.   Such a work
might have been invaluable: but the fragments, preserved by Eusebius, persuade
us that Hegesippus cannot always be followed with safety.

§ Euseb. lib. iv. c. 5.   Le Clerc places this secession in the year 66.   Semler
(sect. 1) fixes the beginning of the Jewish war in 64.   The Christians probably
retired, as the war became more obstinate and advanced nearer to Jerusalem.

whole population may thus have been increased, their actual numbers could not fail to be somewhat diminished, since they could not wholly withdraw themselves from a tempest directed indiscriminately against the whole nation.

During the next sixty years we read little respecting the Church of Jerusalem, except the names of fifteen successive presidents, called " Bishops of the Circumcision :" of these four- Bishops of the Circum-cision. teen only belong to the period in question, since they begin with James; and they terminate at the second destruction of the city, by the emperor Adrian *.   But the precise periods of their successions are extremely uncertain—as the first Christians had little thought of posterity †; nor were any tabularies preserved in their Churches, nor any public acts or monuments of their proceedings. The Church, over which they presided, seems to have perished with them; but there is still reason to believe that it was not numerous; and we may attribute its weakness partly to the continued action of the two causes abovementioned, and partly to the absolute depopulation of the country. Yet it would appear from Scripture, that some sort of authority was at first exercised by the Mother Church over her Gentile children; and that "the decrees ordained by the apostles and elders which were at Jerusalem ‡" found obedience even among distant converts.

On the summit of the sacred hill, out of the ruins which deformed it, Adrian erected a new city, to which he gave the new and Roman title of Ælia Capitolina §—whether he thought to Ælia Capi-tolina.

* Euseb. lib. iv. c. 5.

† This is the complaint of Le Clerc, ad ann. 135. And in fact the two most prominent features in the histories of Christians, during the first three centuries, are their divisions and their persecutions. These subjects we shall examine in separate chapters; and all that can be confidently asserted on other points we are contented to glean from Eusebius and some writers of ambiguous authority who are quoted by him, from the Apologies, Epistles, and Treatises of the early fathers, and from a few fragments of profane antiquity.

‡ Acts xvi. 4.

§ Ecclesiastical writers differ about the date of this event. Semler (cent. ii.) places it in the year 119. Fleury (liv. iii. sect. 24.) mentions Ælia Capitolina as existing previous to the rebellion of Barcochabas, but still as the work of Adrian. Le Clerc (ad ann. 119) seems to waver—(ad ann. 134) decidedly fixes the foundation for that year, and attributes the commotions of the Jews to that cause. Those commotions however broke out in 132, and were soon quelled; and both

erase from all future history the hateful name of Jesusalem, or
that a city with a more civilized appellation would be inhabited
by less rebellious subjects, or that the contumacy of the Jews
was associated with the *name* of their capital. But he employed
besides a more effectual method to secure obedience, by ex-
cluding from his colony all who professed the name, and
practised the rites, of the Jews. This prohibition comprehended, of course, the Christian Church of the Circumcision—
a circumstance which (according to Sulpicius Severus *) was
favorable to the faith,—[since a new church was then established, free from the bondage of the law; and composed either
of Gentiles only, or of those mixed with such Jews as were
willing entirely to abandon the Mosaic rites.] And a strong
proof was afterwards given of the perfect emancipation of this
Church from Judaic prejudices, when it took part with Rome,
against the Asiatic churches, in the Pascal controversy. Marcus,
a Gentile, was raised to the see; and he was followed by a new
succession of Bishops, as obscure and as rapid as that which
we have mentioned. Their names (which is all their history)
are also transmitted to us by the diligence of Eusebius †, but
none with any distinction except Narcissus, the fifteenth in
order, who flourished about the year 180, and of whom some
traditionary miracles ‡ are recorded.

Such are the imperfect accounts which remain to us respecting the early history of the Church in Palestine; but, imperfect
as they are, we are enabled to collect from them, that the progress of Christianity in that stubborn soil was slow, and its

Marginal note: Gentile Church.

Mosheim and Basnage (Ann. Polit. Eccles. 132, vol. ii. p. 72) consider the foundation of the new city to have been immediately subsequent to the rebellion.—See
Euseb. H. E. lib. vi. c. 6. Adrian reigned from 117 to 138.

* Hist. Sacr. lib. ii. c. 31. In such dearth of information, the passage of Severus, though not free from obscurity, is valuable. " Et quia Christiani (those of Palestine) ex Judæis potissimum putabantur (namque tunc Hierosolymæ non nisi ex
Circumcisione habebat Ecclesia Sacerdotem) militum Cohortem custodias in per-
petuum agitare jussit, quæ Judæos omnes Hierosolymæ aditu arceret. Quod quidem
Christianæ Fidei proficiebat : quia tum pæne omnes Christum Deum sub Legis ob-
servatione credebant. Nimirum id, Domino ordinante, dispositum, ut Legis servitus
a libertate Fidei atque Ecclesiæ tolleretur. Ita tum primum Marcus ex Gentibus
apud Hierosolymam Episcopus fuit." Mosheim has some judicious observations
on this passage, De Reb. Gestis ante Const. Secul. ii. s. 38.

† H. E. lib. v. c. 12.   ‡ Euseb. H. E. lib. vi. c. 9.

condition uncertain and fluctuating. And this conclusion is confirmed by the direct assertion of Justin Martyr, a Samaritan proselyte of the second century, our best authority for that age and country, who expressly assures us, that the converts in Judæa and Samaria were inferior, both in number and fidelity, to those of the Gentiles. "We behold the desolation of Judæa, and some from every race of men, who believe the teaching of Christ's Apostles, and have abandoned their ancient customs. We behold ourselves, too, and we perceive that the Christians among the Gentiles are more numerous and more faithful than among the Jews and Samaritans." He then proceeds to account for the fact, "that none of these have believed, excepting some few," by appeal to the prophetic writers[*].

II. From the spectacle of the infidelity and devastation of Palestine, foretold by so many prophecies, and truly designated by Jortin as an "event on which the fate and credit of Christianity depended," we turn to the more grateful office of tracing its advance, and celebrating its success. We may consider the neighbouring Church of *Antioch* to have been founded about 40 A. D.[†] by Paul and Barnabas. It was there that the converts first assumed the name of Christian; and the first act which is recorded respecting them was one of charity to their suffering brethren in Judæa. In a mixed population of Greeks, and natives unfettered by the prejudices of Judaism, our holy faith made a rapid and steady progress. In the residence of the Prefect of Syria, under the very eye of the civil government, it is probable that the infant society was protected against the active hatred of the Jews; and there can be no doubt that its early prosperity was greatly promoted by the zeal of its second bishop, Ignatius. This ardent supporter of the faith, the contemporary, and, as we are informed, the friend of some of the Apostles, presided over the Church of Antioch for above thirty

Marginal notes: Church of Antioch. Ignatius.

---

[*] Apol. i., ch. 68, & seq. Ἰουδαῖοι καὶ Σαμαρεῖς, ἔχοντες τὸν παρὰ τοῦ Θεοῦ λόγον διὰ τῶν προφητῶν παραδοθέντα αὐτοῖς, καὶ ἀεὶ προσδοκήσαντες τὸν Χριστὸν, παραγενόμενον ἠγνόησαν, πλὴν ὀλίγων τινῶν. &c. Sec. ii.

[†] Le Clerc, Hist. Eccl. t. i., p. 347 (ann. 40). Semler places the foundation of the Church in 39. In spite of Scripture (Acts xi. 21, 22, &c.) Baronius claims the honour for St. Peter, and is confuted by Basnage, vol. i., p. 502 (ad ann. 40).

years; and at length, during the persecution of Trajan, and seemingly in the year 107, was led away to Rome, and perished there, a willing and exulting martyr*.

107 A.D.   The narrative of his progress from Antioch to Rome supplies an affecting episode in Ecclesiastical History—it presents, indeed, the picture of an honourable procession, rather than the journey of a prisoner, conducted in chains to execution. He passed from Seleucia to Smyrna; and there he was saluted by a deputation of the bishops of Ephesus, Tralles and Magnesia, which is rendered the more remarkable by the expectation which those pious prelates appear to have held, that he would communicate to them some spiritual gift. He likewise wrote some letters to the churches abovementioned, which we shall notice hereafter. Thence he proceeded to Troas, where he was welcomed with the same respectful reception; and where he composed other letters for the confirmation of the faithful. Thence he was hurried, through Neapolis and Macedonia, to Rome. He arrived, as was apparently designed, during the gladiatorial exhibitions, and on the last day of the games (Dec. 19) he was carried to the amphitheatre, and delivered up to wild beasts, and instantly devoured by them. Some faithful adherents, who had followed him, gathered up his bones and took them back to Antioch, where they were buried near the city gate, amidst the warmest demonstrations of affection and piety.

The fourth bishop in succession from Ignatius was Theophilus, a learned convert from paganism, more justly celebrated for his books to Autolycus in defence of Christianity, than for his attack on the heresies of Marcion and Hermogenes. Under such guidance the Church of Antioch became numerous and respectable; and from the ordinary course of events we may reasonably infer, that the religion which was popular in the

* Le Clerc (ann. 116) fixes this event after the earthquake in 116, which destroyed a great part of the city, and was attributed by the heathen priesthood to the "impiety" of the Christians. Pearson, Pagi, and Fabricius are of the same opinion. But that of Tillemont, Du Pin and Cave, which we follow, is more probable, and is confirmed by Lardner (p. ii. c. v.) But Basnage, after all, is right, when he candidly places "the year of Ignatius's death among the obscurities of chronology."—Hist. Polit. Eccles. ann. 107, sect. 6.

capital of Syria obtained an easy and general reception through-out the province*.

A correspondence between our Saviour himself and Abgarus, Abgarus a prince of Edessa in Mesopotamia, is published at the of Edessa. end of the first book of Eusebius, as copied from the public records of the city. The genuineness of the correspondence has long ceased to find any advocate, and this is probably among the earliest of the many pious frauds which have disgraced the history of the Church: but the existence of the forged record in the archives of Edessa has never been disputed; and, as it is clearly the work of a Christian intending to do honour to the Founder of his religion, it proves at least how early was the introduction of that religion into the province of Mesopotamia†.

III. Of the seven Churches of Asia mentioned in the Revelations, viz. Ephesus, Smyrna, Pergamus, Thyatira, Sardis, Philadelphia, Laodicea, two only (Ephesus and Laodicea) are known to have existed before the death of St. Paul. Of Pergamus and Thyatira little subsequent mention is made in history; the other five, and especially the first two, are distinguished among the most fruitful of the primitive communities. The Church of *Ephesus*, which was founded by St. Paul and governed Church of by Timothy, was blessed by the presence of St. John during the Ephesus. latest years of his long life. Of him it is related, on sufficient authority, that when his infirmities no longer allowed him to perform the offices of religion, he continued ever to dismiss the society with the parting benediction, "My children, love one another!" and there is nothing in the early history of this Church to persuade us that the exhortation was in vain. In fact, the Epistle, which we have mentioned Ignatius to have addressed to the Ephesians, bears testimony to their evangelical purity, and to the virtues of their bishop Onesimus. And it is important to add, that the other Epistles sent at the same period to churches at Magnesia and Tralles (or Trallium), of

---

* Even before his journey to Macedonia we read that " Paul went through *Syria* and *Cilicia*, confirming the Churches."—Acts xv. 41.

† A successor of this Abgarus, who reigned at Edessa from 160—170, is sometimes asserted to have been the first prince who embraced Christianity. He was the patron of Bardesanes, a celebrated heretic of that period,

more recent foundation, prove the continued progress of the faith
in those regions, even after the last of the apostles had been
removed. The date of the foundation of the five Churches, not
established by St. Paul, is not ascertained. But they appear
to have been governed by their several bishops at a very early
period. Nevertheless, they regarded Ephesus as their head—
partly as the metropolis of Proconsular Asia; partly, as having
received the faith from the lips of an Apostle. At the end of
the second century we find that Ephesus still maintained its
supremacy over the Asiatic churches; and we observe its bishop,
Polycrates, conducting them in firm but temperate opposition
to the first aggression of the Church of Rome.

Church of Smyrna. IV. It would appear from the Epistle of Ignatius to the
Smyrnæans, that some in that communion were tainted with
heresies, which appeared unpardonable to that zealous bishop,
and which perhaps might be attended with some danger to an
infant society. But when he designates those schismatics as
"beasts in the shape of men*," we may doubt whether his exertions in this matter were calculated to restore the union of the
Church. A pious bishop, named Polycarp, at that time presided over the Church of Smyrna: he had been appointed to
office by St. John, and continued faithfully to discharge it, until
his aged limbs were affixed to the stake by the brutality of
166 A.D. Marcus Antoninus. "Eighty and six years have I served Christ,
and he hath never wronged me; how then shall I blaspheme
my King and my Saviour?" Such was his reply to the Roman
proconsul, who commanded him to abjure his faith, and curse
his Redeemer; and it will not be out of place here to transcribe
his last beautiful prayer, which has reached us from the pen of
those who witnessed his martyrdom†.

Martyrdom of Poly-carp. "Father of thy beloved and blessed Son Jesus Christ, through
whom we have knowledge of thee; God of angels and powers
and of all creation, and of the whole family of the just who live
in thy presence! I thank thee that thou hast thought me
worthy of this day and this hour, that I may take part in the

---

* Ignat. Epist. Smyrn. sect. 4.
† Epistle of the Church of Smyrna to that of Philomelium. Euseb. iv. 15.

number of the martyrs in the cup of Christ for the resurrection of eternal life, soul and body, in the incorruptibility of the Holy Spirit—among whom may I be received in thy presence to-day in full and acceptable sacrifice, as thou hast prepared, foreshown, and fulfilled, the faithful and true God. For this, and for everything, I praise thee, I bless thee, I glorify thee, through the eternal High Priest, Jesus Christ, thy beloved Son." The martyrdom of Polycarp took place about 166 A.D.*; and some miraculous matters are related in connexion with it, which have no claim to any particular mention. But there is one circumstance in the account of his trial, which should not be passed over in silence. It appears that the Proconsul would not have pressed his execution, if only Polycarp could have persuaded *the people* to listen to him, (πεῖσον τὸν δημόν); and when the sentence was at length pronounced, it was received with the eager acclamations of the multitude, shouting, "This is the teacher of Atheism—the father of the Christians—the destroyer of our gods—who has taught so many to renounce sacrifice and worship!" They then proceeded to prepare with their own hands the materials for his destruction, and the most active of all in this sanguinary office were, as they were wont to be, (ὡς ἔθος αὐτοῖς) the Jews.

The Church of Sardis, whose imperfect faith was rebuked by St. John, may have profited by the reproaches of its founder; for about the year 177 A.D. we again discover it, under the government of a learned and eloquent bishop, named Melito. To this writer we are indebted for the first catalogue of the books of the Old Testament compiled by any Christian author†; and it may be useful as well as curious to quote from Eusebius the titles of some of his works :—' Two Books concerning Easter —Rules of Life and of the Prophets—Concerning the Church— Sardis

---

* This is the opinion of Du Pin, Tillemont, Archbishop Usher, Lardner, (p. ii. 1. 6) and others. Eusebius and Jerome also place the event in the time of M. Antoninus. Bishop Pearson (Op. Post. Diss. 2. c. 15, 16, 17), however, argues that it took place under Antoninus Pius in 148. Le Clerc advocates as late a year as 169 : vol. i. p. 724—730.

† Fleury, lib. iv. sect. 3. Melito was, by many ancient Christians, accounted a *prophet*—in the sense, no doubt, of an inspired teacher. See Jortin, Rem. Eccl. Hist. book ii. part i. end.

A Discourse of the Lord's Day—Of the Nature of Man—Of
the Obedience of the Senses to Faith—Of Baptism—Of Truth
and of Faith, and the Generation of Jesus Christ—Of Prophecy—Of Hospitality—Of the Devil—Of the Revelation of
St. John—Of the Incarnation of God.'   And least of all should
we omit to mention the 'Apology for Christianity *,' which he
addressed to M. Antoninus.

Before we take leave of the Asiatic Churches, we must
remark that the early establishment of Christianity was not
confined to the shores of the Ægean†, or to places little removed
from it.   Hierapolis, an important city of Phrygia, contained a
Christian society, over which Papias presided in the beginning
of the second century.   Papias was an industrious collector of
all reported acts and sayings of the Apostles, and has been
justly designated the Father of Traditions.   He may have been
a feeble and credulous man; but it is enough that his mere
existence as Bishop of Hierapolis proves the very early progress
of the religion towards the interior of Asia.   Claudius Apollinaris was bishop of the same church, in the reign of M. Antoninus: "a man of great reputation," as says Eusebius, and
celebrated for his 'Apology for Christianity,' and his 'Books
against Jews and Pagans.'

The province of Bithynia was situated at the south-western
extremity of the Euxine Sea.   We have no record of any Apostolical Church here founded; but we are accidentally furnished
with proof that, in the very beginning of the second century, a
great portion of the population were Christians—proof which
has never been disputed, because it is derived from the annals
of Pagan history.

Testimony
of Pliny.

Pliny the younger, a humane and accomplished Roman, was
governor of Pontus and Bithynia for about eighteen months,

---

* Fragments of this are preserved by Eusebius. H. E. lib. iv. c. 26. He
boldly censured the Emperor's decree against the Christians, as one 'which ought
not to have been promulgated even against barbarous enemies.' And, therefore,
he expressed a loyal doubt whether it really proceeded from the councils of the
Emperor. Le Clerc supposes the Apology to have been published in 169; Fleury
(l. iv. 1) in 170.

† "We know from certain documents that the Christian religion was firmly
established among the Arabs in the second century." Semler, sec. ii. c. 2.

during the persecution of Trajan; and on that subject, in the year 107* A.D., he addressed to the Emperor his celebrated 107 A.D. Epistle†. This being justly considered as the most important document remaining to us in early Christian history, we shall here transcribe some portion of it—the more willingly, as we shall have occasion hereafter to refer to it.

After mentioning the difficulty of his own situation, and his perplexity in what manner to proceed against men charged with no other crime than the name of Christian, the writer proceeds as follows :—" In the mean time, in respect to those who have been brought before me as Christians, I have followed this plan. I ask them, *Whether they are Christians?* and if they confess, I ask them a second and a third time, threatening them with punishment : if they persevere I condemn them. For I cannot doubt, whatever may be the guilt of their confession, that their perversity and inflexible obstinacy deserve punishment. There were others, inflicted with this madness, whom I discovered to be Roman citizens, and consequently sent them to the city. Presently, the evil (as is wont to happen) spread more widely from being probed and handled, and many forms of it presented themselves. An anonymous 'Libel' was published, containing the names of many who denied that they were, or had been, Christians, and invoked the gods, as I prescribed, and prayed to your image, with incense and wine, and, moreover, blasphemed Christ —none of which things those who are true Christians can (it is said) be compelled to do. So I thought proper to dismiss them. Others were named by an informer, who at first confessed themselves Christians, and afterwards denied it : the rest said that they had been Christians, but had abandoned the religion, some three years ago, some longer, and one or more above twenty years. They all worshipped your image, and the statues of the gods : these also reviled Christ. They affirmed that the whole of their fault or error lay in this—that they were wont to meet together on a stated day before it was light, and sing among themselves alternately a hymn to Christ, as to God; and bind themselves by an oath, not to commit

* Lardner, Test. of Anc. Heathen. Some prefer a later date.
† Lib. x. epist. 97.

any wickedness, not to be guilty of theft, or robbery, or adultery; never to falsify their word, nor to deny a pledge committed to them when called upon to return it. When these things were performed, it was their custom to separate, and then to come together again to a meal, which they ate in common without any disorder; but this they had forborne since the publication of my edict, by which, according to your commands, I prohibited assemblies.

"After receiving this account, I judged it the more necessary to examine, and that by torture, two female servants, which were called ministers (deaconesses); but I have discovered nothing, beside a bad and excessive superstition. Suspending, therefore, all judicial proceedings, I have recourse to you for advice: for it has appeared to me matter highly deserving consideration, especially upon account of the great number of persons who are in danger of suffering; as many of all ages, and every rank, of both sexes likewise, are accused, and will be accused. Nor has the contagion of this superstition seized cities only, but the lesser towns also, and the open country: nevertheless, it seems to me that it may be restrained and corrected. It is certain that the *temples, which were almost forsaken,* begin to be more frequented; and the sacred solemnities, after a long intermission, are revived. Victims likewise are everywhere bought up, whereas for a time there were few purchasers. Whence it is easy to imagine what numbers of men might be reclaimed if pardon were granted to those who repent."

So few * and uncertain are the records left to guide our inquiries through the obscure period which immediately followed the conclusion of the labours of the Apostles, that the above testimony to the numbers and virtues of our forefathers in faith becomes indeed invaluable. No history of the Church of Christ can be perfect without it; and its clear and unsuspected voice will be listened to by every candid inquirer in every age of truth and history. At present our only concern is with the

* Ecclesiastical history discovers to us no important event between the death of St. Peter and St. Paul, and that of St. John, excepting the rise of the Gnostic heresy, which Le Clerc places in the year 76.

concluding paragraphs, which show us how extensively the religion was disseminated within seventy-five years from the death of its founder, in a province very distant from its birthplace, and where no apostle had probably penetrated*; and certainly it is not unfair to infer, that, in other provinces more favourably situated, and more industriously cultivated, as rich a harvest may have grown up of faith and piety, though unnoticed by the pen of the Roman officers, whose mere duty required nothing more from them than its extirpation.

V. From the churches of Asia we proceed to the description of those of Greece, and among these our first notice shall be directed to *Athens*. A vain, and light, and learned city, the Church of theatre of lively wit and loose and careless ridicule, the school Athens. of intellectual subtlety and disputatiousness, the very Pantheon of Polytheism, where the utmost efforts of human genius had been exhausted to celebrate a baseless and gaudy superstition —such, assuredly, was not a place where the homeliness of the Gospel could hope to find favour. More curious in the pursuit of theories than in the investigation of facts, the Athenian philosopher (of whatever sect) would not readily embrace a faith, which required him to believe so much and allowed him to speculate so little; and we may add, that he would bring to the inquiry a mind either hardened by previous habits of universal scepticism, or fraught with some sort of theistical notions, inconsistent with the truths he was called upon to receive. For these, and similar reasons, Christianity made, for some years, very trifling progress at Athens. We read, indeed, of a succession of bishops, beginning with Dionysius the Areopagite, the convert of St. Paul. But it appears that Quadratus, on his accession in Adrian's time, after the martyrdom of his predecessor, Publius, found the church in a state verging on apostacy†, and to him, perhaps, may belong the honour of restoring, if we should not rather say, of establishing it. After that period, we find it more flourishing; and we have the authority of Origen,

---

* It should be mentioned that, according to some traditions, the Apostle Andrew had preached the Gospel there, as well as in Pontus.

† Dionys. apud Euseb. iv. 23. The age of Quadratus is well discussed by Le Clerc, H. E. ad ann. 124.

in his second book against Celsus, for believing that, about the middle of the second century, the Christians of Athens were eminent for their piety; and their industry, if not learning, is attested by the publication of three apologies for their faith. Two were written by Quadratus and a contemporary philosopher named Aristides*, and were presented, or dedicated, to Adrian. The third was published in the year 166, by another philosopher, named Athenagoras, and is still extant. It was entitled ' An Embassy on behalf of the Christians,' and is supposed to have been presented (though not, perhaps, till the year 177) to the emperors M. Aurelius and L. Verus. This work sufficiently assures us of the sufferings and the calumnies to which the Christians were subject—and when it is asserted that the magistrates were insufficient to hear the cases brought before their tribunals, we necessarily infer the great number of the converts.

To the Philippians an epistle was addressed by Polycarp, about 108 A.D., attesting, at least, the permanence of that apostolical Church; and that the Church of Thessalonica had also been perpetuated, and another subsequently established at Larissa, is proved by the circumstance that Antoninus Pius addressed copies of his ' Order of Toleration' to the governors of those cities.

Church of Corinth.　VI. Tracing the footsteps of the Apostle of the Gentiles from Athens, we proceed to *Corinth*. We still find ourselves surrounded by graceful temples and statues, consecrated to the deities of Paganism. We observe the same elegance of opulence, the same abandonment to fastidious luxury; but there is this difference, that the character of the people, with less renown for wit, vanity, and ambitious pretension, is even more distinguished for immorality. Not so warmly attached to the keen and fruitless contests of the schools, the Corinthians

---

* These Apologies, certainly that of Aristides, were extant in the time of Eusebius (l. iv. c. 3) and St. Jerome (Catal. Script. Eccles.).—See Fleury, lib. iii. sect. 22. On Athenagoras see Le Clerc, ad ann. 166 (vol. i. p. 702—710), and Fleury, lib. iii. sect. 47. Bayle (vie Athenag.) mentions with surprise that that writer was unknown to Eusebius, Jerome, and most of the ancient fathers. He appears to have held some erroneous opinions, and is noticed by Epiphanius, Adv. Hær, num. 64, p. 544, t. 1.

rather sought their happiness in the vulgar excitements of sensuality. It is easier to remove many moral imperfections, than to convince the self-sufficiency of wit. And this may have been one of the reasons which decided St. Paul to select Corinth as his principal residence in Greece. The early years of this Church are not free from reproach; but we observe that they are distinguished rather by the spirit of dissension and contumacy, than by that of immorality—it retained the vices * of the Greek character, after it had thrown off those of the Corinthian. Cephas and Apollos divided the very converts of the apostle; and, about fifty years afterwards, the disunion had so far increased, as to call for the friendly interference of the Church of Rome. About 95 A.D.†, St. Clement, the bishop, addressed to them his first and genuine Epistle, which has fortunately been preserved to us, and is probably the most ancient of uninspired Christian writings‡. The author is related to be the same Clement mentioned by St. Paul as one " of his fellow-labourers, whose names are in the Book of Life§." The dissensions of the Corinthians seem to have entirely regarded the discipline, not the doctrine, of the Church; they had dismissed from the ministry certain presbyters, as St. Clement asserts, undeservedly, and much confusion was thus introduced. For the purpose of composing it, five deputies were sent from Rome, the bearers of the Epistle. And as this circumstance has sometimes been advanced to prove the original supremacy of Rome, it is proper to observe, that the Epistle is written in the name of " the Church sojourning at Rome," not in that of the Roman bishop; that its character is of exhortation, not of authority; and that it is an answer to a communication originally made by the Church of Corinth.

* They are thus enumerated by St. Clement, c. 35: ἀδικία, ἀνομία, πλεονεξία, ἔρεις, κακοήθειαι τε καὶ δόλοι, ψιθυρισμοὶ καὶ καταλάλιαι, θεοστυγία, ὑπερηφανία, ἀλαζονεία καὶ κενοδοξία.

† There are very wide differences among historians respecting this date. Lardner (part i. ch. 2.) appears to us to have selected the most probable opinion.

‡ *Perhaps* we should except the Epistle ascribed to St. Barnabas.

§ " Ancient writers, without any doubt or scruple," assert this. Lard. Cred. G. H. p. ii. 1. 2.

The episcopal form of government was, in our opinion*, clearly not yet here established—probably as being adverse to the republican spirit of Greece. This spirit, naturally extending from political to religious affairs, may have acted most strongly in the most numerous society; and to its influence, so dangerous to the concord of an infant community, we may, perhaps, attribute the evils of which we have spoken. At what precise moment the converts of Corinth had the wisdom to discover that their unity in love would be better secured by a stricter form of Church government, we are not informed; but, about seventy years after these dissensions, we find them flourishing under the direction of a pious and learned bishop, Dionysius. This venerable person is chiefly celebrated for his seven Epistles called, by Eusebius†, Catholic: two of these were addressed to the Churches of Rome and Athens; two others to those of Nicomedia and Amastris with the other churches in Pontus; two to those of Gortyna and Gnossos in Crete, and one to that at Lacedæmon. It is thus, incidentally, that we are furnished with our best evidence of the gradual growth of Christianity. From Athens we proceed to Corinth, from Corinth to Lacedæmon; established in the capital, we advance into the towns and villages ‡; and we doubt not that, at that early period, the wild mountaineers of Taygetus received that faith, which they have through so many centuries of trial so devotedly preserved, and which is, at length, confirmed to them for ever.

Church of Rome.

VII. In the Annals of the historian Tacitus (xv. 44), after the description of a terrible fire at Rome, we read with sorrow

Testimony of Tacitus.

and indignation the following passage:—"To suppress the common rumour, that he had himself set fire to the city, Nero procured others to be accused, and inflicted exquisite punishments

---

* As the question has occasioned much controversy, we may refer the reader to a Note at the end of the second chapter of this Work.

† H. E. l. iv. c. 23. In his letter to Pinytus, Bishop of Gnossos, he exhorted him not to impose upon his flock too severely "the heavy burden of chastity." Pinytus, in reply, calls for stronger spiritual nourishment, and disdains the tender infantine food offered by the Bishop of Corinth.

‡ Κατὰ κωμὰς καὶ ἐπαίλεις, Origen. Cels. iii. p. 119. Clem. Ep. ad Cor. 42. Κατὰ χώρας καὶ πόλεις κηρύσσοντες, &c.

upon those people who were held in abhorrence for their crimes,
and were commonly known by the name of Christians.   They
had their denomination from Christus, who, in the reign of
Tiberius, was put to death as a criminal by the procurator
Pontius Pilate.   This pernicious superstition, though checked
for a while, broke out again, and spread not only over Judæa,
the source of this evil, but reached the city also, whither flow
from all quarters all things vile and shameful, and where they
find shelter and encouragement.   At first those only were
apprehended who confessed themselves of that sect; afterwards
a vast multitude was discovered by them, all of whom were condemned, not so much for the crime of burning the city, as for
their enmity to mankind.   Their executions were so contrived
as to expose them to derision and contempt.   Some were
covered over with the skins of wild beasts, and torn to pieces by
dogs; some were crucified; and others, having been daubed
over with combustible materials, were set up as lights in the
night time, and thus burnt to death.   Nero made use of his own
gardens as the theatre upon this occasion, and also exhibited
the diversions of the Circus, sometimes standing in the crowd
as a spectator, in the habit of a charioteer, at others driving a
chariot himself; till at length these men, though really criminal
and deserving exemplary punishment, began to be commiserated,
as people who were destroyed, not out of regard to the public
welfare, but only to gratify the cruelty of one man."

This passage, which will scarcely be deemed creditable to the
philosophy of its author even by those who most extol it, and
which is most deeply disgraceful to his historical accuracy, to
his political knowledge, and to his common humanity, was
written at the end of the first century, about thirty-six years
after the persecution* which it so vividly describes.   It was in

* That event is placed in the year 64, by the general consent of Christian antiquity.   It is also commonly agreed that St. Peter, as well as St. Paul, suffered
martyrdom under Nero. (Euseb. l. ii. c. 25, on the authority of Caius an ecclesiastic, and Dionys., Epist. to Romans.) But there are differences as to the exact
time of that suffering. Le Clerc (vol. i. p. 447, A.D. 68) places it at the end of
Nero's reign in the year 68 ; but the general opinion refers it to the persecution.
The doubt as to fact rests rather on the martyrdom of St. Peter than of St. Paul,
but the authority appears to us sufficient historically to establish the violent end
of both.

the midst of this awful scene that St. Peter and St. Paul are believed to have suffered. We shall not pause to investigate the arguments for this opinion, but rather confine our attention to the testimony here afforded, as to the number of Christians existing at Rome even at that very early period. *A vast multitude* was discovered by the eye of persecution; and the compassion excited by their sufferings would naturally awaken an attention which had never before been directed to them. The assault of Nero was furious and probably transient. Such is precisely the method of aggression which fails not in the end to multiply its objects; and if from this evidence it be probable that, before the end of the first century, the Church of Rome surpassed every other in power and consideration, we may rest assured that these were rather augmented than diminished during the century following. To this belief we are persuaded, partly by the greater facility of conversion offered by the size of the city, and the multitude of the inhabitants; partly by the consideration, that the force of opinion would naturally lead the feeble Christian societies throughout the empire to look for counsel and protection to the capital, as we know the church of Corinth to have done; and partly by the fact, that frequent pecuniary contributions were transmitted by the faithful at Rome to their less fortunate brethren in the provinces. In this, then, consisted the original superiority of Rome; in numbers, in opinion, in wealth: to these limits it was entirely confined, and it was not until quite the conclusion of the second century that we hear of any claim to authority.

Dispute respecting the celebration of Easter.

The circumstances of that claim arose from a very early difference in the Church respecting the celebration of Easter. It was shortly this: the Christians of Lesser Asia observed the feast, at which the Paschal lamb was distributed, in memory of the Last Supper, at the same time at which the Jews celebrated their passover—that is, on the 14th day of the first Jewish month*; and three days afterwards they commemorated the resurrection, without regard to the day of the week. The

---

* Neander discovers a disposition to Judaism in this observance. We have mentioned that the Church of Jerusalem, being now Gentile, took the opposite side.

Western churches observed the anniversary of the resurrection on the first day of the week, and kept their Paschal feast on the night preceding it.   Hence arose some inconveniences; and we find that Polycarp visited Rome about 100 A.D. for the purpose (as we learn from Irenæus) of arranging the controversy.   The conference was amicable, but not successful; and about ninety years afterwards (A.D. 196, Fleury, l. iv. c. 44), as the difference still continued, Victor, Bishop of Rome, addressed Conduct of to the Asiatics an express order to conform to the practice of Rome. Rome.   But this was not a question to be thus decided.   Both parties defended their respective practices by immemorial usage and apostolical authority; and if the names of St. Peter and St. Paul were arrayed on the one side, those of St. John and St. Philip were advanced with equal confidence on the other. The great majority of the churches did indeed take part with Rome.   The whole West was unanimous; and even in the East, where the opposite opinion originated, and where alone it found any public supporters, Cæsarea in Palestine, Jerusalem, Tyre, and Alexandria were favourable to the Roman observance.   But on the other hand, the independence of the several churches was strongly asserted and universally acknowledged; and a respectable minority of the Christian world was not prepared to submit to the arbitrary dictates even of the See of Rome.

Polycrates, Bishop of Ephesus, assembled a synod of bishops, Synod of and temperately communicated to Victor their firm adhesion Ephesus. to the practice by them deemed holy.   Besides the authority of the two apostles, he pleaded the venerable names of Polycarp, Thraseas, and Sagaris, martyrs to the faith; of Papirius and Melito; and even of seven among their own kinsmen, who had held the episcopal office—and then he added—" For my own part, my brethren, I who have lived five and sixty years in the Lord, who have conversed with my brethren dispersed over the whole world, who have read through the whole scriptures—am nothing moved by the terrors that are held over us.   For I know that it has been said, by those who are greater than I am, that it is better to obey God than man."

Offended by this declaration, Victor would have persuaded

his party to remove the dissentients from their communion— but he could not prevail: a more charitable spirit animated the Christians of that age, and the rising flame of intolerance was yet confined to the bosom of Rome. Alone he ventured to

Excommu- break the bond of peace, and at once excommunicated all the *nication* brethren of Asia Minor*. This is remarkable as being the first *of the* *Asiatics.* aggression of a Roman bishop on the tranquillity of the Church of Christ. It was displeasing to many of those who agreed with him in opinion; and there were some, as Eusebius assures us, who rebuked him with severity. Of these the most distinguished was Irenæus, who, in the name of his brethren of Gaul, reminded the intemperate Roman, that, notwithstanding the differences in their Paschal regulations, Christians had hitherto lived together in peace towards each other; and that their discrepancies respecting ceremonies were more properly the means of setting forth in a brighter light their agreement in faith. The address of this truly Christian bishop is said to have had some effect in restoring the unity of the church; but the question in controversy was not finally decided till the Council of Nice, in 325.

The Con- Our first authentic knowledge of the establishment of Chris-*version of* tianity in France is derived from its calamities. During the *Gaul.* persecution of Marcus Antoninus, the churches of Vienne and Lyons sent a relation of their sufferings to those of Asia and Phrygia, which is by some ascribed to the pen of Irenæus†. It is written with simplicity and beauty, and is one of the most affecting passages in the ancient history of Christianity. This persecution appears to have arisen in the first instance from the hostility of the multitude. The magistrates then interfered, and the number of prisoners was presently so great as to make it necessary to apply for instructions to the emperor. His rescript was—" to spare those who retracted, and to execute the contumacious." This answer seems to have inspired the Christians with new ardour and unyielding constancy. They endured the most barbarous torments with fixed and even joyous resignation, and presented to their brethren and their posterity a memorable

---

* Ἀκοινωνήτους ἄρδην πάντας τοὺς ἐκεῖσε ἀνακηρύττων ἀδελφούς. Euseb. v. 24. See Mosh. De Reb. gestis ante Constant. sec. ii. §. 72.

† It is preserved by Eusebius, lib. v. cap. 1.

example of faithful endurance. Pothinus, the bishop, died in
prison—and as soon as the storm abated, Irenæus (so lately
and so honourably mentioned by us) succeeded to the dangerous
eminence. Under his prolonged and vigilant protection Christianity took deep root and spread widely, and fixed itself, beyond
further fear of extirpation, in the soil of France.

According to the best authorities he died in the year 202*.
The persecution had taken place about twenty-five years earlier ;
and it is a common opinion that Pothinus, who was a missionary from the East, had first introduced the religion into Gaul. The
names of the martyrs who perished with him are for the most
part Greek; and the communication of their sufferings was
addressed to their Oriental brethren. Sulpicius affirms that it
was late before the faith was received in the Transalpine pro-
vinces† ; and Lyons is the only church in Gaul which can show
an unquestionable succession from the second century. Besides
which, it seems very probable, from an agreement of their early
Liturgies, that the original service of Gaul was derived from
Ephesus, rather than from Rome. These circumstances, if they
will not lead us altogether to disregard the traditions, which
ascribe to an earlier period the conversion of Gaul, will at least
convince us that the faith had made little progress there, and
established itself with no firmness till the mission of Pothinus.

St. Clement asserts in his celebrated Epistle, that St. Paul Of Spain.
carried his preaching " to the boundary of the West‡ ;" and
though it seems to us rather more probable that, by this expression, the writer intended only to designate Italy (Hesperia),
some have understood him to speak of Spain, and others even

* That he died a martyr is a common belief. But as the fact is not mentioned
either by Tertullian or Eusebius, we may be allowed to suspect it—in spite of
Tillemont, vol. iii. p. 94.

† " Tum primum (on the occasion just described) inter Gallias martyria visa;
serius trans Alpes Dei religione suscepta." Histor. Sacr. l. ii. c. 32.

‡ The passage is in the fifth chapter. Ὁ παῦλος . . κῆρυξ γενόμενος ἐν τῇ ἀνατολῇ καὶ
ἐν τῇ δύσει . . δικαιοσύνην διδάξας ὅλον τὸν κόσμον, καὶ ἐπὶ τὸ τέρμα τῆς δύσεως ἐλθὼν,
καὶ μαρτυρήσας ἐπὶ τῶν Ἡγουμένων, οὕτως ἀπηλλάγη τοῦ κόσμου. It is worth remarking,
that the mention of the apostle's martyrdom, which unquestionably took place
at Rome, immediately follows the vague expression cited in the text—which is
immediately preceded by another equally vague—" that he taught lessons of
righteousness to *the whole world*." Upon the whole, we think it impossible to draw
any certain conclusion from this passage.

of Britain.   Respecting Spain, there is a passage in Irenæus
expressly declaring that the Gospel was established there when
he wrote, though the time and method of its introduction are
not mentioned.   Whatever that time may have been, and whoever may have been the original teacher of the faith, one thing
seems certain—both from the comparison of the ancient Liturgies and from the later history of the church—that the early
Communion of Spain was more closely allied in rites and discipline to that of Gaul, than to that of Rome.   And in so uncertain a matter, we think it the least improbable opinion that
the converts of Lyons transmitted to Spain, soon after the
middle of the second century, the light which they had received
from the East.

Of Britain.   The earliest history of the Church of Britain is involved in
the same obscurity with that of Spain.   For if we disregard the
traditionary journeys of Peter and Paul; and reject the legend
which describes Lucius, King of Britain, as sending for religious
instruction to Eleutherus, Bishop of Rome; and discredit the
vague assertion of Eusebius*, that Britain had been visited by the
apostles—our attention is first arrested by the strong expression of
Tertullian, in his book " Against the Jews*."   After asserting
that Christianity was already embraced by " the Parthians, the
Medes, and the Elamites; by those who dwell in Mesopotamia,
Armenia, Phrygia, Cappadocia; by the inhabitants of Pontus,
of Asia, and Pamphylia; by those who sojourn in Egypt and
the regions of Africa beyond Cyrene (he wrote from Carthage);
by Romans, Jews, Getulians, Moors, and all the boundaries of
Spain, and divers nations of Gaul—to which list he afterwards
adds Sarmatians, and Dacians, and Germans, and Scythians,
and many nations, provinces, and islands not enumerated, because not known"—he furthermore declares, " that some parts
of Britain, inaccessible to the Romans, were subject to Christ."

The confidence which we are desirous to place in this assertion
is shaken by the rhetorical exaggerations which encumber it.

* Dem. Evangel. iii. 5.

† Chap. vii. " Britannorum inaccessa Romanis loca, Christo vero subdita."
Mosheim is prolix on the supposed origin of the British Church, and ends with
the probable conclusion, that it was founded from Lyons, while Eleutherus was
Pope.   Rel. Christ. A. C., Sec. ii. s .3.

But we are bound to recollect that it is not in itself improbable, nor is it contradicted by any evidence whatsoever. So that we may infer thus much from it with great safety—more it does not much concern us to infer—that before the end of the second century our ancestors were numbered among the followers of Christ.

Respecting the source whence they derived their faith, nothing is certainly known. But the differences which were found to exist between the British and Roman Churches, when they first came in contact in the seventh century, persuade us that it was not from Rome that their first instructions were derived; and the fact, that those differences in a great measure concerned the celebration of Easter, is a strong proof of an original connexion between Britain and Ephesus. From these circumstances the natural conclusion seems to be, that Britain, like Spain, received the elements of her early Church, her rites, her Liturgy, and her ordination, from Gaul. And if so, it must have been before Irenæus declared his adhesion to the Roman party, in the Paschal controversy.

About the end of the second century, Tertullian, in the beginning of his " Apology," bears testimony to the sufferings and the power of the Christians; and it seems to be particularly in reference to Carthage that he makes the heathen exclaim—" That the whole country was beset with Christians—that the fields, the fortresses, the islands, were full of Christians—that every sex, and age, and condition, even to the highest rank—were passing over to this denomination*." Here again we are without any information respecting the introduction of the religion into this part of Africa—nor indeed have we any faithful record of its existence there, until the time of Tertullian. But from his writings, confirmed by the fact, that a council held at Carthage in the year 215 was attended by not less than seventy bishops, we infer its general prevalence, then, if not its early propagation. There can

Of Carthage.

---

* The passage in the 17th chapter of the same work is a stronger, but a more general, testimony of the consequence of the Christians. Yet in both we should make some allowance for the author's constitutional love of exaggeration. " Hesterni sumus, et vestra omnia implevimus—urbes, insulas, castella, municipia, conciliabula, castra ipsa, tribus, decurias, palatium, senatum, forum, Sola vobis relinquimus templa."

be little doubt that it was originally received from Rome. The close connexion and perpetual intercourse between the two capitals—the identity of the language of their writers—the intimate communication afterwards subsisting between the churches—and the general agreement between their Liturgies, afford very strong presumptive evidence of that fact—nor is there any opposing testimony.

Church of Alexandria. VIII. It was an early belief that St. Mark first preached his gospel at *Alexandria*, and founded churches there; and he is expressly mentioned by Eusebius* as the first bishop of that city. The same writer asserts that a multitude of converts, both men and women, listened to his instructions, from their very first delivery. The evidence which he brings for this fact is not quite conclusive, but other circumstances render it highly probable. The population of Alexandria was very numerous, and composed of every variety of race and superstition—so that no general prejudice against the introduction of a new religion could exist there; it was commercial, and therefore enlightened; and it was also remarkable for the ardour with which it cultivated every branch of literature, the facility with which it admitted and reconciled philosophical tenets the most dissimilar, and the freedom which it indulged to every novelty of truth or speculation. Again, through the number of Jews originally established there at the foundation of the city, and continually increased by their domestic calamities; through the moderation and even liberality of those Jews, as compared to their brethren in other countries; and especially through the Septuagint translation of the Old Testament, which was there chiefly circulated, and studied by the learned of every sect, the knowledge of the true God was more generally diffused in Alexandria than in any other Gentile city, and the minds of men in some degree prepared to receive the second Covenant. We do not pretend to assert that they received it in entire purity, or with a perfect comprehension of its true character and inestimable advantages; but we doubt not that a vast number believed and were baptized,

---

* H. E. l. ii. c. 16 and 24. St. Luke is also believed to have visited this city, and the Acts of the Apostles to have been written and thence diffused over the Christian world. Semler, c. i. ch. 5.

and constituted, under the holy guidance of the Evangelist and his successors, a repectable and powerful community. St. Mark was succeeded by Anianus; and the Latin names of many of the bishops who followed, persuade us that the same intercourse subsisted between the ecclesiastical, as between the civil, governments of Rome and Alexandria.

Vopiscus, an historian who flourished about 300 A.D., has preserved (in his life of Saturninus) a letter, written by the Emperor Adrian in the year 134, immediately after his visit to Alexandria.   It contains the following expressions:—" I have found Egypt in every quarter fickle and inconstant, and moved by every impulse of absurd report—the worshippers of Serapis are Christians, and those are devoted to Serapis who call themselves Christian Bishops.   There is no ruler of the Jewish synagogue, no Samaritan*, no presbyter of the Christians, no mathematician, no soothsayer, no anointer; even the patriarch himself, should he come into Egypt, is compelled by some to worship Serapis, by others Christ—a most seditious and turbulent sort of men; most vain and insolent.   However, the city is rich and populous, and no one lives there in idleness. . . . They have one God : him the Christians, him the Jews, him all the Gentile people worship; and I would that this city were of purer morality, since it merits by its magnitude the supremacy of Egypt." We need not be surprised or offended by the insolent levity with which the profligate imperial philosopher places the religion of Serapis on a level with that of Christ, while, through the numerous misrepresentations so obvious in these sentences, one important truth may be descried.   They mani-

The Epistle
of Adrian.
134 A. D.

---

* Le Clerc (H. E. ann. 129) thinks it possible that Adrian was deceived by his informers, who may have mistaken the Gnostics, many sects of whom were then found at Alexandria, for the Orthodox Christians : but it is remarkable that both Simon Magus and Menander were natives of Samaria ; and that the Samaritans are in the emperor's letter distinguished from the Christians.   At any rate the supposition is not necessary ; the very style of the passage argues inaccuracy and exaggeration, if not indifference.   The emperor erected a number of temples, *without statues,* which he intended, no doubt, to be consecrated to himself.   Hence, some afterwards imagined that they were built for the Christians, but with little reason.   Lampridius, Vit. Alex. Ser. ch. xliii.   Eusebius, however, (Præp. lib. iv. c. 17,) asserts, that it was particularly in the reign of Adrian that Revelation made progress.

festly prove, that, within a hundred years from the resurrection of Christ, his worshippers formed at least an important part of the inhabitants of the second city of the empire; and, perhaps, it is not unfair from this record to conclude, that they were as numerous as those who remained attached to the indigenous superstitions.

There is another circumstance which increases the importance we should attach to the early prosperity of the Alexandrian Church. Before the birth of Christ, a very great proportion of the learning of the Eastern world had been transferred from the schools of Greece to those of Alexandria. Not that Athens was entirely abandoned by disputants, or even by philosophers; but the uncertain renown which it still maintained was surpassed by the splendid institutions of a city, whose literary triumph was preceded, and perhaps occasioned, by its commercial superiority. The early Christians felt the necessity of education, though they differed as to its proper limits and object. We are told that St. John erected a school at Ephesus, and Polycarp at Smyrna, and even that St. Mark originally established the Catechetical School at Alexandria*. There can be no doubt that those schools, by whomsoever established, were useful in the propagation of religion: but it was long before any of them produced any persons of great literary merit; and we know few particulars of the history of the Alexandrian Church before the middle of the second century, except the titles of its bishops, recorded by Eusebius.

Pantænus.   Pantænus, a convert from stoicism, who flourished about 180 A.D., directed and adorned for several years the Catechetical School. And while he conducted it, some persons are related to have arrived at Alexandria from *India*, to pray that teachers of Christianity might be sent into that country. The country thus designated is variously understood to have been Æthiopia, Arabia Felix, or the shores of the Ganges. The messengers may possibly (as Mosheim conjectures) have been Jews, since many were settled even in those remote regions, and they were least of all men likely to be indifferent to the religious divisions

---

* Schmidius de Schol. Catech. Alex. Jerom. de Vir. illust. c. 36.

which were now agitating the Roman empire, and which had their origin in Judæa.

Pantænus listened to their appeals, and proceeded in person His mission to the South. to effect their conversion. We are not certainly informed with what success his exertions were attended—but if they were confined, as some believe, to the upper regions of the Nile, we have evidence at least that the Thebais contained numerous converts towards the close of the century—who were visited by the sword of Severus, and whose splendid martyrdom (λαμπρὰ μαρτύρια) is recorded by Eusebius (vi. 1.). St. Jerome, in his "Catalogue of Writers" (cap. 36), affirms that Pantænus found, on his arrival in those regions, "that the Apostle Bartholomew had already preached there the coming of Jesus Christ, according to the Gospel of St. Matthew, which he brought back* to Alexandria, written in Hebrew."

Pantænus was succeeded by Clemens, commonly called the Alexandrian, whose writings are justly considered as opening a new period in the history of Christian literature; and Clemens by the celebrated Origen. Their fame, however, more properly belongs to the third century. It is only necessary here to observe, that those learned Christians being tinctured with certain philosophical notions, which they were desirous to reconcile with the Gospel, and influenced by the society of those professing them, have very frequently misrepresented the features of their religion†.

Such are the facts which may be related with most certainty respecting the first propagation of Christianity; and to such we have determined to confine this history. It is an easy and

* From Euseb. H. E. l. v. c. 10, and Orig. Epist. l. vi. c. 19, Le Clerc infers that Pantænus resumed his scholastic office after his return from Ethiopia (India), vol. i. p. 757 (ad ann. 179). Lardner fixes the earliest date of his return in 192 (p. ii. c. 21).

† It is a remark of Neander, that the Epistle to the Hebrews, that ascribed to Barnabas, the Egyptian Gospel, in which the Alexandrian theosophic taste showed itself, and the Gnosticism of the first half of the second century, are proofs of the influence that Christianity exerted over the Jewish philosophy of Alexandria. The influence was reciprocal, and the most sincere and zealous believers of that age could never entirely escape from it. Mosheim does not hesitate at once to ascribe to Ægypt *all* the corruptions of the ancient innocence and chastity of Christianity—all the evils, "quæ invaserunt Rem Christianam." Rel. Christ. A. C., Sec. ii, s. 33.

amusing task to adventure (as some are wont) into the spacious
fields of conjecture; to trace the possible origin of obscure traditions, or legendary narratives; to pursue a flattering theory
through every colour of the most remote probability, and draw
substantial inferences from the merest shadows of truth.   But
we have not observed that such ingenious researches convey to
ordinary minds satisfactory or lasting impressions, or that the
fruit which they bear is at all proportionate to the learned
labour employed on them.

CHAPTER II.

On the Numbers, Discipline, Doctrine, and Morality of the
Primitive Church.

I. General view of the extent of the Church—Facility of intercourse favourable to
Christianity—Other circumstances—Miraculous claims of the Church—To
what limits they ought to be confined.   II. Government of the Primitive
Church—During the time of the Apostles—After their Death—Deacons—
Distinction of Clergy and Laity—Earliest form of Episcopal Government—Independence of the first Churches—Institution of Synods—Their character and
uses—The evil supposed to have arisen from them—Metropolitans—Excommunication—Supposed community of property—Ceremonies of religion—Feasts
and fasts—Schools.   III. Confessions of faith—The Apostles' Creed—Baptism—The Eucharist—The Apage.   IV. Morality of the first Christians—
Testimonies of St. Clement—Pliny—Bardesanes—Chastity—Exposure of infants—Charity—The earliest Converts among the lower Orders—The progress
of the faith was upwards—Testimony of Lucian in the history of Peregrinus—
Suffering courage—Justin Martyr—On the early Fathers—Note on the government of the Church of Corinth.

Extent of
the Pri-
mitive
Church.

I. FROM a review of the preceding chapter we find, that before the year 200 A. D. the religion of Christ had penetrated
into most of the provinces of the Roman empire, and was
widely diffused in many.   The very evidence of Pagan antiquity, rarely and incidentally as it is presented to us—the
testimony of Tacitus; and that of Lucian, which we shall presently mention; the Epistles of Pliny, of Adrian, and the various
Imperial Rescripts regulating the policy to be observed towards

the Christians—these various monuments might demonstrate, had we no stronger proof, the prevalence of the name of Christ, and the stability of his religion.

It is, indeed, a mournful truth, that, by one of those dispositions of Providence which it is not given us perfectly to comprehend, the people, to which the truth was immediately addressed, was that most reluctant to receive it. Its earliest and its bitterest enemies were the Jews—and of all the Apostolical churches the least flourishing was that of Jerusalem. But the hand of Heaven protected the infancy of the faith, and proved its legitimacy, and avenged its wrongs—for the fulfilment of holy prophecy, and an eternal testimony to all generations. The spectacle of " the desolation of Judea" is advanced by Justin Martyr among the motives which led him to conversion; and the chastisement of a single nation became the means of dispersing through every quarter of the world the Gospel of life.

It is worthy of mention, that the Jews of Alexandria were less hostile to Christianity, than those of Greece and Asia. And this peculiarity we may attribute, not so much to any general disposition then prevalent to engraft foreign superstitions on the national worship, as to the fact, that the Alexandrian Jews were much more enlightened by foreign literature and Platonic philosophy, than the rest of their race. It was also another, and a principal cause of their greater moderation, that they had been allowed to build for themselves a temple at Leontopolis, near Alexandria, which tended to disconnect them from Jerusalem, and thus abate their exclusiveness, and soften their prejudices.

During the few earliest years of Christianity, the most flourishing church seems unquestionably to have been that of Antioch. In the wider progress of the Gospel, it was indeed surpassed by the superior power and populousness of Rome and Alexandria; but it still maintained its pre-eminence among the churches of Syria. In the same manner the supremacy of Ephesus was long acknowledged by the Christians of Asia Minor.

From Syria to the shores of the Black Sea, throughout the rich provinces of Asia Minor, Cilicia, Phrygia, Galatia, Pontus,

Bithynia, and along the whole coast of the Ægean Sea, a considerable proportion of the inhabitants were Christians, and we find them established in all the leading cities of Greece. From the cities, in each instance, the religion was silently derived and distributed among the surrounding towns and villages and hamlets, purifying morality, and infusing hope and happiness; and thus every Church was surrounded by a little circle of believers, which gradually enlarged, according to the zeal and wisdom which animated the centre.

There is another important circumstance attending the early history of Christianity which is seldom pressed upon the reader with sufficient force. We are perpetually reminded of the obscurity of the earliest converts, and of the slight and transient notice which they have received from contemporary heathen writers. It is argued, (in spite of the general assertions of Tertullian,) that none can positively be shown to have obtained any political celebrity, or reached any distinguished rank in the army or the court. At the same time their numbers are not disputed, nor the rapidity with which they spread, nor the constancy with which they suffered.

The first Christians were of the middling and lower Classes.   The difficulty is easily resolved. The first Christians undoubtedly consisted of the middling and lower classes of society. It was among the ranks removed below the possession of opulence, or power, or learning, that the religion first fixed itself and spread deeply its indestructible tendons. The promises of the Gospel are better adapted to the understanding and the wants of the simple and the needy, than to the astute vanity of the Sophist, or the ordinary habits of the wealthy. And the artizan and the peasant had already heard and believed, when the very name of Christ had scarcely reached the mansions of the great. In the mean time it was the learned and the great who wrote and who ruled—and the obscure believer in Christ was stigmatized by the one, and tortured by the other, as a vulgar and contemptible malefactor. This is a most important feature in the history of primitive Christianity—and must be perpetually borne in mind by all who would form a correct view of its character, and understand aright the reasons of its obscurity, and the sources of its strength.

Le Clerc, a judicious and thoughtful writer, ascribes (ann. Causes of 102-3) the rapid propagation of the religion during the second the propagation of century to four causes: first, some remaining miracles per- Christianity. formed by the last disciples of the apostles; second, the open confutation of heathenism by the Christian apologists; third, the constancy of the martyrs; fourth, the morals of the Christians. Respecting the last three of these, and the many other human circumstances which have contributed to the same end, we shall not engage in any particular investigation. Instances enough will present themselves in the course of this history, and some even in the present chapter. It would be neither wise nor consistent to dispute their existence, or disparage their efficacy; or to assert that Providence, which condescends to effect its other earthly purposes by the agency of man, has wholly neglected such means in effecting its great purpose, the propagation of Christianity.

A very general facility of intercourse, rendered still easier by Facility of the diffusion of the Greek language through the Eastern pro- intercourse. vinces, and by the knowledge of the Latin, which was universal in the West, prevailed throughout the Roman Empire: for the conquerors well knew that, without great rapidity of communication by sea and by land, so vast a compound of discordant materials could not long be held together in one mass. This was the most beneficial result of their political speculations; and hence proceeded their great diligence in the formation of roads and the construction of bridges. The means, which were intended to advance the progress of armies, and perpetuate the duration of slavery, were also converted to the more honorable purposes of commerce and civilization; and more than that, they became serviceable to a purpose, which was least of all contemplated by their authors—the dissemination of Christianity. They speedily became so; and it was thus that the weak were enabled to obtain support from the more powerful, the poor from the more wealthy, the ignorant from the more enlightened brethren; that the churches in distant provinces could maintain an easy and rapid intercourse; that the East could send missionaries to the West; and the more recent con- verts hold fearless correspondence with the establishments of the Apostles *. The devoted zeal of the primitive missionaries, the pure and austere morals of their converts, and the union and discipline of the church, are universally admitted. By these and similar considerations we are led to believe, that, at least throughout the Eastern provinces of the empire, in Syria, Egypt, Asia Minor, and Greece, a respectable proportion of the people were Christians, even before the end of the second century †. Assuredly there is strong reason for supposing the religion to have been already so firmly rooted in those parts, that its extirpation by any domestic persecutor would even then have been wholly impossible. This, at least, is our opinion; if true, it is an important service to have established it from the fair examination of such imperfect records as remain to us: for infidel writers are fond of insinuating that Christianity emanated from the court of Constantine, and had nowhere assumed any permanent or consistent form, until its character was fixed and its stability decided by the policy of an emperor.

In order to rest on ground which will not be disputed, we have been contented to seek our proofs of the early strength and security of Christianity in the ordinary records of history, made probable by natural circumstances and human operation. But

Miraculous claims. we should treat the subject imperfectly, if we were to make no mention of those higher powers, which have been so generally claimed for the primitive Church; not merely through the interposition of Divine Providence at such moments as seemed fit to His omniscience, but as a gift confided by the Most High to the uncertain discretion of his ministers on earth, and placed, through a succession of ages, at their uncontrolled disposition. The chain of historical evidence, on which this claim rests, is continued from the days of St. Irenæus to those of St. Bernard

* As in the case of the Church of Lyons, which seems to have been established by a Greek missionary, Pothinus, and continued in correspondence with the Churches of Asia.

† The great number of councils assembled about the years 195 and 196, on the controversy about Easter, proves, as Tillemont (vol. iii. p. 114) observes, the tranquillity of the Church: it proves also its prosperity; (and the authority of Tertullian has persuaded that historian that the Christians formed at that time almost the majority of the inhabitants;) and it is, moreover, an additional proof of the easy intercourse subsisting among the various members of the Christian communion.

(and even much later) with much uniformity of confident assertion and glaring improbability; it is interwoven in inseparable
folds throughout the whole mass of ecclesiastical records; and
the links which compose it so strongly resemble each other both
in material and manufacture, that it appears absolutely impossible to break the succession, or to distinguish which of the portions were fabricated by the wisdom of God, which by the impiety of man*. Various writers have assigned various periods
for the cessation of supernatural aids; but they appear for the
most part to have been rather guided by their own views of
probability, than by critical examination of evidence, which
would have led them equally to receive or equally to reject the
claims of every age, excepting the first. The powers, which
were undoubtedly communicated by the Apostles to some of
their immediate successors, probably continued to enlighten and
distinguish those holy persons to the end of their ministry, and
were eminently serviceable in the foundation of the faith†; but
it is a reasonable opinion that, after their departure, the possession of miraculous aids was no longer vouchsafed to the Church
as a community, or to any individuals *as its ministers*. All
miracles, which are related to have taken place after that period,
must be separately subjected to the usual tests‡, and must stand
or fall on their own merits, according to the degrees of evidence
and probability.

On such a question as this it is vain to appeal to authorities; and we have here no space for a full development

* The performance of a pretended miracle for the purpose of delusion is the
highest imaginable impiety, and the deliberate propagation of accounts of such
performances, with knowledge of their character, is not far short of it. But we
do not intend to impute this guilt to all the ancient Christian retailers of miraculous stories,—far from it;—credulity is the weakness of some minds, as mendacity
is the vice of others; and the former of these qualities, perhaps even more than
the latter, has characterised some Eastern nations in every age. And we should
recollect, that to them we are indebted for the fabrication of most of the tales
which stain the earlier pages of ecclesiastical history, and for the example which
led to them all.

† Mosh. Hist. Gen., c. i. p. i. ch. 4.

‡ Thus, when fairly tried by these tests, the once popular miracle of the Thundering Legion appears at length to have fallen into universal discredit. One or
two others will be discussed in the course of this work.—Mosh. Gen. Hist., c. ii,
p. i., ch. 1.

of our reasons. We must be contented, then, to say, that the *argument* by which we are principally moved is this: miracles become improbable in proportion as they seem to be not absolutely necessary; and it appears to us, that through the wonders wrought by the Apostles, and those, their contemporaries, to whom similar power was vouchsafed, some of whom may have survived them forty or fifty years, the foundation of the Christian Church was so firmly established, as to remove the necessity of the further continuance of that power to it. The *facts* which have chiefly decided us are the following:—In the writings of the Apostolical Fathers and those immediately succeeding, we read nothing respecting apostles, prophets, interpreters, or other inspired and extraordinary-gifted ministers: we have no record of the perpetuation of any *office* in the ministry which in its nature and name included the certainty of inspiration and miraculous powers. Again, the fathers who succeeded them, those of the second and third centuries, when they speak of the existence of such powers, confine themselves to the use of general language: they seldom specify an instance of their application; and when they do so, it may usually be classed in that description of miracles which is most liable to misrepresentation or mistake; such as the healing of diseases, or the expulsion of demons. Add to these and similar considerations that, which we do not hesitate to call the historical impossibility of assigning *any* period for the cessation of such gifts in the Church, if we once exceed the barrier which the infallibility of the inspired writers has, in our opinion, clearly marked out. But while, on the one hand, we have ventured to express thus much, we are far from intending to assert, on the other, that Providence withheld His *occasional* assistance from His faithful and afflicted servants; and, perhaps, we may observe generally, that the accounts of His interposition, which we should receive with the least suspicion, are those which describe the supernatural support afforded to missionaries in the prosecution of their holy labours. In the meantime there is one most important consideration which we should always bear in mind—that the truth of Christianity is not at all interested in the decision of this question*.

* See Bishop Kaye on Tertullian, 96—102.

II. We must now proceed to examine the discipline and government of the primitive Church; and, in this inquiry, we shall discover no marks of a loose and passing superstition, but, on the contrary, the surest prognostics of vigour and immortality. There are many reasons which make it necessary, in the treatment of this subject, to distinguish clearly between what is historically known and what is plausibly conjectured; for it is from the confusion of facts with probabilities that most of the difficulties of this question have arisen. In the first place it is certain, that, from the moment in which the early Churches attained a definite shape and consistency, and assumed a permanent form of discipline; as soon as the death of the last of the Apostles had deprived them of the more immediate guidance of the Holy Spirit, and left them, under God's especial care and providence, to the uninspired direction of mere men; so soon had every Church, respecting which we possess any express information, adopted the Episcopal form of government. The probable nature of that government we shall describe presently; but here it is sufficient to mention the undisputed fact, that all the religious communities of the Christian world, whose history is *certainly* known, admitted the superintendence of ministers, called bishops, before the conclusion of the first century*. In the next place it is equally true, that neither our Saviour nor his Apostles have left any express and positive ordinances for the administration of the Church †; desiring, perhaps, that *that*, which was intended for every age and condition of man, to be the associate and guardian of every form of civil government, should have the means of accommodating its external and earthly shape to the various modifications of human polity. It is also certain, that in the earliest government of the first Christian society, that of Jerusalem, not the elders

Margin note: Church government.

Margin note: Episcopal.

* To save the space which would be occupied by an accumulation of authorities, it will be sufficient, perhaps, to remind our readers that this fact is admitted by Gibbon in his 15th chapter. See the note at end of this chapter.

† See Mosh. Gen. Hist., c. i. p. ii. ch. 2, and the translator's impartial note. Also Basnage, tom. i. liv. i. c. 8. Principles are given, but no specific rules. (Hinds' Early Church, vol. ii. p. 100.) After all, no form of Church government now exists, or could exist, accurately framed on the model of the earliest, since *that* was regulated by an inspired ministry, and enlightened by extraordinary gifts. The government which immediately followed that earliest was episcopal.

only, but the 'whole Church'* were associated with the Apostles
—of course, in some degree of subjection to their authority :
and it is even unquestionable, that the terms bishop and elder,
or prebyster, were, in the first instance, and for a short period,
sometimes used synonimously†, and indiscriminately applied to
the same order in the ministry.   From the comparison of these
facts it seems natural to draw the following general conclusions,—
that, during the lifetime of the apostles, they were themselves
the directors, or at least the presidents of the Church ; that, as
long as they remained on earth, it was not necessary, in all cases,
to subject the infant societies to the delegated authority of
a single superintendent—though the instances of Titus and
Timothy prove that it was sometimes done, and though the
appointment of bishops is accounted (on less safe authority‡)
among the holy functions of St. John : and lastly, that, as they
were severally removed from the world, some distinguished brother was appointed to succeed, not indeed to the name and

* Acts xv. 2, 4, 22, 23, &c.   This, according to Mosheim (c. i. p. i. ch. 2), was
the model of all the primitive churches.

† Theodoret (Com. on 1 Tim. iii. 1.), a Father of the fourth century, admits and
explains that circumstance as follows :—" The same persons were anciently called
both bishops and presbyters, while those which are now called bishops were called
apostles ; but, shortly afterwards, the name of apostles was appropriated to those
who were apostles indeed, and then the name bishop was given to those before
called apostles."   (See also a passage from St. Ambrose, cited by Amalarius and
Bingham.)   Whatever value we may attach to this explanation, it is quite certain that bishops began very early to assume the title of " successors of the apostles," which we find to have been done by Firmilian, Cyprian, and other bishops
of Carthage.   See Bingham's Church Antiq., b. ii. c. 2.   Le Clerc, ad ann. 44
(vol. i. p. 358), and ann. 47 (vol. i. p. 449), places the general institution of elders
in the year 47.   Bingham (b. ii. c. 19) and others, admitting the confusion of
names, would still persuade us that there was no identity of office. Bishop Pearson
(Vindic. Ignatianæ) is of opinion that, in some churches, there were bishops and
not presbyters ; in others, presbyters and not bishops—a plausible opinion,
strongly confirmed by the expressions of Clemens and Epiphanius, showing that
in some churches there were bishops and deacons, in others only presbyters and
deacons ; but that the larger communities had all the three orders.   Mosheim,
however, considers " the two terms as undoubtedly applied to the same order of
men" (c. i. p. i. ch. 2) ; and such is the plain interpretation of the Scripture passages.—See Hinds' Early Prog. Christ., vol. i. p. 349, &c.

‡ Eusebius (iii. 23.) refers to Clemens Alexandrinus, in his book entitled
Τίς ὁ σωζόμενος πλούσιος.   The assertion is, that the Apostle went about—ὅπου μὲν ἐπι-
σκόπους καταστήσων· ὅπου δὲ ὅλας ἐκκλησίας ἁρμόσων· ὅπου δὲ κλήρῳ ἕνα γέ τινα κληρώσων
τῶν ὑπὸ τοῦ Πνεύματος σημαινομένων.   A fabulous tale follows—but this does not,
perhaps, affect the truth of the incidental assertion, to which we here refer.

inspiration, but to the ecclesiastical duties of the blessed Teacher who had founded the Church. The concurrence of ancient records confirms this last conclusion; the earliest Church historians* enumerate the first bishops of the Churches of Jerusalem, Antioch, Ephesus, Smyrna, Alexandria and Rome, and trace them in each case from the Apostles. And thus it came to pass, that, for more than twenty years before the death of St. John, most of the considerable Churches had gradually fallen under the presidency of a single person entitled Bishop; and that, *or Elder* after that event, there were probably none which did not speedily follow the same name and system of administration.

Again, for the first thirty years, perhaps somewhat longer, after the ascension of Christ, the labours of the apostles were aided by certain ministers entitled Prophets†, who were gifted **Prophets.** with occasional inspiration, and taught under the influence of the Holy Spirit. This order of teachers was withdrawn from the Church, when their office became no longer necessary for its advancement, and it appears wholly to have ceased before the end of the century; at which period, as we have already observed, ecclesiastical government universally assumed that durable shape which has been perpetuated, and, with certain variations, generally adopted through every age of Christianity.

We have yet made no mention of the deacons, who were the third order in the Episcopal Church. The word deacon **Deacons.** (διάκονος) means minister, and in that sense is sometimes applied to the office of the Apostles; but in a general sense only, since we are assured‡ that the diaconal order was distinct, and instituted for a specific purpose. However, it seems certain that, in the very beginning, the office of the deacons was not confined to the mere ministry of the table, since we read that Stephen disputed publicly on the Christian truth with irresistible wisdom

---

* Euseb. l. iii. c. iv. xiv. xxii. &c. " It is highly probable," says Mosheim, (c. l. p. ii. ch. 2) " that the Church of Jerusalem, grown considerably numerous, and deprived of the ministers and the apostles, who were gone to instruct other nations, was the first which chose a president or bishop: and it is no less probable that the other churches followed, by degrees, such a respectable example." And it is certain that, in at least two instances, such presidents were appointed by an apostle. The Church of Corinth seems, indeed, to have been the only exception. See Hinds' Early Church, vol. ii. p. 163, and Bingham, b. ii. c. 1.

† St. Paul, 1 Cor. xii. 20, &c.; Ephes. iv. 11. Mosheim de Rebus Christ. ante Const. Sæc. l. s. xl. and Gen. Hist. c. i. p. ii. ch. 2.   ‡ Acts vi,

and spirit; and, moreover, that " he did great wonders and miracles among the people." It is equally clear that attendance on the poor was for several centuries attached to it; even after the office of treasurer was held by the bishop, the portion destined to charitable relief continued to pass through the hands of the deacon. It is not so easy to ascertain the extent of their spiritual duties in the earliest Church. Ignatius speaks of them with high respect, and, in one place*, calls them "ministers of the mysteries of Christ." Tertullian distinguishes them from the laity, together with bishops and presbyters. Cyprian asserts that the Apostles appointed them as " ministers of their episcopacy and Church." By the Nicene Council they are designated as servants ($\dot{\upsilon}\pi\eta\rho\acute{\epsilon}\tau\alpha\iota$) of the bishop. It is certain that they were ordained by the bishop alone, without any imposition of hands by presbyters; that in some Churches they were admitted to read the Gospel, and that they universally assisted in the distribution of the Eucharist, without any share in its consecration. Their early acknowledgment as members of the ministry is proved by their occasional presence in the original synods of the clergy†. The Deaconesses, of whom we read in early Church History, may probably have been widows appointed, for the better preservation of the ministry from scandal and calumny, to superintend the charitable distribution made to the female portion of the poor.

Distinction between Clergy and Laity.

The origin of the distinction between the clergy and the laity has given rise to much controversy. Bingham‡ is of opinion that it was derived from the Jewish into the Christian Church in its earliest days. And Clemens Alexandrinus § has expressly declared, "that St. John, after his return from Patmos, ordained bishops, and appointed such men for *clerical* ministers as were signified by the Holy Spirit." That the persons here men-

* Ignat., Ep. ad Trall., c. ii. Δεῖ δὲ καὶ τοὺς Διακόνους ὄντας Μυστηρίων Ἰησοῦ Χριστοῦ κατὰ πάντα τρόπον πᾶσιν ἀρέσκειν. Οὐ γὰρ βρωμάτων καὶ ποτῶν εἰσιν διάκονοι, ἀλλὰ ἐκκλησίας Θεοῦ ὑπηρέται. Tertullian. de Prescrip. Heret., cap. 41. Cyprian. Epist. 65. (ad Rogatian.) Conc. Nic., c. 18.

† On this subject consult Bingham, Eccles. Antiq., b. ii. ch. 20.

‡ Eccles. Antiq., b. i. ch. 5. It is proper here to cite a celebrated passage from Clement's (first) Epistle to the Corinthians, c. 40. Τῷ γὰρ Ἀρχιερεῖ ἴδιαι λειτουργίαι δεδομέναι εἰσι, καὶ τοῖς ἱερεῦσιν ἴδιος ὁ τόπος προστέτακται, καὶ Λευΐταις ἴδιαι διακονίαι ἐπίκεινται· ὁ Λαϊκὸς ἄνθρωπος λαϊκοῖς προστάγμασι δέδεται.

§ Ap. Euseb. H. E. lib. iii., c. 23, κλήρῳ ἕνα γέ τινα κληρώσων τῶν ὑπὸ τοῦ Πνεύματος σημαινομένων, in a passage already cited.

tioned were actually set apart and consecrated to the ministry, and the distinction in question, thus sanctioned by apostolical authority, is an obvious and reasonable inference : yet thus much is not positively asserted.   In the mean time, the separation of the sacred order is so commonly mentioned by the early Fathers, not by Cyprian only, but by his predecessors* Tertullian and Origen, and so invariably treated as a necessary part of the Christian system, that, if its origin was not coeval with the foundation of the system, it is at least unrecorded and immemorial. The fairest supposition respecting this question appears to be, that the *first* converts, those who spread the earliest tidings of redemption before the Apostles themselves had quitted Judæa, were commissioned to preach the name, and diffuse the knowledge of Christ indiscriminately.   But it seems equally certain, that this commission was of very short duration ; and that as soon as in any place converts were found sufficient to form a society or church, a bishop or presbyter† was ordained for life to minister to them.   The act of ordination established the distinction of which we are treating.

According to the earliest form of Episcopal government, it would appear that the bishop possessed little, if any, power in matters of discipline, except with the consent of the council of presbyters ; that the council possessed no sort of power except in conjunction with him‡ ; and that, in affairs strictly spiritual, as the ordination§ of the inferior clergy and

Origin? Polity of the Church

---

* This writer goes so far as severely to censure certain heretics for following the contrary practice. De Præscrip. Heret., c. 41. Among them (he says) " alius hodie Episcopus, cras alius ; hodie Diaconus qui cras Lector ; *hodie Presbyter qui cras Laicus : nam et Laicis Sacerdotalia munera injungunt.*"

† See Epiphan., Hæres. 75 ; Ærian. n. 5, as referred to by Bingham.

‡ We refer to the passages from the Councils of Laodicea, Arles, and Toledo, from Ignatius's Epistles and the Apostolical Canons, and the writings of Tertullian, Jerome, and Ambrose, collected by Bingham, b. ii. ch. 3.

§ When Jerome (Dissert. 85 ad Evagr.) and Chrysostom, in the fourth century (Hom. 2 in 1 Tim. iii. 8), are endeavouring to exalt presbyterial almost to the level of episcopal authority, they agree in considering the power of ordination as constituting the grand, and, as they assert, the only distinction.   It has been argued that the power of preaching was originally confined to the bishops, and from them derived, and by their permission exercised, by the inferior clergy ; the reasons adduced for this opinion are plausible, though not, perhaps, conclusive. —Bingham's Church Antiq., b. ii. ch. 3.

the administration of the sacraments, especially that of baptism*, he acted as some think with original, and certainly with independent, authority. It appears probable (notwithstanding the silence of St. Paul on this subject in his commission to Titus, i. 5) that, in the ceremony of ordination, even in the earliest church, the imposition of hands was performed by certain presbyters, in conjunction with the bishop; but the consecration to the ministry was the act of the bishop only, through the power derived in the first instance from the apostles, and at no time claimed by any inferior order in the church. His office was for life, and the funds of the society were committed to his care and dispensation. Of most of the apostolical churches, the first bishops, where they are recorded to have been at all appointed, were appointed by the apostles: of those not apostolical, the first presidents were probably the missionaries who founded them; but, on their death, the choice of a successor devolved on the members of the society. In this election the people had an equal share with the presbyters and inferior clergy, without exception or distinction; and it is clear that their right in this matter was not barely testimonial, but judicial and elective†.

Independence of the Churches. This appointment was final, requiring no confirmation from the civil power or any superior prelate; and thus, in the management of its internal affairs, every church was essentially independent of every other.

The Churches, thus constituted and regulated, formed a sort of federative body of independent religious communities, dispersed through the greater part of the empire, in continual com-

---

* Mosh. Gen. Hist. (c. i. p. ii. ch. 4. sec. 7 and 8.) When the bishop extended the rite of baptism to presbyters and suffragan bishops (Chorepiscopi), he still reserved to himself the exclusive power of *confirmation.*—Bingham's Church Antiq., p. ii, ch. 3.

† This is made very clear, from the comparison of much contradictory evidence, by Bingham, Ch. Hist., b. iv. ch. 2. sec. 2, 3, 4, &c. There were some variations in the mode of election, according to times and circumstances, since no rule is laid down in Scripture on the subject; but there is a great concurrence of evidence to show that no bishop was ever obtruded on an orthodox people without their consent. Mosheim (c. i. p. ii. ch. 2) attributes a great extent of general power to the people, not only in the election of their teachers, but in the control of their conduct, and even extends it to decision on controverted points and excommunication of unworthy members. We are not aware on what authority he advances these assertions.

munication, and in constant harmony with each other. It is about the middle of the second century that the first change is perhaps perceptible: as the numbers of the believers and the limits of the faith were extended, some diversities in doctrine or discipline would naturally grow up, which it was not found easy to reconcile, except by some description of general assembly. Accordingly, we find the first instances of such assemblies* (unless that which was summoned by the Apostles may be so called) about this period. They were composed, either of the bishops only, or of these associated with a part of the priesthood: those ministers presented themselves as the representatives of their respective societies; nor was any superiority claimed by any of them in virtue of the supposed pre-eminence of particular Churches. These councils were called by the Greek name Councils, Synods, and seem at first to have been provincial, following in or Synods. some manner the political division of the empire. They had their origin in Greece†—the land of public assemblies and popular institutions, of which the memory was fondly cherished there, after the reality had been lost in Roman despotism. Their character was essentially popular; the representatives of equal Churches, elected to their sacred offices by the whole body over which they presided, assembled to deliberate as equals; and we may reasonably indulge the belief, since the exertion of freedom in any one direction makes it more ready to act in every other, that the political emancipation of mankind was promoted, even thus early, by the free and advancing spirit of Christianity.

Such were the principles on which the affairs of the Churches were conducted for some time after the period mentioned by us; and none can be conceived more favourable to the progress of the faith. The government of a single person protected each society from internal dissension—the electiveness of that governor rendered probable his merit—the meeting together of

---

* We believe the view of Mosheim upon this subject to be very nearly correct. C. 1. p. ii. ch. 2.

† " Aguntur per Græcias illa certis in locis concilia, per quæ et altiora quæque in commune tractantur; et ipsa repræsentatio totius nominis Christiani magna veneratione celebratur." Tertullian (De Jejunii, c. xiii.) wrote at the end of this century.

the deputies of the Churches, in occasional assemblies, on equal terms, taught the scattered members of the faith that they were animated by one soul, and informed and dignified by one spirit. Some evil will be expected to arise out of much good; and evils of some importance have been attributed to the necessary frequency of synods. The first was an early addition to the orders and gradations of the hierarchy; for, as it was soon discovered that these provincial Councils required the control of a President, the Bishop of the capital of the province was usually

The Metro-politan. appointed to that office, under the lofty title of the *Metropolitan**. From an occasional office he presently assumed a permanent dignity; and his dignity was insufficient until it was attended by authority. Again, the ecclesiastics who composed them properly appeared there in no other character than as the deputies of their Churches. But it may sometimes have happened, that on their return home they individually assumed some part of the *power* which they had possessed collectively: at least, it is certain that many notions, respecting the exalted and irresistible nature of episcopal authority†, were already floating about the Christian world—and the Bishop was not likely to disclaim the homage which would occasionally be offered to him. But it was not until the habit of acting in bodies made them sensible of their common interest and real power that they ventured to assert such claims, and assumed a loftier manner in the government of their dioceses‡: so that, though these synods were doubtless indispensable to the well-being of Christianity, they seem to have been the means of corrupting the original humility of its ministers; and the method,

---

* Mosh., Gen. Hist., c. ii. p. ii. ch. 2; and De Rebus Christ. ante Const., Secul. ii. sect. xxiii.

† The Epistles attributed to Ignatius are the earliest writings which countenance such claims; and they were afterwards more boldly advocated by Cyprian, Bishop of Carthage. In fact, we should remark that Ignatius exalts the presbyterial with almost as much zeal as the episcopal order, and that his object was rather to increase the authority of the whole ministry, than to elevate any branch of it.

‡ For some ages more properly called *parishes*, παροικιαι. As Eusebius (l. vii. 14), speaking of Anianus, the first Bishop of Alexandria, calls him τῆς κατ' Ἀλεξανδρείαν παροικίας ὁ ὄπρῶτος, et passim; and Eusebius wrote in the fourth century.

which was intended to promote only the eternal interests of the Church, promoted, in some degree, the worldly consideration of the order which governed it.   This change began to show itself towards the end of the second century; and it is certain that at this period, we find the first complaints of the incipient corruption of the clergy.   From the moment that the interests of the ministers became at all distinguished from the interests of the religion, the corruption of Christianity may be considered to have begun.   On the other hand, there can be little doubt that the increased authority and influence of the hierarchy was highly serviceable to the whole body in periods of danger and persecution; and that in those times it was generally exerted to excite the courage, and sustain the constancy of the faithful.

Excommunication was the oldest weapon of ecclesiastical authority.   Doubtless, every society has the right to expel its unworthy members; and this right was of extreme use to the first Christians, as it gave them frequent opportunities of exhibiting to the heathen world the scrupulousness of their moral purity.   But afterwards we know how dangerous an engine it became, when wielded by weak or passionate individuals, and directed by caprice, or interest, or ambition. *Excommunication.*

The question has been greatly controverted, whether an absolute community of property ever subsisted in the Church.   That it did so is a favourite opinion of some Roman Catholic writers, who would willingly discover, in the first apostolical society, the model of the monastic system; and the same, to its utmost extent, has been partly asserted, and partly insinuated by Gibbon.   The learned argument of Mosheim* disposes us to the contrary belief; and if the words of Scripture in one place † should seem to prove that such community did actually exist among the original converts in the Church of Jerusalem, we are obliged to infer from other passages‡, not only that it did not universally prevail as one law of the whole Church, but that *Community of Property.*

---

* Dissertationes ad Hist. Eccl. pertinentes, vol. ii.   Mosheim's object is to prove that St. Luke means community of *use*, not of *possession.*   Some suppose the passage in Acts v. 4 to be at variance with that opinion.

† Acts iv. 32, 34, 35.

‡ Acts v. 4. " After it was sold, was it not in thine own power?"

it gained no favour or footing in the several Churches which were founded elsewhere.   This inference is generally confirmed by the uninspired records of Christianity; and it is indeed obvious that a society of both sexes, constituted on that principle, could not possibly have had a permanent existence.   The truth appears to be this, that the ministers of religion, and the poorer brethren, were maintained by contributions perfectly voluntary, and that a great and general intercourse of mutual support and charity prevailed, as well among the various Churches as among the members of each.

It is probable that the ceremonies of religion had somewhat outstripped their primitive simplicity, even before the conclusion of the second century.   Some additions were introduced even thus early, out of a spirit of conciliation with the various forms of Paganism which were beginning gradually to melt into Christianity; but they were seemingly different in different countries; and it is not easy, nor perhaps very important, to detect them with certainty, or to enumerate them with confidence.   We shall recur to this subject at a future period, when a better acquaintance with the innovations of following ages will enable the reader to form a juster estimate of the earliest[*].

The Lord's Day.
The primitive Christians were unanimous[†] in setting apart the first day of the week, as being that on which our Saviour rose from the dead, for the solemn celebration of public worship. This pious custom was derived from the example of the Church of Jerusalem, on the express appointment of the Apostles.   On these occasions, portions of Scripture were publicly read to the people from the earliest age.

Origin of Festivals.
The two most ancient feasts of the Church were in honour of the Resurrection of Christ, and of the descent of the Holy Spirit. At a period when belief must almost have amounted to knowledge, the first Christians, the companions of the Apostles, perhaps the disciples of our Saviour himself, were so seriously

---

[*] We refer the reader to the thirteenth chapter; to which place we have purposely deferred some facts connected with the earliest ages, and which, taken in conjunction with the first five chapters, will complete our history of the ante-Nicene Church.

[†] Mosh. Gen. Hist., l. i. p. ii. c. 4.

and practically earnest in their belief, and so satisfied of the
generality of that belief, in the truth of those two mighty miracles which have presented, perhaps, the greatest difficulties
to the sceptical inquirers of after ages, as to establish their first
two festivals in solemn commemoration of them.

The only day set apart for public fasting by the primitive Fasts.
Christians was that of the crucifixion.   But we must infer from
a passage of Clemens Alexandrinus *, that both the Wednesday
and Friday of every week were dedicated to that purpose, at
least at Alexandria, before the end of the second century.   The
facts which we learn from Tertullian † on this subject are, that
no Christians fasted on Sunday, not even the Montanists; that
the people were on no occasion prohibited from fasting; and
that the bishops had the power of enjoining general fasts, in
their own dioceses, on particular occasions.   And Justin informs
us, at a still earlier age, that both the convert and the congregation were prepared for the ceremony of baptism by abstinence.
From these circumstances we must infer, that such mortification
was considered, even in the earliest ages, a work of piety; but
that it was exercised with moderation, and partook in no degree
of the superstitious austerity of later times.

Christian schools seem to have existed in the second century, Schools.
at Rome, Ephesus, and Smyrna ‡; but the catechetical school
established at Alexandria was clearly the most important
among the early literary institutions of Christianity.   They
were conducted on the model of the schools of philosophy, and
even the terms, by which the different classes of the faithful
were designated, were borrowed from these latter.   There
appears to have been as yet no costume peculiar to the minis-

---

* Stromatum, lib. viii. p. 744. Edit. Lutet. Clemens is fanciful, or (to use his
own expression) *ænigmatical* on the subject; but the passage proves the *fact.*
Οἶδεν αὐτὸς καὶ τῆς νηστείας τὰ αἰνίγματα τῶν ἡμέρων τούτων—τῆς Τετράδος καὶ τῆς
Παρασκευῆς λέγω· ἐπιφημίζονται γὰρ ἡ μὲν Ἑρμοῦ, ἡ δὲ Ἀφροδίτης, &c.

† De Corona Mil. iii. "Die Dominico jejunium nefas ducimus" and De Jejuniis, passim.

‡ Some infer the existence of a school at Smyrna, under the direction of Polycarp, from the affecting passage of Irenæus ad Florinum ap. Euseb. v. 20—and of
one at Ephesus from that of Irenæus adv. Hæres., ii, xxii. (p. 148. ed. Massuet.)
Neither authority is perfectly conclusive.

ters of religion. The bishops usually adopted the garb of the heathen philosophers.

Canon of Scripture.

III. It is affirmed by Eusebius, that the four Gospels were collected during the life of St. John, and that the other three received the approbation of that apostle *. And though there is great difficulty in ascertaining the precise period, in which all the books of the New Testament were collected into one volume, it is unquestionable, that before the middle of the second century the greatest part of them were received as the rule of faith in every Christian society. We have already noticed the compilation made by Melito about that time. The distinction between the sacred and apocryphal writers which is laid down by Eusebius (lib. iii. cap. 25) is given on the authority of much earlier ages.

Expositions of faith.

The following expositions of faith are found in the works of Tertullian. "We believe in one God—but under the following dispensation or economy—that there is also a Son of God, His Word, who proceeded from him; by whom all things were made, and without whom nothing was made; who was sent by him into the Virgin and was born of her; being both man and God, the Son of Man and the Son of God, and called Jesus Christ; He suffered, died and was buried, according to the Scriptures; and was raised up again by the Father; and was taken up into Heaven, there to sit at the right hand of the Father; and thence to come to judge the quick and the dead; who sent from Heaven, from his Father, according to his promise, the Holy Ghost, the Comforter, the Sanctifier of the faith of all who believe in the Father, Son, and Holy Ghost†." Again— "We have only one rule of faith, single, immoveable, unalterable—to believe in one omnipotent God, the maker of the world; and his Son Jesus Christ; who was born of the Virgin Mary, crucified under Pontius Pilate; who on the third day rose from the dead; who sits on the right hand of the Father; and who

---

* Lib. iii. cap. 24. Τῶν προαναγραφέντων τριῶν ἑστάντας ἤδη καὶ ἐς αὐτὸν διαδιδομένων, ἀποδίξασθαι μὲν φασὶν, ἀλήθειαν αὐτοῖς ἐπιμαρτυρήσαντα. See Mosh., cent. i. p. ii. c. 2.

† Tertull. adversus Praxeam, sect. ii.

will come to judge both the quick and the dead, in the resurrection of the flesh*."

From these expressions, which might be confirmed by others from other writers, we can scarcely avoid the inference, that the early Church maintained the same belief respecting the Trinity, which was inculcated by subsequent councils, and received by the great majority of Christians in all ages.   At the same time it must be recollected, that the first Christians used no written Creed: the Confession of Faith, which was held necessary for Creeds. salvation, was delivered to children or converts by word of mouth, and entrusted to their memory.   Moreover, in the several independent Churches, the rule of faith was liable to some slight changes, according to the opinion and discretion of the Bishop presiding in each.   Hence it arose, that when the creeds of those numerous communities came at length to be written and compared together, they were found to contain some variations.   This was natural and necessary; but when we add, that those variations were for the most part merely verbal, and in no instance involved any question of essential importance, we advance a truth which will seem strange to those who are familiar with the angry disputations of later ages.   But the fact is easily accounted for,—the earliest pastors of the Church drew their belief from the Scripture itself, as delivered to them by writing or preaching, and they were contented to express that belief in the language of Scripture.   They were not curious to investigate that which is not clearly revealed, but they adhered firmly and faithfully to that which they *knew* to be true; therefore their variations were without schism and their differences without acrimony.   The creed which was first adopted, and seemingly in the very earliest age, by the Church of Rome, was that ingly in the very earliest age, by the Church of Rome, was that which is now called the Apostles'. Creed; and it was the general opinion, from the fourth century downwards, that it was actually the production of those blessed persons assembled for that purpose. The evidence † is not sufficient to establish that fact, and some

The Apostles' Creed.

---

* Tertull. De Virgin. Veland. sect. i.

† Ignatius, Justin, and Irenæus make no mention of it, but they occasionally repeat some words contained in it, which is held as proof that they knew it by heart.—See Cent. Magdeb., cent. i. lib. ii. c. 4.

writers * very confidently reject it.   But there is reasonable
ground for our assurance, that the form of faith which we still
repeat and inculcate was in use and honour in the very early propagation of the religion.   The original form of worship appears,
generally, to have been as follows.   First, prayers were offered
in common; then some portion of Scripture was read by a deacon;
then followed the sermon by the bishop or presbyter, which was
followed by prayer.   And afterwards, if any " prophet" felt himself divinely moved to address the congregation, he was permitted
to speak.   This simple form was altered on the subsequent
division of the converts into faithful and catechumens†.

The Sacra-
ment of
Baptism.

The sacraments of the primitive Church were two—those of
Baptism and the Lord's Supper.   The ceremony of immersion
(the oldest form of baptism) was performed in the name of the
three Persons of the Trinity; it was believed to be attended by
the remission of original sin, and the entire regeneration of the
infant or convert, by the passage from the land of bondage into
the kingdom of salvation.   " I will tell you (says Justin Martyr, Apol. A. s. 79) in what manner we consecrate ourselves to
God, being renewed through Jesus Christ.   .   . Whosoever
have faith, and believe that our teaching is true, and promise to
live conformably to it, are instructed to pray and with fasting to
ask of God the remission of their sins, while we pray and fast
along with them.   Then they are led by us to some place where
there is water, and are made regenerate even as ourselves were
regenerated; for they are immersed in this water, in the name
of the Father, Lord of all things, and of our Saviour, Jesus
Christ, and of the Holy Ghost."   The practice of anointing the
baptized with oil, as a part of the sacred ceremony, may have been
much older than the time of Tertullian, though it is first mentioned by him (De Baptismo, l. vii).   "Immediately after baptism
(he says) we are anointed with the blessed unction, according to
the ancient discipline by which men were anointed, from the
horn, to the priesthood."   So (Cyprian Ep. 70) expressly says,
while speaking in the name of a synod, "that it is *necessary* for the

---

* As Mosheim, cent. i. p. ii. ch. 3; admitting, however, (c. ii. p. ii. ch. 3) that the
first teachers inculcated no other doctrines than those contained in what is commonly called the Apostles' Creed.

† Mosh. Reb. Christ. Ant. Const. sec. i. s. 47.

baptized to be anointed—to the end that he may be made God's anointed and receive the grace of Christ." The source of this custom sufficiently appears from these passages—and it seems to have proceeded on the fanciful notion, that every Christian was consecrated at his baptism into a sort of spiritual priesthood.

A great proportion of those baptized in the first ages were, of course, adults; and since the Church was then scrupulous to admit none among its members, excepting those whose sincere repentance gave promise of a holy life, the administration of that sacrament was in some sense accompanied by the remission, not only of the sin from Adam, but of all sin that had been previously committed by the proselyte—that is to say, such absolution was given to the repentance necessary for admission into Christ's Church. In after ages, by an error common in the growth of superstition, the efficacy inherent in the repentance was attributed to the ceremony, and the act which washed away the inherited corruption of nature was supposed to secure a general impunity, even for unrepented offences. But this double delusion gained very little ground during the first two centuries *.

Justin Martyr proceeds, in the lxxxvth section, to describe the celebration of the Eucharist †, which then followed baptism. *The Eucharist.* "After having thus baptized the convert, we lead him to the assembly of those whom we call brethren; and to offer up our common prayers, both for ourselves, and for him who is regenerated (τοῦ φωτισθέντος) and for the whole body of the faithful, that we may be found worthy, through our knowledge of the truth, and our practice of good works, and our observance of the commandments, to obtain eternal salvation. After prayers, we salute each other with a kiss. Then the president (προεστὼς) of the brethren brings to him bread and a cup of water and wine. He takes it, and offers up praise and glory to the Father of all things, through the name of his Son and of the Holy Ghost; and a long thanksgiving *(Eucharist)*, that he has thought us

---

* For instance, Tertullian (De Pœnitentia, ch. vi.) expressly says—"Lavacrum illud obsignatio est fidei: quæ fides a pœnitentiæ fide incipitur et commendatur. Non ideo abluimur, ut delinquere desinamus, sed quia desiimus—quoniam jam corde loti sumus."

· † We shall defer any general account of the earliest liturgies till the xiiith chapter: because the consideration of that subject will require in the reader some acquaintance with the events and characters of ages later than the second.

worthy of this blessing. When he has finished the Prayer
and the Eucharist, all the people assent, saying Amen . . .
Then those, whom we call Deacons, distribute to every one
present a portion of the consecrated (εὐχαριστηθέντος) bread,
and cup of wine and water, and carry part away to the
absent. This nourishment (τροφή) is by us called Eucharist;
and no one can partake of it, except those who believe that our
doctrine is true, and who have been baptized for the remission of
sins and regeneration, and *who live according to the commandments of Christ**."

The Agape   The celebration of the sacrament of the Eucharist was origi-
or Love   nally accompanied by a meeting which somewhat partook of a
Feast.
hospitable, or at least of a charitable character, and was called
Agape, or a Feast of Love.   Every Christian, according to his
circumstances, brought to the assembly portions of bread, wine,
and other things, as gifts, as it were, or oblations to the Lord.
Of the bread and wine such portion as was required for the administration of the sacrament was separated from the rest, and
consecrated (as we have perceived) by the bishop or president
alone; its distribution was followed by a frugal and serious repast.
The character of the Agape is described with some minuteness
by Tertullian, and vindicated from the calumnies which even
in his time were cast upon it.   Its very name, he says, signifies
affection: it is very far indeed from costly; and the little cost
that is made, is made in the cause of piety, since it becomes the
means of relieving the poor.   Such being the object of the
feast, its nature may be thence inferred.   It admits nothing
vile, nothing immodest; and it is preceded by a prayer to God.
There is no indulgence inconsistent with decency, and with the
prayers which are afterwards to be offered—no conversation
which is not intended for the ears of God.   When supper is
over, every one is invited to sing praises to God, either from
Holy Scripture or from his own genius, each according to his

---

* The passage which follows, as it has been differently interpreted, we shall
give in the original. Οὐ γὰρ ὡς κοινὸν ἄρτον, οὐδὲ κοινὸν πόμα, ταῦτα λαμβάνομεν·
ἀλλ' ὃν τρόπον διὰ Λόγου Θεοῦ σαρκοποιηθεὶς Ἰησοῦς Χριστὸς, ὁ Σωτὴρ ἡμῶν, καὶ σάρκα
καὶ αἷμα ὑπὲρ σωτηρίας ἡμῶν ἔσχεν, οὕτως καὶ τὴν δι' εὐχῆς λόγου τοῦ παρ' αὐτοῦ εὐχα-
ριστηθεῖσαν τροφὴν, ἐξ ἧς αἷμα καὶ σάρκες κατὰ μεταβολὴν τρέφονται ἡμῶν, ἐκείνου τοῦ
σαρκοποιηθέντος Ἰησοῦ καὶ σάρκα καὶ αἷμα ἐδιδάχθημεν εἶναι.

ability.   And when they separate, it is not for any purpose of impurity or lasciviousness, but with the chaste and decorous deportment of men, who have made their temperate meal an instrument of moral discipline*.

The above is probably, for the most part, a faithful representation; and if so, there can be no question that those assemblies acted not only as excitements to piety, but also as bonds of strict religious union and mutual devotion, during the dark days of terror and persecution.   It was probably on those occasions, more than any other, that the sufferers rallied their scattered ranks, and encouraged each other, by one solemn act of brotherly communion, to constancy in one faith and association in the same afflictions.   We observe moreover, that, as the dangers passed away from the Church, that more social form † (if we may so express it) of eucharistical administration gradually fell into disuse.

As in the earlier ages the necessity of constant communion among the members of every Church was strictly inculcated, the sacrament was administered every day.   And even in the first half of the third century there was a treatise written by the learned Hippolytus on the question—"Whether a man ought to communicate daily, or at stated seasons."   But after some time the sacrament was confined to the Sunday worship.   It was likewise this same anxiety for universal communion, which gave occasion to the custom of sending the consecrated elements to the absent brethren.   And it was a practice usual, though not perhaps peculiar, to the Church of Carthage, to communicate infants immediately after baptism—which we are to disposed to ascribe to the same cause.   Though some attribute it to a false notion, which they suppose to have prevailed even in the first ages, that the outward participation of the Lord's supper comprehended all that is said in John vi. of eating the flesh and drinking the

---

* Apologet. chap. 31.   After his apostacy to Montanism, Tertullian (De Jeju_niis, c. 17) vented in one very gross sentence what is generally understood to be a charge against these Feasts.   The passage is obscure.   And at any rate, a single passionate expression cannot be weighed against the particular and deliberate evidence conveyed in the text.   Doubtless, there is also some exaggeration in his eulogy—but we can scarcely question that the substance was, *in his, age,* true.

† Acts ii. 42.   Hinds' Early Ch., vol. ii. p. 211, &c.

blood of Christ, and was consequently entirely necessary for the attainment of salvation*.

Marriage.

That the rite of Marriage was a religious solemnity from the earliest times is proved by an injunction of Ignatius in his epistle to Polycarp †:—" It is meet that the parties enter into the union with the sanction of the bishop; that their marriage may be after God, and not after their lusts." The bride and bridegroom then received the communion, and offered a common gift to the Church. And then, in the prayer of the Church, connected with the communion, a blessing was invoked on the marriage. That such was the practice at the end of the second century we have the authority of Tertullian ‡. " How shall we describe the happiness of that marriage, which is concluded by the Church, and confirmed by the Communion, and sealed by the Benediction ? which angels register; and our Father ratifies in Heaven?"

The Morality of the Primitive Church.

IV. The morality of the primitive Church is a subject to which we proceed with high confidence and unalloyed satisfaction; for since, in the various history on which we are entering, our admiration of the excellence of Christianity will be sometimes interrupted by sighs for the degeneracy of its professors, it is delightful to pause on that period when the faith, yet fresh from Heaven, did really carry practice and devotion along with it—a period which preceded the birth of intestine persecution, and was undisturbed by the furious contests of sectaries; which did not witness the superstitious debasement of the Church, nor the vulgar vices of its ministers, nor the burning passions of its rulers. We are taught, indeed, humbly to believe, that at some future, and probably distant period, the whole world will be united in the true spirit and practice of Christianity; but in reviewing the history of the past, we are compelled to confess, that the only model at all approaching to that perfection is confined to the first two centuries, and that it began to fall off in excellence even before the conclusion of that period. But

* See Neander's excellent account of " the several Rites of the Christian Religion," sect. iii. (d).

† Sect. v. πρέπει δὲ ταῖς γαμοῦσι καὶ ταῖς γαμουμέναις μετὰ γνώμης τοῦ Ἐπισκόπου τὴν ἕνωσιν ποιεῖσθαι, ἵν ὁ γάμος ἦ κατὰ Θεὸν καὶ μὴ κατ᾽ ἐπιθυμίαν.

‡ Lib. ii. Ad Uxorem. s. v. " Quod Ecclesia conciliat, et confirmat Oblatio, et obsignat Benedictio : Angeli renunciant ; Pater pro rato habet."

transient as it was, we still recur to it with pious satisfaction, and we rejoice, both as men and as Christians, that our nature has been found capable of such holy exaltation, and that our religion was the instrument which exalted it.

Certainly the character of the first Christians, and we are not without guides who make us acquainted with it, presents to us a *singular* spectacle of virtue and piety, the more splendid as it was surrounded by very mournful and very general depravity. We cannot read either St. Clement's description of the early condition of the Church of Corinth, or Origen's panegyric on that of Athens, without recognising a state of society and morality such as all the annals of paganism do not discover to us, and such as its principles (if it had any fixed principles) could not ever have created. The following lines are a quotation from the former. "You were all humble in spirit, nothing boasting, subject rather than subjecting, giving rather than receiving. Contented with the food of God, and carefully embracing his words, your feelings were expanded, and his sufferings were before your eyes—so profound and beautiful the peace that was given to all of you, and so insatiable the desire of beneficence, and so abundant the effusion of the Holy Spirit which had reached you all. You contended night and day for all the brotherhood, that the number of the elect might be completed. You were sincere and pure, free from all revengeful spirit. Every division, every schism was detestable to you; *you wept over the failings of your neighbours;* you thought their defects your own, and were impatient after every good work," &c. It is true that soon after the period celebrated by this glowing description, some dissensions disturbed the peace, and possibly the morality, of the Church of Corinth; but we have no reason to believe that they were of long duration, or left any lasting consequences behind them.

The above passage refers to the Christians of Greece; and there is a sentence in the letter of Pliny to Trajan, already cited, which gives still stronger testimony to the virtues of the Asiatics. "They bind themselves by an oath, not to the commission of any wickedness, but not to be guilty of theft, or robbery, or adultery,—never to falsify their word, nor to deny a pledge committed to them, when called upon to return it."

Testimony of St. Clement.

Of Pliny.

Of Barde-
sanes.

Bardesanes, a learned Christian of Mesopotamia, who lived in the time of Marcus Antoninus, has the following passage, preserved to us by Eusebius. "Neither do Christians in Parthia indulge in polygamy, though they are Parthians; nor do they marry their own daughters in Persia, though Persians. Among the Bactrians and the Gauls, they do not commit adultery; but, wheresoever they are, they rise above the evil laws and customs of the country." This is not only a very powerful, but almost an universal testimony in favour of Christian morality; and there are some to whom its truth will appear the less questionable, because it comes from the pen of a heretic.

The virtue of chastity, which however it may have been celebrated in the heroic ages of paganism, was certainly little reputed in the East during the more enlightened rule of philosophy, was very rigidly cultivated by the primitive converts. This truth,

Of Justin
Martyr

which is generally attested by the passages above quoted, is made the subject of peculiar exultation by Justin Martyr*. Howbeit the continence of the first Christians did not degenerate into any superstitious principle in the ages immediately subsequent, the simple practice of the Gospel began to be unreasonably exaggerated; and somewhat later the progress of monasticism was forwarded by the exalted value placed on that virtue. So that excess of admiration blinded enthusiasts as to its real nature and character, and led them to invest it with perfections and pretensions, which were at variance with the advancement and happiness of human society.

The heathen governments, even the Roman, in its highest civilization, tolerated, and perhaps encouraged, the unnatural practice of exposing infants, who in that condition were left, as it might happen, to perish from cold or starvation, or to be preserved for the more dreadful fate of public prostitution. This practice was held in deserved detestation by the followers of Christ†.

Benefi-
cence of

Charity was the corner-stone of the moral edifice of Chris-

* C. 18. Apol. A. Πολλοί τινες καὶ πολλαὶ, ἑξηκοντούται καὶ ἑβδομηκοντούται, οἱ ἐκ παίδων ἐμαθητεύθησαν τῷ Χριστῷ, ἄφθοροι διαμένουσι. καὶ εὔχομαι κατὰ πᾶν γένος ἀνθρώπων τοσούτους δεῖξαι. Origen (Contr. Cels. l. vii. p. 365, ed. Cantab.) is more diffuse on the same subject.

† Justin Martyr, Apol. A., c. 36, edit. Cantab.

tianity, and its earliest characteristic; and as this is still the virtue by which it is most distinguished, both publicly and privately, from every false religion, so we need not hesitate to avow, that this of all its excellences was the most efficient under Divine providence in its original establishment. Every Christian society provided for the maintenance of its poorer members; and when the funds were not sufficient for this purpose, they were aided by the superfluities of more wealthy brethren. In this generous rivalry we must not forget to assign the foremost station and the highest praise to the Church of Rome. The greater means, which greater wealth and numbers conferred on her, were employed as became her apostolical origin, and her claims of supremacy—claims which were indeed placed on their surest foundation when they rested on the gratitude of the faithful. It is in the following expressions that Dionysius, the distinguished Bishop of Corinth*, addressed the Roman Church about the year 156. "This has been your custom from the beginning, to confer benefits on all the brethren, and to send relief to various churches in every city. By which means, while you assist the indigent, while you relieve the brethren who are in the mines, and continually persist in such donations, you persevere, like Romans, in the hereditary usage of Romans. And this practice your excellent Bishop Soter not only preserves, but extends, by making generous donations to the saints who come to him from abroad, and edifying them by excellent discourse, as an affectionate father treats his children." It would appear, indeed, that on the occasion of any extraordinary calamity the Bishops caused collections to be made, which they distributed at their own discretion; and that Christians, who were condemned to the mines, or banished, or imprisoned, or shipwrecked, were considered as peculiar objects of charitable relief.

The same spirit, which preached the Gospel to the poor, extended its provisions to their temporal necessities; and so far from thinking it any reproach to our faith that it first addressed itself, by its peculiar virtues as well as precepts, to the lower orders of mankind, we derive from this very fact our strongest

* Apud Euseb. iv. 23.

argument against those who would persuade us that the patronage of kings was necessary for its establishment: it rather
becomes to us matter of pious exultation that its progress was
precisely in the opposite direction.   It cannot be too frequently
repeated, that by far the majority of the early converts were
men of low rank; and their numbers were concealed by their
obscurity, until they became too powerful to dread persecution.
Every step which they took was *upwards*.   Until the middle
of the second century, they could scarcely discover among their
thousands one learned man.   From the schools they advanced
into the senate, and from the senate to the throne; and they
had possessed themselves of every other office in society, before
they attained the highest.   It is important to attend to this
fact, that we may not be misled; it is important to observe, that
the basis from which the pyramid started up was the faith and
constancy of the *common people*—the spirit of the religion, and
the earliest government of the Church, was popular; and it is
in its earliest history that we find those proofs of general moral
purity, on which we now dwell with the more pleasure, because,
in succeeding pages, the picture will never again be presented
to us.

We will make one short extract from the writings of a very
witty pagan of the second century, which throws great light on
Testimony of Lucian. the character of the Christians of that age.   Lucian, who considered every form of worship as equally an object of ridicule,
tells a story of one Peregrinus, who had been expelled from his
country, Armenia, for the most horrible crimes; who thence
wandered into Palestine, became acquainted with the doctrine
of the Christians, and affected to embrace it.   Being a man of
talents and education, he acquired great influence among their
illiterate body; and, in consequence, he soon attracted the notice of the Roman governor, and was thrown into prison for
being a Christian.   In prison he is represented to have been
consoled by the pious charity of the faithful:—" There came
Christians, deputed from many cities in Asia, to relieve, to encourage, and to comfort him : for the care and diligence which
the Christians exert on these occasions is incredible—in a word,
they spare nothing.   They sent, therefore, large sums to Pere-

grinus, and his confinement was an occasion of amassing great riches : for these poor creatures are firmly persuaded they shall one day enjoy eternal life; therefore they despise death with wonderful courage, and offer themselves voluntarily to punishment.   Their first lawgiver has taught them that they are all brethren, when once they have passed over and renounced the gods of the Greeks, and worship that Master of theirs who was crucified, and regulate their manner and conduct by his laws.   They despise, therefore, all earthly possessions, and look upon them as common, having received such rules without any certain grounds of faith.   Therefore, if any juggler, or cunning fellow, who knows how to make his advantage of opportunity, happens to get into their society, he immediately grows rich; because it is easy to abuse the simplicity of these silly people." We have no reason to complain of such a description from the pen of an adversary; for, on the one hand, it attributes to our ancestors in faith boundless charity, zeal inexhaustible, brotherly love, contempt of death and of all earthly possessions, and a steady adherence to the faith and precepts of Christ; on the other hand, it lays no charge against them except simplicity, the usual associate of innocence.

There is one quality mentioned in the above passage which we shall take occasion to notice hereafter, without entirely over-looking it now; the suffering courage of the persecuted.   We consider it a strong proof of the lively faith of the sufferers in the atoning merits of their Saviour—since it could seldom pro-ceed from any other conviction, than that the change which they were about to undergo would lead them to a state of recom-pense; a confidence which seems scarcely consistent with the consciousness of unrepented sin.   Such, at least, we know to have been the impression sometimes produced on the more en-lightened, even among the heathen spectators.   The ancient author of the Second Apology, attributed we think truly to Justin Martyr, urges this proof with much fervour and rea-son*; and the conversion of Justin himself is, in a great degree,

---

* Cap. 12.   καὶ γὰρ αὐτὸς ἐγὼ τοῖς Πλάτωνος χαίρων διδάγμασι, διαβαλλομένους ἀκούων Χριστιανοὺς, ὁρῶν δὲ ἀφόβους πρὸς θάνατον, καὶ πάντα τὰ ἄλλα νομιζόμενα φόβερα, ἐνενοοῦν ἀδύνατον εἶναι ἐν κακίᾳ καὶ φιληδονίᾳ ὑπάρχειν αὐτούς.

ascribed to the persuasion of Christian excellence and sincerity, wrought in him by those awful spectacles.

Of Justin Martyr.

We shall here insert a short quotation from his First Apology (c. xvii.):—" We who formerly rejoiced in licentiousness, now embrace only chastity; we who made use of magical arts, now devote ourselves to the unbegotten God, the God of goodness; we who set our whole affections upon wealth and possessions, now bring into the common stock all our property, and share it with the indigent; we who hated each other, and slew each other, and who, owing to diversity of customs, would not partake of the same hearth with those of a different race, now, since the appearance of Christ, live together, and *pray for our enemies,* and endeavour to persuade those who unjustly hate us, that, by leading a life conformed to the excellent precepts of Christianity, they may be filled with the good hope of obtaining the same happiness with ourselves from that God, who is Lord above all things *."

ON THE EARLY FATHERS.

As we have made frequent mention of the principal writers, commonly called Fathers, of the ancient Church, we shall subjoin to this chapter a very short account of some of the earliest among them. We do not profess any blind veneration for their names, or submission to their opinions; but we are very far removed from the contempt of either. For if we are to bend to any human *authority* (as in such matters some of us must always do, and all of us sometimes), those are assuredly the safest objects of our reverence who stood nearest to the source of revelation, and received the cup of knowledge from the very hands of the Apostles. They were erring and feeble mortals, like ourselves; much inferior in intellectual discipline, and vitiated by early prejudices necessarily proceeding from the oblique principles and perverse systems of their day. Nevertheless, they were earnest and ardent Christians; in respect at least to their religion they had access to infallible instructors, and the lessons which they have transmitted to us, howsoever imperfectly transmitted, should be received with attention and respect.

* See also Lactant. Div. Inst., lib. iii., c. 26.

The Apostolical Fathers are those who were contemporary with the Apostles; some of whom are known, and all of whom may be reasonably believed, to have shared their conversation, and profited by their instruction. These are Barnabas, Clement of Rome, Hermas, Ignatius and Polycarp. They were all (excepting probably Clement) natives of the East, and all originally wrote in the Greek language. The works which have reached us under their names are not numerous; and though the genuineness of some of them has been justly suspected, there is no reason to doubt the very high antiquity of all. They were composed with various objects, according to the dispositions or circumstances of their writers. The design of the epistle attributed to Barnabas was to abate the respect for the peculiar rites and institutions of the Jewish laws, and to show that they were not binding upon Christians. The ' Shepherd of Hermas ' consists of three books, in the first of which are four Visions, in the second twelve Commands, in the third ten Similitudes. The first and third parts are of course very fanciful, yet were they not perhaps unsuited to the genius of the countries and age to which they were addressed; the second contains some excellent moral precepts; and all abound with paraphrastical allusions to the books of the New Testament.

Barnabas.

Hermas.

During the journey from Antioch to Rome, which ended in his martyrdom, Ignatius addressed seven epistles to the Churches of Smyrna, Ephesus, Magnesia, Philadelphia, Tralles, and Rome; and to Polycarp of Smyrna. Five other Epistles were for some time received as his composition, which are now admitted to be spurious; and the seven, of which he was really the author, were, in the dark and wicked ages of the church, so enlarged, corrupted, and interpolated, that the original expressions remained only as a basis for impudent and interested forgeries. It was not till the year 1646 that Isaac Vossius published the genuine Epistles, from a MS. which he found at Florence—for their genuineness is now acknowledged beyond dispute by the general consent of the learned. They are extremely valuable documents—not as putting forth any complete form or summary of faith, or any elaborate exposition of the earliest government of the Church—

Ignatius.

His Epistles.

but as containing many incidental expressions, which illustrate both those subjects; and abounding besides with various warm expressions of unaffected piety.

His Eccle-
siastical
Principles.

Ignatius is generally represented to have been the first Christian writer who exalted beyond its just rank the episcopal dignity; whether truly so, will be best ascertained by citing some of his most remarkable expressions on the subject of the ministry of the Church. " All of you (he says to the Smyrnæans, s. viii.) obey the Bishop, as Christ obeyed the Father; and the Presbytery, as you would reverence the Apostles*; and the Deacons, as the commandment of God. Let no one undertake any ecclesiastical matter without the Bishop. Let that be held an authorized (βέβαια) thanksgiving, which is under the personal administration of the Bishop, or of some one to whom he may commit the office. Wheresoever the Bishop may appear, there let the multitude assemble: even as the Catholic Church is there where Christ Jesus is. It is not lawful either to baptize, or to celebrate an *Agape* without the Bishop: but whatsoever he shall approve, that is likewise well pleasing to God." Again, c. ix. " He who honours the Bishop is honoured by God: he who acts without the knowledge of the Bishop, is in bondage to the devil." In the Epistle to the Ephesians (s. ii.), he tells them " to be perfect in subjection—subject to the Bishop and the Presbyters—that they may be sanctified in all things." In the fourth section of the same, he compares the harmonious relation of the Presbytery with the Bishop to that of the chords with the harp; and in that following, he exhorts the Ephesians to obey the Bishop, as the means of obedience to God. And immediately afterwards he says, that " it is their manifest duty to look up to the Bishop, as to *the Lord himself*." In many other places he unites the Presbytery and the Deacons in honour with the Bishop—as in the fourth and seventh sections of the Epistle to the Philadelphians; the second and seventh of

---

* This idea is frequently repeated elsewhere, and in some places nearly in the same words. Ad Magnes. s. v. vii. xiii.; Philadelph. v.; Trall. s. ii. iii. It is remarkable, that his Epistle to the Romans is free from such lofty exhortations to ecclesiastical obedience; and abounds chiefly with expressions of his resignation, or rather of his eager anxiety for the crown of martyrdom.

that to the Trallians, &c.—Upon the whole, it appears to have been the principal object of this pious man to preserve the churches in strict union and discipline, during the persecution which then threatened their destruction, by subjecting the faithful in rigid obedience to every order of their priesthood, but most especially to the highest. The days were then approaching, and were already come, in which some severe system of subordination was absolutely necessary (under God's providence) for the preservation of the Church*.

An Epistle to the Philippians is still extant, under the name Polycarp. of Polycarp, and its genuineness has scarcely been questioned†. It was written soon after the death of Ignatius, and is animated by the charitable spirit of Christian piety. It is likewise valuable from containing many scriptural expressions, and frequent quotations of the recorded words of Christ. But the most important monument of this apostolical age remaining to us is " The Epistle of the Church of Rome to the Church of Corinth," written about the year 96, A.D. by Clement, Bishop of Rome. Clement of Rome. We have mentioned it already, and shall have occasion presently to recur to it. Its object was to allay some internal dissensions of the Corinthians; and it aims to effect it by the exposition of many moral truths, in a spirit purely Christian, and in powerful and even eloquent language.

Those pious persons wrote before any association had taken place between philosophy and religion, and were better instructed in the knowledge of Scripture than in the lessons of the Schools; and their method of reasoning, no less than their style, attests the want of profane education. Still their style possesses a persuasive simplicity well suited both to the character of the writers, and the integrity of their faith. The fundamental doctrines of Christianity are clearly and scripturally inculcated by them; and these are every where so interwoven with the highest precepts of morality, as to prove to us that the belief of those men was inseparable from their practice, and that it had not ever occurred to them to draw any verbal distinction between these. They delivered the truths which had been entrusted to them, and

* Some account of Ignatius and his Epistles is given by Eusebius, l. iii, cap. 36.
† See Lardner, Credibility of Gospel Hist. n. ii. ch. vi.

associated their moral and doctrinal instructions as inseparable parts of the same scheme. This perhaps is the most peculiar feature in their compositions, and that in which they most resemble the inspired writings. Another is the utter neglect of formal arrangement in the display of their arguments, or the delivery of their rules of conduct; a neglect which unquestionably exposed them to the contempt of the philosopher, who sought in vain for a *system* in their lore, but which well accorded with the plain and unpretending character of truth. But that merit by which they have conferred the most lasting advantage on Christianity, (at least the three last of them,) and which will make them very valuable monuments, in every age, is their frequent reference to almost all the books of the New Testament, such as we now possess them. Thus they furnish us with decisive evidence of the genuineness of those books; and their testimony is liable to no suspicion, because it was not given with any such view.

Justin
Martyr.

The principal Greek writers, who immediately succeeded the apostolical Fathers, were Justin Martyr and Irenæus. Justin Martyr was a learned Samaritan, of Gentile parents, who, after having successively attached himself to the Stoics, the Peripatetics, the Pythagoreans, and the Platonists, discovered the insufficiency and emptiness of philosophy. His attention seems to have been called to Christianity by the sufferings inflicted upon its profession, and the firmness with which he had beheld them endured. He inferred that men so contemptuous of death were far removed from the moral degradation with which they were charged; and that the faith for which they died so fearlessly must stand on some foundation. He examined that foundation, and discovered its stability[*]. The sincerity of his conversion is attested by his martyrdom. He was executed by the Emperor, whose philosophy he had deserted; and he perhaps never was so strongly sensible of the superiority of that which he had preferred, as at the moment when he died for it[†].

[*] See Jortin—Remarks, &c. b. ii. p. 1. A.D. 150. Supra, p. 57.

[†] It has been often asserted, and we believe without contradiction, that no man ever died in attestation of the truth of any philosophical tenet. But those who lay much stress on this fact should show, that an opportunity for martyrdom has ever been afforded to any philosophical sect.

He wrote two apologies for Christianity, the first addressed to Antoninus Pius, the second probably to Marcus ;—and a dialogue with a Jew named Trypho. This last contains many weak arguments, and trifling and even erroneous interpretations of Scripture, mixed up with some useful matter. The two former are more valuable compositions; they were so in those days—because they contained the best defence of religion which had then been published, maintained by arguments very well calculated to persuade those to whom they were addressed : and they are still so, because we find in them many quotations from the same four Gospels which we now acknowledge; they relate many interesting facts respecting the religious customs and ceremonies of the Christians of those times ; and they prove the general acceptance of all the fundamental articles of our belief.   As Justin flourished only one century after the preaching of Christ, (his conversion is usually placed at the year 133 from the birth of our Saviour,) we are not extending the value of tradition beyond its just limits, when we consider his opinions as receiving some additional weight from their contiguity to the apostolical times.   And if it were possible to mark by any decided limit the extent of traditionary authority, we should be disposed to trace the line immediately after his name.   For admitting that Irenæus, who presently succeeded him, by his oriental birth and correspondence may have received some uncorrupted communications transmitted through two generations from the divine origin, we shall still find it very difficult to distinguish these from the mere human matter with which they may be associated.   This difficulty will increase, as we descend lower down the stream; so that we may safely detach the notion of peculiar sanctity or conclusive authority from the names and writings of the succeeding Fathers, though they contain much that may excite our piety, and animate our morality, and confirm our faith.

Irenæus was Bishop of Lyons, about the year 178 A.D.   He is chiefly celebrated for his five books ' Against Heresies;' containing confutations of most of the errors which had then appeared in the Church.   Though the language which he employs in this contest is not always that best adapted either to persuade or to conciliate, his sincere aversion from religious dissension is

Irenæus.

not questioned. It is proved indeed by the epistle which he addressed to Victor, Bishop of Rome, on his insolent demeanour in the controversy respecting Easter, and which breathes a generous spirit of Christian moderation. And in good truth the individual exertions of Churchmen against the progress of unscriptural opinions were in those days the more necessary, and their warmth the more excusable, as there were yet no articles of faith to trace out the limits of orthodoxy, nor any acknowledged head, nor any legally established system of ecclesiastical government. The unity and purity of the Church were chiefly preserved by the independent labours of its most eminent and influential ministers, divided as they were both by language, and manners, and distance, and entirely unsupported by any temporal authority. So that, if we should be disposed to feel surprise at finding (as we shall presently find) numerous forms of heresy very near both to the time and place in which the Revelation was delivered, the above considerations would tend to remove it; while they certainly teach us, that such errors cannot permanently or generally prevail against scriptural truth, as long as they are steadily opposed by temperate and reasonable argument, and by no other weapon than argument only.

NOTE ON THE CHURCH OF CORINTH.

There are some few persons who attach so much importance to the controversy respecting the original government of the Church of Corinth, that we may, perhaps, be excused if we here mention the grounds on which, in our opinion, it really rests. And as we shall entirely abstain from ingenious conjectures, and nice distinctions, and subtle inferences, a very moderate space will suffice for all that remains.

1. There is no direct and positive information from ancient writers on either side. It is no where expressly asserted that any Apostle appointed a Bishop at Corinth—nor is it any where expressly denied.

2. Eusebius is in many places very diligent in recording the

successions of the Bishops, from the apostolical times, in several Eusebius. of the original Churches—as Rome, Jerusalem, Alexandria, and Antioch *—and where he does not trace the succession (as in the cases of Athens, Ephesus, the Cretan Churches, and Smyrna) he at least mentions the name of the first Bishop (Hist. c. iv. 14) according to such records as have reached him.   But he is entirely silent as to any succession of Bishops in the apostolical Church of Corinth; and even as to the existence of any Bishop there in the earliest times.

3. Hegesippus (ap. Euseb. l. iv. c. xxii.) relates, " that the Hegesip-Church of the Corinthians remained orthodox as late as the pus. episcopacy of Primus (μεχρὶ Πρίμου ἐπισκοπεύοντος); and it appears from the context that this Primus was contemporary with Anicetus of Rome, who ruled the Church from 156 A.D. to 168 A.D. This is the first mention (so far at least as our knowledge extends) of any individual as Bishop of Corinth; and the first express and certain assurance of the existence of episcopacy in that Church.   On the other hand, there are two inferences which *cannot* be drawn from this passage—either that Primus was actually the *first* Bishop of Corinth, or that the Church fell away from orthodoxy *after* his time.   The language of Hegesippus does not justify either conclusion. There may doubtless have been Bishops of Corinth before the year 160; only this happens to be the first express mention of any one of them.

4. To ascend higher than this. St. Clement's Epistle was St. Clement probably written in the year 96.   Can we gather from it what of Rome. was the government of the Church to which it was addressed? The following are the passages which bear most directly on the question.   " The Apostles appointed the first-fruits of their converts, when they had proved them by the Spirit, to be *Bishops* and *Deacons* of the future converts. And what wonder is there, if those who were commissioned to this office in Christ by God appointed the aforesaid? . . .   Our Apostles knew, through our Lord Jesus Christ, that there would be contention about the name of the *Episcopacy* (ἔρις περὶ τοῦ ὀνόματος τῆς ἐπισκοπῆς). Wherefore with certain foreknowledge they appointed the above-

---

* H. E. l. iii. c. 4, 11, 14, 22; l. iv. c. 1, 4, 5, 10, 19, 20, &c.

mentioned, and consulted how, when they should have fallen
asleep, there should be a succession of other approved men to
the ministry. Those, then, who were appointed by them, or
afterwards by other men of consideration, with the consent of
the whole Church, and who have ministered without blame to
the flock of Christ, with humility, peace, and liberality—and
who can give abundant evidence of their excellence—those men,
I say, have not been justly ejected from their ministry. For it
is no slight offence in us, if we eject from *the Episcopacy* (ἐὰν τῆς
ἐπισκοπῆς ἀποβάλωμεν) those who have contributed their (spiritual) gifts without blame and with holiness. Blessed are the
Presbyters of former days (μακάριοι οἱ προοδοιπορήσαντες πρεσ-
βύτεροι), who have received a full and perfect dissolution. For
they have no fear of being removed from their appointed situation; as we observe you to have removed certain men of good
life from their honourable office." These expressions are found
in chapters 42, 43, and 44. In 47 are the following:—"It is
very shameful, my beloved, and unworthy of your Christian
discipline, that the most established and antient Church of
Corinth should, on account of one or two persons, be in revolt
against its *Presbyters* (στασιάζειν πρὸς τοὺς πρεσβυτέρους)." In
the fifty-fourth, Clement advises those ministers who had been
the occasion of this discord to withdraw from their offices, and
to say,—" If I have been the cause of dissension and schism, I
retire, and do what is prescribed by the people (τὰ ὑπὸ τοῦ
πλήθους προτασσόμενα): only let the fold of Christ be at peace
with its appointed *Presbyters* (μετὰ τῶν καθισταμένων πρεσβυ-
τέρων):" and again in section fifty-seven, " Do you then, who
have been at the bottom of the dissension, be subject unto your
Presbyters (ὑποταγῆτε τοῖς πρεσβυτέροις), and be disciplined
unto repentance."

From the comparison of these passages one thing is certain,
—that St. Clement applied the terms *Bishop* and *Presbyter* to
the same men, *i. e.* to the ministers ejected by the Corinthians:
and if it be not an absolutely necessary inference, that two
orders only (that of Bishops or Presbyters, and Deacons)
then existed at Corinth, at least there is no passage in the
Epistle from which any one can fairly infer the existence of

three*. If again it shall be conjectured, that the Letter was addressed (not to " the Church abiding at Corinth" only, but) to all the Bishops of all the Churches of the province (and it is no more than conjecture), still the synonymous use of the two terms is not thus affected, and the (supposed) " Bishops" of Achaia cannot even then escape the appellation of " Presbyters."

5. Tertullian, ' De Præscript. Hæret.' xxxvi., says, " Run Tertullian. through the Apostolical Churches, in which the very chairs of the Apostles still preside in their own places (apud quas ipsæ adhuc Cathedræ Apostolorum suis locis præsident), in which the very Letters from their own hands are recited, echoing the voice and representing the face of every one of them. If Achaia be nearest to you, you have Corinth. If you are near to Macedonia, you have Philippi, &c." Some would willingly understand this passage to express the opinion of Tertullian, that a succession of Bishops had occupied, from the earliest ages, the " Chair" of St. Paul. In another section, thirty-two, of the same work, the author asserts generally, that the Apostolical Churches traced their succession to Apostles, or Apostolical men; and he particularizes Polycarp, as ordained by St. John, to Smyrna, and Clement, by St. Peter, to Rome†.

Such, as far as we know, and as fairly as we can state them, are the real merits of this controversy. The particular and

---

* *Half* a passage, from the first chapter, is sometimes cited for this purpose. Speaking of the admirable moral condition in which the Christians of Corinth had heretofore lived, St. Clement says,—ὑποτασσόμενοι τοῖς ἡγουμένοις ὑμῶν καὶ τιμὴν τὴν καθήκουσαν ἀπονέμοντες τοῖς παρ' ὑμῖν πρεσβυτέροις· (and here learned writers stop short, and at once proceed to the conclusion, that ἡγούμενοι must mean *Bishops*,—the very following words will seem, to some, to overthrow that supposition). ΝΕΟΙΣ τε μέτρια καὶ σεμνὰ νοεῖν ἐπετρέπετε. ΓΥΝΑΙΞΙΝ τε ἐν ἀμώμῳ καὶ σεμνῇ καὶ ἁγνῇ συνειδήσει πάντα ἐπιτελεῖν παρηγγέλλετε, &c. This passage is illustrated by another in the twenty-first chapter, τοὺς προηγουμένους ἡμῶν αἰδεσθῶμεν· τοὺς πρεσβυτέρους ἡμῶν τιμήσωμεν. τοὺς νεοὺς παιδεύσωμεν . . . τὰς γυναῖκας ἡμῶν ἐπὶ τὸ ἀγαθὸν διορθωσώμεθα . . τὰ τέκνα ἡμῶν τῆς ἐν Χριστῷ παιδείας, &c. And if it be still doubtful whether these passages do not refer to the civil, rather than the ecclesiastical, subordination of the Faithful, we refer to the fifth chapter, in which St. Paul is said to have suffered martyrdom ἐπὶ τῶν Ηγουμένων—an expression which some translate " under the Emperors"—others, " under the Prefects"—and which of course refers to the civil authorities.

† Clement, by the way, is commonly considered to have been the *third* Bishop of Rome.

contemporary evidence of St. Clement leads us to one conclusion; the more vague expressions of Tertullian may suffice to
incline some to the opposite; and the general silence of antiquity will furnish abundant and easy arguments and inferences
to both parties. But howsoever the reader may decide, he will
do well to bear in mind at least thus much,—that the Apostolical ordination and succession of the ministry are, in the
above passages, expressly asserted, before the end of the first
century, by a faithful writer—whose admirable Epistle continued long afterwards * to be read, on the Lord's Day, to the
Congregations of Corinth.

CHAPTER III.

The Progress of Christianity from the year 200 A. D. *till the*
Accession of Constantine, A. D. 313.

Incipient corruption of the Church—Reasons for it—Its extent—External progress
of religion in Asia and in Europe—Claims, character, and prosperity of the Church
of Rome—That of Alexandria—Clemens—Origen—His character—Industry
—Success—Defect—The Church of Carthage—Tertullian—His character—
Heresy—Merits—On the works and principles of Cyprian—Government of
the Church—Increase of episcopal power, or, rather, influence—Degeneracy of
the Ministers of Religion exaggerated—Institution of inferior orders—Division
of the people into Faithful and Catechumens—Corruption of the sacrament of
Baptism—Effect of this—The Eucharist—Dæmons—Exorcism—Alliance with
philosophy—Its consequences—Pious frauds—Their origin—Excuses for such
corruptions—Eclectic philosophy—Ammonius Saccas—Plotinus—Porphyry—
Compromise with certain philosophers—Millennarian opinions.

RESERVING for subsequent consideration the persecutions and
the heresies by which the early Church was disturbed, we shall
now pursue its more peaceful annals as far as its establishment
by the first Christian emperor. We have found it almost necessary to separate, and indeed widely to distinguish the events of
the first two from those of the third century; for nearly at this
point are we disposed to place the first crisis in the internal

---

* Dionys. ap. Euseb. iv. 3, 23.

history of the Church.   It is true that the first operations of corruption are slow and secret, so that it is hard to ascertain the precise moment of its commencement.   But a candid inquirer cannot avoid perceiving that, about the end of the second and the beginning of the third century, some changes had taken place in the ecclesiastical system, which indicated a departure from its primitive purity.   Indeed, such a state of society, as that which we have recently described, could scarcely hope for permanent endurance, unless through a fundamental alteration in human nature and in the necessary course of human affairs. In addition to this, the very principles of Christianity prevented it from remaining stationary; the spirit of the faith is active, penetrating, and progressive; and thus, as it expanded itself in numerical extent—as it rose in rank, in learning, in wealth—as it came in contact with the people of all nations, and with all classes of the people, a great variety of human passions and motives was comprehended by it, which had no place in its early existence.   As it increased in the number of converts, the zeal of brotherly love and ardent charity became more contracted, since these could no longer be universally exerted.   As it rose in rank, it lost that perfect equality among its members which formed the very essence of its original and best character—false learning corrupted its simplicity, and wealth undermined its morality.   If it gained in prosperity and worldly consideration, it resigned the native innocence and freshness of childhood.

We are far from intending to assert, that any sudden demo- ralization or violent apostacy from its first principles took place in the Church during the third century—far from it—we feel even strongly assured, that it still continued to embrace the greater proportion of whatever was truly virtuous and excellent in the Roman empire.   " Who will not confess (says Origen in substance to Celsus*) that even the worst members of the Church are much more virtuous than those who compose the popular assemblies?   The Church of God, at Athens, if you will, is tranquil and peaceable, searching only to do God's plea- sure: the Assembly of the Athenians is seditious, and bearing no

---

* Lib. iii. sect. 30.

comparison to it. The same is true of the Churches of Corinth and Alexandria, contrasted with the popular assemblies of those cities..... So that, if we compare the senate of the Church with the senate of every city, we shall find the members of the former worthy to govern the city of God; while the others have nothing in their morals which fits them for their rank, or places them above the ordinary qualities of citizens. And, if we carry the comparison farther, we shall observe the immense moral superiority of the most dissolute and imperfect of the bishops and presbyters over the civil magistrates."

But in closely attending to its history, we observe that it becomes thenceforward the history of men, rather than of things; the body of the Church is not so much in view, but the acts of its ministers and teachers are continually before us. We read little of the clergy of the first two centuries; they appear to have discharged their pastoral duties with silent diligence and disinterested piety. We learn their character, for the most part, from the effects of their labours; and we find its ample and indisputable record in the progress of their religion, and in the virtues of their converts.

Progress of Chris-tianity.

The progress of religion, indeed, continued, under easier circumstances, with equal rapidity; and we have reason to believe that, before the time of Constantine, it was deeply rooted in all the eastern * provinces of the Roman, as well as in the Persian empire. Gibbon † has candidly acknowledged his error in attributing the conversion of Armenia to the reign of that emperor; and perhaps a more impartial reflection on the mission of Pantænus, which we have no reason to believe fruitless, would have led him to doubt his own accuracy, when he makes a similar assertion respecting Æthiopia. The light of Christi-

---

* Dionys. ap. Euseb., H. E., vii. 5. Dionysius was Bishop of Alexandria during the middle of the third century. Tillemont (vol. iii. p. 405), on the authority of Origen, asserts that the Christians, before the middle of the second century, not only had built a number of churches, but had ventured in some places an assault upon temples, altars, and idols.

† Vindication, p. 74. We give him credit for this admission, because the error was of his own discovery. He adds, "The seeds of the faith were deeply sown here during the last and greatest persecution. Tiridates may dispute with Constantine the honour of being the first Christian sovereign."

anity had certainly penetrated, with varying splendour, among the Bactrians, the Parthians, the Scythians, Germans, Gauls, and Britons; the Goths of Mysia and Thrace were converted by missionaries from Asia, and laid aside, on the reception of the faith, the primeval barbarity of their manners*.

Before the middle of the third century, every city in every province, at least of the eastern empire, appears to have had its congregation and its Bishop. And numerous documents attest, that the leading prelates were in constant and active communication. During the suspension of persecution, in the reign of Commodus, many great and opulent families were converted; and in a Synod assembled at Rome, in the year 251, to pronounce upon the schism of Novation †, sixty bishops and a still greater number of presbyters and deacons were present, though the rustic pastors in the other districts held their separate meetings on the same subject. Later in this century, before the beginning of Diocletian's persecution, we have the authority of Eusebius ‡ for believing, not only that the religion had made very general progress both "among Greeks and Barbarians," but also that it had risen into great estimation and dignity at Rome. Not only did Christians occupy high and favourite stations about the Imperial court, surrounded by their domestics, wives and children, likewise Christians, but they were allowed publicly to profess their faith, and almost publicly to make their boast of it. Their ministers were treated with respect and kindness not by individuals only, but by the governors of provinces. And such multitudes thronged to their worship, that their ancient Churches no longer sufficed, and new and ample buildings were constructed for their reception§. Thus

* Mosh. Gen. Hist., c. iii., p. i., ch. 1. The progress of Christianity in Gaul was not rapid. Even as late as the reign of Decius, we observe that it was necessary to send fresh missionaries from Rome for the complete conversion of that country.

† Euseb., H. E., vi. 43. See Tillem., vol. iii. p. 433 to 493.

‡ H. E., l. viii. c. 1.

§ Mosh., c. iii., p. i., ch. 1. The emperors during this age who were most favourable to Christianity were Caracalla, Heliogabalus, Alexander Severus, Gordian, and his two successors, the Philips. Respecting the first of these two, a great mass of authorities is adduced to prove that he had actually, though secretly, embraced the religion.

the services of religion were no longer performed as it were by stealth* with the connivance of the civil magistrate—but avowedly and publicly, in perfect toleration, and with as much security as is consistent with the necessary capriciousness of despotism.

Church of Rome. While the Church of Antioch maintained, after the fall of Jerusalem, a nominal supremacy among the Christians of the East, and while the faithful continued, for the most part, to derive from Alexandria the rudiments of their learning, Rome did not lose her pre-eminence in numbers, in wealth, and in the munificence of her charity. We find in Eusebius †, on the authority of Cornelius, that in the middle of the century the ministers in this "Catholic Church" consisted of forty-six presbyters, seven deacons, seven subdeacons, forty-two acolyths, besides exorcists, and readers, and doorkeepers, to the number of fifty-two. We shall presently notice the introduction of these new and unscriptural appellations into the service of the Church. At present we proceed more willingly to the succeeding passage in the epistle of the Bishop, in which he informs us, that there were likewise more than fifteen hundred widows and mourners ‡, all of whom the Church, through the grace and lovingkindness of the Lord, perpetually supported.

This honourable supremacy—in resources and philanthropy—was possessed and exercised by the Church of Rome. But not **Its ambitious claims.** contented with this, she continued to advance, as occasions presented themselves, certain vague assertions of spiritual authority. Soon after the middle of the third century, we observe her bishop

---

* It is a probable opinion that excavations, used as cemeteries, were not uncommon places of worship among the early Christians. And the first recorded instance of the construction of a Church was in the earlier part of the reign of Alexander Severus—about 225 A. D. Origen labours hard, about the same time, to justify the contempt of the Christians for every inanimate place of worship—the body of every Christian was a temple of purity, consecrated to the Divinity, &c. &c. —Contra Celsum.

† H. E., lib. vi. cap. 43.

‡ Χήρας σὺν θλιβομένοις ὑπὲρ τὰς χιλίας πεντηκοσίας· οὓς πάντας ἡ τοῦ Δεσπότου χάρις καὶ φιλανθρωπία διατρέφει. See Semler, vol. i. p. 66. It appears from Cyprian's 60th epistle, that the Christians of Carthage had contributed readily, universally and bounteously for the redemption of some brethren, who were captives in Numidia.

Stephanus tracing the footsteps of his predecessor Victor, in a controversy of still less importance; and striving to impose the tradition of the Roman Church, as an invariable rule for the rest of the Christian world. His aggressions were resisted with the same independent spirit which characterized the last age; and he proceeded, as before, to remove the refractory Churches from his communion.

One of those was the Church of Carthage—and it was at that time governed by Cyprian, the most distinguished churchman of the third century. We shall presently make some general mention both of his character and his works. It is sufficient here to say, that he repelled with vigour and firmness the encroachments of Rome; that he asserted in the plainest language * the independence of individual bishops in the administration of their Churches ; and rejected the authority of tradition when unsupported by the written words of Christ and his apostles.

Resisted by Cyprian,

These principles are the more remarkable and valuable from the pen of Cyprian, because in other places he has voluntarily declared, that "the Primacy was given to Peter;" and has even designated the chair (or see) of Peter as "the Principal Church, whence the Sacerdotal Unity proceeded †." He acknowledged the Primacy, and denied the authority of Rome. In an assembly of all the bishops of Christendom he would have given the precedence to the bishop of Rome—but at the same time he

---

* "Whence is that tradition ? Is it deduced from the words of the Lord, and the authority of the gospels, or from the teaching and the epistles of the apostles ? Custom, which has crept in with some people, must not prevent truth from prevailing—for custom without truth is nothing but inveterate and antiquated error." Epist. liv. See likewise his Epistle to Quintus, an African bishop (Epist. lxxi.) : "We are not to be governed by custom, but overcome by reasoning—even as Peter himself, in his differences with Paul, displayed no arrogance ; and asserted no primacy, &c."

† Lib. De Unitate Eccl. "Hoc erant utique et cæteri Apostoli qnod fuit Petrus, pari consortio præditi et honoris et potestatis : sed exordium ab Unitate proficiscitur, *et primatus Petro datur*, ut una Christi Ecclesia, et Cathedra una monstretur." And Epist. lv. *Ad Cornelium.* "Post ista . . navigare audent, et ad Petri Cathedram, atque ad *Ecclesiam Principalem, unde Unitas Sacerdotalis exorta est,* &c." In collecting the true sense of these passages, the first clause of that first cited must never be lost sight of.

temperately rejected the notion of any other superiority than that of rank. Addressing Stephanus, in the name of a synod*, as a brother and an equal, he used the following expressions:— "These things have we communicated to you, dearest brother, in virtue of our common dignity and sincere love, in the belief that, through the truth of your religious faith, you will take pleasure in what is religious and at the same time true. We know, indeed, that some are loth to lay aside their principles or their purpose; but retain some peculiarities once adopted, without any violation of harmony. In which matter we neither lay force nor impose laws on any one: since every prelate has a right to the exercise of his own free will in the administration of his Church, under responsibility to God."

and Fir-
milianus.

Firmilianus, bishop of Cæsarea in Cappadocia, in a letter addressed to Cyprian†, expresses with greater warmth his indignation at the conduct of Stephanus, in prohibiting the reception at Rome of the African deputation. He accuses the professed successor of Peter of destroying, by his ambitious uncharitableness, the rock of unity on which the Church was built. He asserts that the traditions of Rome are in many instances at variance with those of other churches, also apostolical; and that these last have not on that account interfered to interrupt, in their differences, the bond of Christian peace.

Appeals to
Rome, and
to Car-
thage.

Another circumstance occurred, nearly at the same time, which indicated even more strikingly the character of Rome, and gives us a stronger foretaste of her future usurpations. Two Spanish bishops, Basilides and Martialis, had been deposed by a synod; and the provincial bishops, with the Church over which Basilides presided, had chosen another in his place.

---

* The passage concludes the lxxiind epistle, edit. Paris. He has likewise the following: *Præf. in Concil. Carthag. De Hæret. baptiz.* "Neque enim quisquam nostrûm episcopum se esse Episcoporum constituit aut tyrannico terrore ad obsequendi necessitatem collegas suos adigit: quando habeat omnis Episcopus pro licentia libertatis et potestatis suæ arbitrium proprium, tamque judicari ab alio non possit, quam nec ipse poterit alterum judicare."

† Published among Cyprian's works, epistle lxxv. ed. Paris. This Firmilianus is mentioned by Jerome (Catalog. Scrìpt. Eccles.) to have given great proofs of respect for Origen, and to have received from him instructions in the interpretation of Scripture.

The two delinquents went to Rome and *appealed to Stephanus.*
He reversed the sentence, and restored them to their offices.
This led, of course, to a contest in Spain between the parties—
and an appeal was then made to the Church of Carthage.   Cyprian did not hesitate to annul the decision of Stephanus—and
to declare the sentence, which had deposed the bishops, to be
just, and that unjust which had reinstated them.   It should be
observed, however, that in this epistle Cyprian did not examine
whether or not such right of interference rested with the Roman
see.   He merely asserted, that the offences of the bishops had
merited deposition, and that their successors had been legitimately elected.   But as he claimed no "authority" for himself,
in consequence of the appeal to his own see, so neither, according to his avowed principles, could he acknowledge any such in
the see of Rome.

Somewhat later in this century, in the year 269, a council of
Oriental bishops deposed for heresy Paul bishop of Samosata.
His successor was formally appointed: but Paul, having great
authority in the city, and being likewise supported by the celebrated Zenobia, refused to resign his dignity.   This schism
continued, until Aurelian happened to come to Antioch, after
his victory over the queen of Palmyra.   The Catholic party then
stated to the emperor their inability to enforce their own decision,
and invited him to lend his power to aid them.   Thus, for the
first time in the history of the Church, was the civil authority
invoked to interpose its ambiguous services in the defence of
orthodoxy.   Aurelian replied, that, whichever of the rivals was
in communion with the bishops of Italy and Rome, the same
should be established in the disputed see *.   The decision was
fair and natural, in a pagan and an emperor; and little could he
dream what mighty pretensions and usurpations would hereafter
seek a precedent and justification in that simple proceeding †.

Affair of Paul of Samosata.

---

* τούτοις νεῖμαι προστάττων τὸν οἶκον, οἷς ἂν οἱ κατὰ τὴν Ἰταλίαν καὶ τὴν Ῥωμαίων πόλιν
ἐπίσκοποι τοῦ Δόγματος ἐπιστέλλοιεν.   Euseb. vii. 30. See Pagi, ann. 271. n. 3. 4.
It appears that Paul likewise held some civil office in the city: but the reference
of Aurelian to the *bishops* of Italy sufficiently proves, that his interference respected
the ecclesiastical character of the delinquent.

† "He was the first (says Baronius, ann. 314. s. xxxv.) to point out that imperial

Church of   Clemens, surnamed the Alexandrian, a presbyter of the
Alexandria   Church, succeeded his preceptor Pantænus in the direction of
the " Catechetical School," towards the conclusion of the second
Clemens.   century, and adorned his office by the extent and variety of his
learning *.   The works which have come down to us perhaps
justify the opinion of his contemporaries—and among them (besides his "Admonition to the Gentiles" and his "Pædagogus")
is the more celebrated "Stromates" (Στρωματεῖς).   The appellation indicates the character of the composition—consisting of
a great variety of substances, carelessly sown together, without
regard to uniformity in quality, or harmony in colour.   These
writings profess indeed to inculcate the Christian doctrines, and
recommend the Christian morality; and denounce with strong
censure, and expose by very plain and particular description,
the foul and lascivious mysteries of heathen profligacy.   They
dilate too upon the mythological depravity of the old superstition, and unveil the consecrated scandals of Mount Olympus.
Nor are there wanting some warm and unaffected expressions of
rational piety.   But the mixture of dissociable matter which
pervades the whole; and the great number of illogical inferences, irrelevant arguments and inapt illustrations, render the
works of Clement of little value, in these days, for purposes
either of reason or edification.   They are a mass of mingled
Christianity, philosophy, and mythology, in which the two latter
greatly predominate.   Classical fancies and Christian truths are
heaped together without any discrimination.   Jupiter and Jeho-
vah, Plato and Christ are thrown into the same miscellany,
almost as if they were of equal authority and equal holiness;
and the very morality, which is sometimes well enforced, might
have proceeded, for the most part, from the pen of a heathen.   So
that though the effect of the works of Clemens might possibly be
to raise Christianity to the level of philosophy, they are scarcely
calculated to exalt it much higher.   We may likewise add, as

authority should be called in to chastise those who do not acquiesce in episcopal
decision, &c."
    * Hieronymus ad Magnum.   " Clemens Alexandrinus, presbyter Ecclesiæ, meo
judicio omnium eruditissimus.   Quid in illius libris indoctum ? immo, quid non
è media philosophia ?"

more immediately in connexion with our own researches, that they are peculiarly barren of any particulars which throw light on the doctrine, government or discipline of the early church.

The best history of the Church of Alexandria, during the first half of the third century, is furnished by the life of Origen. That extraordinary person, the most eminent among the early fathers, was a native of Egypt, the son of one Leonidas, who suffered martyrdom in the year 202. When in prison he received an epistle from his son, of which one sentence only is preserved to us. "Take heed, father, that you do not change your mind for our sake." Origen was then about seventeen years old—his religious instructions he had received from Clemens Alexandrinus, his philosophical lore from Ammonius Saccas; and such proficiency had he made in both those studies, that he was called to preside over the "Catechetical School" at the age of eighteen. He filled that office for nearly thirty years, and discharged its duties with zeal and genius so distinguished, with such fruitful diligence of composition, such persuasiveness of oral eloquence, such assiduity in the distribution of the Scriptures, as to make it a question whether Christianity was ever so much advanced, in point of numbers, by the mere intellectual exertions of any other individual. He merited the honour of persecution ; and had the double fortune to be expelled from his chair and country by the jealousy of the Bishop Demetrius, and to be pursued in his old age by the brutality of a Roman emperor. It is mentioned as the cause of the bishop's hostility, that Origen was ordained Presbyter, not at Alexandria*, but by the bishops of Cæsarea and Jerusalem. And it is certain that, during his exile, Cæsarea (in Palestine) was the place of his residence, where he found protection and patronage, till he was cast into prison by Decius, and remained there till the death of that tyrant. He survived him by one or two years, and died at Tyre, probably in 252.

Origen.
185—252,
A. D.

---

* Origen (in this instance adopting the literal sense of Scripture) is recorded to have made himself an eunuch for the kingdom of heaven. Eusebius relates the circumstances, l. vi. c. 8. Περὶ τοῦ τολμηθέντος Ὠριγένει. It is supposed that Demetrius may on this account have considered his ordination as illegitimate, and therefore persecuted him.

The literary labours of Origen were proportionate to the extent of his talents and the vigour of his character: and whatever irregularities of composition and of reasoning may be found to disfigure some parts of them, they bear the indelible mark of a bold and comprehensive mind, burning with religious warmth, unrestrained by vulgar interests or prejudices, and sincerely bent on the attainment of truth. They were, besides, extremely numerous: it is recorded that they amounted to six thousand volumes; that several short-hand writers were always in attendance, while he dictated, by turns relieving each other's labour, and that multitudes were employed besides in copying his works. These traditions at least attest his indefatigable diligence; of which, indeed, no inconsiderable monuments still remain to us.

His Work against Celsus. That most commonly in the hands of learned men is his celebrated ' Defence of Christianity against the Attack of Celsus.' Celsus was the first deliberate literary antagonist of Christianity. He seems to have written during the age of the Antonines, and he designated his book the 'Word of Truth' (Ἀληθὴς Λόγος). But the simplest circumstances of his history were not known even to his inquisitive opponent; and the nature of his philosophical opinions is a subject of uncertainty with learned men to this present moment. Howbeit, whatever may have been his character and his tenets, it is evident, even from the fragments of his work which are cited by his adversary, that he possessed great general powers of expression, especially of sarcasm and of rhetoric; that he was skilful in the selection of the points for attack; and that he possessed too that wicked talent of perverting truth and insinuating falsehood, of suppressing largely and inventing discreetly, and confounding established facts with rumoured calumnies—which so commonly marks the distinguished controversialist. But Origen presented to his aggression an ardent and generous spirit, repelling his assaults, confuting his sophistry, and exposing his inconsistency; and setting forth the excellence of his own profession in language, which even now cannot be read without emotion.

But the most important work of Origen—that on which he justly set the greatest value, and on the compilation of which he is related to have employed eight and twenty years—was his

edition of the 'Septuagint.' Many errors, during 400 years of Edition of the Septuagint.
repeated transcription and, perhaps, interpolation, had crept
into the received version; and it was a task worthy of the genius of Origen to remove them. Accordingly, having collected,
with great labour, three other translations from the Hebrew,
those of Aquila, Theodotion, and Symmachus, (all produced
within a century from his time,) he published these, together
with the Septuagint, in the same volume, in four parallel
columns; and this was called his Tetrapla. He subsequently
added two other columns: one of the original Hebrew, the
other of the same in the Greek character; and this composed
his Hexapla. And still later he discovered, and published with
the rest, two other Greek translations; and this last compilation
was, for the same reason, called his Octapla. These various
versions he compared both with the Hebrew and with each
other in such a manner as to show that his critical talents were
scarcely surpassed by his industry. This extraordinary work
has reached posterity in fragments only.

But when Origen applied himself to the interpretation of
Scripture, it was not with the same success. He failed, however, not through want of genius, but through want of judgment,
and a compliance with the fanciful system which already existed
in his age, and in his school. He fell into the error of the
allegorists, and even carried it much farther than any who had
adopted it before him. From the simplest passages of Scripture he extracted a mystical, or spiritual, sense, to the general
exclusion of the literal—just as the later Platonists affected to
veil the fabulous history of the gods of Greece; and even as the
Jews of Alexandria deviated into a dangerous misinterpretation
of the Sacred Writings. Such, indeed, was the hold which philosophy had acquired on the mind of Origen, that he sought its
principles in the Bible, and applied all the ingenuity of his fancy
to discover them even there. His error, so fascinating to the
loose imaginations of the East, was rapidly propagated by
numerous disciples; nor do we find that it encountered any
serious opposition from the Church till the time of Jerome, the
end of the fourth century.

The fame of Origen was not confined to his native country,

nor to the schools of philosophy, nor to the professors of the
faith. Mammæa, the mother of the Emperor Alexander,
sought a conference with him in Syria; he was held in high
repute at Rome; his personal exertions were extended to Greece;
and among the most fortunate efforts of his genius we may be
allowed to mention, that, when a numerous synod was twice
convoked in Arabia on two occasions of heresy, Origen, who was
present by invitation, was twice successful in convincing his
opponents*. His school gave birth to a number of learned men,
Plutarch, Serenus, Heraclides, Heron, who proved their sincerity
and multiplied the followers of their religion, by the industry
with which they adorned life, and the constancy with which
they quitted it.

This great man "was followed (says Tillemont†) by the same
fate after his death, as during his life. The saints themselves
were divided on the subject. Martyrs have made his defence,
and martyrs have written his condemnation. The one party
has regarded him as the greatest doctor possessed by the
Church since the time of the Apostles: the other has execrated
him as the parent of Arius and every other heresiarch." Both
parties, as is common in extreme opinions, were wrong. The
genius of Origen, though vast and penetrating, was also rash
and irregular, and he was in many respects an erring doctor
and a dangerous guide. Nevertheless, the heresies of Arius
and his successors would still have defiled the Church, (as did
the heresies of his numerous predecessors,) even though Origen
had never opened to theologians the slippery paths of alle-
gory.

Dionysius
of Alex-
andria.

His most distinguished successor in the Catechetical School
was Dionysius; and he was elevated to the see of Alexandria
in the year 247. He was thus the contemporary, and the occasional correspondent of Cyprian; like Cyprian, he was driven
into exile in the persecution of 258, and endured even a longer

---

* Euseb. H. E., vi. 19 and 37. Origen had also the credit of converting various other heretics, especially one Ambrosius, whose errors had some celebrity at
the moment, and at whose instance he afterwards wrote his Books against Celsus.

† Mem., vol. iii. pp. 494, 495. Tillemont takes the favourable side; and the
reader will find there a very satisfactory account of the Life and Writings of
Origen. We may likewise refer to Dr. Burton's twenty-fourth Lecture.

trial of seclusion and indignity. But in this he was more fortunate, that he finally escaped the last infliction, and died in
possession of his office in the year 267. Some few of his writings
are preserved by Eusebius, of considerable merit, and wearing
much less of the philosophical character, than those of his predecessors Clemens and Origen. He was zealously opposed to
the opinions of Novatian : but the controversy, by which he is
best known to posterity, was occasioned by the errors of Sabellius, which first appeared in his diocese. It is true, that in
his ardour to confute this Heresiarch he made use of some
unguarded expressions, which the Arians were afterwards
willing to torture into a profession of their own tenets—but
without justice. For if his language in various passages be
compared, with a due consideration of the circumstances under
which he wrote, it may be pronounced with little hesitation,
that he held the doctrine afterwards promulgated at Nice*.

The Latin Church of Carthage attained little celebrity till Church of
the end of the second century, when it was adorned by Tertul- Carthage.
lian; but we have observed that, about that period, Christianity,
which had already scattered its blessings along the banks of
the Nile, and into the adjacent deserts, was very generally established along the northern coast of Africa. In his deprecatory
Address to Scapula, Proconsul of Africa, Tertullian uses the
following expressions, where exaggeration could have served no
purpose but to throw contempt on his whole exhortation.   "If
you begin a general persecution here, what will you do with so
many thousands, both men and women, of every sex, age, and
dignity†, when they shall come to offer themselves for martyrdom ? What flames and swords will be necessary ! What
will Carthage itself suffer, when *you shall decimate it*—when

---

* We refer the reader to Dr. Burton, Lect. xxvii, where the subject is well
treated.

† Origen, some twenty years later, uses the following more moderate expressions. (Cont. Cels. l. iii. p. 11, 7.) Νὺ μὲν οὖν τάχα, ὅτε διὰ τὸ πλῆθος τῶν
προσερχομένων τῷ Λόγῳ καὶ πλούσιοι καὶ τίνες τῶν ἐν ἀξιώματι καὶ γυναῖα
τὰ ἁβρὰ καὶ εὐγενῆ ἀποδέχονται τοὺς ἀπὸ τοῦ Λόγου, &c. A few pages later he
repels, with great power and eloquence, the sarcasms of Celsus on the low and
vulgar condition of many of the converts.

every one shall recognize his kinsman and comrades among the victims—shall observe men and matrons, it may be, even of your own rank, and all the principal persons, and either the relatives or friends of your own friends! Spare yourself, then, if you feel no mercy for us—Spare Carthage, if you feel no mercy for yourself! Spare the whole province, which is liable, through your project, to military and intestine confusion . . . But do what you will, this sect will never fall away: in fact it is never rising so rapidly, as when it appears to be suffering. For then it is, that every one, who beholds its exemplary endurance, becomes scrupulous, and anxious to enquire into the foundation of the matter; and when he has ascertained the truth, becomes himself too a convert."

Tertullian.   Tertullian was a presbyter of the Church of Carthage; and he appears to have received ordination about the year 192 A. D., at the age of forty-five. He is described by Jerome as a man of eager and vehement character*, and the works, which have reached us from his hand, attest the truth of that description. Thirty-one of these are still extant, and their various objects were, to defend the Faith against the calumnies and oppression of the heathen; to secure its purity from the pollution of heresy; and to establish the discipline and amend the morality of the faithful. His 'Apology' stands without question among the most valuable monuments of early Christianity: and his moral writings must have been eminently serviceable to converts who had been educated in no fixed principles; and whose habits

* " Acris et vehementis ingenii."—Catalogus Script. Eccles. We acknowledge great obligations to Bishop Kaye for the manner in which he has brought within the reach of ordinary readers of theology the works of Justin and Tertullian. Whoever shall imitate his example in the treatment of the other principal Fathers, examining with the same learning, judgment, and moderation their merits and defects, and sifting from the various contents of their folios what is really valuable to the history and right understanding of religion, will complete an undertaking of incalculable use in the study of early Christianity. And at the same time he will perform a secondary, but not unworthy, office—that of placing those writers in their just rank in literature—a rank from which they are equally far removed by the enthusiasm of those who reverence them too highly, and by the ignorance of the more numerous party who scorn them altogether.

could scarcely have escaped the general contagion of profligacy. Respecting the literary merits of his compositions—whatever censure it may be necessary to express on the abruptness of his periods, the frequent inaccuracy of his inferences, and the predominance of his irregular and African imagination—though we may sometimes smile at his rhetoric, and sometimes distrust his historical assertions—we cannot forbear every where to recognize his power. The strength and conciseness of his phraseology, the severity of his sarcasm, and his rude and fearless eloquence, indicate a vigour and vehemence, which we find in no other Antenicene writer.

With this very vehemence was connected his inconstancy. *His Montanism.* After writing many tracts against various heresies, he suddenly adopted the opinions of the least rational, perhaps, of all heretics—the Montanists. St. Jerome ascribes this apostacy "to the indignity and contumely with which he had been treated by the clergy of Rome." But this sinister excuse will only save his reason at the expense of his moral principle. It is, however, certain that, after his desertion*, he published much bitter and exaggerated declamation both against the practices of the Church and the deportment of its ministers.

It was likewise the fortune of Tertullian to become himself, *Sect of Tertullianists.* and as it seems unintentionally, the founder of a sect. He held a peculiar opinion concerning the nature of the soul. Without disputing its immortality, he maintained that it was corporeal†, and even carried this opinion so far, as to assert, that such also was the nature of the Divinity, though it was not expressed by any outward form. This doctrine found some adherents, who were called Tertullianists, and of whom a small remnant still existed in the age of St. Augustine. But what is more remarkable, and gives some insight into the spirit of those early times, is this, that the stigma of heresy was not affixed to Tertullian

---

* Learned writers do not profess to have ascertained with confidence which of Tertullian's treatises were written before, which after, his apostacy. The testimony of St. Jerome (Catal. Eccles. Script.) is, however, express as to the following having been written after *De Pudicitia, De Persecutione, De Jejuniis, De Monogamia, De Ecstasi Libros sex & septimum, quem adversus Apollonium composuit.*

† "Animam dicit immortalem quidem, sed eam *corpus* esse contendit : neque hanc tantum, sed ipsum etiam Deum corporeum esse dicit, licet non effigiatum."—Augustin. lib. de Hæres.

G 2

on account of this metaphysical error, but "because (as are Augustine's expressions) he went over to the Montanists, whom he had before assailed, and condemned second marriages as contrary to the apostolical doctrine; and afterwards seceded from them too, and established conventicles of his own."

Cyprian.

The fame of Tertullian was succeeded in the same Church, at no long interval, by that of Cyprian, whose works furnish matter even more important to the historian of this century. Cyprian was an African and a heathen, and in his earlier years acquired great celebrity as a teacher of rhetoric. Pontius, the deacon, his partial biographer, throws a veil over all the circumstances of his life preceding his conversion*, an event which is ascribed to the persuasions of a presbyter named Cæcilius. He immediately assumed an eminent station in the Church of Carthage. It is the expression of Pontius, that "he was elected, while yet a Neophyte, to the office of the priesthood, and to the episcopal rank;" and it appears probable, that less than three years intervened between his baptism and his elevation to the see of Carthage. This last event seems to have taken place in 248. It is said that he was exalted to that dangerous dignity rather by the popular importunity of the Church, than by his own inclination: it is certain, that he possessed it for ten anxious years of usefulness to his people, and immortal reputation to himself; and that he then suffered martyrdom, with great fortitude, in the reign of Valerian.

The account of his suffering will be given in a later page. At present, we shall shortly consider his ecclesiastical character, as exhibited in those works which remain to us. His Epistles contain several passages in which the episcopal name and dignity is held up to the very high veneration of the people. "We are not ignorant (Epist. 46.) that as there is one God and one Lord Jesus Christ and one Holy Ghost, so should there be one Bishop in the Catholic Church." In the 55th Epistle he

---

* Augustine (Serm. 311) is less discreet. " Mutati sunt postea etiam plurimi Senatores; mutatus est Cyprianus, cujus hodie memoriam frequentamus . . . Ipse scribit, ipse testatur, cujus vitæ fuerit aliquando, quam nefariæ, quam impiæ, quam improbandæ, ac detestandæ." We must remark, however, that we have not observed in Cyprian's works any "Confessions," which at all justify the strong expressions of Augustine.

declares that one who resists a bishop, who has been legitimately elected, passes sentence not so much on the Bishop as on God himself—indeed, in the same Epistle, he plainly represents that he ought to be considered the Vicegerent of God*. In the 69th (ad Florentium Pupianum) he says, " Whence you should know that the Bishop is in the Church, and the Church in the Bishop; and that, whosoever is not with the Bishop, is not in the Church†."

Now we cannot question that it was the effect of these very strong expressions, both on those to whom they were addressed and on succeeding generations, to exalt the episcopal dignity far above its original modesty; and therefore it is, that Cyprian has been loudly eulogized by some as the champion of the venerable hierarchy—and condemned by others as the corruptor of the apostolical humility of the Church. In the mean time, when we look closely into the writings of this Father, we cannot avoid observing—(1) that he sometimes applies to the whole sacerdotal order general terms of reverence not very dissimilar to those in which he elevates the Bishop: (2) that he expressly disclaims for himself and for his order every sort of despotic authority in the government of their several dioceses.

For (1) in Epist. 55, it is of the priesthood generally that he says " not to believe that they are ordained of God, this is to renounce the faith by which we live—this is to refuse honour to God." The 69th Epistle contains similar expressions respecting the *Sacerdotes Dei,* and so do several others. We shall likewise refer to the 65th, addressed to Rogatianus, of which the object is to exhort that prelate to chastise a refractory deacon. After praising the moderation of Rogatian in referring the question to higher authority, rather than punishing the offender himself, as he had lawful power to do, by deposition or suspension, he proceeds to exalt the *Sacerdotal* authority by reference to many passages in the Old Testament, and by mention of the

---

* " Neque enim aliunde hæreses obortæ sunt . . quam inde quod Sacerdoti Dei non obtemperatur, nec *unus* in Ecclesia ad tempus Sacerdos et ad tempus judex *vice Christi* cogitatur : cui si secundum magisteria divina obtemperaret fraternitas universa, &c. . . ."

† " Unde scire debes Episcopum in Ecclesia esse et Ecclesiam in Episcopo : et siquis cum Episcopo non sit, in Ecclesia non esse."

respect which Christ himself had shown for the sacred order.
He then, however, proceeds to infer the inferiority of deacons,
from the circumstance that they were not instituted till after the
Ascension, "whereas the Lord himself had chosen Apostles—
that is Bishops and Prelates (Præpositos);" and asserts besides,
that the relation of the Deacon to the Bishop *who made him,*
implies the same degree of subordination as that of the Bishop
to God himself*—who is the fountain of episcopal authority.

(2.) The word præpositus is used on that occasion, not presbyter. And there is a passage in the fifth Epistle which to
some will seem to illustrate the above, but which is more
important as throwing light on the ecclesiastical polity of the
third century.

" As to what our Brother-presbyters (*Compresbyteres*), Donatus and Fortunatus, Novatus and Gordius, have written me,
I am unable *alone* to return any answer; since it has been a
rule with me, from the very beginning of my episcopacy, never
to act on my own private judgment, without your *counsel,* and
the *consent* of the people†. As our common honour requires,
we will deliberate in common." His thirty-third Epistle proves
that he continued generally to adhere to this rule. It is addressed to " The Clergy and People," and is written purposely
to excuse an exception which he had made to his general rule
of consulting *them* as to the merits of every candidate for the
ministry. In this one instance he " and his colleagues who
were present" had ordained one Aurelius a Reader (ἀναγνωστής,
lector) without their consent; and he mentions in some detail
the peculiar merits of the candidate, which justified this innovation. Such then being the " Rule" of Cyprian, and such his

---

* "Quod si nos aliquid audere contra Deum possumus, qui Episcopos facit,
possunt et contra nos audere Diaconi, a quibus fiunt."

† " Nihil sine consilio vestro et sine consensu plebis mea privatim sententia
gerere." Ecclesiastical historians in citing this passage sometimes (inadver-
tently no doubt) omit the words " et sine consensu plebis." But there are numerous other passages to the same purpose, as in Ep. xiii., " Hoc et verecundiæ et
disciplinæ...convenit, ut Præpositi cum Clero convenientes præsente etiam stan-
tium plebe...disponere omnia consilii communis religione possimus." So Epist.
xxviii., when called upon to decide a point of discipline, relating to two sub-dea-
cons and an acolyth, he replies—" Cui rei non potui me solum judicem
dare, &c." So again Ep. xxiv., &c.

practice, it is unjust to plead his authority in defence of the
episcopal usurpations of later ages.

As he respected the independence of the clergy and people in Episcopal
the government of his Church, so he perpetually recognised election.
their authority in episcopal election. In his sixty-eighth Epistle
(*Ad Clerum et Plebes in Hispania consistentes*) he justified the
public election of Bishops by the law of Moses, and by apostolical authority; he asserted its almost universal observance,
and upheld it by exhortation and argument*. So likewise (as
we have already observed) he maintained the independence of
the several sees, and their perfect equality in spiritual power,
against the rising ambition of Rome.

Reflecting on all these circumstances, we cannot consider Treatise on
Cyprian as the mere advocate of episcopal despotism (as some the Unity
of the
have done), whether in oppressing the Presbyters, or overruling Church.
the people. His general object was not so much to exalt any
order in the ministry at the expense of the rest, as to elevate
the whole ministry in the eyes of the faithful; and to teach
them an unbounded veneration for *the Church.* This is the
spirit which really shows itself in many of his Epistles, as the
leading principle of his conduct; but to see its full development
we must advance to his celebrated Treatise " On the Unity of
the Church," from which we shall cite some few passages; because the principles contained in them, however familiar they will
hereafter become, were now for the first time promulgated with
authority in the Catholic Church. " Whosoever separating
himself from the Church becomes connected with an Adulteress

---

* " Coram omni Synagoga jubet Deus constitui sacerdotem : id est, instruit ac
ostendit ordinationes sacerdotales non nisi sub populi assententis conscientia fieri
oportere ; ut plebe præsente vel detegantur malorum crimina vel bonorum merita
prædicentur, et sit ordinatio justa et legitima, quæ omnium suffragio et judicio
fuerit examinata. Quod postea, secundum divina magisteria, observatur in
Actis Apostolorum. . . Nec hoc in Episcoporum tantum et Sacerdotum sed et
in Diaconorum ordinationibus observasse Apostolos animadvertimus . . Propter quod diligenter, de traditione divina et Apostolica, servandum est et tenen-
dum quod apud nos quoque et fere per provincias universas tenetur, ut ad ordinationes rité celebrandas, ad eam plebem, cui Præpositus ordinatur, Episcopi
ejusdem provinciæ proximi quique conveniant, et *Episcopus deligatur plebe præsente,* quæ singulorum vitam plenissimè novit."

is separated from the promises of the Church : nor will he attain the rewards of Christ, who has deserted the Church of Christ. He is a stranger, he is profane, an enemy. He cannot have God for his father, who has not the Church for his mother. It is no more possible that any man shall escape destruction, who is without the Church, than that any one could have escaped the Deluge, who was without the Ark of Noah*. No one will hold that those can possibly be good, who depart from the Church.

" He can be no martyr, who is not in the Church. He can never attain the kingdom, who abandons her who will be its queen. Christ has given us peace; he has told us to be in harmony and of one mind; he has commanded us to preserve inviolate the bonds of affection and charity. Now no man can present himself as a martyr, unless he has maintained brotherly charity. . . . Those cannot remain with God, who have not chosen to be of one mind in the Church of God. Let them be delivered up and burnt by fire and flame, or be cast to the beasts and so perish; that will not be the crown of their faith, but *the punishment of their perfidy;* nor will their death be the glorious departure of religious excellence, but the destruction of despair.

" Such a man is to be abhorred and avoided, whosoever shall be separated from the Church. Such a one is perverse, and a sinner, and self-condemned. Can he have any part in Christ, who turns against the Priests of Christ, and distinguishes himself from the society of his clergy and his people? He carries arms against the Church, he struggles against the dispensation of God. An enemy of the altar, a rebel against the sacrifice of Christ, a traitor to his faith. . . . ."

Cyprian concludes this Treatise with a mournful lamentation for the falling away of the Christians of his time from the apostolical unanimity and profusion of eleemosynary charity, which

---

* This expression, as synonymous with " The Church," became afterwards in great favour with Roman Catholic writers—and consistently so, for it insinuated one of the avowed maxims of their Church, viz., that there was no salvation out of the Church. When Protestant churchmen use it, it is, doubtless, through inattention to the meaning really conveyed by it.

distinguished the primitive believers—and exhorts them to return to those principles in pious and rational language.

Such then was the sort of Christian " Unity" which Cyprian inculcated as necessary for salvation, and such the limits of his " Charity." It was the unity—not of Christendom—but of the Church. Was there any holiness? It was only to be found within the precincts of the Church. Any hope of eternal salvation? It was forfeited by secession from the Church. In the inexhaustible treasures of God's mercy there was nothing reserved for the man who dissented from the creed, or practice, or discipline established by the Church. Such were the limits of his charity. Those who *conformed* preserved the spirit of Christian concord—but those who differed were consigned, as the foes of unanimity, to everlasting wrath. So early was the spirit of the Gospel forgotten in the spirit of the Church—and so disastrous the influence which the principles of Cyprian exerted over the churchmen of succeeding generations.

At the same time, it is proper to distinguish between the guilt of Cyprian, and that of his imitators in after ages. They had nothing to plead but the zeal of sordid interest, or the mere pusillanimity of bigotry. But in the time of Cyprian, many of the prevalent heresies were so far removed both from Scripture and from reason, that it was difficult to extend to them so much as the name of Christian: and the deadly persecutions which were then raging, and which perpetually threatened the very existence of Christianity, created a strong necessity for a visible unity, enforced by a rigid and exclusive discipline.

Cyprian was the Ignatius of the third century: he lived in the same tempestuous times; he maintained (though in much greater variety and extent) the same sort of ecclesiastical principles; he perished by the same barbarous fate *, and endured it with the same constancy. But if we should compare him with Origen, who was his contemporary †, or with his imme-

---

* It is worth remarking, that while Polycarp and many others were rather the victims of popular madness, both Ignatius and Cyprian fell beneath the deliberate vengeance of the government.

† Origen seems indeed to have been driven away from public life before Cyprian entered it—yet the latter survived him very few years.

diate predecessors Clemens of Alexandria and Tertullian, we should perceive at once how the character of his works was affected by his office in the Church: how much less he engaged in philosophical speculations, or moral investigation, or any general argument—how much more he was compelled to be conversant with the practical interests of the Church *, and the means of consolidating and supporting the external fabric. Hence it is, that in reading his works we find our attention continually fixed upon "the Church." The "nuptials of Christ with the Church;" the "spiritual sword of the Church;" the "discipline of the Church;" the "power and vigour of the priestly office (Sacerdotii vigor);" the "ark of Noah"—these and similar expressions perpetually remind us both of the station of the writer, and the ruling character of his principles. A great proportion of his pages is likewise occupied by ecclesiastical disputes of very transient importance; and the fury with which he pursued the schismatics and heretics of his day, though by no means peculiar to himself, perhaps surpassed the violence of any preceding father. But together with all this matter, we discover without surprise many expressions of fervent Christian piety, and many zealous exhortations of faith and constancy to his afflicted or trembling brethren. For he had fallen on evil times; and in his anxious desire to preserve his religion both from corruption and overthrow, he adopted such measures as to him appeared suited to the necessities of the moment, without altogether neglecting those which proceeded from the true spirit of the faith and were adapted to its perpetual service.

Government of the Church.

Respecting the general government of the Church during the third century some particulars may be collected from the preceding pages. It appears that the more important Churches were severally superintended by a bishop, possessed of a certain, but not very definite degree of authority; and that he ruled in concert with the body of presbyters; and even consulted on

* Neander would establish a general distinction between the χάρισμα διδασκαλίας and the χάρισμα γυβερνήσεως—supposing the former to be equally the office of every believer, and that the latter only was peculiarly that of the minister. It is connected with his notion of an universal priesthood, and is, in our opinion, purely fanciful.

matters of great moment the opinion of the whole assembly. The provincial synods, of which we have spoken, composed of those bishops, assisted by a few presbyters, now began to meet with great regularity, in the spring and autumn of every year*, and to publish canons for the general administration of ecclesiastical affairs. The Metropolitans gradually rose in consequence. Their dignity seems to have been conferred for life; but their legitimate power was confined to the calling and presiding in councils, and the fraternal admonition of offenders. Still it was the natural consequence of this system, that these occasional presidents should insensibly assert a general pre-eminence over the other bishops, which it would become their next step to dispute with each other; and that the other bishops, being now constantly distinguished from their presbyters by these synodical meetings, should assume both over them and the people a degree of ascendency not originally acknowledged, but which it would not be difficult by degrees to convert into authority. If we could bestow on any individual the credit of having accomplished a change so natural and so gradual, that distinction might possibly be due to Cyprian; though, in as far as the episcopal dignity is concerned, his writings had more effect in exalting it in following ages, than during his own. It seems clear, indeed, from several of his epistles †, especially that addressed to Rogatian, that bishops possessed in his time, or at least in his Church, the power of suspending or deposing delinquents among the clergy; yet even this was liable to some indefinite restrictions as to circumstance and custom, and to a

---

* " Qua ex causa necessario apud nos fit, ut per singulos annos Seniores et Præpositi in unum conveniamus, ad disponenda ea, quæ curæ nostræ commissa sunt, ut, siqua graviora sunt, communi consilio dirigantur." Firmiliani ad Cypr. (Epist. 75. Edit. Paris.)   See too Cyprian, Ep. 53, whence we may infer a customary assembly of the bishops at Carthage after Easter.

† Bingham, Ch. Antiq. b. ii. ch. 3. The apostolical canons confirm these pretensions, and so do certain canons of the councils of Nice, Sardica, Antioch, Chalcedon, and others; but, according to the first and second councils of Carthage, the consent of three bishops was necessary for the censure of a deacon, of six for that of a presbyter, of twelve for that of a bishop. "Reliquorum Clericorum causas solus Episcopus loci agnoscat et finiat."—Conc. Carth. iii. Can. 8.   See Mosh. (De Reb. Christ. ant. Const. sec. iii. sect. xxiii. xxiv.) for a full examination of the principles and conduct of Cyprian.

direct appeal to a provincial council.   And it does not appear
that such power was frequently exerted without the consent of
the presbyterial college, or "senate of the Church."   From
these facts, compared with the assertions afterwards made by
Jerome and Chrysostom, (which we have already mentioned,)
we infer that the actual progress of episcopal authority, during
the third century, was much less than some have imagined—or
at least, that the power of the bishops grew chiefly through the
growth of their *influence*, and was not yet publicly acknowledged by the constitution of the Church.   And we are disposed
to attribute much of this increase of influence to a cause not
sufficiently attended to by ecclesiastical writers,—the judicial,
or rather arbitrative, authority originally vested in the bishops
by the consent of their people, and which would naturally
extend its limits, as it was confirmed by time and usage.

Degene-
racy of the
Clergy.
    We admit, however, with sorrowful reflection, that the indi-
vidual conduct of some, perhaps many, among the directors of
the Church, during the course, and especially towards the
conclusion, of this century, deserved the reprehensions of contemporary and succeeding writers *.   Some assumption of the
ensigns of temporal dignity—the splendid throne, the sump-
tuous garments, the parade of external pomp—indicated a
departure from apostolical simplicity ; and a contentious ambition succeeded to the devoted humility of former days.   And
though we believe this evil to have been exaggerated by all the
writers who have dwelt upon it, since the abuses which we have
noticed could scarcely be carried to violent excess by an order
possessing no legally recognised rights or property, we may
still be convinced, by the institution of certain inferior classes

---

   * Origen. Comm. in Matthæum, par. i. App. p. 420, 441, 442 ; Euseb. H. E.
l. viii. cap. 1. Cyprian himself rates his contemporary prelates with great severity.
(Laps. p. 183. Edit. Paris.) " Episcopi plurimi . . . divina procuratione con-
tempta, procuratores rerum secularium fieri, derelicta Cathedra, plebe deserta, per
aliquas Provincias oberrantes negotiationis quæstuosæ nundinationes aucupari," &c.
&c. &c. The language of Mosheim, who is always extremely violent on this subject, will not bear careful examination. Gen. Hist. cent. iii. p. ii. ch. 2. See also
Tillem. vol. iii. p. 306. The praise which Origen has bestowed on Christians
generally, may be contrasted with his censures on the clergy, and they will serve
to moderate each other.

in the ministry, such as subdeacons, acoluthi, readers, exorcists, and others, that the higher ranks had made some advances in luxurious indolence*. Of these new offices, that of reader is presumed to have been the oldest, as it is mentioned by Tertullian †. But the others must have followed soon afterwards; for though the first place in which they are mentioned together is in the epistle of Cornelius, bishop of Rome, (251 A. D.) cited by Eusebius, we find frequent and familiar notice of the acolyths in the writings of Cyprian.

This deterioration in the character of the ministers was attended by a corresponding change in the ceremonies of the Church. The division of the people into two classes, the Faithful and the Catechumens, was the practice, if not the invention, of the third century; and it seems to have been borrowed from the pagan principle of initiation. The outward distinction between those classes was this: after the performance of public worship, the latter was dismissed, while the former, the true and initiated Christians, remained to celebrate the *mysteries*‡ of their religion; and this term is by some thought to have expressed not only the administration of the sacraments, but also the delivery of some doctrinal instructions.

Indeed Origen expressly asserts that the spiritual food prepared for the converts was of two descriptions; and that their teachers only advanced the most excellent and holy doctrines when they were surrounded by intelligent, or initiated §, hearers—concealing the deeper truths from the common assembly, which required more tender and infantine nourishment. Whether or not the distinction here intended by Origen be that above-men-

Faithful and Catechumens.

---

* Mosh., de Reb. Chr. ante Const. sec. iii. sect. 23.

† Præscript. Hæret. c. 41.

‡ The term *mystery* is in the Greek Church synonymous with *sacrament*. See Semler, cent. iii. p. 63; and particularly Le Clerc, cent. ii. ann. 101. and 118. Neither were the Catechumens allowed to use the Lord's Prayer, which was even denominated εὐχὴ πιστῶν, the prayer of *the Faithful*. Chrysost. Hom. ii. in 2 Cor. p. 740, and Hom. x. in Coloss. For other references, see Bingham, Ch. Antiq. b. i. ch. 4.

§ Ὅτ' εὐποροῦμεν συνετῶν ἀκροατῶν· ἀποκρύπτομεν δὲ καὶ παρασιωπῶμεν τὰ βαθύτερα τοὺς συνερχομένους καὶ δεομένους λόγων τροπικῶς ὀνομαζομένων γάλα. Lib. iii. Adv. Cels. (p. 143. Edit. Cantab.)

tioned, may appear uncertain; but the fact of this two-fold instruction is at any rate important and worthy to be recorded.

False notions on Baptism. It is, however, certain that that distinction was closely connected with the office of baptism. The original simplicity of that sacrament had already undergone some corruption. The symbol had been gradually exalted at the expense of the thing signified, and the spirit of the ceremony was beginning to be lost in its form. Hence a belief was gaining ground among the converts, and was inculcated among the heathen, that the act of baptism performed in communion with the Church and by imposition of the hands of the clergy *, gave remission of all sins committed previously to it.

There are some passages in the writings of Cyprian which unreservedly and without any modification assert this doctrine†. And though there are many others, in which the nature of the spiritual regeneration is explained with great clearness, and some where he declares the efficacy of baptism ‡ to that effect to be annulled by subsequent relapse into infidelity or transgression, yet enough exists, even in his enlightened compositions, to account for the origin of that notion. It was not fit, then, that so important a rite should be hastily performed or inconsiderately received ; and, therefore, the new proselytes were, in the first instance, admitted into a probationary state under the name of Catechumens, whence they were chosen, according to their progress in grace, into the body of the faithful. As long as they remained in that class, great care was taken to instruct them in the important truths, and especially in the moral obligations, of religion; yet doubtless there would be some among them, in whom the love of sin survived the

---

* " Quod nunc quoque apud nos geritur, ut qui in Ecclesia baptizantur Præpositis Ecclesiæ offerantur, et per nostram orationem et manus impositionem Spiritum Sanctum consequantur, et signaculo Dominico consummentur." Cypr. Epist. 73.

† Epist. 76. Ed. Paris. "Nam cum in baptismo unicuique peccata sua remittantur, probat et declarat in Evangelio suo Dominus per eos solos peccata posse dimitti, qui habeant Spiritum Sanctum, &c." Also Ep. 73. &c. Euseb. H. E. vii. s. 8. Mosh. c. iii. p. ii. ch. 4. Compare Cyprian's language with the passage of Justin Martyr on the same subject.

‡ "Parum est baptizari et Eucharistiam accipere, nisi quis factis et opere proficiat." Lib. Testimoniorum, iii. 26.

practice of superstition *, and such would naturally defer their baptism and their pardon until the fear of death, or satiety of enjoyment, overtook them.   We should remember, however, that baptism was not supposed to bestow any impunity for future sins; on the contrary, the first offence committed after it required the expiation of a public confession, (called ἐξομολόγησις,) and the second was punished by excommunication.   And if the hope and easy condition of pardon for the past tended, as it may have done, to fill the ranks of the catechumens, we may reasonably indulge the belief, that the great majority were amended and perfected by the religious instruction which was then opened to them.

   An opinion at this time became prevalent in the Christian Exorcism. world, that the demons, the enemies of man, were, in fact, the same beings whom the heathen worshipped as gods, who inhabited their temples and animated their statues.   It became, therefore, the duty of the soldiers of Christ to assail them under every form, and expel them from every residence.   That, indeed, which they are related most frequently to have occupied was the body of man †, and from this refuge they were perseveringly disturbed by the pious exorcisms of the clergy; and this practice was carried to such superstitious excess, that none were admitted to the ordinance of baptism until they had been solemnly delivered from the dominion of the Prince of Darkness.   The first unequivocal trace of the ceremony of exorcism, as essentially connected with baptism, appears in the Cyprianic age.   In the council of Carthage held in 256, and composed of eighty-five bishops, the bishop of Bilta mentions exorcism among the ordinary parts of the ceremony.   And Cyprian him-

* Origen, however, assures us, that among his converts there were more who had previously led a moral life than of the opposite description—a fact which may serve as an answer to one of Gibbon's insinuations.   Contr. Cels. l. iii. pp. 150, 151.   Tillem., Mem., vol. iii. p. 116.

† Celibacy, though under no circumstances considered as a duty either by clergy or laity, acquired some unmerited honour during this age, through the absurd, but general persuasion, that those who had wives were peculiarly liable to the influence of malignant demons.   At least Mosheim (cent. iii. p. ii. ch. 2) asserts this on the authority of an enemy—Porphyry, περὶ Ἀποχῆς, l. iv. p. 417. In the time of Irenæus, (l. i. c. 24.) the profession of celibacy was a heresy.

self, in the lxxvith epistle, after stating how "the Devil was flagellated, burnt and tortured by the exorcists, with human voice but power from above," proceeds to say that, "when the convert comes to the waters of salvation and the sanctification of baptism, we ought to know and trust that the Devil is then oppressed, and the man, dedicated to God, is through divine indulgence set at liberty.   For as serpents and scorpions, so powerful on dry ground, retain not their poison when cast into the water, so neither can the evil spirits remain in the human body, when, through baptism and sanctification, the Holy Spirit enters thereinto."   The general use of exorcism among the Christians of this age is sufficiently proved by the existence of the office, and the testimony of the best writers * ; and this was only the continuation of an older practice: but its connexion with the baptismal service may be ascribed to the first half of the third century.

The sign of the Cross.

We may here mention, that the sign of the cross was already in much honour in the time of Tertullian †, and was held to be of great effect in the expulsion of Dæmons, and other miracles. And we find it proposed, as one of the Theses in 'Cyprian's Book of Testimonies' ‡, "that in this sign there is salvation to all who receive it on the forehead."   It is not probable that the enlightened prelate intended this expression to be interpreted literally : yet was it a dangerous abuse of language and fraught with abundant evil in after times, to confound the mere symbol with the spiritual regeneration signified, and exalt them in the same lofty terms, and propose them as objects of equal reverence to an ignorant and superstitious people.

The Eucharist.

It is commonly asserted that, at about the same time, and from causes connected with the misapprehension of the real nature of baptism, and the division of the converts, a vague and mysterious veneration began to be attached to the other sacra-

---

* Origen (Contr. Cels. lib. i. c. 34.) asserts that traces of the Holy Spirit were yet preserved among Christians—"who *exorcise evil spirits* (ἐξεπᾴδουσι δαίμονας) and perform many cures, and have some foresight, through the will of the Word, of things to come." See chap. xiii.

† De Corona, cap. iii. " Frontem Crucis signaculo terimus."

‡ Lib. ii. s. 22.

ment: that its nature and its merits were exaggerated by those who administered and partook of it: that it was regarded with superstitious curiosity by those to whom it was refused, while reports were propagated of the miraculous efficacy of the consecrated elements.   It is proper to examine how far these notions were justified by the deliberate expressions of the two great fathers of that century.   Origen * speaks of " the bread, which is presented with thanksgiving and prayer, as being made by the prayer a holy body, sanctifying those who use it with wholesome purpose."   Cyprian declares, that the eucharist is taken as a protection to those who receive it—to the end that they may be *safe against the assaults of the adversary,* being armed with the defence of the Lord's feast†."   In another place ‡ he gives a singular reason for the *daily* celebration of the sacrament.   "We who are in Christ daily receive the eucharist as *the food of salvation,* lest being prohibited through the commission of any gross offence from communion and *the heavenly bread* (cœlesti pane), we should be separated from the body of Christ."   The language of Origen afforded no manner of pretext for any superstitious notion ; but the more vague expressions of Cyprian were sure to receive from the ardent imaginations of the people a wild and extravagant interpretation §.

A regular form of penance was imposed upon the offender, before he could be restored to the communion, or, as it is commonly called by Cyprian, the peace, of the Church (pax

Penance and Confession.

---

* Contra Cels. lib. viii. p. 393. Edit. Cantab.   Σῶμα ἅγιον καὶ ἁγιάζον τοὺς μεθ' ὑγιοῦς προθέσεως αὐτῷ χρωμένους.

† "Munimento dominicæ saturitatis." Epist. 54. Ad Cornelium.

‡ *Liber de Dominica Oratione,* p. 209. Edit. Paris.   In the book *De Lapsis* he calls the cup—"Sanctificatus in sanguine Domini potus"—and in Epist. 56. the reason he gives for "the daily drinking of Christ's blood" is, that "Christians may be in perpetual readiness to pour out their blood for Christ."

§ In his *Liber de Lapsis* Cyprian tells a story, on his own personal knowledge, of a female child, which, during the persecution, had been compelled to swallow some of the sacrificial food.   She was afterwards brought to the Lord's table—and when, after many struggles, the deacon at last poured some of the cup down her reluctant throat, she immediately vomited it out.   "In corpore atque ore violato Eucharistia permanere non potuit . . . . . Tanta est potestas Domini, tanta majestas, &c."

Ecclesiæ). The frequency of this practice is proved by the common mention of it in the writings of that, and even of the preceding, age. "The power of remitting sins (says Firmilianus, bishop of Cæsarea in Cappadocia, to Cyprian *) was given to the Apostles, and to the Churches which they founded, and to the bishops who by vicarious ordination have succeeded them. Wherefore, in our periodical councils, besides other important matters, we seek by means of penance a remedy for our brethren who have fallen away after baptism—not as if the remission of sins proceeded from ourselves, but that they may be turned by us to a knowledge of their sins, and make ampler satisfaction to God." "Let every man confess his sins (says Cyprian) while he is still in the world .... and while the satisfaction and remission made to the Lord by his priests may be still acceptable." This penance, even in minor offences, included public confession. "In smaller sins, the sinners do penance for an appointed time; then, according to the order of discipline, they come to the *Exomologesis* †", and then, by imposition of hands of the bishop and clergy, they receive the right of communion ‡". This was the ordinary practice of the Church and extended to all the faithful. But, "there were some of more commanding faith and more scrupulous excellence §, who, though entirely free from the commission of sin, yet because they had so much as thought of it, confessed this very thought with sorrow and simplicity to the priests of God, and made an exomologesis of their conscience."—These however were rare and voluntary acts of devotion, not yet enforced by the precepts, or necessary to the power of an ambitious priesthood.

Christian discipline.

We shall conclude our account of these practices with the description of the Christian discipline given by Origen in his Third Book against Celsus. "The Christian teachers pre-

---

* Epist. Cypr. 73.

† "Exomologesis est, qua delictum Domino nostrum confitemur, non quidem ut ignaro, sed quatenus satisfactio Confessione disponitur, Confessione Pœnitentia nascitur, Pœnitentia Deus mitigatur."—*Tertullian de Pœnitentia*, § ix. Tertullian is more spiritual: Cyprian more ecclesiastical.

‡ Cyprian, Epist. ix. See also Epist. xi. and the Liber de Lapsis.

§ Liber de Lapsis.

examine, as far as possible, the souls of those who wish to hear them, and privately gain mastery * over them before admission.   And when the hearers appear to have given sufficient proof of their desire to lead a good life, before they are received into the public assembly, then they introduce them: making one class of those who are novices, and have not yet received the symbol of purification; another of those who have, as far as may be, made good their profession, and proved that they have no inclinations adverse to the statutes of the Christians. Over these there are persons appointed to investigate their lives and morals, that they may exclude from the common assembly those who do things forbidden; and embrace with their whole soul such as are otherwise disposed, and establish them in the daily progress of improvement.   How severe again is their discipline in regard to sinners, especially the incontinent, whom they expel from communion . . . . . The respectable school of Pythagoras used to erect cenotaphs to those who deserted the sect, accounting them for dead.   But the Christians hold those as perished and dead to God, who are subject to lust or any other evil passion—and these they bewail as departed souls: yet in such manner, that, if they give proofs of sincere repentance, again, after a longer trial than was imposed on their first introduction, they at length receive them back, as if they were risen from the dead.   At the same time, they exclude such, as have thus fallen, from all power and dignity in what is called the Church of God."

Christians had been divided during the second century, as to the propriety of adopting, in their contests with the heathen, the weapons of philosophy; and the difference was finally Philo-decided, at least at Alexandria, by the talents of Clemens and sophy. Origen, and the superior loquacity of the philosophical party. By this condescension the advocates of the faith gained great advantages in the display of argument, in subtilty of investigation, in plausibility of conclusion, in the abuse and even in the use of reason ; but they lost that manly and simple integrity of

---

* Κατ' ἰδίαν αὐτοῖς προσπάσαντες.   We have given what appears to us the general meaning of this expression.   Ἐξιπάδειν is, in Origen, to exorcise.

disputation which well became, in spite of its occasional rusticity, the defenders of truth.   It is to this alliance * that some are

Pious Frauds. disposed to trace the birth of those pious frauds which stain the face of ecclesiastical history.   Howbeit, the original source of this evil was at least innocent.   It had long been a practice among ancient philosophical writers to ascribe their works to some name of undisputed authority, in order to secure attention to their opinions, though the opinions were well known to be only those of the writer;   and this might serve a good purpose, when opinions only were propounded, and not truths;   and when those opinions too were merely speculative, and did not at all involve the hopes or the interests of mankind. But when the same practice was introduced into the service of Christianity, it had no other effect than to generate distrust and contention;   to pollute its present purity;   and prepare the way for future and more abominable corruptions.   Numerous apocryphal Gospels† were published in the second and third centuries.   Acts and Revelations were so multiplied, that there is scarcely one among the apostles whose name has not been affixed to some such forgery.   Books, written in later ages, were zealously circulated as the writings of the Apostolical Fathers‡.   The works of these last were altered or interpolated,

---

* Le Clerc adjudges to an earlier year (ann. 122) the celebrated forgery, under the name of Hermes Trismegistus, of which the object was to trace the doctrine of Christ to a much higher period than his incarnation, and thus to increase its sanctity. The interpolation of the Sibylline Books is referred by the same historian to the year 131.   This latter imposture, as foolish as shameful, was warmly patronised by a host of Fathers, including Clemens Alex., Tertullian, Eusebius, Jerome, Augustin, &c. and thus occasioned much scandal to Christians in general among their enemies in that age, and no little disrepute to its ancient patrons among candid writers of every age.   See Le Clerc, vol. i. p.106.   Jortin, Remarks, &c. vol. i. p. 188.

† As the Gospel of the Infancy of Jesus, the Gospel of Nicodemus, the Gospel of Jude, the Gospel of Peter, the Preaching of Peter, the Acts of Paul and Thecla—all of which probably existed at the middle of the second century.   The last four of these are respectively mentioned by Irenæus (i. 31), Serapion (ap. Euseb. vi. 12.), Clemens Alexandrinus (Stromates, vi.), and Tertullian. The "Testimony of the Twelve Patriarchs" was probably published about the same time—and a multitude of others might be mentioned—for indeed it was the fashion of that age to produce such romances.

‡ Such, in the second century, were the celebrated Apostolical Canons; and, in the fourth, the Apostolical Constitutions, attributed to the diligence of Clemens

according to the notions of after times, or the caprices of the interpolator; but usually for the purpose of proving the antiquity of some new opinion, some innovation in discipline, some usurpation of authority. The practice was justified by the detestable, but popular principle, " that truth may be defended by falsehood ;" it was encouraged by the difficulty of detection in ignorant ages; and it continued for more than six centuries to disgrace the Roman Church. And it was the same principle, pushed a little farther, which has infected the writings of some among the early Fathers with statements at least doubtful, if not with palpable falsehood. On the other hand, we should ever recollect, that Christianity in those days was chiefly in the hands of Greeks and Africans*—men of subtle intellects and violent passions, whose habits and whose climate too often carried them into the extreme either of metaphysical sophistry or wild enthusiasm—men who could speculate on their faith, or who could die for it, but who were little calculated for the tranquil equanimity of sober and reasonable belief. We should recollect also, that some of our best and commonest principles of action were then unknown or partially received; and that, in fact, many of them are the result of the patient operation of Christianity on the human character, through a long succession of ages. We shall never do justice to the history of our religion, unless we continually bear in mind the low condition of society and morals existing among the people to whom it was first delivered.

During the concluding part of the second century, a philosophical sect arose at Alexandria, which professed to form its own tenets, by selecting and reconciling what was reasonable in the tenets of all others, and rejecting what was contrary to rea-

---

Romanus; and such were the False Decretals in the eighth.—Mosh., G. Hist. c. i. p. ii. ch. 2. Le Clerc (sec. i. ad ann. 100) supposes the Canons to be of the third, the Constitutions of a later age. Jortin, supposing that the Canons may have been forged, some in the second and some in the third century, refers the Constitutions to some period after Constantine.—Vol. i. pp. 152, 185.

* It is certainly very remarkable that, for the first three centuries, Rome produced no ecclesiastical writer of any merit, excepting Clement; and the western provinces not one of any description: Rome was very nearly as barren during the three which followed.

Sect of the
Eclectics.

son—its adherents were called the new Platonics, or Eclectics *. What they professed respecting philosophy, they easily extended to religion, since with them religion was entirely founded on philosophical principles. At the very beginning of the follow-

Ammonius
Saccas.

ing age, Ammonius Saccas applied his distinguished talents to place this sect on a substantial foundation, and delivered for nearly thirty years his eloquent lectures. Exactly at the same time Origen presided over the Catechetical School; and the youth of Alexandria were divided between the rival professions of Eclecticism and Christianity. The genius of the teachers was equal; their manner of teaching was in many respects the same; and even their principles were not entirely opposite : for Origen, by an unfortunate compromise of the genuine character of the faith, admitted, in a certain sense, the Platonic origin of the Logos and the Trinity. This gave a pretext to his opponents to represent Christianity as a mere corruption of Platonism—a degenerate and spurious description of philosophy. Ammonius Saccas had been educated in Christianity, and it seems possible that he never entirely abandoned the *name*† of the religion; but neither this circumstance, nor the similarity of his principles, prevented him from waging incessant warfare against its tenets, and establishing a powerful school, for the perpetuation of his doctrines, his learning, and his enmity.

A sect, which was founded on the seductive principle of universal concord, soon made extraordinary progress. In his

Plotinus.

eminent successor Plotinus, Ammonius left a follower not inferior to himself in subtlety of genius and the power of profound and abstruse investigation. But the field of disputation was now transferred to the West. About the year 245 Plotinus opened a school at Rome, and continued to lecture there till his death in 270.

---

* Mosh. Gen. Hist., c. ii. p. ii. ch. 1. Mémoires de Tillem., tom. iii. p. 279.

† Porphyry asserts that Ammonius deserted Christianity, Eusebius that he adhered to it. To these two opinions, variously advocated by most modern divines, others have added a third, that Eusebius mistook a Christian writer of the same name for the heathen philosopher; and this is warmly maintained by Lardner. (Collection of Heathen and Jewish Testimonies.) The question was not worth one page of controversy; and, in our mind, Christian writers would act a more politic, as well as a more manly part, if they at once disclaimed their *ambiguous* defenders.

It was in 262 that he first numbered among his disciples the Porphyry. celebrated name of Porphyry.   That powerful adversary of the faith was a native of Tyre*; and having first studied under Longinus the Platonist, at Athens, he proceeded to Rome. There he passed six years in the schools of Plotinus, and thence retired to reside in Sicily. Næander well describes this eminent Theosophist "to have recast an oriental spirit in a Grecian mould."   Had it so happened that he had engrafted his peculiar notions on Christianity, he would have become a sort of Gnostic.   But having learnt in the schools of Plotinus to take the Grecian Paganism as the basis of his Theosophy, he became the bitter enemy of a religion, which recognized as truth no scheme but one, and had nothing in its exclusive nature which gave any favour to Eclecticism.   His more open attack upon the Gospel was an elaborate work, consisting of one and twenty books, of which some fragments only have escaped the zeal of the Christian emperors.   But that which, being more insidious, may have been more pernicious was his "Life of Pythagoras."   Early in the third century, one Philostratus†, a rhetorician at Rome, had composed a fabulous account of Apol- Life of Apollonius lonius of Tyana, a celebrated philosopher and magician; and so Tyaneus. wrought out the supposed extraordinary incidents of his life, as to establish a close resemblance between them and the miracles of Christ.   Porphyry imitated this example; and he represented the peaceful Pythagoras as having worked by his own power Pythago- ras. many stupendous prodigies—and having, moreover, imparted the same power to his principal disciples, Empedocles, Epimenides, and others.   Such is the sort of weapon, which, as it proceeds from the imagination, and addresses the imagination, and eludes the grasp of reason, has proved at all times the most dangerous to Christianity—and doubtless it was then efficient in retarding its progress.   At the same time it should be mentioned, that, as Origen and his scholars, on the one hand,

---

* See Euseb. l. 6. s. 9.

† We observe that Origen (l. 6. c. Cels. p. 302), speaks of "The Memorials of Apollonius Tyaneus, magician and philosopher, written by Mæragenes." The work is generally ascribed to Philostratus, who is said to have composed it at the suggestion of Julia, wife of Septimus Severus.

adopted into the service of religion some of the peculiar principles of their adversaries, so, on the other, certain disciples of
Plotinus assumed the name and professed the faith of Christians, at the same time that they retained some favourite
opinions of their master*; an accession which was only valuable in so far as it swelled the body and increased the lustre of
the church†.

Minucius
Felix.

We shall here very shortly mention two Latin writers, of less
celebrity in ecclesiastical literature—Minucius Felix, and Arnobius. The former was a lawyer of some eminence, who lived
at Rome. He was a Christian, and wrote a dialogue, entitled
'Octavius,' at the very beginning of the third century. In this
short composition he repels with indignation the calumnies,
then so commonly propagated by the heathen against the Christian name; he describes in glowing colours of eulogy the actual
virtues of the faithful; and retorts the charges of immorality
upon the Pagans and their gods.

Arnobius.

Arnobius was a native of Sicca, in Africa, a convert from
heathenism, and once a persecutor of the faith. By profession
he was a rhetorician, and is related to have given lectures to
Lactantius. About the year 310, probably somewhat earlier, he
published seven books 'Against the Heathen,' which are still
extant. They contain some strong arguments in confutation of
Paganism and in defence of the gospel, mixed with some inac-
curacies, the consequence of his recent conversion. Both these
works contain some faithful pictures of the condition of the
Christians, at the periods when they were respectively composed,
and attest the sufferings which they endured, and throw light
on their moral character and the marks which distinguished

---

* The passages of Augustin (Epist. 56, or 118, ad Dioscor.) referred to by
Mosheim (Cent. iii. p. 2. ch. i.), do not fully justify the assertion in his text.
They are in sect. 21, 32, and 33 of that Epistle.

† To give some idea of the nature of Christian literature in this age, it may be
worth while to mention the subjects of some of the most celebrated productions:—
On Temptations—The Baptism of Heretics—Promises—Chastity—The Creation
—The Origin of Evil—The Vanity of Idols—The Dress of Virgins—The Unity
of the Church—Circumcision—Clean and Unclean Animals—The Lapsed, or
those who had fallen from the Faith during Persecution—The Millennium; besides numerous books against heretics.

them from their persecutors; and this alone it is which gives them any historical value.

Cyprian, in his 66th Epistle, mentions it as a Canon *long ago* enacted in a council of Bishops, that no Clerk or Minister of God should be guardian or executor under any will, "since those who are honoured with the divine priesthood ought to undertake no other service than that of the altar and the sacraments, and to be perpetually at leisure for prayer and supplication." In other places he alludes in like manner to the statutes of former synods. We read of two important councils having met at Carthage before his time—the first, in 215, respecting the baptism administered by heretics, whether it was valid or not in the estimation of the Church—the second, in 240, composed of ninety bishops, for the purpose of condemning one Privatus, of whose offence nothing is expressly known. Doubtless, these councils did not confine their deliberations to the single object proposed to them, but legislated, as was usual in after times, for the general interests of the Church. In 231 a council was held at Iconium, for the same object with the first of Carthage. During the prelacy of Cyprian five numerous synods were assembled at Carthage. They were chiefly occupied by the controversy concerning "the Lapsed," the "Baptism of Heretics," and the contumacy of Novatian. Then follows a long interval in the history of the African Church, distinguished by no monument of ecclesiastical exertion, till we find mention of a considerable assembly held at Cirta, in the year 305. In 251 was the celebrated council of Rome, for the examination of the principles of Novatian; and in 265 and 269 the heresy of Paul of Samosata was twice condemned at Antioch.

But of the numerous Antenicene councils, that which most attracted the notice of later ages was the synod of Eliberis in Spain. It consisted of nineteen bishops, many of whom were confessors—and this may account for the peculiar severity of its Canons* against "the Lapsed"—under no circumstances

Marginal notes: Various Councils. Council of Eliberis.

---

* " Lxxxi Canones Concilii Eliberini" are published, with ample Commentaries, along with the Books of Optatus of Milevi. Edit. Paris, 1731. They relate generally to marriages, divorces, adulteries, &c., as well as to fasts, and other matters of ecclesiastical discipline.

would it readmit them to communion, not even at the hour of
death. Its enactments against idolatry were dictated by the
same spirit; and not only were all paintings in churches expressly prohibited, but even the use of tapers, during worship
in the cemeteries, was likewise forbidden—it was stigmatized
as a heathen practice, partaking of the character of superstition.
But this council is still more remarkable for a Canon respecting
the celibacy of the Clergy, which went so far as to order any
Bishops, Presbyters, Deacons, and Subdeacons, who might happen to be married, to live separate from their wives. This subject was brought, twenty years afterwards, under the consideration of the council of Nice—but we have not observed that it
expressly received the attention of any ecclesiastical assembly
previous to that of Eliberis.

Millen-
narian
notions.

It has been too hastily asserted by some historians, and too
readily admitted by others, that the expectation of the Millennium, or presence of Christ on earth to reign with his elect, was
the universal opinion of the ancient church. The fair statement
of that much-disputed question appears to be this:—Eusebius *
informs us that Papias, "among certain parables and sermons
of the Saviour, and other seemingly fabulous records which he
professed to have received traditionally, said, that there would
be a thousand years after the resurrection of the dead, during
which Christ was to reign bodily upon the earth; in which I
think that he misunderstood the apostolic narrations, not penetrating what was mystically spoken by them; for he appears to

---

* H. E., lib. iii. c. 39.—On this important subject see Whitby's excellent
'Treatise on the Millennium,' at the end of vol. ii. of his 'Commentaries.' This
obscure doctrine was probably known to very few except the Fathers of the
Church, and is very sparingly mentioned by them during the first two centuries.
And there is reason to believe that it scarcely attained much notoriety even among
learned Christians until it was made matter of controversy by Origen, and then
rejected by the great majority. In fact, we find Origen himself, in his Prolego-
mena to the Canticles (69 B.), asserting that it was confined 'to those of the
simpler sort;' and, in his Philocalia (c. xxvi. p. 99) he directly declares that the
few ($\tau\iota\nu\grave{\epsilon}\varsigma$) who held it did so with such secrecy, that *it had not yet come to the
ears of the heathen*.........In all fairness, then, we must consider the opposite declarations of Origen and Eusebius either to have been applied to different parts of
Christendom, or to qualify each other: always recollecting that the latter is confined to ecclesiastics, while the former extends to all classes.

have been very limited in understanding (σμικρὸς τὸν νοῦν), as one may conjecture from his discourses." The historian then proceeds to attribute the general reception of this opinion among ecclesiastics, and particularly by Irenæus, to their respect for 'the antiquity of the man.'* To Papias, then, we may attribute the origin of the belief. It was first adopted by Justin Martyr,† next by Irenæus, and connected by both of them with the resurrection of the flesh. But the passage of the latter‡ plainly declares " that there were some in the church, in divers nations and by various works, who, believing, do consent with the just, who do yet endeavour to turn these things into metaphors;" which proves that even the orthodox were divided on the question at that early age, though the names of the disputants have not reached us. The first distinguished opponent of the doctrine was Origen, who attacked it with great earnestness and ingenuity, and seems, in spite of some opposition, to have thrown it into general discredit; and we shall scarcely have occasion to notice the opinion again, until we arrive at the tenth century.

Dr. Whitby expresses his belief that the Fathers who adopted that doctrine " received it from the traditions and notions of the Jews;" and he proceeds very truly to assert that that error " will not invalidate their authority in any thing delivered by them as witnesses of what they have seen, or declared to have been then the practice of the Church of Christ." In these points, indeed, consists a great portion of the direct value of their works. But they are also greatly, perhaps principally, useful to us, as they prove, by numerous quotations, the early existence of the books of the New Testament *as we now read them,* and their reception in the primitive Church. The Apologies§ for Christianity,

---

* The words are these—πλὴν καὶ τοῖς μετ᾽ αὐτὸν πλείστοις ὅσοις τῶν ἐκκλησιαστικῶν τῆς ὁμοίας αὐτῷ δόξης παραίτιος γέγονε, τὴν ἀρχαιότητα τἀνδρὸς προβεβλημένοις· ὥσπερ οὖν Εἰρηναίῳ καὶ εἴ τις ἄλλος τὰ ὅμοια φρονῶν ἀνεπέφηνεν.

† Dial. cum Tryph.

‡ Adv. Hær. l. v. c. 33.

§ They were very numerous—to those of Justin, Athenagoras, Tatian, Melito, Quadratus, Aristides, and Tertullian, already mentioned, we may add others by Clemens Apollinaris, and Theophilus of Antioch.—Mosh. G. Hist., c. ii., p. ii. ch. 3. Fleury, 1. iv. sect. 4, &c.

published by the early Fathers, however imperfect as specimens
of reasoning or even as representations of religion, were probably, *at the time*, the most useful of their labours, not only
because they brought Christianity into notice, and challenged
examination, and put forward some of its leading excellencies,
but also because they publicly assaulted the tottering temples
of Paganism, and exposed to indelible contempt and contumely
its origin, its rites, its morals, and its mythology.

CHAPTER IV.

Persecutions of several Roman Emperors.

Claims of Roman Paganism to the character of tolerance—examined—Theory
of pure Polytheism—Roman policy—Various laws of the Republic—continued
under the emperors—Mecænas—Remarks—The ten persecutions—how many
general—That of Nero—its character—Of Domitian—The grandsons of St.
Jude—The epistle of Pliny to Trajan—His answer—Real object of Trajan—
Letter of Serenius Granianus to Hadrian—Antoninus Pius—Marcus Antoninus—Gibbon's partiality—Real character of this persecution compared with
those preceding it—His principles and knowledge, and superstition—His
talents and virtues—Connexion of his philosophy and his intolerance—Commodus—Decius—His persecution—accounted for—its nature—Valerian—
Martyrdom of Cyprian—Persecution of Diocletian—Its origin and motives—
Influence of Pagan priesthood—Progress of the persecution—Its mitigation by
Constantius, and final cessation at the accession of Constantine.—General
Remarks—Unpopularity of the Christians—accounted for—Calumnies by
which they suffered—Their contempt of all false gods—Change in the character of their adversaries—Philosophy—Excuses advanced for the persecutors
—their futility—General character of persecuting emperors—Absurd opinions
on this subject—Effect of the persecutions—upon the whole favourable—For
what reasons.

CERTAIN writers have industriously exerted themselves to display the mild and tolerant nature of the religion, which prevailed in the Roman world at the introduction of Christianity;
and then, when its seeming claims to this excellence have been
established, they have placed it in contrast with the persecuting
spirit, which has occasionally broken out from the corruptions
of our faith; insomuch that some persons may possibly have
been persuaded that there was some latent virtue in that super-

stition, which Christianity does not possess. We shall not here pause to show, what none can seriously deny, that the intolerance of Christians, like all their other vices, is in spite, and not in consequence, of their belief; but it is worth while shortly to examine the pretensions of Polytheism to one of the virtues in which we are most disposed to exult, and which we are accustomed to consider most peculiarly our own.

The religion called Polytheism means "the worship of many gods." Now the observation which first occurs to us is this— that, when the number of gods is not limited, the easy reception of an additional divinity does little more than satisfy the definition of the word; it is not the endurance of a new religion, but the slight extension of that already established. The intrusion of one stranger would scarcely be noticed in the numerous synod of Mount Olympus; the golden portals were ever open— useful virtue or splendid vice gave an equal claim to admission; and the policy or servility of Rome bowed with the same pliancy to the captive gods of her enemies, or the manes of her imperial tyrants. This was not a virtue, but a *part* of Polytheism; the new deities became new members of the same monstrous body; they assisted and sustained each other; and the whole mass was held together by ignorance, and animated by the gross spirit of superstition. It seems, indeed, that a Pagan statesman, who may have permitted additions to the calendar of his gods, deserves no higher description of praise than that which we should bestow on a pope, who has been zealous in the canonization of saints. For one idol will presently become as holy as another idol; nor could there be any reason why Jove should scorn the society of Serapis, since their respective divinity was founded on the same evidence, and their worship conducted on the same principles.

Such is the real theory of pure Polytheism. But we should be doing it much more than justice, if we were to confine ourselves to its abstract nature, without mention of the political uses to which it was converted; and which, indeed, subjected it to so much restraint and limitation, that we shall be unable to discover in its practice even that ambiguous virtue which some have supposed to be inherent in it.

[margin: Nature of Polytheism.]

The belief or infidelity of the statesmen of antiquity, who were left to wander over the fields of conjecture, with no better guide than reason, may have varied in individuals, according to the understanding, or the passions, or the wishes of each; but those were certainly very rare, who admitted into their closet the various and irrational worship which they encouraged in the people. They supported religion only as one of the easiest means of governing; and valued devotion to the gods as they supposed it naturally connected with obedience to man—a just supposition, in a case where the gods were little removed from the nature, and generally tainted with the vices of humanity. Our short inquiry into the manner in which the ancients wielded this engine of state shall be confined to the History of Rome, as being immediately connected with the subject of the present chapter.

Religious Polity of Rome.

Cicero (de Legibus, c. ii. s. 8.) gives us the following extract from the most ancient laws of Rome. " Let no one have any separate worship, nor hold any new gods; neither to strange gods, unless they have been publicly adopted, let any private worship be offered; men should attend the temples erected by their ancestors," &c. From Livy (b. iv. c. 30.) we learn that about 430 years before Christ orders were given to the Ædiles to see " that none except Roman gods were worshipped, nor in any other than the established forms." Somewhat more than 200 years after this edict, to crush certain external rites which were becoming common in the city, the following edict was published, " that whoever possesses books of oracle, or prayer, or any written act of sacrifice, deliver all such books and writings to the Prætor before the Calends of April; and that no one sacrifice on public or sacred ground after new or foreign rites." But it may seem needless to produce separate instances, when from the same historian (b. xxxix. c. 16.) we learn, that it had been customary in all the early ages of the republic to empower the magistrates " to prevent all foreign worship, to expel its ministers from the forum, the circus, and the city, to search for and burn the religious books (vaticinos libros), and to abolish every form of sacrifice except the national and established form."

The authority of Livy is confirmed by that of Valerius
Maximus, who wrote under the emperor Tiberius, and bears
testimony to the jealousy with which all foreign religions were
prohibited by the Roman republic (b. i. c. 3). That the same
principle, which had been consecrated by the practice of seven
hundred years, was not discontinued by the emperors, is clearly
attested by the historian Dio Cassius* (p. 490-2). It appears
that Mecænas, in the most earnest terms, exhorted Augustus
" to hate and punish" all foreign religions, and to compel all
men to conform to the national worship; and we are assured
that the scheme of government thus proposed was pursued by
Augustus and adopted by his successors.

Now, from the first of the passages before us, it appears that
all right of private judgment in matters of religion was expressly forbidden by an original law of Rome—which never
was repealed. We know not what stronger proof it would be
possible to adduce of the inherent intolerance of Roman Polytheism. The four next references prove to us that the ancient
law, subversive of the most obvious right of human nature, was
strictly acted upon during the long continuance of the commonwealth. The established form of Paganism might not be violated by individual schism or dissent; the gods, whom the
government created, the people were compelled to worship
according to the forms imposed by the government. Under
the early emperors the same was still the maxim of state; and
if the influx of idolaters from every nation under Heaven made
it difficult to preserve the purity of the Roman religion, that
religion became more domestic, and (let us add) more Roman
by the successive and easy deification of some of the most
vicious of mankind.

These few lines may suffice for the present to disprove the
plausible theory of the tolerance of Paganism, and they may
lead us, perhaps, to discover the true reason why the worship
of Christ was forbidden in that city which acknowledged the
divinity of Nero. At least, we shall have learnt from them,
that the religion which Christianity supplanted was very far

* In the year U. C. 701, the temples of Isis and Osiris were destroyed by order
of the Senate (B. 40.)

from possessing the only point of superiority, which its admirers have ever claimed for it. And we shall not forget, in the following pages, to direct to the religious system of Rome some portion of the abhorrence, which is usually confined to the individuals who administered it.

The number of persecutions. Hitherto we have followed the progress of Christianity through nearly all the provinces of the Roman empire, and some countries without its limits, as if we had been attending a triumphal procession. The less pleasing duty remains to describe its difficulties and its afflictions. And in so doing it is not easy to ascertain the precise path of truth, entangled as it is, on one side, by the exaggerated fictions of enthusiasts, and perplexed, on the other, by the perversity of scepticism.

Early, though not the most ancient, ecclesiastical historians, followed by many moderns, have fixed the number of persecutions at ten; and if we thought proper indiscriminately to designate by that name every partial outrage to which Christians were subjected from the reign of Nero to that of Constantine, perhaps even this number might be considerably extended.* On the other hand, Gibbon has so carefully palliated the guilt, and softened down the asperity of those successive inflictions, that in his representation not one of them wears a serious aspect, excepting that of Diocletian; though he admits that some transient excesses may be charged upon Nero, Domitian, Decius, and perhaps one or two others.

Differing in many respects from that author in our view of this portion of history, and animated, perhaps, by a more general and impartial humanity, we are still willing, in this matter, to make some concessions to his opinion; and though other occasions to prove the sincerity and constancy of Christians were abundantly presented, yet we are not disposed to

---

* Mosh. Gen. Hist., Cent. i. p. i. ch. 5. Idem de Reb. Chr. ant. Const. Sæc. i. sect. xxvi. The number of ten persecutions was an invention of the fifth century, derived from arbitrary interpretation of prophecy rather than historical evidence. Lactantius, in the fourth age, enumerates only six. Eusebius specifies no number, though he appears to mention nine. The same number is adopted by Sulpicius Severus, in the fifth century, who prepares his readers, however, for the infliction of the tenth and last by Antichrist at the end of the world; from his time *ten* became the popular computation.

impute the shame of deliberate unrelenting persecution to more
than four or five among the emperors; but in one important
respect our estimate of these events will still differ from that of
the philosophical historian, as we shall bestow a much greater
share of attention on the conduct of Marcus Antoninus. Our
reasons will appear in the progress of the narrative.

The persecution of Nero was the first to which the Christian   Nero.
name was subjected, and the best account which has reached us
respecting it is that of the historian Tacitus, which we have
translated in a former chapter. From his description, it appears
that the sufferings of the Christians did not originate in any evil
that had been committed by them, nor even in the general
calumnies which blackened their character*, but in a specific
charge, which was notoriously false, that they had occasioned
the destructive conflagration so generally attributed to the madness of the Emperor himself. The nature of their tortures is
related, and the very spots particularized on which they were
inflicted. But their duration is not mentioned, nor the extent
to which the persecution prevailed (if it at all prevailed) in other
parts of the empire. The fact, that it arose in the first instance
from a charge which was necessarily confined to the inhabitants
of Rome, is certainly not a conclusive argument that it might
not afterwards spread beyond the boundaries of the city; and
yet both the words and the silence of Tacitus are such as indirectly persuade us, that the calamity which he is describing
was both local and transient. The imperfect account of Eusebius † throws little more light on these questions, which have
in vain divided the opinions and exercised the ingenuity of a
multitude of critics ‡. For our own part, if that were sufficiently

---

* Suetonius, Vit. Neronis, cap. 16., mentions the same event, in the midst of
some trifling details of sumptuary restrictions, in these few words—"Afflicti sup-
pliciis Christiani, genus hominum superstitionis novæ et maleficæ." But we must
follow the circumstantial narrative of Tacitus.

† Euseb. H. E., lib. ii. c. 25.

‡ In this question, which involves the historical accuracy of Tertullian, compare the reasoning of Semler (sæc. i. cap. 6.) with that of Mosheim (Gen. Hist.
Cent. i. p. 1. ch. 5.) The forgery of the Lusitanian inscription, according to
which Nero "purged that province of the new superstition," is now universally
admitted.

proved which is continually asserted, that the persecution lasted for four years, until the death of Nero*, we should very readily admit the probability that it was general. But whatever uncertainty may rest on this point, the expressions of the Pagan historian unhappily convey sufficient evidence, that the assault was exceedingly destructive and attended by every circumstance of barbarity.

Much difference has also existed respecting the laws supposed to have been enacted by Nero against the Christians, and their continuance or repeal † by subsequent emperors. And this question is so far at least connected with the preceding, that the mere existence of any general edicts against Christians *as such,* proves that the particular charge on which the persecution was founded had been gradually lost in more general accusations, which had been followed by general inflictions. But even in this case, it becomes a question, whether Nero's edicts‡ proceeded any further than to enforce against Christians specifically the ancient statutes universally directed against religious innovation—whether it was not rather a precedent which that emperor established, than a law which he enacted—a precedent which would be followed or disregarded by his successors, as

---

* In the year 68. Mosh. de Reb. Christ. ante Const. sæc. i. sect. xxxiv.

† Some declare them to have been repealed by the Senate (Mosh. de R. Christ. ante Const. sæc. ii. sect. viii.), and Tertullian (lib. i. ad Nationes, c. 7.) asserts that while all Nero's other institutes were repealed, that against the Christians alone remained.

‡ Tertullian (lib. i. ad Nationes, c. 7.) calls Nero's edict Institutum Neronianum, and in other places (as Apol. cap. 5 and 6,) speaks of *laws* existing, and occasionally enforced against Christians ; still we suspect him of error, if he intended to attribute to Nero the invention of those laws—an error very naturally rising from the fact, that that emperor was the first who applied them to Christianity. See, however, Bishop Kaye on this subject, (Lec. on Tertull. pp. 115, et seq.) Certainly Gibbon is rather presumptuous in his manner of concluding, "that the effects, as well as the cause, of Nero's persecution were confined to the walls of Rome, and that the religious tenets of the Christians were never made a subject of punishment or even of inquiry." (Chap. 16.) Still we are disposed to assent at least to the first of his conclusions, as we are aware of no express authority for the contrary opinion earlier than the fifth century. (Sulp. l. ii. p. 146; Oros. l. vii. c. 7, &c.) And if, on the one hand, Tillemont enumerates a great variety of martyrs who perished in that persecution (tom. ii. p. 71, et seq.); on the other, Le Clerc has anticipated Gibbon in both his positions, and argues very plausibly in favour of them. (Hist. Eccles. ad ann. 64.)

their character and religious policy might lead them to execute or suspend the standing statutes of the empire. At least it is strange that, when his other laws were repealed, that against the Christians should alone remain in force, unless we conclude that that alone had existed before his time, and had been applied or perverted, but not enacted, by him.

After this first affliction, the Christians passed about thirty Domitian. years in the silent and undisturbed propagation of their religion. In the year 94 or 95, they again attracted the attention of the civil power, by exciting, as it would seem, the political fears of the emperor. Domitian was no doubt acquainted with an ancient prophecy prevalent throughout the east, and probably an imperfect adumbration of the prophecies of the Old Testament, that the imperial sceptre was destined one day to pass into the hands of a Jew. This led to some inquiries into the actual condition of the royal family of Jerusalem ; and the grandsons of St. Jude the Apostle, the brother of the Saviour, are said to have been brought before the throne of the tyrant : but his jealousy was disarmed by their poverty and simplicity, —their hands were hardened* with daily labour,—and their whole property consisted in one small farm of about twenty-four acres. And when the emperor inquired respecting the nature of their prophetic hopes, and the character of the monarch who was to rise up from among them, he was informed, " that his kingdom was not of earth, but heavenly and angelical ; and that in the completion of time he would come in glory to judge both the living and the dead, according to their merits." They were dismissed without injury ; and soon after this event, some severities, which had lately been exercised against the Christians, were suspended by the prudence† or the death‡ of the emperor.

* Hegesippus apud Euseb. iii. 20. Le Clerc, who is generally and justly suspicious of the authority of Hegesippus, is persuaded of the truth of this narrative, by its simplicity and candour.—Hist. Eccl. ad ann. 96.

† Tertull. Apol. c. 5. This author is the rather to be believed on this point, because it does not go to support his favourite theory, that the only persecutors were the bad emperors—a fancy to which he has unfortunately sacrificed many indisputable facts. See also Heg. ap. Euseb. loc. cit.

‡ Mosheim (Gen. Hist. c. i. p. i. ch. 5.) In another place, after adducing the authorities of Lactantius (cap. iii. De Hist. Persec.), and Xiphilinus in Nerva

Trajan.   The celebrated epistle of Pliny to Trajan was written ten or
twelve years afterwards, and proves that the Christians in Bithynia (and probably in every province of the east) were subjected
to many vexations and sufferings. The emperor's answer
amounted to this—"that the Christians are not to be sought
for, nor molested on anonymous information; but that on conviction they ought to be punished."* From a comparison of
these two documents, we collect, first, that the spirit of persecution in this instance† originated rather in their heathen fellow-subjects than in the character of the emperor; and, secondly,
that the laws by which they were punished were not any recent
edicts issued by an express act of legislation against Christians,
but the original statutes of the republic continued and applied
to them. From the moment that a precedent existed for the
application of those statutes to the religion of the Christians,
their condition must at all times have been very precarious, as
being dependent not only on the policy of the emperor, but on
the caprice of the provincial governors; since it would naturally
seem to rest at their discretion to enforce, or not, the standing
laws against a sect which had already felt their severity. The
object of Trajan, in this rescript, was their mitigation; it is
probable that he knew little respecting the nature and evidence
of the new religion, but was desirous somewhat to soften the
practical intolerance of his own; but the effect was not in the
end favourable to the Christians‡, since it gave a sanction to
legal persecution, and established on high authority the fatal
maxim, that the mere profession of Christianity was a criminal
offence §.

The truth of the first of the above conclusions is confirmed
by the annals of succeeding reigns. About the year 120, Serenius Granianus, Proconsul of Asia, wrote to Adrian, "that it

(D eReb. Christ. ante Const. sæc. i. sect. xxxvi.), he leaves the question doubtful.
—Gibbon follows the opinion which shortens the persecution.

* Tertull., Apol. c. ii., exposes with great vehemence and reason the injustice
and inconsistency exhibited in this rescript. If Christians deserved condemnation,
they should be sought after; if not sought after, they should not be condemned.
"Si damnas, cur non et inquiris; si non inquiris, cur non et absolvis?"

† Euseb. H. E., lib. iii. c. 32., confirms this position.

‡ Mosh. de Reb. Christ. ante Const. sæc. ii. sect. x.

§ "Illud solum expectatur, confessio nominis, non examinatio criminis."—
Tertull. Apol. c. ii.

seemed to him unreasonable that Christians should be put to death merely to gratify the clamours of the people, without trial and without any crime proved against them." And there is a rescript of the emperor, addressed to Minucius Fundanus, in which this letter is noticed, and in which it is enjoined that Christians should not be sacrificed to the *clamours* of the multitude.

During the long reign of Antoninus Pius (from 138 to 161 A. D.), no deliberate injuries were inflicted upon the Christians; and it appears that they suffered much more from the violence of popular tumult than from the operation of the ancient laws. It became common about this time to attribute national calamities of every description to the contempt of the national religion exhibited by the Christians. "If the Tiber has overflowed its banks," (exclaimed Tertullian in the next generation,) "or the Nile has not overflowed; if heaven has refused its rain; if the earth has been shaken; if famine or plague has spread its ravages, the cry is immediately raised—Away with the Christians to the lions* !" The emperor, influenced, as some have supposed, by the Apologies of Justin Martyr, published one, possibly two †, edicts for their protection against such outrage; and during this reign especially they grew and extended in dignity as well as number, and became more generally known by writings not devoid of energy and eloquence. Pius was succeeded by Marcus, of whom Gibbon has said, that "during the whole course of his reign he despised the Christians as a philosopher, and *punished them as a Sovereign.*"

It seems singular, that an historian, who makes great profession of candour and universal humanity, should almost have excepted from the number of persecutors the only name (as far at least as this part of our inquiry) to which that ignominious designation appears justly and certainly to belong: for under all the preceding emperors, the injuries inflicted upon the Christians had either been occasional, as arising from some casual circum-

Antoninus Pius.

Marcus Antoninus.

---

* Tertull. Apol., cap. 40.

† That mentioned by Justin Martyr at the end of his 1st Apol., and by Eusebius, l. iv. c. 13, (if it could establish its claims to be genuine,) would, with much more probability, be ascribed to Pius than to M. Antoninus.

stance, or staining only a portion of their reign; or partial, as confined to a few provinces, or perhaps cities of the empire. Moreover, they had been sometimes excited, and generally encouraged, by popular irritation; they had been directed against a small and obscure and calumniated sect, through the operation, and according to the seeming intention, of the ancient statutes. And the efforts of individual emperors were, for the most part, turned rather to the suspension or mitigation of those statutes than to the rigid enforcement of them. In addition to this, let us not forget, that those individuals possessed little means or opportunity to inform themselves respecting the peculiar principles, doctrines, or habits of Christians; still less to examine the foundation of their belief, or even to understand that it had any foundation :—if they permitted the work of destruction to proceed, it was in ignorance and blindness. On the other hand, Marcus Antoninus undertook the task of "punishment" or persecution among the earliest * of his imperial duties, and he continued to fulfil it with unremitting diligence throughout the nineteen † years of his splendid administration. He acted on deliberate principles, and his principles were not of partial or local operation, but were equally applicable to every province of his empire. And thus he everywhere enforced the laws in their full severity; the lives‡ and the property of the convicted were forfeited by the most summary process of justice; and the search§ which was made after the suspected, and which the uninformed humanity of Trajan had so nobly discouraged, sufficiently proves the activity of the pursuit, and

* Mosh. de Reb. Ch. ante Const. sæc. ii. sect. xv., xvi.

† From 161 A. D. to 180.

‡ Euseb. H. E., lib. v. c. l.—'The Emperor's edict was, that those who denied the charge of Christianity should be spared, but the rest put to death by torture.'

§ Moyle on Marcus Antoninus. We do not accuse him of promulgating any new laws against the Christians, though Melito tells us of a violent persecution in this reign "by new edicts." In fact, such a step was perfectly unnecessary, for the original statutes, to which the Christians were made liable, contained every penalty. His letter to the Assembly of Asia seems indeed to be a forgery. Moyle certainly makes out this point, and Jortin is of the same opinion. It is attributed by Eusebius to Antoninus Pius, and his rescript it must be, if it be genuine at all. We should add, that Moyle believes Adrian's letter to Fundanus to be "as arrant a juggle as that of Antoninus, though the conveyance be a little more cleanly," but he does not *proves* this opinion.

the earnestness of the pursuer. But the most important point of distinction is probably this: Marcus Antoninus knew much better the nature of the evil which he was committing: he was acquainted, to a certain extent at least, with the opinions of the Christians, and the innocence of their character; and it is not likely that he had entirely neglected to examine the grounds of their faith. He watched the process of his own inflictions, and when he perceived the fortitude with which all endured, and the eagerness with which many courted them, he coldly reproved the unphilosophic enthusiasm of the Martyrs*. And yet, perhaps, his own philosophy was not quite devoid of enthusiasm, or, at least, it was not strictly regulated by reason, when it led him to labour for the destruction of the most moral and loyal portion of his subjects, only because they disclaimed the very superstitions which he placed his pride in despising. Nor again was his practice consistent with his professed contempt of these: for it is said, and seemingly on good foundation, that Marcus Antoninus was frequent in consultation with the Chaldæan sages, deeply conversant with the mysteries of astrology, credulously attentive to oracular prophecy, obedient to the premonitions of dreams, which he believed to descend from Heaven —assertions not incredible, nor inconsistent with his studies or his principles; and there is ground to hesitate whether we should not rather convict him of superstition than hypocrisy. But it is certain that his understanding was of the broadest and most comprehensive description; that it was enlightened by every worldly knowledge, and fortified by frequent meditation; that his character was founded in excellent dispositions, confirmed by the best principles which were known to the Pagan world. His general regard for justice has never been questioned; even his humanity is commonly celebrated; and if the representations of history be not exaggerated, he reached as high a degree both of wisdom and of moral excellence as

---

* B. xi., sec. iii. He asserts that men should meet their death, "not through mere ostentation as do the Christians, but considerately and with dignity, and without theatrical display." Μὴ κατὰ ψιλὴν παράταξιν, ὡς οἱ Χριστιανοὶ, ἀλλὰ λελογισμένως, καὶ σεμνῶς, καὶ ἀτραγῴδως. The word which we have rendered ostentation, parade (παράταξιν), is in this passage usually interpreted obstinacy.

is attainable by the unassisted faculties of man—and yet this prince polluted every year of a long reign with innocent blood.

In our natural anxiety to honour every form of human excellence, we search for his excuse in the religious policy so long established in the empire. But we find that those of his predecessors who were disposed to soften or suspend its operation upon Christians, possessed the power to do so; and we cannot doubt that the despotic authority of Marcus would have enabled him to revise or repeal those oppressive statutes, if he had learnt from the books of his philosophers the virtue or the meaning of toleration. This, indeed, is the real and only ground of his defence; and we shall regard his conduct with less indignation, if we reflect how feeble were the mightiest principles of conduct with which he was acquainted; on what a loose and shifting foundation they rested; how large was the class of virtues which they did not comprehend, and how imperfect were the motives which they proposed for the practice of any. And thus considered, we shall discover, perhaps, some trace of heavenly providence in the circumstance, that the imperial philosopher, flourishing in the maturity of his science, and deficient in nothing which nature or man could bestow, was armed with the highest temporal authority and permitted to direct it against the *infancy* of our faith. From the splendid imperfection of Marcus Antoninus, from the perseverance of his powerful enmity, from its final failure, we may learn what narrow limits have been assigned to the virtue and wisdom and power of unassisted man; and we derive a new motive of gratitude for that heavenly aid, which has fixed our social happiness on a certain and eternal foundation.

The greatest prince of antiquity was succeeded by a son, who neither inherited his virtues, nor imitated his crime; so far from this, that we might almost imagine it to have been the object of Commodus to redeem his numerous vices by his humanity towards the Christian name.

Septimius Severus. Septimius Severus ascended the throne in the year 193, and is represented by Tertullian* to have bestowed testimonies of

---

* Tertul. ad Scap., cap. iv. " Sed et clarissimas feminas et clarissimos viros

approbation on several distinguished Christians, and openly to have withstood the popular fury which assailed the sect. But this account will apply only to the earlier part of his reign; for in the year 202 (about the time of the publication of Tertullian's Apology) he issued an edict, which indirectly occasioned a variety of inflictions, the most barbarous of which appear to have been perpetrated in Egypt. The professed object of that edict was only to prevent conversion either to Judaism or Christianity; for the fears of the emperor began to be awakened by the extraordinary progress of the latter. Its effect was to oppress and torture the most zealous ministers of the faith, and to inflame the prejudices of the people against all believers. This enactment continued in force for about nine years, until the death of Severus; and from that period, if indeed we except the injuries inflicted by Maximin * (from 235 to 238 A. D.), and directed chiefly against the instructors and rulers of the churches, the Christians, though occasionally liable to popular outrage, had not much reason to complain of the injustice of the government until the accession of Decius, in the year 249.

Decius, like Marcus Antoninus, is also ranked, and justly ranked, among the most virtuous of the emperors. The virtues of a pagan were usually connected with his philosophy, and his philosophy taught him to despise every form of worship. Perhaps, too, an imperial eye might view with natural distrust the free and independent principles of Christianity, which were now spreading into more general operation and notice—principles which acknowledged an authority superior to the throne of man; and though they devoted the body to Cæsar, yet set apart the soul for God. It would be observed, too, with some jealousy, that the progress of that worship was rapid and universal, in spite of ancient law, popular opposition, and imperial edict. Its *truth* was seldom investigated, because it was not yet suf-

Decius.

Severus sciens hujus sectæ esse non modo non læsit verum et testimonio ornavit, &c." His affection for the Christians is attributed to a cure formerly performed on him, by the application of oil, by a Christian named Proculus. We must be careful not to confound this medical use of oil with the practice of extreme unction, which did not then exist.

 * Euseb., H. E., lib. vi. c. 28. Tillem., tom. iii. p. 305.

ficiently distinguished from surrounding superstitions, which laid no claim to truth, nor even professed to rest on any evidences; and thus the prejudices of the schools at once assumed that the worship of Christ was no better founded than those of Jove and Serapis. In the entire pagan scheme (could we properly consider it as one scheme), religion and philosophy together professed to furnish that which Christianity supplies to us: the mysteries, which also held the place of doctrines, the ceremonies, and the name were provided by the religion; the ethics by philosophy. We need not particularize the numerous points of advantage which both branches of the Christian system possess over the corresponding departments of paganism. But the distinctions chiefly to be remarked are, that *the religion* demanded no belief, proposed no creed, inculcated no *faith*, but was, in fact, identified with its ceremonies, procession and sacrifice; and that *the philosophy* which undertook the whole charge of morals, in vain proposed an elaborate series of barren rules and lifeless exhortations, since it possessed no substantial motive whereby to enforce them. When we reflect how essential are these distinctions, we shall see cause sufficient for the jealousy with which Christianity was assailed both by the one and the other. But their incongruity and incoherence with each other formed the most striking and hopeless deformity of the system; for philosophy lived in open warfare with her senseless associate, and employed a great portion of her diligence and her wit in exposing the multiform absurdities of polytheism*.

These various reasons, carefully considered, will partly account for the peculiar suspicion which armed itself against the " Christian superstition," and at the same time will exhibit to us the motives, from which some of the wisest and best among the emperors unhappily numbered themselves among our adversaries †.

The persecution of Decius proceeded on a broader principle

---

* " Quinimo et Deos vestros palam destruunt.... laudantibus vobis !"—Tertul. Apol., c. 46.

† Eusebius (H. E., lib. vi. c. 39.) very concisely attributes the persecution of Decius to the hatred borne by that emperor to his predecessor Philip. Cyprian considers it as a divine chastisement for the sins of the Church.

than that of Severus, as it pretended no less than to constrain all subjects of the empire to return to the religion of their ancestors * ; it was also strictly universal, as neither confined to particular provinces nor classes, but extending from the lowest confessors to the highest authorities of the Church. Several were consigned to exile or death : Fabianus, bishop of Rome, Alexander of Jerusalem, Babylas of Antioch, were among the latter ; and the celebrated Origen was subjected to imprisonment and perhaps torture †. At Alexandria, in the year preceding the accession of Decius, some Christians had been massacred through the hatred or the avarice of the Pagan mob ; and as such fatal outrages, in addition to authorized injustice, were rather tolerated than promptly repressed by the government which succeeded, it was much more calamitous to the faith than its short duration of three years would lead us to apprehend. Indeed, the unusual number of Lapsed, or Apostates, by which this persecution is distinguished from those preceding it, is a sufficient proof of its intolerable barbarity‡.

We pass over the comparatively lenient inflictions of Gallus and Volusianus ; but the sceptre of Valerian was more darkly Valerian. stained by the blood of Cyprian §, bishop of Carthage, a man of learning and eloquence and piety, whose blameless life and final calmness and constancy have escaped the censure and almost the sarcasm of history. It will be instructive, as well as interesting, to transcribe the simple narrative of his martyrdom.

On the 13th of September, 258, an officer with soldiers was Martyrdom sent to Cyprian's gardens by the proconsul to bring him into his of Cyprian. presence. Cyprian then knew his end was near ; and with a

* Tillemont, vol. iii. p. 310, on the authority of Greg. Nyssensis, who gives a very vivid description of the effects of the edict.

† Alexander and Babylas died in prison. Some of the sufferings of Origen are particularized in Eusebius, loc. cit. ; and those of the most celebrated martyrs who perished on this occasion occupy above a hundred pages in the Mémoires de Tillem., vol. iii. p. 325—428. Ed. 2.

‡ The fable of the Seven Sleepers of Ephesus belongs to this persecution ; the supposed martyrdom of the Theban legion to the reign of Diocletian.

§ It appears from Cyprian's Epistles that, in his Church, at least, the full severity of the persecution scarcely raged for more than one year. See Tillem., vol. iii. p. 324.

ready and constant mind and cheerful countenance he went without delay to Sexti, a place about six miles from Carthage, where the proconsul resided. Cyprian's cause was deferred for that day. He was therefore ordered to the house of an officer, where he was detained for the night, but was well accommodated, and his friends had free access to him. The news of this having been brought to Carthage, a great number of people of all sorts, and the Christians in general, flocked thence to Sexti; and Cyprian's people lay all night before the door of the officer, thus keeping, as Pontius expresses it, the vigil of their bishop's passion.

On the next morning, the 14th of September, he was led to the proconsul's palace, surrounded by a mixed multitude of people and a strong guard of soldiers. After some time, the proconsul came out into the hall, and Cyprian being placed before him, he said, "Art thou Thascius Cyprian?" Cyprian the bishop answered, "I am." Galerius Maximus the proconsul said, "The most sacred emperors have commanded thee to sacrifice." Cyprian the bishop answered, "I do not sacrifice." Galerius Maximus said, "Be well advised." Cyprian the bishop answered, "Do as thou art commanded; in so just a cause thou needest no consultation." The proconsul having advised with his council, spoke to Cyprian in angry terms as being an enemy to the gods[*] and a seducer of the people, and then read his sentence from a tablet, "It is decreed that Thascius Cyprian be beheaded." Cyprian the bishop said, "God be praised!" and the crowd of his brethren exclaimed, "Let us too be beheaded with him!"

This is the account given in the Acts of Cyprian's passion, and that of Pontius (in his Life of Cyprian) is to the same purpose[†].

Diocletian. For nearly fifty years after this outrage, the peace and progress of religion were not seriously interrupted. The earliest portion even of the reign of Diocletian was favourable to its security, and it was through the weakness of that prince, rather

---

[*] " Inimicus Diis Romanis et sacris legibus."

[†] Lardner, vol. iii. p. 141. The more usual date of Cyprian's martyrdom is 257.

than his wickedness, that his name is now inscribed on the tablets of infamy as the most savage among our persecutors. Two circumstances may be mentioned, as having engaged his tardy consent * to the commencement of a plan, into which he appears to have entered with the most considerate calmness; though it is also true that during its progress some incidents occurred which enlisted his passions in the cause, and even so inflamed them that, in the height of his madness, he certainly proposed nothing less than the extermination of the Christian name. The influence of the Cæsar, Galerius, who was animated, from whatsoever motive, by an unmitigated detestation of the worshippers of Christ, and who thirsted for their destruction, was probably the most powerful of those circumstances. But the second must not be forgotten. In the disputes, now become general, between the Christian ministers and the Pagan priests, the teachers of philosophy are almost invariably found on the side of the latter; and, as it is not denied —not even by Gibbon—that those learned persons directed the course and suggested the means of persecution, we need not hesitate to attribute a considerable share in the guilt of its origin to their pernicious eloquence.

Diocletian published his first edict in the February of 303. Three others of greater severity succeeded it; and, during a shameful period of ten years, they were very generally and rigorously enforced by himself, his colleagues, and successors. It is needless to particularize the degrees of barbarity by which those edicts were severally distinguished; the substance of the whole series is this†. The sacred books of the Christians were sought for and burnt; death was the punishment of all who assembled secretly for religious worship; imprisonment, slavery,

---

* Galerius represented to him that the permanence of the Roman institutions was incompatible with the prevalence of Christianity, which should therefore be extirpated. Diocletian proposed the subject to a sort of Council, composed of some eminent military and judicial officers. They assented to the opinion of Galerius; but the emperor still hesitated, until the measure was sanctioned and sanctified by the oracle of the Milesian Apollo.

† Nearly the whole of Eusebius's 8th book is devoted to this subject; on which he possesses, indeed, the authority of a contemporary, as he is believed to have been born about the year 270 A.D. See, too, Lactant. de Morte Persecut., cap. 13.

and infamy were inflicted on the dignitaries and presidents of the Churches; every art and method was enjoined for the conversion of the believers, and among those methods were various descriptions of torture, some of them fatal. During the preceding ninety years, the Church had availed itself of the consent or connivance of the civil government to erect numerous religious edifices, and to purchase some landed property; these buildings were now demolished, and the property underwent the usual process of confiscation. A more degrading, but less effectual, measure attended these: Christians were excluded from all public honours and offices, and even removed without the pale of the laws and the protection of justice—liable to all accusations, and inviting them by their adversity, they were deprived of every form of legal redress. Such were the penalties contained in those edicts; and though it be true that in some of the western provinces of the empire, as in Gaul and perhaps Britain, their asperity was somewhat softened by the character and influence of the Cæsar, Constantius, we are not allowed to believe that their execution even there was generally neglected; while we have too much reason to be assured that it was conducted with very subservient zeal throughout the rest of the empire. In process of time the sufferings of the Christians were partially alleviated by the victories of Constantine;

Accession of Constantine. but they did not finally terminate till his accession. That event, which took place in the year 313, and which marks the first grand epoch in ecclesiastical history, ended at the same time both the fears and the sufferings of the followers of Christ, and established his worship as the acknowledged religion of the Roman empire.

As the account here given of the persecutions of the early Christians differs in some respects from the views usually taken of this important portion of our history, it may be proper to close this chapter with a few additional remarks.

Causes of the unpopularity of the early Christians. 1st. Contemporary evidence obliges us to admit, that the Christian name was for many years (so late at least as the reign of Decius) an object of decided aversion to many of those who did not profess it; whether of the learned, who scorned the origin, were ignorant of the principles, and feared the progress, of the new religion, or of the vulgar, who believed the calumnies so industriously propagated against its professors. Hence proceeded those popular tumults, which, during the first two centuries (if we except from them the reign of Marcus Antoninus), may have destroyed as many victims as the deliberate policy of the emperors, or the established system of religious government. Still it must appear singular that a body of persons, distinguished by the moral qualities which are almost universally attributed to the first Christians, should have incurred the hatred of their fellow-subjects, rather than the admiration, or at least the sympathy, which was claimed by the character of their virtues. There are several reasons by which we may account for this strange circumstance. The prejudices and passions of mankind were opposed to the new religion; it contradicted their received ways of worship, the dictates and practices of their forefathers, their own indulged lusts and evil habits. Even the fame and semblance of peculiar sanctity are ever objects of bitter jealousy to those who are incapable of its practice, and who consequently dispute its reality. Again, when it was observed that Christians were not contented with mere inactive profession, but were animated with industrious zeal for the extension of their faith, a disposition to suspect and resist it, as it were in self-defence, was excited among many; and those who might have tolerated an indifferent or merely speculative superstition, armed themselves against the active and converting spirit of Christianity. Another, perhaps the most effective, and certainly the original cause of that aversion, was the persevering hostility of the Jews to the name of Christ. In some of the more populous and commercial cities, the Jews formed no inconsiderable portion of the inhabitants, and they were scattered in smaller numbers over the whole face of the East. The destruction of their capital increased the crowd of exiles, and inflamed the angry spirit by which they were animated. It is true that, in their attempts at open outrage, they were sometimes restrained by the civil power; but they were more successful in their secret endeavours to excite against the rising sect the contempt or malice of the heathen. To their malignity we may probably attribute those monstrous calumnies which tainted the Christian name, at the very period when its professors were farthest removed from corruption. It was rumoured and believed that the religious meetings of the faithful were polluted by alternate excesses of superstition and debauchery; the mysteries especially were invested with the most revolting character; the Eucharist was said to be celebrated by the sacrifice of an infant, and the Feast of Charity was represented to be a revel of cannibals *. These stories contained nothing incredible to a pagan, whom the external piety of the new religionists rendered still more suspicious of their private conversation. Without difficulty he believed in the perpetration of rites which bore some resemblance to the darker parts of his own superstition; and his belief was followed by insult and outrage.

The notorious malevolence of the Jews did not prevent the prevalence of another very early and very injurious opinion respecting Christianity—that it was merely a form, and a rejected form, of Judaism. This was a natural error—since the religion proceeded from Judæa, and many among its original preachers, and all its most active enemies, were Jews: it was indeed gradually, though slowly, removed by the writings of the early fathers, and the progress of the faith; but the prejudice arising from it was the chief cause of that contempt with which the worship was regarded for above one hundred years both by philosophers and statesmen.

Again, in the scenes of public festivity, in the temples, and at the sacrifices of the gods, the Christian was never present; he partook not in triumphs and rejoicings of which religion formed any portion, and appeared not at the sports of the amphitheatre, except as a victim. This seclusion from the amusements of his fellow-countrymen was mistaken for indifference to the happiness and interests of his country; it was mistaken for disaffection to the government, for moroseness or misanthropy; its real motive was never estimated or even conceived: for the careless temper of polytheism was unable to comprehend an exclusive religion, or to understand why the worship of Jupiter was not consistent with that of Christ.

* See Justin Martyr, Apol., i. 35, ii. 14.

Another difficulty was created by the spiritual nature of our religion. It was in vain that the Roman magistrate inquired for the images and statues of the God of the Christians, for the altars and temples consecrated to him. Unwilling, or unable, to believe that an Invisible Being could be the immediate object of adoration, he pronounced that to be atheism, which differed so widely from the general appearance of theism; and thus, among the ignorant at least, the Christians were liable to the double imputation, not only that they repudiated the national divinities, but that they substituted none other in their place. It was probably this last charge which inflamed and envenomed the rest; for the same moral enormities which were pardonable in the devotee of Apollo became infamous in those who partook of no devotion, and the worshippers of every idol under heaven united their clamours against the impiety of the atheists; and unhappily, among the impassioned natives of the East, clamours are seldom unattended by violence, and violence is only satisfied with blood.

There is, perhaps, no characteristic by which Christianity was so early and so strongly distinguished, as the pious horror of every approach to idolatry*: this singularity would be more commonly forced on the attention of pagans than any other, and no doubt, in the opinion of the vast majority, with whom the image was in fact the object of worship, it would be sufficient alone to constitute irreligion. Again, it led them into a second and scarcely less dangerous imputation, that of disloyalty; since the image of the emperor, which was usually exalted among the standards and in public places, was not honoured by the devout salutation of the Christian; and this omission naturally gave pretext to a *political* charge.

As another cause of the early unpopularity of the Christians, we may mention the unceasing opposition of all, whose personal interests were concerned in the support of paganism. The magnificent temples and gorgeous ceremonies of that superstition were a source of unfailing profit, not only to a numerous

---

* This extreme aversion from every form of idolatry is ascribed to a prevalent belief, that the statues were actually animated by those supposed beings whom the pagans worshipped as gods, and whom the Christians abominated as devils.

race of priests and hierodules, of architects and statuaries, but to multitudes of citizens, who lived, like the craftsmen of Ephesus, on the treasury of the temple, and were engaged by their most immediate necessities to maintain the worship; and not these only, but the whole mass of the populace were in some degree gainers by the sacrificial profusion which distinguished their religion; to say nothing of the share which they took in those splendid processions and rites, which converted the practice of religion into mere sensual enjoyment and careless festivity. When, in the place of this pompous pageantry, it was proposed to substitute a simple spiritual worship, recommended, not by the display of external ceremony, which it scorned, but by inward purity and the sanctity of moral excellence, in opposition at the same time to the passions of all men, and to the immediate interests of many, it would have been strange indeed if the popular voice had not been raised against it.

To the many causes of excitement already mentioned we may add one more—the substantial motive of avarice; since we invariably find that the Christians, who were the objects of these popular commotions, sustained, among other injuries, the loss of their property. And we must not forget that, in many instances*, the Roman police tolerated, perhaps encouraged, excesses which it might possibly consider as an innocent exercise of popular feeling, or as a part of a religious ceremony.

The evils which we have here noticed, or at least the causes which produced them, were most prevalent in the earliest age of the religion, and seem gradually to have died away during

---

* During the whole course of these persecutions, with the exception of those few in which the emperor pronounced his will by an express specification of the penalties, very much rested on the discretion of the magistrates, and, undoubtedly, many among these were guided by the common feelings of humanity. But the clamours of an importunate populace also demand more than common firmness, to be invariably resisted. Gibbon, in his endeavour to exaggerate the humanity of the Roman magistrates, has forgotten his own:—"They were far from punishing with death *all* those who were convicted of an obstinate adherence to the new superstition: contenting themselves for the most part with the *milder* chastisements of imprisonment, exile, or *slavery in the mines*, they left the unhappy victims of their *justice* some reason to hope for a prosperous event—the accession, the marriage, or the triumph of an emperor, which might restore them by a general pardon to their former state."—Chap. xvi.

the third century.   For they were chiefly founded in ignorance
of the real principles of Christianity, aided by contempt for the
weakness of its professors—circumstances which were gradually
removed, as the members of the Church advanced in numbers
and its ministers in learning.   But this progress of the faith
(as we have had occasion to observe) did not immediately
reconcile or disarm its adversaries, but rather changed their
character and their weapons.   For instance, during the first Pagan
ages we do not observe that the pagan priesthood were dis- Priests and Philoso-
tinguished by any systematic exertions against the new worship, phers.
and they may possibly have despised and overlooked it; but
presently their seeming indifference was changed into suspicious
jealousy, and then into active and persevering hatred*; and we
may be assured that the influence which they possessed over the
people (whatsoever that may have been) was exerted to the
prejudice of the rival religion.   In the next place, Philosophy
descended from the contempt, with which she had professedly
viewed the earliest efforts of Christianity, and proceeded to distinguish it from all other "superstitions" by her malice and
enmity; and she knew not in so doing how honourable a distinction she had conferred on it.   This coalition of philosophy
with paganism, though strange, was not unnatural; nor would
any evil consequences have followed it, had it not engaged the
concurrence, and advanced under the banners, of civil authority†.
And if it be true that from her numerous chastisements and
inflictions our religion may have somewhat profited in purity,
we must admit that she learnt one hateful lesson in the school
of adversity, which in after ages she did not forget to practise;
it was deeply ingrafted on her infancy by her sufferings, and it
brought forth in her maturity the bitter fruits of crime and
misery.   However, the poisonous plant was not the native of
her own vineyard, and it is now, for the most part, rooted up

* See Mosh. de Reb. Christ. ant. Const. Sæc. iv. sec. 1.

† There seems reason to believe that this alliance was fortified by the powerful addition of the Roman bar; at least we are assured that the proconsuls felt
themselves so interested in the defence of ancient laws, during Ulpian's time,
as to endeavour to excite Alexander Severus against an illegal religion.   This
took place about 223.   Baron. Ann. t. ii. pp. 367, 369.

and cast away; and she accounts it the severest among the wrongs of her pagan oppressors, that they instructed her in the maxims, and accustomed her to the spectacle, of persecution.

Pretext for persecution. II. As an excuse for the rigour of the Roman government, it has been argued that the Christians were not punished for their worship of Christ, but for their refusal to sacrifice to the gods of their ancestors and their government[*]; and that the crime for which they suffered was not in fact their religion, but their contumacy; and some set great value on this argument. In our opinion it amounts to nothing more than this: the laws of Rome punished all religious dissent with death; openly to oppose those laws was sedition; and thus the punishment was inflicted on the sedition, not on the dissent. This is foolish and unworthy sophistry; and its utmost consequence could go no farther than to excuse the individual who executed the laws, and to throw the whole odium upon the system[†]. But to allow it even this weight is too much concession; for we perceive, by the very different manner in which the law was

---

[*] The dialogue, which is supposed to have taken place during the reign of Septimius Severus (about 200) between Saturninus, proconsul of Africa, and Speratus, one of the famous Scillitan martyrs, whether genuine or not, is very ancient and perfectly consistent with probability. "You may hope for the pardon of the emperors our masters, if you come to your senses and observe the ceremonies of the gods." "We have never done any evil, nor partaken in injustice. We recollect not to have injured any one; on the contrary, when we suffer we render thanks to God: in which respect we obey _our_ Emperor, who has ordained that rule for us." "We also have a very simple religion; we swear by the genius of the emperors, and make vows for their health; you must do as much." "If you will listen to me calmly, I will tell you the mystery of Christian simplicity." "Dicente te de Mysterio, non inferam mala. Swear rather by the genius of the emperors our masters." "I recognize not the genius of the emperor of this world, but I serve the God of Heaven, whom no man hath seen or can see. I have never committed any crime punishable by the laws." They were remanded, and on the following day brought up again. "Do you persevere in being a Christian?" "Yes, I persevere: I call you all to witness—I am a Christian." All those who had been arrested with him heard him, and cried, "We also are Christians." "You will neither deliberate, then, nor receive pardon." "We need no pardon with justice on our side; do what you will; we die with joy for Jesus Christ," &c. &c. Act. Mart. Scill. pp. 86, 87. Ed. Amstel.

[†] Precisely of the same value is another excuse, derived from the admission that it was difficult or impossible for a pagan to comprehend even the _meaning_ of toleration, according to the latitude which we give to it. Its only effect can be to turn away our indignation from the individuals upon the system, which made them tyrants and persecutors.

enforced by different emperors, that they possessed, in fact, an authority superior to it, and power to suspend or revise it; and that there was not one of whom it can be truly said that he was barbarous on compulsion.   But on the other hand, if any will persist to justify the personal character of certain emperors at the expense of the religious policy of the empire, they give us only additional reason to rejoice at the triumph of Christian principles over the inherent depravity of the pagan system.

Another and a very fruitless dispute has been raised respecting the general virtues or vices or fortunes of those sovereigns who are most remarkable for severity towards the Christians; and while some have asserted that the persecutors are to be found only among the most odious and vicious of the emperors, and while others endeavoured to establish a sort of temporal retribution which overtook, by violent or untimely deaths, all who were hostile to the name,—there are again other writers who have been willing to insinuate that the wisest and most virtuous monarchs were those most sensible of the necessity to repress the growing religion.   All these writers are almost equally remote from truth.   The former are obliged to qualify the unrelenting injustice of Marcus Antoninus out of respect to his various virtues and his natural end; and the last must extenuate the outrages not of Nero only, or Domitian, or Maximin, but of Galerius and the stupid barbarian Licinius.   But if the insinuation were really founded in fact, the only important conclusion which could be derived from it is one which we are not anxious to dispute; that the noblest human wisdom was not exempt from shameful folly, and that the highest principles of justice discoverable by man permitted the perpetration of revolting enormities.   In the mean time, the truth appears to be nearly this: that, in the want of any fixed and substantial rule of action, the imperial character fluctuated between the extreme limits of depravity and (what was called) *virtue;* that the motives of all our enemies (except M. Antoninus and Diocletian) and of many of our protectors are to be sought either in accidental circumstances or in their own caprices; and that in both those classes we may number princes of the highest moral and intellectual excellence and of the lowest imaginable turpitude.

Character of the persecutors.

Number of
Martyrs.

Another question has been raised concerning the probable number of the martyrs; and this has led to wider difference, as it is less capable of accurate determination*. The spirit of exaggeration or credulity on the one hand has excited that of disparagement or scepticism on the other; and the truth, if it could be ascertained at all, would be found to lie between them. It is certain, however, that when Gibbon estimates the whole number of Diocletian's victims throughout the provinces of the Eastern empire according to the trifling portion who perished in Palestine, he infers neither very fairly nor very consistently; for in other places he is forward enough to acknowledge the narrow limits and to extenuate the population of Palestine, and he is not ignorant that even the *proportion* of Christians in that country was less than in any other province. Semler (sec. 1. c. 6.) inclines to the opinion of Dodwell, admitting the difficulty of the question; and Bishop Kaye† remarks, that "though the number may have been greater than Dodwell was willing to allow, it is certain that his opinion approaches much nearer to truth than that of his opponents." It has been one cause of the exaggeration, that the term martyr (witness) was in the early Church indiscriminately extended to all whose religion had exposed them to *any* infliction, as loss of property or liberty—a class of sufferers afterwards more usually called confessors.

III. Without giving our universal assent to the popular paradox, that the effect of persecution is to nourish that which it seems to consume, we may admit that the pagan persecutions were not, perhaps, upon the whole unfavourable to the progress of religion‡. Among many reasons for this opinion, there are three which appear to us important.

Result of
the perse-
cutions.

(1.) The first of these is the nature of the persecutions themselves; which, in the first place, were usually of short duration, and relieved by longer intermissions, if not of security, at least of repose and hope, so that the survivors had space to refit their shattered vessel against the tempests which were still in the

* Dodwell, Dissert. in Cypr. XI. Ruinart. Præf. Act. Martyr.
† Lect. on Tertull. p. 138.
‡ The same was the professed opinion even of Tertullian himself.

horizon; and which, in the next, were generally signalized by such extreme barbarity, and such obvious injustice as civil punishments, as not only to revolt whatever humanity might be found among the spectators, but to harden and fortify the obstinacy of the sufferers.   (2.) The noble and devoted constancy with which martyrdom was generally endured excited the admiration of the best portion of the Gentile world; and not their admiration only, for those who reflected on what they beheld were persuaded, first, of the piety of the sufferers, and next of their sincerity: and this persuasion led some among them to examine the foundation of those motives and principles, which seemed to infuse an original energy into the human soul.   If a new crime was invented for the affliction of the Christians, a new virtue appeared to be sent down to them for their support; and it became a serious question, whether that virtue could otherwise have sustained them, than by the direct interference of Heaven.   (3.) Several, driven from their country by persecution, carried with them into distant and barbarous exile the faith of the Christian, and the zeal of the missionary and the martyr.   And thus the victims of man's blind and insensate impiety became instruments in the scheme of Providence for the advancement of his great purposes in the propagation of faith and knowledge*.

* We might divide the first 313 years of the Christian æra into three periods, in respect to its internal history.   The first century was the age of Christ and the Apostles, of miracles and inspiration inherent in the Church; the next fifty years we may consider as that of the Apostolical Fathers, enlightened by some lingering rays of the departed glory, which were successively and insensibly withdrawn; the third was the period of severe probation and bitter anxiety, unalleviated by extraordinary aids, and so far removed from human consolation, that the powers of the earth might seem to have conspired with the meanest of its progeny, in order to oppress and desolate the Church of Christ—yet even this was not without the Spirit of God.

CHAPTER V.

On the Heresies of the first three Centuries.

Meaning of the word Heresy—Charges of immorality brought against Heretics—
Their treatment by the early Church—Number of early Heresies—Moderation
of the primitive church—Three classes of Heretics. (1.) Two kinds of Philosophy—Gnosticism—Origin and nature of that doctrine—its association with
Christianity—Moral practice of the Gnostics—Their martyrs—Various forms
of Gnosticism—Basilides—Carpocrates—Valentinus—Cerdo and Marcion—
Tatian and the Encratites. (2.) The Ebionites—Eusebius's account of them—
Conclusions from it—The Heresy of Artemon—revived by Paul of Samosata—
his sentence and expulsion—how finally enforced—Heresy of Praxeas—Doctrines of the Church stated by Tertullian—Sabellius—his opinions—Patropas-
sians. (3.) Simon Magus—Montanus—his preaching and success—On the Life,
pretensions, and doctrines of Manes, and the discipline of his followers—Their
unrelenting persecution by the Church—Controversy on the Baptism of Heretics—The Novatians—their schism and opinions—Conclusions respecting the
general character of the early Heresies, and the manner of opposing them.

Usage of
the word
Heresy.

THE original meaning of the word heresy is *choice;* it was long
used by the philosophers to designate the preference and selection of some speculative opinion, and in process of time[*] was
applied without any sense of reproach to any *sect*—a term with
which it thus became nearly synonymous. From philosophy
it passed into the service of religion, and we find it applied
both by St. Luke and Josephus[†] to the Pharisees and Saddu-
cees, with no imputation of censure or error. Next we observe
that it was employed by the Jews to distinguish the new opinions of the Christians ; St. Paul is accused of being the " ring-
leader of the heresy of the Nazarenes," and confesses that he
" worships the God of his fathers, after the way which they call
heresy"—an expression which indicates that some reproach had
been intended by the term. The word was then adopted by

---

[*] Cicero. (Paradox I. vol. vii. p. 845. Ed. Oxon.)　Philo Judæus (Fram. e lib.
II. in Exod.);　Burton, Bampt. Lect. I.　See too Clem. Alex. (Strom. vii. p. 755.)
Ἐν μόνῃ τῇ ἀληθεῖ καὶ τῇ ἀρχαίᾳ Ἐκκλησίᾳ ἥτε ἀκριβεστάτη Γνῶσις, καὶ ἡ τῷ ὄντι ἀρίστη
Αἵρεσις.

[†] Acts of Apost. v. 17; xv. 5.　Joseph. Antiq. xiii. 5. 9.

Christians; and though it still continued for some ages to be used, in its first and most general sense, to designate every denomination, not only of sects but of false religions*, yet for the most part it was employed in speaking of those who, professing Christianity, had departed from the doctrine which was taught by the Apostles. In the mouth of an orthodox Christian it could not, in any of these senses, be a term of indifference; since, according to the necessary exclusiveness of our principles, the faith which was revealed through Christ and interpreted by his Apostles is alone truth—every other belief is error.

We next observe, that the notion of wilfulness and perversity (perhaps a much worse notion) was very early attached to it; and even by the writers of the New Testament it is sometimes so used, that a somewhat indefinite idea of evil appears to have been affixed to it. Some, indeed, have supposed that it was understood by early Christian writers to contain the imputation of immorality [†], and thus we may partly account for the exceeding zeal with which many of them laboured for its extirpation, and the language which they applied to those who had deviated into it. Charges, indeed, or insinuations of the grossest impurities are sometimes thrown out by the orthodox writers against the early heretics [‡], but we are bound to receive them with great caution: because the answers which may have been given to them are lost; and because they are not generally justified by

* Epiphanius, in his Book on Heresies, mentions Βαρβαρισμὸς, Σκυθισμὸς, Ἑλληνισμὸς, Ἰουδαϊσμὸς, Σαμαρειτισμὸς, all under the name of heresy. Balsamon (Comment. 14th Can. Council of Chalcedon) expresses himself thus:—" Heretics are divided into two kinds: 1. Those who receive the Christian religion, but err in points, who, when they come over to the Church, are anointed with oil; 2. those who do not receive it at all, and are unbelievers, such as Jews and Greeks; and these we baptize." See Burton's Bampt. Lect. I.

† The argument amounts to this: heresy is opposed by St. Paul to faith, and is commensurate with it; and as faith comprehends as its essence and sends forth as its emanation purity of heart and excellence of conduct, so heresy must contain, of necessity, the contrary qualities.

‡ Thus Clem. Alex. (Strom. iii. p. 430. D. Ed. Lutet.) retails, against the Carpocratians, the rumour propagated by the Heathen against all Christians, of universal prostitution in their Agapæ. In another place (Strom. vii. p. 757) he says, " As one is transformed from man to beast by Circe's drugs, so one ceases to belong to God .... who rejects the ecclesiastical tradition, and bounds off (ἀποσκιρτήσας) into heresy." . The same sort of language is perpetually recurring in his writings, as well as in those of Tertullian and Cyprian.

any authentic records which we possess respecting the lives of those heretics. The truth appears to be this,—that some flagrant immoralities were notoriously perpetrated by some of the wildest among their sects, and that these have given colouring to the charges which have been thrown upon them too indiscriminately.

But whatsoever uncertainty may rest on this inquiry, it cannot be disputed, first, that the Apostolical Fathers, following the footsteps of the Apostles themselves, regarded with great jealousy the birth and growth of erroneous opinions; and next, that they did not authorize, either by instruction or example, any severity on the *persons* of those in error. They opposed it by their reasoning and their eloquence, and they avoided its contagion by removing from their communion those who persisted in it; but they were also mindful that within these limits was confined the power, which the Church received from the Apostle who founded it, over the spiritual disobedience of its members.

Variety of early Heresies.

The heretics or seceders from the primitive Church were extremely various, at least in name, and there is no period in ecclesiastical history in which dissent has appeared under so many denominations as the earliest. But it seems doubtful whether many of those sects had very numerous adherents, or were at all generally dispersed over the surface of Christendom. Some of them were merely local, scarcely extending beyond the spot which gave them birth, and others were chiefly confined to the controversial writers; as the difference was on points too abstruse to create much interest in those days among the body of the people. Many, again, have left behind them no traces of their existence, and their very names have only been preserved through the labours of their adversaries; so that we may fairly presume, in spite of the display and parade of denominations, that the great majority of the early Christians remained attached to the primitive faith. In the mean time, the mere fact of the existence of so many different forms of Christianity certainly proves, not only the zeal, but also the *numbers* of the early converts: for if these had been inconsiderable, we should have heard little either about dissenters from the orthodox body, or of their divisions among themselves. The paucity and weakness of the faithful would have been a sufficient guarantee for their unanimity.

That many of those errors gained footing at a very early period, long before the conclusion of the first century, has not been disputed with any probability*; and their origin is ascribed with great appearance of truth to the twelve or perhaps fifteen years which intervened between the ascension of Christ and the departure of the Apostles from Judæa. During this period, partly through the dispersion of the converts after the martyrdom of Stephen, partly through the periodical religious communications of foreign Jews with their native country, some imperfect accounts of the history and doctrine of the Saviour were spread abroad, even before the fulness of the truth was delivered by the Apostles. This circumstance will assist us in accounting for the great variety of forms in which error presented itself, especially if we consider the vast extent of country and the widely separated regions over which the faith was diffused. But the cause, to which we should more directly attribute the multiplicity of heresies, is the philosophical subdivisions of the heathen world, and the facility of combining opinions the most incongruous. Thus, while all parties were desirous to adapt the particular tenets of Christianity to their own preconceived opinions, which again materially differed in different sects, the forms created by such associations were necessarily very numerous, and frequently very monstrous.

Again, the manner in which the differences between the Church and those at variance with it were conducted was not free from violence of feeling and invective; the contrary would have been wonderful indeed, when we consider the situation and character of the parties. For, in the first place, as we shall presently see, a very large proportion of the early heresies were divided from the doctrine of the Gospel, not by slight or partial

Opposition of the early Fathers.

---

* Tittman, ' De Vestig. Gnosticorum,' &c. has, in our opinion, entirely failed in his learned attempt to fix the origin of the Gnostic heresies in the second century. The passages which seem most in his favour are Clem. Alex., Strom. l. vii. p. 764, Ed. Sylburg., Hegesipp. ap. Euseb. l. iii. c. 32 ; but the general voice of history is on the other side.

deviations, but by delusions so extravagant and irrational, as to place them almost in direct opposition to the true spirit of Christianity. But this was not all; in themselves they were pitiable and pardonable, but in their effects on the Church they were fraught with injury and danger: because the real character of the religion was not yet generally comprehended, and the heathens formed their estimation of it according to the specimens which were presented to them; and when they observed that absurdities were professed, and perhaps immoralities practised, in the name of Christ, they extended their contempt and indignation to the whole body of his followers*. The individual expression of those sentiments would naturally retard the progress of the faith; but neither was this the whole evil: for calumnies springing from that origin not only tainted the Christian name, but contributed to call down upon it, during the moments of its most perilous weakness, those visitations of popular fury and imperial injustice, which threatened to crush and exterminate it. Under such circumstances we shall scarcely condemn that intemperance of expression into which the early defenders of the apostolical doctrine were occasionally betrayed. At the same time we may remark, that as the controversies of those days were at least exempt from personal infliction, so religious dissent, being unrepressed by civil penalties, was less rancorous, as well as less consistent and less permanent.

The great multitude of those heresies was not only reconcilable with the moderation of the primitive Church, but may, in some degree, have proceeded from it. For as the imperfection of human nature will not allow us to hope, under any circumstances, for perfect unanimity in religious opinion, so the *names* of dissent will generally become more numerous as its expression is less discouraged. But as the differences of dissenters from each other are generally greater than their deviations from the Church, from which they branch out in all

* See Orig. Contr. Celsum, lib. iii. p. 119. l. v. p. 271. Le Clerc, H. E., ad ann. 83. Notwithstanding, Gibbon supposes the exertions of the heretics to have promoted, upon the whole, the progress of Christianity; because (as he thinks) the heathen, to whom they communicated an imperfect knowledge of the faith, subsequently threw off their errors and melted into the body of the Church.

directions as from a common centre, so any lasting coalition is little to be apprehended, and least so when no temporal authority is exerted to chastise, and by chastisement to multiply and unite them.

It would be tedious and unprofitable successively to enumerate all the heresies and dissensions of the early Christians; and it is very difficult to classify them with accuracy—for several, which were distinct in their origin, arrived by different roads so nearly at the same conclusions, that they may there seem to be identified; while others are so obscure in their own nature, or from defects in our information, as to make it neither very certain, nor perhaps very important, to which class they most properly belong.

Mosheim distinguishes three classes of early heretics:— Their Classifications by Mosheim; (1.) those who associated Christianity with Judaism, who were the Nazarenes and Ebionites; (2.) those who engrafted some of its doctrines on the system of the oriental philosophy, among whom are accounted, of the Asiatic school, Elxai, Simon Magus, Menander, Saturninus, Cerdo, and Marcion; of the Alexandrian, Basilides, Carpocrates, and the perfecter of the system, Valentinus; (3.) those who endeavoured to explain certain of the Christian mysteries by the principles of the Grecian philosophy, among whom are placed Praxeas, Artemon, Theodotus, and others. It has been objected to this division, that it is not supported by the authority of the ancient fathers, who, in no instance, derive the opinions which they combat from the oriental philosophy. Tertullian, indeed, expressly calls the philosophers the parents or "patriarchs of the heretics;" but it is to the Grecian school that he intends to confine that charge, and especially to the sects of Pythagoras and Plato, against which he constantly alleges it. Other writers hold the same language, and Irenæus goes so far as to derive the doctrine of the succession of Æons, promulgated by Valentinus, from the Greek Theogonies, not from the speculations of the eastern sages. From this circumstance we are at liberty to infer, either that the eastern philosophy had no share in the origin of the early heresies, or that those fathers were entirely unacquainted with its existence.

A different view is taken of this subject by Dr. Burton*. He ascribes the rise of all the oldest heresies to the Gnostic philosophy. But at the same time, under that comprehensive name, we understand him directly or indirectly to combine almost every form of philosophy which was professed through-out the whole extent of the eastern and western empire. The three sources which contributed to form this heterogeneous mix-ture, were, (1.) the eastern doctrine of the two principles; (2.) the Jewish Cabala; (3.) the Platonic philosophy: the last of these, under its various modifications, supplied the most abundant stream; and the point of their conflux and commix-ture is naturally supposed to have been that vast emporium of commerce and literature, Alexandria. In this city principally Gnosticism, such as it is here described, is believed to have been amalgamated into one substance, and hence distributed over the various provinces of the Roman empire not very long before the birth of Christ.

We have no space to state the learned arguments by which that opinion is supported, nor those which might reasonably be urged against it; but the fact is indisputable, that, before the period of which we are treating, the theological speculations of the eastern philosophers had been received in Europe with favour and attention, insomuch that even the worship which was founded on them was in very common practice. But whether we should still continue to distinguish the Grecian from the Oriental, as if the latter were peculiarly the Gnostical philosophy, or whether we should employ the term Gnosticism to designate a single system formed from their union, is a question which it is not necessary for us to discuss, since it is admitted that Gnosticism, in its more extended sense, embraced a multitude of ill-assorted opinions, impregnated more or less deeply with the character of the soil out of which they respectively rose.

For our own part, in the concise view which we here propose to present of the multiform family of heresies, we shall rather be directed by their subject than by their supposed origin—by the common character which runs through them, than by the source whence that character may possibly have been derived.

* See Bampt. Lect. II. and III. and note 7.

And with this intent, we shall *first* mention those wherein some of the Christian doctrines were corrupted by association with that extended philosophical system, which took its root in the vain curiosity respecting the Origin of Evil; *secondly,* we shall notice those which laid the foundation of the great controversies respecting the Trinity and Incarnation, which broke out in succeeding ages; and, *lastly,* we shall mention one or two of those which appear to have been excited by mere individual enthusiasm or madness. In the mean time, we readily admit the imperfection of this division in the light of an absolute distinction, since some of the opinions held by those, whom we shall place in the second class, might be traced to the principles which will be treated in the first; and there is so much wildness in the ravings* of certain in both those classes, that they might perhaps, without much error, be adjudged to the third.

I. The Oriental philosophy, which is commonly confounded with Gnosticism†, proceeded from the hopeless inquiry into the nature and origin of evil. Convinced that this could not possibly be ascribed to the divine agency, the speculators embraced what appeared to be the only alternative, and attributed it to matter—thence their first inference, that matter was eternal. And then, when they proceeded to consider the various forms of matter, senseless and animal, exhibited in the visible world, and their seeming imperfections, they found it impossible to account for so many modifications of evil, except by the supposed agency of some being, superior indeed to man, but subordinate to the Author of all good. At this point ceased the uniformity of the fanciful theory, and it branched off into inquiries like the following: What *was* this mighty, though inferior, being?—of what origin, power, attributes?—one and alone, or assisted or served by others, equal or inferior? *On the Gnostic Heresies.*

All these points were disputed; all however agreed as to the independent existence of the two principles, good and evil; and nearly all that the latter was the Creator of the world. Such

---

* See Irenæus, lib. i. c. 29, et seq. Le Clerc, H. E., ann. 76.

† The word is derived from γνῶσις, signifying merely knowledge, erudition. But its later sense among Christian writers implies some acquaintance with mysterious doctrines or occult interpretations, not possessed by ordinary persons. See Le Clerc on the subject of Gnosticism, Hist. Eccl. ad ann. 76.

were the philosophical notions of these persons; and such was their attachment to them, that, even when they became persuaded of the divine mission of Christ, they were unwilling entirely to sacrifice them, but rather strove to associate them with the doctrines, and engraft them on the history, of the Bible. The first consequence of so perverse a misapplication of reason was the monstrous conclusion that the God of the Jews was the evil principle, and that Jesus Christ was sent down by the good principle to put an end to his reign on earth; that the former was the God of the Old, and the latter that of the New Testament. At this point the philosophy of the Gnostics ended, and their heresy began; and the errors which we have mentioned speedily led them into others: after rejecting—such was the necessary consequence of their opinions—the inspiration and authority of the Old Testament, they applied themselves to the misrepresentation of the New. They denied the humanity of Christ, asserting that he came not in the flesh; that he suffered not, that he died not; that what seemed to be material in his nature was a fantastic, incorporeal substance. The same principles obliged them also to dispute the resurrection of the body, a substance too gross for an eternal destiny. This opinion again variously affected their moral practice; for while there were undoubtedly some who mortified the sensual portion of our nature, for the greater perfection of the soul, there are also said to have been others, of more violent enthusiasm or fiery temperament, who permitted every license of impurity to that which lay so far beneath consideration and respect. It is chiefly to the Gnostic heretics of Egypt (who were distinguished from their brethren by greater wildness in their speculations) that these excesses are attributed—we cannot now determine how truly. But, on the other hand, it is just to mention that, in professing the Christian name, those heretics did not always shrink from the dangers which surrounded it; and we have evidence that many among them encountered persecution with the same courage which distinguished their brethren of the Church, and endured it with the same unbending constancy*.

* In Diocletian's persecution, Peter and Asclepias, the former a member of

Among the Gnostic heretics (thus we shall continue to deno- Simon
minate those who associated, however variously and diversely, Magus.
the Eastern or Persian system with some belief in Christ) it is
usual to account the followers of Simon Magus, a Samarian*,
the first corrupter of the Christian doctrine : these are said to
have been numerous, especially at Rome ; though Origen †
asserts, that in his time scarcely thirty were to be found in the
whole world.   Certainly the celebrity of their master has been
considerably increased by the assertion of Justin Martyr, repeated by several of the fathers, that a statue had been erected
(and existed at his time) inscribed to the honour of the deified
heresiarch‡.   Nicolas, one of the seven deacons mentioned in Nicolas,
the Acts, is asserted to have misled the sect called Nicolaitans.

the Church, the latter a Marcionite Bishop, were burnt.   "*Peter*," says Tillemont,
"*went to heaven, and Asclepias to hell-fire.*"   That intemperate bigot might have
taken a lesson of moderation even from the language of Eusebius:—"With
Peter suffered Asclepias ; through a zeal, as he thought, for piety, but not for
that which is according to knowledge ; however, they were consumed in one and
the same fire."—Jortin, Rem. Eccl. Hist., book ii. p. ii.

    * "Simon Magus taught in Samaria that he was the Father, in Judæa that
he was the Son, among the Gentiles that he was the Holy Spirit." Iren., i.
c. 20, (or 23.)   So Tertullian: "Simon Magus ausus est summam se dicere virtu-
tem, i. e. summum Deum, post hunc Menander, discipulus ipsius, eadem dicens
quæ Simon ipse."   According to Origen, he professed to be the Δύναμις Θεοῦ;
and he is said to have denied that any one could be saved unless baptized in his
name.   At the same time we are bound to add, that Beausobre (the author who
has investigated these subjects most profoundly) holds most of what we read
about Simon to be purely fabulous—treating with no great respect the authority
either of Irenæus or Tertullian.   He seems, indeed, to consider Simon as the
"Hero of the Romance of Heresies," though he dares not directly to venture on
so bold an expression.

    † C. Cels. lib. i., and again lib. vi. p. 282.

    ‡ Bearing the Latin inscription *Semoni Deo Sancto*.   We should mention that
in 1574 a stone was discovered in the Island of the Tiber, inscribed "Semoni Sango
Deo Fidio Sacrum;" and many have hence inferred that Justin had mistaken a
statue dedicated to a Sabine Deity for that of the Heresiarch.   This stone bore
some resemblance to the pedestal of a statue, but was probably too small even to
have served that purpose.   This is the account of Baronius (ann. 44); and if we
believe this, we are likewise bound to believe Justin.   Otherwise we must suppose
that Father to have called that a *statue*, which was no part, or even support, of a
statue, but a mere rude stone, consecrated to a Pagan divinity.   Justin Martyr,
Apol. 4. s. 34 and 72.   In the latter passage Justin expressly asserts that Simon,
when he came to Rome in the time of Claudius, so astounded the senate and the
people of Rome, that they adscribed him, by a public vote, to the list of their gods,
and honoured him, like other gods, with a statue.

Menander,
Saturninus,
Basilides,
Carpo-
crates,
Cerinthus.

Menander, the pupil of Simon, perpetuated his teacher's errors, and through him they were transmitted to Saturninus, who disseminated them in the Asiatic school, and to Basilides*, who may have introduced them into the Egyptian. In this prolific soil, equally favourable to the growth of evil and of good, they became, among the gross disciples of Carpocrates†, the principles of deliberate immorality, while they received from the ingenuity of Valentinus ‡ such refinement, as to call on that writer the particular attention both of Irenæus and Tertullian§. The name of Cerinthus is usually coupled with that of Carpocrates, among the original Gnostics. Carpocrates was a Greek, and possibly an Alexandrian Platonist; and he flourished in the beginning of the second century. Cerinthus was a Jew, who lived perhaps twenty years earlier; and his history is connected, by ecclesiastical tradition, with that of St. John. There are some who go so far as to conjecture, that the object of that Apostle's visit to Ephesus was not so much to superintend the metropolis of Asia Minor, as to assail the heresy of the Gnostics in its strongest hold, and even that his gospel was written with that view. And a story‖ is handed down to prove the pious aversion with which the heretic was regarded by the apostle.

Cerdo,
Marcion.

Cerdo, and after him Marcion, the most distinguished among

* See Le Clerc, H. E., ad ann. 78 and 118.

† Iren., lib. i. c. 25. Euseb., lib. iv. c. 7. This reproach is shared with the Nicolaitans. Burton, Bampt. Lect. V., conclusion.

‡ Le Clerc places Carpocrates at the year 120 A. D., and Valentinus in the year following—aut non multo serius.

§ Our information respecting Gnosticism is chiefly collected from the writers who opposed Valentinus, and especially from Irenæus.

‖ St. John is related to have encountered Cerinthus one day in the public baths at Ephesus. He immediately hurried away, exclaiming, " Let us escape hence, lest the bath should fall to pieces, while Cerinthus, the enemy of truth, is in it ! " In a similar manner the pious Polycarp, according to another tradition, treated the heretic Marcion. They met at Rome—and when the latter courted a recognition from Polycarp, the bishop indignantly replied, " I recognize thee as the first-born of Satan." The stories are probably fabulous; and those who invented them for the purpose of doing honour to the memory of the Apostle whom Christ loved, and of the venerable martyr of Smyrna, as well as those who have retailed them with the same, or with any other view, seem to us to have strangely mistaken the character of those holy persons, as well as the charitable spirit of their religion.

the heretics of his day, introduced the same delusion, with certain* variations, into Rome, during the reign of Antoninus Pius. Here the doctrines† were immediately disclaimed by the prelates of that Church, and confuted by the ablest Christian writer, Justin Martyr. They were afterwards made the subject of a separate treatise by Tertullian. It has been inferred, from the discovery of some Gnostic medals in France, that the heresy was at one time generally disseminated in the western provinces. But this fact, liable as it is to some dispute, is not sufficient to counterbalance the silence of history, confirmed by the certainty of the early disappearance of the sect. In the mean time we do not dispute that the *philosophy* of the Gnostics had some prevalence throughout that part of the empire during the first and second centuries; but it was not until the end of the second that Christianity can be said to have made any progress there.

Soon afterwards, in the year 172, Tatian, a man of some learning, and a disciple of Justin Martyr, built on the basis of Gnosticism the heresy of the Encratites. These sectarians professed the simplest principles of the monastic life, meditation and bodily austerity. It may be said, perhaps, that under the names of Essenes and Therapeutæ such enthusiasts existed in the very earliest age of Christianity, and even before its foundation: but it is certain that it was at this period, and under this designation, that they first attracted serious attention; and it is not disputed that they met with utter discouragement and condemnation from the Church. For the birth of monachism was not destined to take place in an age of piety and sincere devo-

The Encratites. [marginal note]

---

* Cerdo and Marcion appear to have asserted the doctrine of the two principles with more boldness than the Valentinians; but both parties agreed in teaching that the Father of Jesus Christ was not the Creator of the world, nor the God of the Old Testament. Tertull. c. Marc., lib. i. c. 15, 16. Iren., lib. i. c. 47. Burton, Bampt. Lect., p. 50.

† It appears that one of the grounds on which Marcion resisted was the refusal of the Church to make any concession to the Jews, or conciliate them by any compromise of the pure faith. This appears to prove that the principal success of the Gnostic heresy had been among the Jewish converts. Probably it was most prevalent in Judæa and Egypt; but we also learn that the Church of Ephesus was early tainted by it, and probably it had gained some footing throughout Asia Minor. Marcion was a native of Pontus. The work of Justin is lost.

tion; and when at length it was produced, its growth was still irregular and unequal, keeping pace with the corruption of religion and the degradation of the Church.

The Phantastics, or Docetæ.   It is a strong, but scarcely exaggerated expression of St. Jerome*, that the body of our Lord was declared to be a phantom while the Apostles were still in the world, and the blood of Christ was still fresh in Judæa. The Phantastics, under the denomination of Docetæ, were, indeed, a sect of very early origin, and we connect their opinions with one peculiarity of the Gnostic system, which we have not yet mentioned. Certain among those philosophers, in order to remove the Author of good to an immeasurable distance from the contact of matter, imagined a vast succession of created but superhuman beings, as the agents of communication between the Supreme God and the world, or at least its Creator. These were emanations from the Deity; and they appear, when their office was discharged, to have been restored to the Pleroma, to the presence of Him who sent them—these beings were called Æons. Among them a very high rank, possibly the highest, was assigned to Christ; but from this point the Gnostics broke off into two different and almost opposite theories : many imagined that Jesus was a mere man, and maintained that the æon Christ descended upon the man Jesus at his baptism, and left him immediately before his crucifixion, so that Christ was not, in fact, subjected to pain and death : while others held that the body, with which Christ appeared to be invested, was not really human and passible, but unsubstantial, or ethereal, or at least immaterial. These last were called Docetæ. At the same time, both parties alike misunderstood that which the Church considered to be the peculiar doctrine and object of Christianity : for they agreed in believing that the mission of Christ had no further intention than to reveal the knowledge of the true God; they denied the resurrection and the final judgment, and by explaining away the death of Christ, they deprived his religion of the doctrine of the Atonement.

* Advers. Lucif., c. viii. vol. ii. p. 203. "Apostolis adhuc in sæculo superstitibus, adhuc apud Judæam sanguine Christi recenti, Phantasma Domini corpus designabatur."

From the above brief and very general outline of the Gnostic Heresies—which differed again widely from each other in many subordinate opinions—we perceive how very far they were removed from the precincts of reason and truth. Indeed, they retained so much more of Gnosticism than they assumed of Christianity, that it was only in the ancient and very broad acceptation of the term that they could be fairly denominated *Heresies ;* and thus we are less disposed to censure the severity of those Fathers who refused them the name of Christian. For however cautious we should be in withholding that appellation from those whose errors are founded on the mere perversion of reason, we may safely disclaim our fraternity with men, who substitute, for the fundamental doctrines and the clearest truths of the Gospel, wild visions and theories which have not any ground or existence, except in vain and lawless imagination. And we might do well to conclude this subject in the words of Le Clerc—one of the most rational and faithful among our historical guides. " I am weary of the Valentinians, (thus he begins his account of the year 145,) and so I imagine are my readers ; but the history of the second century is so crammed with them, and the Fathers, both of those and of later times, so often refer to them, that it is necessary to expose monstrous opinions, which in themselves do not merit one moment's attention." In truth, their principal, if not their only claim on our attention, is, that the Books of the New Testament appear to contain some allusions to them, which it is our duty to examine and understand *.

Howbeit, there is one Heresy, belonging to this School, on which it is proper to bestow a somewhat less superficial notice ; because it acquired much more general prevalence than any of the others, and an importance too, which recommended it for a long series of centuries to the jealousy and persecution of the Church, both in the East and in the West. Manes†, the most

History of Manes ;

---

* Any one desirous of more ample details respecting the Gnostic Heresies may safely consult the learned author in the Encycl. Britan., pp. 24, 25, 26., and Dr. Burton's Bampton Lectures, and Eccles. History of the Early Church. But if he wish to study their principles profoundly, he should have recourse to Beausobre's History of Manicheism.

† The original document, whence the Western accounts of Manes are generally,

distinguished of all Heresiarchs, was born in Persia about the year 240 A.D.   He professed Christianity, and is believed by some to have received ordination; but he was expelled at an early age from the catholic communion. At the same time, he held most of the tenets of the Magians; though he seems to have belonged to one of those sects which had not embraced the Reformation of Zoroaster.

Thus heterodox in both his professions, he applied himself to unite, and by uniting to perfect them. And this he proposed to accomplish by retaining just so much of both as he might hope to reconcile, without too flagrant a violation of reason. *His profession,* This purpose required authority. Accordingly, he presented himself as an inspired apostle, superior in rank to those who had preceded him: enlightened and directed by the Holy Ghost, and commissioned to disclose those secret truths which the Saviour had withheld from his disciples; to purify the Sacred Books; to purge away the judaism which corrupted Christianity; and to complete, according to the promise of Christ, the work of Revelation. This office, (for his pretensions aspired no higher*,) by assuming his infallibility, placed him above the necessity of giving any reasons for his doctrines; and he was thus contented to claim the privileges of the spiritual man, "who judgeth all things, yet he himself is judged of no man†."

if not entirely, drawn—viz. " Acta Disputationis Archelai, Episcopi Mesopotamiæ, et Manetis Heresiarchæ," appears to be supposititious. Beausobre, whose arguments on this subject are to us perfectly conclusive, has had recourse to the more copious and credible authorities of Oriental writers—and it is from the elaborate work of Beausobre that the following account is for the most part derived. The *name* of the heretic of course furnished matter for sarcasm to the ignorant malevolence of the Greeks—μίσει μὲν πάντας αἰρετικοὺς· ἐξαιρέτως δὲ τὸν τῆς Μανίας ἐπώνυμον—is the amiable injunction of Cyril of Jerusalem; and the pun is diversified in a variety of forms.   But the probability is, that his name was really Menahem, or Manaem—a term signifying *Comforter*—and this approaches nearer too to his common denomination, Manichæus.   Such at least is the conjecture of Archbishop Usher (founded on a passage of Sulpicius Severus, Hist. Sacr., l. i. p. 49), and it is confirmed by Beausobre.

* The Manicheans seem to have regarded their founder much in the same light in which the Unitarians regard Christ—as a mere man, authorized to reveal to his fellow-creatures the mysteries of heaven.

† 1 Corinth. ii. 15.

As he had been rejected by the Christian Church for his imperfect Christianity, so did his corruption of Magianism subject him to vexations from the established powers in Persia. He was imprisoned; he is stated to have passed a considerable period in exile; and he finally atoned for his dangerous innovations by death. The day of his execution (or martyrdom) is commonly asserted to have been the sixth of March, 276 or and death. 277 : the anniversary was long celebrated by his disciples, but the year has not been fixed with equal certainty. The author of his punishment is supposed (for this too is disputed) to have been Varanes I.: and the fatal offence appears, without much doubt, to have been his general proselytizing invasion of the established religion of his country—while the particular tenet, which excited the highest indignation and raised the loudest cry against him, was his denial of the resurrection of the flesh. It was not for the profession of Christianity that he suffered. As long as he was no more than an excommunicated heretic, he lived without any molestation. But when he began to proclaim a heavenly commission, and to collect disciples, and to promulgate doctrines, and to send forth missionaries, he presently incurred the jealousy of the Persian government ; and when it was ascertained besides, that his scheme embraced not only the revelation of a purer Christianity, but also the reformation of the Zoroastrian system, and the diffusion of unauthorized tenets, it was thought expedient at once to extinguish so dangerous an innovator. A public disputation was accordingly appointed between Manes and the Magians, in the presence of prejudiced judges : the arguments of the latter were pronounced to be victorious ; and the reformer was condemned and led away to execution.

To the question, whether Manes was an impostor or a fanatic, the only reasonable answer is, that he was probably both: for there has seldom been a successful heresiarch, who has not contrived to combine craft and enthusiasm. The more useful inquiry would be—if even that were useful—*which* may have predominated in the mixture ? It seems at least certain that the character of Manes, such as it is universally described, was far removed from that vulgar fanaticism, so closely connected with ignorance. It

His character.

is affirmed that he was the most learned man in the Persian empire; that he was acquainted with the Greek language; that he was versed in the various arts and sciences, in music, mathematics, geography, astronomy, and astrology, painting and medicine; that he was thoroughly familiar with the scriptures, both of the Old and New Testament, and initiated in all the mysteries of the Eastern philosophy. The accounts which we have of his dress and ordinary bearing are such as indicate rank and distinction. He aspired, like Zoroaster, to reform his religion; and he rested his lofty pretensions, not on any miraculous gifts, to which he laid no claim, but on his own extraordinary supereminence in knowledge and wisdom. And in the histories of his life, a circumstance is incidentally mentioned, which proves that he wanted neither resolution nor piety. Several of his disciples came to visit him when he was in prison; and while they were exhorting him to have some regard for his personal safety, "he told them to be of good cheer, and rose and betook himself to prayer." His ambition may have been to surpass the renown of Zoroaster; but the result is different —for while the memory of the latter is transmitted to universal celebrity with every expression of gratitude and veneration, Manes was convicted of a *double* apostacy, persecuted by one party and fiercely stigmatized by the other, unpitied and *unpardoned* by either.

On the doctrines of Manes.

The works of Manes are lost. They consisted of his "Revelation or Gospel of Life (Τὸ ζῶν Εὐαγγέλιον); "The Treasure of Life;" "The Book of Chapters or Fundamentals (τῶν Κεφαλαίων);" and the "Book of Mysteries." There were also "Collections of his Letters," and of his "Memorable Sayings and Actions." His immediate followers appear to have used a liturgy or prayer book; but this composition is not with any certainty ascribed to Manes. It is from the fragments of these works (especially the "Book of Mysteries") and from some controversial writings of the early fathers (particularly Augustine[*]), that we glean most of our imperfect knowledge of the

---

[*] The work of Faustus, an African Bishop and a Manichean, which is preserved and confuted by Augustine, contains the best exposition and the most ingenious defence of *some* of the Manichean doctrines. The controversy is very

principles, opinions, and observances of Manes and his followers.

It may be necessary to remind our readers that the ancient Magi were, in the strictest sense, Dualists: they believed in two original coeternal principles; both gifted with perception, thought, and active power—God and matter. They believed, that there was a prince or ruler in this region of matter, possessed of might nearly equal to that of the prince of good in his own region: and that when God made this world in the region of matter, the two principles of good and evil, light and darkness, became necessarily mixed and confused together. This doctrine prevailed in Persia, until it was for the most part supplanted by the purer theism of Zoroaster. He taught the existence of only *one* original principle—which created light and darkness: that good and evil proceeded from these respectively, and the world from their mixture. In this manner the reformer removed the offensive notion of two original conflicting beings; but in so doing, he indirectly introduced another tenet, which, to some, was scarcely less offensive—that God was the author and creator of evil.

Manes succeeded; and he so far agreed with the old Magi, in opposition to the Zoroastrian scheme, as to assert matter to be eternal, endowed with sense, and the parent of the evil spirit —but he denied, notwithstanding, that matter was God[*]. According to his definition, God was an eternal, intelligent, pure light, mixed with no darkness, and susceptible of no change. His being was indeed corporeal, and consequently not infinite:

powerfully dissected by Beausobre—a writer who unites more intellect with more candour, than we have hitherto seen applied to ecclesiastical history. In this instance he does indeed, at first sight, appear unconsciously to advocate the cause of the heretic—as if, himself an exile, he sympathized with the exile and the martyr, or was well pleased to enter the lists against the great patriarch of a persecuting Church. This may have been so too. But we should reflect likewise, that in those numerous cases, where we receive the opinions of a heretic entirely, or chiefly, from the pen of his adversary, it becomes an historical duty to receive them with suspicion—to examine the charges, and detect the misrepresentations, and separate the truth, if possible, from the mass of controversial calumny.

[*] This distinction is held by many, and Mosheim (Reb. Gest. ante Const. sec. iii. s. 41. p. 765) among the rest, to be delusive—on the ground, that an original, self-existent, sensible principle, call it by what name you will, is still a God. We need not enter into this verbal difference.

but the infinitude, which Manes withheld from the person of the Deity, he ascribed to his attributes. He was single, indivisible, immortal, impassible; perfect in mercy, holiness, and justice—in independence, power, and wisdom*. Matter was nothing more than the "Sovereign Evil," the "Sovereign Imperfection,' and the earth, the place of matter, was the land of darkness.

This last subject Manes more fully treated in his "Book of Mysteries": he there explained his theory of the creation of the world and the formation of man—how souls came to be mixed with matter, and how they might be delivered from it. From the disorders of this sublunary world he concluded, that so irregular a work could not be the effect of a perfectly free design, formed by the wisdom and executed by the power of God; but that some second cause must have interposed in the creation, and that that cause was matter.

The theological error, which naturally and immediately flowed from these principles, was the entire rejection of the authority of the Old Testament. In respect to this question, Manes was compelled by his adoption of the Oriental philosophy to reject the theosophy of the Jews. He was, in the fullest extent, an eclectic—for in endeavouring to accommodate Christianity to magianism he only chose those portions either of the one or of the other which it seemed possible to reconcile. It was a favourite text with his disciples, perhaps with himself, to "examine all things and hold fast by that which is good;" and they extended its arbitrary application even to the books of the New Testament. Those which they seem to have rejected altogether, were the Acts of the Apostles, and the Epistle to the Hebrews; that of St. Jude, the second of St. Peter, the third and fourth of St. John, and the Revelations. The rest they did in substance retain; but they charged them with many interpolations—they even denied that the Gospels were written by

---

* "Sanctus atque illustris Pater, in sua sancta stirpe perpetuus, in virtute magnificus, magnitudine incomprehensibilis . . natura ipsa verus, æternitate propria exultans, semper continens apud se sapientiam et sensus vitales . . in sua laude præcipuus . . . Ita autem fundata sunt ejus splendidissima regna, ut a nullo unquam aut moveri aut concuti possint." Manich. ap. Augustin. contr. Ep. Tuad. cap. xii. God is likewise described as surrounded by "gloriosa secula," or Æons. See Beausob. p. ii. l. iii. ch. iv.

their professed authors, and ascribed them to a later age. By this supposition they did in fact deprive them of all their authority: but they forgot (as Augustin has observed) that while they were thus subverting Christianity, they subverted Manicheism also—since this latter rests entirely on a promise recorded in those suspicious and corrupted compositions!

At the same time they proclaimed their belief in the perfect divinity of Christ, and admitted without any equivocation the doctrine of the Trinity. They asserted likewise the consubstantiality of the Father and the Son, and even ranked among the orthodox in the controversy of Nice. They received the sacraments of Baptism and the Lord's Supper, and followed in their administration the rites of the Church, except in respect to the cup, where they used water instead of wine. But when they came to consider Christ's human nature, their peculiar principle led them into error: for, as matter was essentially the source and cause of evil, to invest the Redeemer with flesh was in fact to impute sin to him. Consequently, they adopted the notion of the Phantastics. They denied the incarnation, circumcision, baptism, and temptation; and maintained that the crucifixion and resurrection were not real, but apparent only. Connected with this opinion was their disbelief in the resurrection of the flesh*, and (as it would likewise seem) in the eternity of punishments. Not that they doubted the last judgment, or the threatened infliction by fire—but they held that it would be purgatory and temporary, rather than penal and everlasting.

Such, as far as we are able to pronounce with any certainty, were the principal doctrines of Manes and his followers. They celebrated the festivals of Easter, and of the Ascension; and probably of the descent of the Holy Spirit. They observed the Lord's Day as a rigid fast. They had no places peculiarly dedicated to worship; and rejected, on the same principles, temples and altars, images and incense. They were divided into two classes—the Elect and the Hearers. The former were, for the

Certain observances of his followers.

---

* Origen had previously fallen into the same error; but he guarded it (for a time at least) by a subtle distinction—while he denied the resurrection of the flesh, he asserted that of the *body*. The opinion of Manes was a dangerous apostacy both from Zoroaster and from Christ. See Beausob., p. ii. l. viii. c. v.

most part, the ministers of religion—though not exclusively so*;
the latter comprehended all the secular Manicheans.   Both
were baptized—so that this distinction was not in imitation of
the usual division of Christians into Faithful and Catechumens.
To the "Elect" was prescribed the rigid rule of abstinence† and
celibacy—the absolute mortification of the corrupt and sinful
flesh.   But as to the "Hearers," those severe observances were
recommended by counsel rather than command; it was not
attempted to enforce them.   In regard to their alleged worship
of the sun, they admitted that, when they prayed, they did indeed direct their eyes to that luminary, as they deemed it to be
the abode of Christ, and their piety was excited by the contem-
plation: but the prayers were in fact addressed, not to the place,
but to the immortal Being who dwelt therein; and this explanation should have been satisfactory to the Roman Catholics of
later days, since they defended their own veneration for images
by a very similar distinction.   Lastly, the Manicheans maintained the apostolical institution of the three orders of the
priesthood; but at the same time, they did not permit them to
possess property—and this was indeed a heresy, which could
not fail to subject its adherents to the displeasure of the Roman
hierarchy, in the 12th and 13th centuries.

Howbeit, there was not any century, nor any church which
looked with favour upon the opinions, or with mercy upon the
persons, of the Manicheans.   In Persia, their master perished
by a barbarous death.   They had scarcely gained footing in
the Roman empire, when they were assailed by a sanguinary
edict of Diocletian‡.   Priscillian was persecuted and suffered

---

* "Sed et ipsi *Auditores* ante *Electos* genua figunt, ut iis manus suppliciter
imponantur, non a solis Episcopis, vel Presbyteris, vel Diaconis eorum, sed a qui-
buslibet Electis."   August. Epist. 74.   "Auditoribus vestris, quos tanquam dis-
tinctos a genere sacerdotum, &c."   Aug. Faust. xxx. 5.

† "Secularibus vero vulgo concedantur omnia quæ qui possunt;" and again, "Nos
quidem ex plebe sacerdotum genus censemus a carne abstinere debere."   Aug.
Faust. l. xvi. 6 and l. xxx. i.   See Beausob. p. ii. l. ix. c. x.

‡ From some expressions in this edict it would seem that Diocletian's hostility was *national*, at least as much as it was religious.   In fact, at so very
early a period the new sect could scarcely have become sufficiently odious as
a sect to call forth so much indignation.   "Audivimus Manichæos nuperrime,
velut nova inopinata prodigia, in hunc mundum (Proconsular Africa) de Persica

under that title. They were numbered among the proscribed
in the Theodosian code.   They were pursued by the eager*
orthodoxy of Leo the Great.   As Paulicians, they became
afterwards the objects of fierce aggression from the Eastern
court, ending in destruction or exile.   And lastly, under the
various appellations of Cathari, Gazari, Publicani, Paterini,
they were hunted by the myrmidons of triumphant papacy :
such too was the popular horror attached to the name of this
heresy, that the mere imputation was fatal in those bad ages ;
and among the earliest victims of the inquisition numbers were
sacrificed—with what justice we know not—to the charge of
Manicheism.

II. We have observed, that among the earliest corrupters of Heresies
the Christian doctrines, there were some who disputed the hu- respecting
man nature of Christ. It appears to us equally clear that there of Christ.
were also others who denied his divinity.   The oldest and perhaps the most numerous among these were the Ebionites.

Tertullian considers them as a sect of Judaizing Christians, The Ebion-
named from their founder Ebion, who strictly maintained the ites.
observance of the ceremonial law, and rejected the miraculous
conception and the divine nature of the Saviour†.   Eusebius,
in his Ecclesiastical History, (book iii. c. xxvii.) describes them
in these words :—

et *adversaria nobis gente* progressa, vel orta esse . . . Verendum est ne forte, ut
fieri adsolet, accedente tempore, conentur ad execrandas *consuetudines* et *inces-
tas leges Persarum* innocentioris naturæ homines, Romanam Gentem . . . . vene-
nis suis inficere." We may remark, on the other hand, that Christianity was not
much persecuted in Persia, until it became dominant in the Roman Empire.
Then it became an acknowledged portion of the institutions of an enemy—till
then, being persecuted by the powers at home, it might well be tolerated by a
hostile government.

* One of the peculiarities by which he detected them was their refusal to partake of the *Wine* at the holy sacrament.   We refer to chap. ix. of this history.

† De Præscript. Hæret. c. 33.; De Virgin. Veland. c. 6.   "Quam utique Vir-
ginem fuisse constat, licet Ebion resistat."   De Carne Christi, c. 14. 18, 19.
" Poterit et hæc opinio Ebioni convenire, qui nudum hominem et tantum ex semine
David—id est—non Dei Filium, constituit Jesum."   The Ebionites are classed
by Mosheim among the Judaizing sects; and Ebion, if he existed at all, was
probably a Jew : the numbers and influence of those sects diminished so rapidly
during the second century, after the promulgation of Adrian's Edict, and are consequently so little noticed by the fathers of the third and following ages, that it
seems unnecessary to bestow a separate notice on them.

"The Ebionites were so called from the poverty and mean-
ness with which they dogmatized concerning Christ; for they
considered him as a mere man born of the connexion of a man
and Mary.   And they thought too that the ceremonial law
(νομικὴ ϑρησκεία) was to be followed; as neither faith in Christ,
nor the life led through that faith, was sufficient for salvation.
But there were others* bearing the same appellation, who
escaped the extravagant absurdity of these former, since they
did not deny that the Lord was born of a virgin and the Holy
Spirit.   But neither did these, acknowledging his pre-existence,
and that he was Logos and Sophia, (the Word and the Wisdom,) turn entirely away from the unrighteousness of the former, chiefly because they too were careful about the bodily
service (σωματικὴν λάτρειαν) of the law.   These then did not
receive the epistles of the apostle, calling him an apostate from
the law, and only used the gospel according to the Hebrews;
but they observed Sunday in commemoration of the resurrection, keeping the Jewish sabbath.

This description agrees in all material points with the account of Tertullian; and without proceeding to deeper investigation, we may safely infer from it two historical truths : that
the peculiar opinions of the Ebionites were confined (or nearly
so) to the Jewish converts—and that they were neither wholly
nor in part the doctrines of the ante-Nicene Church.

It is well known that the high antiquity of the opinions of
the Ebionites has been held by some to be an evidence of their
truth; but the same inference might be drawn, with the same
reason, respecting the delusions of the Phantastics, which had
at least as early an origin.   The Ebionites probably arose after
the publication of three of the gospels†.   The Gnostic errors

---

* So Origen (C. Cels. l. v. p. 272) Οὗτοι δ᾽ εἰσιν οἱ δισσοὶ Εʼβιωναῖοι· ἤτοι ἐκ Παρθένον
ὁμολογοῦντες, ὁμοίως ἡμῖν, τὸν Ἰησοῦν—ἢ οὐκ οὕτω γεγενῆσθαι ἀλλ᾽ ὡς τοὺς λοιποὺς ἀνθρώπους.

† Le Clerc distinguishes the early from the more recent Ebionites, placing
them respectively at ann. 72 and 103.   The former he considers, on the authority
of Jerome, to have been merely Judaizing Christians—who, as that Father remarks, in their wish to be both Jews and Christians, were neither.   Le Clerc considers the Nazarenes to have been the same sect as the early Ebionites, ann. 72.
Mosheim (De Reb. Christ. ant. Const. Sec. i., sect. lviii. and Sec. ii., sect. xxxix.,
xl. &c.) refers the rise of the Ebionites to the second century.

of the Docetæ may even have preceded the preaching of the Apostles; they were certainly contemporary with it. Again, if it be admitted that the Apostles were the interpreters of God's word, and if it be not proved that the sect of the Ebionites was founded by any one of them, and if it be certain that the fathers who subsequently directed the Church, and explained its doctrine, did invariably disclaim that sect, we may fairly conclude that its opinions were neither favourably received, nor at all commonly adopted. On the other hand, it is endeavoured, by confounding the Ebionites with the Gnostic Heretics, to make them in some degree accountable for all the absurdities of the latter; and these, it is truly urged, had all a tendency to the opposite extreme, to spiritualize the body rather than to degrade the divine nature of Christ. And it is hence inferred, that it was *Jesus* alone to whom the Ebionites attributed a human nature, while they acknowledged the uncontaminated divinity of *Christ*. It is possible that there were some, calling themselves Ebionites, who were in fact merely Gnostics. But in the face of our direct authorities we cannot admit the hypothesis in question. What Tertullian and Eusebius* expressly tell us to have been the Ebionitical opinions respecting *Christ*, we cannot suppose to be meant of Jesus as *opposed to Christ*. And we feel obliged to believe, that those are as far removed from truth on the one hand, who dispute the early *existence* of the Unitarian opinions, as those are, on the other, who assert their early reception by the Church; they have existed from the beginning, and from the beginning they have been condemned.

Again, the doctrine of the mere humanity of Christ, separated from the Judaism of the Ebionites, was advanced towards the end of the second century by Theodotus and Artemon; and during the episcopacy of Victor, the former was expelled from the Church of Rome for that error. Eusebius in this place designates him as the '*father* of a *godless* apostacy'—(ἀρχηγὸν καὶ πατέρα ταύτης τῆς ἀρνησιθέου ἀποστασίας)—and in so far as he had divested the old opinion of its judaism, and advanced it nakedly in the very face of the Church, the assertion is true. That it had

Theodotus and Artemon.

---

* See also respecting the opinions of the Ebionites, Irenæus, lib. i. c. 26. lib. iii. c. 21. lib. iv. c. 50. Ed. Paris; and Epiphanius. Hæres. 30.

not hitherto found any admittance at Rome, or in any of the European Churches, is sufficiently proved by reference to the writings of Justin, and Miltiades, and Tatian, and Clement, and Irenæus, and Melito, "by all of whom (says Eusebius) the divinity of Christ is asserted *."

Paul of Samosata.

In the next century the heresy of Artemon (it became more generally known by his name) was revived by Paul of Samosata, Bishop of Antioch †. A synod of Bishops, Presbyters and Deacons was convoked at Antioch (for the second time) in the year 269, to take cognizance of the offence; and Eusebius notices the eagerness with which they hurried "from all directions against the defiler of Christ's flock." From the numerous provinces of Western and middle Asia deputies presented themselves at the appointed time, and the ecclesiastical world, from Pontus to Arabia, was thrown into commotion. In the meantime it does not appear that any bishops attended from the west; and the prelates of Italy, to whom the dispute was finally referred, were neither present nor even represented in the councils of Antioch.

It was a bold resolution in those days to expose and condemn the heresy of a bishop of Antioch—for the See was still regarded as possessing the Primacy of Asia. The difficulty was increased by the personal power and arrogance of Paul. He is represented to have appeared in public with a great parade of guards and other attendants (an early deviation from the Apostolical humility); and to have sought safety, not only in ingenious and subtle argument, but also in the physical force of his protectors and adherents. Nevertheless, he was condemned by the Council, and the act of his deposition was subscribed by no less than

---

* ἐν οἷς ἅπασι Θεολογεῖται ὁ Χριστός. Last chap. of lib. v.

† We follow in this statement the authority of Eusebius, and the opinion almost universally received. But it is fair to mention that Dr. Burton ingeniously argues, from a careful examination of contemporary evidence, compared chiefly with the assertions of Athanasius, that "Paul believed *Jesus* to be a mere human being, but conceived him to become *Christ*, by being united to the eternal *Logos* of God."—(Bampt. Lect., viii. notes 99. 102.) It does not appear that the contemporaries of the Heretic placed that construction upon his doctrine. And Eusebius (H. E. L. vii. c. 27) expressly says—τούτου δὲ ταπεινὰ καὶ χαμαιπετῆ περὶ τοῦ Χριστοῦ παρὰ τὴν ἐκκλησιαστικὴν διδασκαλίαν φρονήσαντος, ὡς κοινοῦ τὴν φύσιν ἀνθρώπου γενομένου, &c. &c. See Mosheim, De R. Christ. ante Const. Sæc. iii. sect. 35.

seventy Bishops. How he resisted the execution of the sentence, and in what manner it was finally enforced, has been related in a former chapter. At present we shall refer to a more important matter, the exposition of faith which was published by the councils. It is contained in a letter to Paul, which is still extant; and it asserts in the plainest expressions the essential divinity of Christ, his eternal pre-existence and his miraculous incarnation—that he is related to God, not as a creature, but as a Son; and that the world was created by his hands. The doctrine of Antioch was essentially the same with that of Nice; but there was a *verbal* discrepancy, which some have laboured to magnify into a real difference. The word " Consubstantial" does not appear in the confession of Antioch; and in avoiding unscriptural terms, calculated to create and multiply causes or pretext for controversy, those Fathers exhibited a judicious forbearance, which was not always imitated by their successors.

The controversy respecting the nature of Christ's existence on earth, which presently so branched out, as to involve the doctrine of the Trinity as well as the Incarnation, may be said to have first assumed a tangible form under the pen of Praxeas, a writer of the Grecian school. He published his opinions about the year 200 A. D., and was answered very soon afterwards by Tertullian. The opinions of Praxeas (as is natural in a question capable of so much metaphysical subtilty) are variously represented*; but the doctrine of the Orthodox is very clearly stated in the expressions of his antagonist, which we have already cited. In fact, it is to us the principal advantage derived from these controversies, that they open the clearest insight we possess into the original doctrine of the Church †. *Heresy of Praxeas,*

The heresy of Praxeas was succeeded, in the course of about fifty years, by that of Sabellius, or perhaps we should rather say, *and of Sabellius.*

---

* They are chiefly to be divined from the treatise written against him by Tertullian. It should be mentioned also, that Praxeas had declared very strongly against *Montanism*, before Tertullian attacked him.

† It appears too from the examination of Irenæus' writings against the Valentinians, that that more ancient Father maintained, as far as he particularizes them, the same opinions. It has been observed, that Tertullian was the first author who used the words Trinitas and Persona in the theological sense.

revived in it. Both proceeded, in appearance, from the difficulty of reconciling the Trinity with the Unity of the Godhead—
in reality, from our human and necessary incapacity to comprehend the nature of the union. But Greek philosophy was
too vain to admit any limits to the human comprehension, and
too disputatious to quit so fine a field for sophistry, as was
opened by an abstruse and inexplicable question. And certainly that philosophy lost nothing either in minuteness or pertinacity, when it ascended to the climate, and employed the
genius of Africans*. Sabellius was an African, and seemingly
either Bishop, or Presbyter at Barce, the capital of the Cyre-
naica : he denied the distinct personality of the second and third
persons of the Trinity, and maintained that a certain energy
only, proceeding from the supreme Parent, or a certain portion
of the Divine nature, was united to the son of God, the man
Jesus †. And in the same manner he considered the Holy
Ghost to be a portion of the everlasting Father. This error,
into which he was led by an excessive fear of Tritheism, (the
acknowledgment of three Gods,) was liable to the inference,
that the Being who suffered on the cross was in fact the Father ; hence his followers were called Patripassians. He was
confuted by Dionysius, Bishop of Alexandria.

The Mon-
tanists.

III. We shall not dwell upon the varying shapes of mere
frenzy. The deliberate errors of an informed and serious mind,
however in appearance remote from reason, always merit some
sort of consideration ; but the dreams of an ignorant fanatic
can have no claims on our time or reflection. Perhaps we
should place under this head some of the wilder of those heresies usually called Gnostic ; and some would refer to the same
origin the opinions of the Manichæan sect ; but we shall here
confine ourselves to those of the Montanists. About the year
170 A. D., a vain and superstitious enthusiast, named Montanus,

* See Mosheim, De R. Christ. ante Const. Sæc. iii. sec. 33. The different opinions, or rather the different shades of the same opinion, which have been ascribed
to Sabellius, are there accurately treated.

† We perceive how nearly this opinion approaches to the old Gnostic heresy,
which considered Christ as an Æon or Divine Emanation united for a time to
the man Jesus—but for a time only—the Gnostics withdrew the Æon before the
Crucifixion, and thus avoided the conclusion charged against the Patripassians.

began to prophesy in Phrygia and other provinces of Asia Minor—he professed, like Manes afterwards, and like Simon, perhaps, before him, to be inspired * by the Holy Ghost, and to be the messenger whose appearance on earth before the second coming of Christ, for the purpose of completing the divine Revelation, was expected by many of the faithful; and his trances, and extatic raptures, and fanatic ravings, were probably regarded by the credulous and wondering multitude as the surest signs of divine inspiration. Certainly there were many in those regions who followed him; and his success was promoted by his association with two prophetesses, named Maximilla and Priscilla, who confirmed his mission, and shared his spirit. Another cause of the temporary fame of Montanism was the severity of the morality inculcated by it. The strictest celibacy and the most rigid fasts were exacted from the proselytes; and this circumstance threw an appearance of sanctity round the sect, which seems to have deadened the penetration of Tertullian—for he presently professed himself its advocate. To that circumstance perhaps this heresy may be indebted for most of its celebrity. It was condemned by certain Asiatic councils at the time of its eruption; and it appears to have made very little progress after the second century, and at no time to have found general reception beyond the precincts of its birth-place, though some remains of it subsisted there for two or three ages †.

Before we quit the subject of Heresy, we must mention a controversy which divided the Church during the third century, respecting the form of receiving a converted heretic into the number of the orthodox. The Churches of the west ‡ were, for

On the baptism of Heretics.

---

* See Bishop Kaye on Tertullian, p. 23, et seq. Beausob. Hist. Manich., p. ii. l. i. c. ii. It is the deliberate opinion of Mosheim, that he professed *to be* the Paraclete, sent down to complete the Christian system; but that he distinguished between the Paraclete and the Holy Ghost. Bishop Kaye, however, certainly shows that this distinction has no foundation. " Hoc unum significavit Tertullianus, Paracletum Spiritum Sanctum *per* Montanum multa docuisse." Petav. Dog. Theol. Incarn. l. iv. cap. 14. The same difference has arisen concerning Manes, and the same was probably the truth.

† We observe the name of Montanism among the heresies stigmatized in the Theodosian Code.

‡ We may account for this greater moderation of the western Churches, by their having escaped some of the most extravagant among the early heresies:

M 2

the most part, of opinion, that the baptism of Heretics was valid, and that the mere imposition* of hands, attended by prayer, was form sufficient to solemnize their introduction within the pale; whereas the less moderate Christians of Asia decided in council at Iconium, that their admission must be preceded by repetition of baptism : this obligation had been previously advocated by Tertullian in powerful language; it had been inculcated by a council of seventy Bishops assembled at Carthage in 215; and it was finally approved, and enforced by Cyprian in the Churches of Africa. Stephen, Bishop of Rome, who was at the head of those who held the contrary opinion, conducted his opposition with injudicious violence*, and by emulating the uncharitable intemperance of Victor†, afforded a second precedent of arrogance, for the imitation of his distant successors. The mention of this controversy is important, at least on one account, as it affords an additional proof of the very serious view in which Heresy was regarded by the Churchmen of those days, and the scrupulousness of their care to preserve the purity of the faith.

On the re-admission of the Lapsed.

In the beginning of the third century it seems to have been the general practice of the Church to re-admit to communion, after a prescribed course of penance, those who had *lapsed* from the faith during persecution. But in the time of Cyprian, the "Confessors," though laymen, were permitted to assume one privilege, of a character strictly ecclesiastical, viz., that of granting to their weaker brethren some remission of penance, or even of restoring them at once to communion‡. Cyprian

these, as they chiefly originated in the wild imaginations of the east, were for the most part confined to those regions. The grand council of Carthage held by Cyprian, on this question, was in the year 256. It consisted of 87 bishops, whose opinions, delivered *seriatim*, are still extant and published with Cyprian's works.

* Thus much was deemed necessary even by the most indulgent party—on the ground, that, though the Heretic might have been duly baptized in the name of the three Persons, he could not possibly have received the Holy Ghost.

† This controversy resembles, in two points, that before mentioned, respecting the celebration of Easter. The Roman was right perhaps in the principle, but overbearing and insolent in the *manner*.

‡ The confessor gave a *libellus* or certificate to the lapsed brother, and on presenting this to the priest, he claimed to be restored to communion. Those so re-

was not favourable to this innovation in the discipline of the Church—yet was he far from wishing to withhold communion from the sincere penitent; and in the councils, which he held on this subject in 251 and 252, it was his object to preserve this moderate system.

In the mean time, a schism had divided the Church of Carthage, which originated in the opposition made by certain Presbyters to the election of Cyprian. One Novatus, a Presbyter, had been active in fomenting it; and accordingly we find him described, in the writings of Cyprian, as the most degraded of mankind. He went to Rome in 251; and is represented as having there excited a Presbyter of Rome, named Novatian*, to a similar opposition to the newly-elected Bishop Cornelius. Whatever may have been the vices of the African schismatic, it is not disputed that Novatian at least was a man of talents and learning and severe and immaculate character.

The schism of Novatian.

He failed, however, in his opposition to Cornelius, and then immediately propounded his rigid system of ecclesiastical discipline. He entered first into the particular controversy of the day, and contended, that the lapsed ought not at any time, or under any circumstances, to be restored to the Communion of the Church †. Presently he found, that consistency compelled him, first, to extend to *all* transgressors the principle which he at first applied only to one sort; and next, to justify this universal severity of exclusion, by denying the *temporal* efficacy of repentance : this denial involved the rejection of the prac-

stored were called *Libellatici*. This is one explanation of the term. Mosheim (Reb. Gest. a. Const. sec. iii. s. ii.) concludes, from the comparison of some obscure passages, that the libellus was a *certificate of sacrifice* given by the civil magistrates to lapsed Christians—supposing at the same time that it was often given without any sacrifice at all, through interest or humanity. In either case the Libellatici were the weaker brethren.

* Euseb. l. vi. c. 43. Jerome De Vivis Illust. c. 70. See too Cornel. ap. Cypr. Ep. 50 (or 48), and Cyprian, passim. He is asserted to have been a convert from some sect of philosophy, probably the Stoic. It is singular that Eusebius and the Greek writers generally (not always, Clem. Alex. ap. Euseb. l. c.) call him Novatus, and Lardner imitates them—not, however, at all confounding him with his unworthy (or calumniated) associate the Presbyter of Carthage. The reader may consult Tillem. Mem. H. Eccles., vol. iii. c. pp. 433, 435. ann. 251, and Næander, sect. ii. part iii.

† It is worth remarking, that to this extent the opinions of Novatian were afterwards adopted by the orthodox council of Eliberis.

tice of penance, as being a temptation to sin and useless for purposes of reconciliation, and thus deprived the Church of the inherent power of absolution. But this he had no reluctance to do; since he considered the genuine Church of Christ to be a society, where virtue and innocence reigned universally, and refused any longer to acknowledge those as its members, who had even once degenerated into unrighteousness. His followers were called Cathari, or Puritans, and they comprehended many austere and independent Christians, in the east* no less than in the west. But this endeavour to revive the spotless moral purity of the primitive faith was found inconsistent with the corruptions even of that early age: it was regarded with suspicion by the leading prelates, as a vain and visionary scheme; and those rigid principles, which had characterized and sanctified the Church in the first century, were abandoned to the profession of schismatic sectaries in the third.

Though the Novatians are sometimes stigmatized as Heretics by ecclesiastical writers, they are not accused of any express doctrinal difference with the Church. On the great question of the Trinity they zealously co-operated with the orthodox; and when Dionysius† of Alexandria expresses his "justifiable aversion for Novatian, because he had divided the Church, and carried some of the brethren into impiety and blasphemy," his subsequent expressions disclose to us the extent of that guilt: "that he had calumniously represented our blessed Lord Jesus Christ as unforgiving; that he had disparaged the holy Baptism, and subverted the faith and the *confession* which precede it; and denied the Holy Spirit to many, who might have hoped, either that it would have abided with them, or returned to them." As Novatian is no where deliberately accused of any error respecting the nature or efficacy of Baptism, we may, perhaps, consider the above representation as merely an amplification of the schismatic's real offence, which was his secession from the Church.

* Especially, as it would seem, in Phrygia—where their rigid practices brought them into danger of being confounded with the Montanists. (Mosh. c. iii. eno. Lardner, Cred. Gosp. Hist. p. ii. ch. 47.) They were excepted, on better information, by Constantine from his General Edict against Heretics, into which, on its first publication, their name had been hastily inserted.

† Ap. Euseb. l. vii. c. viii.

From a review of what has been written on this subject, some General observations. truths may be derived of considerable historical importance; the following are among them: (1.) In the midst of perpetual dissent and occasional controversy, a steady and distinguishable line, both in doctrine and practice, was maintained by the early Church, and its efforts against those, whom it called Heretics, were zealous and persevering, and for the most part consistent. Its contests were fought with the " sword of the Spirit," with the arms of reason and eloquence; and as they were always unattended by personal oppression, so were they most effectually successful—successful, not in establishing a nominal unity, nor silencing the expression of private opinion, but in maintaining the purity of the faith, in preserving the attachment of the great majority of the believers, and in consigning, either to immediate disrepute or early neglect, all the unscriptural doctrines which were successively arrayed against it. (2.) The greater part of the early heresies was derived from the impure mixture of profane philosophy with the simple revelation of the Gospel. Hence proceeded those vain and subtile disputations about things incomprehensible, which would indeed have been less pernicious, had they exercised only the ingenuity of men, without engaging their passions. Their bitter fruits were not fully gathered until a later age; but they served, even in their origin, to perplex the faith and disturb the harmony of many devout Christians. (3.) No public dispute had hitherto arisen respecting the manner of salvation; for the conclusions deducible from the Gnostic hallucinations are not worthy of serious consideration. The great question respecting Predestination and Grace had not yet become matter of controversy, nor had any of the fundamental doctrines of Christianity been assailed, excepting the Trinity and the Incarnation. (4.) There was yet no dissent on the subject of Church government. It was now universally and undisputably Episcopal. Even the reformer Novatian, after his expulsion from the Church, assumed the direction of his own rigid sect under the title of bishop. And if any dissatisfaction had arisen as to the established method of directing the Church, it would certainly have displayed itself on the occasion of a schism which entirely respected matters of practice and discipline. In the same manner, we observe that the disciples of Theodotus and Artemon adopted the Episcopal government; and Cyprian incidentally mentions, among other charges against Heretics, that they appointed their bishops independently of the Church.

END OF PART I.

PART II.

FROM THE ACCESSION OF CONSTANTINE TO THE DEATH OF CHARLEMAGNE.

CHAPTER VI.

Constantine the Great.

Victory of Constantine over Maxentius—his supposed conversion—the miracle of the luminous Cross—evidence for and against it—the latter conclusive—The Edict of Milan—its nature and effects—union of the whole Empire under Constantine—His moral character—sincerity of his conversion—unjustly disputed —Remarks on his policy—power of the Christians—Alterations introduced into the constitutions of the Church—Its nature at Constantine's accession— spiritual and temporal power—union and strength of the early Church—how cemented—View of the Church probably taken by Constantine—he sought its alliance—Three periods of the ecclesiastical life of Constantine—How circumstanced with regard to the state in which Constantine found the Church—He assumes the supremacy—Rights of the Church—Its *Internal* administration— little altered in theory—permission to bequeath property to the Church—Independent jurisdiction of the Bishops—on what founded—*External*—subject to the Emperor—what particulars included in it—General observations—Constantine usurped nothing from the Church—Indeterminate limits of the civil and spiritual authority—Alterations of the titles and gradations of the Hierarchy—pre-eminence unattended by authority—Conclusion—Note on Eusebius.

DURING the early part of Diocletian's persecution, Constantius Chlorus ruled, with as much humanity as circumstances permitted him to exercise, the provinces of the West. On his death, at York, in the year 306, the army proclaimed Constantine, his son, Emperor. In the mean time, the provinces eastward of Gaul were distracted by the dissensions of rival emperors, which favoured the growing strength of Constantine. In 311, Galerius, the fiercest among the assailants of Christianity, died, and his dominions were divided between Maximin and Licinius ; Maxentius had already usurped the government of Italy and Africa. Presently Constantine, justified, as most assert, by sufficient provocation, marched into Italy and overthrew Maxentius in the immediate neighbourhood of Rome ; that tyrant (as all admit him to have been) was drowned in the Tiber, and his dominions were added to the possessions of the con-

queror. This event took place in the year 312; and it has
been usually assigned as marking the period of Constantine's
conversion to Christianity. A miraculous story* is connected
with this epoch in our history. As the Emperor was marching
toward Rome, at the head of his army, he beheld a luminous
Cross, suspended about noonday in the air, and inscribed with
the following words—Τούτῳ νίκα—' By this conquer.' The
phenomenon confirmed his uncertain faith, and afforded him
the surest omen of victory. But this was not all: during
the ensuing night the form of Christ himself presented itself
with the same Cross, and directed him to frame a standard
after that shape. And it is certain that, about that period, and
possibly on that occasion, a standard was so framed, and continued for many following years to be displayed, whenever it
became necessary to excite the enthusiasm of the Christian
soldiers—but the extraordinary appearances to which its adoption is ascribed demand the most rigid examination.

In the first place, the story which we have shortly given is
related by no contemporary author, excepting Eusebius; next,
it is related in his life † of Constantine, and not in his Ecclesiastical History; it is related in the year 338, or six-and-twenty
years after the supposed appearance; it is related on the authority of Constantine alone, though it must have been witnessed by his whole army, and notorious throughout his whole
empire; and lastly it was published after the death of Constantine. In an age, wherein pious frauds had already acquired
some honour; by a writer, who, respectable as he undoubtedly
is, and faithful in most of his historical records, does not even
profess those rigid rules of veracity which command universal
credit‡; in a book, which rather wears the character of partial

---

* In the relation of this story we have ventured to omit the dream published
by the uncertain author of the book " De Mortibus Persecutorum," as well as
Nazarius's army of divine warriors. We confine ourselves to that which appears
under the more respectable authority of Eusebius. See Gibbon, chap. xx.

† Euseb. Vit. Const. l. i., c. 28, 29, 30, 31.

‡ Eusebius says, that Constantine related the story to himself on oath. May
we not believe Eusebius in this? And may we not also suppose, that the Emperor deceived him in some moment, when enthusiasm, or indisposition, or mere
human weakness had brought him first to deceive himself? He may really have

panegyric, than of exact and scrupulous history—a flattering fable might be published and believed; but it can claim no place among the authentic records of history, and by writers, whose only object is truth, it may very safely be consigned to contempt and oblivion*.

The defeat of Maxentius was followed by a conference between Constantine and Licinius, which led to the publication, in the March of 313, of the celebrated Edict of Milan.

This Edict was a proclamation of universal toleration; but its advantages were of course chiefly or entirely reaped by the Christians, as theirs had been the only religion not already tolerated. It gave back to them the civil and religious rights of which they had been deprived; it restored without dispute, delay or expense, their places of worship which had been demolished, and their lands which had been confiscated—and free and absolute power was granted to them, and to all others, of following the religion which every individual might think proper to follow. We may likewise remark, that from this time forward, the term *Catholic* was invariably applied, in all official documents, to the Church.

Immediately afterwards, Licinius, who was no friend to Christianity, overthrew the Eastern Emperor Maximin, who had been its savage adversary, and became master of the empire of the East. A war followed between the conqueror and Constantine, which terminated, in 315, to the advantage of the latter, who on that occasion extended his empire to the eastern limits of Europe: eight years of peace succeeded, which were employed by the Christian Emperor in securing the real interests and legislating for the happiness of his subjects. This

Margin note: Edict of Milan. 313 A.D.

recollected some uncommon appearance about the sun, not strongly noticed at the moment, but which the imagination of memory, heated by exciting events, or by passion, or by feverish sickness, may have converted into a miracle. The story of the vision (which stands indeed on *rather* better authority) might be merely the exaggeration of a dream. At least this supposition has nothing in it unnatural; and it is the only supposition which can save both the *intention* of the Emperor and the veracity of the historian. See Note at the end of the chapter.

* It is somewhat singular that, on this same occasion, Maxentius is related by the Pagan historian, Zosimus, (who makes no mention of the Christian miracle, lib. ii.) to have carefully consulted the Sibylline books, and credulously applied to his own circumstances a prediction which he found there.

period of rare tranquillity was succeeded by a second war* with Licinius, which terminated in 324 by his submission and death, and by the consequent union of the whole empire under the sceptre of Constantine.

Character and faith of Constantine.

The year which followed the final success of Constantine was disgraced by the execution of his eldest son; and it is not disputed that the progress of his career was marked by the usual excesses of intemperate and worldly ambition. Some of his laws† were severe even to cruelty, and the general propriety of his moral conduct cannot with any justice be maintained. Hence a suspicion has arisen as to the sincerity of his conversion—chiefly, as it appears to us, or entirely, founded on the inadequacy of his character to his profession. But is there any page in Christian history, or any form of Christian society, which does not mournfully attest the possibility of combining the most immoral conduct with the most unhesitating faith? Or is this a condition of humanity, from which monarchs are more exempt than their subjects? We should recollect, moreover, that the character of Constantine, notwithstanding its grievous stains, will bear a comparison with some of the best among his pagan predecessors; while it was free from those monstrous deformities which distinguished not a few of them, and which have indeed been rarely paralleled in Christian history. But even had his conduct been more reprehensible than in truth it was, it would have furnished very insufficient evidence against the sincerity of his belief.

Again, it was usual in those days, in continuance of a practice of which we have mentioned the cause and origin, to defer the sacrament of baptism until the approach of death, and then once to administer it, as the means of regeneration and the as-

---

* This is considered by Eusebius (Vit. Constant. lib. ii.) almost in the light of a religious war—the first, if it was so, among the many by which the name of Christ has been profaned.

† Nevertheless, the general spirit of his laws was decidedly humane and favourable to the progress of civilization: he made decrees tending to the termination of slavery; he abolished some barbarous forms of punishment, as branding, for instance; he restrained exorbitant usury, and endeavoured to prevent the exposure of children, by relieving the poor. See Jortin, Eccl. Hist., book iii. Fleury, Hist. Eccl. L. X. Sect 21. Baronius, ad ann. 315. sect. 30.

surance of pardon and grace.   In compliance with this custom*
the emperor was not baptized (seemingly he did not even become
a Catechumen†) until his last illness; but no argument can
hence be drawn against his sincerity, which would not equally
apply to a large proportion of the Christians in his empire.   In
his favour the following facts should be observed.   For many
years he had publicly and consistently professed his belief in
Christianity: in a long discourse, which is still extant, he even
expatiated on its various proofs; he began his reign by protecting the believers; in its progress he favoured and honoured
them; he inscribed the cross on the banners of the empire; he
celebrated the festivals of the Church; he associated in the
closest intimacy with Christian writers‡ and prelates; he inquired into all the particulars of their faith, and displayed what
some have thought an inconsiderate zeal for its purity.   By such
reasons, according to every fair principle of historical inference,
we are precluded from any reasonable doubt on this subject;
nor need we hesitate for a moment to acquit a wise and, in
many respects, a virtuous prince of the odious charge of the foul-
est description of hypocrisy§.

* Constantius in like manner put off his baptism till his last illness, (Athanas.
lib. de Synodis;) so did Theodosius the Great until the illness which he mistook
for his last.   Socrat. l. v. c. 6.

† From Euseb. de Vit. Const. lib. iv. c. 61, it appears that the emperor, just
before his baptism, received for the first time the imposition of hands, usual in
making a Catechumen.   But in the same work (lib. i. c. 32), it would seem that
he was κατηχηθεὶς on his first profession of Christianity, immediately after the
vision.   We are disposed to attach greater credit to the former account.   See
Fleury, l. xi. sect. 60.

‡ Lactantius possessed his confidence, while his command was confined to the
West, and Eusebius enjoyed throughout his life great influence at the Court of
Constantinople.   The respect which he paid to the festivals of the Church, his
"diligence in prayer," the issuing of medals throughout the empire, in which he
is represented in the attitude of devotion, are facts mentioned by Euseb., Vit. Const.
l. iv. c. 15 and 22.

§ A vain dispute has been raised as to the probable moment of his conversion,
into which we shall not enter, because the truth is not discoverable, and if it
were, would still be unprofitable.   Gibbon *affects* to set some value on it, because
he would willingly prove that Constantine was no real proselyte.   Two facts he
mentions in support of his suspicion—that Constantine "persevered till he was
near forty years of age in the practice of the established religion," especially
in the worship of Apollo; and that in the same year (321) he published two
edicts, the first of which enjoined the solemn observance of Sunday (Euseb. Vit.

At the same time, we are willing to admit that his conduct to the Christians was strictly in accordance with his interests; and it is very probable, that the protection with which he distinguished them may, *in the first instance,* have originated in his policy. But this is perfectly consistent with his subsequent conversion. And we may here remark, that those who assign policy as his chief or only motive, bear the strongest evidence to the power and real importance which the Church of Christ had acquired before his time; they attest, that its stability had not been shaken by the sword of Diocletian; that by its own unassisted and increasing energy it had triumphed over the fury of the most determined of its persecutors, and that its claims on the justice and respect of the Throne, though only urged by perseverance in suffering, could no longer be overlooked with safety. And this fact is of much greater historical importance than the motives or sincerity of any individual can possibly be.

Let us now proceed to ascertain what was the condition and constitution of the Church, as Constantine found it; what were the principal alterations introduced by him, and in what form and attitude he left it.

The Constitution of the Church, before Constantine. We have already described the free and independent constitution of the primitive Church; the bishops and teachers were chosen by the clergy and people; the bishop managed the eccle-

---

Const. l. iv. c. 18.), and the second directed the regular consultation of aruspices. Both are literally true; but the inferences drawn from both are false: Constantine did not profess his religion, perhaps he did not adopt it, until the campaign against Maxentius in 312—he had previously protected and favoured the Christians, but till then he did not proclaim, nor could he perhaps safely have proclaimed, his own belief; but he seized the earliest moment to do so, and during the twenty-five following years, he maintained his profession with ardent and active perseverance. By bringing forward the second fact as an argument against his belief, the historian has forgotten that the edict of Milan was an edict of *universal* toleration, protecting all Pagan, as well as all Christian, ceremonies; so that the two proclamations, which he is willing to expose as inconsistent, were only the necessary consequence of that generous policy, which had been so little understood by the Pagan emperors. Before we quit this subject we should mention, that Zosimus (lib. ii.) attributes Constantine's change of faith to the persuasion, instilled into him by one Ægyptius, a Spaniard, that the remission of sins attended the act of conversion to Christianity. Thus it appears, at least, that the Pagan historian did not doubt the reality of the conversion, though he may have mistaken its motive.

siastical affairs of his diocese, in council with the Presbyters and " with a due regard to the suffrages of the whole assembly of the people." Again, the great ecclesiastical divisions of the empire appear from the earliest period naturally to have followed the political; and thus far the regulation of matters relating to the interests of a whole province, whether they were religious controversies, or the forms and rites of divine service, or other things of like moment, the bishops of the Province assembled in council, and deliberated and legislated.

We have also remarked, that during the course of the third century this constitution was so far changed, that the episcopal authority was somewhat advanced, at the expense of that of the inferior ministers, and the people. But in all other respects the government of the Church remained in reality the same, and perhaps even in this respect it was apparently so ; for the forms of the lesser or diocesan councils were still preserved, though the relative influence of the three parties composing them had undergone a change.

And here it will be proper to examine how far those are correct who consider the Church at that period, as a separate republic or body-politic distinguished from the empire. In the first place—the synods which we have mentioned, local as well as provincial, assumed the office and power to arrange ecclesiastical affairs, and to punish ecclesiastical offences. But neither was their power acknowledged by the civil government, nor were their awards or censures enforced by it. Again, the bishop, through an authority which professed to be derived from Scripture, and which may certainly be traced to the earliest age, exerted a kind of mediative interference throughout his diocese, in the civil disputes of the Christians, to which they very frequently appealed, and admitted his decisions as conclusive ; but no such jurisdiction was recognised by the Government, nor were any such decisions legally valid. Moreover, some of the Churches had become possessed, as corporate bodies, of considerable property, in land or buildings purchased from the common fund, and applied to the purposes of the society ; but the Government never formally acknowledged the legality of those acquisitions, and availed itself, as we have already seen, of the first pretext to confiscate them.

Distinction between spiritual and temporal power.

It is in this condition of ecclesiastical affairs, that we may discover perhaps the earliest vestige of the distinction, which will hereafter become so familiar to us, between spiritual and temporal power—though in the present indefinite shape and imperfect development of the former, we can scarcely trace any intimation of its future proportions and magnitude. We perceive, also, on how strange and irregular a foundation the security of the early Church was established:—in fact, to a statesman of those days, before the force of religious union and the intensity of religious attachment were generally known and understood, the society or communion which rested not on a political basis, would naturally appear to possess no principle of stability. To the eye of a Pagan its strength was imperceptible, as the elements which composed it were concealed from him; and it was this circumstance which encouraged Diocletian to an aggression, of which the barbarity indeed shocked him, but of which he never, perhaps, doubted the success, since the power which resisted it was unseen and incomprehensible. In the mean time, the public discipline, which had been made necessary by the neglect of the civil power, was cemented and fortified by its opposition; and the private sincerity of belief, which could not be understood by a Pagan, because Paganism had nothing to do with truth, was animated into contumacy by the sense of injustice and injury.

Effect of the episcopal government.

It is even probable that the union of the scattered Churches was facilitated by the increase of the episcopal authority in each; for they thus acquired that decision and steadiness of continuous exertion which marks individual superintendence, and which would scarcely have been so constant and uniform had the government of the dioceses retained, in its utmost strictness, its original popular character. The power of the bishops made them formidable only to the persecutor; their interests demanded their union; and their union was then the only security for that of the whole Church, and thereby (without the direct interposition of Providence) for its actual preservation.

To us, indeed, it seems nearly certain that these powerful but latent principles of ecclesiastical stability, which repelled the assault of Diocletian, would have preserved the Church through a much severer trial, if the genius of Constantine had not discovered its real strength, and courted its friendship and alliance. It is true, that in becoming acquainted with its strength, he also discovered its virtues; in the excellence of the Christian system, he perceived a great omen of its perpetuity: he saw too, that, as a rule for civilized society, it was more efficient than any human law, because more powerful in its motives to obedience; and perhaps he remarked also, that the energy of Christians had hitherto been confined to submission and endurance—to unoffending, unresisting perseverance—and this outward display of loyalty might lead him to overlook that free spirit, which pervaded both the principles of the religion and the government of the Church, and which in later ages was so commonly found in opposition to civil despotism.

Constantine admired the morality of the Christians, he loved their submission to arbitrary power, and he respected that internal and advancing vigour, which had triumphed over so many persecutors. These, we doubt not, were the motives which induced him to seek the alliance of the Church, and to confer on it advantages, not more substantial, perhaps, than those which he received from it.

We are disposed to divide the ecclesiastical life of Constantine into three periods. In the first of these he confined himself, at least ostensibly, to the impartial toleration of all religions, though he legally established that of the Christians. This extends from the Edict of Milan to the Council of Nice in the year 325. His next occupation was to define the doctrines, and thus to preserve the unity of the Church, which he had established. It was not till the third and latest period of his life, that he attacked the superstition of his forefathers, by edicts directly levelled against Paganism. The Arian controversy and the overthrow of Paganism will form the subjects of separate chapters—at present we shall endeavour to point out the most important alterations introduced during this reign into the constitution of the Church, and their immediate effects upon its ministers and members.

Constantine found the Church an independent body, a kind of self-constituted commonwealth, which might some- *Changes introduced by Constantine.*

times be at peace, and sometimes at variance with the civil government, but which was never acknowledged as any part of the whole body politic; it had a separate administration, separate laws, and frequently (through the perversity of its persecutors) separate interests also. The Christian, as a citizen of the empire, was subject of course to the universal statutes of the empire—as a member of the Church, he owed a distinct allegiance to the spiritual directors of the Church; and though this allegiance was never inconsistent with his civil obedience, except when that obedience would have deprived him of his religion, it was founded on more commanding motives, and was one from which no earthly authority was sufficient to absolve him. Thus far, and thus far only, his ecclesiastical divided him from his civil duties: to this extent they placed him, at all times, in divergency from the State, and, in times of persecution, in actual opposition to it. And so long as the Church which he honoured was disclaimed as a part, or associate, of the State; so long as the space between them was broad and distinguishable, so long the limits of his allegiance to either were very clearly marked. Constantine comprehended the nature, and perceived the inconveniences and the danger of this disunion; and he therefore employed the earliest exertion of his power and policy to acknowledge the existence, to consolidate the elements, to establish the authority, and to diminish the independence of the Church. To accomplish the first of these three objects, he received that body into strict alliance with the state—to effect the last, he so received it, as to constitute himself its director as well as its guardian, and to combine in his own person the highest ecclesiastical with the highest civil authority. His right to this authority (if he condescended to consider that point) he might derive with some plausibility from the original institutions of Rome. From the earliest ages of its history, the chief magistrate of the nation had been entrusted with the superintendence of the national religion; and it seemed fair that he should impose the same, as the condition of the *establishment* of Christianity. And yet a great distinction is to be observed even in this point. For, according to the principles of Polytheism, the most sacred functions of religion might be performed by the hands of the civil magistrates; but the consecration of a separate order to those purposes by the Christian system excluded the Emperor from the administration of the rites of religion; and the Prince and the Priest became henceforward characters wholly distinct, and independent. It was perhaps by this restriction, that the first avowed and legal limitation was imposed upon the authority of the former; and it was not a trifling triumph, to have obtained from a Roman emperor the acknowledgment of any right in a subject, or any restraint upon himself.

Notwithstanding this assumption of ecclesiastical supremacy by the Emperor, the Church retained in many respects its separate existence, or at least the freedom of its autonomous constitution—indeed, had not this been so, the term Alliance, which is used to designate the union of Church and State under Constantine, as it implies a certain degree of independence in both parties, would be unmeaning and out of place. Some immediate advantages were also reaped by the Church; much that it had formerly held by sufferance, it now possessed by law; many privileges, which had hitherto existed through the connivance only, or the ignorance, of the government, were now converted into rights, and as such confirmed and perpetuated.

Constantine divided the administration of the Church into (1.) Internal, and (2.) External.

(1.) The former continued, as heretofore, in the hands of the prelates, individually and in council—little or no alteration was introduced into this department; and it comprehended nearly every thing which was really tangible and available in the power of the Church before its association with the State, now confirmed to it by that association. The settlement of religious controversies was recommended to the wisdom of the Hierarchy*; the forms of Divine worship, the regulation of customary rites and ceremonies, or the institution of new ones, the ordination and offices of the priesthood, which included the unrestrained right of public preaching, and the formidable

The internal administration of the Church.

---

* A rescript of Constantine to the Provincial Bishops on the disputes between Athanasius and Eusebius of Nicomedia, admits—" Vestri est, non mei judicii, de eâ re cognoscere." See Baronius ad ann. 329, sect. 8.

weapon of spiritual censure were left to the exclusive direction
of the Church. The freedom of episcopal election was not
violated; and the bishops retained their power to convoke legislative synods twice a year in every diocese, uncontrolled by the
civil magistrate. We have already mentioned, that, by the
Edict of Milan, the possessions of the Church were restored,
and its legal right to them for the first time acknowledged;
and this act of justice was followed, in the year 321, by another
Edict, which permitted all subjects to bequeath property to
that body*. Exemption from all civil offices was granted to
the whole body of the clergy †; and, perhaps, a more important privilege, about the same time conferred on the higher orders,
was that of independent jurisdiction, even in capital charges,
over their own members: so that the bishop, alone among the
myriads of the subjects of the empire, enjoyed the right of
being tried by his Peers. This was not granted, however, with
any intention of securing his impunity; for, though degradation
was the severest punishment which could be inflicted by a spiritual court, the penalty was liable to increase, after condemnation, by the interference of the secular authority. While we may
consider the free trial of the bishops, in a political light, as
another important inroad into the pure despotism of the imperial
system, we are also assured that on the body, thus exclusively
possessing it, it conferred no inconsiderable advantages. But
another privilege, even more valuable than this, and one which
will more constantly be present to us in the history of succeeding ages, is traced with equal certainty to the legislation of
Constantine. The arbitration of bishops in the civil differences
referred to them in their diocese was now ratified by law; and
their decisions, of which the validity had formerly depended on
the consent of the parties, were henceforward enforced by the
civil magistrate‡. On this foundation was imperceptibly esta-

---

* Constantine's personal generosity to the Church, as well as his deference to
the Episcopal Order, is mentioned by Eusebius, (Vit. Const., lib. i. c. 42, lib. ii.,
and Hist. Eccles., 1. x.) and was continued throughout his whole reign. The Pagan Zosimus (lib. ii.) remarks on the profusion which he wasted upon " useless
persons."

† Baronius, ad ann. 319, sect. 30.

‡ Fleury, Hist. Eccl., l. x. sect. 27, on authority of Sozomen (l. i. c. 8 and 9) and

blished the vast and durable edifice of ecclesiastical jurisdiction; from this simple legalization of an ancient custom, in
process of time, the most substantial portion of sacerdotal power
proceeded, and the most extravagant pretensions of spiritual
ambition.   But those consequences convey no reflection on the
wisdom of Constantine, since they were produced by circumstances which he could not possibly foresee; and which, besides,
never influenced, to any great extent, the eastern division of
Christendom.

In the separate view, which we have taken of the internal
constitution of the Church, we perceive a powerful, self-regu-
lated body, armed with very ample and extensive authority,
and supported, when such support was necessary, by the secular arm.   Let us proceed to the second division, or the external
administration of the Church.

(2.) Of this department the Emperor assumed the entire *Its external
economy.*
control to himself*.   It comprehended every thing relating to
the outward state and discipline of the Church; and was understood to include a certain degree of superintendence over such
contests and debates as might arise among the ministers, of
whatsoever rank, concerning their possessions, their reputation,
their rights and privileges, as well as their political, or other
offences against the laws of the Empire.   Even the final decision of religious controversies was subjected to the discretion of
judges appointed by the Emperor†: the same terminated any
differences which might arise between the bishops and people,
fixed the limits of the ecclesiastical provinces, took cognizance
of the *civil* causes subsisting between ministers, and lent his
power to the execution of the punishment due to their criminal
offences.   And though the right of convoking local and provincial synods remained with the Church, that of assembling a
General Council was exercised only by the Prince.

When we consider in succession these articles of imperial

Const. Apostol. (lib. ii. c. 46). Baronius, ad ann. 314, sect. 38, with reference to
Cod. Theodos.

* The authority assumed by the Emperors appears, under various titles, in the
16th book of the Theodosian Code, as also in the Code of Justinian.

† Mosheim, Cent. iv. part. ii. ch. ii.

supremacy, we perceive, in the first place, that Constantine did not transfer to himself from the Church any power which had before belonged to it : most of the cases, there provided for, must by necessity have always fallen under civil cognizance —for whenever it happened either that the external encroachments of the Church, or the differences among Christians, or their ministers, proceeded to endanger public tranquillity, such offences fell, of course, under the cognizance of the secular, which was then the only acknowledged, jurisdiction.

Power of convoking General Councils.

There appear, indeed, to be two cases in which the Emperor assumed a power not before belonging to the State—interference for the arrangement of religious controversies by the appointment of judges, and the convocation of General Councils. Respecting the *first* of these—which proved indeed the least effectual part of his ecclesiastical authority—it was not probable that the Emperor would be anxious to exert it, unless called upon to undertake the office by one or both of the parties in controversy. If invited to enforce the sentence of the Church against a condemned Heretic, he might reasonably plead the interference of Aurelian in the affair of Paul of Samosata; if solicited to decide between two opinions dividing the body of the Church itself, he would naturally have recourse to the *second* of the methods intrusted to him, the calling of a General Council. But the authority to do so was not the usurpation of a power before possessed by another, but the creation of a new power. For as a General Council of all the leading ministers of the Church neither had been, nor could have been, assembled in times when the Church, if haply not persecuted, was at least unacknowledged, so the new condition of its establishment gave birth to new circumstances, for the regulation of which a new authority was necessary; and that authority was properly vested in the highest civil magistrate.

In the next place, in comparing the privileges remaining to the Church with those assumed by the Emperor in his connexion with it, and in tracing the consequences to which either might be extended, we cannot fail to observe, that their limits are often vague and indeterminate; and that, when they are not so, the points of contact and intersection are very numerous, offering frequent means and temptations to mutual innovation. We shall see that, in after ages, they led to much aggression and injustice in both parties ; but as matters then stood, with so large a portion of the population still unconverted, and even adverse to the Faith, under an Emperor possessed of undivided and seemingly unbounded authority, we should be surprised, perhaps, to find so many privileges confirmed to a distinct religious community, if we were not acquainted with the bold and vigorous character of Constantine, and also persuaded of his attachment to Christianity.

We should not omit to mention some changes at that time introduced into the titles and gradations of the Hierarchy, in order to associate their administration more intimately with that of the civil officers. To the three Prelates of Rome, Antioch and Alexandria, who enjoyed a certain degree of pre-eminence in the Church, was added the Patriarch of Constantinople—these four corresponded with the four Prætorian Prefects then also created. After these followed the Exarchs*, who had the inspection over several provinces, and answered to the appointment of certain civil officers of the same name. The Metropolitans had the government of one province only, and under them were the Archbishops, whose inspection was confined to certain districts. The Bishops were the lowest in this gradation, but many of them possessed ample extent of authority and jurisdiction. Their number at this time was one thousand eight hundred, of whom a thousand administered the Eastern, eight hundred the Western Church. In this whole body, the Bishop of Rome possessed a certain indeterminate precedence, or pre-eminence, unattended by any authority; and this precedence is attributed, first, to the Imperial name of Rome, and next to the superiority in wealth, which he seems to have acquired at a very early period; to the splendour and extent of his religious administration, and the influence naturally rising from these causes.

The simple establishment of the Church, such as we have now described it, without anticipating the measures of State

Changes in the form of the Hierarchy.

Observations.

---

* Mosheim, loc. cit.

afterwards applied, or misapplied, to the support of it, was favourable not only to the progress of Christianity, but also to the concord of Christians: the former has never been disputed; as to the latter, we have seen by what a cloud of heresies the religion was overshadowed before its establishment; and no one can reasonably doubt, that the additional sanction given to the Gospel by imperial adoption, and the greater dignity and influence and actual power thus acquired by its regular ministers in every province of the Empire, would conduce to dissolve and disperse them. They did so—but while the numerous forms of error, of which we have treated, fell for the most part into silence and disrepute, there was one, of which we have yet made no mention, which grew up into such vigour and attained so much consistency, that there seemed to be danger lest it should possess itself of the high places, and occupy the sanctuary itself. Its progress, and the means adopted to oppose it, form the subject of the following chapter. We shall conclude the present with one or two observations.

It is one favourite opinion of most sceptical writers, that Christianity is entirely indebted for its general propagation and stability to the imperial patronage of Constantine; it is another, that the establishment of the Church led to the disunion of its members, and its prosperity to its corruption. The first of those theories is falsified by the history of the first three centuries—during which we observe the religion to have been gradually but rapidly progressive throughout the whole extent of the Roman Empire, in spite of the persecution of some emperors, the suspicious jealousy of others, and the indifference of the rest. We need not dwell longer on this fact; especially as it is virtually admitted by those same writers, when it suits them to attribute Constantine's *pretended* conversion to his policy. The second of their assertions has a greater show of truth, but is, in fact, almost equally erroneous. A fairer view of that question, and, if we mistake not, the correct view, is the following: the *establishment* of the Church was in itself highly beneficial both to the progress of religion, and to the happiness of society: the mere pacific alliance of that body with the State was fraught with advantage to the whole Empire, with danger

to no member of it. Many evils indeed did follow it, and
many vexations were inflicted by Christians upon each other in
the perverse zeal of religious controversy. But such controversies, as we have sufficiently shown, had existed in very great
abundance, very long before Christianity was recognised by law;
and the vexations were not at all the necessary consequence of
that recognition. They originated, not in the system itself, but
in the blindness of those who administered it; they proceeded
from the fallacious supposition—that which afterwards animated the Romish Church, and which has misled despots and
bigots in every age—that unanimity in religious belief and practice was a thing attainable ; and they were conducted on a notion equally remote from reason, that such unanimity, or even
the appearance of it, could be attained by force. Many ages of
bitter experience have been necessary to prove the absurdity of
these notions, and the fruitless wickedness of the measures proceeding from them. But a candid inquirer will admit that they
were not at all inseparably connected with the establishment of
the Church; and that that body would not only have continued
to exist and to flourish, without any interference of civil authority to crush its adversaries, but that it would have subsisted
in that condition with more dignity, and more honour, and
much more security.

The prosperity of the Church was unquestionably followed
by an increase in the number and impurity of its corruptions.
But unhappily we have already had occasion to observe, that
several abuses had taken root in all its departments, during at
least that century which immediately preceded the reign of Constantine—to the fourth age we may undoubtedly assign the extravagant honours paid to Martyrs, and the shameful superstitions which arose from them. But we should also recollect, that
many among the Romish corruptions are of a much later date,
and that several may be directly referred to the influence of
expiring Paganism, not to the gratuitous invention of a wealthy
and degenerate priesthood. Indeed, we should add, that in respect to the moral character of the clergy of the fourth century,
they seem rather chargeable with the narrow, contentious, sectarian spirit, which was encouraged and inflamed by the

capricious interference of the civil power, than with any
flagrant deficiency in piety and sanctity of life.

NOTE ON EUSEBIUS.

The name of Eusebius has been so frequently referred to in this
History, that, being now arrived at the age in which he flourished, we are bound to give some account of his life and character. He is believed to have been born at Cæsarea in Palestine, about the year 270; he was raised to that See about 315,
and died in 339, or 340; being thus (within two or three years)
contemporary with his emperor, and his friend, in the three circumstances of his birth, his elevation to dignity, and his death.
He was extremely diligent and learned, and the author of " in-
numerable volumes*."   And among those which still exist, his
Ecclesiastical History, and his Life of Constantine, furnish us
with the best lights which we possess respecting his own times,
and with our only consecutive narrative of the previous fortunes of
Christianity. Eusebius admits, in the first chapter of his History,
that he has " entered upon a desolate and unfrequented path;"
and in gleaning the scattered records of preceding writers, and
presenting them for the most part in their own language and on
their own authority, he has indeed very frequently discovered to
us the scantiness of the harvest and the poverty of the soil. Still
in that respect he has faithfully discharged his historical duties,
and has rescued much valuable matter from certain oblivion.
In this indeed consists one peculiar merit of his History, that it
unfolds to us a number of earlier memoirs, written immediately
after the events which they describe, and on all of which we are
at liberty to exercise our critical judgment, as to the credit
which may be due to them, without also involving that of Eusebius in our conclusion. But respecting the historical candour
of the author, when he speaks in his own person, and the fidelity
with which he has delivered such circumstances as were well
known to him, a few words are necessary, because the question
is not usually stated with fairness.

* Jerome, de Vir. Illust. c. xxxi.

In describing the sufferings of the Christians during the last His histori-
persecution, Eusebius* (H. E. lib. viii. c. ii.) admits "that it cal charac-
does not agree with our plan to relate their dissensions and thority.
wickedness before the persecution, on which account we have
determined to relate nothing more concerning them than may
serve to justify the Divine Judgment. We have therefore not
been induced to make mention, either of those who were tempted
in the persecution, or of those who made utter shipwreck of
their salvation, and were sunk of their own accord in the depths
of the storm; but shall only add those things to our General
History, which may in the first place be profitable to ourselves,
and afterwards to posterity." And in another passage he asserts, that the events most suitable to a ' History of Martyrs'
are those which redound to their honour. From these two passages it appears that Eusebius, in his relation of that persecution,
has suppressed the *particulars* of the dissensions and scandals
which had prevailed among the faithful, because he judged such
accounts less productive of immediate edification and future
profit, than the celebration of their virtues and their constancy.
We may remark that, in this determination, his first error was
one of judgment—if indeed he imagined that the great lessons
of history were more surely taught by the records of what is
splendid and glorious, than by the painful, but impressive story
of human imperfection, and of the calamities which man has
gathered from his own folly and wickedness. But his second
and less pardonable deviation was from principle—there is a
direct and avowed disregard of the *second* fundamental precept
of historical composition. However, the crime is less dangerous because it is avowed, and more excusable because less
dangerous; and at any rate, if we shall perceive, in the general
course and character of the work, a disposition to investigate
diligently, and represent faithfully, we shall be disposed to confine our doubts to those portions only, which the writer has not
even professed to treat with entire fidelity; and in the vast multitude of circumstances, in which the honour of the martyrs is
not concerned, we shall approach our only fountain of information with a confidence not *much* impaired by a partial derelic-
tion of principle, which is fairly admitted.

* In Vit. Constant. cap. ix., he makes the same sort of profession.

But that delinquency of Eusebius which we have just mentioned is confined to the suppression of truth—it does not
proceed to the direct assertion of falsehood: we shall now
notice a still more serious suspicion, to which he has rendered
himself liable. The thirty-first chapter of the twelfth book of
his Evangelical Preparation bears for its title this scandalous
proposition*—"How it may be lawful and fitting to use falsehood as a medicine, for the advantage of those who require
such a method." We have already deplored, with sorrow and
indignation, the fatal moment, when fraud and falsehood were
first admitted into the service of religion. Philosophy, in the
open array of her avowed hostility, was not so dangerous as
when she lent to her undisciplined adversaries her own poisoned
weapons, and placed them in unskilful hands, as implements of
self-destruction. It was disgraceful to the less enlightened
fathers of the second and third centuries, that, even in the
midst of trial and tribulation, they borrowed a momentary succour from the profession of falsehood—but the same expedient
was still more shameful to Eusebius, who flourished during the
prosperity of the Church, whose age and more extensive learning left him no excuse in ignorance or inexperience, and whose
great name and unquestionable piety gave sanction and authority to all his opinions. There can be no doubt then, that

---

* We purposely copy the language of Gibbon. (Vindication, p. 137, 2d ed.)
Still we should fail in doing perfect justice to Eusebius, if we did not publish,
together with the proposition, the very short chapter in which it is treated. It
begins with a quotation from Plato. (De Leg. 2.) "A legislator of any value—
even if the fact were not such as our discourse has just established it—if in any
case he might make bold to deceive young persons for their advantage—could he
possibly inculcate any falsehood more profitable than this, or more potent to
lead all without force or compulsion to the practice of all justice?" "Truth, my
friend, is honourable and permanent; but not, it would seem, very easy of persuasion." To this somewhat hypothetical passage of Plato, Eusebius adds—"You
may find a thousand such instances in the Scriptures, where God is described as
jealous, or sleeping, or angry, or liable to other human affections, so expressed for
the advantage of those who require such a method (ἐπ' ὠφελείᾳ τῶν δεομένων τοῦ
τοιούτου τρόπου.)" This is all that is said on the subject, and it shows us perhaps
to what limits Eusebius intended to confine the application of his proposition. And
thus Gibbon's account of the chapter, though it may be literally true, is calculated
to mislead. "In this chapter (says he) Eusebius alleges a passage of Plato,
which approves the occasional practice of pious and salutary frauds; nor is he
ashamed to justify the sentiments of the Athenian philosopher by the example of
the sacred writers of the Old Testament."

the publication of that detestable principle in any one of his writings, however modified and limited by his explanation, must, to a certain extent, disturb our confidence in the rest: the mind which does not profess to be constantly guided by truth possesses no claim to our implicit reliance. Nevertheless, the works of Eusebius must at last be judged by the character which severally pervades them, not by any single principle which the author has once only laid down; to which he has not intended (as it would seem) to give general application, and which he has manifestly proposed rather as a philosophical speculation, than as a rule for his own composition. At least we feel convinced, that whoever shall calmly peruse his Ecclesiastical History will not discover in it any deliberate intention to deceive: in the relation of miraculous stories, he is more sparing than most of the Church Historians who succeeded him, and seemingly even than those whom he has copied; and upon the whole, we shall not do him more than justice, if we consider him as an avowed, but honest *advocate,* many of whose statements must be examined with suspicion, while the greater part bear direct and incontestable marks of truth*.

---

* Dr. Jortin (vol. i. p. 209) has corrected a mistake of Dr. Middleton, who had attributed to Eusebius an absurd respect for the Erythrean Sibyl—which seems, in fact, to have been entertained by Constantine.

CHAPTER VII.

The Arian Controversy.

Controversies among Christians—their origin—how distinguished from philosophical disputations—their character—accounted for. Constantine's conduct towards Heretics, and origin of the Arian controversy—Alexander—Arius—his opinions—followers—Interference of the Emperor—Council of Nice—various motives of those assembled—their proceedings and decision—Proposal of Eusebius of Cæsarea—Gibbon's account of this Council—Temporal penalties—to what extent carried. Conduct of the successors of Constantine—Constantius. Athanasius—his history—twice exiled—his triumphant restoration—contests with Constantius—methods taken by the latter to secure success—remarks on them—third banishment of Athanasius—Council of Rimini—progress of Arianism.—Theodosius—Council of Constantinople. Arianism of the Northern Barbarians—the conquerors of the West—its effects. Justinian—Spain—Council of Toledo. Termination of the controversy. Observations—examination of Arian claims to greater purity of faith—to greater moderation—Progress of Arianism in the West—to what cause attributable—confusion of sectarian and national enmity—conduct of Catholics and Arians under persecution—Note on certain Christian Writers.

Some preliminary observations.

WHEN Constantine established Christianity as the religion of the empire, he probably did not foresee how soon he should be called upon to interpose his authority, in order to prescribe and define the precise tenets of that religion which he had established. Doubtless he was well informed, how numerous were the opinions by which Christians had ever been divided; but he saw that, in spite of them, the body had continued to advance in vigour and magnitude with the show of health and unity. The Church was strong in the midst of heresy, as well as of oppression—and when he gave her his protection against the latter, he imagined, perhaps reasonably, that she could have nothing to apprehend from the former. But, whether it was, as some suppose, that the evil passions of Christians were inflamed by their present security, or, as we rather believe, that the expression of dissent had been softened by the impunity which attended it during former reigns, it is certain that scarcely ten years from the Edict of Milan had elapsed, before the Christian world beheld the beginning of a convulsion, which continued for some time to increase in violence, and which was not finally composed without a long and desolating struggle.

It had been the vice of the Christians of the third century to involve themselves in "certain metaphysical questions, which, if considered in one light, are too sublime to become the subject of human wit; if in another, too trifling to gain the attention of reasonable men*." The rage for such disputations had been communicated to religion by the contagion of philosophy; but the manner in which it operated on the one and on the other was essentially different. With the philosopher, such questions were objects of the understanding only, matters of comparatively dispassionate speculation, whereon the versatile ingenuity of a minute mind might employ or waste itself. But with the Christian they were questions of truth or falsehood, of belief or disbelief; and he felt assured that his eternal interests would be influenced, if not decided by his choice. Hence arose an intense anxiety respecting the result; and thus the passions were awakened, and presently broke loose and proceeded to every excess.

From the moment that the solution of these questions was attempted by any other method than the fair interpretation of the words of Scripture; as soon as the copious language of Greece was vaguely applied to the definition of spiritual things, and the explanation of heavenly mysteries, the field of contention seemed to be removed from earth to air—where the foot found nothing stable to rest upon; where arguments were easily eluded, and where the space to fly and to rally was infinite; so that the contest grew more noisy as it was less decisive, and more angry as it became more prolonged and complicated. Add to this the nature and genius of the disputants; for the origin of these disputes may be traced, without any exception, to the restless imaginations of the East. The violent temperament of Orientals, while it was highly adapted to the reception of religious impressions, and admitted them with fervour and earnestness, at the same time so closely intermingled passion

* Warburton, Post. to 4th ed. of the Alliance of Church and State.

with piety, as scarcely to conceive them separable. The
natural ardour of their feelings was not abated by the natural
subtilty of their understanding, which was sharpened in the
schools of Egypt; and when this latter began to be occupied by
inquiries in which the former were also deeply engaged, and
when the nature of those inquiries assumed an indeterminate
and impalpable form, it was to be expected that many extravagances would follow. We must also mention the loose and
unsettled principles of that age—principles, which had prevailed
before the appearance of Christianity, and had been to a certain extent adopted by its professors—those, for instance, which
justified the means by the end, and admitted fraud and forgery
into the service of religion. From these considerations we perceive, that disputations on such subjects, conducted by minds
such as have been described, and on the worst principles, could
not possibly hope for moderation, and could not speedily terminate : and it is not useless to have premised them to our account
of those controversies, for thus we shall neither attribute them
(as some have done) to mistaken causes; nor be so much scan-
dalized by their intemperance, as to take any offence against
religion itself, because such evils have been done in its name.

Constantine appears to have enlisted himself very early under the banners of the Church which he had established : very
soon after the Edict of Milan, we find him publishing laws
against heresy, which went so far, in menace at least, as to
transfer the property of heretical bishops or ministers to the
orthodox. In the list of the proscribed we find the followers of
Paul of Samosata, the Unitarians of those days; we find the
Montanists, who were the Enthusiasts, the Novatians, who
were the Reformers, and two denominations of Gnostics* : but
the opinions of the Arians were not yet attacked; perhaps
they had not yet assumed a tangible form, or at least were not
distinguished and stigmatized by a name.

---

* The Marcionites and Valentinians. See Sozomen, lib. ii. c. 32; and the beginning of Gibbon's 21st chapter. We should rather conclude, however, from
Eusebius's account (Vit. Const. l. iii. c. 63—66), that Constantine's edict against
those heretics was posterior to the council of Nice. Sozomen asserts (not very accurately) that the effect of the edict was the destruction of all excepting the Novatians, against whom it was not seriously enforced.

In the freedom exercised by individual opinion on abstruse mysteries under the early Church, it is possible that many may have held the doctrine afterwards called Arian; but the *controversy* seems to have been awakened about the year 319, by the zeal of a bishop of the Church; and the scene of its explosion was that hotbed of heresy and dissension, Alexandria*. Alexander was the bishop, Arius a presbyter, in that city; and the former, in an assembly of his clergy, felt it his duty both to interrogate† them on their sentiments respecting the nature of the Godhead, and strongly to impress on them his own: and he maintained, among other things‡, that the Son was not only of the same eminence and dignity, but also of the same essence with the Father. Arius disputed this doctrine, and this dispute led him to the promulgation of his own opinions: they were these, or nearly these§:—that the Son had been created by the Father before all things; but that time had existed before his creation, and that he was therefore not co-eternal with the

Beginning of the Arian controversy.

---

* Even after the Council of Nice we learn from Eusebius (Vit. Const. l. iii. c. 23) that "while all the rest of the world was disposed to concord, among the Egyptians alone there prevailed immitigable dissension."—Some anecdotes respecting the character of this people, which had engrafted Greek principles on African character, are given by Jortin. Eccl. Hist., book iii. A. D. 364.

† Socrat. l. i. s. 5. Constantine was likely to be well informed on this subject, and he thus expressed himself in his pacific Epistle to the disputants (Euseb. Vit. Const. ii. 69):—"I learn that the foundation of this controversy was thus—When you, Alexander, inquired of your presbyters what each of them severally held concerning a particular passage in the written law (ὑπὲρ τινος τόπου τῶν ἐν τῷ νόμῳ γεγραμμένων), or rather about some vain portion of a controversy; and when you, Arius, inconsiderately advanced what you ought never to have imagined, or having imagined, never to have uttered—thence discord arose and the council was assembled, and the faithful were divided, &c."

‡ The opinions of Alexander himself have not escaped the charge of heresy: his notions respecting the distinct persons of the Trinity were so imperfect, that Arius accused him, with seeming justice, of inclination to the error of Sabellius. And again, some of his expressions respecting the *nature* of the second person place him upon the very borders of the error subsequently denominated *semi*-Arianism: so difficult was it in those days even for the most pious prelate to discover, and preserve undeviatingly, the precise path of orthodoxy.

§ Mosh. Gen. Hist. c. iv. p. ii. ch. 5. Maimb. Hist. Arian. book i. p. 16. Gibbon, chap. 21. The original materials from which the history of Arianism is chiefly composed, are Eusebius's life of Constantine, the writings of Athanasius (particularly the first volume), and the Ecclesiastical Histories of Socrates, Sozomen, and Theodoret. We may also mention the 69th (or 49th) Heresy of Epiphanius.

Father; that he was created out of nothing; that he was not co-essential with the Father; that, though immeasurably superior in power and in glory to the highest created beings, he was still inferior in both to the Father. These opinions found many and respectable advocates* in Asia as well as Egypt, among the clergy as well as the laity, and even in the highest ranks of the clergy; and their number was probably increased, when the bishop, after condemning the tenets of Arius two councils in held at Alexandria, pronounced against him the sentence of excommunication.

Appeal to Constantine,

The quarrel now became so violent, that it was judged necessary to invite the interference of the Emperor. Constantine viewed the whole question as trifling and utterly unimportant†; he regretted that the peace of the Church should be so vainly disturbed; he lamented that the harmony of Christians, who were united on so many subjects of infinite weight, should be interrupted by such unprofitable speculations—and in the Epistle containing those sentiments he enjoined peace to both parties. Constantine knew not the nature‡ of the tempest which was excited, for neither experience nor history had yet presented to him anything resembling it. However, he had adopted the only measure which offered any hope of appeasing it; and had he persisted in his neutrality, it is probable that the Arian controversy, after some noisy debates and angry invectives, would have discharged its passion in words, and the heresy itself would have fallen into dishonour, almost into oblivion, like

---

* Sozomen i. 15. iii. 18.

† Constantine's epistle appears in Euseb. Vit. Const. l. ii. c. 64—72. In c. 71 the Emperor rebukes the parties for disputing ὑπὲρ μικρῶν καὶ λίαν ἐλαχίστων— 'about trifling, and most truly insignificant matters.' This account is, upon the whole, confirmed by Sozomen, H. E. l. i. c. 15 and 16. Socrates, H. E. lib. i. c. 7,

‡ It would appear indeed from the following passage in his Epistle, that he was very imperfectly informed even respecting the nature of the question controverted. 'Wherefore, says he, let an unguarded question, and an inconsiderate answer mutually excuse each other—for neither does the cause of your contention regard the chief among the commandments of the law, nor *has any new heresy been introduced* by you respecting *the worship of God*, but *both of you hold one and the same opinion*—so that there is nothing to prevent your concord and communion.' Vit. Const. l. ii. c. 70. There was nothing, indeed, to prevent their concord and communion—yet the opinions which they held were widely and essentially different.

so many others*.   But the firmness of the Emperor was not proof against the importunity of the orthodox prelates, seconded, as some think, by his own theological vanity; a General Council was suggested as the only remedy for the evil, and the Emperor would, of course, preside over its deliberations.   Still the matter was some little time in suspense; and *that* was perhaps the most critical moment in ecclesiastical history, in which Constantine determined to convoke the Council of Nice.

In the year 325 A. D. about three hundred and eighteen† Bishops assembled at Nice (Nicæa) in Bithynia, for the purpose of composing the Arian Controversy.   "The flower of the Ministers of God from all the Churches, which fill Europe, Africa and Asia, now met together.   Our house of Prayer, as if divinely enlarged, contained, under the same roof, Syrians and Cilicians, Phœnicians and Arabians, men of Palestine and of Egypt, Thebans and Libyans. Mesopotamia, Persia, Scythia, Galatia, Pamphylia, the various provinces of Greece, and even

Council of Nice, 325, A. D. Eusebius.

* Jortin has suggested another method in the following very rational passage— (Eccles. Hist. B. iii.)   ' If, when the quarrel between Alexander and Arius was grown to such a height as to want a remedy, the Fathers of the Church had, for the sake of peace, agreed to draw up a Confession of Faith in words of Scripture, and to establish the divinity of Christ on the expressions used by the Apostles, every one might have assented to it, and the Arian party would most certainly have received it.   The difference of sentiments, indeed, and of interpretation, would not have ceased, but the controversy would have cooled and dwindled away, after every champion had discharged his zeal upon paper and written to his heart's content.   The Arian notion that the *Son was created in time*, and that *there was a time when he existed not*, would probably have sunk, as not being the language of the new Testament; and the Macedonian notion, that the *Holy Ghost was created in time*, would have sunk with the other, for the same reason; at least these opinions would never have been obtruded upon us as Articles of Faith.'

† ' Persons not more widely separated and diversified in sentiments, than in person, residence, and race, here met together; and one city received them all, as it were an ample garland of priests, variegated with beautiful flowers.'   Such is the light in which this assembly appeared to Eusebius, who was one of its members.   Vit. Const. l. iii. c. 6.   Respecting the number of bishops, Eusebius, as the passage has come down to us, makes it *more than* two hundred and fifty.   Socrates (lib. i. c. 8.) professing to follow Eusebius, describes it in one place as above three hundred, in another as three hundred and eighteen.   And this number is generally received by modern writers, on the additional authority of Athanasius, Hilary, Jerome, and Rufinus.

Spain, sent their holy contributions to the Council . . . which had the appearance of an assemblage of Apostles. Of the ministers of God who were present some were distinguished for their wisdom; others for the austerity of their morals and their laborious constancy; others for the urbanity of their manners. Some were venerable through their great age; others were flourishing in the vigour of manhood; while some had scarcely entered into the ministry." This is the description of Eusebius. On Dr. Jortin. the other hand, Dr. Jortin diligently enumerates all the sad variety of base or wicked motives, by which the mind of man may be warped from rectitude—servility, prejudice, the thousand forms of timidity, personal interest, insolence, intolerance, vanity, ambition, resentment, indolence, and so many others— and would thus disparage the result of these deliberations. Such remarks, however, will apply with almost equal force to every description of large assembly. And if to a certain extent they may have been true in this case, it is at least as manifest, on the other hand, that among such numbers assembled, many there must have been of sincere intention and earnest piety, and assuredly several well instructed in the learning of the age: and the excellence of these persons doubtless so influenced the general character of the Council, that, though unable to repress the intemperate violence of some of its members, they were sufficient to conduct it to that decision, which has now been followed by the great majority of Christians for fifteen centuries.

The bishops began with much personal dissension, and presented to the Emperor a variety of written accusations against each other; the Emperor burnt all their libels and exhorted them to peace and unity. They then proceeded to examine the momentous question proposed to them. It was soon discovered that the differences, which it was intended to reconcile, might in their principle be reduced to one point, and that that point might be expressed by one *word*—and thus the question appears to have been speedily simplified (as indeed was necessary, that so many persons might come to one conclusion on so mysterious a subject) and reduced to this—whether the Son was, or was not, *consubstantial* with the Father. . . . Many of the leading bishops hesitated, or even held in the first instance the negative opinion, and among them were Eusebius * of Cæsarea, the historian of Constantine, and Eusebius of Nicomedia, from whose hands the Emperor afterwards received baptism. The former proposed to the assembly a Creed, in which the word consubstantial † (Homoousian) was omitted; but in which he anathematized *every impious heresy*, without particularizing any. His advice was not followed. Then arose subtile disceptations respecting the meaning of the word‡, "about which some conflicted with each other, dwelling on the term and minutely dissecting it: it was like a battle fought in the dark; for neither party seemed at all to understand on what ground they vilified each other §." However, the result was perfectly conclusive: they finally decided against the Arian opinions, and established, respecting the two first persons of the Trinity, the doctrine which the Church still professes in the Nicene Creed.

Gibbon's account of this Council does not rest on evidence sufficient to counteract its improbability. He divides the Christian world, as represented at Nice, into three classes or parties, all Heretical—Arians, Sabellians and Tritheists; and then he asserts that the two last (professing opinions diametrically opposite to each other) combined against the Arians. Without affecting to believe that the majority of the Nicene

Gibbon's account examined.

---

* Jortin (Eccl. Hist. b. iii.) has discussed the religious opinions of Eusebius very reasonably.

† He objected to the term as *unscriptural*—and to the use of such terms he attributed nearly all the confusion and disorder of the Churches. (See Socrates, lib. i. c. viii. near the end.) We may observe that this was the most tenable ground in which the Arians of every denomination entrenched themselves in the course of their subsequent disputes with the Consubstantialists.—See Maim. Hist. Arian. b. iv. (vol. i. p. 223.) The distrust of tradition which they ventured to express even in that early age, was closely connected with it—yet it proved also, that the early tradition of the Church was favourable to the catholic opinion.

‡ St. Ambrose asserts that the word was maintained by the Orthodox, as an unsheathed sword for the decapitation of the Heresy. "Hæc Epistola (Eusebii) cum lecta esset in Concilio Niceno, hoc verbum posuerunt Patres, quia id viderunt adversariis esse formidini; ut, tanquam evaginato ab ipsis gladio, ipsorum nefandæ caput hæreseos amputarent." Ambros. De Fide, lib. iii. cap. xv.

§ See Socrates, l. i. c. xxiii. This passage has rather reference to the differences on the same subject which continued after the Council; but it well describes the nature of the disputations. "Sit ista in Græcorum levitate perversitas qui maledictis insectantur eos a quibus de veritate dissentiunt."

Bishops would have explained the mystery of the Trinity in the precise language of the Athanasian Creed, we think it very irrational to suppose, that there were none (that there were not many) among them, impressed with notions of the Trinity very far removed either from Sabellianism or Tritheism. Those, who know the pertinacity with which men adhere to their own previous notions on such matters will not easily believe that two numerous parties, professing opinions not only contrary, but adverse, should immediately waive those opinions, and assume, and persist in, other opinions essentially different from either, and then unite, merely for the sake of outvoting a third party, against which they were not inflamed by any personal animosity. It is possible that there may have been some Sabellians as well as Tritheists among the members of the Council, notwithstanding the repeated condemnations of those heresies by the Church writers; but it is impossible to believe, that the opinions, which were finally sanctioned by the great majority of the Bishops, and were ever afterwards followed as the rule of orthodoxy, were not previously very general among the ministers of the Church.

Their labours being completed, the Bishops dispersed to their respective provinces:—besides the solemn declaration of their opinion, on a most important point of doctrine (since it established the equal Divinity of the Son), they finally set at rest the question respecting the celebration of Easter, and enacted some profitable regulations relating to Church discipline*. Thus far, then, we can have no just reason to condemn the result of their meeting, or to pronounce such assemblies either pernicious or useless. The doctrine of the majority of Christendom was proclaimed by a public act, on a subject hitherto uncontroverted, and henceforward it was reasonably considered the doctrine of the Church. And if matters had rested here, perhaps the dissentients would either have concealed their opinions, or gradually melted away into the mass of the orthodox.

* The three written monuments of this Council were the Rule of Faith—a number of Canons—and the Synodical Epistle which was addressed to the Churches on its dissolution. Socrates, E. Hist. lib. i., c. ix. See Semler, Cent. iv. cap. iii. De Conciliis. Mosheim, E. H. Cent. iv. p. ii. c. v.

But Constantine thought the work of ecclesiastical legislation incomplete, until the spiritual edict was enforced by temporal penalties. Immediate exile was inflicted on those who persisted in error; and the punishment of a Heretic by a Christian Prince was defended by the same plea of rebellious contumacy, which is urged by the apologists of his Pagan predecessors to justify the execution of a Christian*.

In justice, however, to the character of Constantine, we must admit, that he was animated throughout these perplexing dissensions not by any private or sectarian animosity against the Arian party, but by a sincere desire to restore peace to the Church. It was his object to correct and chastise the perversity of the Heretics, and thus to force them into communion with the great body of his Christian subjects; but he had no wish for their extermination. And as soon as he discovered that his first severities were ineffectual; that the Arians, under the episcopal guidance of Eusebius of Nicomedia†, lost little strength in Asia, and even maintained the contest in Alexandria itself; and that they were not without support in his own Court and Household, he perceived the inutility of his measures, and chose rather to retrace the steps which he had taken, than to advance more deeply into the paths of persecution. He therefore recalled Eusebius in the year 330, and six years afterwards Arius himself, after presenting to the Emperor a modified profession of faith, was released from the sentence of banishment‡. That Heresiarch perished soon afterwards by a

* In a formal Edict addressed to the " Bishops and People," Constantine compares the blindness of Arius to that of Porphyry, and commands his followers to be designated by the ignominious name of Porphyrians. He then proceeds to consign the books of Arius to the flames, nearly in the following terms:—' If any man be found to have concealed a copy of those Books, and not to have instantly produced it and thrown it into the fire, he shall be put to death. The moment he is convicted of this he shall be subjected to capital punishment. The Lord continue to preserve you.' Socrates, Hist. E., lib. i. p. 32.

† Philostorgius, the Arian historian, attributes miracles to this Eusebius; and Athanasius (Orat. 2.) seems to consider him rather as the master than the disciple of Arius. See Tillemont, Sur les Ariens, Art. vi.

‡ It is another, perhaps a more probable, opinion, that Eusebius was recalled in 328, and Arius even sooner; but that the Emperor did not invite Arius to Constantinople until 336. Mosh. Ecc. Hist., Cent. iv. p. ii. c. v. See also Tillem. loc. cit., who dates the real rancour of the contest from the refusal of Athanasius still to communicate with his adversary.

Death and character of Arius.

sudden, but probably a natural, death—and so far from joining in the anathemas, which are commonly heaped upon him, we shall perform a more grateful office in bearing testimony to the purity of his moral life, and the probable sincerity of his religious opinions. Respecting the less important circumstances of his manners and conversation, we shall be contented to adopt the language of a writer, who has seldom treated either him or his followers with any show of candour or justice*. 'Arius made use of the advantages he was master of, by art and by nature, to gain the people—for it is certain that he had a great many talents, which rendered him capable of nicely insinuating himself into their good opinion and affections. He was tall of stature and of a very becoming make, grave and serious in his carriage, with a certain air of severity in his looks, which made him pass for a man of great virtue and austerity of life. Yet this severity did not discourage those who accosted him, because it was softened by an extraordinary delicacy in his features that gave lustre to his whole person, and had something in it so sweet and engaging, as was not easily to be resisted. His garb was modest, but withal neat, and such as was usually worn by those who were not men of quality as well as learning. His manner of receiving people was very courteous, and very ingratiating, through his agreeable way of entertaining those who came to him upon any occasion. In short, notwithstanding his mighty seriousness, and the severity and strictness of his mien, he perfectly well understood how to soothe and flatter, with all imaginable wit and address, those whom he had a mind to bring over to his opinion, and engage in his party.'

Constantius and Constans.

On the death of Constantine in A. D. 336 the empire was partitioned among his sons. Constantius occupied the eastern throne, and Constantine and Constans divided that of the west. These two princes (in compliance perhaps with the inclinations of their subjects) supported the Nicene faith in their dominions; but Constantius loudly proclaimed his adhesion to the Arian or Eusebian† doctrine; and, perceiving that a numerous sect

* Maimbourg, Hist. Arian., b. i. It is a flattering amplification of a passage in Epiphanius, Hæres., 69.

† Eusebius of Nicomedia died in the year 342, after gaining some advantages over his great antagonist Athanasius.

already professed it, he proceeded by every art to impose it upon the body of his people. It is admitted that Constantius possessed a "vain and feeble mind, alike incapable of being moderated by reason or fixed by faith*. Instead of reconciling the parties by the weight of his authority, he cherished and propagated by verbal disputes the differences which his vain curiosity had excited." And it is the complaint of Ammianus, a contemporary historian, that the highways were covered, and the establishment of posts almost exhausted, by the troops of bishops, who were perpetually hurrying from synod to synod. These measures served only to animate dissension; and the evils and the odium which it produced are more justly charged upon the prince, who inflamed, than upon the parties who blindly engaged in it.

In the year 350 Constans was assassinated, and soon afterwards Rome and Italy, with a great part of the western empire, fell into the hands of Constantius. Hitherto the Churches of the West had not been deeply agitated by the controversy, but having willingly embraced, had steadily maintained, the doctrine of Nice; but the first attention of the emperor was directed to the disturbance of their repose and their faith.

In the mean time, an adversary, dangerous to the opinions, and not wholly subject even to the power, of the sovereign, had been raised up in the person of Athanasius. That great champion of Catholicism, the most distinguished among the Fathers of the Church, not by his writings only, but by his adventures and his sufferings, steadily defended the Nicene doctrine during forty-six years of alternate dignity and persecution†. He succeeded Alexander in the see of Alexandria in the year 326; he succeeded also to his enmity against the opinions and person of Arius, and boldly raised his voice against his recall from banishment by Constantine. Some intemperance in his zeal seems soon afterwards to have given a pretext to the Asiatic

Atha-nasius. 326, 373, A. D.

---

* Gibbon, c. 21. Yet when Gibbon talks of "reconciling parties by the weight of authority," what can he mean to recommend, but persecution? and at last, when were religious differences ever reconciled by *authority?*

† His character is admirably described by Gibbon (chap. 21), and the history of his constancy and his misfortunes is written with splendour and impartiality, even when Julian becomes his persecutor.

bishops, many of whom were still Arian; and in a synod held
at Tyre,* they pronounced the sentence of degradation and
exile, which was enforced by the emperor. At the end of
twenty-eight months, soon after the death of Constantine, he
was restored; but in 341 he was once more exiled by the synod
of Antioch†, acting under the influence of Constantius. The
place of his former banishment was France; that of his second
was Italy, and chiefly Rome; so that he became familiar with
the language of the West, with the discipline and primates of
its Church, and with the court of its emperor. He profited
by all these advantages, and availed himself so effectually of
the last, that Constans at length prepared to interfere with
arms in his favour. He was probably encouraged to this
resolution by the decision of the celebrated council held at
Sardica in Thrace in 347, in which the great majority were
Catholics. Threatened by the horrors of a religious war, Constantius reluctantly consented to his restoration‡. In the year
349 he re-occupied his former throne. " The entrance of the
archbishop into his capital was a triumphal procession; absence and persecution had endeared him to the Alexandrians;
his authority, which he exercised with rigour, was more firmly
established, and his fame was diffused from Æthiopia to Britain, over the whole extent of the Christian world."

It was immediately after this event that Constantius succeeded to the Western Empire; and in his zeal for the pro-

* It was held in the year 335. The most important of the charges brought
against Athanasius were manifestly confuted, and the justice of his sentence is
at least very questionable.

† At this time, or soon afterwards, the Arians drew up a creed, in which they
omitted the offensive word consubstantial; but the terms which they applied to
the Son, calling him ἄτρεπτόν τε καὶ ἀναλλοίωτον τῆς θεότητος, οὐσίας τε καὶ βουλῆς
καὶ δυναμέως καὶ δόξης ἀπαράλλακτον εἰκόνα, καὶ πρωτότοκον πάσης κτίσεως—are such
as might have been subscribed by the most zealous Catholic. See Le Clerc, ap.
Jortin, E. H. b. iii.; and Tillemont, Sur les Ariens, Article xxxii. Also, Sozomen, l. iii. c. v ; and Athanas. de Synodis.

‡ It was on this occasion that Constantius requested Athanasius to grant to
the Arians one Church at Alexandria. This request the patriarch answered by
another, proposing a similar concession to the Catholics at Antioch. From this
conference we learn not only what high ground was assumed by the prelate, in
his transactions with the emperor, but also with what different success the measures of the latter had been attended in the capitals of Syria and of Egypt.

pagation of Arianism he presently renewed his attacks on Athanasius. He summoned* councils of the Western bishops; he menaced and caressed and corrupted the bishops whom he had summoned, and at length (in the year 356) with great difficulty succeeded in deposing for the third time his spiritual adversary.

This struggle must not be passed over with slight notice, since it presents to us an event, of which there had yet been no experience in the history of the Church, or in the history of Rome, or perhaps in the history of man. Hitherto, or at least a very short time previous, the Church had been a despised and seemingly defenceless community, subject, as a body, to the capricious insults of every tyrant, and liable, in its individual members, to his arbitrary inflictions.   Until very lately, the emperor of the Roman world possessed authority uncontrolled over the liberty and life of his subjects, undisputed by any, except as rebels, or rivals for the throne.   And certainly the monstrous evils of despotic government have never been more signally displayed, than during the dreary interval which separated Augustus and Constantine.   Still at the end of that period the rules of government remained the same as at the beginning—no civil revolution had assigned limits to the authority of the prince, or introduced any counteracting power—no political change had given weight to popular opinion or honour to free principles.   And yet scarcely forty years from the accession of Constantine had elapsed, when we behold his son and successor reduced to the employment of intrigue and artifice, for the deposition of a magistrate whom he detested.   The singularity of this circumstance is even increased by two other considerations—one of which is, that the emperor had the cordial support of a considerable portion of his subjects, the Arian party, in this contest—and the other, that his adversary was not sus-

His contest with Constantius.

---

* The most numerous council assembled on this occasion appears to have been that of Milan in 355, which was attended by above 300 Western as well as many Eastern bishops. (See Maimb., Hist. Arian., b. iv. vol. i., p. 174 et seq.) In the same year Liberius, bishop of Rome, was banished for his faithful attachment to the doctrine and cause of Athanasius ; but he was presently recalled, through the intercession first of the matrons, and afterwards of the populace, of Rome. Sozom., lib. iv. c. ii, Theod., lib. ii. c. xvii,

tained by any armed force of soldiers or followers; nor is it probable even that his violent execution would have been followed by any serious insurrection*. Yet Constantius, with a prudent respect both for the spiritual authority of the bishop and the rights of the Church, proceeded to the accomplishment of his object by indirect, and tedious, and unworthy methods. Such circumstances become, indeed, familiar to us in the pages of later history; but we should not for that reason overlook their first occurrence, nor fail to record with pleasure and gratitude the earliest proof we possess of the political effect of Christianity in moderating the despotism with which it was associated.

The third banishment of Athanasius lasted six years, until the death of his persecutor in 362†. They were passed in the deserts of Upper Egypt, in concealment and dependence; and they were consoled by the pious exertions of the exile for the opinions for which he suffered—exertions, which the vigilance of the Imperial police could neither prevent nor neutralize. After his final restoration he enjoyed his see without interruption for eleven years, and at length died in peace and dignity.

Divisions of the Arians.

In the mean time, as is natural among those who indulge in any laxity of speculation respecting mysteries really inscrutable, the Arians were divided among themselves almost as widely as the more moderate among them varied from the Church. The original and pure Arians, following the opinions of their founder, maintained not only that the substance of the Word was different from that of the Father, but that it did not even resemble it; while others, pretending the authority of Eusebius of Nicomedia, denied with equal confidence the Consubstantiality of the two Persons, but at the same tine affirmed their *perfect likeness*. These last are commonly called Semiarians; and their doctrine appears to have been first proclaimed at the Synod of Ancyra in Galatia, held by Basil, the Bishop of that

---

* It is true that some popular commotions did at last attend the execution even of the legal order for the deposition of the bishop, which were suppressed by force; but they were of very short duration, and entirely confined to Alexandria.

† It is asserted by Tillemont (Sur les Ariens, Art. 103) that during the neutrality of Julian, the Catholics gained considerable ground upon their adversaries.

place, in the year 358; but the Council of Seleucia, by which Council of Seleucia. 359, A. D. their tenets were sanctioned in the following year, holds a more prominent place in ecclesiastical annals*.   They were very numerous during the reign of Constantius, who was their protector, and, as is supposed, their proselyte; but they afterwards yielded in some measure to the pure Arianism of Valens and his patriarch, Eudoxius.

Again, the Semiarians were not themselves entirely united: several among them maintained the pre-eternity of the Word; while others believed that, though it had subsisted before all ages, it had once had a beginning.   And that party † was not inconsiderable which, admitting a *general* likeness between the Father and the Son, denied that there was any similarity of substance‡.   Athanasius, in his epistle respecting the Synods of Seleucia and Rimini, exposes the great variety of the Arian Creeds, and the subject has been enlarged upon by Catholic historians §, to show the inevitable perplexities of those who have once permitted themselves to deviate from the established doctrine.

Having succeeded in his attack on the Consubstantialists,

---

* In the fourth century were held thirteen Councils against Arius, fifteen for him, and seventeen for the Semiarians; in all forty-five. Jortin, Ecc. Hist., b. iii.

† It would appear that Constantius himself belonged to this sect of the Semiarians. See Gibbon, chap. 21.

‡ The Consubstantialists are known in history by the Greek term HOMOOUSIANS; those who asserted the similarity of the substances by the name of HOMOIOUSIANS; those who denied any sort of resemblance were called ANOMOIANS ; and, to complete the confusion, the last-mentioned Sectarians are sometimes denominated— from the name of one of their most popular teachers—Eunomians. The unimportance of the verbal difference has provoked the ridicule of some, who would have done better to reflect with sadness, how much the angry application of those terms tended to prolong and embitter the controversy. See Semler, cent. iv. chap. iv., ad finem.

§ The distinction which Tillemont (Sur les Ariens, Art. 66) draws between the Arians and Eusebians refers rather to their situation in *respect to the Church* than to their doctrine. "By the Arians we mean those who were expelled from the Church by the Council of Nice—by the Eusebians those who remained in communion with the Church, but who bent themselves insidiously to ruin its doctrine by the invention of new formularies, who endeavoured to expel Athanasius, and who communicated with the original Arians. So that these two formed only one sect in intrigue, and perhaps in belief too—though the one party appeared in the Church, and the other was visibly separated from it." The word ὁμοούσιος is interpreted—habens simul essentiam, *i. e.* eundem essentiam.

(and, we might add, on the pure Arians) of the East, Constantius removed the scene of action to the Western provinces, and

Council of
Rimini. convoked a council at Rimini in the year 360; by nearly the
same arts which he had employed to procure the condemnation
of Athanasius*, supported by a moderate, but firm exertion of
the civil authority, he succeeded in influencing the members to
the subscription of a creed, containing some expressions capable
of heretical interpretation. "The whole world groaned (says
St. Jerome) and wondered to find itself Arian!" But this
conversion was neither sincere nor lasting; of the four hundred
prelates assembled at Rimini eighty only were Arians; and
however opinions may have been divided in the East—for even
there, though the majority of the bishops† followed the faith
of the Emperor, there is reason to believe that many among
the people remained catholic‡—we may safely infer from the
small number of Arian prelates who were found willing to proclaim that doctrine, even under an Arian Emperor, that it had
yet made little progress in the Latin Church. For we should
always bear in mind, that any sudden change in the opinions
of the vulgar respecting an abtruse mystery must necessarily
be *preceded* by the same change in their spiritual directors.

Valens.   The path of intolerance, which had been pointed out and
abandoned by Constantine, but so steadily followed by his
heretical successor, was trodden with equal diligence in the

---

* He directed Taurus, the governor of the province, to confine the bishops, until they should be all of one mind, that is, until they should be all of the Emperor's
mind. The conditions of concord on which they at length agreed amounted to
this: the Catholics conceded the offensive term (Consubstantialism), and the
Arians to all appearance the doctrine; at least all parties agreed in anathema-
tizing the name of Arius, while they professed, as it would seem, the Semiarian
opinions. Sulpic. Sever. lib. ii. p. 420. Edit. Lugd. Batav. Maimb. Hist.
Arian., b. iii. Gibbon, chap. 21. Some *British* bishops appeared at this synod,
and a trait of their poverty and discretion is told by Sulpicius.

† The throne and principal churches of Constantinople were occupied by Arian
patriarchs from the year 342 till their restoration to the Catholics by Theodosius
nearly forty years afterwards. Semler, Epit. sec. iv.

‡ At Antioch at least the dissent of the people from the established Arianism
was strongly and violently expressed; and at Constantinople itself, the very citadel
of the heresy, in spite of the savage edicts of Constantius, some very sanguinary
tumults still proved the steady perseverance of many Catholics. In one of these
3150 persons were killed.

Eastern empire by Valens.   That prince, who is believed to
have been converted to Arianism by the influence of his Empress* Dominica, in the year 367, permitted considerable
licence against the catholics to his patriarch Eudoxius, even
during the beginning of his reign, and proceeded, after a few
years, to more direct and intemperate measures†.   Alexandria,
by whose pernicious fertility the controversy was first engendered, remained, however, through the influence of Alexander
and Athanasius, strongly attached to the Nicene faith.   It
became the scene of frightful disorder, as soon as the civil
authorities added strength to the malignity of the Arians, and
proceeded again to expel Peter, the orthodox patriarch.   The
calamities thus occasioned were undoubtedly heightened by the
zealous interference of the Jews and Pagans, who derived their
best argument against christianity from the furious dissensions
of its professors, and who were, on all occasions, anxious from
other motives to join in the assault on the stronger and wealthier
party.   On the other hand, the Monks, a new but numerous
body, continued faithful to the doctrine of Athanasius, and
loved it the more because they suffered for it.   Peter avoided
the tempest by a hasty retreat to Rome, and the success of the
Arians does not appear permanently to have increased either
their numbers or their popularity.   However, there can be no
doubt that the profession of Arianism was common, and even
general, throughout the East, during the reign of Valens, and
that in some of the Asiatic provinces, especially Syria, such

---

* The Arians had no cause to blush at the obligations which they likewise
owed to two preceding empresses.   Constantia protected their infancy and their
misfortunes during the reign of Constantine, and Eusebia promoted their prosperity
under the sceptre of Constantius.   The Catholics could also boast of similar
patronage; but Maimbourg (book vi.) establishes a very broad distinction as to
the agency by which such aid was in each case administered; "as the devil (says
that very rigid Catholic) had employed the assistance of princesses to introduce
Arianism into the court of Constantine, of Constantius and Valens, so God made
use of the empress Ælia Flaccilla in order to prevent it from creeping into the
court of Theodosius."   In a later page (b. xii. A. D. 590) the same author again
alludes to the diabolical agency "which introduced the Arian heresy into the
East by the means of three women," and which was afterwards compensated by
the divine benevolence in raising up three princesses, Clotilda, Indegonda, and
Theodelinda, for the purification of France, Spain, and Italy.

† They are enlarged upon by Tillemont, Sur les Ariens, Art. 115.

may have been the real belief of the majority; but its progress was attended with perpetual tumults, and at the death of Valens in 378 it had reached the highest point of prevalence which it was destined in those regions to attain.

Theodosius the Great.

Two years afterwards, Theodosius the Great proclaimed his adhesion to the doctrine of Nice, and immediately prepared to establish it as the creed of his subjects. "I will not permit (thus he addressed certain Arians in the year * 383) throughout my dominions any other religion than that which obliges us to worship the Son of God in unity of essence with the Father and Holy Ghost in the adorable Trinity—as I hold the empire of Him, and the power which I have to command you, he likewise will give me strength, as he hath given me the will, to make myself obeyed in a point so absolutely necessary to your salvation, and to the peace of my subjects." The peace of his subjects was not indeed the immediate reward of his violent measures, but, on the contrary, general confusion and much individual suffering were occasioned by them. Still, as he persevered inflexibly, as he was supported even in the East by the more zealous, and, in some places, the more numerous party, and as he was seconded almost by the unanimity of the Western Empire, his severities were attended by general and lasting success, and the doctrine of Arius, if not perfectly extirpated, withered from that moment rapidly and irrecoverably throughout the provinces of the East.

Second General Council, 381, A.D.

The work of Theodosius was considerably promoted by the council which he assembled at Constantinople A. D. 381, and which stands in the history of the Church as the Second General Council. Its object, besides the regulation of several points of ecclesiastical discipline, was to confirm the decision of Nice against the Arians, and especially to promulgate the doctrine of the Divinity of the Third Person, against the Macedonian †

---

* See Maimb., Hist. Arian., b. vi.

† Macedonius, in common with other Arians (or rather Semiarians), denied the Consubstantiality, and affirmed the likeness of the two first Persons; but he positively asserted that the Holy Ghost was κτιστὸν, created. He is said to have published this notion twenty years before the General Council which condemned it. Le Clerc, Compend. Hist., ap. Jort., b. iii. Mosh. H. E., Cent. iv., p. ii., ch. v.

Heretics. The doctrine on those fundamental points, which was then established, is the same (if we except the manner of the holy procession) which is still professed in our Church: by the Oriental Church it has been unceasingly maintained, without any variation, to the present moment.

We turn to the consideration of the Western Empire. While Valens was disturbing his subjects with fruitless persecution, the Western Empire was administered by his brother Valentinian with justice and moderation. Those, and they were few in number, among the Western Bishops, who had openly deserted to the faith of Constantius, were now concealed in obscurity, or removed by death; Damasus, the Bishop of Rome, was an ardent supporter of the Nicene doctrine, and the Church preserved the general appearance, if it could not quite secure the reality, of concord. At Milan, during the reign of Theodosius, the celebrated St. Ambrose exerted his genius in the same cause, and at the end of the fourth century the proselytes of Arianism formed an inconsiderable and a declining party. Suddenly it received a new and extraordinary impulse from a quarter which could not have been suspected, from accidents which could not be averted, nor immediately controlled, and which prolonged the existence of that heresy beyond the duration which seemed otherwise to have been assigned to it. During the course of the fifth century numerous tribes of Barbarians, Goths, Huns and Vandals, Suevi and Alani and Salii, overran and occupied the provinces of the West. Of these some had been previously converted to Christianity in their native forests, before their emigration to the south: the rest for the most part adopted the religion of the vanquished; but while they professed generally the name of Christianity, they followed in its particular tenets the faith of their prince or leader. Now it so happened that all these tribes, excepting probably the Salii, imbibed in the first instance the notions of Arius. *Arianism of the Barbarians.*

This circumstance is thus accounted for:—The Goths, who were the earliest and most zealous among the converts, were directed in their religious creed by their bishop Ulphilas, a man of great talents and influence. This prelate, in the course of *Ulphilas.*

two missions to Constantinople, during the reigns of Constantius and Valens, accommodated his opinions (whether sincerely or not, is questionable) to those of the imperial court, and he returned, at least from his second embassy, the zealous proselyte of Arianism. This doctrine he rapidly propagated among his compatriots, and diffused it through the whole nation. The example of the Goths was respected by the leaders of tribes of subsequent invaders and converts: in embracing the religion of the provinces which they conquered they preferred that form of it which was professed by their predecessors in conquest; and thus the tenets of Arius were disseminated among the barbarian colonists in every province of the western empire. Other means of spreading those tenets were the persecutions of the orthodox emperors, especially Theodosius: by scattering the followers of the heretic among distant and populous nations, they diffused to the same extent the knowledge of his doctrine, and multiplied the number of its professors.

Again, those of the barbarian princes who embraced Christianity after their success, when they saw the great controversy by which the Christian world was divided, would be guided also by political motives as to the side they chose in it, and one of these would probably be opposition to the Eastern throne; and, as they were little versed in the arguments by which the question was contested, and probably blind even to its real nature and importance, the mere effect of their ignorance would be to direct them to what might seem the simpler creed. Their soldiers and followers, still more ignorant than themselves, naturally acquiesced in their belief; and even among the vanquished natives, the many who were indifferent would turn to the same profession. On the other hand, the Church remained firm; the exertions of its most eminent directors were bent almost without exception on the maintenance of the Nicene faith, and with such success, that the great majority of zealous and influential Christians probably retained, even under foreign and Arian rule, their attachment to the established doctrine.

Extinction of Arianism.

This re-action in favour of Arianism, as it was sudden and somewhat violent, was not of long duration; indeed we may fairly consider the sixth century as having brought about its termination. The conversion of Clovis to the Catholic faith in the year 496, and his subsequent zeal in its favour, are commonly mentioned as having first opened the path to the conclusion of the dispute; and as it is sometimes the pleasure of Divine Providence to select the vilest instruments for the accomplishment of His mysterious designs, so we may believe without astonishment that He deigned to bring about a great good even by the impure and flagitious ministry of Clovis. A more effective agent in the same work was Justinian. That Emperor began his long and active reign in 527, and his rigid orthodoxy was disgraced by the most violent proceedings against every description of heresy. His victories extended his means of extirpation into the West, and before his death he had very generally strengthened, though he had not universally restored, the authority of the Church.

The Arians still retained a very powerful party in Spain, In Spain which was not destined to be otherwise extinguished than by the 589, A. D. accession of an orthodox monarch. In the year 585 Recared assembled the leaders of the two parties in a conference, which concluded in the triumph of the Catholics; and that prince pursued his victory both in Spain and Narbonese Gaul, with so much diligence and rigour, that, after some sanguinary tumults and barbarous executions*, the great body of his subjects ranged themselves under his doctrine, and never afterwards relapsed into heresy. The celebrated Council of Toledo, which was held by the same king in 589, may be considered as having completed the extirpation of Arianism from the soil of Spain.

In Italy the victories obtained by the generals of Justinian Among the gave strength and confidence to the Catholic Church, and Lombards, weakened the opposition of its adversaries; and the heresy appears to have been falling into discredit, when it received a fresh but momentary impulse from the invasion and triumphs of the Lombards. Those Arian warriors crossed the Alps in the year 569, and presently became masters of the greater part of

---

* Maimb. Hist. Arian., b. xi. The fact is admitted and justified by Mariana, Hist. Hispan., lib. v., ch. xiv. See Bayle's Dict., Arius. The facility with which the Arians yielded to this persecution has given great matter of exultation to Catholic writers.

the country. Their conquests were attended by unusual circumstances of barbarity, and the necessary horrors of uncivilized
warfare were inflamed by sectarian animosity. But the sufferings of the Catholics were not of long duration; they were
speedily and effectually terminated by the conversion of the
conquerors. This event is ascribed, in the first instance, to the
diligence and fidelity of the orthodox Bishops*, who availed
themselves of the first moments of tranquillity to recommend
the Nicene doctrine to the conscience of the victors. It is at
least probable that their exertions prepared and facilitated the
success of a Catholic Queen, Theodelinda, who appears to have
completed the overthrow of Arianism, even among her Lombard subjects, before the conclusion of the sixth century. The
triumph of that princess may be read by the Catholic without
a blush, and recorded by the historian without a sigh; since it
was accomplished, if not by the process of rational conviction,
at least without the savage inflictions by which sudden religious
changes are usually effected.

It was thus that this lamentable controversy, after perplexing
the faith, and animating the malice, and disturbing the happiness
of the Christian world for more than two hundred and fifty
years, was at length extinguished; and at this moment the
very name of Arius is almost forgotten in the Eastern world;
while in the West his opinions are confined to the breasts of a
very inconsiderable proportion of the Christian community.

Observa-
tions.
We shall close this account with a few additional observations. The Arians have laid claim to the greater moderation,
both in the origin and in the conduct of this controversy; and
they moreover assert that their communion was free from many
of the superstitious corruptions, which, at that time, were growing up so rapidly in the Catholic Church. This latter assertion is, at least, founded in probability; because the principle
of their faith, by disparaging the dignity of the Redeemer, removed them farther from religious excess. Their tendency was
rather towards too little, than towards too much, belief; and
we can readily suppose that those who were so averse from the

* Maimbourg (Hist. Arian., b. xii.) is the more to be believed in this point, as
he mentions the fact almost incidentally.

worship of Christ, would certainly refuse any adoration to the Virgin or other created beings. But notwithstanding this, we find that Constantius had a superstitious veneration for relics, and was the first to encourage their transfer from place to place, with the miraculous qualities attached to them; and when that Arian disturbed the (real or supposed) bodies of Timothy, St. Andrew, and St. Luke, and conveyed them to Constantinople, he assuredly introduced into the Church of Christ one of its most degrading corruptions*.

But their claims to superior moderation are still more disputable, except, indeed, as far as it might be the fruit of their weakness. In the East, the reign of Constantius was the era of their triumph, and it was polluted by constant and sanguinary persecution. That of Valens was not less distinguished by the same spirit and principle, and the same oppression; and as the Arian Bishops were then exceedingly numerous and powerful, at least in Asia, it would be unfair to impute the whole criminality to the Emperor. Athanasius, the continual object of their hostility, has the following passage concerning them: 'Whenever any man differs from them, they have him before the governor or the general; him whom they cannot subdue by reason and argument, they take upon them to convince by whippings and imprisonments; which is enough to show that their principles are anything rather than religion; for it is the property of religion not to compel, but to persuade.' On the other hand, Athanasius himself either had not yet learnt, or had wholly forgotten, this excellent truth, when he appealed to Constantine against the recall of Arius; nor was it generally either practised or acknowledged afterwards by the Catholic Emperors of the East†. Gradually the faith of the prelates submitted itself to the injunctions of those monarchs; the people were, upon the whole, always favourable to Catholicism; and thus before the middle of the sixth century the Nicene doctrine was very firmly established throughout that part of the Empire.

* This took place in 336. See Jortin, Eccl. Hist., vol. iv., p. xii.

† There is one distinction, however, which to a certain extent is true, that the Arians were more lenient in their treatment of other Heretics; whereas the Catholics persecuted universally. See the Theodos. Code. The Edicts of Justinian.

In the West, Arianism would never have taken any deep root, except through the influence of the barbarian conquerors; for the Church was steadily and zealously opposed to it, and so was the most religious, if not the most numerous, part of the conquered. It was probably confined to the courts of the victors, to their armies, and to such of the natives as were in most immediate intercourse with them. In Gaul, in Spain, and in Italy, the Gothic Princes appear seldom to have persecuted their Catholic subjects, except in retaliation for some outrage exercised against the Arians by the Catholic Emperors of Constantinople. But in Africa the Vandal Arians were guilty of horrible excesses during the last half of the fifth century, which were not terminated until their expulsion by Belisarius in the year 530. On the other hand, in all those provinces the Catholic population, whether persecuted or not, seems always to have been equally disposed to rise in favour of a Catholic invader. But we should here recollect that the distinction of Arian and Catholic was in general so entirely identified with that of Barbarian and Roman, conqueror and conquered, that we can scarcely say how much of this we should attribute to religious, how much to national, animosity. Upon the whole, we have little reason to give the praise of moderation, or even humanity, to either party; much depended on the personal character of the Princes on either side, and on the principles or prejudices in which they had been educated. But in as far as the *sectarian* feeling was concerned, we may discover on both sides an equal disposition to give loose to it.

The Arian was more flexible, the Catholic more rigid under persecution*; the former finally submitted to conversion; the latter would probably never have yielded to any infliction short of extirpation. This distinction is attributed by some to the undoubted circumstance, that it is easier to extend the belief of

* Bayle (in his Life of Arius) observes this inconsistency in Roman Catholic writers, that they urge generally the obstinate perversity of Heretics as a proof of their errors; and yet press their flexibility in particular cases to the same conclusion. Yet the Roman Catholics endeavoured to accommodate their practice to both their suppositions; which, indeed, could only be reconciled by the assumption, that Heretics were obstinate *until* they were persecuted, and no longer; and on this ground they erected the Inquisition.

the multitude, than to contract it; a circumstance which proceeds from the false but prevalent notion, that too much belief is at least an error on the safe side, and that Jesus Christ would more readily intercede for those who might have paid Him excessive honour, than for those who had fallen short in their worship. Others imagine that the Arian always felt in his heart some latent consciousness of error, which undermined his constancy in the hour of trial, and deprived him of that energy of invincible endurance which is inconsistent with the very shadow of insincerity.

NOTE ON CERTAIN EARLY ECCLESIASTICAL HISTORIANS.

THREE Greek writers, Socrates, Sozomen, and Theodoret, take up the annals of the Church about the time of its establishment by Constantine nearly where the history of Eusebius terminates, and carry them on as far as the reign of Theodosius the younger, through a space of about one hundred and twenty years. It is necessary to give a short account of them.

1. *Socrates* was a native of Constantinople; he was carefully instructed in grammar and rhetoric, and presently assumed the profession of a scholastic or advocate. Much time, however, and very considerable diligence he directed to the compilation of his historical materials, and no scanty judgment is shown in their arrangement and composition. The epistles of Bishops, the acts of Councils, the works of preceding or contemporary ecclesiastics, are consulted with care, and seemingly cited with fidelity, and the principal events are chronologically distinguished by olympiads or consulates. His impartiality is so strikingly displayed, as to make his orthodoxy questionable to Baronius, the celebrated Roman Catholic historian; but Valesius in his life has clearly shown that there is no reason for such suspicion. We may mention another principle, which he has followed, which in the mind of Baronius may have tended to confirm the notion of his heterodoxy—he is invariably adverse to every form of persecution on account of religious opinions—' διωγμὸν δὲ λέγω τὸ ὁπωσοῦν ταράττειν τοὺς ἡσυχάζοντας'—and I call it persecution to offer any description of molestation to

those who are quiet. Some credulity respecting miraculous stories is his principal failing.

2. *Hermias Sozomen* was also an advocate, resident at Constantinople; but he was a native of Palestine, born near Gaza, and was educated in a monastery in that country. In his writings we perceive a great ardour for the monastic life, and a concomitant tendency to superstitious extravagance. Superior in style to his contemporary, he is below him in judgment and discrimination: still his work contains much valuable matter; though some of it was probably borrowed from that of Socrates, which seems to have been published some little earlier.

3. *Theodoret,* like Sozomen, received a monastic education; but he entered into the ecclesiastical profession, and became Bishop of Cyrus, in Syria. He was remarkable, not only for his learning and piety, but for his absolute and voluntary poverty. ' I was ordained Bishop against my will; for twenty-five years (says he, in an epistle still extant) I have so lived in that station, as never to be at variance, never to prosecute any one at law or to be prosecuted. The same I can say of all the pious clergy who are under my inspection, none of whom was ever seen in any court of justice. Neither I nor my domestics ever received the smallest present from any person, not even a loaf or an egg. My patrimony I gave long ago to the poor, and I have made no new acquisitions. I have neither house, nor land, nor money, nor a sepulchre where my friends may lay my body when I die. I am possessed of nothing save the poor raiment which I wear.' As a writer, however, he is inferior to his two fellow-labourers, both in judgment and moderation; he is more violent against schism and heresy, more bigoted, and more absurdly credulous. Yet he did not himself escape the charge of heresy, and was certainly attached to the party, probably to the opinions, of Nestorius. His style is pronounced by Photius to be clear and lofty without redundancy.

To this list we may venture to regret that we cannot add the name of *Philostorgius.* This writer was an Arian; his history extended from the year 300 to 425, and he had witnessed much of what he described. But of his works nothing remains, except an epitome by Photius, and some fragments. Photius assures us that he betrayed great partiality for the sect to which he belonged, and this appears indeed to have been so; yet even such a narrative we would willingly confront with the probable misrepresentations of his adversaries.

We have also referred to the authorities of Epiphanius, Hilary, Rufinus, and Sulpicius Severus, but have been very sparing in our use of them. *Epiphanius* was bred a monk, and became bishop of Salamis, in Cyprus. He was the author of a voluminous book against all the heresies which had hitherto arisen. But his work is disfigured by so many marks of levity and ignorance, that we can follow him with no general confidence. *Hilary* was bishop of Poictiers, for the most part a copyist of Tertullian and Origen, but celebrated for " Twelve Books concerning the Trinity," written against the Arians. *Rufinus* was a Presbyter of Aquileia, a translator, and not always a faithful one, of Origen and other Greek writers. He was engaged in a violent contest with St. Jerome, and was assailed by the virulence of that intemperate writer ; and he had the additional misfortune of being excommunicated by Anastasius, the Bishop of Rome, for his attachment to the opinions of Origen. Contemporary with Rufinus was *Sulpicius Severus,* a native of Aquitania, and a man of rank and learning. He received ordination, and was extremely attached to the person and character of Martin, the venerable Bishop of Tours. He lived to become his biographer, and besides his " Vita Beati Martini," he wrote Three Epistles also relating to that prelate. But his principal work was his " Sacra Historia :" it consists of Two Books, of which the contents extend from the time of Adam to the end of the fourth century. The only valuable portion of it is the conclusion, which contains some interesting contemporary information.

CHAPTER VIII.

The Decline and Fall of Paganism.

Condition of the two Religions on the accession of Constantine—Progress of Christianity during his reign—His successive measures against Paganism—Remarks on them—Proceedings of his sons—Accession of Julian—Reasons given for his Apostacy—His enthusiasm for Paganism—his character compared with that of M. Antoninus—his policy contrasted with that of Constantine—his successive measures against Christianity—his attempts to reform Paganism—directed to three points—his attack on the truth of Christianity—in the attempt to rebuild the Temple of Jerusalem—defeated—by what means—whether miraculous or not—examination of a late opinion—his death. Rapid decline of Paganism—Valentinian I.—Gratian.—Theodocius I.—his edict against Paganism—extremely effectual. Imperfect faith of many of the Converts—corruptions introduced from Paganism. Synesius. Arcadius and Honorius—abolition of Gladiatorial Games. Theodosius II.—subversion of Paganism—in the East—in the West. Note on certain Pagan writers.

FROM the dissensions of Christians, and the calamities occasioned by them, we turn to a more pleasing subject—the final triumph of the Faith over the superstition which had heretofore prevailed throughout the Roman empire. In proceeding to this investigation, that which first strikes us as most remarkable is, that the very period during which the Christian world was most widely and angrily divided by the Arian controversy, the middle and conclusion of the fourth century, was that precisely during which the Religion, as if invigorated by internal agitation, overthrew her most powerful adversary—a circumstance the more to be remarked, as strongly indicative of her own heavenly energy, because the spectacle of Christian dissension has afforded to infidels in every age, as it does at this moment, the most plausible argument for unbelief. Let us endeavour then to trace the measures by which this extraordinary revolution was brought about.

Progress of Christianity.

At the accession of Constantine, the Christians, though very numerous, formed no doubt the smaller portion of his subjects, since the multitude, who were in fact of no religion, were accounted among the votaries of Paganism. Besides, among the lower classes, the parade of a splendid superstition was more attractive than the simplicity of the true worship, to persons both ignorant and incurious about the truth of either ; and in many others, a latent inclination towards the new religion would be repressed by the sight of the worldly afflictions which so frequently pursued it.   The conversion of the emperor was naturally followed by a great increase in the number of nominal* Christians; the faith of many, who were nearly indifferent, would be decided by that event ; and many also, of more serious minds, would thus be led to examine with respect to the nature of the religion, which in its adversity they had contemptuously neg-lected. Honour and emoluments were annexed to the dignities of the Church, which were thus made objects of ambition to the noble and the learned; and since many, through the exercise of the religion, would gradually imbibe those sentiments and principles of piety, which they had not perhaps carried into it, we may believe that, while the name of Christianity was rapidly extended over the Roman world, its essential doctrines and moral influence made a considerable, though by no means an equal, progress.

Constantine's first measure was the famous edict of universal toleration, which established Christianity without molesting any other religion ; and as late as the year 321 he published a pro-clamation favourable to the maintenance of one of the grossest impostures of Paganism, the art of divination. Until this period, and perhaps for some few years longer, he held with tolerably equal hand the balance of the two religions† ; and in the rivalry thus established between them Christianity was daily gaining some weight at the expense of its opponent. This crisis was, indeed, of short duration, and the attentive eye of the emperor immediately perceived to which side the victory was inclining. It was then that he threw into the preponderating scale the de-

Policy of Constantine.

---

* See a note on Dr. Arnold's seventh Sermon, p. 88.

† In book iii. of Eusebius's Life of Constantine, the 44th and 45th chapters mention some prohibitions against sacrifice and idol-worship, addressed first to the Pagan magistrates, and then to the people ; but in his prayer, or doxology, published in the 55th and following chapters, he accords alike "both to believers and those in error, the enjoyment of peace and tranquillity ; as such friendly communion has most tendency to lead men in the straight path."

cisive addition of his civil authority. In the year 333 he began[*]
to overthrow the temples of the idols of the Gentiles, and to
invade their property; he suppressed some of the writings most
hostile to Christianity, and proclaimed his opposition to the
sacred rites of Paganism. He condemned them as detrimental
to the state; and whatever may have been the sincerity of his
faith, he was at least convinced that forms of worship, so contrary to each other in all their principles, could not long co-
exist in the same empire, and he gave his support to that which
most conduced to the virtue and happiness of his subjects.

The sons of Constantine followed their father's footsteps.
During the Arian rule of Constantius the severity of the laws
against Paganism was rather increased than relaxed, and sacrifice, together with idolatrous worship, was visited with capital
punishment. This system lasted until his death; so that, for
a space of about thirty years, the antient superstition was
restrained by perpetual discouragement, and afflicted with frequent persecution. The number of its followers was thus considerably reduced: but the triumph was not yet complete, and
many were there still in every province of the empire, who
hailed the accession of Julian.

Julian.　　Julian, who is commonly mentioned in history by the name
of Apostate, was the nephew of the Great Constantine; he abandoned in early youth the faith in which he had been educated,
and betook himself with great zeal to the practice of Paganism.
The motive, to which this change is usually attributed, is the
hatred that he indulged towards the name and sons of Constantine, owing to the cruelties they had inflicted on his family
—hatred which a young and impetuous disposition might easily
extend to their religion. Another reason alleged is, that when
he saw the dissensions of the Christians, and their rancour
against each other, his faith was perplexed; he found it hard
to distinguish the excellence of the religion from the vices of

---

[*] Semler, tab. sec. quarti, on orthor. of Julian, Orat. 7. Mosheim (cent. iv.,
p. i. c. i.) dates the exertions of Constantine from the overthrow of Licinius. See
Euseb. Vit. Const. lib. iv. c. 23, 25, &c. Fleury (lib. xi., sect. 33) assigns the
destruction of the temple of Venus, in Syria, and of Æsculapius and Apollo, in
Cilicia, to the year which followed the Council of Nice. See Euseb. Vit. Const.,
lib. iii., chap. 54; and Sozomen, Hist. Eccl., lib. ii., c. 5.

those who professed it, and was unable to prevent his judgment from being blinded by his indignation. Both of them may be true; for it is clear, from some part of his subsequent conduct, that his enmity to Christianity was founded on passion more than on reason, and his hatred of the faith is more prominent than his disbelief of it*. Hence it is that, having renounced one religion, he flew with ardour to the exercise of the other, and sought its aid and alliance against the common adversary. This enthusiasm for Paganism carried him into some ridiculous excesses. It is true that the affection which he professed for processions and ceremony, and the profuse splendour of his sacrifices, may have proceeded from a wish to seduce and allure the vulgar; but his private devotion to magical rites and the practice of divination, in which his sincerity is not doubted, has no such excuse, and could only have proceeded from an irregular and superstitious mind. Yet to this weakness he united many extraordinary qualities—" he was eloquent and liberal, artful, insinuating, and indefatigable; which, joined to a severe temperance, an affected love of justice†, and a courage superior to all trials, first gained him the affections, and soon after the peaceable possession of the whole empire." A strong attachment to literature distinguished his character, and may have tended to nourish his heathen prejudices; and the passion for glory which sometimes misled him was probably the strongest of his passions, and his leading motive of action.

If we compare the character of Julian with that of the other great enemy of the religion, Marcus Antoninus, we shall find all the advantages of a thoughtful, consistent, and sober understanding on the side of the latter. His conduct was invariably guided by his principles, and his principles were the best which heathen philosophy could suggest to him. His knowledge of Christianity was too partial, and the power of its professors too inconsiderable, to command his belief or respect; and he was too deeply sensible of the absurdities of Paganism to feel any

Compared with M. Antoninus.

---

* See Note at the end of the chapter.

† The passage is from Warburton; but we have no reason to question the sincerity of that principle in Julian, though it was sometimes overpowered by his religious antipathy.

regard for that worship; so that he was contented rigorously, but not intemperately, to maintain that which happened to be the established religion.   But Julian had more of passion than philosophy in his constitution and in his principles; and even his philosophy (that of the new Academy) tended much more to speculation than to practice.   Indifference, to which his temperament would never have led him, was precluded by the situation of the empire.   Impetuous, and restless, and fearless, he converted into love for the one religion that which at first was only hatred for the other, and he proceeded daringly to accomplish what he ardently projected: yet his daring was tempered by so much address and knowledge, that it was not far removed from consummate prudence.

With Constantine.   But if we had space for such disquisitions, more interesting and perhaps more profitable contrast might be drawn between the situation and conduct of Julian and of Constantine. Both arrived at the possession of unlimited power, through great difficulties, chiefly by means of their personal talents and popularity; both, on reaching the throne, found the religion of the state different from their own, and followed by the majority of their subjects; and both determined to substitute that which himself professed.   The grand difference was this—the religion of Constantine (we may be permitted for one moment to treat the subject merely politically) was young and progressive ; it stood on principles which proved its excellence, and ensured its durability; the only weakness which it acknowledged was that of immaturity.   The religion of Julian had for ages been held in derision by all reasonable men ; its energy had long passed away from it, and its feebleness was the decrepitude of old age.   So that the one led on to certain victory an aspiring assailant ; the other endeavoured to rally a shattered, undisciplined, dispirited fugitive.

Progress of Julian in the practice of persecution.   Let us next examine the manner in which Julian proceeded to the accomplishment of his hopeless enterprise.   His first step was in direct imitation of the first act of Constantine.   He published edicts which established the religion of the emperor as that of the state, and which tolerated every other.   By such decrees he placed Christianity in a very similar situation to that in which, about fifty years before, his uncle had placed Paganism ; and he further increased this resemblance by inviting the most eminent philosophers to his court, admitting them to his confidence, and raising them to the highest dignities and offices in their religion.   His second step was the natural consequence of the first ; he took away the immunities, honours, and revenues, which had been bestowed on the Christian clergy, and transferred them to the service of the established religion—and though great individual injustice was thus perpetrated, no one can reasonably complain of the *principle* of this transfer, since such advantages are necessarily conferred by the state on those who profess the religion of the state.   His first edicts, while they restored to Pagans their civil rights, do not appear to have violated those of the Christians : but by a subsequent regulation he disqualified the Christian laity from office in the state.   This measure was attended by another, founded on a deeper principle, and of much more dangerous consequence—*he forbade any Christian to lecture in the public schools of science or literature;* and this prohibition not only obliged the Christian youth to have recourse to Pagan instructors, but also deprived them of one of the greatest encouragements to proficiency. Julian was sufficiently instructed in the nature of his project, to perceive that it would be of little avail to oppress the dissentients by vexatious restraints, unless at the same time he could degrade them by ignorance*.   His last measure (for which we have the authority of the historian Socrates) was the direct imposition of a tax on all who refused to sacrifice to the gods of the empire.

Considering that the reign of Julian lasted not two years, we must admit that, while he developed a perfect knowledge of the theory of persecution, he made very rapid progress in the practice of it ; and had he been suffered by Providence much longer

---

* A contemporary Christian writer (Gregory Nazianzen) tells us of another method adopted by Julian in order to bring the religion into disrepute, which proves how low his enmity was contented to descend, for the sake of inflicting one additional and ignoble wound. He commanded by edict (νομοθετήσας) that Christians should no longer be called Christians, but Galileans. There was some art in this attack; for the value of a *name*, which is every where of some influence, has especial importance among orientals.

to persist in his aggression, with proportionate increase of severity, it is probable that the final triumph of Christianity would not otherwise have been achieved, than by means of a religious war. But the provinces of the civilized world were saved from that severest infliction by the death of the emperor.

His reform of Paganism.

As Julian was either too sincere a religionist, or at least too wise a politician, to wish to deprive his subjects of all religion, he accompanied his labours for the subversion of Christianity by some judicious attempts to render paganism more durable. But this scheme could scarcely have hoped for any great success, even had it been undertaken at an earlier period, when the vices of that religion had been less openly exposed and acknowledged: when its shrines were less generally deserted; and when the mere moral superiority of its rival was less manifestly and notoriously exhibited. He appears to have directed his exertions to three points:— 1. To conceal or disguise the absurdity of its origin and nature by moral and philosophical allegories; 2. To establish ecclesiastical discipline and policy on the model of the Christian Church; 3. To correct the morals of the priesthood.

For the first of these purposes he found materials already provided by the philosophers of his own sect, the Platonists; who had been employed, especially since the appearance of Christianity, in refining the theology of paganism. In pursuance of the second, he planned an establishment for readers in that theology; for the order and parts of the divine office; for a regular and formal service, with days and hours of worship; and with respect to the third, he enjoined to the priesthood (whom he seemingly would have established as a separate order), as well as to their household, great severity of personal behaviour, and strictly to withhold themselves from all vulgar amusements and ignoble professions. While he imitated the discipline of the Church, he was willing also to emulate her moral excellencies; and therefore he decreed the foundation of hospitals and other charitable institutions, and particularly recommended to the ministers of religion the virtues of charity and benevolence. He did not live to complete, or probably to mature, these designs; but the above sketch is sufficient to prove the extent of the beneficial influence which Christianity had already exerted, even over those who were not persuaded of its truth; and to show that the only art by which its formidable adversary could affect to supplant it, was by an ungraceful endeavour to resemble it*.

But Julian, with all his authority and address, could scarcely hope to substitute that which was known to be a shadow, for that which was believed to be real and substantial. It therefore became necessary for his design to overthrow the foundations on which Christianity rested, or at least to disclose their weakness. One of the most important and influential of these was the accomplishment of so many ancient prophecies, tending, as it were to a common centre, to the establishment of its truth. Among those prophecies, there was no one which excited such general admiration, and so strangely perplexed the unbelieving, as that which related to the destruction of the Temple of Jerusalem; not only as it had been once and signally fulfilled by the arms of Titus, but as the consequent dispersion of the nation and abolition of the law had already continued for nearly three hundred years to be a subject of appeal and triumphant argument with the defenders of Revelation. Julian doubtless perceived that if he could remove that ground of faith, many would be persuaded that the ancient books of the Christians had no better title to divine inspiration than the Homeric rhapsodies, or the Orphic hymns; and that the exclusive claim to TRUTH, which distinguished the religion from every superstition, had in fact no solid foundation. We can scarcely be mistaken in considering this to have been his leading object, when, in the year 363, he undertook to rebuild the Temple.

This was indeed to attack Christianity on the only ground on which any lasting advantage could be obtained, or on which its overthrow could possibly have been effected. The persecution of its professors was certain to terminate in a re-action

His attempt to rebuild the Temple of Jerusalem,' 363, A. D. (margin note)

---

* Julian has not, after all, the credit of originality in this attempt. It had been previously made, on a smaller scale, by Maximin—who established priests in all the principal towns, and a high priest in every province. The high priest was to be a man of superior rank, and it was his office to appear and sacrifice, dressed in white and surrounded by soldiers, &c. See Euseb. viii. s. 14. et ix. s. 4. et Lactantius de Mort. Penit. c. 36.

favourable to them; the reform and adornment of paganism was only a ridiculous and contemptible mockery; but the falsification of one prophecy would have reduced the worship of Christ, as far as its origin was concerned, to a level with that of Jove: so that we need not wonder at the ardour with which its adversaries engaged in this attempt, at the suspicion with which some wavering Christians beheld it, at the joy of anticipated triumph which it excited in true believers*.

Extraordinary obstacle.

The historical facts are simply these:—the work was undertaken with some parade, under the superintendence of Alypius, an officer of rank and reputation, a pagan, and a personal friend of the emperor; and the workmen were proceeding to clear away the ruins, and lay bare the old foundations, when an earthquake and tempest, accompanied by fire from below, and a strange appearance in the heavens, tore the foundations asunder, destroyed or dispersed those engaged in the labour, and consumed the materials; and this, it clearly appears, not once only, but on repeated attempts. Many of those who survived bore about with them lasting marks of fire, and the work was immediately suspended, and never afterwards renewed. These facts are the result of the combined evidence of four contemporary authors†, one of whom, Ammianus Marcellinus, was

* Twice previously, during the reigns of Adrian and Constantine, the Jews had expressed a disposition to rebuild the Temple with their own hands; but the Imperial permission was withheld from political causes in the first instance, and from religious, or from both, in the second.

† Ammian. Marc., lib. xxiii., c. i. Ambrose, Epist. xi., t. ii. Chrysostom adv. Jud. et Gentiles. Gregory Nazianzen, Orat. iv. adv. Julian. The passage of Ammianus at least requires insertion; and we should observe, that *alone* it does not go to the full extent of the account which we have given. "Diligentiam ubique dividens imperiique sui memoriam magnitudine operum gestiens propagare, ambitiosum quoddam apud Hierosolymam Templum, quod post multa et interneciva certamina obsidente Vespasiano posteaque Tito ægrè est expugnatum, instaurare sumptibus cogitabat immodicis; negotiumque maturandum Alypio dedit Antiochensi, qui olim Britannias curaverat pro præfectis. *Cum itaque rei idem fortiter instaret Alypius, juvaretque provinciæ Rector, metuendi globi flammarum prope fundamenta crebris adsultibus erumpentes fecere locum exustis aliquoties operantibus inaccessum; hocque modo elemento destinatius repellente cessavit inceptum.*" The epistle of Ambrose is addressed to the emperor Theodosius, and Chrysostom was not far distant from the spot when the event took place. Both these writers speak of it with brevity, as notorious and undisputed. But Gregory enters into more detail; and, besides the circumstances mentioned in the text,

a pagan, a zealous admirer of the emperor, and resident with his master at Antioch when the event took place.   To the circumstances above narrated others of a more extraordinary nature were at different periods * appended, some of which are indeed consistent with physical probability, but others are manifestly the superstitious exaggerations of later ages.   The truth of the outline which we have given cannot reasonably be contested, nor is it at all affected by some variations in the details, implying diversity, but no contradiction.

But, though the facts be undisputed, the question has still been moved and argued with much ingenuity, whether the convulsion in question was a phenomenon merely natural, or occasioned by divine interposition; and as that question is usually proposed, the fairest method of stating it appears to be this. In a very critical period of the history of Christianity, the highest earthly authority, having declared against it, proceeded to apply the severest test, not only to the constancy of its professors, but to the truth of the faith itself; (and in this respect the attempt of Julian differs in character from those of any preceding persecutor.)   The trial was made in the most public manner, in the very birth-place of the religion, in the eyes of the whole civilized world; and as the world was still divided (and perhaps not very unequally divided) between the rival religions, the result would be necessarily expected with attentive anxiety by the votaries of both.   Under these circumstances Julian undertook to falsify the prophecies of God, and thus most assuredly to overthrow the belief which rested on them. Again, the mountain on which the Temple of Jerusalem had stood was not so constituted, as either from its frame or situation to be probably the scene of a natural eruption; history speaks but of one other commotion, confined particularly to that hill, which took place at another critical conjuncture, the moment of the Crucifixion; and from the days of Julian to

Attempts to account for it.

relates a miraculous closing of the doors of a church in which the workmen would have taken refuge, and the impression of the figure of the Cross on the dress and persons of those present.   This last phenomenon is very ingeniously and even probably explained by Warburton.

* The miracle is related about half a century afterwards, with the addition of various particulars, by Rufinus, Socrates, Sozomen, and Theodoret.

this time, the convulsion has not ever been repeated. It remains then for us to consider, whether it be less improbable,
that God should have interposed for the confirmation of his
religion at the moment when its truth was put to a most public
and insulting proof; than, that a mountain hitherto quiescent,
and ever since so, should have undergone a natural convulsion,
and thrown forth destructive fire from physical causes, at that
very crisis (and at that crisis only) when the test was applied,
and the insult offered; that the eruption should have been confined to the particular spot in question; that it should have
continued as long as the attempts were repeated; and that it
should have ceased when they ceased, when its seeming purpose was effected, for ever: and thus we might fairly leave it
to any unprejudiced mind to decide, whether such a concurrence
of fortuitous circumstances *at such a conjuncture* were more or
less credible than a miracle.

But the question is not yet exhausted; a very plausible explanation of the phenomenon has been recently published, and
received with an attention, of which, perhaps, it is not undeserving*. The greater part of the city of Jerusalem was
undermined by very extensive subterranean vaults and passages †, which were used as cisterns, or magazines, or places of
refuge, or sepulchres, according to political circumstances, or
their own form and situation. We learn that the cisterns alone
furnished water during the siege to the eleven hundred thousand
inhabitants, for whom the fountain of Siloa was insufficient; and
we find, that when resistance became hopeless, the most active
among the insurgents formed the project of secreting themselves
in those recesses until the Romans should have evacuated the
city. Some remains of such excavations may still be observed
both in the city and in the adjacent mountains. Now it may
reasonably be supposed, that during the long period of deso-

---

* It appears to have been first proposed by Michaelis, quoted by Guizot in his
translation of Gibbon's History. It is very reasonably treated by the judicious
writer in the Encyclop. Metropol. (Life of Julianus), and still more lately has been
adopted, with too little hesitation or comment, by the author of " The History of
the Jews."

† See Tacit. v. 12.   Dio, 66. p. 747.   Josephus, Bell. Jud. vii. 2., and Antiq.
Jud. xv. c. xi. sect. 7.

lation which intervened between Titus and Julian, those vast caverns, being obstructed by rubbish and ruins, would remain untenanted, and probably unexplored; and thus the workmen of Alypius, when they proceeded with torches to examine and penetrate the gloomy labyrinths, might be terrified and expelled by frequent explosions of inflammable air. On a spot singularly congenial to superstitious apprehensions, under circumstances peculiarly calculated to awaken and encourage them, such natural detonations might readily be ascribed, even by some of those who witnessed them, to extraordinary interposition; and certainly the multitude of the Christians who heard the story, being as familiar with miraculous tales as they were ignorant of the mysteries of nature, would receive it unhesitatingly, as an especial proof of divine protection. Such might naturally be the case; and suspicious as we should always be of any attempt to substitute plausible conjecture for facts historically proved, how marvellous soever their character, we are not prepared to reject the above explanation, though by no means impatient to embrace it. At least we should observe, that, if it satisfies the description of Ammianus, it is not applicable to some of the circumstances mentioned by the Christian authorities; so that these must be condemned and sacrificed to it, and our belief entirely confined to the pagan account. And even then it will remain with many a matter of wonder, that Alypius, a dignified and enlightened pagan, assisted by the presence of the governor of the province, and acting almost under the eyes of the Emperor himself, should have finally abandoned a project esteemed by his master of immense importance, through a fortuitous impediment, of which the cause could scarcely be concealed from him, or the facility of overcoming it. And after all, it will remain at least questionable, whether the gases generated in those caverns were not of a nature more likely to extinguish, than to produce, combustion.

A few months after this event Julian was killed in battle; and the succession of Christian Emperors was then restored, and never afterwards disturbed. Henceforward the advance of religion upon the receding ranks of paganism encountered little resistance, and was conducted with singular rapidity; still we do not observe in the religious policy of the immediate successors of Julian any violent disposition to direct the pursuit.

Valentinian.

Valentinian I. placed his pride in the most impartial and universal toleration.   We may have observed indeed that some of the pagan Emperors commenced with the same professions a reign which ended in persecution;   and we have seen that both Constantine and Julian hastened to deviate from the generous principles which they first proclaimed.   But Valentinian is scarcely, if at all, liable to this reproach ; and though in other matters he was guilty of some passionate exertions of unnecessary severity, and though he neglected to restrain the Arian intolerance of his brother Valens, which afflicted the Catholics in the East, he appears himself to have maintained throughout the whole Western empire a perfect civil equality, as well between the religions which divided it, as among the sects of each religion*.

The short reign of Gratian, which likewise commenced with great professions of moderation, was rather remarkable for some laws against Heretics, than for any deliberate attack on Paganism.   Nevertheless that worship was unable to survive the political patronage by which alone it had so long subsisted; it seemed to have lost its only principle of existence as soon as it ceased to form a part of the system of Government† ; left to its own energies it discovered the secret of its decrepitude, and so easy and uninterrupted was the process of its dissolution, that it seemed patiently to await the final blow from any hand disposed to inflict it.

Theodosius the Great.

Theodosius I. is the Emperor to whom that achievement is

---

* " Inclaruit hoc moderamine principatus quod inter religionum diversitates medius stetit, nec quenquam inquietavit, neque ut hoc coleretur imperavit, aut illud ; nec interdictis minacibus subjectorum cervicem ad id quod ipse coluit inclinabat, sed intemeratas reliquit has partes, ut reperit."—Ammianus Marcellinus. Was there any emperor of those days (if we except the short rule of Jovian) who can share this honour with Valentinian ?

† We may remark that, by some of the earliest laws against Paganism, Divination was permitted, while Magic was forbidden ; because the former was a public ceremony, instrumental for political purposes, while the latter was the private and individual exercise of a similar description of art.   The object of both was superstitious deception, but the government would not permit the people to be deceived except by itself.

usually, and, if to any individual, justly, attributed. He ascended the throne in the year 379, but he does not appear to have published his famous law until thirteen years afterwards. It was to this effect—" that no one, of whatever rank or dignity or fortune, whether hereditary or acquired, high or humble, in what place or city soever he may dwell, shall either slay a victim to senseless images; or, while he addresses in private expiation the Lar, the Genius and the Penates, with fire, or wine, or odours, light torches, or burn incense, or suspend garlands in their honour; but if any one shall immolate a victim in sacrifice, or consult the panting entrails, that any man may become his informer, until he receive competent punishment, &c. &c." The execution of this law, and of others to the same effect, was no doubt much facilitated by the zeal of Christian informers; and there could be few who would suffer martyrdom for a religion*, which, as it rested on no evidence, could offer no certainty of recompense; and, therefore, the consequence of the Edict of Theodosius was a vast diminution in the number of professed Polytheists. This change was most immediately perceptible in the principal cities of the empire, throughout which the superstition for the most part disappeared; thenceforward it was chiefly confined to the small towns and villages (or *pagi*); and about that time it was that the name *Pagan* (or Rustic, Villager) was first adopted to designate those who adhered to Polytheism.

The prohibitions contained in the above edict are impartially levelled against every condition of Heathen; yet their weight and efficacy must clearly have fallen upon the lower classes: for among the higher and better informed, though there might be many who had not yet embraced Christianity, there could at

---

* The bold resistance of an officer of high rank and character, named Gennadius, to a very impolitic edict of Honorius, has been produced as a solitary instance even of the *disposition* to suffer in the cause of Paganism. Honorius had forbidden any except Christians to wear a girdle or sash at court, and Gennadius in consequence declined to present himself there. The emperor then expressed himself willing to make a particular exception in favour of an officer who was at the moment necessary to him, but Gennadius refused that distinction, and persevered in his opposition so resolutely, that the emperor finally repealed the invidious law. See Zosimus, lib. v.

that time have been extremely few, who either felt or affected any ardent attachment to a worship, which professed no moral principles, and offered no temporal advantages*. The vulgar persevered in it somewhat longer, from habit, from prejudice, and from ignorance; but these motives were not sufficient long to sustain them against the laws of the empire, and the authority of their superiors, and the example of their neighbours, all combining to propagate a more excellent and more reasonable faith.

But we are not to imagine that the number of real converts to Christianity was at all in proportion to that of the seceders from paganism; for persons who are forced out of any sort of faith will not readily throw themselves into the arms of that whence the compulsion has proceeded. However, time and patience might have remedied this disinclination, and led those converts (or at least the succeeding generation) to a sincere affection for a pure religion, if the purity of that religion had not been already corrupted by the intemperate zeal of its own professors.

Horror of Idolatry among the early Christians.

We have noticed indeed certain abuses which had already shown themselves even in the iron days of Christianity, and there are others yet unnoticed by us, of which the earliest vestiges and indications may probably be discovered in the practice of the ante-Nicene Church, or in the writings of its Fathers; but among these idolatry certainly is not one. The ancient Christians continued to shun with a pious horror, which persecution exasperated, and which time did not mitigate, every approach to that abomination; and while they truly considered it essentially and distinctively Pagan, the reluctance which they felt to bow before any image was aggravated by the firm belief, that the images of the Pagans represented the implacable adversaries of man and God. So definite and so broad was the

---

* A celebrated Pagan, Libanius, published even in this age an apology for his religion. His work was not suppressed, nor himself removed from one of the most important offices in the state, which he then held. While the emperor was engaged in destroying the *practice* of Paganism, he might easily accord to a favourite subject the innocent indulgence of writing its defence; for he knew that it was not by reason but by habit that the worship would subsist, if it could possibly subsist at all.

space which in this point at least separated the two religions, that it seemed impossible that either of them should overstep it, or that any compromise could ever be effected between principles so fundamentally hostile. Yet the contrary result took place; and a reconciliation, which in the beginning of the fourth century could not easily have been imagined, was virtually accomplished before its termination.

Let us trace the progress of this extraordinary revolution. Veneration for Martyrs. On the first establishment of their religion, it was natural that Christians should look back from a condition of unexpected security on the sufferings of their immediate predecessors, with the most vivid sentiments of sympathy and admiration. They had beheld those sufferings, they had beheld the constancy with which they were endured; the same terror had been suspended over themselves, and their own preservation they attributed, under the especial protection of divine Providence, to the perseverance of those who had perished. The gratitude and veneration thus fervently excited were loudly and passionately expressed; and the honours which were due to the virtues of the departed were profusely bestowed on their names and their memory. Enthusiasm easily passed into superstition, and those who had sealed a Christian's faith by a martyr's death were exalted above the condition of men, and enthroned among superior beings. Superstition gave birth to credulity, and those who sat among the Powers of heaven might sustain, by miraculous assistance, their votaries on earth; and credulity increased the food on which it fed, by encouraging the detested practice of forgery and imposture. Under these dangerous circumstances it became the duty of the fathers and the leading ministers of the Church to moderate the violence of popular feeling, and to restrain any tendency towards vicious excess. But, unhappily for the integrity of the Catholic faith, the instructors were themselves carried away by the current, or, we should rather say, united their exertions to swell and corrupt it. The people we may excuse and compassionate: but we blush when we discover the most distinguished writers of the fourth century, Athanasius, Eusebius the historian, Gregory Nazianzen, Chrysostom, Jerome, and Augustine, engaged in shameful conspiracy against their religion, while they exaggerate the merit of the martyrs, assert or insinuate their immediate sanctification, and claim for them a sort of reverence which could not easily be distinguished from worship. In this age, and from this cause, arose the stupid veneration for bones and relics : it was inculcated and believed that prayer was never so surely efficacious as when offered at the tomb of some saint or holy person ; the number of such tombs was then multiplied ; at all of them miracles, and prophecies, and prodigies, and visions, were exhibited or recorded ; and the spirit of the Gospel was forgotten in the practice of forbidden ceremonies, and the belief of impious fables.

Compromise with Paganism.

Such were the first unworthy advances which were made by Christianity, and encouraged by her leading ministers, with a view to reconcile at least her external differences with Paganism*. And, no doubt, they were very effectual in alluring those easy Polytheists, whose piety was satisfied with numerous festivals in celebration of the exploits of mortals deified; for with them the change was only in the name of the Deity, not in the principles of the religion. At the same time, it must be observed that the Pagans on their side made the concession of sacrifice, or at least of immolation, which was the centre of their whole system. They were indulged with a sort of Polytheism of saints and martyrs ; and even sensible objects of worship were not withheld from them. But those Beings and Images were to be approached only with prayer and supplication; and if it was presently found expedient to permit *offerings* to be made to them, their shrines were never contaminated by the blood of victims. By this degrading compromise the Church was filled by numerous converts, who believed, and who were

* In the year 410, Synesius, a Platonic philosopher of Cyrene, was ordained Bishop of Ptolemais by Theophilus of Alexandria. Synesius remonstrated against this election, declared himself to be a Platonist, and specified several points in which his speculative opinions differed from those of the Christians. But as he was an agreeable orator, and had much influence in the province, his objections were overlooked, and after receiving baptism he entered upon his episcopal functions. This is far from being the only instance of the pliancy of the early Church, at a period too when it had no excuse from fear or persecution.

probably taught to believe, that the worship which they had deserted was by no means essentially dissimilar from that which they had embraced, and who continued, after their admission, to perpetuate and exaggerate those corruptions by which alone the resemblance was created.

Here then we discover the root of several of the abuses of Papacy; they were concessions made during this critical period to the genius of paganism, in order to delude its votaries into more speedy apostacy, and to accelerate the dissolution of the one religion into the other.   The immediate object was accomplished—to diminish the numerical display of Polytheism, and prematurely to crowd the churches and processions with nominal Christians; and this was merely to anticipate the tardy but certain operation of irresistible causes, and to effect that in appearance, which in the next generation would have been surely consummated.   But the lasting result has been, to darken and disfigure the features of Christianity, not in one race only, or for one age, but through a period, of which fourteen centuries have already been accomplished, and of which we cannot yet foresee the termination.

Arcadius and Honorius succeeded respectively to the thrones of the East and West, and they followed the steps of Theodosius in his warfare against paganism, as well as heresy.   Arcadius was more distinguished in the latter contest, though he proceeded to some extremities against the temples and idols of Phœnicia.   Honorius is more honourably celebrated by the law which abolished the Gladiatorial Games.   This institution, the most barbarous that ever disgraced a civilized nation, was the genuine offspring of the character and morals of Pagan antiquity; and it was supported through the extinction of human feeling, and the contempt of human life.   It was not suppressed until the year 404, or about ninety years after the first establishment of Christianity—so slow is the influence of the most perfect moral system to undermine any practice which time and use have consecrated.   But at length it sank before the gradual prevalence of happier and more natural principles; and while we record its subversion, as marking an important epoch in the

Abolition of Gladiatorial Games, 404, A.D.

history of human civilization, we readily assign to it a corresponding rank in the annals of Christianity.

Severities exercised against the Pagans.

Theodosius the younger succeeded Arcadius in the empire of the East; and we may consider him as having completed, as far as the limits of his authority extended, the task transmitted to him by his father, and his grandfather. And whether from greater moderation of temper, or because extreme rigour was judged no longer necessary against a fallen adversary, he somewhat mitigated the severity of the existing laws; and was satisfied with inflicting upon the few, who still persisted "in their accursed sacrifices to dæmons," the milder punishments of confiscation and exile, " though the crime was justly capital*." From the flexible character of Polytheism, and the rare mention of Heathen martyrs, we are perhaps justified in drawing the consoling conclusion, that those oppressive laws were seldom enforced to the last penalty. Yet we cannot doubt that many less direct, but not less effectual, modes of persecution were diligently exercised; we are assured that numbers must have suffered in their persons or property for a blind but conscientious adherence to the worship of their fathers; and we should have celebrated with greater satisfaction the final success of our religion, if it had been brought about by less questionable measures.

Extinction of Paganism.

In the West, the expiring struggles of Paganism continued perhaps a little longer. Though the exhibition of gladiators had been abolished, the games of the circus, and the contests of wild beasts were still permitted; and though the essence of the Pagan religion was virtually extinguished, when the act of *Immolation,* in which in truth it consisted, was finally abolished, yet those spectacles were so closely associated with its exercise, if they were not rather a part of it, that they served at least to keep the minds of the converts suspended, by seeming to reconcile with the principles of Christianity the barbarous relics of the old superstition. And thus, though the number

---

* The Theodosian code is a collection of the constitutions of the Emperors from Constantine to Theodosius II., published by the latter in 438.

who professed that worship was now exceedingly small, yet its practice in some measure survived its profession, and it continued to linger in the recollections, and usages, and prejudices of men for some time after its name was disclaimed and repudiated. Still from the historical survey of this subject, it is manifest that the mortal wound was inflicted by Theodosius I.; and whatever fleeting vestiges we may discover in succeeding reigns, the superstition was in fact extinct from the moment that the Emperor called upon the Senate of Rome to make their election between that and Christianity. This celebrated assembly was convened in the year 388; Christianity was established by the voice, and probably by the conscience of a very large majority; and the religion of Julian did not in reality survive its enthusiastic votary and reformer for more than twenty-five years.

Christianity established by the Roman Senate, 388, A. D.

NOTE ON CERTAIN PAGAN WRITERS.

1.—The first whom we propose to mention (first in time and personal distinction rather than in literary merit) is *Julian.* His " Lives of the Emperors," his predecessors, in which we find many pointed remarks and illustrations of their several characters, and especially of their defects, though possessing neither the fulness nor impartiality of history, must nevertheless be considered his most important work. That next in celebrity bears the singular name of the Misopogon, or Beardhater. The imperial satirist seems to have been excited to this composition by the appearance of certain anapæsts, published in ridicule of his personal rusticity, among his lively subjects of Antioch or Daphne. He admits the justice of their ridicule, he affects even to exaggerate the cause of it, and condescends to visit his own shaggy exterior with much humorous severity. But through the levity of his self-condemnation some traces of suppressed asperity are occasionally discernible; and the wit, which had dared to trifle with an emperor, was not recommended to Julian by the general belief, that it had proceeded from the pen

The Emperor Julian.

of a Christian. Besides these two works, several epistles and
rescripts are extant, which are of greater historical importance.

That Julian's feeling towards the Christians was not the contempt of a philosopher, but the angry malevolence of a Pagan
and a rival, appears from several passages in his works, and
from those especially which are directed against Athanasius.
In his Epistle to Ecdicius, Eparch of the Egyptians, we find
these passionate expressions,—" I swear by the great Serapis,
that unless Athanasius, the enemy of the gods, shall be wholly
expelled from Egypt before the calends of December, I will
impose a fine of a hundred pounds of gold on the troops under
your command; and you know that if I am slow to condemn,
I am still more so to relax the sentence. For it does exceedingly afflict me, that all the gods should be contemned through
his means ; nor is there anything that I would so willingly behold or hear accomplished by you, as the expulsion of Athanasius from the regions of Egypt—the scoundrel who has dared,
and in my reign too, to persecute some distinguished Grecian
ladies, till they submitted to baptism." Again, in a decree
addressed to the Alexandrians, the emperor declares, "that he
had recalled the Galilæans, who had been banished by Constantius*, not, *to their churches*, but only to their countries;
while I understand, (he adds) that Athanasius, with the extreme insolence and audacity which is characteristic of him,
has taken possession of what they call the episcopal throne."
He then decrees his exile. In a subsequent letter, (Edit. Par.
p. 330.) addressed to the same people, he expresses his hatred
both of the persons and doctrines of the Galilæans in the most
powerful and passionate language. On the other hand he acknowledges, in more than one passage, the charitable attention
which those same Galilæans bestowed upon the poor, and
ascribes much of their success to that virtue ; and the general
spirit of his instructions respecting their treatment, while it
enjoins a preference to the worshippers of the gods†, decidedly
discourages unprovoked severities against the persons of " the

---

* In a very kind epistle to Ætius, a celebrated Arian bishop, and formerly his
friend, Julian mentions the same fact.

† Προτιμᾶσθαι μεντοι τους θεοσεβεις και πανυ φημι δειν.   Epistle to Astabius.

Atheists." At the same time, he seems very readily to have availed himself of the offences of the Christians, in order to plunder them, and that too with perfect impartiality. In an epistle to Ecebolus he complains that the Arians of Edessa, exulting in their opulence, had made an assault upon the Valentinians; and he adds, " that with a view to assist them in effectuating the instructions of their own admirable law, and that they might more easily travel to the kingdom of heaven, he had ordered all the possessions to be taken away from the Church of Edessa; distributing the money among the soldiers, and confiscating the fixed property."

A passage in the Misopogon proves either the abject super- His superstitiousness of the author, or his impudent and prejudiced stition. hypocrisy; and though we believe the former to be the more probable charge, we are willing to leave the decision to his most devoted admirers. The story is well known of the religious disappointment which he experienced at Daphne; how he entered the temple with extraordinary parade and solemnity, for the purpose of presiding at a public and splendid sacrifice, and how he was reduced, by the universal desertion of the votaries of the gods, to the performance of an imperfect, and almost solitary act of devotion. In his relation of this story, in which his angry embarrassment is almost ludicrously depicted, he unreservedly asserts, and invokes the sun to attest his veracity, that, at the moment of his entrance into the temple, the statue of the god indicated to him what was to take place*.

His celebrated epistle respecting the reformation of Paganism His atis addressed to Arcadius, the chief priest of Galatia; it is the tempt to reform Pamost remarkable monument of the religious policy of Julian, ganism. and it is also an evidence of the great and general influence which Christian principles had acquired even over the conduct of unbelievers. The progress of "impiety or Atheism" is ascribed by the emperor chiefly to three causes: to the charitable or hospitable philanthropy of its professors; to their provident care respecting the sepulture of the dead; to their parade and affectation of a holy life: and he enjoins the vo-

* Επεσήμηνέ μοι εἰσελθόντι πρῶτον τὸ ἄγαλμα. p. 112. Ed. Paris.

taries of the ancient worship to imitate the first of these pretensions, and to realize the last.   On the priests especially, as well
as their families and their servants, he imposes a rigid attention
to their religious duties, and he forbids them at the same time
the amusement of the theatre, the conviviality of the tavern, and
the exercise of every vulgar profession; the disobedient are to
be removed from the ministry.   The emperor then proceeds to
order the foundation of numerous establishments (Ξενοδοχεῖα)
in every city, for the humane purpose of hospitality and charity:
" for it is shameful to us, that no beggar should be found among
the Jews, and that the impious Galilæans should support not
only *their own poor, but ours also ;* while these last appear
destitute of all assistance from ourselves."   And that Pagan
authority may not be thought wanting to justify his philanthropy, he cites a passage from Homer in praise of hospitality.
He concludes with some instructions to regulate the intercourse
and define the respective dignities of the religious and civil
authorities.

Ammianus
Marcelli-
nus.

2. The name of *Ammianus Marcellinus* deserves, even at the
hands of the ecclesiastical historian, more elaborate mention
than can here be bestowed upon it.   A native of Antioch, of
noble family, he devoted his youth to military service, and
attended Julian, his patron and friend, in his fatal expedition
against the Persians.   During the reign of Valentinian and
Valens he appears to have withdrawn to studious repose in his
native city, and under Theodosius he finally fixed his residence
at Rome.   It was here that he composed his history in the
Latin language, and published it with the general applause of
a people, among whom the admiration of literary merit had
survived its possession.   The work consisted of thirty-one books,
comprising the affairs of the empire from the beginning of the
reign of Nerva to the end of that of Valens.   The first thirteen
are lost, and those remaining have escaped to us as from a shipwreck, torn and mutilated*.   Respecting the religion of the
author, there can be no serious doubt that he adhered to Pagan-

---

* See the Life of Ammianus Marcellinus by Valesius, which we have chiefly
followed in this account.

ism; though the impartiality, with which he commonly treats the deeds and character of Christians, has led some writers to suspect his attachment to their faith. The suspicion is at least honourable to the historian; and a more faithful imitation of his example would have removed many stains from the pages of ecclesiastical annalists, and spared much perplexity to those who search them for information and truth.

3. The history of *Zosimus* extends from the time of Augustus Zosimus. to the second siege of Rome by Alaric: it consists of five books, and the fragment of a sixth, into the first of which the reigns of the predecessors of Constantine are compressed. Zosimus was a prejudiced, and, as some miraculous descriptions attest, a superstitious Pagan; and he treats with severity, perhaps with injustice, the character of some of the Christian emperors. Julian is his great hero, and Constantine the principal object of his censure. Respecting the latter, it has been observed, that we may safely believe any evil that has escaped from Eusebius, and any good that has been extorted from Zosimus. But these combined would furnish very scanty materials for the delineation of a great character. We must believe much more than these; and in this matter the panegyrics of the Christian are not, perhaps, more liable to suspicion than the aspersions of the Pagan writer. Howbeit, by far the greatest proportion of his attention is bestowed on the details of military enterprise, and it is not often that he crosses the more peaceful path of the ecclesiastical historian.

CHAPTER IX.

From the Fall of Paganism to the Death of Justinian.
(388 . . . 567.)

I. Conversion of the Goths—of Clovis and the Franks—of other Barbarians—
causes of its facility—Miraculous interpositions. II. Internal condition of the
Church—Symeon and the Stylites—Pope Leo the Great—Papal aggrandisement—private confession—Justinian, his orthodoxy, intolerance, and heresy.
III. Literature—its decay not attributable to Christianity—three periods of its
decline—Religious corruptions—Barbarian conquests—Seven liberal arts—Justinian closes the Schools of Athens—early connexion of Philosophy with Religion—Morality—of the Clergy—of the People—general misery—Note on certain Fathers of the fourth and fifth centuries.

THAT we may treat with some perspicuity the long period over
which the two following chapters are extended, we shall separate
in each of them the external progress and reverses of Christianity
from the internal conduct and condition of the Church, and the
character of those who ruled and influenced it.

Conversion
of the Bar-
barians.
I. Christianity had scarcely completed its triumph over an
ancient superstition, refined and embellished by the utmost
human ingenuity, when it was called upon to dispute the possession of the world with a wild and savage adversary. Almost
at the very moment when Julian was labouring for the re-
establishment of Paganism, Ulphilas*, who is commonly called
the apostle of the Goths, was diffusing the knowledge of the Gos-

---

* Ulphilas is believed to have been the descendant of a Cappadocian family
carried into captivity by the Goths, in the reign of Gallienus. His conversion to
Arianism is referred to his embassy to the court of Valens in 378, and on his return home he diligently diffused that heresy. It would appear, however, that
his method of seduction was to assure the Goths, that the disputes between the
Catholics and Arians were merely verbal, not at all affecting the substance of
the faith—so that his success was gradual, and at first imperfect : thus, for instance, in the time of Theodoret, the Goths avowed their belief, that the Father
was greater than the Son ; but they were not yet prepared to affirm that the Son
was created—though they continued to communicate with those who held that
opinion. Fleury, H. E. liv. xvii. sect. 36. Tillem. (Sur les Ariens, Art. 132, 133)
pronounces an eulogy upon his virtues, in spite of his heresy ; and yet he adds,
" Voilà comment un homme entraîna dans l'enfer ce nombre infini des Septen-
trionaux, qui avec lui et après lui ont embrassé l'Arianisme."

pel with great rapidity among that young and powerful people: so that the first invaders of the empire had previously learnt in their own land to profess, or at least to respect, the religion of the empire.   The Goths then were early and easy proselytes to Christianity; and the example of their conversion, as well as of their invasion, was followed by the various hordes of barbarians who presently overran and occupied the West.   The Burgundians in Gaul, the Suevi in Spain, the Vandals in Africa, the Ostrogoths in Pannonia, and others, as they successively possessed themselves of the Roman provinces, during the fifth and sixth centuries, successively adopted the religion of the conquered; and if Rome, in her days of warlike triumph, received from vanquished Greece some taste in arts, and attainment in science, and skill in philosophical disputation, she repaid her private obligation with more solid and extensive generosity in the days of her decline, when she instructed her own conquerors in those lessons of religious truth and moral knowledge, of which the principles can never change, nor the application ever be limited.

It is impossible to trace with any certainty the exact moment Of Clovis. and circumstances of the conversion of so many tribes.   That of Clovis, king of the Franks, has attained the greatest historical celebrity, and many of the particulars respecting it wear great appearance of probability*.   In the year 493 Clovis espoused Clotilda, niece of the King of the Burgundians, a Christian and a Catholic.   He tolerated the religion of his bride, and showed respect to its professors, especially to St. Remi, Archbishop of Rheims; but he steadily refused to abandon his hereditary idols on the importunity either of the prelate or queen.   At length he found himself in a situation of danger. In the heat of an unsuccessful battle, while his Franks were flying before the Alemanni, Clovis is related to have raised his weeping eyes to heaven, and exclaimed, "Jesus Christ † ! thou

* Those which we select, together with many others, are related on the authority of Gregory of Tours, and Hincm. Vita San. Remigii. See Fleury, liv. xxx. sect. 46.

† "Jesu Christe, quem Chrotechildis prædicat esse Filium Dei vivi, qui dare auxilium laborantibus, victoriamque in te sperantibus tribuere diceris, tuæ opis gloriam devotus efflagito: ut si mihi victoriam … indulseris .. credam tibi, et

whom Clotilda asserts to be the Son of the living God; thou, who art said to succour those in difficulty, and to give victory to all who trust in thee! I implore thy succour. If thou wilt give me the victory, I will believe in thee, and be baptized in thy name." At that moment the King of the Alemanni was slain; his soldiers immediately fled, and abandoned the field to Clovis. The victor was not unmindful of the God of his adversity. On the conclusion of his expedition he caused himself to be publicly baptized; about three thousand of his soldiers attended him to the holy font with joy and acclamation, and the rest of his subjects followed without any hesitation the faith of their prince. The conversion of Clovis took place in 496; and though it had not the effect of amending the brutal character of the proselyte, it made a great addition to the physical strength of Christianity*; and it was attended by a peculiar circumstance which places it among the important events of ecclesiastical history. The numerous barbarian conquerors who then ruled the Western empire had embraced, without any exception, the heresy of Arius; Thrasamond, King of the Vandals, in Africa; Theodoric, of the Ostrogoths, in Italy; Alaric, of the Visigoths, in Spain; Gondebaud, of the Burgundians, were all Arians; and, as if to complete the heterodoxy of the princes of Christendom, even Anastasius, the Emperor of the East, was involved in the Eutychian heresy. Clovis alone adopted the Catholic faith; and this accident (we are taught to attribute it to the orthodoxy of his wife) was probably the earliest cause of that close connexion between the Court of Burgundy and the See of Rome, of which some traces may be discerned even thus early, and which, in a later age, was confirmed by Pepin and established by Charlemagne.

in nomine tuo baptizer, &c." *Gregorius Turonens.* Historia Francorum, lib. ii. s. 30. ann. 496. Gregory's History extends from the creation to the year 591: it is continued by Fredegarius, a Burgundian, and probably a Monk, to 768. Both compositions are nearly barren of any valuable ecclesiastical information. Gregory was born at Auvergne about 540. A. D. His History is in Ten Books; and he wrote besides, Four Books, " De S. Martini Miraculis," and a great number of " Vitæ Patrum."

* Clovis, immediately after his baptism, made some considerable donations of land to St. Remi, who applied them to the use of divers churches, and the foundation of the bishopric of Laon.

The success of the Roman arms during the reign of Justinian, which began about thirty years after the baptism of Clovis, does not appear to have disinclined the barbarians to the religion of their enemies. It might even naturally produce the contrary effect; and we do not read of any of their tribes which, after settling in a conquered province, were disposed long to resist the influence of the Gospel.

Respecting the *natural* causes which facilitated this powerful accession to the body of Christianity from a quarter whence the darkest danger was portended, it is proper to suggest a few brief observations, that we may be enabled calmly to consider, whether or not they are sufficient to account for the phenomenon without the intervention of miraculous assistance. The wild and warlike Polytheists of the north, who estimated excellence by power, and power by extent of military sway, and who ignorantly applied to the gods the rules by which they judged of men, approached with respectful predisposition the Deity of the Roman empire*. And if it be true that their own successes gradually tended to abate this respect, yet is it not possible that they could fail to observe, or observe without some sense of reverence and humiliation, the superiority in arts and sciences, the high intellectual pre-eminence of the people whom their mere sword had overthrown; nor would they hesitate to infer, from such sensible indications, both the wisdom and beneficence of the protecting Divinity. Again—The form of idolatry which they professed was most peculiarly characterised by a superstitious veneration for their priesthood;—it had no written law, nor any fixed principles, nor any very attractive immemorial solemnities. In a foreign country, in the licence of a military expedition, the reverence for their native, and for the most part

Probable causes of their conversion.

---

* The conversion of the Burgundians, early in the fifth century, is thus related, with no improbability. Harassed by the continual incursions of the Huns, and incapable of self-defence, they resolved to place themselves under the protection of some God; and considering that the God of the Romans most powerfully befriended those who served him, they determined, on public deliberation, to believe in Jesus Christ. They therefore went to a city in Gaul, and entreated the Bishop to baptize them. Immediately after that ceremony they gained a battle against their enemies, and continued zealous in faith ever afterwards—ἐξ ἐκείνου τὸ ἔθνος διαφόρως ἐχριστιάνισιν. Socrat. vii., cap. 30.

absent ministers, would gradually abate in fervency and fidelity; and then (such is the nature of superstition) it would
change its object, and swell into devout respect for the ministers of the unknown religion, by whose more imposing rites
they were now surrounded and dazzled. By this process, being
insensibly weaned from an ancient worship, chiefly perhaps
endeared to them by its association with that home which they
had now deserted for ever, they would join in the splendid
processions, and bend in the stately temples of the Christians.
Of such advantages as these the clergy were not slow to avail
themselves; and their own great superiority in penetration and
learning, joined with a zealous and interested activity*, enabled
them to convert the mass of the invaders; while the Prince, as
illiterate as his subjects, was often influenced by the address,
and often by the piety, of the prelates who had access to his
court. The same work was still further facilitated by the example of the Goths, who had opened the gates of Christianity
to succeeding conquerors. Nor should we by any means pass
over the exertions of the missionaries, who had previously introduced into the native forests of the invaders a favourable
opinion, and even a partial profession, of the religion of the
empire which they were destined to subvert.

Claims to
miraculous
aid.

These reasons are probably sufficient to account for the facility with which the various invaders of the western provinces
adopted the religion which they found established there, even
without any deep examination into its merits or its truth; but
the histories of those times are so abundant in preternatural
tales of extraordinary conversions everywhere wrought by the
continual interposition of Providence, that we must not quite
overlook this consideration. However, we can here entertain

---

* At a Council supposed to have been held at Braga, or Braccara, in Portugal,
in the year 412, on the irruption of an idolatrous or Arian host of Alani, Suevi and
Vandals, the Bishops prepared themselves to resist at every risk the destructive
torrent. For this purpose they appear to have adopted two measures, which,
taken together, are strongly indicative of the state of religion in that age and
country. The first was to publish an abbreviation of the Creed of the Catholic
church; the second, to conceal in the securest recesses and caverns the invaluable relics of their saints. Fleury, H. E. lib. xxiii., sect. 6. Concil. tom. ii.,
p. 1508.

little doubt, or feel any strong hesitation to affirm, that the very great proportion of those miraculous stories is wholly and unquestionably fabulous*. But we must be careful that our indignation at the impiety, which fabricated so many wicked impostures, and the diligent mendacity, which has retailed them, do not so far prevail as to hurry us into an entire disbelief of *any* divine intervention in those ages. To pronounce so sweeping a sentence, in the confusion of contemporary evidence, and our necessary ignorance of the dispositions of Providence, would approach too near to presumption; and we shall, therefore, do better to leave this subject where the judicious moderation of Mosheim † has placed it :—

'How far these conversions (he says) were due to real miracles attending the ministry of those early preachers is a matter extremely difficult to be determined. For, though I am persuaded that those pious men who, in the midst of many dangers, and in the face of obstacles seemingly invincible, endeavoured to spread the light of Christianity through the barbarous nations, were sometimes accompanied by the more peculiar favour and succour of the Most High; yet I am equally convinced, that the greatest part of the prodigies recorded in the histories of this age are liable to the strongest suspicions of falsehood or imposture. The simplicity and ignorance of the generality in those times furnished the most favourable occasion for the exercise of fraud ; and the impudence of impostors in contriving false miracles was artfully proportioned to the credulity of the vulgar, while the sagacious and the wise, who

* Unbelievers and heretics were closely associated in the language and opinion of the Catholics of those days, and were consequently subjected to the same mode of cure. In the fourth century even the great St. Ambrose condescended to adopt the miraculous method of argument for the conversion of the Arians. He used, in his disputes with those Heretics, to produce men possessed with devils, who, on the approach of certain Catholic relics, were obliged by preternatural compulsion to acknowledge with loud cries that the doctrine of the Council of Nice was true, and that of the Arians both false and of most dangerous consequence. This testimony of the Prince of darkness was regarded by St. Ambrose as unquestionable and conclusive (Mosh. c.iv., p. 2., c. 3), nor was it easily answered by adversaries who made less pretension to influence in the other world.

† Cent. v., p. 1. c. 1.

perceived these cheats, were obliged to silence, by the danger which threatened their lives and their fortunes, if they detected the artifice. Thus does it generally happen in human life, that when the discovery and profession of the truth is attended with danger, the prudent are silent, the multitude believe, and the impostors triumph."

Changes within the Church. II. While the profession of Christianity was thus extending itself among so many nations, the changes which were gradually taking place within the Church were by no means favourable to its purity. We have already mentioned the copious transfusion of heathen ceremonies into the Christian worship which had taken place before the end of the fourth century, and, to a certain extent, paganized (if we may so express it) the outward form and aspect of religion : those ceremonies became more general and more numerous, and, so far as the calamities of the times would permit, more splendid in the age which followed. To console the convert for the loss of his favourite festival, others of a different name, but similar description, were introduced ; and the simple and serious occupation of spiritual devotion was beginning to degenerate into a worship of parade and demonstration, or a mere scene of riotous festivity. Various were the forms assumed, and numerous the excesses occasioned, by religious corruption ; which was by no other circumstance more plainly evidenced, or more effectually promoted, than by the growing prevalence of the monastic spirit.

Symeon the Stylite. It is contrary to our general purpose to call much attention to instances of the passing fanaticism of the day—those transient eruptions of superstition, which have left no deep traces in history, or in their moral consequences; nevertheless, we cannot forbear to record one very extraordinary shape which the phrensy of those times assumed. About the year 427, one Symeon, at first a shepherd, afterwards a monk, of Syria, invented a new method of penitential devotion. Dissatisfied with the insufficient austerities which were practised in his convent, he retired to a mountain in the neighbourhood of Antioch, where, by solitary self-inflictions and extreme abstinence, he obtained great provincial celebrity; but his piety or his ambition were not thus easily contented, and accordingly he devised an original and more difficult path to sanctity. He caused a pillar to be erected, of which the height was gradually increased from nine to sixty feet; thereon he established his residence. His ordinary occupation was prayer; and habit and exercise enabled him to take, without risk or difficulty, the different postures of devotion. Sometimes, especially on great solemnities, he assumed an erect attitude, with his arms outstretched; sometimes he bent forward his body, attenuated by continual fasting, till the forehead touched the feet; and he repeated those inclinations with marvellous flexibility*. He passed the whole night and a part of the morning in worship; one slender meal in the course of a week sufficed for his sustenance, and a coarse vestment of skin, which wrapt his whole body, was his only covering: in this situation he endured the returning inclemencies of thirty seasons, and at length died, without descending from his column.

It is no matter of reasonable astonishment, that the passionate enthusiasts of the east thronged eagerly round the pillar of Symeon from the most remote provinces, and regarded the self-devoted martyr with feelings partaking of adoration. Nor are we, in any degree, surprised to read, that he converted to Christianity the inhabitants of Libanus and Antilibanus, and an entire tribe of Arabs, together with several Jews and heretics, by miraculous aid and operation. Nor, perhaps, have we cause to think it strange, that this popular fanaticism was rather encouraged than disclaimed by the Church †; and that it has

---

* " A curious spectator (says Gibbon), after numbering 1244 repetitions, at length desisted from the endless account." Theodoret, who had frequently seen and conversed with him, wrote an account of his life during its continuance. That author himself entertained some doubts as to the credibility of his narration: although (says he) I have for my witness, if I may so express myself, every man in existence, yet I fear that to posterity my account may appear a groundless fable; for what is passing here is above humanity, and men are wont to proportion their belief to the powers of nature, and all which surpasses those boundaries appears falsehood to such as are not familiar with things divine.

† It is true that when Symeon first ascended his pillar some opposition was made to the *innovation* by some monasteries both of Syria and Egypt; but as their objections were confined to the novelty of the scheme, and did not proceed from its absurdity, they speedily disappeared, and Symeon was restored with unanimity to the bosom of the Catholic church.

descended to posterity without any ecclesiastical stigma of schism or heresy. But our amazement is reasonably excited, when we learn that Theodosius II. seriously consulted Symeon the Stylite on the most important concerns of Church and State*; and that the Emperor Leo particularly solicited his advice respecting the council of Chalcedon—whether those princes really shared the popular madness, and considered him as a soothsayer or prophet, to whom bodily mortification, and a loftier residence had disclosed a nearer prospect of the secrets of futurity; or whether they were only willing to gain credit with the silliest among their subjects by encouraging their most absurd superstition. However this may be, Symeon became the founder of a sect of fanatics called "Stylites" (or Pillar-men); who, under the names of "Holy Birds" and "Aërial Martyrs," peopled the columns of the east; and, after imitating (so far as their physical powers permitted them) the ascetic gesticulations of their master, have escaped, in more fortunate oblivion, the sinister celebrity which still attends his name.

Leo the Great. 440 A.D. We have now traced the history of the Roman See to the middle of the fifth century, and our attention has not hitherto been arrested by the character of any individual who has occupied it. Not one man remarkable for commanding genius, or profound acquirement, or even great ecclesiastical energy, had, up to this period, distinguished the chair of St. Peter. We have no cause to lament this circumstance. The truly episcopal duties of devotion and charity are usually performed in silent unobtrusiveness; and the highest interests, and the truest happiness of the human race, have commonly been best promoted by those, of whom Fame has made least mention. But this long period of comparative obscurity was at length terminated by Leo, surnamed the Great. That prelate ascended the chair of St. Peter in the year 440, and occupied it for one and twenty years. At his accession, he found the eastern Church still agitated by the receding tempest of the Nestorian controversy;

---

* Gibbon, chap. xxxvii. Fleury, liv. xxix, sect. 9. The Emperor Marcian is also said to have indulged his curiosity by a secret visit to the Holy Pillar in the throng of his miserable subjects.

and the heresy of Eutyches, immediately succeeding, introduced fresh disorders, which continued to disturb his long pontificate. In the west, the success of the barbarians in Africa and Gaul presented a new and extensive field for ecclesiastical exertion; while we are taught, at the same time, to believe that the internal lustre of his Church was darkened and endangered by the prevalence of the Manichæan heresy. The zeal of St. Leo was directed to all these points; and, perhaps, if he had evinced less eagerness in the discovery* and pursuit of his domestic adversaries, the very circumstance of their existence might never have been known to us. It is a singular fact, however, and worthy of notice, that one of the tests which he employed for their detection, was their refusal of the *cup* in the sacrament of the Lord's Supper. Indeed, Pope Gelasius very shortly afterwards published a decree, which shall here be recorded †, on the same subject. But in justice to Leo, we are equally bound to praise his firm co-operation with the eastern church for the peaceful repression (had such been possible) of the perverse notions which perplexed and divided it; nor are there wanting many salutary expositions of doctrine and reasonable rules of discipline, scattered throughout his numerous writings ‡.

* Baronius (chiefly ad ann. 443) gives several proofs, from the Chronicon of Prosper and St. Leo's own writings, of the diligence of that Prelate in tearing those heretics from their hiding-places, and publishing their infamy. It also appears that until that period it had been usual for all Christians to direct their prayers to the East; but as this form was with the Manichæans essential, with the orthodox only matter of ceremony, he directed the latter to discontinue the practice, in order that the perverse might be distinguished and detected by their perseverance. In the year 444 he even held a Council at Rome against them, and made a speech against the abominable sect, "in qua lex est mendacium, Diabolus religio, sacrificium turpitudo." There is also a passage (in his 95th epistle) in which he advocates the unsheathing of the temporal sword in vindication of the doctrines of the Church. "Profuit diu *ista districtio* ecclesiasticæ lenitati, quæ, etsi sacerdotali contenta judicio cruentas refugit ultiones, severis tamen Christianorum principum constitutionibus adjuvatur, dum ad spiritale non-nunquam recurrunt remedium, qui timent corporale supplicium."

† "Comperimus quod quidam, sumpta tantummodo Corporis Christi portione, a Calice sacri Cruoris abstineant: qui proculdubio . . aut integra Sacramenta percipiant, aut ab integris arceantur: quia divisio unius ejusdemque mysterii sine grandi sacrilegio non potest provenire." We are not aware how the Roman Church, for the last six centuries, has got rid of this charge of *sacrilege,* proceeding from so venerable an authority.

‡ One hundred and forty-one Epistles and ninety-six Sermons still remain to us,

The circumstances of the times were favourable to another object, which, with Leo, indeed, may possibly have been secondary, though it occupied the foremost place in the attention of so many of his successors—the aggrandisement of the Roman See. In the East, it happened about that time that the patriarch of Constantinople, by the assumption of some additional power*, had alienated the Bishops of Alexandria and Antioch, and that these last appealed to Rome for succour and justice. Of course, the authority, which such appeal might seem to imply, was at no time recognised by the patriarch—it was even decided, during this very pontificate, by the twenty-ninth canon of the council of Chalcedon†, that the "See of New Rome should have the same advantages with that of Antient Rome in the ecclesiastical constitution;" but, nevertheless, the influence of the latter was extended, for the moment at least, among the subjects of the former, by the dissensions which severed them from their head. And, again, the accidents which placed the Bishop of Rome in familiar and almost independent correspondence ‡ with the emperor, could not fail to exalt his name and elevate his dignity. In the western provinces, the increase of Papal authority was owing to other causes. The declining power, the indolence and the absence of the emperors, left little civil control over the authority of the bishop who presided in

though several of both are lost. Upon the whole they indicate great talents, and an improved and exercised mind. Respecting their genuineness, see Dupin, t. iii. p. 2.

* Mosh. cent. v., p. ii. c. ii.

† Held in 451. The substance of the enactment is as follows:—"That the Fathers did reasonably accord its privileges to Antient Rome, *because it was the imperial city;* and for the same reason the hundred and fifty Bishops here assembled have decided that New Rome, which is honoured with the empire and the senate, shall have the same advantages with Antient Rome in the ecclesiastical constitution, and *be the second after it*"—meaning, obviously, that the two Sees were to be independent in power and equal in privilege; but that in rank and precedence the superiority was due to the more ancient. This Canon has given birth to the most voluminous contentions. Fleury, liv. xxviii. sect. 30. Baron. ann. 451. Sect. 148.

‡ Some Epistles are still extant, addressed by St. Leo to the Emperor Theodosius, on the subject of the Eastern controversies; and one of them begins in the following terms:—Quantum præsidii Dominus ecclesiæ suæ in fide vestræ clementiæ præpararit, his etiam literis, quas ad me misistis, ostenditur: ut vobis non solum regium, sed etiam sacerdotalem animum esse gaudeamus, &c."

the imperial city; and the incursions and triumphs of the barbarians rather contributed to advance than to restrain his rising dominion.　For the chiefs of the invaders, whose principal solicitude was to give stability to their government, when they perceived the great deference paid by the multitude to the hierarchy, courted even the inferior members of that body, but naturally offered the most obsequious respect to the highest in rank.　From these and similar causes a variety of advantages spontaneously flowed, and they were seized and perpetuated by the genius and ambition of Leo.

One innovation in the discipline of the Church was introduced by that pontiff, which deserves more attentive notice than is usually directed to it.　It had been the custom for the more grievous offenders to make the confession of their sins publicly, in the face of the congregation; or at least for the ministers occasionally to proclaim before the whole assembly the nature of the confessions which they had received.　Leo strongly discouraged that practice; and permitted, and even enjoined with some earnestness, that confession should rather be private, and confided to the priest alone.　The evil most obviously proceeding from this relaxation was the general increase, or, at least, the more indecent practice, of the mortal sins, and especially (as Mosheim* has observed) of that of incontinence; unless, indeed, we are to suppose that the original publicity of confession was abandoned, from its being no longer practicable in a more numerous body and corrupt age.　But another consequence which certainly flowed from this measure, and which,

Institution of private confession.

---

* Cent. v. p. 2. ch. iv.　The epistle containing this ordinance is the 136th, addressed (on March 6, 459) to the Bishop of the March of Ancona and Abruzzo. Dupin, Nouv. Biblioth. tom. iii. par. ii.　The words of the decree are given by Baronius, ann. 459. sect. ult., and should be cited.　" Illam contra Apostolicam regulam præsumptionem, quam nuper cognovi a quibusdam illicita usurpatione committi, modis omnibus constituimus submoveri—*ne de singulorum peccatorum genere libellis scripta professio publicè recitetur*—cum reatus conscientiarum sufficiat *solis sacerdotibus* indicare *confessione secreta* . . . . Sufficit enim illa confessio, quæ primum Deo offertur, tum etiam *sacerdoti, qui pro delictis pœnitentium precator attendit.*　Tum enim demum plures ad pœnitentiam poterunt provocari, si publicis auribus non publicetur conscientia confitentis."　We should observe, that even in introducing this innovation St. Leo is not ashamed to plead the apostolical usage.

in the eye of an ambitious Churchman, might counterbalance
its demoralizing effect, was the vast addition of influence which
it gave to the clergy.   When he delivered over the conscience
of the people into the hands of the priests,—when he consigned
the most secret acts and thoughts of individual imperfection to
the torture of private inquisition and scrutiny,—Leo the Great
had indeed the glory of laying the first and corner-stone of the
Papal edifice—that on which it rose and rested, and without
which the industry of his successors would have been vainly
exerted, or (as is more probable) their boldest projects would
never have been formed.

Justinian,   From the name of St. Leo we may proceed without interruption to that of Justinian*; who ascended the throne of Constantinople in the year 527, and occupied it for nearly forty
years.   This emperor is most honourably known by his legislative labours, and the digest of a code of laws, which, in a
later age, obtained general and durable reception throughout
Europe, and which are not in all places obsolete at this moment.   A different and secondary description of celebrity is
reflected on him by the success of his generals, Belisarius and
Narses, against the invaders of the West; but, for our own part,
we are not disposed to think, that he would have made any
addition to the extent, or improvement in the nature, of his
reputation, had he deserted the pacific duties for which he was
well qualified, to place himself at the head of armies† without
disposition or experience for command.   He deputed to his
soldiers the sanguinary task of conquest, and confined his own
talents to those offices, which he justly considered to be more
truly imperial.   Among the first and favourite of these he
placed the regulation of the religious affairs of his subjects.
His own faith was distinguished by the most rigid orthodoxy;
and his theological studies had at least conducted him to sound

* Of the jurisdiction of the clergy, which was the most acknowledged exercise
of their power and the most direct cause of their influence, it will be better to
defer all mention until we come to treat of the acts of Charlemagne.

† The trumpet of Gibbon (upon the whole a humane historian) is too often
and too loudly sounded in celebration of military prowess, and the pomp of camps,
and the virtues of heroes—the favourite themes of vulgar minds, and the easiest
incentives to vulgar enthusiasm.

doctrinal conclusions. But he had studied with more success the tenets, than the history, of his religion; or he would have learnt from the sad experience of two centuries, that neither the canons of councils, nor the oppression of civil power, are sufficient to restrain the wanderings of human opinion. He devoted a large portion of his long reign to the extinction of his intole-heresy; he waged war with equal fury* against the remnant rance, of the Arians, the Nestorians, and the Eutychians; he expelled them from their churches, which he transferred, together with their public possessions, to the Catholics; and, finally, he descended to individual persecution, and confiscated the private property of many. Whatever ambiguous excuses may be found for his other proceedings, the guilt of this last robbery is usually attributed to his sordid avarice. In spite of those measures (shall we not rather say, in consequence of them?), the fifth General Council (assembled at Constantinople during his reign) conferred upon him the title of "The Most Christian Emperor;" not foreseeing that, by one of those strange dispositions of Providence which seem to mock at human calculation and consistency, the very monarch whom they had exalted by that glorious distinction—due, indeed, to the purity of his faith, but forfeited by his intemperance and bigotry,—was destined to die a heretic! † A foolish dispute had been raised at that time, whether the body of Christ on earth was or was not liable to corruption; and this divided Oriental Christians into the two sects of Corruptibles and Incorruptibles. The latter were obviously involved in the heresy of the Phantastics; and yet Jus- and heresy. tinian, in the blindness of old age, adopted that opinion; and it is even believed, that he was preparing to persecute all who differed from him, when he fell sick and died.

---

* He appears to have taken pains to search for them—a detestable exaggeration of persecution. He assailed with the same ardour both pagans and astrologers; and his severities against the Samaritans, who had obtained a place in the long list of heretics, excited and justified their rebellion; and it was not suppressed without horrible carnage. On the other hand, he exerted himself with equal vigour against various forms of impiety and immorality (Fleury, liv. xxxii. sect. 27.); and was no less zealous in the conversion of the Heruli and other barbarian tribes to the belief in the Gospel, than in oppressing all who did not interpret that Gospel as he did.

† The history of Henry VIII, of England furnishes an instance at first sight similar to this.

Our censures on the religious policy of Justinian, though at variance with the usual language of ecclesiastical historians, require no justification—but it is proper to clear that emperor from the more odious imputation of having created the system, which he so zealously administered. The sentence of banishment pronounced by Constantine against Arius and his followers, however speedily regretted and revoked, was the grand and authoritative precedent to which every Catholic persecutor of after-times appealed with pride and confidence. That which was an experiment—an injudicious and fruitless experiment— with Constantine, became a principle or a habit with most of his successors, each of whom enacted such penalties as seemed suited to repress the errors of the day; but it was reserved to Theodosius II. to complete the work, and to confirm and embody the scattered edicts of bigotry and despotism. There is no space here to enumerate the severe laws against heretics, which may be found in the Theodosian code*; it may suffice to say, that they extended to almost every denomination of dissent, and menaced the contumacious with confiscation, intestation, exile, as the ordinary punishments—while the " last and *inexpiable* penalty" was suspended over the most formidable innovators. More than this—that emperor actually

Severe laws of Theodosius II.

---

* The following are extracts :—" Quid sensibus excæcatos Judæos, Samaritas, Paganos, et cætera hæreticorum genera portentorum audere cognoscimus! Quod si ad sanitatem mentis egregio legum edicto revocare conemur, severitatis culpam ipsi præstabunt; qui duræ frontis obstinato piaculo locum veniæ non relinquunt. Quamobrem, cum sententia veteri desperatis morbis nulla sit abhibenda curatio, tandem, ne ferales sectæ in vitam, immemores nostri sæculi velut indiscreta confusione, licentius evagentur, hac *victura in omne ævum* lege sancimus—Neminem Judæum, neminem Samaritam, neutra lege constantem, ad honores et dignitates accedere; nulli administrationem patere civilis obsequii, nec defensoris fungi saltem officio. Nefas quippe credimus, ut supernæ majestati et Romanis legibus inimici, ultoresque etiam nostrarum legum surreptivæ jurisdictionis habeantur obtentu et acquisitæ dignitatis auctoritate muniti adversum Christianos, et ipsos plerumque sacræ Religionis Antistites, velut insultantes fidei nostræ judicandi vel pronuntiandi quid velint, habeant potestatem," &c. Again :—" Hinc prospicit nostra Clementia Paganorum quoque et gentilium immanitates vigiliam nostram debere sortiri, qui naturali vesania et licentia pertinaci religionis tramite dissi_ dentes nefarios sacrificiorum ritus occultis exercere quodammodo solitudinibus designantur—quos non promulgatarum legum mille terrores, non denuntiati exitii pœna compescant, ut si emendari non possint, *mole saltem criminum* et *illuvie victimarum* discerent abstinere. Sed prorsus ea furoris peccatur audacia, &c. &c." Leg. Novell. Div. Theod. A. Lib. These enactments of the first, con rmed by the second Theodosius, are in every sense *barbarous*.

appointed *Inquisitors* for the detection of certain specified offenders, and enjoined the most diligent and penetrating search * for the purpose of unmasking them.   It has been observed, that Pope Leo the Great adopted this method for the extinction of the Manichæans; and it is some excuse for the eagerness of the bishop that the mighty footsteps of the emperor lay traced before him.   It would not be just to attach to his name very deeply the guilt of intolerance; nor would we defraud even Justinian himself of such plea as may be found for him in the penal system previously established, in the spirit of the times, in the practice of his predecessors.   Yet should we distinguish—a churchman may be more leniently censured, if he enforce the laws already enacted for the protection of his Church, and calculated, as he may ignorantly imagine, for that purpose.   But a legislator should look more deeply into the records of history and the constitution of human nature; and if, among the venerable statutes of his ancestors he observes one which is founded in manifest injustice, which in its immediate operation occasions confusion and misery, and which in its general efficacy has been proved by long experience to miss the end proposed—to re-enact and perpetuate that statute is not error, but deep and inexpiable crime.

III. We shall conclude this Chapter with a few remarks respecting the literature and morality of the period on which we are employed: for though it may seem impossible to treat so extensive a subject in such contracted limits with adequate fulness, or even with profitable precision, there would be still greater ground of reproach were we to neglect it altogether.

---

* " Summa exploratione rimetur, ut, quicunque in unum Paschæ diem non obsequenti religione convenerint, tales indubitanter, quales hac lege damnamus, habeantur." This seems to have been levelled against the remains of the Quartadecimans. The Encratites, Saccophori, and Hydroparastatæ, are the names which are threatened " summo supplicio et inexpiabili pœna." A law was also enacted to prevent the meetings of the Tascodragitæ—a denomination of persons " who made their prayers inwardly and silently, compressing their noses and lips with their hands, lest any sound should transpire." Basnage, iii. 82. Jortin, vol. iv. ad ann. 381. That any danger either to Church or State could for an instant have been apprehended from such abject and pitiful enthusiasm might have been pronounced impossible, if the history of persecution in every age, howsoever modified and disguised by time and circumstance, did not incessantly attest it to be both credible and probable.

Decline of
Literature.

The decline of Roman literature, between the age of Augustus and that of the Antonines, in chasteness and delicacy of
thought and expression, and even the decay of the language
itself, are instantly perceptible to the classical reader; yet was
it still animated by some of the fire of ancient genius. It had
availed itself of the progress of science and the increased knowledge of man, and it applied that knowledge with immortal
success to history as well as philosophy. But from the reign
of Antoninus to that of Diocletian the fall was sudden and pre-
cipitate. In the barren records of the third century we find no
names of good, few even of indifferent writers; and if the works
of the ancients were more generally diffused and studied than
formerly (which seems uncertain), they were at least much less
diligently imitated, and not an effort was made to surpass them.
It is of importance to remark this fact; because there have been
some so unjust in their hostility to Revelation, or so perverse in
their estimation of history, as to attribute the decay of literature
to the prevalence and influence of the Christian religion. This
charge is very far removed from truth—indeed it is easy to
show that literature had already fallen into deep and irre-
trievable ruin, before Christianity began to exercise any control
over the refinements of society. At the beginning of the third
century, during the parting struggles of learning, the Christians,
numerous as they were, and irresistible in strength, were principally confined to the lower and middle ranks; and even at
the beginning of the last persecution, though they held some
high offices in the court of Justinian, it will scarcely be asserted
that they formed a sufficient proportion of the higher and educated classes, to affect in any great degree the literary character
of the empire*. A very general *moral* improvement they had
undoubtedly introduced among the lower orders: some influence
on the civilization of the people, and even on the policy of the

* The effect which Christianity may have produced on the literature of the
Roman empire in the third century bears some resemblance in character (though
it was far inferior in degree) to that exerted by Puritanism on the literature of
our own country. And if it is true, that the immediate influence of both was, to
a certain extent, hostile, their ultimate operation was certainly to invigorate and
renovate. Some of the fathers of the fourth and fifth centuries write better than
any profane author after Tacitus.

government, they may also have exercised; but complete revolutions in national literature do not originate in those quarters; and even had it been otherwise, we have seen, that, more than a century before that period, the downfall of taste and learning had been irrevocably decreed.

While they speculate on the secondary causes of singular phænomena, historians are sometimes too prone to neglect such as are plain and obvious.   In the present instance these were certainly no other than the prolongation of unmitigated despotism, and the civil confusion, which, in addition to its customary attendants, it so commonly introduced in the succession to the throne.   It is unnecessary to search after remote reasons for the degradation of any people which has been subjected for three centuries to the abuse of arbitrary rule.   And though it be true that Trajan and the Antonines for a moment arrested the torrent of corruption, they were but accidental blessings; and if their personal excellence partially remedied the monstrous depravity of the system, their influence lasted not beyond their life.   Presently the tide resumed its downward course, and its natural and necessary progress was scarcely accelerated either by the crimes of Severus, or the calamities of Decius.   Whether, then, it be reasonable to consider the first period of the decline of literature as closing with the reign of the Antonines, or whether we shall extend it over the barren period, which intervened between the death of Marcus and the establishment of Christianity, it is clear that it proceeded from causes quite independent of that religion.   The second line we may venture perhaps to draw after the fourth council of Carthage, and the third at the expulsion of the Athenian philosophers by Justinian.

During the *second* period, Constantine, Julian and Theodosius successively proposed encouragements to learning, and bestowed personal honours on those possessing it.   If Julian confined his rewards to Pagan, and Constantine to Christian, literature, the greater effect (owing to the longer duration of his reign) was produced by the latter—the same is true of the exertions of Theodosius; consequently, during the last half of the fourth and the beginning of the fifth century, the Church abounded with prelates of splendid talents, and laborious industry, and such learning as was then thought most necessary. The Christian writings of this period, to whatsoever objections they may be liable, constitute the best part of its literature. And in so far as they are censured (and justly censured) for the occasional display of vain speculation about things not determinable, of unfair representation, of perverse disputatiousness, of absurd or unworthy arguments, it is a question, whether the lucubrations of the schoolmen and rhetoricians of Rome or Greece give less ground for the same reproaches : for in a mere literary point of-view, it matters little, whether it be the inscrutable in nature or revelation on which the wayward imagination wastes itself ; and as these latter researches are more likely to deviate into a moral character, so is there a better prospect of their utility. And in justice to most of the Fathers of this period we should add, that there are many splendid illustrations of scripture, and many generous bursts of moral exhortation, which enrich and ennoble their works, and which surpass the ardour, if they do not rival the elegance, of profane philosophy.

Fourth Council of Carthage. 398 A. D. A canon of the council held at Carthage * in the year 398 forbade the study of secular books by bishops ; and we have therefore selected this as a crisis in the history of *Christian* literature. Assuredly a deplorable dearth of learning very soon followed this crisis, and our *third* period is distinguished by scarcely two or three names respectable for talents or acquirements. However, we do not at all intend to attribute this rapid defection to the injudicious ordinance in question ; since

* The celebrated canon in question appears in the midst of several others, generally respecting the episcopal office and duties : their substance is as follows :—" The bishop should have a small residence near the church ; his furniture should be of small price, and his table poorly supplied ; he should sustain his dignity by his faith and his holy life ; *he shall read no profane books,* nor those of the heretics, unless by necessity. He shall take no concern in the execution of wills, nor any care of his domestic affairs, nor plead for any temporal interests. He shall not himself take charge either of the widows, orphans, or strangers, but commit that office to the chief priest—he shall have no other occupation than reading, prayer and preaching. He shall perform no ordinations without the counsel of his clergy, and the consent of the people." See Fleury, liv. xx., sect. xxxii. We are not to suppose that the above canons were everywhere received, or perhaps strictly enforced any where.

its authority was not universal, and since injunctions of that description are seldom obeyed, except by such as are previously disposed to receive them. It was an index, rather than a cause, of the altering spirit of the Church, and as such we record it. The real reasons of that sudden defection, and of the darkness which followed it, are two: the first of these, which alone perhaps might gradually have completed the extinction of sound learning, was the internal corruption of Christianity, and the spreading influence of monachism. An age of prodigies and relics and Stylites was not proper for the growth of genius, or the cultivation of knowledge; and the little of either, which survived in the East, may have owed its existence to the dissensions of the Christians, as much as to their virtues. The second reason was the frequent irruption and final settlement of the barbarian conquerors. This cause was indeed confined almost entirely to the provinces of the West; but the wounds which it inflicted there were deeper and of more extensive influence, than might at first have been apprehended. It afforded a fearful prospect, that those hordes of colonists were wholly uninstructed in literary acquirements, and even generally prejudiced against them. Theodoric himself, the wisest, as well as the best, among their princes, while he respected the superior civilization of the vanquished, despised and disclaimed *that* art, which seemed to be employed for no other end, than to inflame and perpetuate religious controversy. He could never be prevailed upon to learn to read. But the cause which increased and prolonged that mischief, and created many others, was the superstitious disposition which the invaders brought with them. They had learnt, as the rudiments of their own religion, a subservient reverence for their priesthood, and this principle accompanied them into the Christian Church; the priesthood received without reluctance the unbounded homage which was offered to them; their authority grew with that obsequiousness, and their ambition swelled with their authority; and when they found how easily this could be maintained and extended over a credulous people, and how certainly credulity is the offspring of ignorance, they became interested in perpetuating blindness and prejudice.

Subjects of Education.

Some schools indeed still subsisted, and the youth were instructed in what were called the *Seven Liberal Arts;* but these, as we learn from Augustin's account of them, consisted only in a number of subtile and useless precepts; and were consequently more adapted to perplex the memory than to strengthen the judgment. The arts in question were grammar, rhetoric, logic, arithmetic, music, geometry, and astronomy; and those were very rare among the scholars whose studies extended beyond the three first. Moral exhortations began now to be commonly confined to the public reading of "Books of Martyrs" and "Lives of Saints," by which the passions of the vulgar were excited, and their imaginations prepared for the belief of any imposture which it might be expedient to practise upon them. Such were the materials of Christian literature during the fifth and sixth centuries, and such they continued with very little alteration until the eleventh.

The Edict of Justinian, which closed the Schools of Athens, 529 A.D.

Some remnants of the philosophy of ancient Greece still lingered at Athens; and a few degenerate descendants of Plato, Aristotle or Zeno, still exhibited in their half deserted schools the shadow of the lore of former ages. Those teachers had been encouraged by M. Antoninus and Julian, and tolerated by the Christian emperors, and they may have constituted the wisest, and probably the most virtuous portion of the Pagan population; but they had gradually dwindled away into obscurity and insignificance. Nevertheless, Justinian considered their existence as inconsistent with the principles of his government, and consequently issued (in the year 529) that celebrated edict which closed the schools of Athens for ever. The historian of the Church of Christ need not fear to celebrate *any* judicious exertions to enlighten and dignify mankind. And in as far as the genius of philosophy has been employed in the discovery of moral truth, and in effectual exhortations to virtue and magnanimity; in as far as it has taught the science of government on sound and practical principles; in as far as its researches have had no other object than truth, and truth which was convertible to the service and improvement of society—so far we respect its exertions and honour its name, and disdain

the narrow policy which completed its extinction.   But we are
bound to admit, that, long before the period in question, the
abuse of reason had so far supplanted its proper exercise, and
perverted its noble character and purposes, that it constituted
in fact the most active portion of the systems then called philosophical—just as the abuses of religion were then beginning to
form the most conspicuous part of the Catholic system.   To
the connexion of Christianity with philosophy several of those
abuses may be attributed; for at the first moment of their contact, while religion was yet pure, philosophy was already deeply
and vitally corrupted; and the infection of bad principles, whether of reasoning or morality, was too easily communicated.
And thus religion, which is indeed the friend of that true and
useful philosophy whose object is the advancement of society
and the happiness of man, became stained and degraded by its
alliance with controversial sophistry.

There is also another reflection which lessens the indignation so naturally excited in every generous mind by the edict
of Justinian.   The philosophers had declared war against
Christianity at an early period; to their malignity the last and
severest persecution may be partly attributed, and the more dangerous aggressions of Julian were conducted by their spirit, if
not by their counsel; so that, if we cannot excuse the severe
retaliation, which Christianity, in her time of triumph, more
effectually inflicted, at least our compassion for the sufferer is
diminished by the recollection of its hostility and its vices. The
exiled philosophers (seven in number) at first took refuge at the
court of Persia; but finding none of the moral advantages, which
they professed to expect under a different form of government
and worship, they were presently contented to return, on certain
stipulations, and terminate their days under a Christian monarch.

We can scarcely believe that the character of Christian literature was so deeply affected by that act of Justinian, as some
imagine.   Mosheim* appears to consider it as having occasioned

* Cent. vi., p. ii., c. i.   In another place he seems inclined to attribute the
same result (and perhaps with rather more probability) to the decision of the fifth
General Council, by which some of the opinions of Origen, who was a New Pla-
tonician, were condemned.

particularly the extinction of the New Academy, (the descendant of the Platonic school,) and the substitution of the system of Aristotle. It is, indeed, well known that about this period the latter philosophy was gradually gaining ground upon the former in the Christian schools, probably because it was better suited to the contentious spirit of the age; and whatever evils had heretofore been occasioned in the Church by too great reverence for the authority of Plato, and by the boldness of his followers, much wider and more durable calamities were afterwards inflicted upon the Christian world by the universal submission of the human mind to the name of Aristotle. But we are not persuaded that this change was brought about violently: or that the edict, which silenced a few obscure Pagan philosophers, at all generally influenced the learning of Christians; or that any act of legislation could suddenly have effected so general an alteration in the studies and intellectual pursuits of an extensive empire. These mighty changes usually result from the patient operation of general principles upon the morals and habits of a people—the caprice of a monarch has no power to create them; and, perhaps, it is the commonest mistake of historians to attribute too much to the edicts of sovereigns, and too little to the unceasing movement and agitation of civilized society.

Morality of the Clergy and People. Respecting the condition of morals during this period it is impossible to speak with equal definiteness; some indeed do not hesitate to describe them as exceedingly depraved, and in no respect better upheld by the clergy than by the laity[*]: and true it is, that certain laws were enacted, with the specific object of securing the morality, and even of punishing the offences, of the priesthood; indeed when we consider the sort of immunity from civil tribunals which that body in those times enjoyed, we are not surprised that too great general indulgence led to the imposition of occasional and particular restraints. But these by no means prove its universal corruption.

The increased wealth of the Church is mentioned as another and a necessary reason of its increased degradation. But we should not be too indiscriminate in our inference of evil from

* Mosheim, cent. vi., p. ii., c. ii.

that cause.   The ill effects of ecclesiastical wealth, which is generally diffused among the clergy with very great inequality, would be chiefly confined to the more elevated and ambitious members of the hierarchy, and would scarcely extend to the lower and more numerous ranks of the ministry ; besides which we should recollect, that it is at least as common an effect of wealth to enlarge and exalt, as to debase, the character of its possessor.   Even were this not so, the Church, in the sixth century, had certainly not arrived at any dangerous degree of opulence, since the sources, which in after ages so profusely supplied it, were scarcely yet opened.   At the same time, the steady progress of religion, the general conversion of the barbarian conquerors, and the devotion of the converts to their priesthood, are scarcely consistent with the gross immorality, and even total contempt of decency, with which Mosheim charges that order*.   And therefore, without advocating its perfect moral purity, we need not hesitate to believe, that the great majority of its members continued with zeal, though in silence, to execute their offices of piety, and that, though stained by individual scandal, the body was very far removed from general degradation, either in the Eastern or Western empire.

Hitherto we have spoken of the clergy only, and the general morality of the age would to a great extent be regulated by the conduct of that body.   But the political prostration of the Western provinces, overrun by so many savage tribes—the rapid dissolution of the old governments without any stability in those which succeeded them—the subversion of legal security, the substitution of military and barbarous license—these and

---

* " Whence so many laws to restrain the vices and preserve the morals of the ecclesiastical orders, if they had fulfilled even the obligations of external decency, or shown, in the general tenour of their conduct, a certain degree of respect for religion or virtue ?   Be that as it will, the effects of all these laws and edicts were so inconsiderable as to be hardly perceived ; for so high was the veneration paid at this time to the clergy, that their most flagitious crimes were corrected by the slightest and gentlest punishments : an unhappy circumstance, which added to their presumption, and rendered them more daring and audacious in iniquity." These are Mosheim's words ; and some will think that they carry their own confutation with them.   At least we may safely believe, that the flagrant offences of a few notorious individuals have been darkly reflected upon the whole body ; and such has been the misfortune of the Christian priesthood in every age.

other circumstances, aggravating the usual miseries of conquest, occasioned, wheresoever they extended, more absolute wretchedness, both individual and national, than had hitherto been recorded in the history of man; insomuch, that among those who beheld and shared those inflictions, there were many who regarded them as special demonstrations of divine wrath. And as men are ever prone to attribute such chastisements to the most striking revolution of their own day, and as the subversion of the temples of their ancestors was still recent in their memory, some there were, who ascribed the anger of the gods to the establishment and prevalence of Christianity. Since the appearance of that impiety (they said) the Roman power has incessantly declined. The gods, the founders and protectors of that empire, have withdrawn their succour, as their service has been neglected; and now that their worship has been entirely suppressed, now that their sanctuaries are closed, and their sacrifices, auguries and other propitiations rigorously prohibited, they have at length abandoned us wholly, and left the once victorious Rome to be a prey to barbarians*. This foolish delusion was immediately and successfully combated by the eloquence of St. Augustin. In his noble composition, "The City of God†", he confuted the error by irrefragable arguments, and conclusive appeals to the evidence of profane history; and inculcated the more reasonable opinion, that the temporal afflictions which God permitted to devastate the empire were chastisements‡ inflicted by a just Providence for the

---

* Fleury, H. E., liv. xxiii., sect. vii.

† The work was published in 426, after thirteen years had been employed in its composition. It consists of twenty-two books, of which the first ten are devoted to the confutation of the various errors of Paganism, and among others of that which we have now mentioned; while the last twelve establish the truth of Christianity.

‡ Thirteen years afterwards Carthage was sacked by the Vandals: Salvian, a Presbyter of Marseilles, a contemporary author, also considers that event as a signal example of divine justice; and he enlarges with great fervour on the exceeding corruption of that great city. " It seemed as if the inhabitants had entirely taken leave of reason—the streets were filled with drunkards crowned with flowers and perfumes, and infested with every possible snare against chastity; adulteries, and the most abominable impurities were the commonest of all things, and they were publicly practised with extreme impudence. The orphans and widows were oppressed, and the poor were tortured to such despair, that they

correction, not for the destruction, of his creatures.   The error was indeed confuted, and presently died away; but the general dislocation of society, which occasioned it, must have suspended for a time the moral energies of man: and the period of his severest suffering may also have been that of his deepest depravity.

NOTE ON CERTAIN ECCLESIASTICAL WRITERS OF THE FOURTH AND FIFTH CENTURIES.

1. It is probable that LACTANTIUS was a native of Africa, since his first lessons were received from Arnobius, whose school was at Sicca, in that country; but the truth is not positively known, nor the year of his birth.   It is only certain, that he witnessed and survived the persecution of Diocletian, and was selected, in his old age, as preceptor to Crispus, the son of Constantine. He was the most learned Christian of his time ; and the record of his necessitous and voluntary poverty may at least persuade us, that his habits were influenced by the spirit of Christian philosophy which adorns his writings.

prayed God to deliver the city to the barbarians. Blasphemies, too, and impiety reigned there ; many, though professedly Christians, were at heart Pagans, and worshipped the celestial goddess with entire devotion.   Besides which (he adds), the people had an extreme contempt and aversion for the Monks, however holy they might be."   The description is probably exaggerated—yet ecclesiastical historians almost universally admit the corruption of Christians to have been the cause of their chastisement.   Baronius adds another reason—the prevalence of heresy.   At the year 412, he asserts—" Barbari prævalent ubi hæreses vigent." He in other places (ann. 410, 428) declares, that the former might easily have been subdued, if the latter could have been expelled ; and ad ann. 406, 407, he more expressly affirms, that Providence sent the invaders into Gaul for the mere purpose of destroying the heresy of Vigilantius, and that the greatest devastations were committed in the districts where those errors were most deeply rooted. By an opposite, but not less extravagant error, Theodosius, legislating nearly at the same time, attributed even the unseasonable severities of the skies to the prolonged existence of Paganism.   " An diutius perferimus mutari temporum vices irata cœli temperie ? quæ, Paganorum exacerbata perfidia, nescit naturæ libramenta servare.   Unde enim ver solitam gratiam abjuravit ?   Unde æstas messe jejuna laboriosum agricolam in spe destituit aristarum ?   Unde intemperata ferocitas ubertatem terrarum penetrabili frigore sterilitatis læsione damnavit—nisi quod ad impietatis vindictam transit lege sua naturæ decretum ?   Quod ne posthac sustinere cogamur, *pacifica ultione,* ut diximus, pianda est supremi numinis veneranda majestas."

The "Divine Institutions," his most important work, contain a powerful confutation of Paganism, in a style not uninspired with the genius of antiquity. "Lactantius (says St. Jerome*) is as a stream of Ciceronian eloquence; and I would that he had been as successful in confirming our own doctrine as in overthrowing that of others." He was liable indeed to that reproach, and he shared it with all the apologists who had preceded him; his arguments are often feeble, his assumptions sometimes false, and his conclusions not always sound : but his style deserves great praise; and if his diction occasionally rivals the elegant exuberance of Cicero, (and he is commonly compared, and sometimes preferred, to that orator,) the Christian has reached, through the more elevated nature of his subject, a sublimer range of thought and expression, in the field of moral as well as divine philosophy. A nobler conception of the Deity, and a deeper knowledge of his works and dispensations, have occasionally exalted, above the Roman's boldest flights, a genius clearly much inferior both in nature and cultivation.

There is another work still extant, called "The Death of the Persecutors," first printed in 1679, and by many attributed (though probably not with truth) to Lactantius. It is of undisputed antiquity†, and contains some valuable facts not elsewhere recorded ; but it is still more remarkable for an attempt to vindicate the temporal retribution of Providence, by asserting the violent ends of the various persecutors. But an endeavour to pervert, with whatsoever promise of temporary profit, the eternal truths of history, can produce no other lasting effect, than to stain the character of the author, and to throw discredit on the cause which is advocated by falsehood.

Gregory Nazianzen. 2. *Gregory,* son of the Bishop of *Nazianzus,* was born about 320. He was animated by a strong natural love for literary and religious seclusion, and a disinclination to ecclesiastical dignities, of which we are compelled to acknowledge the sin-

* Epist. 13, addressed to Paulinus, bishop of Nola. See Dupin, Nouvelle Biblioth., Vie de Lactance. The Institutions were dedicated to Constantine, *probably* during the conclusion of the last persecution (between 306 and 311), and may possibly have influenced his religious opinions.

† Probably published about 315.

cerity, though it so happened that he occupied, in succession, the sees of Sasimi, of Nazianzus*, and Constantinople. His learning, his eloquence, and his religious zeal preserved him from obscurity, and raised him, in his own despight, from independence and privacy. On a visit to Constantinople, about the year 376, he found the Churches, with only one exception, in the possession of the Arians. In the adversity and humiliation of the Church, he raised his voice against the predominant heresy with boldness and success. Several are believed to have been converted by his arguments; and he continued to instruct and govern the Catholic party, until the accession of the orthodox Theodosius. He was then raised by the command of the emperor and the affection of the people to a dignity which he neither coveted, nor long retained. Some discontents which followed gave him a pretext for resignation, and he died in 389 in the retirement of his native city.

There remain to us about fifty of his Discourses and Sermons, of which the language and sentiments alike argue a moderate temper and a cultivated mind. The most celebrated among them are the third and fourth, which are directed against the emperor Julian. In the seventeenth discourse, delivered on the occasion of some seditious disturbances at Nazianzus, in presenting himself as a mediator between the people and the civil officer, he exalts the authority of the Church in very lofty language. He thus addresses the governor of the city:—"The law of Christ subjects you to my power and to my pulpit; for ours is the authority—an authority greater and more excellent than that which you possess, unless, indeed, spirit is to be subject unto flesh, and heaven unto earth† : you command with Jesus Christ; it is He with whom you exercise your authority; it is He who has given you the sword which you wear, not so much for the chastisement of crime, as for its prevention by terror and by menace." It is curious to reflect, that these principles were thus publicly promulgated (in the year 372) within sixty years

* He was raised to a share of this see, as a kind of *Coadjutor* to his father, and on his death fled from the city, lest the undivided responsibility should then be forced upon him.

† Dupin, a liberal Catholic, throws into his translation of this passage the words *Church* and *Princes,* neither of which came from the lips of Gregory.

from the establishment of Christianity, and within nine from the death of Julian. Yet the character of Gregory was mild and forbearing; his twenty-sixth discourse contains some temperate injunctions respecting the treatment of heretics; and both in that and in other places, while he laments the distractions of the Church, and while he proclaims his own attachment to the Catholic doctrine, he is never so unjust as to ascribe the whole evil to the opposite party, nor so partial as to conceal or to spare the vices and scandals which disgraced his own*.

Gregory of Nyssa.

Gregory is celebrated for his friendship with St. Basil, the father of oriental monachism; and the brother of St. Basil was another *Gregory*, Bishop of *Nyssa*, in Cappadocia. This last was the author of five orations on the Lord's Prayer, besides various Commentaries on Scripture, and discourses on the mysteries, and moral treatises. But the work by which he is most known is his oration on the life of St. Gregory, surnamed Thaumaturgus, or the Wonder-worker. That renowned prelate (he was Bishop of Neocæsarea) flourished about one hundred and twenty years before his namesake of Nyssa; so that the stupendous miracles, which are so diligently recorded of him by his credulous panegyrist, can have no claim on our serious consideration.

St. Ambrose.

3. *St. Ambrose* was born in Gaul, about the year 340, of Roman and noble parents†; he was educated in Italy, and his talents and conduct early raised him to a high civil appointment. In 374, on the vacancy of the see of Milan, a violent dissension arose between the Catholics and the Arians; the bishops of both parties assembled in great numbers, and the tumultuous divisions of the people not only violated the unity of the Church, but seriously threatened the repose of the state. Ambrose was then Governor-General of the province, and he

---

* It should be observed, that in his sixth Discourse (delivered before Gregory of Nyssa) he exalts the honour of the martyrs, and even attributes to them the office of mediators.

† Dupin, Nouv. Biblioth., Vie St. Ambrose. While the infant was one day sleeping in his father's palace, a swarm of bees surrounded his cradle, and after reposing on his lips, suddenly ascended high into the air, and disappeared. Ambrose had been anticipated by Plato—yet the Roman Church has shown no disinclination to adopt the profane miracle.

proceeded in person to compose the disorders. The people were assembled in the principal church, and there he addressed them at length on their civil duties—on social order and public tranquillity. His eloquent harangue produced a very different effect from that which had been (at least professedly) proposed by it, for it was followed by the unanimous acclamatory shout—" We will have Ambrose for our bishop."

Ambrose was *not yet baptized**—what religious instruction he may have received in the schools of the Catechumens is uncertain, and it appears to have been exceedingly slight; but he had not yet been admitted to the communion of the faithful. Yet no difficulty seems to have arisen from this obstacle. Again—the consent of the emperor was necessary for his translation from a civil to an ecclesiastical office. That consent was granted with immediate alacrity. Still there remained one unforeseen impediment to be overcome—the persevering repugnance of Ambrose to the proposed elevation. But the perseverance of the people was not less obstinate. It was in vain that the bishop elect, in order to disqualify himself in their eyes for a sacred office, publicly committed some acts of judicial cruelty and flagrant immorality. The people exclaimed— " Thy offence be upon our heads." It was in vain that he escaped from the city and concealed himself at the residence of a faithful friend; he was discovered and conducted in triumph to Milan. At length, conceiving that the will of God was thus irresistibly declared against him, he submitted to assume the ungrateful dignity.

After having passed through the necessary ecclesiastical gradations he was ordained bishop on the 8th day after his baptism, at the age of 34. His first act was to make over the whole of his property to the Church or the poor; and it should be remarked, that the same charitable disposition continued afterwards to distinguish him. He immediately declared in favour of the Catholic against the Arian doctrine; and though the fury, with which the contest was at that time conducted, reached and infected him, we cannot justly accuse him of hav-

His sudden elevation to the See of Milan.

---

* See Fleury, liv. xvii., sec. xxi., &c.

ing wantonly inflamed it. The Empress Justinia, the widow
of Valentinian, was an Arian, together with her soldiers and
her court; the great body of the people were on the side of
Ambrose; and in the year 385 some violent disputes arose, in
which the bishop maintained his spiritual privileges with a courage and a confidence not unworthy of the brightest ages of
papacy*. From a contest with a passionate woman, he advanced to measure his strength with a wise and powerful emperor. Theodosius the Great had very barbarously avenged
the murder of some imperial officers at Thessalonica by the
massacre of the inhabitants; and as the bishop of Milan had
previously interfered in their favour, he boldly condemned the
sanguinary execution. Theodosius pleaded in his defence the
example of David. " Since then you have imitated his offence
(rejoined the prelate) imitate also his penitence." It appears,
that for the period of eight months the emperor was denied all
access to the holy offices of the Church—the consolation which
was afforded to the lowest of his subjects was refused (as he
complained†) to himself. Finally, after some public humiliation, to remind him of the essential distinctions between the
priest and the prince‡, and the spiritual inferiority of the latter,
he consented to the performance of public penance, as the condition of reconciliation with the Church. This extraordinary
event took place in 390§; and if we have already remarked

---

* The great influence which Ambrose is shown to have possessed over the populace, not to excite only but to compose its tumults, attests the vigour of his character more certainly, than it proves either his virtues or even his eloquence—
though we have no reason to doubt either.

† See Fleury, liv. xix., sect. xxi. The power "to bind and to loose," as delegated by Christ to his ministers on earth, is a favourite theme with St. Ambrose,
and asserted by him in a sufficiently extensive sense.

‡ See Theodoret, book v., c. xviii. Sozomen, lib. vii., cap. 25. "Stop (said
Ambrose to the emperor, as he was entering the sacred precincts) ἐπίσχες. It is not
meet that a man, profane with sin and polluted with unjust blood, tread on the
holy threshold, and enter into communion of the divine sacraments, until he has
done penance—πρὸ μετανοίας."

§ Six years earlier (according to Fleury) St. Ambrose addressed to Valentinian
a letter, in which he strenuously opposed the restoration of the altar of Victory at
Rome, so warmly pressed by Symmachus. It contains these bold expressions—
" What answer will you make, then, when a bishop shall say to you, The Church
cannot receive your offerings, since you have given ornaments to the temples of
the gods ? The altar of Christ rejects your gifts, since you have made an altar for

upon the boldness with which Gregory Nazianzen proclaimed (about eighteen years earlier) the ghostly supremacy of the Church, we must not here omit to observe, that from the conclusion of Diocletian's persecution fourscore years had not yet elapsed, ere a successor of that lawless despot was compelled, by the mere influence of opinion, to humble himself before the unarmed minister of that religion, which his predecessor had designed to exterminate.

Many works of St. Ambrose remain, which exhibit no great indications of literary genius; but they abound in useful moral lessons, which are plentifully interspersed with exhortations to fasting and celibacy, and the other superstitions of the day. It is also recorded, that he performed many astonishing miracles; stories that throw disgrace on an elevated character, which really needed not the aid of imposture to secure respect, and even popularity. He died in 397; and after enjoying universal celebrity during his life, throughout the whole extent of Christendom, he has deserved from succeeding generations the equivocal praise, that he was the first effectual assertor of those exalted ecclesiastical pretensions, so essential to the existence of the Romish system, and so dear to the ambitious ministers of every Church.

4. *St. John*, surnamed, from his eloquence, *Chrysostom* (*i. e.* the Golden Mouthed), was a native of Antioch, of a noble and opulent family. In the year 374, while he was still young, he had acquired such distinction, that the neighbouring prelates elected him to a vacant see; but it is generally affirmed that he refused that dignity, and fled to an adjacent mountain, where he passed four years in the society of an ancient solitary; thence he changed his residence to a frightful cavern, which witnessed for the two following years his rigid austerities. Having completed this preparatory discipline, he entered upon the offices of the ministry; and after edifying his native city for eighteen years by the most animating instructions, he was at once exalted, without solicitation, and even

John Chrysostom.

idols. It was your voice, your hand, your signature—the whole work was yours. The honour which you offer to Jesus he refuses and scorns, since at the same instant you offer adoration to idols. No—you cannot serve two masters," &c. Epistle 17.

against his professed wish, to the see of Constantinople. Chrysostom carried with him to that dangerous eminence not only the fervour of Christian eloquence, but the severity of monastic virtue; and he thought it little to move the affections and raise the admiration of his audience, unless he could reach their practice and quell their vices. Had he confined his exhortations to the mass of the people, he would have produced less effect perhaps, but he would have excited no odium—but the intrepid and earnest orator rose in his vehement denunciations from the people to the clergy, and from the clergy to the court, without excepting even the empress herself from his reproaches*. To the keenness of his censures he added the weight of ecclesiastical jurisdiction, and both were zealously employed against episcopal licentiousness†, no less than against the vices and scandals imputed to the priesthood, and especially to the monastic orders.

But in the tedious and delicate office of ecclesiastical reform, that zeal which is not tempered with moderation, and qualified by due regard for existing circumstances, will commonly ruin the advocate, without benefiting the cause. The disposition of Chrysostom was naturally choleric and impatient, and his noblest intentions were frustrated by his passionate imprudence. Two powerful parties united for his overthrow; and though their first triumph was instantly reversed by an insurrection of the populace, whom his ardent eloquence, the beneficence of his charitable habits and institutions, the austerity of his morals, and the very bitterness of his rebukes, had bound and devoted to him, yet a subsequent condemnation was more effectual; and after a tumultuous rule of six years, Chrysostom was dismissed into exile to a desolate town named Cucusus, among the

* Eudoxia, after failing in her first attempt to displace Chrysostom, renewed her hostilities; and it was then that the bishop delivered the sermon (if indeed he did at all deliver it) beginning with the celebrated words—" Herodias is again furious; Herodias again dances; she once again requires the head of St. John." "An insolent allusion (says Gibbon) which, as a woman and a sovereign, it was equally impossible for her to forgive." Chap. xxxii. The whole account of St. Chrysostom, given by that author, is written with learning, eloquence and fairness.

† In his visitation through the Asiatic provinces he deposed thirteen bishops of Lydia and Phrygia, and passed a very severe censure upon the whole order.

ridges of Mount Taurus.   Still his expulsion was not effected without popular commotions, which led to the conflagration of the principal church and the adjoining palace.   In that remote residence he passed three years, the last, perhaps the most glorious of his life—for his virtues were more eagerly acknowledged in his absence, and his genius was endeared, and his errors were obliterated, by his misfortunes.   About thirteen years afterwards his relics were removed to Constantinople, and his name has assumed an eminent place among the saints of the Church : and it is proper to add, that the justice, which was so abundantly bestowed on the memory of Chrysostom, should in a great measure be attributed to the perseverance of the bishop of Rome; whose sympathy had consoled him in his adversity, and whose influence, had his life been much prolonged, might eventually have restored him to his dignity*.

The works that remain of St. Chrysostom are for the most part Sermons and Homilies, and are nearly a thousand in number.   Their style is not recommended by that emulation of Attic purity which adorns the writings of Basilius, or Gregory Nazianzen; but it is elevated and unconstrained, pregnant with natural thoughts and easy expressions, enriched with metaphors and analogies, and dignified by boldness and grandeur.   And, what is more important, the matter of his discourses, while it declines the affectation of subtlety, and avoids the barren fields of theological speculation, is directly addressed to the common feelings, and principles, and duties of mankind.   The heart is penetrated, the latent vice is discovered, and exposed in the most frightful colours to the detestation of Christians.   Such was the character of that eloquence which, by captivating the people and scandalizing the great, occasioned such tumultuous disorder in the metropolis of the East.   Yet the historian finds much more to admire in the bold and impetuous enthusiasm of the orator, than to censure in his indiscretion.   One object alone filled his mind and animated his efforts—and that the noblest object to which the genius of man can be directed—to

The style of his eloquence.

---

* A letter from Chrysostom to Innocent, written in 406, is still extant, in which, with many expressions of gratitude, he exhorts that pope to continue his exertions to succour him, without being discouraged by the want of success.

warm the religion, to purify the morals, and to advance the virtue and happiness of those whom he influenced.

At the same time, it is not asserted that St. Chrysostom was exempt from the errors and abuses of his day; he exalted the merit of celibacy; he strongly inculcated the duty of fasting, and the sanctity of a solitary and ascetic life; he encouraged the veneration for saints and martyrs: but the practical nature of his piety sometimes shone through the mists of his superstitious delusion. If any, for instance, engaged in a pilgrimage to the holy places, he assured them that their principal motive should be the relief of the poor—if any were bent on offering up prayers for the dead, he exhorted them to give alms for the dead also*.

His doctrine. With respect to his doctrine, the three points which have been most warmly disputed are, his opinions on the Eucharist, on Grace and Original Sin, and on Confession. Regarding the first of these, his expressions are both vague and contradictory; since some of them would lead us to believe, that he very nearly approached, if he did not actually reach, the belief now held by the Roman Catholic Church; while in another passage, where he affirms the real presence, he also (and incidentally) asserts that the nature of the bread is not changed. Upon the whole, it is clear that he held very elevated notions respecting the sacrament, and it is probable that his deliberate opinion was in favour of that which we call Consubstantiation. But regarding the nature of penitence, it is quite plain, in spite of some seeming inconsistencies, which Roman Catholic writers have detected, or imagined, that his direct assertions inculcate the sufficiency of penitential confession to God in prayer, without any necessity for the mediation of his ministers. As to the

---

* See Dupin, Nouv. Biblioth., Art. St. Jean Chrysostom. The latter part of the fourth century, and the beginning of the fifth, from the death of Julian, for instance, to the conquest of Africa by the Vandals, is a very important and a deeply interesting period of Christian history; and there is no method perhaps by which its peculiarities could be so distinctly painted, as by detailed accounts of St. Ambrose, St. Chrysostom, and St. Augustine—accounts, which should reject all that is fabulous and absurd in the records respecting those fathers, while they embraced the most characteristic and striking *particulars* of their private, as well as public, conversation, their writings and their doctrine.

second point, we shall refer to the probable opinion of this father, when we shall arrive at the description of the Pelagian controversy.

5. *St. Jerome* was born at the city of Strigna or Stridona, on the confines of Pannonia and Dalmatia, about the year 345. His family was honourable, his fortune abundant, and his youthful studies, under the celebrated Donatus*, had improved and fortified his literary taste. But the deep religious feeling†, which took early possession of his soul, led him to consecrate his labours and his learning to that, which he deemed the service of Christ. An excessive admiration of monastic excellence, and ardour for the habits which conferred it, constituted the ruling principle of his life : and whether it was, that the solitudes of Europe were not yet sufficiently sanctified to satisfy his passion for holy seclusion, or that the celebrity attending on ascetic privations was still chiefly confined to the eastern world, he bade adieu to his native hills, to his hereditary property, to pontifical Rome herself, and transferred his library, his diligence, and his enthusiasm to a convent at Bethlehem. In a retreat, so well qualified to nourish religious emotion even in the most torpid heart, the zeal of Jerome did not slumber, but rather seemed to catch fresh fire from the objects and the recollections which surrounded him. From that wild and awful abode he poured forth the torrent of his lawless eloquence, and thundered with indiscriminate wrath against the enemies and the reformers of his religion. And if in that peaceful, and perhaps sinless solitude, it was excusable that he should exaggerate the merits of mortification, and fasting, and celibacy, and pilgrimage, and disparage the substantial virtues, which he could rarely witness, and which he could never practise ; on

St. Jerome,

retires to Bethlehem.

---

* The commentator on Virgil and Terence.

† In his twenty-second letter, in order to divert his correspondent (Eustochium) from the study of profane authors, St. Jerome recounts, that formerly, during the access of a violent fever, he had been dragged in spirit to the tribunal of Jesus Christ, where, after receiving severe chastisement for his attachment to those authors (Cicero and Plautus are specified), he had been forbidden to read them more. Moreover, he assures Eustochium, that that story is no dream, and invokes the heavenly tribunal before which he had appeared, to attest his veracity. See Dupin, Nouv. Bibl., vie S. Jerome.

the other hand, it was some aggravation of his intemperance, that in the birth-place of Christ, at the very fountain of humility and peace, he vented, even against his Christian adversaries, a malignant and calumnious rancour. Rufinus, Jovinian, and Vigilantius, successively sustained the bitterness of his indignation; and lastly, towards the close of his life, the opinions of Pelagius again excited that violence, which even old age[*] had been unable to moderate.

In the mean time St. Jerome was not himself exempt from error, and such too as called for the reprehension even of St. Augustine. The former has somewhere expressed an opinion, that the difference between St. Paul and St. Peter, described in the Acts, was not real, but only feigned—for pious purposes; an opinion which the bishop of Hippo most justly condemned as false in itself, and of very dangerous consequence[†]. St. Jerome also ventured a prophecy respecting the Millennium— but this indeed was a safer field for speculation, since his prediction was not the object of conclusive reasoning; and thus it continued in honour for about six hundred years, until the patience of time at length falsified it.

But while we censure both the superstitious and contentious spirit of St. Jerome, we must also recollect how great a compensation he made for evils thus occasioned, by his great work, the Latin translation of the Old Testament. And we must add, that a considerable knowledge of Hebrew, much general learning, and long application, qualified him, far above any contemporary, for the most important undertaking hitherto accomplished by any father of the Roman Church.

And here let us pause, to observe for one moment the *immediate* effect of his various labours. His theological philippics were hailed by the body of the Church with triumphant acclamation; his exhortations to seclusion and celibacy peopled the desert places with monks and hermits; but his translation of the Bible was ill received by the Church; "it was considered as a rash and dangerous innovation[‡];" even St. Augustine dis-

---

[*] St. Jerome died in the year 420.
[†] See note on St. Augustine in the eleventh chapter.
[‡] Dupin, Nouv. Biblioth., loc. cit.

approved, and held that it was more prudent to abide by the text of the Septuagint, than to risk the confusion and scandal which a new version might create. This senseless clamour was sufficient, even in those days, to prevent the immediate diffusion of the work; and almost two hundred years afterwards, we learn, that it only divided with its rival the diligence of St. Gregory; in later times it spread into wider circulation, and finally obtained very general possession of the Latin church*.

As the name of Athanasius more properly belongs to the Arian controversy, so that of *Augustine* is closely connected with the history of the Donatists and Pelagians, and that of *Basil* with the rise of Monachism. Those who may desire more extensive information respecting the lives and countless writings of the fathers here mentioned, and of the more numerous and obscure associates whom we have no space to notice, may apply, though with different degrees of confidence, to the compilations of Lardner, Dupin, Cave, and Tillemont.

* Of all the works of St. Jerome, his "Catalogue of Ecclesiastical Writers" is that which is now most frequently referred to.

CHAPTER X.

From the Death of Justinian to that of Charlemagne.
567 to 814.

I. The external fortunes of Christianity—its Restoration in England by St. Austin—its progress in Germany—among the Tartars—Its reverses—Mahomet and his successors—their conquests in Asia—in Egypt—facilitated by Christian dissensions—in Africa—Carthage—in Spain—in France—their defeat by Charles Martel—Treatment of Christian subjects by the Saracens—Charlemagne—forcible conversion of the Saxons and Pannonians.—II. The internal condition of Christianity—method of this History—Pope Gregory the Great —his character and conduct—worship of Images—Purgatory—Relics—Ceremonies—the Gregorian Canon—Gregory the creator of the Papal system— Title of Œcumenic Bishop—Power of the Keys—Apocrisiarii and Defensores —Changes in the seventh and eighth centuries—Orders of the Clergy—The Tonsure—Unity of the Church—Councils—Metropolitans—Increase and abuse of Episcopal power—Pope Zachary consulted as to the deposition of Childeric —his conduct how far blameable—the Lombards—the Donation of Pepin— confirmed by Charlemagne—His liberality to the Church, and the motives of it—His endeavours to reform the Church.

CHRISTIANITY had obtained a very early and perhaps general reception in Britain, when it was suddenly swept away, with the language itself, by the invasion of the Anglo-Saxons in 452, and almost entirely obliterated. Towards the end of the sixth century some circumstances occurred favourable to its restoration. Ethelbert, King of Kent, the most considerable of the Anglo-Saxon princes, married Bertha, daughter of the King of Paris, a Christian. Some clergy appear to have followed her to England, and to have softened the pagan prejudices of the king. Gregory the Great, who was then Bishop of Rome,

Mission of St. Austin into England, 596 A. D.

availed himself of this circumstance, and in the year 596, he sent over forty Benedictine monks, under the conduct of Augustine (commonly called St. Austin), prior of a monastery of that order. The king was converted, and most of the inhabitants of Kent followed his example; the missionary then received episcopal ordination from the primate of Arles, and was invested, as Archbishop of Canterbury, with power over the

British Church. The religion, thus established, spread with great rapidity; six other Anglo-Saxon Kings embraced the faith of Augustine and Ethelbert; and it was very generally propagated throughout the whole island before the conclusion of the seventh century.

The miraculous assistance, by which this work was accom- *Miraculous power ascribed to him.* plished, is acknowledged in a letter addressed by the pope himself to his missionary. " I know that God has performed through you great miracles among that people; but let us remember that, when the disciples said with joy to their divine Master, ' Lord, even the devils are subject unto us through thy name,' he answered them—' Rather rejoice, because your names are written in heaven.' While God thus employs your agency without, remember, my dear brother, to judge yourself severely within, and to know well what you are. If you have offended God in word or deed, preserve those offences in your thoughts, to repress the vain glory of your heart, and consider, that the gift of miracles is not granted to you for yourself, but for those whose salvation you are labouring to procure." An increased acquaintance with the character of Gregory, which we shall presently acquire, will diminish the weight of his testimony on this matter; which many indeed will be strongly predisposed to doubt, from the circumstance, that the apostle of England was never supernaturally gifted with any knowledge of the language of the country, but was obliged, in addressing the people, to avail himself of the imperfect service of an interpreter. But (little as those stories may be entitled to credit) it is certain that God vouchsafed one heavenly blessing on the mission of St. Austin, though displayed in a manner less popular with Roman Catholic historians—the work of conversion was accomplished without violence or compulsion: the sword of the Spirit was found sufficient for the holy purpose, and the ruins of our Saxon idolatry were not stained by the blood of one martyr.

It is not pretended, that the religion thus hastily introduced was a pure form of Christianity, nor even that it differed very widely, in its first appearance or operation, from the superstition which it succeeded. There even exists an epistle from

Gregory, in which he permits the ceremonies of the former worship to be associated with the profession of the gospel; nor is it possible even for the most perfect law at once to change the habits and correct the morals of a savage people. But the consent of history assures us, that, during the century following, the nation gradually emerged from the rudest barbarism into a condition of comparative civilization, and that the principles and motives of Christianity extended their salutary influence over the succeeding generations.

Many historians affirm, that St. Austin neglected the lessons of humility which he had received from his master, and proceeded to assert with great insolence the spiritual supremacy of Rome, not only over his own converts, but also over that faithful portion, who still maintained among the Cambrian mountains the doctrine and practice transmitted from their forefathers. It appears indeed that those simple believers, having been long severed from the body of Christendom, ignorantly preserved the original oriental rite in the celebration of Easter, which had been so long proclaimed schismatic: they were still involved in the error of the Quartadecimans: and they continued to persevere both in that and in the rejection of papal authority, even after they had been enlightened by the exhortations of St. Austin. It is recorded, and is probable, that they were deterred by the imperious conduct of that prelate from uniting with his church; and thus far we need not hesitate to condemn him; but some more serious charges which have been brought against him stand on very slight foundation*.

* Jortin (Eccl. Hist., vol. iv., p. 417) says, "The Christianity which this pretended apostle and sanctified ruffian taught us, seemed to consist principally in two things, in keeping Easter upon a proper day, and to be slaves to our Sovereign Lord God the Pope, and to Austin, his deputy and vicegerent. Such were the boasted blessings and benefits which we received from the mission and ministry of this most audacious and insolent monk." This is passionate and unjust abuse. St. Austin was indeed the missionary of a Pope—but his conversion of the mass of the inhabitants of this island was perfectly independent of his endeavours to bring over to the Church of Rome the few and obscure schismatics of Wales; and let us recollect that his exertions, in both cases, were directed only to *persuade*. The evidence respecting the massacre of the twelve hundred monks of Bangor is very fairly stated by Fuller; and it seems upon the whole probable, that the event took place after the death of St. Austin. But at any rate the crime was committed in the heat of battle, apparently without design or premeditation—so

It is next our duty to record the labours of Succathus, a Succathus and Columban.
Scotsman, to whom is usually ascribed the glory of having converted the Irish, and established among them the Episcopal
Church; and also of Columban, an Irish monk and missionary,
who diffused the religion among the Gauls and various Teutonic
tribes, about the end of the sixth century. It is not easy, at
this distance of time, to calculate the precise effect of mere individual exertion in so difficult an enterprise, or to separate
what is fabulous in such records from that which may reasonably be received. But the progress of St. Austin is much more
intelligible—since he was aided by the immediate support of
Pope Gregory, and since one of the earliest among his proselytes was a king.

It appears probable, that at the beginning of the eighth cen- Winfrid the apostle of the Germans, 715 A. D.
tury Christianity had made very little progress in Germany;
at least its reception had been confined to provinces immediately
bordering on the Roman empire*. In the year 715, Winfrid†,
a noble Englishman, who was afterwards known by the name
of Boniface, undertook the labours of a missionary. His first
attempt was fruitless; but presently returning, under the auspices and by the authority of Pope Gregory II., he preached
among the Frieselanders and Hessians with considerable suc-
cess‡. In 723 he was consecrated a bishop, and being joined
by many pious Christians, from France as well as England, he

---

that it is absurd to charge it upon a person, who, even if he was living, was certainly not present at the scene.

* Fleury (l. xxxviii., sect. lviii. on the authority of the "Benedictine Acts")
mentions three monasteries as having been founded at Tournay and Ghent about
the middle of the seventh century.

† We are not to confound this missionary with St. Wilfrid, another Englishman, who also gained some reputation both in France and at Rome, from about
660 to 710. The vast quantity of relics which he brought home from his first
expedition to the continent is mentioned by historians.

‡ Mosheim, Cent. viii., p. i., c. i. Milner takes great pains to exculpate Boniface from the various charges of violence, arrogance, fraud, &c., which Mosheim
very liberally heaps upon him, and to prove him, from his own correspondence, to
have been a mere pious, unambitious missionary. There is *some* reason in the
defence; and Mosheim may very probably have been prejudiced against Boniface
by that absolute devotion to the Holy See which he professed, and by which he
profited. Some of the acts (real and imaginary) of this saint are retailed at the
end of Fleury's 41st Book.

established numerous churches throughout the country. His immediate recompense was advancement to the archiepiscopal See of Mayence, and to the primacy of Germany and Belgium. To posterity he is more generally and more gloriously known as the *Apostle of the Germans*. And the additional title of *Saint* was due not only to his zeal, but also to his martyrdom —for, returning in his old age to Frieseland*, that he might terminate his labours where he had begun them, he was massacred by the savage inhabitants, together with fifty ecclesiastics who attended him. (A. D. 755.)

Conversion of the Tartars, 790 A. D.

To the eighth we may also refer the introduction of Christianity among the Tartars, the inhabitants of those regions which now constitute the southern Asiatic provinces of the Russian empire. This spiritual conquest was achieved under the auspices of an heretical bishop, Timotheus the Nestorian, about the year 790. On the other hand, for the chastisement of a corrupt Church and a sinful people, the extensive tracts of central and southern Asia had been already overwhelmed by the fiercest enemies who have ever been raised against the Christian name, the fanatic followers of Mahomet; and to their mention we cannot proceed perhaps with a better augury, than after recording that obscure fact, which planted the banner of Christianity in a Russian province.

---

* That country was for some years the scene of the successive exertions of St. Wilfrid, St. Vulfran, St. Villebrod, and lastly St. Boniface. It was the second of those missionaries whose injudicious answer to Radbod, the king of the Frieselanders, retarded the progress of the new religion. That prince was standing at the baptismal font, prepared for the ceremony—only one point remained, respecting which his curiosity was still unsatisfied —" Tell me," said he to the holy bishop, " where is now the greater number of the kings and princes of the nation of the Frieselanders—are they in the paradise which you promise me, or in the hell with which you menace me ? " " Do not deceive yourself," replied St. Vulfran ; "the princes, your predecessors, who have died without baptism, are most assuredly damned ; but whosoever shall believe henceforward, and be baptised, shall be in joy eternal with Christ Jesus." Upon this Radbod withdrew his foot from the font, and said—" I cannot resolve to relinquish the society of the kings, my predecessors, in order to live with a few poor people in this heavenly kingdom. I cannot believe these novelties, and I will rather adhere to the ancient usages of my nation." It was not until after the death of this prince that St. Boniface gained any footing in the country. Vit. S. Vulfran, Tom. iii. Act. S. S. Bened., p. 361. Fleury. l. 41. s. 35.

During the fourth century of our history we were occupied in observing the destruction of the ancient paganism of Greece and Rome; during the fifth and sixth we marked the success of Christianity in supplanting the rude superstitions of the Celtic invaders of the empire, and subduing those savage aggressors to the law, or at least to the name, of Christ. But the seventh century was marked by the birth of a new and resolute adversary, who began his career with the most stupendous triumphs, who has torn from us the possession of half the world, and who retains his conquests even to this moment. Mahomet was born *about* the year 570; we are ignorant of the precise period of the nativity of that man who wrought the most extraordinary revolution in the affairs of this globe, which the agency of any being merely human has ever yet accomplished. His pretended mission did not commence till he was about forty years old, and the date of his celebrated flight from Mecca, the Hedjirah, or era of Mahometan nations, is 622 A.D. The remainder of his life was spent in establishing his religion and his authority in his native land, Arabia; and the sword, with which he finally completed that purpose, he bequeathed, for the universal propagation of both, to his followers. His commission was zealously executed; and, in less than a century after his death, his faith was uninterruptedly extended by a chain of nations from India to the Atlantic.

The fate of Persia was decided by the battle of Cadesia, in 636. In Syria, Damascus had already fallen, and after the sanguinary conflict of Yermuk, where the Saracens for the first time encountered and overthrew a Christian enemy, the conquerors instantly proceeded to the reduction of Jerusalem; that grand religious triumph they obtained in 637. In the year following, Aleppo and Antioch fell into their hands, which completed the conquest of Syria. Thence they proceeded northward as far as the shores of the Euxine and the neighbourhood of Constantinople.

The invasion of Egypt took place in 638, and within the space of three years, the whole of that populous province was in the possession of the infidels. Alexandria was the last city which fell; and in somewhat more than a century after the

Margin notes:
Mahometan conquests.

Of Persia and Syria.

Of Egypt.

expulsion of philosophy from Europe by a Christian legislator, the schools of Africa were closed in their turn by the arms of an unlettered Mahometan.

Coalition betweenthe Mahometans and Jacobites.

The success of the Saracens was not inconsiderably promoted by the religious dissensions of their Christian adversaries. A vast number of heretics, who had been oppressed and stigmatized by Edicts and Councils, were scattered over the surface of Asia; and these were contented to receive a foreign master, of whose principles they were still ignorant, in the place of a tyrant, whose injustice they had experienced. But in Egypt especially, the whole mass of the native population was unfortunately involved in the Jacobite heresy; and few at that time were found, except the resident Greeks, who adhered to the doctrine of the Church. The followers of Eutyches formed an immediate alliance with the soldiers of Mahomet against a Catholic prince; and they considered that there was nothing unnatural in that act, since they hoped to secure for themselves, under a Mahometan, the toleration which had been refused by an orthodox government. We should remark, however, that this hope, the pretext of their desertion, was with many the suggestion of their malice : that, besides the recollection of wrongs, and the desire to escape or revenge them, they were influenced as furiously as their persecutors by that narrow sectarian spirit, which is commonly excited most keenly where the differences are most trifling; and which, while it exaggerated the lines that separated them from their fellow Christians, blinded them to the broad gulf which divided all alike from the infidel.

Carthage,

From Egypt the conquerors rushed along the northern shore of Africa; and though their progress in that direction was interrupted by the domestic dissensions of the Prophet's family, even more than by the occasional vigour of the Christians, they were in possession of Carthage before the end of the seventh century. Thence they proceeded westward, and after encountering some opposition from the native Moors, little either from the Greek or Vandal masters of the country, they completed their conquest in the year 709.

and Spain.

Hitherto the Mahometans had gained no footing in Europe; and it may seem strange that the most western of its provinces should have been that which was first exposed to their occupation. But the vicinity of Spain to their latest conquests, and the factious dissensions of its nobility, gave them an early opportunity to attempt the subjugation of that country. Their success was almost unusually rapid. In 711 they overthrew the Gothic monarchy by the victory of Xeres; and the two following years were sufficient to secure their dominion over the greatest part of the Peninsula.

The waters of this torrent were destined to proceed still a little farther. Ten years after the battle of Xeres, the Saracens crossed the Pyrenees, and overran with little opposition the south-western provinces of France—" the vineyards of Gascony and the city of Bourdeaux were possessed by the Sovereign of Damascus and Samarcand ; and the south of France, from the mouth of the Garonne to that of the Rhone, assumed the manners and religion of Arabia." Still dissatisfied with those ample limits, or impatient of any limit, these children of the desert again marched forward into the centre of the kingdom. They were encamped between Tours and Poitiers, when Charles Martel, the Mayor or Duke of the Franks, encountered them. It is too much to assert that the fate of Christianity depended upon the result of the battle which followed; but if victory had declared for the Saracens, it would probably have secured to them in France the same extent, perhaps the same duration, of authority which they possessed in Spain. Next they would have carried the horrors of war and Islamism into Germany or Britain; but there other fields must have been fought, against nations of warriors as brave as the Franks, by an invader who was becoming less powerful, and even less enthusiastic, as he advanced farther from the head of his resources and his faith. Indeed, if we had space to speculate more deeply on the probabilities of this question, we should rather be led to consider this effort against France as the last wave of the deluge now exhausted, and about to recede within more reasonable boundaries.

The final struggle of the Saracens was scarcely worthy of their former triumphs. During six days of desultory combat the horsemen and archers of the East maintained indeed an Defeat of the Arabs by Charles Martel.

indecisive advantage; but in the closer onset of the seventh day,
the Germans, more eminently powerful in limb, and strong in
heart as well as hand, instantly extinguished the Arabs with
iron arm and overbearing chest*.   The chief of the Saracens
fell in the conflict; the survivors fled to their encampment, and
after a night passed in the dissension usual to the vanquished,
they dispersed, and evacuated the country.   This battle was
fought in the year 732; the advantages were slowly but resolutely pursued by the conqueror, and presently ended in the
final expulsion of the invader from the soil of France.

**Religious
policy of
the Sara-
cens.**

In less than one century from the preaching of Mahomet,
his disciples had obtained military possession of Persia, Syria,
and the greater part of central and western Asia, of Egypt, and
the long extent of the northern coast of Africa; and lastly of
the kingdom of Spain.   The propagation of their religion furnished to all the pretext, and to many the sincere motive, of
aggression; and as the most violent means were not forbidden
by their law, and as religious wars are seldom distinguished by
mildness and humanity, we may believe that many revolting
cruelties were occasionally perpetrated by them.   However,
upon the whole they found it more politic to tolerate than to
exterminate: with the heretics of the East they formed early
and friendly relations through a common enmity; and in
Africa and Spain they generally proffered the alternative of
the Koran or tribute†; so that Christianity was not immediately extirpated from any of the conquered countries, and
even at this moment it continues to linger, however degraded
by adversity and oppression, in almost all of them.   The country in which it suffered the most immediate and perfect prostration was the northern coast of Africa; and those two fruitful
nurseries of religion and religious men, Alexandria and
Carthage, which fill so eminent a station in the early Catholic

---

* Gibbon, c. lii.   Roderic Toletan. c. xiv.   " Gens Austriæ membrorum pre-
eminentia valida, et gens Germana corde et corpore præstantissima, quasi in ictu
oculi manu ferrea et pectore arduo Arabes extinxerunt."

† The Mahometans drew a broad distinction between those infidels who had a
Book of faith, and those who had none.   Among the former they placed the disciples of Zoroaster, and therefore showed them great mercy—but they had no
compassion on the Pagan.

Church—names which are so closely associated with all the various fortunes of rising Christianity, with its most honourable and holy triumphs, with its afflictions and reverses, with the zeal, the genius, and the eloquence of its professors, with their dissensions and intolerance—those two powerful Churches were from that time forward obliterated from history. It is true, indeed, that the former still preserved a title, but it was without power; and a dignity, but it was without independence: she lost her learning and her industry, and all her excellence and energy departed with them. But at Carthage the actual extinction of Christianity very speedily followed the success of the Mahometans; and the labours of Tertullian, Cyprian, Lactantius, Augustin and so many others were spurned and execrated, if indeed their very names were not rather forgotten, by a faithless and blaspheming posterity.

The most eloquent account of the progress of the Saracens, *Gibbon's account of the Mahometan conquests.* which has yet been composed, is that of Gibbon—yet we may here be permitted to observe, that, with all its splendour, it is in truth the least philosophical portion of his whole work. As if he were blinded by the brilliancy of the Mahometan conquests, or by his dislike for the religion at the expense of which they were principally gained, he overlooks not only the misery immediately occasioned by them, but their fatal influence on the progressive and permanent improvement of man. History is philosophy teaching by example; and the lessons of history are then indeed noble and profitable, and then only, when philosophy casts away her pride and her pedantry, and condescends to *rise* into philanthropy.

The victory of Charles Martel was soon followed by the re- *The zeal of Charlemagne.* establishment of a more effective government in France; and precisely forty years after the battle of Tours, we find Charlemagne engaged in a sanguinary war against the Saxons, for the purpose of converting them to the Christian religion. It seemed, indeed, as if that zealous prince was for a season possessed by the spirit of the Arabian, and that he imitated the fury of his armed apostles; and, as if Christianity had not already sufficiently suffered by adopting the vices of other systems, he dragged into its service the most savage principle of

Islamism.   After eight years of resistance and misfortune the Saxons were compelled to take refuge in the profession of the Gospel*; and the Huns of Pannonia were soon afterwards driven by the same victorious compulsion to the same necessity.

When we behold the limits of Christendom extended by the writings of its ministers, or the eloquence of its missionaries, we record such conquests with pure and grateful satisfaction: when we observe a mass of Pagans, or other unbelievers, suddenly, but peacefully, melting into the bosom of the Church, we question their motives, we lament the stain which they may bring with them, and we censure any unworthy compromise which has been made to conciliate them; yet we are consoled to reflect that no immediate misery has been occasioned by a change, pregnant at least with future improvement.   But when we see the sword employed to propagate a religion, of which the very essence is peace, we are at once disgusted and revolted by the cruel and impious mockery.

THE INTERNAL CONDITION OF CHRISTIANITY FROM THE REIGN OF JUSTINIAN TO THAT OF CHARLEMAGNE.

In an endeavour to compress into a few chapters the ever-varying records of fifteen centuries, it might, perhaps, be thought sufficient to exhibit a mere chronological series of events and names; but we consider it a more profitable, as it is certainly a more attractive employment, to select and illustrate what is material and consequential, and to pass, as it were, from eminence to eminence, dwelling for some short space on each, and delineating its features with some exactness, though we may thus be compelled to treat with little minuteness the periods intervening.   But it is certain that there are many secondary

---

* Charlemagne was occasionally troubled by the *contumacy* of his converts, even to the end of his reign; and in the civil wars among his grandsons, we find Lothaire proclaiming *liberty of conscience* to the Saxons of the succeeding generation (in 841).   Many of them eagerly cast away the mask of Christianity, and flew to his standard.   Compulsion has filled the world with hypocrites, but it has never made a true convert to any faith, or any form of faith. See Millot, Hist. Fran,

names, and many occurrences of mere temporary importance, which may be consigned to silence without any danger to the integrity and usefulness of history. On this principle we shall proceed, without delay, from the death of Justinian to the accession of Gregory the First to the pontifical chair. That prelate presided over the Church of Rome from the year 590 to 604; and he illustrated that short period by so many splendid qualities, and pursued his various purposes with such bold and successful exertion, that he has acquired, and perhaps deserved, the deep and faithful veneration of the Catholic Church. At least it has been found so difficult to estimate his character with moderation, and there is so much intemperance, both in the eulogies and the insults* offered to it, that its mere strength and energy, which are thus sufficiently proved, assert its claim to a more considerate and impartial examination.

Two prominent vices overshadowed and counteracted the numerous excellencies of Gregory—superstition and ambition. For the former of these some excuse may be found in the spirit and principles of the age in which he lived: the latter was the produce of the same vigorous nature which gave birth to his virtues; and it went to an excess in him, which it would not have reached in a feebler mind. His virtues were his own, and those of his religion; and if we should discredit, as affected, that humility which preferred the cloister to the chair of St Peter, and so long rejected the proffered mitre†, at least we must praise the generosity which led him, in early life, to bestow his large possessions on the Church, and we must admire his ardent piety, and sincere, though often misdirected, devotion. The extreme severity of his moral practice has not been

Character of Gregory the Great. 590—604 A. D.

---

* " Pope Gregory the Great, called St. Gregory, was remarkable for many things; for exalting his own authority, for running down human learning and polite literature, for burning classic authors, for patronizing ignorance and stupidity, for persecuting heretics, for flattering the most execrable princes, and for relating a multitude of absurd, monstrous and ridiculous lies, called miracles. He was an ambitious, insolent prelate, under the mask of humility." Jortin, Remarks, vol. iv. p. 403. Most, though by no means all, of the above charges are true; but the counterpoise of good and powerful qualities is left almost entirely unnoticed by their author.

† Baron. ann. 590, sect. vii. &c. &c.

contested, nor his honest endeavours to enforce the same practice in every rank and order of his clergy. Circumstances, political as well as religious, had introduced abuses into the system of ecclesiastical discipline, which a weak and narrow mind might have thought it expedient to protect, but which Gregory knew that it was wiser to reform. Indeed we may observe, that the best friends of every Church in every age, and those whose services are most gratefully acknowledged by posterity, however ungraciously they may be accepted by interested contemporaries, are men who dare to distinguish between the system and its corruptions, and to administer those vigorous measures of renovation which are necessary for its health and perpetuity. And thus would it have been still happier for the fame of that pope, had he taken a still bolder view of the imperfections of his Church, and applied to the cure of its deeper and spiritual diseases the remedial attention which he confined to its discipline and its ceremonies.

The character of Gregory was distinguished by the fervour of his charity: the virtue which surrounded his palace with crowds of sufferers of every rank and profession, and distributed for their relief * the funds, which with little scandal might have been lavished on selfish purposes, has never been disputed, and ought never to have been disparaged. Nor was he contented to exercise this alone, but strove, on the contrary, to extend its practice by powerful exhortations among his episcopal brethren —" Let not the bishop think that reading and preaching alone suffice, or studiously to maintain himself in retirement, while the hand which enriches and fructifies is closed. But let his hand be bountiful; let him make advances to those who are in necessity; let him consider the wants of others as his own; for without these qualities the name of bishop is a vain and empty title†." We should also remark, that this pope exerted himself on more than one occasion to redeem Christian prisoners from captivity, and to alleviate their sufferings during it.

He was diligent in his efforts to propagate the Catholic faith.

---

* See Baronius, ann. 591, sect. iii. xxiv. &c.; ann. 592, sect. ii.; ann. 596, sect. viii. Fleury, l. xxxv. sect. xvi. Gibbon, chap. xlv.

† Lib. v., Epist. 29, apud Baron. ann. 592, sect. xvi.

His most important spiritual conquest was that of England; and if it be a reproach to him that he there permitted the first converts to retain, under other names, the substance of some of their superstitious practices*, in France, where the longer and more general diffusion of the religion left less excuse for such a concession, he zealously endeavoured to extirpate the remains of idolatry†. The conversion of the Jews‡ was another favourite object with him ; and in one respect he adopted the most promising means for that purpose, by treating them with mildness and humanity; in another he insulted their principles, while he disgraced his own, by the direct offer of gain, as the reward of their apostacy. His zeal for the unity of the Church is a very ambiguous excellence; but it was warmly, and (as Roman Catholic historians assert) successfully exerted, both against the remnant of the Donatists, and against certain schismatics who had seceded from the Church on the controversy respecting the Three Chapters§. We may add to this, that his activity in ennobling the services of religion, and adding splendour to its ceremonies, however unworthy a method of recommending a spiritual religion, found some excuse in the degenerate principles of the sixth century.

Through the disturbed condition of Italy, the aggressions of the Lombard invaders, and the weakness of the imperial power, the direction of the political interests of Rome devolved for the

---

* " Altaria destruantur, *relliquiæ ponantur*." He allows even sacrifices on *Saint's* days—substituting, however, a convivial, for a superstitious motive—" nec diabolo tam animalia immolent, sed ad laudem Dei in esu suo animalia occidant," &c. Baron. ann. 601. xxii.

† He complains of immolations to idols, worship of trees, sacrifices of the heads of animals, &c.—" Quia pervenit ad nos quod multi Christianorum et ad Ecclesias occurrant, et (quod dici nefas est) a culturis dæmonum non discedant." See Baron. ann. 597, xviii. Fleury dedicates the 22nd chapter of his 35th book to the Saints, and the 23rd to the Impostors, of Gaul. It appears that St. Ivrier " cured several by making the sign of the cross upon them, and in like manner performed many miracles "—yet St. Ivrier is classed among the *former*.

‡ Baron. ann. 594, sect. viii. ann. 598, sect. xiv.

§ The subject of the fifth general council. (See chap. xi.) One of these schismatics, named Stephanus, came to Rome, and offered to Gregory to return to the Church, if the bishop would take upon himself the risk of his soul, and intercede with God as his sponsor and fidejussor, that his return to the Catholic Church should be sanctioned in heaven ; which Gregory undertook without any hesitation—quod Gregorius minimè facere cunctatus est. Baronius. ann. 590. sect. xxvi.

most part upon Gregory. It appears not that he sought that charge, so eagerly grasped by many of his successors, but rather that he entered with reluctance upon duties which, if not at direct variance, were at least little in accordance with a spiritual office. But, having once undertaken them, he discharged them with the ability and in the spirit which became his character and his profession; he presented himself as a mediator and pacificator, and by his faithful ministry to the God of peace*, he succeeded in averting the arms of his enemies, and in preserving his country from servitude.

He professed to reject from the service of religion that profane learning, of which his writings prove him to have been ignorant; and hence probably proceeded the charge so commonly believed, though insufficiently† supported, that he burnt the Palatine library, and destroyed some of the most valuable remains of classical antiquity. But it is admitted that he was inferior to none in the learning of his own age‡; and his diligence and energy are abundantly attested by the voluminous and even vigorous compositions which he has left behind him§.

He protected images. We shall proceed to point out some instances in which Gregory deviated even farther than his predecessors from that ancient faith and practice, of which his see, since it now claimed exclusively the denomination of apostolical, professed a peculiar observance. Before the end of the sixth century,

* The following is his boast to Sabinianus, his Apocrisiarius or Envoy at Constantinople. " Unum est quod breviter suggeras serenissimis Dominis nostris : quia (that) si ego servus eorum in mortem Longobardorum me miscere voluissem, hodie Longobardorum gens nec regem, nec duces, nec comites habuisset, atque in summa confusione esset divisa. *Sed quia Deum timeo, in mortem cujuslibet hominis me miscere formido.*" See Baronius (ann. 595, sect. xviii.), who details his various negociations with the Lombards very accurately.

† There seems to be no authority for this accusation older than the twelfth century. See Bayle, Vie de Grég. I.

‡ " Disciplinis vero liberalibus, hoc est grammatica, rhetorica, dialectica, ita a puero est institutus, ut quamvis eo tempore florerent adhuc Romæ studia literarum, tamen nulli in urbe sua secundus putaretur." Paul Diac. Vit. St. Greg. Gibbon. c. xlv.

§ There are greater remains of the works of Gregory than of any other pope; and a diligent and judicious study of his epistles might still throw much new light on the early history of his Church. Baronius attributes the rudeness of his style to the barbarism of the age in which he lived.

the dangerous usage, which had originated in the fourth*, of exposing images of saints, of the Virgin, and even of Christ, in places consecrated to worship, had taken deep root, as well in the Western as in the Eastern Church. Serenus, the bishop of Marseilles, observing that the people worshipped such images, removed or destroyed them, and complaint was made to Gregory. The pope addressed to him two epistles, in which he praised the zeal, that had combated any show of idolatry, but at the same time maintained the propriety of filling the Churches with idols: "for there is a great difference," he says, "between worshipping an image, and learning, from the history represented by it, what it is that we ought to worship; for that which writing teaches to those who can read, painting makes intelligible to all who have eyes to see. It is in such representations that the ignorant perceive what they ought to follow; it is the book of the illiterate. On this account it is of great service to the barbarians; to which circumstance you, who are placed in the midst of barbarians, ought to be particularly attentive, so as to cause them no scandal by an indiscreet zeal." This passage probably discloses the principal motive of that attachment to the cause of images, which was afterwards so warmly manifested by the Church of Rome. At least it teaches us, that the places which they had gradually usurped, during the three preceding ages, were at length confirmed to them, and secured by the highest authority. And we may pause once more to condemn the sophistry, which distinguished between the use and the worship, and coldly forbade the ignorant barbarian to adore an object, which could not seriously be placed in *his* hands for any other purpose.

The belief in the fire of purgatory was seriously inculcated by the same pontiff; and to him, more justly than to any individual, we may attribute the practical system to which that speculative opinion gave birth. He also exalted the merit of pilgrimages† to the Holy Places; but the superstition which he most ardently sustained, was, a reverential respect for relics,

---

* We shall treat this, as well as purgatory, and some other of the Roman Catholic corruptions, more fully in the thirteenth chapter.

† Baronius, ann. 592, sect. xix.

founded for the most part on their miraculous qualities. The deep and earnest solemnity, with which one of the greatest characters of his age and church was not ashamed to enforce so very gross a delusion, cannot so well be depicted to the reader as in his own language.

Showed great reverence for relics. The empress Constantina, who was building a Church at Constantinople to St. Paul, made application to Gregory for the head of that apostle*, or at least for some portion of his body. The pope begins his answer by a very polite expression of his sorrow " that he neither could nor dared to grant that favour; for the bodies of the holy apostles, Peter and Paul, are so resplendent with miracles and terrific prodigies in their own Churches, that no one can approach them without great awe, even for the purpose of adoring them. When my predecessor, of happy memory, wished to change some silver ornament which was placed over the most holy body of St. Peter, though at the distance of almost fifteen feet, a warning of no small terror appeared to him. Even I myself wished to make some alteration near the most holy body of St. Paul, and it was necessary to dig rather deeply near his tomb. The superior of the place found some bones which were not at all connected with that tomb; and, having presumed to disturb and remove them to some other place, he was visited by certain fearful apparitions, and died suddenly. My predecessor, of holy memory, also undertook to make some repairs near the tomb of St. Lawrence: as they were digging, without knowing precisely where the venerable body was placed, they happened to open his sepulchre. The monks and guardians who were at the work, only because they had seen the body of that martyr, though they did not presume so much as to touch it, all died within ten days; to the end that no man might remain in life who had beheld the body of that just man. Be it then known to you, that it is the custom of the Romans, when they give any

---

* Baronius, who cites the pope's reply with considerable admiration, attributes the empress's exorbitant request to ecclesiastical ambition,—to a desire to exalt the see of Constantinople to a level with that of Rome, by getting into her possession so important a portion of so great an apostle. Fleury quotes the letter chiefly in proof that the *transfer* of relics was forbidden in the Roman Church, while that abuse was permitted in the East.

relics, not to venture to touch any portion of the body; only they put into a box a piece of linen (called *brandeum*), which is placed near the holy bodies; then it is withdrawn, and shut up with due veneration in the Church which is to be dedicated, and as many prodigies are then wrought by it, as if the bodies themselves had been carried thither; whence it happened, that in the time of St. Leo, (as we learn from our ancestors,) when some Greeks doubted the virtue of such relics, that pope called for a pair of scissors, and cut the linen, and blood flowed from the incision.   And not at Rome only, but throughout the whole of the West, it is held sacrilegious to touch the bodies of the saints, nor does such temerity ever remain unpunished.   For which reason we are much astonished at the custom of the Greeks to take away the bones of the saints, and we scarcely give credit to it.   But what shall I say respecting the bodies of the holy apostles, when it is a known fact, that, at the time of their martyrdom, a number of the faithful came from the East to claim them?   But when they had carried them out of the city, to the second milestone, to a place called the catacombs, the whole multitude was unable to move them farther,—such a tempest of thunder and lightning terrified and dispersed them. The napkin, too, which you wished to be sent at the same time, is with the body, and cannot be touched more than the body can be approached.   But that your religious desire may not be wholly frustrated, I will hasten to send to you some part of those chains which St. Paul wore on his neck and hands, if indeed I shall succeed in getting off any filings from them.   For since many continually solicit as a blessing that they may carry off from those chains some small portion of their filings, *a priest stands by with a file;* and sometimes it happens that some portions fall off from the chains instantly, and without delay; while, at other times, the file is long drawn over the chains, and yet nothing is at last scraped off from them."

The pages of Ecclesiastical History are so full of such idle fables, that the repetition even of the smallest portion of them is a task as tedious, as it is unworthy of a reasonable mind; but when such absurdities are propagated and dignified by the pen of Gregory the Great—of him whom the Roman Church reveres almost as the first among her saints, and whose writings for so many centuries directed, and even still direct, the principles of her ministers—it would be a neglect of historical duty to pass them over in complete silence*.

Dignified
the ceremo-
nies of the
Church.

The public worship of God was still celebrated by every nation in its own language; but its forms were enlarged from time to time by new prayers and offices, as well as hymns and psalmody, and such other additions as were found proper to enliven devotion. Gregory introduced a more imposing method of administering the Communion, with a magnificent assemblage of pompous ceremonies. This institution was called the Canon of the Mass; and such as it appears in the Sacramentaries of St. Gregory, such, word for word (says Fleury†), we say it still. After regulating the prayers, the pope descended to the modulation of the chant; and to give some permanency to his success in this matter, he established a school of chanters, which subsisted for at least three centuries after his death‡.

* The Dialogues of Gregory abound with miraculous narratives; and Fleury excuses this practice by pleading that he had not philosophers for his antagonists, who needed argument for confutation, but that the Pagans then to be found were chiefly peasants, serfs, or soldiers, and were more moved by a miraculous story than by the most conclusive syllogism. In process of time, Gregory, from being the relater, rose to be the performer of miracles. About one hundred and eighty years after his death, Paulus Diaconus records, that a Roman lady, on some occasion, receiving the Communion from Gregory, and hearing him say the customary words, could not forbear smiling, when he called that the body of Christ which she had made with her own hands—for at that time the people used to bring to the Communion their own bread, which was a small, round, flat cake. The Pope, perceiving her behaviour, took the bread out of her hands, and, having prayed over it, showed it to her turned into flesh in the sight of the whole people. This story is only valuable, in as far as it shows that, in the time of Paulus Diaconus, the belief in Transubstantiation was not uncommon.

† H. E. lib. xxxvi., s. xix. Fleury describes the alterations of Gregory at length and clearly. The great pains which the Pope took in these matters, and especially in the composition of his celebrated chant, are zealously related by Maimbourg, in his History of St. Gregory.

‡ Fleury, lib. xxxvi., sect. xxi. "In the time of John the Deacon (about 900), the original of his Antiphonarius was preserved with great respect, as well as the couch on which he reposed while chanting, and the whip with which he menaced the children." Pope Gelasius (says the same historian in sect. xv.) had made a collection of the office of the masses, into which St. Gregory introduced many changes and additions. He collected the whole in one volume, which is his Sacramentarius, for so they formerly called the book which contained the prayers used in the administration of the Sacraments, and chiefly of the Eucharist. All

Other alterations were made by the same pontiff in the distribution of the parishes, the calendar of festivals, the order of processions, the service of the priests and deacons, the variety and change of sacerdotal garments ; and as most of them were permanent, we may consider the system properly called Roman Catholic as having assumed its peculiar character at this time. And thus, while the antiquity of the universal Church may justly be regarded as having ceased at the accession of Constantine, it is not a fanciful position that its middle age—that indistinct period during which the principles that were hereafter to give it a more lasting and definite form were collecting strength, but were not yet developed—was brought to a close by the splendid pontificate of Gregory.

The foregoing remark has reference to the doctrinal and cere- Elements monial structure, rather than to the *papal* polity of the Church, of Papacy. which scarcely displayed its real shape till the reign of Gregory VII. Nevertheless, it will be reasonably inquired what elements existed, or, at least, what indications may be discovered, in the sixth century, of the monarchical government, which formed the characteristic of the Communion in later ages ? We shall, therefore, proceed to point out such of these as were most perceptible during the time of Gregory I. We have noticed an early jealousy subsisting between the Sees of Rome and Constantinople, and the sort of superiority which was conferred upon the former by the council of Chalcedon. It appears, too, that St. Leo was addressed by certain Oriental correspondents by the title of Œcumenic, or Universal Patriarch, though his Title of immediate successors refrained from adopting that lofty appel- Universal lation. Matters rested thus till the year 588, when the Emperor Maurice conferred that same title upon his own patriarch John, commonly called the Faster*, an austere and ambitious

that was to be chanted was marked in another volume, called the " *Antiphonaire*, parce que l'on chantoit alternativement; d'où vient le nom d'antiphones ou antiennes (anthems) comme il a été expliqué."

* John the Faster, disputing an unmeaning title with Gregory, is assimilated by Baronius (ann. 595, sect. xxvii.) to the apostate angel rising against the Most High God—a comparison not far removed from blasphemy. In more than thirty sections, which that historian devotes to the subject, he labours to depress the See of Constantinople even below that of Alexandria, and continually advances

prelate. Pope Pelagius opposed those pretensions; and, eight
years afterwards, the contest was much more vigorously renewed by Gregory. In 595, he addressed five epistles on this
subject to John himself, to the Emperor and Empress, and to
the rival Patriarchs of Alexandria and Antioch; in all vehe-
mently inveighing against the arrogance of the Faster, and professing the very purest spirit of Christian humility. In his letter to the Emperor he declares that the public calamities are
to be ascribed to no other cause than the ambition of the
bishops. "We destroy (he says) by example that which we
preach in word; our bones are consumed with fastings, and our
soul is puffed up with pride; beneath the meanest garments
we conceal a haughty heart; we repose on ashes, and we pretend to grandeur; under the aspect of the sheep we nourish the
fangs of the wolf." He proceeds—"The direction and primacy of the whole Church has been given to St. Peter; nevertheless we do not call him the Universal Apostle, and yet the
holy man John, my brother, is ambitious to be called the Universal Bishop*." To Constantina he mournfully complains of
the insult which has been offered to the See of Rome; and
while he humbly confesses "that the sins of Gregory have
merited such chastisement," he reminds the Empress that St.
Peter at least is sinless, and undeserving the outrage which
had been offered him.

Primacy of
St. Peter.

From these and others, even among the few passages which
we have cited from Gregory's writings, it appears that the
ground, on which the Church of Rome rested its assertion of
supremacy, was already changed very essentially. In its early
days the sort of superiority which it endeavoured to assume
was founded for the most part on its imperial name and dignity; but when that basis was overthrown by the conquests of
the barbarians, another was substituted, of a purely spiritual

the obtrusiveness of Rome, as a proof of her rightful authority. However, it is
true enough that the power of Rome was now growing real and substantial—a fact
much more easily shown than either its antiquity or legitimacy.

* St. Gregory could not foresee that, within twelve years from that in which he
was writing, the same title would be proudly worn by a successor to the chair of
St. Peter (Boniface III.), though granted to that pontiff by an Emperor who disgraced human nature.

nature, and thus better calculated to impose upon the ignorant proselytes. The name of St. Peter became more venerable than that of Augustus or Trajan; and his chair, as it was occupied by the successors of the apostle and the vicars of Christ, inspired a deeper awe into the blind and superstitious multitude, than the throne of all the Cæsars. This change, no doubt, was gradual—it cannot entirely be ascribed to Gregory, nor to any other individual; indications of that pretension may even be discovered in very early ecclesiastical writers; but that Pope exerted himself more than any of his predecessors to confirm it, and to give to that uncertain ground-work a stability, which has enabled it to support the mighty papal edifice for so many ages.

It has also been observed that Gregory was the first who *The power of the keys.* asserted the power of the keys, as committed to the successor of St. Peter, rather than to the body of the Bishops; and he betrayed on many occasions a very ridiculous eagerness to secure their honour. Consequently he was profuse in his distribution of certain keys, endowed, as he was not ashamed to assert, with supernatural qualities; he even ventured to insult Anastasius, the Patriarch of Antioch, by such a gift. " I have sent you (he says) keys of the blessed Apostle Peter, your guardian, which, when placed upon the sick, are wont to be resplendent with numerous miracles.*" We may attribute this absurdity to the basest superstition, or to the most impudent hypocrisy; and we would gladly have preferred the more excusable motive, if the supposed advancement of the See, which was clearly concerned in these presents, did not rather lead us to the latter.

Two descriptions of papal agents rise into notice during the *Papal Envoys, or Legates and Advocates.* pontificate of Gregory—the Apocrisiarii (Correspondents), who

---

* " Amatoris vestri, beati Petri Apostoli, vobis claves transmisi, quæ super ægros positæ multis solent miraculis coruscare." He addresses nearly the same words to one Andreas, a nobleman, with a similar present. And in another epistle (to Theotistus) he coolly relates a prodigy which had once been performed by one of those keys upon a Lombard soldier. Baronius, ann. 585, sect. iv., ann. 597, sect. xiv., ann. 591., sect. vii., viii., The historian (in the first of those places) eagerly attaches to the keys the notion and omen of *possession,* which probably did not occur to a Pope (not even to Pope Gregory) in the sixth century.

acted as envoys or legates at the Court and at the See of Constantinople; and the Defensores, or Advocates, who, besides
their general commission to protect* the property of St. Peter,
appear to have been vested with a kind of appellative jurisdiction, which might sometimes interfere with that of the bishops.
The former of these appointments tended to raise the external
dignity of the See; the latter to extend its internal influence.
Again, we find sufficient evidence, in the records of this age,
that a practice which afterwards proved one of the most fruitful
sources of Papal power, was already gaining ground—that of
appeal from episcopal decision to the Roman See. It does not,
indeed, appear that it was founded on any general law, civil or
ecclesiastical; but it proceeded very naturally from the *prejudice* attached to the name of Rome, and the chair of St. Peter;
and it was carefully encouraged by the See, whose authority
was insensibly augmented by it. Before we quit the subject of
papal aggrandisement, we shall mention one other circumstance only†. Great relaxation in the monastic discipline of
the age justified the very sedulous interference of Gregory to
restrain it; and so much address did that pontiff combine with
his diligence, as not only to reform the order, but also to secure
and protect it. For, while he enforced the severity of the
ancient rules with judicious rigour‡, he took measures to shelter it from episcopal oppression, and taught it hereafter to look
to Rome for redress and favour. As none are ignorant how firm
a support to papal power was furnished in later ages by the
devotion of the monasteries, it is important to record the origin

Connexion
of the Pope
with the
Monaste-
ries.

---

* Baron. ann. 598, sect. xv. xix. Gibbon (chap. xlv.) considers them to have
possessed not a civil only, but a criminal jurisdiction over the tenants and hus-
bandmen of the Holy See.

† "The bishops of Italy and the adjacent islands acknowledged the Roman
Pontiff as their special Metropolitan. Even the existence, the union and the
translation of episcopal seats was decided by his absolute discretion; and his successful inroads into the provinces of Greece, of Spain, and of Gaul, might countenance the more lofty pretensions of succeeding popes. He interposed to prevent the abuses of popular elections ; his zealous care maintained the purity of
faith and discipline ; and the apostolic shepherd assiduously watched over the
faith and discipline of the subordinate pastors." Gibbon, chap. xlv.

‡ Fleury, H. E. lib. xxxvi. sect. 33 and 34, has condensed the original information contained in the third and following epistles of Gregory.

of that connexion; and it is difficult to discover any earlier trace of it than that which we have mentioned.

Gibbon, who has drawn with vigour and impartiality the character of Gregory, has much over-rated his qualities when he designates him as the *greatest* of that name. It is very true that the mixture of simplicity and cunning, of pride and humility*, of sense and superstition, which singularly distinguished him, was happily suited both to his station and to the temper of the times; and it might perhaps be pleaded, that he did no more than yield to that evil temper, when he gave sanction to opinions and usages which were at variance with the spirit of Scripture. But this was to consult his present convenience or popularity, not his perpetual fame. Those who follow the stream of prejudice may be excused or pitied, but they can establish no claim to greatness, no title to the respect or gratitude of a posterity to which they transmit, without correction, the errors or vices of their ancestors. So far as he applied himself to remedy those vices or imperfections, so far as he reformed the discipline and repressed the avarice of his clergy, and introduced such improvements into other departments of the system as were consistent with the Gospel truth on which it stood, his name is deservedly celebrated by every honest Christian; but his eagerness in the encouragement of superstitious corruptions (for he was not even contented to tolerate, still less did he make any effort to repress them) must not be treated with indifference or indulgence; because the diffusion of error† has a far more

The various qualities of Gregory.

---

* His humility sometimes descended to baseness. The abject adulation with which he courted Phocas, the usurper of the Eastern Throne, the most execrable parricide in history, proves (as Bayle has malignantly remarked) that those who prevailed with him to accept the Popedom, knew him better than he knew himself. " Ils voyoient en lui le fonds de toutes les ruses et de toutes les souplesses dont on a besoin pour se faire de grands protecteurs, et pour attirer sur l'Eglise les bénédictions de la terre." The motive of his flattery was jealousy of the Patriarch of Constantinople. He addressed, with the same servility, Brunehaud, a very wicked Queen of France, and again found his excuse in the interests of his Church.

† In his epistle to the King of England, Gregory (cited by Baronius, ann. 601, sect. xix.) thus expresses his own millennarian opinions. " Besides, we wish you (vestram gloriam) to know, as we learn from the words of Almighty God, in the Holy Scriptures, that the end of the present world is already near, and the kingdom of the Saints is at hand, which can know no end. But as the end of the

pernicious consequence in religious than in other matters. A mere speculative falsehood will mislead the understanding of the studious, but it will not reach his principles of action; a wrong political axiom will unquestionably influence for a time the happiness of a nation; but on the discovery of its falsity, it is not difficult to modify or reject it, because it can seldom become rooted in the habits or the prejudices of the people. But the religious impostures which were authorized and propagated by Gregory affected not the belief only, but the conduct and character of the greater portion of Christendom through a long succession of ages; and while their certain and necessary tendency was to debase the mass of believers, and to deliver them over in blindness and bondage to a spiritual tyranny, their final and most disastrous effect has been, to enlarge the path of infidelity, by dissociating the use of reason from the belief in Revelation.

At the same time it is proper to mention, that the religious compositions of that age, though containing frequent indications of the growing superstition, were not destitute of excellent precepts and pious exhortations; and it will not be out of place here to present to the reader a short specimen of the discourses, which were delivered to a Christian people in the age of its darkest ignorance.

A sermon of St. Eligius.

St. Eligius, or Eloi, bishop of Noyon and contemporary with Gregory, was celebrated for his ardour in searching after the bodies of martyrs, and his miraculous sagacity in discovering them—yet his sermons to the people contain some of the purest admonitions of Christian morality*. "Wherefore, my brethren,

---

world is now approaching, many things hang over us which before were not,—to wit, change of atmosphere, and terrors from Heaven, and unseasonable tempests, war, famine, pestilence, and earthquakes,—which however shall not all fall out in our days, but will certainly follow afterwards." The caution of the concluding sentence would almost prove the Pope's distrust in his own prophecy.

* See the life of Eligius in the Spicilegium Dacherii, vol. v., p. 147—304. Our reason for selecting this passage is, that it has been most grossly and unpardonably mis-represented by Mosheim (cent. vii., p. ii., c. iv.) That writer has been so exceedingly unjust both to St. Eligius and his Church, as to select from the bishop's sermon certain passages (which we have put in italics) and string them together, without any notice of the context, and thus present them as a fair specimen of the compositions of that age, and of the sort of piety inculcated by the hierarchy. And as the historian has been at the pains to weed

love your friends in God, and love your enemies on account
of God, for he who loveth his neighbour (saith the apostle)
hath fulfilled the law; for the man who would be a true
Christian must observe the precepts, since he who observes not
circumvents himself.   He, then, is a good Christian, who believes not in charms or inventions of the devil, but places the
whole of his hope in Christ alone; who receives the stranger
with joy, as though he were receiving Christ himself; since it
was He who said, ' I was a stranger, and ye took me in;' and
' inasmuch as ye have done it unto the least of these my brethren, ye have done it unto me.'   *He, I say, is a good Christian,*
who washes the feet of the strangers, and cherishes them as his
beloved parents; who gives alms to the poor in proportion to
his possessions; *who goes frequently to church and makes his
oblations at God's altar; who never tastes of his own fruit
until he hath presented some to God;* who has no deceitful
balances, nor deceitful measures; who has never lent his money
on usury; who both lives chastely himself, and teaches his
children and his neighbours to live chastely and in the fear of
God; *and who for many days before the festivals observes strict
chastity, though he be married, that he may approach the altar
with a safe conscience; lastly, who can repeat the Creed and
the Lord's Prayer,* and teaches the same to his children and
his family.   He who is such as this, without any doubt is a
true Christian, and Christ dwells in him.

   " Behold! ye have heard, my brethren, what sort of people
good Christians are; wherefore strive as much as you are able,
with the help of God, that the name of Christ may not be false
in you; but to the end that ye be true Christians, always pon-
der the precepts of Christ in your mind, and also fulfil them in
your practice. *Redeem your souls from punishment whilst you*

out the original expressions and give them with a direct reference to the Spicilegium, he has imposed for a while upon the confidence of some following writers.
In the mean time, the impression which he conveys to his readers is wholly
false: and the calumny thus indirectly cast upon his author is not the less reprehensible, because it falls on one of the obscurest saints in the Roman calendar.
If the very essence of all history be truth, and if the deliberate violation of truth
be sinful in the profane annalist, still less can it deserve pardon or mercy in the
historian of the Church of Christ.

have it in your power; give alms according to your means; keep peace and charity; recall the contentious to concord; avoid lies; tremble at perjury; bear not false witness; commit no theft; *offer your free gifts and tithes to the churches; contribute towards the luminaries in the holy places;* repeat the Creed and the Lord's Prayer, and teach it to your children; instruct and correct even your god-children, and recollect that you are their sponsors with God. *Repair frequently to church, and humbly implore the protection of the saints;* observe the Lord's day, through reverence for Christ's resurrection, without any bodily work; piously celebrate the solemnities of the saints; love your neighbours as yourselves, and do as you would be done by; and what you wish not to be done to yourselves, that do to no man. Observe charity before all things, because charity covers a multitude of sins; be hospitable, humble, placing all your solicitude in God, since he hath care of you. Visit the infirm, seek out those who are in prison, take charge of strangers, feed the hungry, clothe the naked. Despise jugglers and magicians; be just in your measures; require of no man more than your due; and on no account exact usury. *If you observe these things, you may appear boldly at God's tribunal in the day of judgment, and say, Give, Lord, as we have given;* show compassion even as we have shown it; we have fulfilled what thou hast commanded, do thou now reward us as thou hast promised."

Ecclesiastical History is not distinguished by any character of very great eminence for the period of above a hundred and fifty years, which separates Gregory from Charlemagne; nor is that period marked by any single occurrence of striking importance, except the separation of the Roman states from the Eastern empire, and the donation made by Pepin to the Holy See. Yet very considerable changes were gradually taking place in the constitution of the Church, which it is the more necessary to detect and notice, because they are not discovered without some care, and have indeed commonly escaped the observation which is due to them. The conquest of the Western empire by the barbarians, its subdivision into numerous principalities and provinces, and the prevalence of the institu-

Changes from Gregory to Charlemagne.

tions and habits of the conquerors, could not fail to influence, in many respects, the religious establishment of those countries. And hence it is that the distinction between the Eastern and Western Churches, which may be traced in name, at least, to the division of the empire, was afterwards extended and widened by many substantial points of difference. In the former, indeed, very few alterations took place after the time of Justinian, even in the form of administering the Church, and none in the principles of its constitution: if some new privileges, or additional revenues, seemed to swell the importance of the clergy, yet the emperors maintained so firmly their undisputed supremacy*, and exerted, moreover, such frequent interference in spiritual affairs, that the power of the hierarchy received no real increase, nor did any other circumstances accidentally intrude, to enlarge beyond its just limits their influence over the people. But the policy for the most part pursued by the Western kings was different—they were usually watchful in preserving their temporal rights over the Church, and even in usurping others which they did not possess, especially that of episcopal election: but they abstained from all intervention in matters strictly spiritual; and in committing to the priesthood the entire regulation of doctrine, and consigning to their uncontrolled direction the consciences of their ignorant and uncivilized subjects, they left to that body much larger means of despotic and permanent authority, than any of those of which they deprived it.

In the more enlightened provinces of the East, the discussion of theological subjects was not uncommonly shared by intelligent laymen; but in the West it became exclusively confined to the clergy, and their dictates, howsoever remote from scripture or reason, were submissively and blindly received. Again, in the aristocratical assemblies, by which political affairs were chiefly regulated, the property and intelligence of the bishops acquired for them both rank and influence; and thus also were they placed in a different position from their brethren in the East, where the original spiritual character of the hierarchy was more rigidly preserved. It has been already remarked,

Marginal note: Distinctions between the Eastern and Western Churches.

---

* Giannone, Stor. di Nap., lib. iii., cap. vi.

that the limits of the spiritual and temporal powers were, even from the very establishment of Christianity, liable to some confusion and perplexity.   They were long maintained, however, with tolerable distinctness in the countries which escaped from barbarian invasion; but in the West, from the circumstances just mentioned, and from the unsettled and arbitrary form of the civil governments, the causes of discord and temptations to mutual aggression were incalculably multiplied.

The clergy were very early divided into major and minor orders, of which the latter consisted of the acolyths, porters, **Degrada-** exorcists, and readers.   Between the sixth and eighth century **tion of the** this lost its whole weight and almost name in the Church; and **Western** **Clergy.** even the higher order of subdeacons, deacons, and priests, suffered great degradation.   The kings of the West, in their desire to devote the whole of their free subjects to military service, forbade the ordination of a freeman without their particular consent; and hence proceeded the debasing, but not uncommon, practice of conferring the office of priesthood on serfs of the Church, emancipated for that purpose.   Nor did the bishops contend against this innovation so vigorously as the interests of the Church required, because their own authority was obviously augmented by the humiliation of the order next below them.   Add to this, that the priests were in some places, and perhaps generally, bound, on their ordination, by a solemn obligation to remain attached to the Church to which they were originally appointed—a sort of servitude which subjected even their persons to the authority of the bishop.   No such changes in the constitution of the clergy took place in the Eastern Church.

The Ton- Another order was rapidly increasing in the seventh and **sure.** eighth centuries, which probably exercised more influence in Church matters than is usually attributed to it.   The tonsure was originally considered as a sign of destination for orders, (signum destinationis ad ordinem,) and was given to those only who were intended for the sacred profession; but in aftertimes it was less discriminately administered, and was made the means of connecting with the Church a large body of persons who received some of the immunities without any of the restrictions of the sacerdotal condition, and became clerks without being ecclesiastics. It may be true* that they introduced to a certain extent a sort of lay influence into the ecclesiastical administration; but they had probably a much greater effect in diffusing that of the clergy among the private and sacred relation of domestic life.

The grand principle of the "Unity of the Church"—existing as one mighty spiritual communion undivided by any diversity in place, time, language, government, or other circumstances— though it was broached as early as the third century, did not enter into full operation till the dissolution of the Western empire. Its worst effects had, indeed, been developed before that time in the persecutions to which it gave birth on both sides of the Adriatic. But the good, which it was capable of producing, was not felt until the Western Provinces were broken up into numerous, and independent, and hostile states, with no political bond of union, and little friendly or commercial intercourse. It was then that the notion of one universal religious society contributed to supply the want of international sympathy and co-operation, and, through the means of a common belief, introduced the feeling of common interests, and the exercise of common virtues. Subsequently, during the seventh and eighth centuries, the principle was more rapidly progressive; and it presently gave birth to a second principle, which naturally sprang from it—viz. that the one body could have only one head. The

Unity of the Church.

* Guizot (Hist. de la Civilisation en France, 13 Leçon) mentions four avenues through which the laity still continued, in the seventh and eighth centuries, to exert an influence in ecclesiastical matters. (1.) The distinction between the Ordination and the Tonsure, and the numbers of those who received the latter only. (2.) The founder of a Church or Chapel, whether bishop or layman, possessed the privilege of appointing the minister to serve it. (3.) Chaplains were very commonly resident in noble families for the service of the private oratories. (4.) Certain laymen, under the names of Causidici, Tutores, and Vicedomini, were appointed at an early period for the protection of the Church property. They originated, it would seem, in the African Church; at Rome they were called Defensores, and they were afterwards employed in Gaul, under the title of Advocates. Fleury (end of livre xliv.) mentions that they were originally Scholastics or Lawyers; but that after the barbarian conquests they possessed also a military character—to the end that, in case of necessity, they might also be qualified to defend the interests of the Church by material weapons.

general footing which this acquired, at least throughout the West, contributed in no small degree to prepare and smooth the way to papal despotism.

Councils of Toledo.   Much of the history of this period is collected from the canons of the councils held in all the kingdoms of the West, and especially in Spain—for the ecclesiastical affairs of Gaul * were also in part regulated by these last. Those of Toledo were the most celebrated and influential, and the attention which was paid to their proceedings even by the Roman See sufficiently proves the authority which they held in the Church. The fifteenth of these was assembled in 688, and the *last*, not long before the invasion of the Saracens, in 696. But, upon the whole, the number of councils diminished during the seventh and eighth centuries, and in Gaul especially we find that, whereas fifty-four were held in the sixth, twenty only assembled in the seventh century, and only seven during the first half of the eighth. This gradual disuse of one of the most ancient and legitimate methods of governing the Church, and one of the best guarantees both for its inward purity and external independence, was a proof of its growing corruption, and a fearful omen for its future prosperity. It arose in some measure from a cause which we are about to mention.

Decay of the Metropolitan system.   The early origin and duties of the metropolitans have already been noticed: they were the prelates resident in the capital of the province, and their legitimate office was to preside in provincial councils; but they endeavoured to extend their consequence by usurping a judicial authority in charges against bishops, and other matters properly lying under the cognizance of the council; and they had some success until the sixth century. But from this period we may date their downfall: the ambition of the popes, always jealous of their power, and anxious to transfer it to the Holy See, pressed and assailed them from above: from below, the episcopal order, preferring a distant and indulgent control to the more rigid scrutiny of a do-

---

* The fourth council of Toledo, held in 633, ordains an uniformity of rites and ceremonies, prayer and psalmody, throughout Spain and Gaul—the same office of the mass, and other services. Fleury, l. xxxvii., sect. 46.

mestic censor, were equally eager for their overthrow; and this was greatly facilitated by the minute subdivisions of some of the Western provinces, which in many cases politically separated the metropolitan from the bishops who were placed under his superintendence, and thus at once annihilated his influence. From these causes the metropolitan system fell into decay, so that little more than its name remained at the end of the eighth century—and closely connected with its fall was the disuse of provincial councils.

The steps, by which the popes progressively subverted that system, are so clearly traced by Giannone*, that we shall here give the substance of his account. In the fifth century the title of patriarch was universally acknowledged to belong, in common with the four Oriental prelates, to the bishop of Rome. His ordinary power indeed did not extend beyond the provinces called Suburban (Suburbicarie), those which obeyed the vicar-general of Rome; and to these limits it was confined till the reign of Valentinian. But in process of time, as the prerogatives of *primacy* were united in his person, it was easy to stretch them farther. It belonged to him as primate to have regard and attention; on this ground he began to send into such provinces as seemed to require such superintendence his own vicars; in Illyria first, afterwards in Thessaly and Macedonia, the delegates of the Roman pontiff exercised patriarchal authority. This he presently afterwards extended over the whole of Italy, over Gaul and Spain, as well as over all countries newly converted by his missionaries; so that the Greeks themselves acknowledged him to be sole *patriarch* of the West. The next step of the popes, which occasioned no small disturbances, was to usurp the power of ordaining bishops throughout all the western Church, which was no less than to subvert the rights of all the metropolitans. They proceeded farther, and claimed the office of ordaining the metropolitans themselves.

The method they made use of to usurp the rights of the metropolitans regarding ordination was, to send them the vest

* Storia di Napoli, lib. iv. c. 6.

or *pallium**—for it was by means of this that the metropolitans were invested by the holy pontiff with the power of ordaining the bishops of the province; whence it followed that such power was not possessed by them unless by this grant of the pallium. Here another point was gained—the metropolitans had not the power of exercising all the episcopal functions until they had received the pallium from the pope. The last step naturally followed this—that the pope would not grant the pallium until the metropolitans had taken an oath of fidelity such as he required. Another ground on which he advanced was this—he contrived that appeals from the decisions of the metropolitans, especially relating to disputed elections of bishops, should be brought before himself; that if the electors had been negligent, or the elected unfit, the election should devolve on the pope; that he alone should possess the right of accepting the cessions of sees, of determining translations, and the coadjutorships in the next succession; and lastly, that the confirmation of all episcopal elections should be vested in the Holy See.

Aggrandisement and consequent corruption of the episcopal order. The great result which was brought about by the above circumstances, and which showed itself early in the West—as to the West were also confined the changes which we have mentioned—was the undue aggrandisement of the episcopal order, and its consequent deformity and corruption. From the moment that the princes succeeded in usurping the appointment to vacant sees, the mutual awe and dependence of the bishop and his clergy were at an end. The original method of election, according to which the dignity was generally conferred on some eminent ecclesiastic who had long resided in the diocese, secured at least some degree of deference in the elected to the office and privileges of the priesthood; but the practice of regal appointment broke that tie, and the stranger, who was frequently intruded, with few common interests or affections, gave loose without any restraint to his insolence or his avarice, in an

---

* It was sent in the first instance in token of an honour, to which no condition was attached—but afterwards in attestation of their subjection to the See, and obedience to its canonical commands. The *virtues* of the Pallium are described at great length in an epistle from Pope Zachary to Boniface, Baron. ann. 742, s. v.

age and condition of society in which public opinion had no influence. Accordingly we collect, even from the councils of
those times which were entirely composed of bishops, the
violent excesses to which many members of that order proceeded. "We have learnt (says the council of Toledo, in 589)
that the bishops treat their parishes not episcopally but cruelly,
and oppress their dioceses with exactions. Wherefore, let all
that the bishops would appropriate to themselves be refused,
excepting that which the ancient constitutions grant to them;
and let the clergy, whether parochial or diocesan, who are
tormented by the bishop, carry their complaints to the metropolitan, and let the metropolitan hasten to repress such excesses." Nearly a century afterwards, the fourth council of
Braga (in 675) inveighs against the brutality of certain bishops
who treated honourable men like robbers, and lacerated priests,
abbots, and deacons, with personal chastisement. "Avarice
(says the council of Toledo in 633) is the root of all evils, and
that detestable thirst takes possession even of the hearts of
bishops. Many of the faithful, through the love of Christ and
the martyrs, build chapels in the parishes of the bishops, and
leave offerings there; but the bishops seize them and turn them
to their own use. Hence it follows that clerks are wanting to
perform the divine offices, for they receive not their fees; and
the chapels when dilapidated are not repaired, because sacerdotal avidity has carried away the resources, &c." Besides
these and similar proofs, which might be brought in great
abundance, the tyrannical oppressions of the bishops are sufficiently evinced by the conspiracies or coalitions of the priesthood to resist them, which are sometimes mentioned, of course
with reprehension and menace, by the councils of the sixth and
seventh centuries.

Notwithstanding the measures taken to repress it, the licence
and the demoralization of the episcopal order gradually increased, and towards the close of the eighth century it had
reached perhaps the farthest limit to which it ever proceeded.
The restraint, which had formerly been imposed by the watchful superintendence of provincial councils and metropolitans,
was feebly supplied by the rare, and cautious, and often inef-

fectual interference of the Roman see. The practice of regal
election freed the bishop from any check, with which either respect or gratitude towards his clergy and people might otherwise have supplied him—and the positive degradation of the
clergy itself removed him still farther from any deference to
the feelings, or even the rights of that body. Sole adminis-
trator of the revenues of the Church, he possessed the most
ample means of plunder and usurpation; while his close connexion with political transactions, and the weight, which he
exerted in the most important deliberations of the state, so in-
terwove the temporal with the spiritual office and duties, and
also added to his legitimate authority so much temporal power,
that there were few excesses which he might not hope to commit with impunity. It is therefore without surprise that we
find him at one time advancing to battle* at the head of his
armed attendants, and at another engaged in marauding ex-
peditions from motives of plunder or private hostility. His
habits and his manners alike departed from the ecclesiastical
character, and he grew to resemble the rude barons who surrounded him, both in the extent of his power, and the insolence
with which he exercised it.

The Papal
principle.

We now turn to Rome—the centre to which most of our attention must hereafter be directed—and having shown the progress of the religious aristocracy during the seventh and eighth
ages, let us observe whether any corresponding advance was
made by the monarchical principle. Gregory the Great died
in the year 604; and certainly if his immediate successors
had equalled him in energy and ambition, the yet distant period of pontifical despotism might have been greatly anticipated.
But the fact was so far otherwise, that, through a dreary period
of almost five centuries, the Vatican was never ruled by any
character of sufficient transcendency to assert its single supereminence, and seize the sceptre which was so long presented to
it by superstition and ignorance. But this accident, though it
retarded the maturity of the Roman Church, did not prevent

* It should not be forgotten, however, that this character was sometimes
assumed on royal compulsion; nor was this the only stain which the Church
received from its contact with the wild barbarism of those ages.

the gradual operation of the principles on which it was now firmly founded ; and if it be the province of genius alone to create those commanding situations and circumstances, by which systems are formed or established, a very ordinary mind may turn them to advantage when created and presented. And thus the long succession of obscure pontiffs, who presided in the West for the century and a half which followed, may have profited by such occasions as were offered to extend the authority of the Church and exalt the supremacy of its head. At least we have reason to believe, that both the one and the other of those objects were, upon the whole, advanced during the period in question.

Within fifty years from the death of Gregory, pope St. Mar- tin assembled a council at Rome, in which, among various ex- positions of doctrine, he condemned a certain heresy at that time maintained by Constans, the emperor of the East. That prince, little disposed to pardon the offence, sent his exarch into Italy with orders to seize the person of the pontiff. By the em- ployment of some address he succeeded in his mission; in the year 653 St. Martin was carried away from Rome a captive to Constantinople, and thence, after enduring, according to the Catholic historians, a multitude of insults, he was exiled to the Chersonesus. In the year following (654) he died there; and his successor Eugenius was appointed by the emperor. The singularity of this circumstance has recommended it to our notice, rather than its importance. It was an isolated event, de- pending solely on the political power which the emperor of the day might happen to possess over his Italian subjects, and not at all affecting the influence which the Holy See was now ac- quiring in every quarter of the West—for *that* was the ground on which its battles were to be fought and its conquests gained, and to that they were destined to be confined; and so long as it suffered no reverses in that field, it mattered little what might be the result of an occasional dispute either with the patriarch or the emperor of the East.

We have already mentioned that, during the seventh and eighth centuries, some successful inroads were made by the popes on the privileges of the metropolitans, especially in their

[margin note:] Seizure of Pope Mar- tin by the emperor, 653, A. D.

election or confirmation; and the influence of St. Boniface, the apostle of Germany, was warmly exerted about the year 742 among the bishops of France and Germany, to extend the authority of the see. Another occurrence, which tended much more effectually, though by a very different course, to the same result, took place almost immediately afterwards.

The donation of Pepin, 754 A.D. Pepin, who was mayor of the palace to Childeric III., King of France, was desirous to dethrone his imbecile master, and to usurp the name, after having long exercised the power, of royalty. Accordingly he assembled the states of the realm, and they gave it as their opinion that the bishop of Rome should previously be consulted respecting the lawfulness of the project. In consequence ambassadors were sent to Zachary with a question to the following import—" Whether the divine law did not permit a valiant and warlike people to dethrone a pusillanimous and indolent monarch, who was incapable of discharging any of the functions of royalty, and to substitute in his place one more worthy of rule, and who had already rendered most important services to the state?" The answer of the pope was such as the usurper desired: Childeric was stripped of royalty without any opposition, and Pepin took undisputed possession of the throne.

This occurrence is generally related as the first instance of the temporal ambition of the Vatican, or at least of its interference with the rights of princes and the allegiance of subjects —and therefore the conduct of the pope has commonly been treated (by Protestant writers) with unmeasured reprehension. But certainly if we consider the act of Zachary distinct from those subsequent usurpations, to which in truth it did neither necessarily lead, nor even furnish a plausible precedent—if we consider the act, as historical justice requires of us, with a fair regard to the circumstances of France and Italy, and to the principles of the times, we shall be surprised indeed that a pope of the eighth century should so easily assent to the most popular principle of republicanism, and we may reject perhaps the political axiom which he has laid down; but we shall not accuse him of ambitious or unchristian arrogance for having resolved a difficulty which he did not create—for having answered a question which was proposed to him, as the highest human authority, and proposed without any interference or solicitation on his own part. It is true that the nature of his answer may have been influenced by his manifest interests, and the necessity in which the see then stood of a powerful protector—but this is a consideration quite distinct from the charge of intrusion into temporal concerns—and even in this matter, the mere absence of that splendid disinterestedness, which is rare in every age, and almost impossible in bad ages, is not to be stigmatized as inexcusably criminal, nor to be placed on the same level with the active, intriguing intrusiveness of guilty ambition.

It is not probable that Pope Zachary foresaw all the advantages which soon afterwards accrued to the Holy See from his decision—but pressed by the Greeks on one hand, and the Lombards on the other, he was no doubt glad of the occasion to create a substantial friendship beyond the Alps. The Lombards had gradually possessed themselves of those provinces of Italy which had remained longest attached to the Greek empire, under the name of the Exarchate of Ravenna*; and these warlike foreigners were now projecting the extension of their conquest to the whole peninsula. Stephen II., the successor of Zachary, applied to the court of France for protection; and instantly, Pepin, at the head of a numerous army, crossed the Alps, and overthrew the Lombards, and recovered the Exarchate from their hands. Pepin might have restored this valuable spoil to the throne of Constantinople with great praise of justice; or by the indulgence of ambition he might have retained permanent possession of it himself, without any reproach and with much profit—he did neither; but, mindful of his obligation to the Holy See, and sensible of the advantage of intimate alliance with it, he transferred the sovereignty over the provinces in question to the bishop of Rome. This celebrated *donation* took place in 754-5; and thus we observe that the earliest interference of the Vatican in temporal matters

---

* The strict limits of the Exarchate were included in the territories of Ravenna, Bologna and Ferrara: dependent on it was the Pentapolis, which extended along the Adriatic from Rimini to Ancona, and advanced into the interior as far as the ridges of the Apennines. Gibbon, c. 49.

brought after it, in the course of three years only, a rich and solid reward of temporal power, which has never since been either greatly increased or greatly diminished. The degree of authority which individual pontiffs have exerted in their states has indeed been liable in different ages to extreme diversities: still the authority itself has, in some shape, been perpetuated; and it has survived the splendid pretensions of the spiritual despotism, by whose infancy it was created, whose maturity it assisted to swell and pamper, and whose expiring influence will probably be confined to the same limits with itself.

Charlemagne's liberality to the Church and his motives for it.

The donation of Pepin awaited the confirmation of his son Charlemagne, for in the year 774 the Lombards again threatened the Roman territories; the aid of France was again invoked, and the monarch, who now afforded it, did not pause till he had entirely and finally subverted the empire of those conquerors, and proclaimed himself their king. Charlemagne was so far from disapproving his father's munificence to the pope, that he renewed and even increased the grant by some accession of territory; he drew still closer the bonds which allied him with a bishop, whose power was real and solid, however fanciful may have been the claims on which it stood; and thus he secured the zealous assistance of the See, when circumstances at length allowed him to mature the projects of his own ambition, and to proclaim himself, in the year 800, the Emperor of the West.

Charlemagne did not confine his benefactions to the bishop of Rome, but distributed them among all the orders of the hierarchy. He augmented their wealth, he enlarged their privileges, he exalted their dignity, he confirmed and extended their immunities; and were it not beyond contradiction established, that he was one of the greatest and wisest princes who ever reigned, some writers would not have hesitated to place him among the weakest of mankind. But the motives of his liberality were such as became a magnanimous and a benevolent monarch. Superstition has never been accounted among them, nor any unfounded fears or undue reverence of the ecclesiastical order—from the former he was perhaps more nearly exempt, than would have appeared possible in so rude an age; and in his transactions with the clergy, even with the pope himself, he never forgot, or allowed them to forget, his own supremacy. But he was desirous to civilize his barbarous subjects; he was anxious to influence their rude manners, and correct their vicious morals, by the more general diffusion and comprehension of the Christian truths; and he was willing also to sow the seeds of secular learning, and dispel the ignorance which oppressed his people. As the first step towards this regeneration, he presented to them the example of his own piety and his own learning *. But when he looked round for the means of communicating those blessings, the first and the only one which presented itself was the agency of the clergy. All that was influential among his subjects was contained in the two orders, military and ecclesiastical; and the wild turbulence of the former pointed them out rather as objects than instruments of reformation. The little of literary taste or acquirement which his kingdom contained was confined to the clergy; and there he laboured to encourage its increase, and to distribute it, through the only channel that was open, for the moral improvement of his subjects. It was chiefly with this view that he augmented the power and revenues of the Church, and raised its ministers to a more exalted rank and influence— influence which they subsequently studied to improve by methods not always honourable, but which, as circumstances then existed, it was pardonable if not commendable, it was magnanimous if it was not also politic, in Charlemagne to bestow.

---

* Many writers assert that he yielded not to any contemporary in either of those merits: the former, however, does not appear greatly to have influenced his moral practices; and as to his proficiency in the latter, we may at least venture to prefer to him his own master and preceptor Alcuin, an Englishman, the most celebrated divine of the day; and since we are assured that Charlemagne did not learn to write till late in life, doubtless we might make other exceptions. Alcuin is regarded as the restorer of letters in France, or at least the principal instrument of Charles in that work. In a letter to that prince, he avers that it rested with those two alone to raise up in France a Christian Athens. And his own writings attest his industry in restoring almost every branch of study. The devotion of Charlemagne to the services of religion is not disputed; through his whole life he was a regular attendant on the offices, even the nocturnal ceremonies, of the Church, and his last days were passed in correcting the text of the Gospel with the assistance of certain Greeks and Syrians. Fleury, H. E. l. 45, s. viii. and xviii.

But we shall readily admit that that monarch's munificence would have been very dangerously bestowed, had he not taken vigorous measures to reform, at the same time that he enriched, the ecclesiastical body; and some of those measures, though we had proposed to defer the particulars of his legislation till a subsequent chapter, may be mentioned with no less propriety in the present. In the year 789, at an assembly at Aix-la-Chapelle, Charlemagne published a Capitulary in eighty articles, chiefly with a view to restore the ancient discipline of the Church *. It was addressed to all ecclesiastics, and carried by the officers of the monarch into all the provinces. The instructions which most nearly affected the peculiar abuses of the age were those, perhaps, which exhorted the bishops to select their clergy from free men rather than from slaves; and which forbade bishops and abbots and abbesses to possess dogs, or hawks, or buffoons, or jugglers. At the same time he protected the property of the Church (which he designated as vota fidelium, pretia peccatorum et patrimonia pauperum) from the invasions and usurpations of the laity†.

By the celebrated council of Francfort (sur le Mein) held in 794, it was enacted, among many other wholesome regulations, that bishops should not be translated from city to city; that the bishop should never be absent from his Church for more than three weeks; that he should so diligently instruct his clergy, that a worthy successor might ever be found among them; and that after his death his heirs should only succeed to such portion of his property as he possessed before his ordination—all acquisitions subsequently made were to return to his Church. Other articles regulated the discipline of the inferior clergy. We shall conclude with one additional and very singular instance. Towards the close of the year 803 the emperor held a parliament at Worms, when a petition was presented to him by all the people of his states, of which the

---

* The substance may be found in Fleury, H. E. liv. 44, sect. 46, and liv. 45, sect. 26.

† Five years afterwards we observe that pope Hadrian pronounced all who perseveringly refused restitution guilty of *Heresy.* "Hæreticum eum *pro hujus erroris perseverantia* decernemus." Ap. Baron. ann. 794. s. 50.

following was the substance—"We pray your Majesty that henceforward bishops may not be constrained to join the army, as they have been hitherto. But when we march with you against the enemy, let them remain in their dioceses, occupied with their holy ministry, and praying for you and your army, singing masses, and making processions and almsgiving. For we have beheld some among them wounded and killed in battle, God is our witness with how much terror! and these accidents cause many to fly before the enemy. So that you will have more combatants if they remain in their dioceses, since many are employed in guarding them; and they will aid you more effectually by their prayers, raising their hands to heaven, after the manner of Moses. We make the same petition with respect to the priests, that they come not to the army, unless by the choice of their bishops, and that those be such in learning and morals that we may place full confidence in them, &c." Charlemagne replied as follows—"In our desire both to reform ourselves, and to leave an example to our successors, we ordain that no ecclesiastic shall join the army, except two or three bishops chosen by the others, to give the benediction, preach and conciliate, and with them some chosen priests to impose penance, celebrate mass, take care of the sick, and give the unction of holy oil and the viaticum. But these shall carry no arms, neither shall they go to battle nor shed any blood, but shall be contented to carry relics and holy vessels, and to pray for the combatants. The other bishops who remain at their churches shall send their vassals well armed with us or at our disposal, and shall pray for us and our army. For the people and the kings, who have permitted their priests to fight along with them, have not gained the advantage in their wars, as we know from what has happened in Gaul, in Spain, and in Lombardy. In adopting the contrary practice we hope to obtain victory over the pagans, and finally everlasting life."

CHAPTER XI.

On the Dissensions of the Church from the Age of Constantine to that of Charlemagne.

Division of the subject:—I. *Schism of the Donatists*—its real origin—progress—Circumcellions—conduct of Constantine—and his successor—of Julian—conference of Carthage—St. Augustin—the Vandals—Saracens—real extent of the offences of the Donatists: some account of St. Augustine.—II. *Priscillian*—his persecution and death—probable opinions—the first Martyr to religious dissent—how truly so—Ithakius—Martin of Tours—effect of Priscillian's death on his followers.—III. *Jovinian*—his opinions—by whom chiefly opposed—Edict of Honorius—Vigilantius—his character—abuses opposed by him—St. Jerome.—IV. *Pelagian Controversy*—its importance—and perplexity—Pelagius and Celestius—opposition of St. Augustine—Councils of Jerusalem and Diospolis—reference to Zosimus, Bishop of Rome—perseverance of St. Augustine—and his success—the sum of the Pelagian opinions—opposite doctrine of Fatalism—Semi-Pelagianism—Doctrine of the East—indifference of the Greek Church to this Controversy.—V. *Controversy* respecting the *Incarnation*—early origin—Apollinaris—his doctrine—Nestorius—his rash assertion—Cyril of Alexandria—Council of Ephesus—condemnation and banishment of Nestorius—progress of his opinions—what they really amounted to—Eutyches—the Monophysite heresy—Dioscorus of Alexandria—second council of Ephesus—interference of Pope Leo—Council of Chalcedon—condemnation and subsequent conduct of the Eutychians—Henoticon of Zeno—its object—effect—Controversies leading to the fifth General Council—Errors of Origen—The Three Chapters—Heraclius and the Monothelites—Council of Constantinople—general remarks on this Controversy—apology for those engaged in it—some of its consequences.—VI. *Worship of Images*—its specious origin—its progress in East and West—Leo the Isaurian—effects of his Edict—Constantine Copronymus—Synod of Constantinople—the Empress Irene—second Council of Nice, or Seventh General Council—Remarks on the Seven General Councils—Leo the Armenian—Michel—his Epistle to Louis le Débonnaire—The Empress Theodora—Feast of Orthodoxy—general remarks—John Damascenus—miracles—conduct of secular clergy—of monastic orders—of the common people—of Papal See—contrast between the Italian and French clergy.

THE controversies which occasioned the widest divisions in the Church during the five centuries following its establishment, (we do not refer to the Arian disputes, which have already been treated) principally regarded two subjects—the Incarnation of our blessed Saviour, and the Worship of Images. Indeed, if we except the Pelagian opinions, there were none other than

these, which left any lasting consequences behind them.   Still
we are not justified in confining our notice entirely to those
three, but we must extend it, though more concisely, to some
other dissensions, of less importance and earlier date, which
animated the passions of Churchmen during the interval between the Arian and the Incarnation controversies.   We shall
mention them in the following order :—1. The schism of the
Donatists ; 2. the heresy of the Priscillianists ; 3. the opinions
of the reformers, Jovinian and Vigilantius ; and shall then proceed to the doctrines of Pelagius and Celestius.   To these we
shall limit our curiosity ; for the various disputes, created,
directly or indirectly, by the writings of Origen, and the many
real (or supposed) ramifications of the Manichean heresy, are
not such as to claim a prominent place in this work.

I. On the death of Mensurius, Bishop of Carthage, in 311, Origin of
the clergy and people of that city and district elected in his the schism
place the Archdeacon Cæcilianus, and proceeded to his consecra- of the Donatists, 311
tion without waiting, as it would seem, for the consent of the A. D.
Bishops of Numidia, a contiguous and subordinate province.   Probably custom or courtesy was violated by this
neglect ; but the Numidians considered it also as an infringe-
ment of their right, and hastened to resent it as such.   This
was no doubt the real foundation of the schism—an objection
was indeed taken against the character of Felix, the Bishop
who had consecrated Cæcilianus : he was accused of being a
Traditor *, and the question of the validity of a consecration,
performed by such hands, was repeatedly brought forward in
the course of the controversy, and is continually mentioned by
those who have described it—nevertheless, the objection seems
to us to have been, in the first instance, a frivolous pretext.
The dissentients, headed by a certain *Donatus,* assembled a
Council of their own, condemned Cæcilianus, and appointed
his deacon, Majorinus, for his successor.   Both parties then
proceeded to great extremities ; and as there appeared no other
prospect of reconciliation, they agreed to bring the dispute be-

---

* *i. e.* of having delivered up copies of the Scriptures during Diocletian's persecution,

fore the Emperor Constantine, who had just then proclaimed
the establishment of Christianity.   Constantine inquired into
the affair, first by means of a Synod at Rome, consisting of
three Gaulish and fifteen Italian prelates*, at which the Bishop
of the capital presided ; and presently afterwards, by an inquiry
into the truth of the charges against Felix, before the civil magistrate Ælian, proconsul of Africa, assisted by several lay, and
for the most part military assessors : the decision, on both in-
vestigations, was unfavourable to the Donatists.

They were discontented ; seventy venerable Numidian prelates, assembled in council in the heart and light of Africa,
had rejected the authority of Cæcilianus : could so solemn an
act be superseded by a commission of a small number of obscure Bishops meeting in a different province, and perhaps
ignorant of the leading circumstances ? they submitted the matter to the Emperor's re-consideration. His patience was not yet
exhausted ; he immediately summoned a much more numerous
synod at Arles, in Gaul, and here again, after much serious de-
bate, the Donatists lost their cause.   Still dissatisfied, they had
recourse to the final expedient, an appeal to the personal justice of Constantine.   The Emperor again consented to their
request ; but on this occasion the motive of his indulgence may
be liable to some suspicion, since the very application admitted
the power of the Emperor to reverse the decision of an ecclesiastical council—a right which he might very naturally choose
to assert at that moment : at least it is certain that, in the year
316, he condescended to investigate the affair at Milan, in the
presence of the contending parties.   He deliberately confirmed
the former decisions ; and then, as these repeated condemnations had no other effect than to increase the perversity of the
schismatics, he applied the secular power to their correction.
He drove some into exile ; he is also said to have deprived
them of their churches, and even to have shed some blood.
This measure led to some violent disturbances ; many joined,
as persecuted, those whom they loved not as schismatics ; and

---

* Fleury, lib. x., sect. 11, records the names of most of them, and the order
of precedence.

the confusion thus generally occasioned gave license to a number of lawless ruffians, the refuse of Africa, of no sect, and probably of no faith, to range their weapons and their crimes on the side of the contumacious. These men, the soldiers of the Donatists, were called Circumcellions; and their savage excesses went very far to convert the schism into a rebellion. When the quarrel arrived at this point, it is well worthy of notice, that Constantine, instead of proceeding to extinguish the malcontents by the sword, attended to *the advice of the governors of Africa,* so as to repeal the laws which had been enacted against them, and to allow the people full liberty to adhere to the party which they might prefer. This change in his policy seems to have taken place in 321—after five years' experience of the opposite system. Their contests with the Government and the Catholics.

Not so his successor Constans: during his reign we read of the defeat of the Donatists at the battle of Bagnia, and of thirteen years of tumult and bloodshed, and uninterrupted persecution. These severe measures, which the fury of the Circumcellions could scarcely justify, destroyed many, and dispersed into other countries a still greater number of the perverse schismatics, but converted probably none.

The moment of reaction was not far distant; the numerous and revengeful exiles were restored to their home by the suspicious justice of Julian, and the horrors which they committed on their restoration are very vividly and seriously retailed by Fleury*. They expelled the Catholic people, violated the women, and murdered the children. They threw the Eucharist to the dogs, but the dogs became mad, and turning against their masters tore them in pieces. One of them threw out of the window a phial of the holy ointment, which fell among the stones without breaking. They exorcised the faithful in order to baptize them anew; they washed the walls of the churches, and broke the altars and burnt them—for most of those in

* L. xv., s. 32, on the partial authority of Optatus of Milevi, (lib. ii., p. 54, 55.) and Augustine—" Venistis rabidi, venistis irati, membra laniantes Ecclesiæ —subtiles in seductionibus, in cædibus immanes, &c. &c. Episcopi vestri jusserunt Eucharistiam canibus fundi: non sine signo divini judicii: nam iidem canes accensi rabie," &c.

Africa were then of wood—they broke the consecrated chalices and melted them down, to convert them to other purposes—in a word, they held as profane all that the Catholic Bishops had consecrated. Whatever may be the truth of these particulars, the sect appears to have sprung up, during the few following years, to the highest eminence which it at any time attained. Towards the conclusion of the fourth century Africa was covered with its churches, and its spiritual interests were guarded by a body of four hundred Bishops.

Let us observe the consequence of this prosperity—a violent division grew up among them, respecting some very insignificant person or thing, and opened a breach in their fortress to the persevering assaults of the Catholics. Besides which, the method of assault was now somewhat changed and refined ; the weapons of reason and disputation were now again admitted into the service of the Church ; and they were not without effect, since they were directed and sharpened by the genius of Augustine. The Bishop of Hippo* attacked the Donatists in his writings, in his public discourses, in his private conversation ; and so vigorously exposed their dangerous and seditious spirit, as to lessen their popularity in Africa, and to destroy any sympathy which their former sufferings might have created in the rest of Christendom.

Conference of Carthage, 411 A.D.

From this period they fell gradually into dishonour ; somewhat they still endured from the unjust application of the laws against heresy, of which no one has ever accused them ; but a more dangerous wound was inflicted by the celebrated conference held at Carthage in 411. The tribune Marcellinus was sent into Africa by the Emperor Honorius, with full power to terminate the controversy ; he convoked an assembly of the heads of both parties, and two hundred and eighty-six Catholic, and about two hundred and seventy-nine Donatist, bishops presented themselves in defence of their respective opinions. The most solemn preparations were made to give weight and dignity to this meeting, and its deliberations were watched with pro-

* He seems first to have taken the field while a simple presbyter, in the year 394.

found anxiety by the people of Africa*.   For three days the Tribune listened with respectful attention to the arguments advanced by both parties, and then proceeded to confirm the decisions of the former century, by pronouncing in favour of the Catholics.   Augustine has deserved the glory of this spiritual triumph—and, that no means might be wanting to make it decisive, it was vigorously pursued by the myrmidons of civil authority, who inflicted almost every punishment on the contumacious, except the last.   And even this exception was little more than nominal; for though the infliction of death, as the direct punishment of schism, is not enjoined by the Edict of Honorius, it necessarily followed, as the punishment of contumacy and rebellion.   The edict, however, even without that penalty, was so severe, and threatened to drive the Donatists to such extremities, that the civil magistrate, Dulcitius, hesitated to enforce it, until he should have taken counsel of Augustine. That prelate exhorted him to proceed—" since it was much better (he said) that some should perish by their own fires, than that the whole body should burn in the everlasting flames of Gehenna, through the desert of their impious dissension†."

The survivors took breath under the government of the Vandals, who conquered that part of Africa from the Romans about the year 427; and when it was recovered by Belisarius, more than a hundred years afterwards, the sect of the Donatists was still found to exist there as a separate communion.   It was again exposed to the jealousy of the Catholics, and particularly attracted the hostility of Gregory the Great; but we do not learn that it suffered further persecution.   We are told that it dwindled into insignificance about the end of the sixth century; but it is not improbable that the Saracen invaders of Numidia

* " Let the Bishops (says Marcellinus in a previous proclamation) signify to the people in their sermons to keep themselves quiet and silent.   I will publish my sentence and expose it to the judgment of all the people of Carthage."   St. Augustine himself addressed an epistle or tract on this controversy to the Donatist laity.   The particulars of the conference are retailed with great patience by Fleury in his twenty-second book.   See the " Gesta Collationis Carthagini habitæ inter Cath. et Don., &c." published with the works of Optatus Milev.   Ed. Paris.

† Epist. 61, (204).   Honorius's Edict appears in the Theodosian Code, and a very sufficient specimen of it may be found in Jortin, H. E., ann. 414.

found there, some few years later, the remnant of a sect not ill-disposed to favour any invader, nor unmindful of the sufferings of their ancestors.

The ground of difference.

The Donatists have never been charged, with the slightest show of truth, with any error of doctrine, or any defect in Church government or discipline, or any depravity of moral practice; they agreed with their adversaries in every respect, except one—they did not acknowledge as legitimate the ministry of the African Church, but considered their own body to be the true, uncorrupted, universal Church. It is quite clear that they pushed their schism to very great extremities—even to that of rejecting the communion of all who were in communion with the Church which they called false; but this was the extent of their spiritual offence, even from the assertion of their enemies. The excesses of the Circumcellions lost them much of the sympathy which would otherwise have been bestowed on their misfortunes; but the outrages and association of those outlaws were generally disclaimed by the most respectable leaders of the sect. One strange sin, indeed, they are accused of encouraging, and of indulging with dreadful frequency—an uncontrollable inclination to suicide*. But suicide is the resource of the desperate; and it is unlikely that it found any favour among them, until oppression had persuaded them, that death was not the greatest among human evils.

Observations.

In the fortunes of the Donatists do we not trace the usual history of persecution? In its commencement fearful and reluctant, and, as it were, conscious of its corrupt origin, it irritates without depressing; then it hesitates, and next suspends the attack; thereon its object rises up and takes strength and courage. The same process is then repeated, under circumstances slightly different—with the same result. Then follows the passionate and sanguinary assault which destroys the noblest

---

* Mosheim, cent. v., p. ii., ch. v. An authority for this fact is Augustine, in his Epistle to Boniface, ch. iii. " Quidam etiam se trucidandos armatis viatoribus ingerebant, percussuros eos se, nisi ab iis perimerentur, terribiliter comminantes. Nonnunquam et ab judicibus transeuntibus extorquebant violenter, ut a carnificibus vel ab officio ferirentur. Jam vero per abrupta præcipitia, per aquas et flammas occidere seipsos quotidianus illis ludus fuit."

among the recusants, while the most active and dangerous are preserved by hypocrisy or exile—and thus the sect spreads secretly and widely; it secures a sympathy which it may not have merited by its excellence, and on the first occasion breaks out again with fresh force and fury. Then indeed, if recourse be had to argument, if greater right be on the stronger side, and if the secular sword be only employed to *pursue* the victory of reason, the cause of the sufferers becomes more feeble and less popular—but still, unless the pursuit be carried to absolute, individual extermination, the extinction even of the silliest heresy can only be effected by time—and time itself will complete its work at least as much by calming passion, as by correcting judgment.

The above narrative has introduced us to the name of Augustine, who was the most celebrated amongst the antient Christian fathers, and who deserves even now a more than usual attention, from the influence which his writings have unceasingly exerted in the Roman Catholic Church. But the notice which can here be bestowed upon him must necessarily be confined to the most important points.   He was born in Numidia, in the year 354, and his early youth was distinguished by his aversion from all study, and especially that of the Greek language.   But an ardent passion for poetry at length opened the gate, through which he entered into the fields of general literature.   From profane, he directed his attention to religious subjects ; and when we recollect that Tertullian, the greatest amongst his African predecessors, seceded from the Church in the maturity of his judgment and learning, in order to embrace the visions of a raving fanatic, we are scarcely astonished to learn that the youthful imagination of Augustine was seduced by the Manichæan opinions.   He appears to have retained them for nine or ten years, during which time his rhetorical talents had raised him into notice; and it was not till the year 386 that he was persuaded (as it is said) by the sermons of St. Ambrose, and the writings of St. Paul, to return to the communion of the Church.   His baptism (he was previously a catechumen only) speedily followed his conversion; his ordination took place soon afterwards, and the city of Hippo, in Africa, which owes most

Notice of St. Augustine, 354—430 A.D.

of its celebrity to its association with his name, was that in
which he first ministered as Priest, and afterwards presided as
Bishop.   He died in 430, in the thirty-fifth year of his epis-
copate.

Of cessa-
tion of the
Agapæ.

The first recorded exploit of his ecclesiastical life was the
destruction of an inveterate and consecrated abuse.   We have
mentioned the innocent origin of the Agapæ or feasts of charity, and the good purposes to which, in early times, they contributed.   But as the influx of the Pagan converts grew more
rapid, and as these naturally sought in the new religion for any
resemblance to the popular ceremonies of the old, the solemnity
in question insensibly changed its character under their influence, and degenerated into the licence and debauchery of a
heathen festival.   Augustine, while yet a Presbyter, undertook
the difficult task of *persuading* the people to abandon a favourite and hereditary practice, and by the simple exertion of his
eloquence he succeeded.   Services of reading and chaunting
were substituted in its place; and while the Churches of the
heretics* resounded with the customary revelry, the voice of
devotion alone proceeded from the assemblies of the Catholics.
This change took place in the year 395; and from that moment the reputation of Augustine spread rapidly throughout
the African Church, and thence, as his labours proceeded, was
diffused with no less of splendour to the most distant parts of
Christendom.

His reasons
for adhe-
sion to the
Church.

Besides the faithful discharge of his episcopal and his private
duties, the Bishop of Hippo engaged deeply in the controversies
of the day; and his attacks are chiefly directed against the
Manichæans, the Donatists, and the Pelagians.   His familiarity with the errors of the first may have qualified him more
effectually to confute them—but it is at the same time curious
to observe the motives which he advanced for his own adhesion
to the Catholic Church.   They are the following: the consent of
the people; the authority which began in the faith of miracles,

---

* Epist. 29, ad Alypium.   This is the occasion on which it is recorded, that
as long as his eloquence was honoured only by the acclamations of the listening
multitudes, Augustine was sensible of its imperfection, and despaired of success
—his hopes were only revived by the sight of their tears.

which was nourished by hope, augmented by charity, confirmed by antiquity; the succession in the chair of St. Peter; and the *name* of Catholic so established, that if a stranger should ask *where* is the Catholic Church? no heretic would certainly dare to claim that title for his own communion*. These arguments, and such as these, have been so commonly reported in later ages, that, without at all entering (for such is not·our province) into the question of their real value, we are contented to record their high antiquity, and the sanction which they received from the name of Augustine.

His exertions against the Donatists, which we have already noticed, have attached to the character of that father the stain of persecution.   The maxim (says Mosheim†) which justified the chastisement of religious errors by civil penalties was confirmed and established by the authority of Augustine, and thus transmitted to following ages.   He cannot be vindicated from that charge‡; he unquestionably maintained the general principle, that the unity of the Church should be preserved by secular interference, and that its adversaries should be crushed by the material sword.   But his natural humanity in some degree counteracted the barbarity of his ecclesiastical principles; and there is still extant an epistle addressed by him to Marcellinus (in 412), in which he earnestly entreated that magistrate to extend mercy to certain Donatists, who had been convicted of some sanguinary excesses against the Catholics.   But the misfortune was, that, while his private philanthropy preserved the lives perhaps of a few individuals, the efficacy which he added to the worst maxim of Church policy, not only sharpened the shafts of injustice in his own time, but tempered them for long and fatal service in after ages.

His intolerant principles.

---

* No heretic was so likely to have laid that claim as a Donatist—yet even a Donatist, while he maintained that the true Catholic spirit and purity was alone perpetuated and inherent in his own communion, would scarcely have affirmed, that that was *bonâ fide* the Universal Church, which did not extend beyond the shores of Africa, and which had not the majority even there.

† Cent. iv., p. ii., ch. iii.

‡ Besides the epistle to Dulcitius, see his letter, or rather tract, to Boniface, " de Correctione Donatistarum;" and that to Vincentius (113, alias 48).   The principle is avowed and defended in both—at least provided the *animus* be to correct, not to revenge!

The Pelagians, the third class of his religious adversaries, will receive a separate notice in the following pages. Of the numerous works which he composed, unconnected with these controversies, that entitled "De Civitate Dei" has justly acquired the greatest celebrity. We may also mention his book on the Trinity among his most important productions. He devoted much diligence and judgment to the interpretation of Scripture; and his writings contain many excellent arguments for the truth of the religion, and of the evangelical history; but the mere barren enumeration of his works would convey neither amusement nor profit to the reader, and we have no space for abstracts sufficiently copious to make him familiar with the mind of the author.

Augustine and Jerome compared.

Erasmus has drawn a parallel between Augustine and his great contemporary, the monk of Palestine, which is certainly too favourable to the latter. "No one can deny (he says) that there is great importance in the country and education of men. Jerome was born at Stridona, which is so near to Italy, that the Italians claim him for a compatriot; he was educated at Rome under very learned masters. Augustine was born in Africa, a barbarous region, and singularly indifferent to literary pursuits, as he avows in his epistles. Jerome, a Christian, the child of Christians, imbibed with his very milk the philosophy of Christ: Augustine began to read St. Paul's epistles with no instructor when nearly thirty years of age. Jerome devoted his great talents for thirty years to the study of the Scriptures: Augustine was immediately hurried to the episcopal office, and compelled to teach to others what he had not yet learnt himself. We observe then, even supposing a parity of country, talents, masters, education, how much more learning was brought to the task by Jerome: for it is no trifling matter that he was skilled in the Greek and Hebrew languages; since in those days all theology, as well as all philosophy, was in possession of the Greeks. Augustine was ignorant of Greek*; at

---

* Dr. Lardner makes, we think, a very ineffectual attempt to prove that Augustine knew much more of that language than he even himself professed to know. For a few happy translations of Greek words, and even sentences, he was probably obliged to the learning of a friend or secretary.

least the very trifling knowledge which he possessed of it was insufficient for the study of the commentaries of the Greek writers*." The merit of more profound learning was unquestionably on the side of Jerome, but we cannot justly attribute to him any other superiority; in soundness of reasoning and in natural judgment he certainly yielded to the Bishop of Hippo, and in the only recorded point of difference† between them he was very properly corrected by that prelate. In depth of moral feeling and energy of affecting eloquence the advantage is also due to Augustine; and the natural suavity of his disposition, which forms so strong a contrast with what might almost be designated the ferocity of Jerome, tended to soften the acrimony of religious difference‡, and to throw some sparks of charity into the controversies in which he found himself almost necessarily engaged.

Some particulars relating to his private life are recorded by historians, on the evidence of his own writings, and other respectable authority. His furniture and his dress were plain, without affectation either of fineness or of poverty. He wore, like other people, a linen garment underneath, and one of wool without; he wore shoes and stockings, and exhorted those, who thought better to obey the Gospel by walking with naked feet, to assume no merit from that practice. " Let us observe cha-

Records of his private life.

---

* Erasmus ends his comparison by affirming, " that for his own part he learns more of Christian philosophy from one page of Origen than from ten of Augustine;" and others, perhaps, will add, from their own experience, " and from one page of Augustine, than from ten of Jerome."

† This dispute was on the verse (ch. ii., v. 11.) of St. Paul's epistle to the Galatians : " When Peter came to Antioch, I withstood him to the face, because he was to be blamed." Jerome had published his opinion, that the apostles had this public difference on a previous understanding, and by a charitable artifice; and that St. Paul in fact saw the policy and propriety of St. Peter's adhesion to the Jews, at the moment when he professed to condemn it. According to Augustine, this interpretation goes to overthrow the whole authority of Scripture ; for if it is once allowed to admit there the existence of serviceable falsehoods, and to say that St. Paul in that passage spoke what he did not mean, and treated St. Peter as reprehensible when he did not think him so, there is no passage which may not be similarly eluded. The heretics who condemn marriage would assert that St. Paul only approved it through condescension to the imperfection of the first Christians—and so of others.

‡ Compare, for instance, the manner of his opposition to the opinions of Jovinian with that of Jerome.

rity, he said : I admire your courage—endure my weakness."
His table was frugal, and ordinarily served with vegetables;
meat was seldom prepared, unless for guests or for the infirm,
but there was always wine. Excepting his spoons, which were
of silver, all the service was earthen, or of wood or marble,
not by necessity, but from a love for poverty. On his table
were written two verses, to forbid any scandal to be spoken of
the absent—proving that it was without a cloth, according to
the usage of antiquity. He never forgot the poor, and aided
them from the same fund on which he subsisted with his
clergy; that is, from the revenues of the Church or the oblations of the faithful. He paid great regard to hospitality, and
held it as a maxim, that it was a much preferable error to entertain a rogue, than to refuse an honest man. His usual
occupation was arbitration among Christians and persons of
all religions, who submitted their differences to him. But he
liked much better to decide between strangers than between his
friends—" for of the two strangers I may make one a friend; of
the two friends I shall make one an enemy." He applied himself little to the temporal interests of the Church, but busied
himself much more in study, and in the meditation of spiritual
concerns*.

Priscillian.   II. Priscillian, a Spanish bishop of birth and fortune and
eloquence, was accused by certain other bishops of the heresy
of the Manichæans : he was condemned by a council held at
Saragossa (in 380), and a rescript was then obtained for his
banishment, from the emperor Gratian; but he was speedily
restored to his country and his dignity. Gratian was assassinated, and succeeded by Maximus, a tyrant worthy of the
throne of Domitian; and before him † Idacius and Ithakius,
the two ecclesiastics most persevering in their zeal or malignity, again accused Priscillian. His followers were probably
not very numerous, but they presented themselves to plead
their cause and prove their innocence, before Damasus, Bishop
of Rome, and the celebrated Ambrose, at Milan—from neither

---

* Fleury, liv. xxiv., chap. xxxviii. xxxix.

† Sulpicius Severus mentions Magnus and Rufus as the two bishops who were
finally the successful agents in procuring the condemnation of Priscillian,

of them could they obtain a hearing*.   Perhaps their unfortunate instructor was not more successful at the court of Maximus; at least it is certain that, in the year 384, he was put to
death at Treves, with some of his associates, on no other pretext than his heretical opinions†.

It is now disputed what those opinions were; and it is probable *His pro-*
bable opi-
that the same dispute existed in his own time; since no ancient *nions.*
writer has given us any clear account of them—and none of the
works of Priscillian or any of his followers have reached us.
Sulpicius simply calls them gnostical; and it seems likely that
they made some approaches, perhaps very distant ones, to
the errors of the Manichæans respecting the two principles,
the doctrine of æons, or emanations from the divine nature,
and the creation of the world.   It is possible that they disputed the *reality* of Christ's birth and incarnation—though
they professed to receive the Scriptures both of the Old and
New Testament.   They are stated to have disbelieved the resurrection of the body, and they had some errors concerning the
nature and functions of the soul.   They are blamed for not
consuming the Eucharist at church, and for some irregularity
in the seasons of their fasts; and some of them were charged
besides (strange charges to be brought by Catholic accusers!)
with having deserted their social rank, in order to betake themselves to solitary devotion; and with holding opinions favourable
to celibacy.   For these offences, or such as these, Priscillian suffered death.   And it is a curious reflection, that at the same
moment in which Priscillian was suffering those pangs, for opinions *resembling* the Manichæan heresy, St. Augustine, the destined bulwark of the Catholic Church,—the man whose future

---

* Their opinions may have been adopted by several both among the nobility
and the people, and by a vast multitude of women (as is also asserted) in Spain;
but they obtained no footing elsewhere.   They are said to have been introduced into that country by one Marc, an Egyptian, of Memphis, and a Gnostic.
Augustine (Hæres. cap. 70) calls them a compound of Gnosticism and
Manicheism.   St. Leo brings them nearer to Sabellianism, ap. Maron. ann.
447; but in his epistle (xv.) to Turibius, where he approves of the interference of the "Mundi Principes" on such occasions, he confounds them with
Manicheism.

† We need not pause to notice some monstrous charges of immorality—such as
we have seen so commonly affixed to an unpopular heresy.

writings were to become a storehouse of the true doctrine for so many countries and ages—was actually and deeply involved in the very intricacies of the heresy itself. He returned to reason—but Priscillian, who was much nearer to it than himself, was hastily executed.

His fate has gained him the more celebrity, because it is usual to consider him as the first martyr to religious dissent. Not perhaps truly so—for between the years 325 and 384 many an obscure victim of the Arian heresy must have perished for his opinions, in silence and ignominy—but Arius himself escaped the storm; and it cannot be disputed that Priscillian was the first who atoned with his life for the dangerous distinction of founding a religious sect*. It is some consolation to be enabled to add, that the principle by which he suffered was not yet in favour with the Christian Church. The character of Ithakius, his most active enemy, is thus described by a contemporary historian (Sulpicius Severus†),—"he was a man void of all principle; loquacious, impudent, expensive, a slave to gluttony—so senseless as to represent every holy person who delighted in religious studies, and practised mortification and abstinence, as an associate or disciple of Priscillian."

Martin of Tours.

On the other hand, the persecuted heretic found a powerful protector in one of the most venerable prelates of that age, Martin of Tours, "a man comparable to the apostles." So long as Martin remained at the court of Maximus, his authority was sufficient to prevent the meditated injustice; he had even ventured to represent to that usurper, that it was "a new and unlawful attempt of the civil magistrate to take cognizance

---

* We should mention, perhaps, the distinction that Priscillian suffered death for the opinions themselves—directly and avowedly—not, as thousands before him had suffered, for contumacy in persisting in them,—a distinction which has no real value, except as marking the greater shamelessness of persecution in at length casting off her mask.

† Nearly at the end of his *Sacra Historia*. Sulpicius, though a moderate man, was a bitter enemy to the "doctrina exitiabilis," &c. of Priscillian. Therefore the following description of his personal character is the more valuable :— "Acer, inquies, facundus, multa lectione eruditus, disserendi ac disputandi promptissimus. Felix profecto, si non pravo studio corrupisset optimum ingenium : prorsus multa in eo animi et corporis bona cerneres. Vigilare multum, famem ac sitim ferre poterat, habendi minimè cupidus, utendi parcissimus."

of an ecclesiastical cause"—a boldness consistent with his peaceful virtues, and derived from the now acknowledged dignity of his profession. The deed was perpetrated in his absence, and he then protested against it, and withdrew from the communion of the murderers. The memory of this excellent prelate has been disfigured by the credulous historian, who intended to be his eulogist; and we would willingly believe, that the stupendous miracles, so profusely attributed to him, were created by the veneration of the vulgar, or even by the enthusiasm of the writer, not by the deliberate imposture of a pious Christian*.

Sulpicius proceeds to say, that "the death of Priscillian was so far from repressing the heresy of which he had been the author, that it conduced greatly to confirm and extend it; for his followers, who before had reverenced him as a pious man, began to worship him as a martyr. The bodies of those who had suffered death were carried back to Spain, and interred with great solemnity; and to swear by the name of Priscillian was practised as a religious act." Such were the immediate consequences of his execution; it does not appear, however, that his opinions took any deep or lasting root, or ever again became the occasion of offence or confusion to the Church.

III. The same age, almost the same year, which witnessed Jovinian, the death of one heretic for opinions, of which an undue admiration of bodily austerities and religious seclusion was one, beheld with less surprise the banishment of another heretic, for daring to raise his voice in disparagement of those same practices. Jovinian had received his education in an Italian convent; but the common feelings and principles of nature were not extinguished in him. He left his retirement and published a volume, in which he rashly endeavoured to show, that those

---

* "Men of probity in other respects, and fully persuaded of the truth of Christianity, (and such I take Martin, Paulinus, and Sulpicius to have been,) having found in the populace a strong taste for the marvellous, and no capacity for better proofs, judged it expedient rather to leave them to their prejudices, and to make use of those prejudices to confirm them in the true faith, than to undertake the vain task of curing them of their superstition, and run the risk of plunging them into vice and unbelief. Therefore they humoured the trick, and complied with the fashion, for the good of those who were deceived." Le Clerc, Bibl. Chois., ap. Jortin, ad ann. 402. This seems to be the simplest solution of the difficulty.

who followed the rules of the Gospel, amid the temptations and perplexities of social life, possessed as just a claim to the rewards of futurity, as those who observed the same rules in solitude; that pleasures are not necessarily sins; that temperance is as excellent a virtue as abstinence; and that the chaste enjoyments of marriage are as agreeable to the eye of a benevolent Deity, as the mortifications of unnatural celibacy. He was also charged with the speculative error, that all who have been regenerated by baptism, with perfect faith, were indefectible, and could not fail of their heavenly recompense. He may also have held this opinion—but the points on which the controversy turned were those which much more nearly affected the practice of mankind. Jerome, "the monk of the age," poured out in reply much passionate declamation in praise of the established superstitions, and some calumnious invectives against the person of the reformer; and as the current already ran too strongly in his favour, his clamours were echoed by the zealous multitude, while the wise were constrained to sorrow and silence*. Among the Christian Churches the foremost in the extinction of reason and true Christianity was the Church of Rome. Her impatience to crush the dangerous innovator was emulated by Ambrose at Milan; and the opinions of Jovinian were formally condemned, in the year 390, by a council there held by that prelate. But the work was not yet complete; the emperor Honorius was prevailed upon to interpose the secular authority in the same cause; and the following was his proclamation—"The complaint of some bishops mentions as a grievance that Jovinian assembles sacrilegious meetings without the walls of the most holy city. Wherefore we ordain that the above-mentioned be seized and whipped, together with his abettors and attendants, and confined to some

condemned and banished.

place of banishment; and that the machinator himself be immediately sent away to the island of Boa." Boa was a wretched rock, near the Illyrian coast; and in this exile, Jovinian, during the remainder of his life, expiated the crime of proclaiming in

---

* It should be mentioned that the reply of Jerome was not written till after the condemnation of the offender, in consequence of some progress which the opinions are said for the moment to have made at Rome.

the fourth century truths which no one had dreamed of disputing in the second, and which are defended with almost equal clearness by the authority of reason and revelation.

This example did not prevent another and a bolder attempt Vigilantius. at Reformation—for as the corruptions of that time had not yet subsided into habits; as they could not yet plead prescription and long familiar practice; as they were not yet consecrated by the claims of hereditary reverence, it was natural that the voice of reason should sometimes raise itself in faint opposition to their progress. Very early in the following century, Vigilantius, a native of Gaul, who had performed the functions of presbyter in Spain, and afterwards, by his travels through Egypt and Palestine, enlightened and enriched a vigorous understanding and character, boldly avowed his disgust at the growing abuses of the day. Nor did he confine his attack to one or two points; he directed it against the castles and strong holds of superstition. He denied that the tombstones of the martyrs were proper objects of homage and worship; he denied the holiness of places so sanctified, and censured the pilgrimages that were made to them. He derided the prodigies by which the temples of the martyrs were so much celebrated, and condemned the vigils performed in them; and he even ventured to assert that the custom of burning tapers at their tombs, in the face of day, was a foolish imitation of the Pagan practice. He denied the efficacy of prayers addressed to departed saints, and spoke lightly of fasting and mortifications, and celibacy, and the various and useless austerities of the monastic life. And lastly, he disparaged the merit of that suspicious charity which lavished large sums for devout purposes, in fancied atonement for unrepented sin. The clamorous guardian of ecclesiastical depravity was again awakened by this second invasion of abuses so dear to him; and immediately, from his monastery at Bethlehem, he assailed the reformer with such overbearing vehemence of plausible and popular argument, that the good Vigilantius deemed it wiser to retire from the conflict than to expose himself to unprofitable martyrdom. And in fact we find that this heresy (so it was designated) gained so little ground, that the interference of a council was not required

to extinguish it.   The principal credit of both these triumphs
is due to St. Jerome—than whom the Church, in her whole
history, has not ever listened to a more pernicious counsellor.

IV. The controversy to which we next proceed was on a
subject of the deepest and most permanent importance to the
whole Christian world; and though, through the perverse misapplication of human ingenuity, dissensions have flowed from
it, to the great disturbance of former ages, and to the division
even of the present, we cannot affect either surprise or regret
that a question of so much moment should have agitated thus
early the minds of pious men—for it went to the bottom of the
Christian doctrine respecting the original corruption of human
nature, and the necessity of divine grace, to enlighten the understanding and to purify the heart.

It is in all cases extremely difficult, in the statement of those
ancient controversies, to do justice to the arguments, or even to
the opinions, maintained by either party—because these, in the
process of the dispute, became closely, often inseparably, connected with *consequences* imputed to them by the adversary as
necessary, and disclaimed by the advocate as unfair and arbitrary.   So that those very subtilties of reasoning, which professed to unfold and explain the difference, did in fact only
produce perplexity. In the Pelagian controversy this difficulty
is increased by two causes : first, that we know little of the
opinions of the heretic, except from the writings of his opponents; secondly, that the fear of public condemnation, and
perhaps temporal punishment, occasionally led him into unworthy equivocation; so that his expressions are sometimes
such as seemingly to convey an assertion of orthodoxy at
variance with the whole drift of his previous argument. Again,
the mere facts of the controversy have been variously related,
according as the opinions of the relators have been tinged,
however slightly, by the opposite colours of Pelagianism or
Fatalism. We must endeavour, however, to disentangle the
truth from these intricacies.

Pelagius was a native of Britain, probably of Wales; the
associate of his travels, his heresy, and his celebrity, was Celestius, an Irishman : both were monks; both, too, were men of

considerable talents, and no just suspicions have ever been thrown on the sanctity of their moral conduct.   They arrived at Rome in the very beginning of the fifth century, and remained there in the undisturbed, and perhaps obscure, profession of their opinions till the year 410, when they retired, on the Gothic invasion, the former to Palestine, the latter to Carthage.   Here the peculiar doctrines of Celestius did not long Outline of escape detection; they first attracted the attention of the controversy. deacon, Paulinus of Milan, who arraigned and caused them to be condemned in a council held at Carthage in the year 412.   The errors here charged against Celestius were comprised in seven articles—1. That Adam was created mortal, and would have died, whether he had sinned or not; 2. that the sin of Adam injured himself alone, not the human race; 3. that infants, at their birth, are in the condition of Adam, before his sin; 4. that neither the death nor sin of Adam is the cause of man's mortality, nor the resurrection of Christ of his resurrection; 5. that man may be saved by the Law as well as by the Gospel; 6. that before the coming of Christ there had been men without sin; 7. that infants inherit eternal life without baptism.   Though these were partly disclaimed or explained away, still enough remained to show the real nature of his opinions: we may observe that the words free-will and grace do not yet appear in the controversy.

It does not appear that Augustine assisted at this council, as he was still engaged in pursuing his advantages over the Donatists; however, he did not delay to enter the field against the new adversary, and very soon afterwards assailed the infant heresy, both by his sermons and writings*.   Dissatisfied with

* The natural causes of the opposition of the Church to the Pelagian opinions are ingeniously and reasonably discussed by Guizot (Cours d'Histoire Moderne, Leçon V.)   We shall transcribe one passage, which deserves attention, and which cannot be condensed:—" Augustine, who was the chief among the doctors of the Church, was peculiarly called upon to maintain the general system of its belief.   Now, the notions of Pelagius and Celestius appeared to him to be in contradiction with some of the fundamental points of Christian faith, especially the doctrine of original sin and that of redemption.   He attacked them, then, in three characters;—as philosopher, because their *science* of human nature was, in his view, narrow and incomplete; as practical reformer and governor of the Church, because they weakened, in his mind, the most efficacious method of re-

Exertions
of Augus-
tine.
the easy triumph which attended his exertions in his own
Church, he followed the fugitive into the East, and having
ascertained that Pelagius maintained the same errors in Palestine, he occasioned him to be accused before two councils;
the one at Jerusalem*, the other at Diospolis.   John, bishop
of Jerusalem, was favourable to the cause, perhaps to the tenets
of Pelagius; and thus, partly by his influence, partly from the
absence of any fixed rule of orthodoxy on those particular subjects in the Eastern Church, partly from the very modified
statement of his own opinions delivered to the councils by
Pelagius, that sectarian, in spite of the violent opposition of
Jerome, was acquitted in both.   This event took place in 415;
and in the year following, Augustine, undaunted by this repulse,
again assembled councils in Africa and Numidia, and again
condemned the offensive doctrines.

Conduct of
the bishop
of Rome.
The scene of action was then transferred to Rome, on the
appeal, as it would seem, of the two heretics, and with the hope,
perhaps, (not a reasonable hope,) that the authority of the
Church of Jerusalem would have as much weight at the Vatican, as that of the Church of Carthage.   Zosimus had been
just raised to the pontificate; to him the controversy was referred, with great show of humility, by Celestius; and whether
deceived by the artful composition of the creed presented to
him for approval, or overlooking the importance of a question

form and government; as logician, because their ideas did not exactly square with
the consequences which flowed from the essential principles of the faith.   Observe, then, what gravity the dispute assumed from that moment: everything was
engaged in it—philosophy, politics, and religion; the opinions of St. Augustine,
and his business, his vanity, and his duty.   He abandoned himself entirely to it,
publishing treatises, writing letters, collecting communications which flowed in
upon him from all quarters, profuse in regulations and counsels, and carrying
into all his writings and all his measures that mixture of passion and mildness,
of authority and sympathy, of expanse of mind and logical strictness, which gave
him such singular power."

* On this occasion, being asked if he really maintained opinions which Augustine had condemned, he replied, " What is Augustine to me ? "   Many were offended, for Augustine was the most venerable authority of the age ; and some
immediately proposed to excommunicate the spiritual rebel: but John averted
the blow, and kindly addressed Pelagius,—" It is I who am Augustine here ; it
is to me that you shall answer."   Pelagius spoke Greek, and is said to have thus
obtained some advantages over his accuser Orosius, who was ignorant of that
language.

to which his attention had not previously been much directed, or flattered by the personal appeal to his justice and the acknowledged submission to the chair of St. Peter, or influenced by all these reasons, Zosimus pronounced the innocence of the disputed doctrine.

Augustine was not even thus discouraged; and his ardent religious feelings, as well as his reputation, were now too deeply interested in the controversy to allow him to rest here. Once more he assembled his bishops, and after the public renewal of former declarations, he proceeded to inform the bishop of Rome more clearly as to the real nature and importance of the question; as to the errors which had been actually professed by the heretics; and those which, though disingenuously disavowed, followed of course from them. Zosimus does not appear to have been much moved by these representations; but in the mean time a more powerful avenger had been roused by the perseverance of the Africans. An imperial edict descended from Constantinople, which banished both the delinquents from Rome, and menaced with perpetual exile and confiscation of estates all who should maintain their doctrines in any place. This decisive blow was struck in the March of 418; in the May following, another and still more numerous council* met at Carthage for the purpose of completing the triumph; and then the Bishop of Rome was at length prevailed upon to place, in conjunction with his clergy, the final seal of heresy on the Pelagian opinions. The opinions themselves did not, indeed, expire from these successive wounds, but have frequently reappeared under different forms and modifications; but no further attempts were made to extend them by their original authors.

The sum of those opinions was this:—1. That the sins of our first parents are imputed to themselves alone, and not to their posterity; that we derive no corruption from their fall; that we inherit no depravity from our origin; but enter into the world as pure and unspotted as Adam at his creation. It

The sum of the opinions.

---

* Two hundred and three, or, as some assert, two hundred and fourteen bishops were present.

was a necessary inference from this doctrine, that infant baptism is not a sign or seal of the remission of sins, but only a *mark* of admission into the kingdom of Christ. 2. That our own powers are sufficient for our own justification; that as by our own free-will we run into sin, so, by the same voluntary exercise of our faculties, we are able to repent, and reform, and raise ourselves to the highest degree of virtue and piety; that we are, indeed, assisted by that external* grace of God which has taught us the truths of revelation; which opens to us our prospects, and enlightens our understanding, and animates our exertions after godliness; but that the internal and immediate operation of the Holy Spirit is not *necessary,* either to awaken us to religious feelings, or to further us in our progress towards holiness; in short, that man, by the unassisted agency of his natural perfections under the guidance of his own *free-will,* is enabled to work out his own salvation.

Regarding these doctrines, it is sufficient for a Christian to examine, whether or not they are in accordance with the obvious interpretation of Scripture; and the long experience of a fruitless controversy must at length have convinced us respecting such inscrutable subjects, that if we advance one step beyond the safe and substantial ground of revelation, we become entangled in the mazes of metaphysical disputation. In these matters, we are not to inquire what is probable, but what is *written;* and it has become a question, whether the presumptuous arrogance of reason, which is objected to the system of Pelagius, did not lead his opponents, who believed themselves humble, equally far away from that entire submission to the Gospel, which is the only true humility.

Augustine maintained the Church doctrines of original sin and saving grace with great force and zeal, and the most unaffected sincerity; and his writings on this subject continued for above twelve centuries to distribute the waters of regeneration

---

* Pelagius artfully perplexed the subject, by his assertion of six different kinds of grace; and if there be any of his expressions which may seem to imply more than we here give them credit for, they are, at least, so vague, and we think purposely so vague, as to make it impossible to attach any definite meaning to them.

over the barren surface of the Roman Catholic Church.   But Augustine himself, in the ardour of his opposition to free-will, did he not overstep the just limits of reason, and advance into the contrary extreme of fatalism ?   It is true that he warmly disclaimed that doctrine, when nakedly objected to him as the obvious and inevitable result of those which he professed; but it was not without some sacrifice of logical severity that he declined the formidable conclusion.   Nevertheless, more rigid logicians and more daring theologians were found, who pressed to their utmost consequences the opinions of their master, and deduced from them the predestinarian dogma in its full extent. Again, the publication of the astounding tenet on such authority (for Augustine, as well as his adversaries, was held responsible for the consequences of his positions*) became the occasion of another series of divisions in the Church, which more particularly distracted that of Gaul; so that the discord which grew out of the Pelagian controversy was not confined to the original ground of dispute, but spread with baneful luxuriance over the vineyard of Christ.

Among the opinions to which it gave birth, the most popular, and perhaps the most reasonable, were those of the Semi-Pelagians.   They began to spread in the South of France about the year 428, and are attributed to an Oriental, named Cassian, who resided in a monastery at Marseilles.   These Sectarians† regarded with equal suspicion that absolute independence of the Divine aid, so rashly ascribed to the human soul by the Pelagian system, and its entire prostration and helplessness, as exhi-

The Semi-Pelagians.

---

* In fact, Augustine attributed the progressive sanctification of man to the direct, immediate, and special action of God on the soul; that is, to grace, properly so called ; grace to which man had, by his own power, no title, and which proceeded from the absolutely gratuitous gift and free choice of the Divinity.   His twelve fundamental points of the doctrine of grace are delivered in the epistle (to Vitalis) numbered 217 or 107.

† Guizot has justly observed, that none of these doctrines gave birth to a *Sect*, according to the modern acceptation of the term : those who held them were not formally separated from the Church and formed into a distinct religious society, nor had they any peculiar organization or worship.   The doctrines were pure opinions debated among enlightened men, and varying both in their credit and in the degrees of their deviation from the Church, but never such as to menace a formal schism.

bited by the Fatalists ; and they consequently concluded, that,
by holding a middle course between opposite errors, they should
most nearly arrive at truth.   And so they maintained, on the
one hand, that the Grace purchased by Christ was necessary for
salvation, and that no man could *persevere* or advance in holiness without its perpetual support and assistance : on the other,
that our natural faculties were sufficient for the beginning of
repentance and amendment : that Christ died for all men, and
that there was no *particular* dispensation of his grace in consequence of predestination, but that it was equally offered to all
men ; that man was born free, and therefore capable of receiving its influences, or resisting them.   These doctrines were
generally condemned in the Western Church *.   It is true, they
have continued, with slight variations, to find many advocates
there in every age : but the Church faithfully followed the line
which had been traced by Augustine.   By adopting his doctrines on grace, it condemned the heresy both of the Pelagians
and Semi-Pelagians ; and by rejecting the dogma of the Fatalists, it relieved itself from that which would have proved a perpetual source of internal dissatisfaction and dissent.   But in the
East, if we may judge from the writings of Chrysostom †, and
the general tone of the Greek fathers, the Semi-Pelagian opinions had obtained an earlier and common prevalence, and they
appear to have been maintained, with little interruption or dispute, to the present moment.   The Greeks, however, engaged
with little ardour in the Pelagian disputes ; and the reason may
have been, that the seeds of another contention, even more
suited to the peculiarity of their metaphysical taste, were now
ready to burst forth with abundant fertility.   The great controversy respecting the Incarnation of Jesus Christ, which engaged,
for about two hundred and fifty years, the ingenuity and the
passions of the Eastern world, first discovered itself in the be-

---

* Augustine of Rome died about two years after their birth, but his work
was followed up by Prosper and Hilary, who caused them to be condemned very
soon afterwards by Celestine.   On the other hand, the opinions of the Predesti-
narians were also condemned by the Councils of Arles (in 472), and of Lyons (in
473).

† The opinions of Chrysostom on the subject appear to be fairly discussed by
Dupin, Nouv. Bibl., in his Life of that Father.

ginning of the fifth century, emerging, as it were, from the mists of some early heresies. We shall give as concise an account of it, as is consistent with the illustration of its more important features.

V. The controversy respecting the Trinity was terminated by the Council of Constantinople in the year 381, which established the belief in the personality and divinity of the Holy Spirit, as the true doctrine of the Universal Church. The Arian heresy had been previously condemned; and about the end of the fourth century, the attention of speculative minds began to turn from the momentous consideration of the eternal and celestial nature of Christ, and the consequent degree of worship which is due to him, to a subordinate inquiry into the probable nature of his existence during his temporary residence here on earth. This question had, indeed, been moved in the first ages of the Church, and some of the errors of Marcion, of Cerinthus, Carpocrates, Basilides, and others, are connected with it; but their opinions were so immediately derived from the absurd theories of Gnosticism, that they gained no great or lasting prevalence, nor have any claim on our present attention. And it will seem, indeed, a very singular circumstance, that the first speculations on this subject, which necessarily fix our notice, should have proceeded from the friend and associate of Athanasius. Apollinaris, Bishop of Laodicea, whether carried into excess by his hostility to Arianism, or inextricably entangled in his own unnecessary subtilties, so far lost sight of the moderation of reason, that in asserting the divinity of Christ he denied the reality of his human nature. For he held that the divine nature (the Logos) supplied in Him the place of the spiritual and intellectual principle, and constituted, in fact, *His mind*. In this sense he could not be considered as perfect man; and in effect, the substitution of the Divine essence for the human soul so far confused the two natures of Christ, as to reduce them to " one incarnate nature,"—a doctrine which, indeed, Apollinaris did not disavow. This opinion took deep root in the Egyptian Church, but it was condemned by the clergy of Asia and Syria.

The question, however, not being publicly pursued by the

[margin: The Controversy on the Incarnation.]

[margin: Apollinaris.]

directors of the Church, rested in an unsettled state until the accession of Nestorius to the See of Constantinople in the year 428. That prelate was a native of Antioch, and had been educated in the Syrian schools; and having then been strongly impressed with the *distinction* of the two natures and the dangerous error of confusing them, he inculcated so strongly the difference between the Son of God and the Son of Man, as to seem almost to extend the distinction of natures to a distinction of *persons,* though he avowed no such intention. In consequence of these principles he defended one of his presbyters, Anastasius, who, in a public discourse, had ventured to argue, that the Virgin Mary ought not properly to be called " Mother of God" (Θεοτόκος), but " Mother of Christ" (Χριστοτόκος), or even " Mother of Man" ('Ανθρωποτόκος). Whatsoever may be the most appropriate appellation for the Mother of Jesus Christ, it was assuredly the proof of a narrow and contentious spirit, that the Head of the Oriental Church should in any* way interfere in so vain a dispute. But Nestorius interfered with earnestness and ardour. It also happened, that the opinion which he undertook to protect was at variance with the popular enthusiasm; *that* had already set in the opposite direction, and it was easily urged on and roused into a tempest, when an insult was represented to have been offered to the dignity and holiness of the Virgin. On one occasion, in the midst of a numerous assembly, one Eusebius (then a lawyer, and afterwards Bishop of Doryleum) interrupted the sermon of the patriarch with these words:—" It is the eternal Logos himself who has undergone a second birth according to the flesh, and by means of a woman." The people were excited; the subject occupied universal attention; the passions became inflamed, and Nestorius, in his own capital, was absurdly† accused of reviving the heresies of Photinus and Paul of Samosata.

* In a letter addressed to John of Jerusalem, about two years afterwards, when the matter was inflamed almost beyond hope, Nestorius, indeed, attempts a justification, by saying that he *found* the religious world divided between Theotocos and Anthropotocos; and that his only object was to unite both parties by the intermediate term, Christotocos. But he had then discovered the folly of his attempt.

† In a sermon, delivered in answer to a public attack made by Proclus, Bishop

But it was not among his domestic adversaries that he found his most formidable opponent. That opponent was Cyril, the patriarch of Alexandria—a man of learning and eloquence, and intolerable arrogance. And some jealousy which at that time subsisted, respecting the relative dignity of the two Sees, probably heightened the contention, and is believed by some to have caused it. Whether that be so or not, the two patriarchs anathematised each other with mutual violence; and such troubles were raised, that the Emperor Theodosius the younger deemed it necessary to convoke a General Council for the purpose of appeasing them. It was assembled at Ephesus in the year 431, and stands in the annals of the Church as the Third General Council. Cyril was appointed to preside, and consequently to judge the cause of his adversary; and he carried into this office such little show of impartiality, that he refused even to wait for the arrival of the Bishop of Antioch and others, who were held friendly to Nestorius, and proceeded to pronounce sentence, while the meeting was yet incomplete. To secure or prosecute his advantages, he had brought with him from Egypt a number of robust and daring fanatics*, who acted as his soldiery. And it had been skilfully arranged, that Ephesus should be chosen for the decision of a difference respecting the dignity of the Virgin; since popular tradition had buried her in that city, and the imperfect Christianity of its inhabitants had readily transferred to her the worship, which their ancestors had offered to Diana.

After publishing an unjust condemnation† of the undefended

Cyril of Alexandria.

Council of Ephesus. Third General, 431 A.D.

---

of Cyzicus, Nestorius maintained that it was improper "nakedly to assert, that God was born of Mary; but rather, that God, the Word of the Father, was joined to him who was the Man, and not the Word God, which rose again; the Temple should be distinguished from the God who dwells there." (Fleury, liv. xxv. sect. 2.) It seems very probable, that if Nestorius had abstained from all mention of the Virgin Mary, or merely avoided the imprudence of interfering with the *title* of a Being who was already becoming the object of superstition, the *controversy* would not have taken place at all.

* These were chiefly monks—a race which swarmed with singular fecundity along the banks of the Nile, and in the deserts of the Thebais. The influence which they possessed in the Egyptian Church is proved by the circumstance, that the first attack which Cyril made upon his brother-patriarch appeared in the form of an Epistle General to the Monks of Egypt. Its success was very sensibly displayed at Ephesus.

† The first burst of the unanimous (if it was so) indignation of the Fathers was

patriarch, and causing, through its own dissensions, some sanguinary tumults through the city, the Third General Council was at length dismissed by Theodosius in these words :—" God is my witness, that I am not the author of this confusion. His providence will discern and punish the guilty. Return to your provinces; and may your private virtues repair the mischief and scandal of your meeting." The banishment of Nestorius did not immediately follow his condemnation; and four other years of intrigue and malevolence were necessary before he was dismissed,—first, to his original convent at Antioch, and finally to an island (or oasis) in the deserts of Upper Egypt. There he died; and as he died a persecuted exile, he has a strong and natural claim on our sympathy : but it is lessened by the recollection of his dangerous indiscretion; and we are forbidden to forget or to conceal, that in his days of prosperity, while in the enjoyment of dignity and power, he had not refused to inflict on the Arians and other heretics the calamities which were impending over himself*.

In the mean time his opinions extended themselves rapidly throughout central Asia, along the eastern extremities of Christendom. Through Chaldea, Persia, Syria, and Assyria; in Arabia, India, Tartary, and even China, they took deep root during the fifth and sixth centuries; and the number of their professors, their indignation against the persecutors of Nestorius, and their consequent enmity against the Church and name of Greece, prepared them, in a later age, for alliance with the Mahometan invader†.

---

expressed nearly in these words :—" Anathema to him who does not anathematize Nestorius ; the orthodox faith anathematizes him ; the holy council anathematizes him. We all anathematize the heretic Nestorius ; we anathematize all who communicate with him and his impious belief. All the earth anathematizes the unholy religion of Nestorius. Anathema to him who does not anathematize Nestorius."— Fleury, liv. xxv. sect. 39.

* During his banishment he was carried into captivity by the Blemmyes ; and after his release by them, was hurried about from place to place by the governor of Upper Egypt, so that he had no repose even in exile. " Enfin (says Fleury) il mourut, accablé de vieillesse et d'infirmités ; et on dit, que sa langue fut rongée de vers." Of all Roman Catholic historians, Fleury is the most charitable.

† " The successors of Mahomet in Persia employed the Nestorians in the most important affairs, both of the cabinet and of the provinces, and suffered the pa-

They assembled their councils at Seleucia, and their doc- Doctrine of the Nestorians. trine, as there determined, amounted to this—"That in the Saviour of the world there were two persons or substances (ὑποστάσεις), of which the one was divine, the Eternal Word; and the other, which was human, was the man Jesus: that these two substances had only one *aspect* (barsopa, πρόσωπον) : that the union between the Son of God and the Son of man was not an union of nature or of person, but only of will and affection : that Christ was therefore to be carefully distinguished from God, who dwelt in him as in a temple: that Mary was to be called the mother of Christ, and not the mother of God." From this exposition * of doctrine it has been suspected, and with some appearance of justice, that the difference between the Nestorians and the Orthodox was in fact merely verbal; and that the more rational disputants of both parties were maintaining, with some variation of expression, the very same opinions.

In the history of this controversy, the name of Eutyches im- Eutyches. mediately succeeds to that of Nestorius. This person was the abbot of a convent at Constantinople, and an intemperate opposer of the opinions of Nestorius. He carried the doctrine of the Egyptian school to its extreme interpretation, and appears to have exceeded the obscure limits of the error of Apollinaris†. For that heresiarch affected to draw some distinction between an intellectual and a *sensitive* soul, which, however subtile, may seem to remove his doctrine one step from that of the Monophysites; but Eutyches at once boldly pronounced

triarch of that sect only to reside in the kingdom of Babylon. The Monophysites enjoyed in Syria and Egypt an equal degree of favour and protection." Mosh. cent. vii. p. ii. ch. v.

* It is taken from Mosheim; and the peculiar word Barsopa may perhaps be properly translated *aspect*. Only render it *person*, and omit that same word when it is used synonymously with substance, and even the shadow of the difference is almost removed. It is at least certain that the Monothelites have commonly accused the Catholics of Nestorianism, and have sometimes mistaken the one for the other.

† In the mean time Eutyches was so far from acknowledging this resemblance, that in his letter to St. Leo, and in the presence of the council, he anathematized Apollinaris, together with Valentinus, Manes, Nestorius, and Simon the magician. He had reached his seventy-first year, when his opinions were attacked by the very same man who had first sounded the trumpet against Nestorius— Eusebius, now bishop of Doryleum.

" that in Christ there was but *one** nature—that of the incarnate word." Dioscorus, who had succeeded to the throne of Alexandria and to the character of Cyril, gave his decided support to Eutyches, and as both parties grew violent, Theodosius was exhorted to convoke another council to determine the difference. He did so ; and, as if to prove the inefficacy of experience to confer wisdom, he again appointed Ephesus as the place of the meeting, and again selected the bishop of Alexandria to preside in it. The tumults which had disgraced the Church in 431 were repeated with some additional brutalities in 449 ; the Egyptians again were triumphant; and the assembly at length dispersed, after having sanctioned the doctrine of Eutyches, and acquired the title, by which it has been stigmatized in every age of the Church, as "The Assembly of Robbers." This meeting, we should observe, has not obtained a place among the general councils of the Church†.

Latrocinium Ephesinum. 431 A. D.

The Western bishops had hitherto interfered, not very warmly, in these disputes, which were indeed peculiarly Oriental both in their origin and character. But Leo the Great, sensible of the scandal now brought upon the whole Church even by the temporary establishment of an erroneous doctrine, saw the necessity of more zealous interposition. He therefore prevailed upon Marcian, the successor of Theodosius, to summon another council on the same subject. It met at Chalcedon in 451 ; and the pope's legates (under the usual superintendence of the Imperial Officers) presided there. The proceedings were conducted with greater decency ; Eutyches and Dioscorus were condemned, and the orthodox‡ doctrine of "Christ in one person and two natures" was finally established.

Council of Chalcedon. Fourth General. 451 A. D.

---

* A necessary consequence of this doctrine seems to be the ascription of the passion and sufferings of Christ to the Divine (the only) nature, and this could scarcely be avoided without taking refuge in the heresy of the Phantastics. In fact, the dissensions between the corruptibles and incorruptibles, in the reign of Justinian, were little else than a continuation of the Eutychean controversy, in ITS CONSEQUENCES. These disputes chiefly prevailed in Egypt, the hotbed of the Monophysite heresy.

† " Σύνοδος ληστρική, Conventus Latronum, Latrocinium Ephesinum," are the terms in which it is usually mentioned by the writers of both Churches.

‡ Admitting, as we do, that the opinions of Nestorius were in fact very little, if at all, removed from orthodoxy, we cannot at all assent to the reasoning of Le Clerc, who would persuade us (and who appears to have persuaded both Jortin

As before with the Nestorians, so now with the followers of Eutyches, their energy, and perhaps their numbers, increased on the public condemnation of their opinions. Some monks of that persuasion obtained possession of Jerusalem, and indulged in the most violent excesses; and the Catholic successor of Dioscorus, after a contention of five years with his Alexandrian subjects, was at length sacrificed to their religious fury. Presently afterwards, in the year 482, the emperor Zeno made a fruitless but memorable attempt to extinguish all religious dissension, by the publication of an edict of union, called the Henoticon. In this proclamation he confirmed the established doctrines, and anathematized alike the Arians, Phantastics, Nestorians, and Eutychians; but out of tenderness to the feelings of the last, he avoided any particular mention of the Council of Chalcedon. The more moderate men, both among the Catholics and Monophysites*, (still the two prevailing parties,) subscribed to this decree; but the fruits of their moderation were not such as, by their principles and example, they deserved, and perhaps expected. Among the latter a violent schism arose, and this speedily gave birth to numerous other schisms, which divided into several sects the followers of Eutyches; while among the Catholics very great and general indignation was excited by the omission of the name of Chalcedon, against all who had signed so imperfect a declaration of orthodoxy. And thus it proved, to the disgrace of the disputants, and almost to the scandal of human nature, that an attempt, judiciously conceived by a benevolent prince, to compose the religious differences of his subjects, produced no other effect than to inflame the character, and multiply the grounds of dissension. And that unhappy result was not in this case attributable to the infliction of any civil penalties in the arbi-

(margin) Henoticon of Zeno. 482, A.D.

and Gibbon) that Eutyches also held the same doctrine with both Nestorius and the orthodox—for in this last dispute there is no confusion of *terms;* in the very same words the one party plainly asserts *one*, the other *two* natures of Christ; and the same train and description of argument, which is applied to reconcile this difference, would, in our mind, be equally successful in removing every religious difference.

 * The Eutychians or Monophysites are also known in history by the appellation of Jacobites, from the name of one of their teachers, James Baraddus.

trary enforcement of the decree, but solely to the vehemence of the passions engaged on both sides, which had hardened the greater number against any representations of wisdom or reason, and even against the ordinary influence of human feelings.

The Monothelites.

However, time effected much towards the healing of these animosities, and they were diverted during the reign of Justinian into other channels. Several of the opinions of Origen had been very keenly controverted since the beginning of the fifth century; and some important errors were imputed to him by many churchmen. He was accused of having held (1.) that in the Trinity the Father is greater than the Son; the Son than the Holy Ghost. (2.) That souls pre-existed, and were condemned to inhabit mortal bodies, as a punishment. (3.) That the soul of Christ was united to the Word, before the incarnation. (4.) That the sun and other heavenly bodies were animated and endowed with rational souls. (5.) That at the resurrection all bodies will be of a spherical form. (6.) That the torments of the damned will have a termination. (7.) That as Christ was crucified here, to save man, he will be crucified in the next world, to save the devils. Now, though the adherents of Origen were very powerful in some parts of the East, especially in Egypt and Syria, the opposite party was still more numerous: and thus his offensive opinions had been repeatedly condemned, since the time of Jerome—but they had not yet been subjected to the deliberate examination of a general council.

Errors of Origen.

Again : the Council of Chalcedon had given its sanction to a body of suspicious theology, called the Three Chapters. These consisted (1.) of the writings of Theodore of Mopsuesta. (2.) Of the books which Theodoret of Cyrus wrote against the Twelve Anathemas, which Cyril had written against the Nestorians. (3.) Of the letter, which Ibas of Edessa had written to one Maris, a Persian, concerning the Council of Ephesus and the condemnation of Nestorius. All these were supposed to have a Nestorian tendency—and thus the theological zeal of Justinian was easily excited against them. It would seem, however, that he overstepped the boundaries of ecclesiastical moderation when he presumed to condemn (in 544), on his own authority,

The Three Chapters.

what had been approved by the decision of a general council. Accordingly, many independent prelates, among whom some Western bishops were distinguished, resisted this edict, but the emperor, nothing daunted, confirmed it, in the year 551, by a second. The discord was thus augmented, and two years after- wards Justinian found it expedient to summon the Fifth General The Fifth General Council. 553 A.D. Council. To its deliberations the opinions of Origen (to which the emperor was adverse) as well as the Three Chapters were submitted; and the obsequious prelates (they were almost en- tirely Orientals) pronounced the sentence of condemnation on both.

After the lapse of nearly two hundred years from the Council of Chalcedon, the waves of the incarnation controversy had seemingly subsided, and the differences and even the malevo- lence, which may still have existed, no longer broke out into open outrage. The vain curiosity of the Emperor Heraclius threatened the revival of those evils. On his return from the Persian war in the year 629, that prince proposed to his bishops the unprofitable question—"Whether Christ, of one person but two natures, was actuated by a single or a double *will?*" The Greeks in general favoured the former opinion, but not with their usual impetuosity; indeed they seem at length to have been so far exhausted by such fruitless contests, as to have con- sidered the question trifling and superfluous. And it was not until the year 680, that, through the angry opposition of the Latins to this dogma, the Sixth General Council was assembled Sixth General Council. 680 A. D. at Constantinople, which formerly pronounced that *two* wills were harmonized in the person of Christ. Such is still the doctrine both of the Greek and Latin Churches; and with the establishment of that doctrine the controversy respecting the incarnation, after an interrupted duration of about three hun- dred years, expired*.

---

* Accurately speaking, the Monothelite Controversy was rather a consequence, than a part, of that respecting the incarnation; since those who adopted the doc- trine of one will, did not in consequence reject the decisions either of Ephesus or Chalcedon, but adhered, on the contrary, to both,—so as to unite (in profession at least, if not in reason) the strictest orthodoxy respecting the nature and person of Christ with their perverse opinion respecting his will.

The heretics who advocated the *one will* were called Monothelites, and by this name the dispute is generally known. It lasted
about fifty years; and it is a painful but necessary reflection,
that during its continuance, while the attention of Christendom
was in some degree engaged by it, the Mahometans had found
time to convert Arabia and to complete the conquest of Persia,
Syria, Palestine, and Egypt: the three patriarchal thrones,
Antioch, Alexandria, and Jerusalem had fallen into their
hands; and Carthage itself was already on the point of under-
going the same fate.

Observa-
tions on
these Con-
troversies.
Having treated the conduct of the parties engaged in these
dissensions with unrestrained freedom, we shall conclude with
some considerations not unfavourable to them, and not less just
than our censure. 1. None of the disputants at any time fell
into any heresy respecting the Trinity—the doctrine which had
been established by the first and second general councils was
followed with equal fidelity by those who deviated from the
Church respecting the incarnation, and by those who adhered
to it. 2. As the manner in which this controversy was conducted, exhibited the earnest devotion of all parties to their respective opinions, so the origin of all those opinions may be
traced to an anxiety (oftentimes indeed a very injudicious
anxiety) to acquire accurate notions respecting the Redeemer,
so as neither to exaggerate nor disparage his dignity. It may be
traced to an excéss of the religious feeling, even to a tendency
to superstitious enthusiasm; but at least it was free from the
infection of that cold, indifferent apathy, which sometimes
shelters itself under the name of philosophy, but which, in fact,
is not far removed from scepticism. 3. The very individuals
who, under the excitement of religious dissension and the bustle
of public councils, heated too by the various passions, which
the mere spirit of resistance will create in the calmest temperament, ran loose into scandalous excesses, might very consistently be endued with the purest piety, and habituated, in the
private exercise of their sacerdotal functions, to the fervent discharge of every Christian duty. It argues a very slight or a
very partial view of human nature to infer, from the occasional
extravagance of public feeling, the general destitution of moral

principle or the absence of virtuous habits; and we must be careful not to be misled by those historians, who bid us judge the general character of the Eastern clergy by their conduct at the Councils of Ephesus. Lastly, whatever may have been the original policy of convoking general councils for the suppression of religious difference, it cannot be asserted that such councils were wholly useless—for, besides the particular doctrine which they were called upon to settle, and which on some occasions was fundamentally important, they also published numerous canons and ordinances for the regulation and reform of the Church. These were disseminated and received through every part of Christendom, and very often proved of the highest utility. And even as to the doctrines on such occasions established, we should observe, that after the first tumult of opposition had subsided, they met with general acquiescence; that they were almost universally adopted in succeeding ages, and still constitute the creed of the great majority of Christians*.

VI. We proceed to the contest respecting the worship of images, which claims our careful attention, partly from the extreme agitation which it excited throughout Christendom during the eighth and ninth centuries—partly, because it occasioned (should we not rather say accelerated?) the separation of the Roman states from the Greek empire. Among the various superstitions which had gradually grown up in the Church, and of which the vestiges may, in some cases, be traced to its earliest ages, none had obtained such general influence and firm footing among the lower orders (especially in the East) as Image-wor-

Marginal note: Controversy respecting images.

---

* The Controversy, which we have described, branched out into various theories respecting the *manner* of the union of the two natures, which amused the refined imaginations of the Greeks. But it was reserved for the grosser absurdity of a German to originate the following offensive speculation:—" Eodem tempore aliud ex Germaniâ certamen in Gallias inferebatur de modo quo Sanctissimus Servator ex utero Matris in lucem prodiit. Germani quidam Jesum Christum non communi reliquorum hominum lege, sed singulari et extraordinaria, utero Matris exiisse statuebant. Qua sententia in Galliam delata, Ratramnus eam oppugnabat, atque Christum per naturæ januam in mundum ingressum esse tuebatur. Germanis subveniebat Paschasius Radbertus, libro singulari, &c. &c." Jortin, vol. iv., p. 489. This occurred about the year 840, and it is worthy of notice, if it were only that we find the great patron of Transubstantiation, Paschasius Radbertus, advocating such extravagant and impious nonsense.

ship. It was an idle distinction to uphold a respect for images, as *means* and not as *objects* of devotion, when they were presented to the uninstructed and undiscriminating vulgar. When the understanding has never been enlightened, when the heart has never been informed with the genuine feelings of religion, the devotee will surely address his prayer to the Deity which is placed before his eyes, and turn, in the darkness of his intellect, to that which is perceptible by his mere senses. And it was therefore the greatest among the crimes of the ancient directors of the Church, and that which appears more peculiarly to have brought down upon it the chastisement from Arabia, that they filled the temples with their detested idols, and obtruded them upon the eyes and into the hands of the most ignorant. Nor can their advocates plead the necessity of this conduct; for the example of the Mahometan faith alone has proved, that a people may be barbarous without being idolatrous, when idolatry is discouraged by the ministers of religion. And if any excuse be furnished by the general and deeply-rooted influence of the ancient superstition, it is at least none for those who exerted their power and their talents to extend and perpetuate it. Unhappily, those exertions were attended by too easy success; before the year 600, idolatry was firmly established in the Eastern Church, and during the following century it made a gradual and very general progress in the West, where it had previously gained some footing.

Leo the Isaurian. 726, A. D.

It was not till the year 726 that any vigorous attempt was made to disturb its sway; and then the minds of men were become weakened by long acquiescence in superstitious maxims, even so far as to regard with submissive reverence the sins and follies of their ancestors. Nevertheless, the Emperor Leo, surnamed the Isaurian, a prince of sense and energy, had the boldness to undertake*, in the face of so many difficulties, the purification of the Church; and he began his pious enterprise

---

* Roman Catholic historians attribute Leo's resolution to the sudden appearance of a new island in the Archipelago, from volcanic causes. This phenomenon the superstitious emperor ascribed to the Divine wrath, excited by the idolatrous impiety of his subjects. He is also supposed to have derived his prejudice from the Mahometan religion, to which his attachment is more than insinuated.

by an attack on its most flagrant corruption.   It is disputed, whether the first measure of Leo was prudently confined to the abolition of idolatrous *worship*, and the removal of its objects to higher and more distant situations in the churches, wherein they were suspended; or whether, without any indulgence to prejudice, he entirely concealed them from view, and even destroyed them.   The effect of the edict would rather lead us to the latter conclusion—for it immediately occasioned a civil war, both in the East and in the West.   In the East, the islands of the Archipelago, and even a part of Asia, broke out into a tumultuous insurrection, which however was speedily suppressed; but in the West, the more deliberate resistance of the Bishop of Rome (Gregory II.) encouraged the rebellion of the Italian provinces (in 730), and led to the defeat of the Imperial troops before Ravenna.   The tribute paid to the Eastern Emperor was then withdrawn, and his authority was never afterwards acknowledged in the ecclesiastical states.

This reverse did not abate the zeal of Leo, who proceeded to enforce his resolutions, as far as his power extended; and as he found the strongest opposition to proceed from the monastic orders, he extended his scheme of reformation to them.   And in spite of various tumults, excited partly by their influence, and partly through a popular prejudice in favour of superstition, he persisted in his project, with uncompromising perseverance, and even with some prospect of success, until his death.   In the year 741 he was succeeded by his son Constantine, surnamed Copronymus, who faithfully followed his footsteps.   Thirteen years afterwards that prince assembled a synod in the suburbs of Constantinople, at which three hundred and thirty-eight bishops attended.   They decreed the destruction of images*, and the decision, which has sometimes been attributed to their loyalty, may with equal justice be ascribed to their sense and their piety.   They were called Iconoclasts, or image-breakers; and the execution of their decrees occa-

Constantine Copronymus. 741. A.D

---

* Some of the arguments seriously advanced on this occasion by the Iconoclasts seem intended to surpass the absurdity of their adversaries; according to them, even the very painter is convicted of several, and even the most opposite, heresies.   They may be found in Fleury, liv. xliii., sect. 7.

sioned many calumnies against the emperor's character, and many tumults, which disturbed the peace and even endangered the security of his reign. Nevertheless that reign lasted thirty-four years; and the whole space was perseveringly employed in contention with idols, with the monks who protected them, and with the pernicious influence of Rome, which was active and constant in the support of both.

Seventh General Council, 787 A.D.

Leo, who succeeded, was guided by the principles of Constantine; but he died soon after his accession, and the education of his son, a boy of ten years old, as well as the direction of public affairs, was entrusted to the empress Irene. Immediately the religious policy of the palace was changed; and as fifty years of vigorous opposition had not availed to extirpate corruptions which were the gradual growth of four centuries, the change was hailed with delight by a large proportion of the people. In the year 787, a General Council was assembled at Nice, by which the images were reinstated in their former honours*, through the united exertions of the monks and the mob, and the pope and the empress. This Council, the second of Nice, is accounted in the East as the seventh and last General Council, and its decisions completed the body of doctrine and discipline which constitutes the system of the Greek Church.

Several objects of the seven general councils.

It may be proper, in this place, very briefly to remind our readers of the particular objects for which these seven celebrated Councils were severally summoned; not merely as matters of barren recollection, but because we perceive in them, if we are not greatly in error, an indication of the gradual departure of the Church, first from scriptural simplicity, and then from truth. Between the first and the last of them the space

---

* The following is a part of the confession of faith published with the authority of this Council:—"We receive, besides the figure of the cross, the relics of saints, and their images; we embrace them according to the ancient tradition of our fathers, who have placed them in all the churches of God, and all the places where he is served. We honour and adore them, viz. that of Jesus Christ, of his holy Mother, of the angels,—for though they are incorporeal, they have revealed themselves in a human form; those of the apostles, the prophets, the martyrs, and other saints; because those paintings recall to us the memory of the originals and *make us participate in their sanctity.*" Fleury, liv. xliv., sect. 34.

of 462 years intervened, an interval full of important, and, for
the most part, pernicious changes in the ecclesiastical constitution; but most of these were imperceptibly introduced, especially
into the Western Church, without the authority or cognizance
of any general assembly, and they involved many circumstances
of power, property, or discipline, to which we do not here intend
any reference.   The professed purpose for which the general
councils were in every instance convoked, was to compose the
controversy of the day, and to pronounce a final decision upon
the doctrine which happened to be disputed; and thus, in the
history of those councils, we follow the track of theological investigation, and observe it gradually receding from soberness
and sense.

(1.) The object, for which the first two were assembled, was
to ascertain and promulgate the scriptural doctrine of the
Trinity; and a more important inquiry, and one more worthy
of the deliberate consideration of the directors of Christendom,
was not ever propounded to any religious assembly: and their
decisions respecting this doctrine were in accordance with the
sense of Scripture, as it has been interpreted by the great majority of Christians in every following age.

(2.) The questions proposed for the investigation of the third
and fourth Councils were of less importance to truth, and, in
the same proportion precisely, more difficult to comprehend and
determine,—the nature of Christ's existence on earth.   The
manner in which they were argued was not calculated to diminish this difficulty; and the violence, with which even the
more decorous* of these meetings was disgraced, was such as

---

* We might refer to the whole account of the sessions of the Council of
Chalcedon, even as it is given by Fleury (lib. xx. 8.)   One short passage may
serve as a specimen.   The assembly was divided into two parties: the bishops
of Egypt, Illyrium, and Palestine formed one; those of the East—of Pontus,
Asia, and Thrace—the other.   *Theodoret* was obnoxious to the former party, as
being suspected of the Nestorian heresy.   Nevertheless, he was allowed a seat in
the council by the emperor.   When he took his place the Orientals cried out,
" He is worthy of it."   The Egyptians exclaimed, " Call him not bishop—he is
no bishop ; expel the enemy of God—expel the Jew ! "   The Orientals cried,
" Expel the seditious—drive out the murderers ! "   And they continued for some
time to vent such exclamations on both sides.   At length the magistrates interfered : " These popular cries are unworthy of the episcopal character, and are of

would naturally result from eager disputation on a matter of
mysterious and almost impenetrable abstruseness. The subject
of the labours of the Sixth Council grew out of that which
occupied the third and fourth; and while it surpassed the other
in metaphysical intricacy, it presented even less prospect of any
practical advantage from its decision.

(3.) The matters which employed the Fifth Council were in
a great measure derived from the individual opinions of Origen;
and if these should be thought by some not to have merited by
their importance the cognizance of so solemn a tribunal, they
had at least a greater claim on general attention than the
foolish speculation of the Monothelites.

(4.) The seventh and last established idolatry as the law of
the Christian Church; and thus was completed the structure
of Oriental orthodoxy. It rose from the most solid and substantial foundation; it advanced, by the labours of a busy but
unwise generation, through the mid air and mist of metaphysics,
and terminated in a still blinder age, in clear and manifest superstition.

The same seven Councils are also received by the Roman
Church, but not as a perfect rule either of faith or discipline;
and, indeed, when we consider that they were held, without
exception, *in the East,* on the occasion of controversies originating in the East, and almost confined to it; that their deliberations were closely surveyed and influenced, if not directed, by
the Eastern emperor; and that the prelates who framed them
were almost exclusively Orientals*, we shall be disposed, perhaps, to feel some surprise that the Western Church, with so
many causes of variance with her rival, should have acquiesced
so submissively in their decisions. We might also feel surprise,

no use to either party—allow the paper to be read to you." The Egyptians exclaimed, "Expel that one man only, and we will all listen; our voice is raised
for the Catholic faith," &c.

* At Nice, among 318 members, three were of the Western Church; at Constantinople (1.), among 150, one only; at Ephesus, among 68, one; at Chalcedon, among 353, three; at Constantinople (2.), among 164, six; at Constantinople (3.), among 56, five; and even at the last, among the 377 who assisted, we
can observe no Occidentals, except the pope's legates, a very small number of
Sicilian bishops, and a deputy of the bishop of Sardinia.

were we not accustomed to such phenomena, that the last public act of the united Greek and Latin Communions, the last which was in truth binding on the *universal* Church, was the establishment of the grossest practical corruption which the religion has ever suffered.   And we may likewise remark, that it was established solely on the authority of *tradition*, while it was that, of all others, for which even the traditional authority is most defective, since it cannot be traced higher than the fourth century.

The edicts of the last General Council did not secure immediate obedience.   Leo the Armenian, who reigned from 814 to 820, relapsed into the heresy of the Isaurian.   He fell an early victim to conspiracy; but his successor, Michael, fearlessly proceeded in the same difficult endeavour; and the earnestness of his wishes and the perplexities of his situation are naturally displayed in an epistle addressed by him to the son of Charlemagne, Louis, emperor of the West.   As this document throws great general light on the ecclesiastical history of that age, we shall transcribe it here.

" Many of our clergy and laity, departing from the apostolical traditions, have introduced pernicious novelties. They took down the crosses in the churches and put images in their room, before which they lighted up lamps and burned incense, honouring them as the cross. They sang before them, worshipped them, and implored their succour.   Many dressed the female images with robes, and made them stand godmothers to their children. They offered up hair to them when they cut it off for the first time.   Some Presbyters scratched off the paint from the images and mixed it with the holy Eucharist, and gave it in the communion.   Others put the body of the Lord into the hands* of the images, and made the communicants take it out thence.   Others used boards with pictures painted on them, instead of an altar, on which they consecrated the elements; and

Epistle of the Emperor Michael.

---

* Thus it appears that the distinction at present so broadly drawn by the Greek Church between the worship of *painted* and of *graven* images did not then exist.   The distinction is, indeed, very old in the writings of the Church; but it is probable that it was not practically introduced until after the Mahometan conquest.

many such-like abuses were committed. Therefore, the orthodox emperors and the most learned bishops, assembled in
council, have forbidden these enormities, and have removed the
images to higher places in the church, where they stood formerly, and when they were not worshipped, as they have been
of late, by ignorant people.

"Some of the complainers are gone to Rome to calumniate
us there; but we are orthodox; we believe the Trinity, one
God in three persons, the incarnation of the Word, his two
wills and two operations; we implore the intercession of the
Holy Virgin, the mother of God, and of all the Saints; we reverence their relics; we receive all the apostolical traditions
and the decrees of the six Councils*."

The spirit of appeal and justification, in which the above
epistle is conceived, indicates the weakness of a falling cause;
and so, indeed, it proved; for in the year 842 the Empress
Theodora re-established the authority of the Seventh Council,
Final triumph of the Images, 842, A. D. and replaced the images with so firm a hand, that they have
never since been shaken. In celebration of this achievement, a
new festival was instituted under the name of the "Feast of
Orthodoxy"†, and the most riotous enthusiasm generally
attended the proclamation of idolatry.

The malice of historians has not failed to observe, that as the
first success over the reviving reason and religion had been obtained under the auspices of Irene; so the second and mortal
wound was inflicted by the rashness of a second woman ‡. The

---

* See Jortin, Eccl. Hist. ad ann. 814. From this concluding confession we
observe how many were the abuses to which even a reformer of the Church felt
obliged to publish his adhesion.

† There seems some reason to believe that this feast was not established until
after the Council which was assembled by Photius, in 879, in further confirmation
of idolatry.

‡ In favour at least of the consistency of that sex, we must mention that it
declared itself for idolatry from the very commencement of the contest, and very
strongly too, as will be seen. Leo the Isaurian began his enterprize by an attack
upon a very celebrated image of Jesus Christ, called the Antiphonetes, or Re-
spondent; and he despatched one of his officers, named Jovinus, to break it down.
Several women who were present endeavoured to avert his design by their supplications; but Jovinus, nothing moved by them, ascended a ladder and dealt some
severe blows on the image. On this the women became furious; they pulled

charge is true and remarkable; but the strenuous and systematic exertions of a long succession of Popes in the same cause will easily excuse the blindness of two empresses. Indeed, a general view of history rather tends to raise our astonishment, that so many princes were found wise and bold enough to stem the popular torrent. But this attempt at reformation commenced so late, and under circumstances so unfavourable, that even another century of judicious exertion, continued without pause or vacillation, might scarcely have sufficed for its success.

We shall conclude the chapter with a few additional remarks John Damascenus. on this controversy. The best writer in the Eastern Church during this most critical period in its history,—indeed, the only writer of any reputation even in his own day,—was John Damascenus; and with his name the long list of Greek Fathers may probably be said to terminate. He was a monk, and contemporary with Leo the Isaurian, against whom he vented his indignation with great impunity, as his ordinary residence was the monastery of St. Sabas, near Jerusalem, beyond the limits of the imperial control. His laborious and subtile works (of which the principal are " Four Books concerning the Orthodox Faith," and " Sacred Parallels") are tainted by the infection of the Aristotelian philosophy, and by a strong superstitious tendency; and therefore we are not surprised to observe that his eloquence and influence were zealously engaged in the defence of images*. He possessed considerable learning; and his sophistry, no less than his authority, may really have blinded the reason of some, while many more would nourish under the shelter of his name a previous inclination to idolatry†.

down the ladder, massacred the officer on the spot, and tore him in pieces. The image fell notwithstanding, and the women were led away to execution.

* He condescends to appeal to the authority of older fathers in his defence of images—to that of Basil, Gregory of Nyssa, Chrysostom, Ambrose, Anastasius of Antioch, and others. But we believe that he has not even affected to advance any name of higher antiquity than the fourth century—not, by the way, that his cause would have been much better if he had. He was anathematized by the Iconoclast Council in 754.

† Theodore Studites, a monk and abbot, has acquired great reputation in the history of the Eastern Church by his obstinate defence of the orthodox practice, chiefly during the second contest. Exile was the punishment of his zeal, and severer punishment was very seldom, if ever, inflicted on the contumacious.

We believe it to be true, that of the miracles which are re
corded to have abundantly signalized this prolonged dispute, the
very great proportion, if not the whole, were performed by the
friends of the idols,—a fact which, while it proves the higher
principles of the other party, will also assist in accounting for
their unpopularity. The people in the East were not, indeed,
at this time so stupid and unenlightened as the serfs of the
Western Empire; but they were by nature more disposed to
fanaticism; they were familiar, through long habits of deception, with preternatural appearances, and disposed, by a con-
trolling imagination, to eager credulity.

Conduct of   The Bishops, and, in general, the secular clergy of the East,
the secular
and regular appear to have taken no violent part in the contest. Indeed,
Clergy;   we are persuaded that that numerous body contained many
pious and rational individuals, who were shocked by the degradation of Christianity and human nature, and who watched
with an anxious eye the endeavours which were made to remove
it. But such characters, which are among the best of the sacred
profession, are seldom busy or ambitious; and the anxiety of
those excellent men may have been often confined to their own
bosoms, or at least to the narrow limits of their diocese. On
the other hand, the monastic orders have too generally thrown
discredit on their origin by their alliance with impurity and imposture. And thus in the present instance, they were furious
advocates for a system so necessary to their influence and their
avarice; and it is chiefly, no doubt, to their perseverance that
we are to attribute the evil result of the conflict.

of the peo-   The common people, partly from a natural tendency to a sen-
ple:
sible worship, partly from the inveteracy of long habit, were
strongly disposed to the same party; and that disposition was
effectually improved by the monks, who, from a greater show of
austerity, had the greatest hold upon their minds. Nor is the
circumstance to be slightly noticed, that the contest in this case
was for an intelligible and visible object. Unlike the metaphysical intricacies of some former controversies, it carried a direct
appeal to the understanding of the vulgar, because its subject
was the subject of their senses. If they positively worshipped
the image, its destruction deprived them of their god; and even

where the worship was only relative, it was extremely easy to persuade them that, in parting with the symbols of their faith, with the book of their religion, they were rashly casting away religion itself. Their enthusiasm was heated by false miracles; and when we think of the violence which the populace of the East were wont to exhibit even at their public spectacles, in the frivolous contests of the Hippodrome, we shall understand to what excesses they might be hurried by the agitation of religious excitement.

The Papal Chair perseveringly supported the cause of superstition; and this, perhaps, is the first occasion on which the close alliance of *principle* between the Pope and the monastic orders displayed itself. The Pope's legates were present at the last General Council, and his Italian clergy appear to have given him very cordial assistance. Not so the more rational Prelates of France. Less awed by the presence of the spiritual director, more so by the dictates of real piety, they established, under the guidance of Charlemagne*, a very broad distinction between positive and relative worship; and without entirely disclaiming the authority of the Seventh Council, they endeavoured to obviate, as much as possible, the great practical evil which directly flowed from it. This difference in the conduct of the French and Italian Churches on so great a question is a fact of some importance in history and deserving of attentive notice; and it is but justice to our own ancestors, as well as to the German divines of the age, to admit that they generally endeavoured to follow the same difficult course. But their resistance was not long effectual, nor indeed could it reasonably expect success; because, by permitting the use of images and their presence in the congregations of the converts, they made that first concession to error, of which all the others were remote, perhaps, but necessary consequences †.

of the Bishop of Rome:

of the French Church.

---

* The Council of Francfort, whose deliberations were held under the eye of that monarch, went, indeed, somewhat farther than this, and, though it permitted the images to remain, forbade any sort of adoration to be addressed to them.

† Dupin (Nouv. Bibl. on second Council of Nice) gives a tolerably fair *historical* view of the subject of image-worship. He admits that, during the three first ages and the beginning of the fourth, images were *very rare* among Christians;

CHAPTER XII.

On the Schism between the Greek and Latin Churches.

Preliminary considerations—Political causes—Ecclesiastical—Origin of the Dispute—Dignity and jurisdiction of the See of Constantinople—Council of Chalcedon—Ambition of the Patriarch—Oriental dissensions—profitable to the Pope—Popish legate at Constantinople—Disputes between the two Sees—Title of Œcumenical Bishop assumed by John the Faster—Opposition of Gregory the Great—Emperor Phocas—Limits of papal influence in Greece—Ground of controversy changed—Procession of the Holy Spirit—the original doctrine—Process of the change—Spain—France—Charlemagne—Moderation of Pope Leo III.—Perseverance of the Greeks—Forgery of the Latins—the Patriarch Photius—his character—his excommunication of Pope Nicholas I.—Five heresies charged on the Roman Church—Transfer of several provinces from papal to patriarchal jurisdiction—Bulgaria—Dissensions of the Greeks—Fortunes of Photius—Connexion of Rome with Greek parties—defeat of the designs of the former—Subsequent differences—Michael Cerularius—Anathema of Leo IX. by his legates at Constantinople.

WE have so frequently had occasion, especially in our later pages, to distinguish between the conduct and character of the Greek and Roman Churches, that it becomes necessary to enter still farther into the causes of this distinction, and to trace the differences which had for some time disturbed their harmony, and which ended in their entire separation. In so doing, we must, in the first place, be careful not to confound the division of the churches with that of the empires; for the former, in fact, did not take place until more than a century after the final alienation of the ecclesiastical States from the sceptre of Leo the Isaurian. Nor, on the other hand, should we be

that towards the end of the fifth, pictures and images made their appearance, chiefly in the East, and became common in the sixth; they represented combats of martyrs and other sacred stories, for the instruction of those who were unable to read. The simple vulgar were touched by these representations; and when they beheld the Saints so vividly, and, as it were, bodily presented to them, they could not prevent themselves from testifying, by *exterior signs*, the respect, the esteem, and the veneration which they felt for them. Thus the worship of images insensibly established itself, and it was still further confirmed by the miracles which were attributed to them.

correct in considering these events as perfectly unconnected. Doubtless, political causes had great influence both in opening and widening the spiritual breach. The division of the empire under Arcadius and Honorius, though not immediately affect-ing the unity of the church, operated indirectly to its dis-turbance by weakening the bonds of connexion and destroying the complete community of interests which more naturally sub-sists under a single government. Again, the circumstance, that the seat of the Western Empire was removed from Rome to Ravenna, communicated that sort of independence to the Ro-man Bishop, which though it conferred not, in fact, any tempo-ral authority, failed not to give nourishment to his pride and some countenance to his general claims of supremacy. A further alienation was necessarily occasioned by the barbarian conquest of the West; because this event not only annihilated the former relations and the reciprocal dependence of the two empires, but also produced a great and rapid change in the character of the Western clergy, and even in the principles of the Church.

Causes of the breach between the two Churches.

Lastly, the common violence and mutual insults of Leo the Isaurian and Pope Gregory II., the civil war which broke out between them, the complete triumph of the latter, and the con-sequent transfer of certain jurisdictions in Sicily and the South of Italy from the Roman to the Constantinopolitan See, greatly tended to weaken the spirit which had hitherto identified the Churches, and to remove any notion of their inseparability. These are some of the political causes which undoubtedly pre-pared the way for the grand schism, and contributed to acce-lerate and inflame it. But there are others, of a nature purely ecclesiastical, to which it is more usually ascribed, and which had doubtless the principal share in its accomplishment.

The earliest recorded difference between the Churches was that already noticed by us, respecting the celebration of Easter; and we also remarked the tone of authority which the Bishop of the *imperial* city arrogated even in those days : but their connexion, and even their harmony, was not seriously endan-gered by that dispute ; nor, indeed, can we trace the origin of the fatal controversy with any certainty to an earlier period than the fifth century. On the foundation of the new capital at

Byzantium, the Bishop was, of course, invested with some power and dignity, which gradually increased, through the consent or the neglect of the immediate successors of Constantine; however, the superior rank and precedence of the Roman Pontiff was not yet disputed. But in the beginning of the fifth century the spiritual jurisdiction of the See of Constantinople was much more widely extended: it then comprehended Asia, Thrace, and Pontus, and advanced on the west within the confines of Illyricum; and, in 451, the Council of Chalcedon not only confirmed that jurisdiction, but conferred on the Bishop of Constantinople the same honours and privileges which were already possessed by that of Rome: the equality of the Pontiffs was justified by the equal dignity and lustre of the two capitals. The legates of Leo the Great were present, and had considerable influence in that council; but neither their exertions, nor those of the Pope himself, were able to prevent this affront to his dignity. Having attained so elevated a situation, the patriarch very soon proceeded to exalt himself still higher. The method which he took to extend his authority was, to humble, if possible, his brethren of Antioch and Alexandria*; and thus the same ambition was found to pursue the same course at Constantinople as at Rome. But *there* it was liable to severer mortifications and more effectual control from the immediate presence of the Emperor, from his power and supremacy, and his habitual interference in church affairs.

The Council of Chalcedon, 451, A.D.

Again, the grasping ambition of the patriarch, and the dissensions which, from other causes no less than from that, so continually disturbed the Oriental Church, were productive of great influence to the Pope, not only through the positive weakness occasioned to that Church by such divisions, but chiefly because the injured or discontented party very generally made its appeal to the Roman See, where it met with most willing and partial attention. We may recollect that Athanasius, when persecuted in the East, fled to the Western Church for refuge; and this example was not lost on those

---

* It was not till a little before this time that Juvenal, Bishop of Jerusalem, *usurped* the title of patriarch, which, however, was confirmed to him by Theodosius the Younger.

who thought themselves aggrieved in after-ages. It is true that Roman interference was, on every occasion, indignantly rejected by the rival Pontiff; nevertheless, the habit of interposing would lead many to imagine that it was founded on some indefinite, unacknowledged right; and disaffection was encouraged in the East by the certainty of a powerful protector.

Very soon after the Council of Chalcedon, Leo appointed a resident legate at Constantinople to watch over the papal interests, and to communicate with the Vatican on matters of spiritual importance. That useful privilege, as we have already seen, was not abandoned by succeeding popes: and those ecclesiastical ambassadors, or ‘ Correspondents,’ continued for some time to represent the papal chair in the eastern capital. *Pope's Legates.*

For the next hundred and thirty years, the disputes respecting the equality of the two Sees, as well as the limits of their jurisdiction, were carried on with little interruption perhaps, but with little violence. But in 588, at a Synod called at Constantinople respecting the conduct of a patriarch of Antioch, John, surnamed the Faster, who was then Primate of the East, adopted, as we have observed, the title of Œcumenical, or Universal Bishop. It appears that this title had been conferred on the patriarchs by the emperors Leo and Justinian, without any accession of power; nor was it, in fact, understood to indicate any claim to supremacy beyond the limits of the Eastern Church. But Gregory could not brook such presumption in an Eastern Prelate, and used every endeavour to deprive his rival of the obnoxious title, and at the same time to establish his own superiority. He failed in both these attempts—at least his success in the latter was confined to the Western clergy, and to the interested and precarious assent of the discontented subjects of the Eastern Church. *Title of Universal Bishop, 588, A.D.*

The quarrel proceeded during the seventh century, and Roman Catholic writers confidently assert that the Emperor Phocas (a sanguinary usurper), through the influence of Pope Boniface III., *transferred* the disputed title from the Greek to the Roman Pontiff. It seems probable that he acknowledged the pre-eminence of the latter—and early usage justified him in so doing—without at all derogating from the independence of the former.   But the alliance of the Eastern Emperor with a foreign Bishop against his own patriarch could not possibly be of long duration ; and, accordingly, throughout the controversy about images (which presently followed) we find the Pope in direct and open opposition to the Emperor and to the powerful party in his Church which favoured him.

On the other hand, the ecclesiastical orders in the East were so widely and passionately divided on the subject of this dispute, and the hopes of the weaker and more violent party were obliged for so many years to fix themselves on Rome, that the Pope must again have acquired great influence in that quarter. It was great, but it was temporary only; for the popular prejudice, especially in Greece itself, was still strong and general against any acknowledgment of papal supremacy, and the national vanity was still jealous of the name and ascendancy of Rome.   And thus the actual influence of the Pope was generally confined to those, who stood in need of his assistance, and seldom survived the crisis during which they needed it.

Thus far the disputes between the Pope and the Patriarch were confined almost entirely to the question of supremacy in the Universal Church, pertinaciously claimed by the one, and perseveringly refused by the other; and to this difference we need not doubt that a great proportion of the violence which disgraced the controversy may be ascribed.   But during the eighth century, the contention assumed a different aspect, and took a ground and character less discreditable to either party.

Difference respecting the double Procession. According to the original creed of the Latin, as well as of the Greek Church, the Holy Spirit was believed to proceed *from the Father only ;* and the question, though of great theological importance, does not appear to have been generally investigated until the eighth century—at least to that period we must refer the origin of the controversy respecting it.   It is true that the change in the established doctrine was first introduced into the Church of Spain*, an event which must have

---

* Baronius asserts, that the words *Filioque* were first added by the Council of Toledo, *by the authority of Pope Leo I.*, about the year 447 ; but he confesses that the doctrine was not expressly received by the Roman Church until some ages afterwards.

taken place before the Mahometan conquest. Thence it proceeded into France, and in the year 767 it was agitated in the Council of Gentilli, near Paris; it then received the assent of the French clergy. Soon afterwards, it was warmly advocated by Charlemagne himself; and in the year 809, at the Council of Aix-la-Chapelle*, Pope Leo III. acknowledged the truth of the doctrine, but still objected to making it an article of faith; observing, with great reason, 'that every doctrine which is true should not, for that reason, be inserted in a *creed*:' nevertheless, as it had previously obtained place in the Latin creeds, his authority, or his inclination, was not sufficiently strong to effect its general erasure. It was maintained in France, and its rejection by Rome was feeble and temporary.

But the Greeks obstinately adhered to their original faith, as established by the Council of Constantinople; and what gave them great advantage in the subsequent controversy was, that their adversaries had begun the contest by abandoning the defensible ground of argument: they forgot the authority of scripture, and took refuge under a falsified copy of the Canons of that Council, into which (through that obtuse craft which becomes a principle in ignorant ages) the words *Filioque (and the Son)* had been interpolated. The fraud was instantly detected, and the homage, which they had thus reluctantly offered to the Council in question, was converted into a conclusive argument by an adversary, who rested his own faith on no better ground than its antiquity.

A controversy conducted on such principles could hope for no rational discussion, nor any friendly termination: its only effect was to inflame the enmity already too hotly kindled, and to accelerate the certain hour of separation. This consummation was presently secured by the promotion of a very extraordinary person to the patriarchal throne. In the year 853, Photius†, a layman of splendid talents, unusual extent of eru-

Photius,
853—886
A.D.

* Fleury, Hist. Eccl. liv. xlv. sect. 48, Concil. Tom. vii. The Pope defended his opinion by the argument, that two General Councils, that of Chalcedon and the Fifth, had forbidden any addition to the creed.

† " Photius, than whom Greece, the parent of so much genius, has never produced, perhaps, a more accomplished man, is singularly recommended by talents applicable to every object, sound judgment, extreme acuteness, infinite reading,

dition both secular and theological, and unimpeachable moral
character, was raised to that dignity by the Emperor Michael,
who, with that view, removed and banished the actual bishop,
Ignatius.   The exile appealed to Rome.   And if the jealousy
of the Vatican was excited by the splendid reputation of the
new patriarch, its anxiety might also be awakened by his ambitious and fearless character : therefore Pope Nicholas I.,
who was as proud and aspiring as his rival, listened to the
appeal, and eagerly espoused the cause of Ignatius.   He assembled a Council at Rome * in 862, in which he pronounced
the election of Photius illegal, and excommunicated him with
all his abettors.   The patriarch was not much disturbed by
this violence, and four years afterwards, in a Council summoned
at Constantinople, he retorted the anathemas of his rival, pronounced his deposition, and removed him from the communion
of all Christians.

Five direct
heresies
charged on
the Church
of Rome.

Photius justified this extremely bold measure by a circular
letter addressed to his brother patriarchs, in which, besides
some strong reflections on other grievances, he charged the
Roman Church with five direct heresies.   We shall here enumerate them, both that we may more clearly show what were
held to be the principal points on which the Churches were divided, and also that we may observe how low the malevolence
of controversy will sometimes condescend to stoop : 1. That
the Romans fasted on the Sabbath, or seventh day of the week;
2. That in the first week of Lent they permitted the use of
milk and cheese; 3. That they prohibited their priests to
marry, and separated from their wives such as were married
when they went into orders; 4. That they authorized the
Bishops alone to anoint baptized persons with the holy chrism,
withholding that power from Presbyters; 5. That they had
interpolated the creed of Constantinople by the insertion of the

incredible diligence. He had held nearly all the offices of state, he had thoroughly
investigated all the records of the Church; in his Bibliotheca alone, still extant,
he has brought together nearly two hundred and eighty writers, chiefly ecclesiastical, which he has studied, reviewed, and abstracted, and pronounced a most
accurate judgment on their arguments, style, fidelity, authority.' Cave ap. Jortin, A.D. 861.

* Mosheim, cent. ix. p. ii., c. iii.

words *Filioque,* and held the doctrine of the procession of the Holy Spirit from the Son as well as the Father.

These charges, and the consequent recriminations, embittered as they also were by national animosity, had, of course, no other effect than to exasperate the violence of both parties; but we should be mistaken if we were wholly to attribute that fury to the differences either in doctrine or discipline. Its deepest motive is, perhaps, to be traced to another source. The emperor, with the assistance, and probably through the influence, of his ambitious Primate, had lately and definitively withdrawn from the papal jurisdiction various provinces to the east of the Adriatic, Illyricum, Macedonia, Epirus, Achaia, Thessaly, and either transferred them to the patriarch, or (for the point is disputed) confirmed his previous authority over them; and this, indeed, was an ecclesiastical offence of a description little calculated to find forgiveness at Rome. Moreover, it happened that this sensible injury was immediately succeeded by another of the same nature. The heathen inhabitants of Bulgaria, a province of the Eastern Empire not far distant from Constantinople, had very lately been converted to Christianity by Greek missionaries; or, if it be admitted that some very imperfect efforts had been previously made there by the emissaries of Charlemagne, the Greeks at least had the merit of completing the spiritual conquest *: consequently, Photius placed Bulgaria under his own jurisdiction; nor will the impartial historian blame that prelate for his endeavour to make the limits of the Church co-extensive with those of the empire, and to repel the intrusive invasions of Rome.

Disputed limits of jurisdiction.

But the influence of the pope was still maintained, and nourished by the dissensions of the Greeks; and the flame of controversy had not at all abated, when Basilius, the Macedonian, on his accession to the throne, deposed Photius, and restored Ignatius to his former dignity. This act was confirmed

---

* It appears, indeed, from Roman Catholic historians, that the Pope maintained a sort of communication with the Bulgarians, by means of missionaries, and that their King actually sent his son to Rome in acknowledgment (as those assert) of spiritual obedience. The utmost that can be truly alleged is, that the field, which both parties had exerted themselves to cultivate, was the subject of *equal* claims.

by a council assembled at Constantinople in 869, in which the papal legates had great influence, and which the Roman Church still acknowledges as the *Eighth* General Council. In 878 Photius was recalled, and in 886 again deposed; but neither his recall nor his deposition had the effect of conferring on the papal chair the jurisdiction for which it had struggled so pertinaciously. And, indeed, we may again observe, that throughout her long succession of interferences in the religious affairs of Greece, Rome has, on no occasion, gained any substantial or permanent advantage. In fact, even at the moment when she seemed to be playing her part most artfully, she was little more than a tool in the more artful hands of a Greek *party*, who flattered her as long as their own interests required her support, but were always ready to reject her intervention when they required it no longer.

Eighth General Council of the Roman Church, 869, A.D.

Dispute between Cerularius and Pope Leo IX.

We might have closed the account of this controversy with the mutual excommunications of Photius and Nicholas: indeed the schism did properly commence at that period; and though the popes continued to prosecute, through the two succeeding centuries, their unsuccessful schemes of ambition, they produced little mischief, and have, consequently, little attracted the notice of history. About the middle of the eleventh century the attention of Rome seems to have been particularly directed to the reduction of the Bishops of Alexandria and Antioch under its own supremacy. While the pontiffs were contending for authority, the Churches were debating with extreme ardour a point of difference posterior in origin to the time of Photius, *viz.* whether the bread used at the Eucharist should be leavened or unleavened? The Greek clergy held the former opinion, and objected the latter to the Latins as an unpardonable error*. Michael Cerularius, a man of lofty, perhaps turbulent spirit, was at that time patriarch; and after some angry correspondence between him and Pope Leo IX., the latter pronounced at Rome the sentence of excommunication. Nevertheless, his

---

* Some other abuses are also imputed to them by Cerularius, and they are among the most frivolous which could have been selected out of the long and dark list of their corruptions—a proof that the *spirit* of the Greek Church in that age was as far from the true comprehension of Christianity, as that of its rival.

legates were invited to Constantinople with a view to heal the schism; there they asserted some insolent claims, which Cerularius indignantly rejected.   As the deliberations continued, the differences grew deeper and wider, and at length the legates in the heart of Constantinople, in the church of St. Sophia, publicly excommunicated the patriarch and all his adherents. They then solemnly deposited the written act of their anathema on the grand altar of the temple, and, having shaken off the dust from their feet, departed.

Excommunication of the Greek Church, 1054, A.D.

This event took place in 1054, and confirmed and consummated the separation; and though some degree of friendly intercourse has been occasionally resumed since that time, as political rather than religious exigencies have required it, the imputed errors of the Greeks (of which the most offensive was their independence) have never been seriously retracted by their Church, nor ever pardoned by its rival.

CHAPTER XIII.

WE shall depart from that important position in our history, which is occupied by the acts of Charlemagne, with a clearer view of their nature and a better comprehension of the character of the Roman Church, if we previously throw even a hasty retrospect over some portion of the path which we have traced; and thus, after retouching some parts which may not have been sufficiently illustrated, we shall complete the account which we propose to give of the first eight centuries of the Church. Some particulars will also be introduced, of which all mention has purposely been deferred till this occasion, in order to bring them into contact with those more remarkable events to which they are allied in principle, though separated by time or other circumstances. We shall commence this review from the earliest ages.

I. The primitive assemblies (ἐκκλησίαι) of the converts were called Churches. These, in the first instance, were scattered, as the religion spread itself, in perfect equality and independence, and their affairs were, for the most part, regulated by a body of presbyters, who acted with the consent of the people, and under the guidance of the Apostles. This form of government was, to a certain extent, modelled on that of the Jewish synagogues, and it was natural that it should be so; since most of the first converts were Jews; since Christ himself had not laid down any general rules of ecclesiastical polity; and since his apostles were more intent on enlarging the numbers of the believers, and informing their piety, than on constructing partial laws for the external constitution of a society, which was destined to comprehend every race and variety of man.

The ante-Nicene Church.

Earliest form of government.

Over two at least among the original Churches presidents were apostolically appointed under the name of bishops; and presently, as the apostles were gradually withdrawn, all the principal Churches, respecting which we have any express * information, elected for themselves superintendents under the same name. That custom prevailed very commonly even before the death of St. John, and became almost universal before the end of the first century: still, for a certain time longer, the various Churches continued to conduct their own affairs without any mutual dependence, and with little other correspondence than that of counsel and charity; and the bishop, in almost all matters, acted in concert with the presbytery in the internal administration of each.

Thus, in the unsettled constitution of the primitive Church, we may observe the elements of three† forms of government

---

* We refer to the note at the end of Chapter II. The first bishops were in many instances appointed by the apostles: their successors were chosen by the people; and this practice continued. The following is a curious passage (in Cyprian's 68th Epistle), and should be cited:—" Propter quod plebs, obsequens præceptis Dominicis et Deum metuens, a peccatore præposito separare se debet, nec se ad sacrilegi sacerdotis sacrificia miscere—quando ipsa maximè potestatem habeat vel eligendi dignos sacerdotes, vel indignos recusandi."

† Perhaps we might even say four—at least those, who maintain the sufficiency of the occasional and spontaneous exhortation of any zealous member of any con-

subsisting under apostolical direction, the Episcopal, the Presbyterian, and the Independent. But of these the second scarcely survived the departure of the inspired directors, and immediately subsided into a limited episcopacy; and the third, though it continued somewhat longer, so coalesced with the other two, that the greater part, if not the whole, of the Independent Churches, during the first half of the second century, were ruled by a bishop and a presbytery: that is to say, the various societies which constituted the body of Christendom were so ruled, though as yet they exercised no control over each other.

In a very short time, as new circumstances rapidly sprang up, it was found necessary for the common interest to facilitate a more general communication between societies, which, though separate in government, were united by far more powerful ties. This was most reasonably accomplished by the assembling of Councils or occasional councils, called synods, composed for the most part Synods. of bishops, each of whom represented his own Church, and acknowledged no superiority of power or rank in any of his brethren. These associations of Churches cannot be traced to the first century; but before the time of Tertullian* they were common and extensive, at least in Greece, and the custom rapidly spread over every part of Christendom. The rules or canons enacted by these synods were received as laws *of the Church* throughout the province which had sent its deputies to the meeting; they were frequently published and communicated to other provinces; and the correspondence and co-operation, thus created, united, in a certain measure, the whole body, and combined the many scattered Churches into that *one,* which, even in those early days, was called the *Catholic †* Church. But from this description we observe both the independent equality of the members composing it, and also, that it had no acknowledged chief or head. For though the metropolitans might assume, each in his own province, some superiority in rank, perhaps even in authority, yet these among

gregation for spiritual instruction, also seek their authority in the partial and transient practice of the Primitive Church.

* De Jejuniis.—"Aguntur per Græcias illa in locis concilia ex universis ecclesiis, per quæ et altiora quæque in commune tractantur, et ipsa repræsentatio totius nominis Christiani magna veneratione celebratur."

† See Bingham, Antiq. b. i., c. i., sect. 7.

themselves were equal, and their precedence and power were strictly confined to their own district.

The principal bond, which united the original Catholic Church, was the possession of a common canon or catalogue of sacred books; and thus, when everywhere tried by the same test, the opinions which might be stigmatized as heretical by any one of the Churches were, for the same reason, condemned by the universal Church; and the spiritual delinquents, who were removed from communion by a part of the Catholic body, were consequently repudiated by the whole. It is true, that those who combined and directed this external system of Catholicism were the ecclesiastical ministers, and chiefly the Bishops: it is also true, that the influence of all these over the people, and the power of the latter in the government of their dioceses, were augmented beyond their original moderation by the circumstances, which led the clergy to so general a co-operation. But, on the other hand, it is extremely doubtful whether, without such a confederation, the faith itself, loosely scattered over so broad a space, could have withstood the various tempests which were levelled against it; and it certainly was not possible that any general confederation could have been formed among the Churches, unless by the exertions of their directors—and those, too, in each instance invested with some personal authority. So that, if there are any who inveigh against the original Catholic Church as the first corruption of Christianity, and the parent of all that have followed, they do not sufficiently consider either the simple objects and character of that Church, or the perilous circumstances under which it coalesced, and combined many defenceless members into one powerful body. Under *any* circumstances, a close association and unity among religious societies, possessing the same canon of faith and the same form of administration, would have been natural and desirable; but, under the pressure of common danger and calamity, it was not only reasonable, but necessary.

Semler* considers it to have been the worst consequence of the formation of the early Church as a single body, that it restrained the liberty of individual judgment, or what he calls *in-*

The original Catholic Church.

---

* Observationes Novæ in Historiam iii. primorum sæculorum.

ternal religion; that it imposed certain rules, both of doctrine and discipline, upon the more ignorant and worldly Christians, and discouraged any laxity, or, as he would say, freedom, of interpretation or practice. And on that principle he exalts the character of the bolder and more mystical writers, Clemens Alexandrinus and Origen, who were not partizans of the Church, at the expense of Tertullian, Cyprian, and others, and praises the independence of the heretics in thinking and reasoning for themselves. We are not, however, able to discover that the expositions of Scripture contained in the Alexandrian, are, upon the whole, more sound and rational than those of the Carthaginian, Fathers, while they certainly abound with many fanciful extravagances from which the latter are free; and we have shown that the tenets of many of the early heretics were incalculably remote from the precincts of reason and Scripture. At the same time we are willing to agree with Semler, that it were better far for religion to endure all those irregular absurdities, than to support the Unity of the Church as it was proclaimed in the Roman Catholic sense, and as it was upheld by execution and massacre. But it cannot be asserted that the papal system was the *necessary* offspring of the early Catholic Church; for, if so, it would have arisen in the Eastern as surely as in the Western communion. The worst principles of that system proceeded from causes posterior far to the second century; and the union of the religious societies, which at that time constituted *the Church,* was, in our opinion, an instrument in God's hands both for the preservation of sound doctrine amidst the numerous and irrational deviations of heresy, and also for the association of the faithful in discipline, and in devoted resistance to the attacks of persecution.

The ante-Nicene Fathers.

The writings of the ante-Nicene fathers contain all the most important doctrines of Christianity; but we should vainly search those books for a complete and consistent system of theology. In fact, their writers did not commonly handle the dogmas of faith, unless with a view to the confutation of some new or prevalent heresy*. Thus their arguments were usually directed

---

* " C'est la matière de tous les Sermons des Pères la morale et les hérésies du tems. Sans cette clef souvent on ne les entend pas; ou du moins on ne les

to a particular purpose, and addressed to the views and prejudices of the time or place in which they were published. Many of them were uninstructed in the art of reasoning, and almost all were, in some degree, infected either with the narrow spirit of Judaism, or the loose and speculative genius of philosophy; so that, in correcting the errors of others, they often deviated very widely from sense and truth themselves *. Those controversies, however, though not always conducted with becoming moderation, were not, perhaps, without their use even in those days ; since they warmed the zeal and animated the industry of the parties, without endangering their personal security. And to us their retrospect may bring some increase of charity, if the consideration of the very broad and essential points, on which they turned, should haply lead us to attach less weight to those less momentous differences, which have raised such heats in later times, and which even yet have not entirely lost their bitterness.

It is certain that a very important moral improvement was immediately introduced by Christianity, wheresoever it gained footing. The earliest societies of the converts furnished an example of rigid, but simple and unaffected piety, to which the history of man cannot, perhaps, produce any parallel; and even in the following century we need not hesitate to assert the incomparable superiority of the Christians over their Pagan contemporaries: the principles of their religion, the severity of their discipline, the peculiarity of their civil condition, confirm the evidence which assures us that such was the fact. But the golden days of Christianity were confined to its infancy; and it is a great delusion to imagine that its perfect integrity continued throughout the whole period of its persecution, or to refer indiscriminately to the history of the first three centuries for a model of

Morality of the early Christians.

---

peut goûter. Et c'est encore une utilité considérable de l'Histoire Ecclésiastique. Car quand on scait les hérésies qui régnoient en chaque tems et en chaque pais on voit pourquoi les pères revenoient toujours à certains points de doctrine.'' Fleury, Disc. 1. sur l'Hist. Eccles., s. xiv.

* Even Irenæus, almost the earliest among them, is not exempt from this charge : his errors are enumerated by Dupin, Nouv. Biblioth., Vie S. Irénée, vol. i. p. 73.

Evangelical purity.   We must also be careful not to exaggerate the merits of the early Church, nor to extenuate the abuses which it certainly admitted, nor to exculpate the ministers who created or encouraged them.

The anti-
quity of
some
abuses.

So far, indeed, are we from any such intention, that we consider the present as a proper opportunity to examine with more specific notice the innovations which successively appeared, either in doctrine or discipline: that we may ascribe to its proper age each of the several abuses which at length combined to deform the structure of the Catholic Church; and that we may perceive how gradual was their growth, and how deep and ancient the root from which many of them proceeded.

That to which we shall first recall the reader's attention (for there are few, if any, of which some mention has not already been made) is the claim to miraculous power, as inherent in the Church, which was asserted by several among the early Christians, from Justin Martyr downwards, and asserted (as evidence and reason have persuaded us*) without any

The mira-
culous
claims of
the early
Church.

truth.   According to the Apologists, and other writers of the second and third centuries, the sick were commonly healed, the dead were raised†, and evil spirits cast out, through the

---

* See Chapter II.

† The following is part of the celebrated testimony of Irenæus (lib. ii. cap. 31 or 57), as cited by Eusebius (lib. v. cap. 7):—οἱ μὲν γὰρ δαίμονας ἐλαύνουσι βεβαίως καὶ ἀληθῶς· ὥστε πολλάκις καὶ πιστεύειν αὐτοὺς ἐκείνους καθαρισθέντας ἀπὸ τῶν πονηρῶν πνευμάτων καὶ εἶναι ἐν τῇ ἐκκλησία· οἱ δὲ καὶ πρόγνωσιν ἔχουσι τῶν μελλόντων, καὶ ὀπτασίας καὶ ῥήσεις προφητικάς· ἄλλοι δὲ τοὺς κάμνοντας διὰ τῆς τῶν χειρῶν ἐπιθέσεως ἰῶνται, καὶ ὑγιεῖς ἀποκαθιστᾶσιν. ἤδη δὲ καθὼς ἔφαμεν καὶ νεκροὶ ἐγέρθησαν, καὶ παρέμειναν σὺν ἡμῖν ἱκανοῖς ἔτεσι. Καὶ τί γάρ; οὐκ ἔστιν ἀριθμὸν εἰπεῖν τῶν χαρισμάτων ὧν κατὰ παντὸς τοῦ κόσμου ἡ ἐκκλησία παρὰ Θεοῦ γαβοῦσα, &c. &c.   " Some effectually expel devils, so that the very persons who are cleansed from evil spirits believe and are in the Church ! Others have foreknowledge of the future, and visions and prophetic declarations ; others heal the sick by imposition of hands ; and it has happened (as we have said) that the dead have been raised and continued among us for some years.   It is impossible to enumerate the grace which the Church throughout the whole world has received from God," &c.

We shall here only remark (as Jortin has remarked before us) that in speaking of resurrection, the writer uses the *past* tense, while the other miracles are described as in the actual course of present occurrence ; yet the words σὺν ἡμῖν cannot, without great violence, be understood of any preceding generation, and we doubt not that Irenæus intended to assert that dead persons had been brought to life in his own time.   In a subsequent paragraph, that father also claims the gift

prayers of the faithful in the name of Jesus.   Men of unquestionable piety eagerly retailed, and may possibly have believed,
each other's fabrications.   Visions and dreams became the motives of action or belief, and the commonest feelings and resolutions were ascribed to the immediate impulse and inspiration
of the Deity.   Some nominal converts may thus have been
enrolled under the banners of the Church; but the evil of the
practice overbalanced its profit, even its momentary profit; since
the minds of men were thereby hurried away from the proper
understanding of the Gospel, and the true character of the
religion, to gaze after marvels and prodigies, and prepared to
ascribe to fallacious impressions a belief, which can only be
sound when it is founded in reason.   It is proper, however, to
point out one general distinction between these early miracles
and those which clouded the Church in later ages; for, though
it is insufficient to establish their credit, it may lead us to regard their authors with more charity.   There appears to have
been nothing absurd or superstitious in the *manner* of their
performance, nor base or wicked in their *object*.   They are related to have been usually wrought by the simple invocation of
Christ's name; and it does not appear that their accomplishment directly tended to feed avarice or individual ambition—
neither to augment the power of the clergy, nor to decide religious controversy, nor to subvert any obnoxious heresy, nor to
establish any new doctrine, nor to recommend any foolish practice or superstitious observance*.   We can seldom trace them
to any other motive than an injudicious zeal for the propagation of the faith.

---

of tongues for his age. καθὼς καὶ πολλῶν ἀκούομεν ἀδελφῶν ἐν τῇ ἐκκλησίᾳ προφητικὰ
χαρίσματα ἐχόντων, καὶ παντοδαπαῖς λαλούντων διὰ Πνεύματος γλώσσαις.   After this
passage, there is scarcely any mention made of that gift in ecclesiastical history.
We should observe, that Eusebius makes the above citation in proof of his assertion " that miraculous powers ἐν ἐκκλησίαις τ ι σ ι ν ὑπελίλειπτο, remained in *certain
Churches* as late as the time of Irenæus."   He does not appear disposed to claim
them *for the Church* at any later period.   Origen asserts in various places, that
vestiges (ἴχνη) of the antient miracles were still extant: καὶ εἰ πιστοί ἐσμεν λέγοντες,
ἑωράκομεν καὶ ἡμεῖς. (C. Cels., L. ii., p. 62.)   Again (L. ii., p. 80) Γενναῖον δ' ἔργον
τοῦ Ἰησοῦ, τὸ μέχρι σήμερον θεραπεύεσθαι τῷ ὀνόματι αὐτοῦ, οὓς ὁ Θεὸς βούλεται.

* This subject is very fairly treated by Dr. Jortin in the beginning of his second
book.

The triumphs of the Exorcists over the powers of darkness
are so loudly and perpetually celebrated by the oldest Church
writers, that they may deserve a separate notice.   It seems, indeed, probable that the Jews, especially after their intercourse
with the Chaldeans during the captivity, attributed to the direct
operation of evil spirits a great number of those disorders of
which the causes were not obvious; and such particularly as
were attended by distortion of body, or extraordinary mental
agitation and phrenzy*.   This delusion necessarily created a
large and various multitude of " Dæmoniacs," whose mani-
fold diseases could hope for no relief from ordinary remedies,
as they proceeded not from human accidents.   The language
even of Scripture, when literally understood, appears to sanction such an opinion, and the literal interpretation has had its
advocates among the learned and pious in every age of the
Church.   But the notion of real Dæmoniacal agency was carried to an extreme of absurdity, and led, we fear, to many acts
of deceit in the second and third centuries.   " Oh, could you
but hear (says Cyprian†) and see those dæmons when they are
tortured by us, and afflicted with spiritual chastisement and
verbal anguish, and thus ejected from the bodies of the possessed (*obsessorum*) ; moaning and lamenting with human
voice, through the power divine, as they feel the rods and
stripes, they confess the judgment to come."   " Thence too power
is given, by means of chastity and integrity, a pure voice and
sincere virtue . . to compel to confession foul and erratic spirits,
to urge them with stripes, to prostrate them struggling, moaning and groaning through aggravation of chastisement, to beat
them with stripes and roast them with fire."   " Oftentimes the
devil promises to depart, but departs not ; but when we come
to baptism, then indeed we ought to be assured and confident,
because the dæmon is then oppressed ; and the man is consecrated to God and liberated."   The invocation of Christ, attended
by the sign of the cross, and pronounced by persons formally
appointed to the office, was the method by which those stupen-

---

* See Lightfoot, Horæ Hebraicæ.
‡ Liber ad Demetrianum.   See likewise Epist. i. and Epist. 76.   Both Irenæus
and Tertullian are very animated on the same subject.

dous effects were usually produced ; and one among the many evils, that proceeded from this absurd practice, was an opinion, which gained some prevalence among the less enlightened converts, that the object of Christ's mission was to emancipate mankind from the yoke of their invisible enemy, and that the promised *Redemption* was nothing more than a sensible liberation from the manifest influence of evil spirits*.

Of the literary forgeries which corrupted and disgraced the ante-Nicene Church, we have made frequent and sorrowful mention ; and the great number † and popularity of such apocryphal works seem indeed to prove that the canon of the New Testament, though very early received among the clergy, was not in general circulation among the people.   They arose in the second, even more, perhaps, than in the following age ; and originated partly in the still remaining influence of Judaism, partly in the connexion between Christianity and philosophy, which at that time commenced. Almost all the Church writers partook more or less of one or the other of these tendencies; Justin Martyr, Tatian, Irenæus, and even Tertullian himself, were in some degree tainted by the former infection, while Clemens Alexandrinus and Origen were deeply vitiated by the latter. But we do not intend to ascribe the forgeries in question to those respectable fathers, nor even wholly to any members of the Church, though we admit that some of them received undue countenance from that quarter. We shall here only remark, without pausing again to condemn the principle which created them, that their immediate effect was exceedingly injurious, since they contributed, together with the other abuses just mentioned, to disseminate false and unworthy notions respecting the nature of Christianity.   Foremost among them,

Various apocryphal works.

* Clemens Alexandrinus, on the other hand, (Strom. ii. p. 210, 211) cites the authority of the " Apostolical Barnabas" for the opposite principle ; οὐ γὰρ οἱ δαίμονες ἡμῶν ἀπελαύνονται, ἀλλ' αἱ ἁμαρτίαι ἀφίενται, ἃς ὁμοίως ἐκείνοις ἐπιτελοῦμεν, πρὶν ἢ πιστεῦσαι.   But the grosser opinion obtained footing among the vulgar.

† Among these, besides the Epistle to Abgarus, the works ascribed to Hermes Trismegistus, the Sibylline Prophesies, Hydaspis, the Apostolical Canons and Constitutions, we may mention various apocryphal histories of Jesus, of Mary, and his other relatives—of Tiberius, Nicodemus, and Joseph of Arimathea—o the Apostles, especially St. Peter—the origin of the Apostles' Creed—the Synods of the Apostles—the Epistle of Seneca to Paul—the Acts of Pilate, &c. &c.

the gross millennarian* doctrine, which was the first-born child
of tradition, was supported and diffused by those writings; and
it did not cease to exercise, in various parts of Christendom, a
pernicious and perhaps powerful influence, until it was checked
by the pen of Origen and succeeding writers.

Division
into cate-
chumens
and
believers.

The distinction of the converts into "Catechumens," and
" Faithful," or " Believers," (Πιστοὶ) was introduced after the
age of Justin, and before or during that of Tertullian†.   Its
motive was probably twofold :—first, to prove the sincerity, to
instruct the ignorance, to ascertain or correct the morality of
the ruder proselytes, who were now numerous and eager for
baptism, and so to restrain the indiscriminate performance of
that rite ; next, to conciliate reverence and excite curiosity by
the temporary concealment of the most solemn ceremonies of
the new religion.   To this end the catechumens were only admitted to the previous part of the service, and, before the celebration of the holy sacraments, were *dismissed* ‡ : all that
followed was strictly veiled from them, until the time of their
own initiation.   Even from the above short description it is
easy to discover in this early Christian practice an imitation of

---

* Mosheim (De Reb. Gestis ante Constantinum, sec. iii., 8. 38.) seems to
consider Chiliasm as of Judaistical origin, and goes at great length into the subject.   The following passage of Tertullian (Adv. Marcionem, l. iii., ad finem) deserves to be cited :—" Hæc ratio regni terreni, post cujus mille annos (intra quam
ætatem concluditur sanctorum resurrectio, pro meritis maturius vel tardius surgen-
tium) tunc et mundi destructione et judicii conflagratione commissa, demutati in
atomo in angelicam substantiam, scilicet per illud incorruptelæ superindumen-
tum transferemur in cœleste regnum, &c."

† De Prescrip. adv. Hæret. cap. 41.   He censures the heretics for not making
the distinction in question in their congregations.

‡ " Ite, *Missa* est (i. e. Ecclesia.) Go—it is dismissed."   This seems, upon the
whole, the most probable origin of the words, Missal, Mass ; though many others
have been proposed. (See Bingham, b. xiii. chap. i.) Οἱ ἀκοινώνητοι, περιπατήσατε
—" Non-communicants, depart"—was the Greek form of separating the two
classes.   Bingham is very minute, and probably very faithful, in describing the
nature of the Missa Catechumenorum and the Missa Fidelium, or Communion
Service—though the forms, as he gives them, probably belonged to the fourth
and the subsequent, rather than the preceding, centuries.   But a summary of the
instructions delivered to the catechumens is given by the author of the Constit.
Apostol., lib. vii , c. 39.   It embraces the knowledge of the Trinity, the order of
the world's creation and series of Divine Providence, as exhibited in the Old
Testament : the doctrine of Christ's Incarnation, Passion, Resurrection, and Assumption, and what it is to renounce the devil and to enter into the covenant of
Christ.

the system of Pagan mysteries. These, as is well known, were twofold in number and importance—the first or lesser being of common notoriety, and easy access to all conditions and ages, while the greater were revealed*, with considerable discrimination, to such only as were thought qualified for the privilege, by their rank, or knowledge, or virtue. The name also passed into the liturgies of the Church; and the sacraments, which were withdrawn from the profane eye of the catechumens, were denominated Mysteries.

These mysteries continued for some time, perhaps till the beginning of the fourth century, to be two only, baptism and the eucharist. We have proofs, indeed, that in *that* age the ceremonies, at least of penitential absolution, of ordination, and confirmation,† were concealed from the uninitiated, as carefully as the two original sacraments; and hence no doubt arose the error which has sanctified them by the same name. Regarding the rite of baptism‡, we have noticed, in a former chapter, a misapprehension of its true nature and object, which gained very early footing in the Church; and the consequent abuse of deferring it until the hour of death was clearly customary before the days of Constantine; we need not pause to point out the evils which obviously proceeded from it§. The original simple

Two sacraments or mysteries.

---

* Mosheim treats the *Disciplina Arcani* (which he identifies with the Theologia Mystica) as being of various kinds—admitting, however, the uncertainty of any speculation on the subject. De Reb. Gest., sec. ii., 34.

† The passages which respectively prove these three facts are from Optatus contr. Parmen., lib. ii., p. 57; Chrysostom Hom., 18, in ii. Cor. p. 872; and Innocent I., Epist. i., ad Decentium Eugubin: and are cited by Bingham, Antiq., book x., chapter v. St. Basil (De Spir. Sanct. c. 27) places the oil of chrism among the things which the uninitiated might not look upon; while St. Augustine (Comm. in Psalm ciii., Concio. i.) says, " Quid est quod occultum est et non publicum in Ecclesia ? *Sacramentum Baptismi, Sacramentum Eucharistiæ.* Opera nostra bona vident et Pagani, Sacramenta vero occultantur illis." The practice probably varied in different Churches ; but the whole proves that the *Seven* Sacraments were not yet acknowledged in any.

‡ The following are the instructions delivered by Tertullian (De Baptismo, lib. xx.) " Ingressuros baptismum, orationibus crebris, jejuniis, et geniculationibus et pervigiliis orare oportet, et cum confessione omnium retro delictorum, &c." Mosheim (De Reb. Gest., sec. iv., 7) supposes that there were two impositions of hands—the first, on making the catechumen, the second, at baptism.

§ Gibbon somewhere proposes a question, whether this pernicious practice was at any time condemned by any council of the Church ? And in reply, a learned modern writer appeals to the 12th canon of the council of Neocæsarea :—ἐὰν τὶς νοσῶν φωτισθῇ, εἰς πρεσβύτερον ἄγεσθαι οὐ δύναται· οὐκ ἐκ προαιρέσεως γὰρ ἡ πίστις αὐτῇ,

character of the eucharistical assemblies of the primitive Christians, such as they are described by Justin Martyr, was first exalted by the strong and almost ambiguous language of Irenæus, and still further by the exaggerated though the vague expressions of subsequent writers *. By such means the eucharist gradually rose to be considered the most abstruse and awful of the mysteries. Yet is it still doubtful whether this grew to be a great abuse before the establishment of the Church; though the secrecy and exclusiveness, which sur-rounded its most holy ceremony, offended the open character of the religion, and even lessened its estimation among the wise and virtuous, by introducing an unworthy assimilation to the mummeries of paganism.

Honours
paid to
martyrs.

It was an opinion in the third century, originating, perhaps, with Tertullian, but more expressly declared by Dionysius, "That the holy martyrs were the assessors of Christ and par-ticipators in his kingdom, and partakers in his judgment, sitting in judgment with him†." While we read this extravagant conceit of that early age, we might almost be disposed to praise the moderation of later times, which were contented to invest those holy sufferers with the character of mediators‡. But long even before the age of Dionysius, and probably before any thought had been raised respecting their immediate exaltation or beatification, it had been a natural and even pious custom to celebrate the *birthdays* of those, who had offered themselves

---

ἀλλ' ἐξ ἀνάγκης· εἰ μὴ ταχά, διὰ τὴν μετὰ ταῦτα αὐτοῦ σπουδὴν καὶ πίστιν, καὶ διὰ σπάνιν ἀνθρώπων. The last clause is extremely obscure ; the two preceding seem to contain a general prohibition against the baptism of sick persons, as seeking it rather through a sort of compulsion than by deliberate choice.

* The passages in Irenæus, which have given occasion to the warmest contro-versy, and not wholly without ground, are lib. iv. c. 17 (or 32) and 18 (or 34). and lib. v. c. 2, " Miracula Sacræ Cœnæ vel Cyprianus audet narrare." Semler, Observ. Nov., &c.

† Tertull. de Resurrectione Carnis, cap. 43. "Nemo enim peregrinatus a cor-pore statim immoratur penes Dominum, nisi ex martyrii prerogativa, Paradiso scilicet non Inferis deversurus." And lib. de Anima, cap. 55. Dionys. ap. Euseb., liv. vi., cap. 42. τοῦ Χριστοῦ πάρεδροι, καὶ τῆς βασιλείας αὐτοῦ κοινωνοὶ, καὶ μέτοχοι τῆς κρίσεως αὐτοῦ, καὶ συνδικάζοντες αὐτῷ.

‡ Οὐχ ὡς Θεοὺς αὐτοὺς προσίοντες, ἀλλ' ὡς Θείους ἀνθρώπους ἀντιβολοῦντες, καὶ γίνεσθαι πρεσβευτὰς ὑπὲρ σφῶν παρακαλοῦντες. (Theodoret. ap. Beaus. Hist. Man., p. ii., l. ix., c. iv.) Τῶν ἁγίων μαρτύρων μνημονεύωμεν, ὅπως κοίνωνοι γίνεσθαι τῆς ἀθλήσεως αὐτῶν καταξιωθῶμεν. Constit. Apostol. viii. 13.

up as sacrifices for their religion.   By their birthdays (their γενέθλια) were understood, not the days of their introduction to the sins and afflictions of earth, but of their release from such bondage and their resurrection to glory.   Those days of their nativity to everlasting life were observed (as indeed it was fit) in joyous* commemoration of the piety of the departed, and of the example which they had bequeathed to posterity.   Assemblies were held for this purpose at the tombs of the martyrs, or on the spots where they had perished, and their frequency is attested by Tertullian, Cyprian, Origen, and others of the oldest fathers.   The Μαρτύρων γενέθλια were the Saints' days of the early Christians, and may be traced at least as far back as the execution of Polycarp†; indeed, the expressions bearing on this subject, which the Church of Smyrna addressed on that occasion to the Church of Philomelium, may properly be cited here:—"The heathen know not that we can neither forsake that Christ, who suffered for the salvation of the whole world of the redeemed, *nor can we worship any other*.   We pray to Him; but we love the martyrs, as they deserve, for their exceeding love to their King and Master; and as we also hope to become their companions and fellow-disciples.

"We take up his bones, which are more valuable to us than gold and precious stones, and we lay them down in a becoming place; and God will grant that we may gather them together in peace and joy, and *celebrate the birthday of his martyrdom*, in remembrance of the departed warrior, and for the practice and exercise of those whom the battle awaits."   As the places of meeting were not then consecrated by chapels or sanctuaries, and as the mortal, whose euthanasia was commemorated, was not yet made an object of superstitious adoration, it would be too severe to charge upon those innocent demonstrations of popular reverence the system of idolatrous impiety, which was built in later ages on that foundation.   We do not

---

* In the days of Ambrose this joyousness had degenerated into intemperance. " Sicut illi qui calices ad sepulcra martyrum deferunt, atque illic in vesperam bibunt, et aliter se exaudiri non posse credunt.   Oh stultitia hominum, qui ebrietatem sacrificium esse putant ; qui existimant *illos* ebrietate *placare* qui jejunio passionem sustinere didicerunt."   De Elia. et Jejun. c. xvii.   The words in italics likewise teach us what was the object of those meetings at the end of the fourth century.

† Apud Euseb. lib. iv., cap. 15.

mean that there was no *tendency* to superstition in the honours
paid to martyrs even in the third century. Relics were already
coming into consideration, the blood of the sufferers was eagerly
collected in sponges, and other similar extravagances are recorded ; but these were the natural excesses of popular enthusiasm, and would have ceased with the cessation of persecution,
if they had not afterwards been perpetuated and systematized
by the arts of a corrupt priesthood *.

Prayers
and offer-
ings for the
dead.

The use of prayers and even of offerings for the dead were
earlier than the age of Tertullian† ; nor is it any wonder that
the numerous converts from Paganism should bring over with
them some fragments of their former observances. But there
is no just reason to suspect that the ante-Nicene Church studied
to turn them to its own profit, nor at least that they were made
to minister to the avarice of the clergy. If they were encouraged, it was rather through the hope of increasing by such
indulgence the number of the proselytes.

Fasts.

The mortification of occasional fasting was probably enjoined
in the earliest age. For the ceremony of Baptism, as we learn
from Justin, both the neophyte and the congregation were prepared by abstinence ; and in the time of Tertullian, the bishops,
if he belies‡ them not, found their advantage in increasing the
number of such observances. The first general fast was on
Good Friday, and it does not appear that any others were very
soon added, or at least universally received. Yet there can be
no doubt, that, long before the fourth century, at least some §

---

* Very soon after the establishment of the Church, temples began to be dedicated to martyrs, called *Martyria*, which properly meant altars with relics under
them. And as the council in Trullo (canon xxvii.) prohibited the existence of
any altars without such relics, all Churches presently became Martyria. From
their regal splendour they acquired the name of Basilics. In respect to relics,
they made such rapid progress in popular veneration that, about the end of the
fourth century, they were employed for the miraculous confutation of heretics.
And St. Augustine himself is not ashamed to relate the resuscitation of a virgin,
on the tunic of St. Stephen being thrown over her. " Hac tunica opperuerunt
cadaver ejus parentes, et, recepto spiritu, salva facta est." De Civ. Dei, xxii. 8.

† Tertull. de Monogamia, c. 10.

‡ He may do so ; for in his " Liber de Jejuniis " he is writing in favour of Montanism against the Church. " Bene autem quod et Episcopi universæ plebi
mandare jejunia assolent : non dico de *industria stipium conferendarum ut vestræ
capturæ est,* sed interdum et ex aliqua solicitudinis ecclesiasticæ causa." See
Thomassin, Traité des Jeunes de l'Eglise.

§ The Quadragesimal Fast (τισσαρακοστή) is by some supposed to indicate the

part of Lent was strictly observed, and a partial fast (till three in the afternoon) on the fourth and sixth days of every week, is by some referred to very high antiquity.   Upon the whole it would seem, that, until the establishment of the Church, a great variety prevailed in this department of its discipline, dependent in some measure on the circumstances of particular provinces, and the individual regulations of the bishops presiding there.

When we consider in what countries the religion was revealed, and among what people it first spread, it is natural to search for the oldest forms of its external economy in the Jewish, and for those somewhat less ancient in the Pagan, system;—and thus we find them to have originated, so far at least as the origin of either can be discovered with any certainty.   There can be little doubt, for instance, that the very early distinction between clergy and laity was immediately derived from the corresponding institution of Judaism.   The gradations and offices of the original priesthood, and the power of the Presbytery, proceeded from the same source*, and the subsequent introduction of the more dignified term Sacerdos attested the continuation of the same influence.

Again, "There seems to be nothing more uncontested among learned men than that the Jews had set forms of worship in all parts of divine service, and that the apostles freely used these in all instances in which they thought it necessary or becoming to join with them.   Their ordinary service was of two sorts—the service of the temple and the service of the synagogue.   These differed in many respects; but both agreed in this, that the public prayers in both were offered up in a certain constant form of words †."   To what extent this practice

On antient Liturgies.

---

number of *hours* of abstinence which preceded the festival of the resurrection. But in the time of Chrysostom (who calls Lent "the remedy and physic of the soul") and of Theodosius the Great (who suspended all criminal proceedings and punishments during its continuance) the entire period was unquestionably observed.   See Cave on the Early Church, chapter vii.   It is St. Jerome, who has somewhere declared, that fasting is not so properly to be considered a virtue, as the foundation of every virtue.

* There is a passage in St. Clement's First Epistle to the Corinthians, chap. 40, and cited in a former page, in which the system of Jewish discipline is indirectly proposed as a model for the imitation of Christians.

† Bingham (Church Antiq., Book xiii., chap. v.), in prosecution of this subject, exhibits too warmly the zeal of an advocate.

was imitated in the primitive Church is a question, which has
led to much controversy among learned men ; because the passages in the earliest fathers, which bear directly upon it, are few
and scanty.   In the mean time, those passages are sufficient
to show, that some fixed form, or forms, of prayer did exist in
some of the early churches; though not to teach us what the
particulars of such forms were.   Since this subject, however,
has been very lately examined with great ingenuity by a
learned and candid writer*, it is proper to present to our
readers the most important results of his enquiry. It is one of
no inconsiderable importance—and it does not seem probable,
either that any new facts will hereafter be brought to light for
its better illustration, or that those, which at present exist, will
be handled with greater ability.

Four ori-
ginal
sources.

By a comparison of the various ancient liturgies now existing with each other, and with the references which early Christian writers have made to such services, we may trace them
with great probability to four original sources, viz. :—the Great
Oriental, the Alexandrian, the Roman, and the Gallican.

The Ori-
ental Li-
turgy.

(I.) The first of these comprehends the liturgies of Antioch
and Cæsarea, as well as that falsely ascribed to St. Chrysostom.
That of *Antioch* commonly bears the name of James, the
brother of the Saviour.   And though this pretension may not
be older than the fifth century, the vestiges of the service itself
are traced as high as the second. At least we find in the Apology of Justin Martyr† an outline of the liturgy of his days
and Church, which agrees, as far as it goes, with that of Antioch.   St. Basil became bishop of *Cæsarea* in the year 370—
and he presently published the office, which still bears his
name : it was immediately adopted at Constantinople, and at
this moment forms a part of the ritual of the Greek Church.
It was *probably* the ancient liturgy of Cæsarea, reconstructed
by the prelate whose name it bears : and though it is impossible at this time to distinguish what were the original portions
which he retained, there is at least no reason to suppose that

* Palmer, " Origines Liturgicæ, &c. with a Dissertation on Primitive Liturgies."
Oxford, 1832. We should observe, that in this " Dissertation" the term *Liturgy*
is used in that restricted sense, which it commonly bears in the writings of the
ancients—the service of the celebration of the Eucharist.

† Page 96, 97.

any part of it is posterior to that age. It agrees in substance and the order of its parts with the liturgy of Antioch, as well as with that of *Chrysostom*. This last appears to have been used in the Byzantine Churches as early as the fourth century—but no sufficient reason is given for its usurpation of the name of Chrysostom*. From the general agreement in the outlines of these three liturgies, some learned writers are willing to infer their apostolical origin.

(II.) As St. Basil reformed the ancient service ascribed to St. James, so, as seems most probable, did Cyril of *Alexandria* The Alexandrian. amplify the original liturgy of his own Church. This was naturally attributed to St. Mark, but without any shadow of authority : though there is no doubt of its very great antiquity. It differs in the order of its parts from every other liturgy, except the Æthiopic, which was seemingly derived from it.

(III.) The *Roman* liturgy was revised and enlarged by Gregory the Great; but it is a mistake to consider him as its The Roman. author. Its identity, at least in some principal respects, may be traced as high as the end of the fourth century. The service of Milan (called the Ambrosian) continued to agree with that of Rome, in all substantial points, till the time of Gregory —and there is no reason to disbelieve, what seems at first sight so natural, that it was received in the first instance from the Capital. The African liturgy may be traced (in the writings of the African Fathers) to an earlier age than that of Rome : and the allusions, which we find made to it, may persuade us that it was substantially the same. From this circumstance it is inferred, that the Roman service is of much higher antiquity than can be historically proved. For, since Carthage, according to all likelihood, received the religion from Rome, it would be strange, if it had not received the liturgy likewise. The greater eminence of the early African writers will account for those early references to the African liturgy, during the obscurity of that of Rome.

---

* The liturgy ascribed to St. Clement, in the sixth book of the apostolical constitutions, would more properly belong to the Oriental, than to the Roman communion, if it could properly be considered as a transcript of the liturgy of any Church. It is a mere forgery of the fourth or fifth centuries. Still it has its value; as we must suppose that the author of it had some model not very dissimilar before his eyes.

The Galli-
can.

(IV.) The original *Gallican* liturgy was again different from
any of the three abovementioned; and it may very probably
have been brought from Ephesus by the missionaries who
introduced Christianity into the country: since, from the little
light that remains, respecting the ancient ritual of Ephesus, we
may still collect, that it differed from the Oriental liturgy, and
agreed with that of Gaul.   It naturally assumed the name and
authority of St. John—and it continued to distinguish the
Church of France, until Charlemagne confirmed his connexion
with Rome by imposing *her* service upon his reluctant subjects.
The same sort of coincidence, in the number and order of
the parts, subsisted between the Gallican and Spanish (or
Mosarabic), as between the Roman and African, between that
of Antioch and that of Cæsarea: until the popes of the eleventh
century succeeded in supplanting the Mosarabic, and substituting the Roman in its place.   And, as the early records of
the English Church sufficiently prove, that its original liturgy
differed from that of Rome, it may very probably have been
received, together with the power of ordination and even the
religion itself, from the bishops of Gaul.

Observa-
tions.

A few remarks are necessary, in order that this short sketch
of the earliest liturgical remains may convey a just impression,
and no more than just, to the minds of our less learned
readers.   Of the four original liturgies, of which the existence
seems so probable, not one is now extant, nor, as far as can be
shown, any considerable portion of any one: the language,
the precise expressions—the particulars which filled up the
outline—are entirely lost.   All that can now be done, is to
ascertain, in each case, the substance and order of the parts—
or, if not the substance, at least the order—or if not the order of
every individual part, at least the "main order;" and this order
it is, which essentially and mainly constitutes the identity of
liturgies*.   Thus it is only from a variation in this order that

---

* Palmer, p. 43. Again—"It is only for the antiquity of the main order that
I contend, not for that of every individual part." p. 121.   "As to the very words
of this liturgy (the Gallican) during the primitive ages, or indeed at any time,
we need not attempt to seek for them.   The number and order of the lessons and
prayers, the main substance and tendency of some of them, the words commemo-
rating Christ's deeds and words at the institution, the hymn Ter-sanctus, the
Lord's prayer, and a few minor particulars, seem to be all that was fixed." p. 158.

an original difference can be inferred. So, for instance, where it is observed that the Roman liturgy ordered the kiss of peace to be given *after* the consecration; that all the Oriental liturgies, as well as the Gallican ordered it before; and that the Ambrosian and (according to Tertullian and Augustine) the African agreed with the Roman form; it is inferred that these three proceeded from the same source with each other (whatever that may have been)—and a different source from those which, in so material a point, followed a different order. Again, the chief distinction between the Gallican and Oriental liturgies consisted in this: that the prayers for the living and departed members of the Church occurred after the thanksgiving and consecration, in the latter; while in the former they preceded the salutation of peace and thanksgiving. Besides which, the Gallican had not the three prayers for the faithful*.

Such is the nature of those distinctions and coincidences, which might well be overlooked by a careless eye, but which suffice to conduct the experienced ritualist, in the absence of clearer light, to probable conclusions. The degree of probability, which will be attached to his particular inferences, will depend upon the mind of the student; and that which may almost carry certainty to one, will seem frivolous and fanciful to another. But respecting the general conclusions, which may be drawn from this investigation, there can exist little doubt in any unprejudiced mind. There can be little question, that some regular forms of worship were in use among the primitive Christians—and that these did not proceed (as some have imagined) from one common original, but varied more or less in different Churches. In respect to the question, whether or not they were actually composed by the Apostles, there is no direct evidence, of any value, either way. They were very ancient; they were immemorial—they may, or they may not, have been Apostolical. The practice of the Jews is favourable

---

* Palmer, p. 163. Those three prayers seem to have been introduced into the Oriental liturgy about the beginning of the fourth century—*i.e.* long after Gaul had received its liturgy from Ephesus.

to the supposition, that they were coeval (at least in Syria and Alexandria) with the propagation of Christianity. And the little allusion made to them by the early fathers may be partly ascribed to the peculiar sanctity then attached to the *mysteries* of the faith, and an unwillingness to disclose those awful secrets to the Catechumen, or the Infidel. It should likewise be recollected, that the first liturgies were not committed to writing, but preserved only in the memory of the faithful.

Some ecclesiastical terms and ceremonies.

Many of the early Ecclesiastical terms, and some few ceremonies chiefly of the third century, are usually considered as of Pagan derivation, though some of them may, with equal justice, be ascribed to a Jewish original. A very ancient name for the chancel was θυσιαστήριον, Ara Dei*, or *Altare; oblations* were made there, and "the unbloody *sacrifice*" offered up, and *frankincense* smoked, and lamps were lighted, even during the persecutions of the Church; even *votive* donations (donaria— ἀναθήματα) were suspended in the yet rude and ill-constructed *temples* of Christ. But the simple superstition of the Faithful in those ages did not proceed to more dangerous excesses. It was reserved for the following century to fill those temples with images, and to introduce into the sanctuaries of God the predominating spirit of Paganism.

Various inferences from the above facts.

In reference to the various facts which we have above stated, and which carry with them the plain conclusions to which we proceed, it seems only necessary to observe—*first*, that we are not to attend to those writers who represent the ante-Nicene Church as the perfect model of a Christian society—as the unfailing storehouse whence universal and perpetual rules of doctrine and discipline may be derived with confidence, and followed with submission. The truth is far otherwise; and though we ought assuredly to distinguish the authority of the apostolical from that of the later uninspired writers, still even the works of those first Fathers are not without much imperfection, and furnish, besides, very insufficient materials for the construction or defence of any system; and in the extensive

---

* "Nonne solemnior erit statio tua si et ad aram Dei steteris?" Tertull. De Oratione. It is asserted, however, that the original appellation of the Lord's table was *mensa*.

variety both of opinions and arguments, which distinguishes their successors from Justin to Eusebius, we cannot fail to observe, that the former are sometimes erroneous, and the latter very commonly feeble and inconsequential. From such facts we are compelled to infer, that the true nature and design of Christ's mission on earth were not very perfectly comprehended by the mass of Christians in the second and third centuries. Indeed, it was scarcely possible that it could be otherwise; since they consisted of converts, or the children of converts, many of whom were imbued with the deep and indelible prejudices of Judaism, and the others attached by long hereditary affection to the splendid ceremonies of Paganism. To either of these classes it was necessary to address a *peculiar* form of argument, and to present a peculiar view of the religion, that there might be any just hope of persuading them to embrace it. We should also mention that some of the errors of the third, and even of the second century, may be ascribed to the undue weight already attached to apostolical tradition, and the authority that was blindly attributed to any precept or usage, however obscurely traced to that uncertain source.

But, in the *second* place, we are equally bound to remark, that the fundamental doctrines of Christianity shine with a steady and continuous light through the strange mists in which the ante-Nicene Church has sometimes involved them; it was a great advantage which that age possessed over those which followed, that it confined itself to plain and scriptural expressions, and was contented to deliver the truths of God in the language of the holy writings. Moreover we should add, that among the abuses which we have described, though some were shameful to their inventors, and injurious to the cause, there were many which, in their origin, were comparatively, if not absolutely, innocent; in many instances they arose rather from the circumstances of the converts than from the design of the priesthood, and there were few, if any, among them which might not have been arrested after the establishment of Christianity, if that security, which gave power to the ministers of religion, had conferred wisdom and true piety along with it.

To conclude, then:—a general view of the Church of the

three first ages presents to us a body always unconnected with the state, frequently at variance with it; surrounded by multitudes of heresies, many of them very monstrous, which it combated with the sword of the Spirit alone; under a government in which the gradually-increasing influence of the bishop was still for the most part extremely limited by the power of his presbytery; with a rule of faith not curiously definite on abstruse questions, but simply conceived and scripturally expressed—rising into strength and confirming its consistency, and, finally, making good its long-neglected claims to toleration and respect. A closer examination of the same body discloses to us a number of stains and defects, proceeding at different moments from various causes, and spreading, in some degree, as that advanced in magnitude : but as they had not yet penetrated to its heart, they might still have been checked, and even removed, by an influential and truly Christian priesthood. It is certain that the deep and fatal corruptions of after ages sprang, in many instances, directly from them; but the crime of those consequences must rest, for the most part, with those who combined and perpetuated the first abuses; for these were indeed rather the produce of circumstances than the work of men. We have also observed, in the various conditions of apostolical Christianity, the scattered elements of some forms of government and discipline, which, though they very early melted away into the episcopal system, should not be passed over in silence, since they are still pleaded as precedents and imitated as models by many excellent Christians.

From Constantine to Gregory the Great.

II. Fleury, who is the most moderate and reasonable of the Roman Catholic historians, laments that, after the first six centuries, the brightest days of the Church were passed away*. In his first discourse he represents the brilliancy of that period in vivid and exaggerated colours. The reverence due to the sanctified martyr—the solemn aspect of monastic solitude—the piety and disinterested poverty of the early prelates—the purity of their election—the austerity of their life—the magni-

---

* Discours sur l'Hist. Ecclés. depuis l'an 600 jusques à l'an 1100. "Les beaux jours de l'Eglise sont passés, mais Dieu n'a pas rejetté son peuple, ni oublié ses promesses," &c. &c.

ficence of the offices—the severity of discipline—the venerable
names of tradition* and antiquity—are objects of his warm and
indiscriminate eulogy. But it was an error (for to Fleury we
would not willingly ascribe the intention of deceiving) to confound the three earliest with the three following centuries; as
if the government, discipline, and spirit of the Catholic Church
had remained invariable from the age of St. Clement to that of
St. Gregory. Even the first of those periods was somewhat
removed from apostolical perfection, but in the second the
distance was incalculably increased; and that, not only according to the customary progress of unreformed abuse, but also
through a change of principles in the administration of the
Church, which proceeded from other causes.

At present, before we enter on any general review of the Particular
outward form and position of the Church, or even of its internal innova-
administration, we shall mention, as in continuation of the
subject which has been most lately treated, some particular
innovations in belief and discipline which either began or were
established during the fourth, fifth, and sixth centuries. The
first, and by far the most important of these, was the institution
of the monastic system, of which it cannot be properly said that
there existed any vestige before the beginning of the fourth age,
and which, before its termination, had fixed its roots deeply,
and struck them into the very heart of Christendom. Its origin
and progress will be the object of future inquiry†; at present
we shall confine our notice to a subject very closely connected
with it—the celibacy of the clergy. In the first ages the Church

---

* "It was one of the rules of discipline not to commit it to writing, but to preserve it *by a secret tradition* among the bishops and priests, chiefly that regarding
the administration of the sacraments; and the better to keep that secret, that the
bishops should confide their ecclesiastical letters to the clergy only. So, when
the ancients speak of observing the canons, imagine not that they speak of written
canons; they speak of all that was practised through a constant tradition.
For we must believe, according to the maxim of St. Augustine, that that which
the Church has observed at every time, and in every place, is apostolical tradition.
In fact, from what other source could have come those universal practices, such
as the veneration of relics, the prayer for the dead, the observance of Lent?"
Fleury, Discours sur l'Hist. des Six Premiers Siècles, &c. &c —Of the three practices here instanced, two at least were probably much posterior to the times of the
Apostles.

† See Chapter xix.

writers advocated the universal lawfulness of marriage against the *heretical* rigour of the Encratites, of Saturninus and Basilides, of the Montanists, and even the Novatians—so that any undue respect for celibacy which may have prevailed during the first three ages cannot justly be attributed to the Church: it was also very partial and vague in its nature, and wholly unsupported by canonical regulations. Afterwards, there can be no question that the cause, which first gave impulse to the principle, and carried it into practice, and subjected it to repeated legislation, was the growing prevalence of Monachism, and the popular veneration that was found to attach to excessive austerities. Already at the council of Nice* it was proposed to forbid the marriage of the clergy; but through the opposition of an Egyptian bishop, named Paphnutius, it was only enacted, that all clerks who had been married before they took orders should be allowed to retain their wives, according to the ancient *tradition* of the Church, but that they should not marry a second time †. Such continued both the rule and practice of the Eastern Church; it was confirmed by the council in Trullo in the year 692, with an exception against bishops, who were obliged, on their promotion, to separate from their wives; and this law was never afterwards altered. But in the West, where the spirit of sacerdotal domination more strongly prevailed, many attempts were made in those days to enforce perfect celibacy on all the orders of the ministry; and their constant repetition proves their inefficacy. Siricius, who held the see of Rome from 385 to 398, published some letters or decretals, which have acquired the weight of canons in the Roman Church. One of his great objects was to discourage the marriage of the

---

* Eleven years earlier it was enacted, by the tenth canon of the Council of Ancyra, that when a deacon declared his intention to marry, at the time of his ordination, he might be allowed to do so, but not otherwise. Dupin, Nouv. Bibl., tome ii. p. 312. Bingham, Church Antiq. b. iv. ch. v.—Dupin, Nouv. Biblioth., tome i. (Abrégé de la Discipline), mentions, as the rule of the early (ante-Nicene) Church, that it was permitted to a priest to keep his wife, but not to marry again: on a deacon there was no such restraint. It is impossible to trace that, which is mentioned as being imposed upon the priest, to the first ages; but in the beginning of the fourth century, perhaps somewhat earlier, it was undoubtedly established, that no man who was ordained priest could marry.

† Socrates, lib. i., c. 11. Sozomen, lib. i., c. 23.

clergy, but it does not appear* that his regulations much exceeded the severity of those of Nice. However, it must be
admitted, that the perseverance of his successors was not fruitless, at least so far as their immediate influence extended; and
we are assured that at the end of the fifth century, the rule of
celibacy was very commonly observed by the clergy of Rome†.
But a hundred years afterwards, Gregory, as we have seen, was
still engaged in the same struggle against the natural affections
and the common reason of man, and he transmitted it, still
unfinished, to his distant‡ posterity. His object was clerical
celibacy in the strictest sense; but we should remark that no
ordinance going to that extent had yet been enacted by any
general council, even of the Western Church, and that the
common practice was still in opposition to it; a great number,
probably far the larger proportion, of the German, French,
English, and Spanish clergy continued to avail themselves at
least of that portion of their scriptural right, which the Council
of Nice had left them.

The penitential discipline of the ante-Nicene Church was Penitential
exceedingly severe, even in the season of persecution, and it was discipline
by rigour rather than indulgence that it sought to secure the of the early
fidelity and increase the number of its members. For the space Church.
of fifteen, or sometimes of twenty years, it might be for his
whole life, the repentant sinner was excluded from the precincts
of the Church, and exposed to the reproach or compassion of
every beholder. After this long endurance, when the gates of the
sanctuary were at length unclosed to him, it was only, perhaps,
that he might worship there for some additional years in the
attitude of prostration, muffled and unshaven, fasting and

* Dupin, Nouv. Bibl., Vie de Sirice.

† A distinction in this respect was observed a century earlier between the
Catholic and the Arian clergy; the *laxity* of the latter, who were almost universally married, was made matter of reproach by their more rigid adversaries.

‡ In the ninth century (about the year 860) we observe Hulderic, Bishop of
Augsburg, vigorously resisting the edicts of Pope Nicholas; and two hundred
and twenty years afterwards, when Gregory VII. at length achieved the object,
which had foiled his predecessors for above six centuries, he encountered an
opposition which could scarcely have been surmounted by a less extraordinary
character.

covered with ashes*. A discipline which, in some ages, would be deemed barbarous, if it were not impracticable, was found very effectual in those early times, both in preserving individual morality, and in upholding the external show and dignity of the Church. It seems to have been maintained in its original spirit throughout the fourth century†, and its rigour was still further aggravated by the necessity of public confession. The measure of Pope Leo, which substituted private confession, may have been made necessary by the universal profession of Christianity, and the degeneracy of many who professed it. But not only was it attended by an immediate relaxation in the penitential discipline of the Church (for secret penance very speedily followed secret confession), but it became, in process of time, one of the most abundant sources of sacerdotal influence.

Purgatory. During the first four centuries, there was no mention of any place of Purgatory ‡—neither St. Ambrose, nor even St. Jerome has expressed any belief in such an intermediate state. But St. Augustine§ speaks somewhat more ambiguously; for if, in

---

* Fleury, Discours sur les Six Premiers Siècles, &c. et passim. Cyprian is the most ancient father who has mentioned any sort of system of penance. But some derive such rules from the discipline imposed in the Pagan system previous to initiation in the great mysteries.

† See Dupin, Nouv. Bibl. tome ii. p. 247, Vie de S. Ambroise. 1. Sinners were expected to request that they might be admitted to penance. 2. The circumstance of their doing penance separated them from the communion. 3. They did penance publicly. 4. They practised a number of fastings, austerities, and humiliations during the whole time of penance. 5. They could be admitted to that penance once only. Of course the penance here mentioned was the severest which the Church ever inflicted for the most enormous sins.

‡ The allusion of Origen (C. Cels. l. vi. p. 292, ed. Cantab.) to the passage in Malachi (iii. 2, 3) can scarcely be so considered. He does indeed speak of a sort of purification for *leaden* souls,—τὴν μετὰ βασάνου κάθαρσιν τῶν τοιῶν δὲ ψυχῶν; but he admits that the opinion should be kept secret, seeing how difficult it was to restrain people within bounds, even when you held out to them an eternity of punishment.

§ Mosheim (cent. v. p. ii. c. iii.) remarks that " the famous Pagan doctrine concerning the purification of departed souls by means of a certain kind of fire was more amply explained and confirmed now than it had hitherto been," and he refers to St. Augustine, De viii. Questionibus ad Dulcitium N. xiii. tome vi. De Fide et Operibus, cap. xvi. p. 182. De Fide, Spe, et Charitate, sect. 118, p. 222, Enarrat. Psalm xxxv. s. 3.

some passages, he rejects the supposition as vain and improbable, in others he admits that the truth cannot be certainly
ascertained, but may deserve investigation.　During the two
following ages, the plausible scheme gained some little credit
among the clergy of the West, and especially among the monastic orders; but the credit of establishing it among the unquestionable truths of the Church is due to the superstition or
the craft of Gregory the Great.　In the Fourth Book of his
Dialogues* he maintains the existence of a purgatory for the
expiation of the more venial offences of persons whose general
excellence may have deserved such indulgence.　He then takes
occasion to remark, that many discoveries had lately been made
respecting the condition of souls after death, which had not been
penetrated by antiquity, and for this reason—that as this world
was approaching to its end, men saw more closely into the
secrets of the next †.　A theory which had been tolerated by
St. Augustine, and defended, however absurdly, by St. Gregory,
found easy acceptance in the Western Church; it was eagerly
seized by the Benedictine Monks, and was presently perceived
to be so profitable in its operation on the people, that it soon
became one of the dearest and most necessary tenets of the
Roman Communion.

　The general influence of Paganism on the Christian cere-　Imitations
monies was already discoverable in the second and third ages;　of Pagan-
and the particular practice which, in its abuse, was especially　ism.

---

* Cap. xxxix. and xli. A question is proposed :—" Doceri vellem si post mortem
purgatorius ignis credendus est"—(proving, at least, that there was then no general belief in purgatory); and Gregory, in his reply, advances " Sed tamen de quibusdam levibus culpis esse ante judicium purgatorius ignis credendus est, pro
eo quod Veritas dicit, quia ' Si quis in S. Spiritu blasphemiam dixerit, neque in hoc
seculo remittetur ei, neque in futuro.' In quâ sententiâ datur intelligi, quasdam
culpas in hoc seculo, quasdam vero in futuro posse laxari. Sed tamen hoc de
parvis minimisque peccatis fieri posse credendum est, sicut est otiosus sermo, im-
moderatus risus, aut in non gravibus rebus error ignorantiæ." Then, after
admitting that the passage of St. Paul may be understood of the fire of tribulation in this life, and repeating that his own purifying fire can only be designed
for the expurgation of minor offences, he continues—" Hoc tamen sciendum est,
quia illic saltem de minimis nihil quisque purgationis obtinebit, nisi bonis hoc
artibus in hac adhuc vita positus, ut illic obtineat, promereatur."

† His words are (Cap. 41), " Quantum præsens seculum propinquat, tantum
futurum seculum ipsa jam quasi propinquitate tangitur, et signis manifestionibus
aperitur."

destined to assimilate two forms of worship essentially dissociable, and to bring them together, too, on that very point where their difference had been the widest, may be traced, perhaps, to the early but innocent reverence which was paid to martyrs. During the progress of the fourth and fifth centuries, many new concessions were made, on various and important points, to the popular genius of the old superstition. Expiatory processions and supplications were framed and conducted after the ancient models. The sanctity which had been inherent in the Temples of the gods was now transferred to the Christian Churches *, which began to rival the splendour and magnitude, if they failed to emulate the elegance, of their profane competitors. If any inspiration had been communicated to the devout Pagan by sleeping within the holy precincts, the same descended upon the Convert when he reposed upon a martyr's tomb. If any purity had been conferred by customary lustration, it was compensated by the frequent use of holy water. Other such compromises might be mentioned; and so completely was the spirit of the rejected worship transfused into the system which succeeded it, that the very miracles which the Christian writers of those days credulously retailed concerning their saints and martyrs were, in many instances, only ungraceful copies of the long-exploded fables of heathenism † : so poisonous was the expiring breath of that base superstition, and so fatal the garment which it cast, even during its latest struggles, over its heavenly destroyer. But in no respect was its malice so lastingly pernicious, as when it fastened upon Christianity the badge of its own character by the communication of idolatrous worship. It is true that in the ante-Nicene Church martyrs were reverenced, and even relics held in some estimation; but no description of image, whether carved or painted, was tolerated in the Churches of Christ, and it was through that distinction chiefly that they claimed exclusive sanctity. In the fourth and fifth centuries, the previous veneration for the saints

---

* The ancient privilege of sanctuary was conferred upon Christian churches by Constantine, and afterwards extended by Theodosius II. to the consecrated precincts.

† See Jortin, Eccl.Hist. vol. iv. pp.73, 124, 220, 238, &c.&c.; and Middleton's Letter from Rome, passim.

was exalted into actual worship; their lives and their miracles were recited and devoured with ardent credulity; astonishing prodigies were performed by fragments of their bones or garments; distant and dangerous pilgrimages were undertaken to obtain their ashes, or only to pray at their tombs: and this rage was encouraged by the unanimous acclamation of the ecclesiastical directors.

The first authenticated instance of the erection of images The use of within the consecrated precincts was, probably, the act of Sul- Images. picius Severus, related by his correspondent, Paulinus of Nola*. That pious historian placed the images of St. Martin and Paulinus near a baptistery, situated between two churches, to the end that " to those who were laying aside, through baptism, the old leaven of worldliness, representations of spiritual holiness might be present for their imitation." This was the whole of his innocent object; nor does it appear that any one, even the least considerate among the early writers, warmly and directly advocated the worship, or even the use, of images†; the opinions and practice of some of them were certainly op-

---

* Epist. xii. Martin was dead, and Paulinus wrote, with great modesty, the following distich, as a sort of inscription for the two statues, one of which was his own:—

Hunc peccatores, illum spectate beati!
Exemplum sanctis ille sit—iste reis.

† St. Epiphanius, in his letter to John of Jerusalem, translated by St. Jerome, and written towards the end of the fourth century, writes as follows:—" Having entered into a church in a village in Palestine, named Anablatha, I found there a veil which was suspended at the door, and painted with a representation, whether of Jesus Christ or of some Saint, for I do not well recollect whose image it was; but seeing that, in opposition to the authority of Scripture, there was a human image in the Church of Jesus Christ, I tore it in pieces, and gave order to those who had care of that church to bury a corpse with the veil. And as they grumbled out some answer, that ' since he has chosen to tear the veil, he might as well find another,' I promised them one, and I now discharge that promise." Baronius, Bellarmine, and some others, have disputed the genuineness of this passage by arguments, which have been very easily and candidly confuted by Dupin, Nouv. Bibl. Vie de S. Epiphanie. St. Augustine somewhere praises the religious severity of the ancient Romans, who worshipped God without images. Leo the Great (Serm. viii. In Natal. Domini), speaks of the " Basilica" of St. Peter:—" Quæ uni Deo vivo et vero dictata est:" thus, though the Churches bore the name of the Saint whose ashes were supposed to rest there, they were still dedicated to God. In the same sermon, the pope strongly discommends even the appearance of idolatry.

posed to it. Among the emperors, both Valens and Theodosius enacted laws against the painting or graving the likeness of Christ. Nevertheless, we perceive (from passages in Gregory of Nyssa, St. Cyril, St. Basil, and others) that representations of the combats of the martyrs, and of some scriptural scenes, had already obtained place in some of the churches, though they were not yet in general honour. Thus the seeds were sown, and as they were watered by the enthusiasm of the vulgar, ever prone to some sort of sensible worship, and fondly nourished by the headstrong prejudice of the heathen converts, and as the fathers of the Church did not interpose to root them out, they spread with rapid, though, perhaps, silent growth, and before the end of the sixth century the *use* of images was very generally permitted throughout the Christian world.

From the above review of the principal abuses in doctrine and discipline* which took root in the Church during the three centuries following its establishment, let us proceed to consider that body,—first, in regard to its connexion with the state; secondly, in respect to its own internal administration. As the Pagan system was merely an engine of State, so its entire regulation, even to the performance of its most sacred rights and offices, was consistently and properly intrusted to the control and exercise of the civil magistrate. The power which directed it, the power which its ministers possessed to enforce their decrees, was not distinguished from that with which they were invested for any other purpose,—it was strictly and exclusively temporal. Christianity rose from a very different foundation: it claimed to be a direct revelation from Heaven; its truth, not its utility, was the fact which its professors unbendingly asserted by their arguments and their sufferings; they *believed* that it was the work of God which they were forwarding, and that their souls were placed for ever in his retributive hands. From this lofty ground they were

Marginal notes:
TheChurch in connexion with the State.

Distinction between Temporal and Spiritual Power.

---

* Dupin has collected from the works of Athanasius a sort of summary of the discipline of that age. Among the particulars, we observe, that there were priests, and even bishops, who were married, though in small number; that the people and clergy continued to choose their bishops; that there were no translations; that Lent was observed as a fast; Easter as a solemn festival; that the Gospel was read in the vulgar tongue.

enabled to discern that there was a limit to all human authority, and that there was a power above, which was greater than
the might of Emperors.   That heavenly authority they considered to be, in some degree, communicated to Christ's ministers on earth, and associated with their *spiritual* office.

During the period preceding the accession of Constantine,
the exercise of this authority was confined to preserving the
purity of the apostolical doctrine, to augmenting the number,
enforcing the morality, and preventing the apostacy of the converts.   It was working silently among the faithful, and had
already established a solemn and indissoluble connexion between
the clergy and the lower orders; but it had not hitherto, on
any occasion, been brought into open communication with the
temporal power, either to co-operate or to contend with it; nor,
indeed, was its existence yet acknowledged, or perhaps perceived, by the latter.

Let us now advance one century, and consider the position Growth of
of the Church as it then stood in connexion with the State. ecclesiasti-
Its real substantial weight proceeded, in fact, from one cause, cal influ-
and from one only,—the influence of the clergy over the people. power.
Many circumstances at this time contributed to confirm and
consolidate that influence—the judicial authority and acknowledged dignity of the bishops, the increase in their number and
wealth, the popular character of their election, their public and
commanding eloquence.   Moreover, there can be no question
that even the spiritual control of the ecclesiastics was exerted
with greater confidence, when the civil power was at hand to
support them; while their zeal was warmly and successfully
employed in asserting the vast superiority of that control, and
the interests connected with it, over any that were merely temporal and worldly.   To these considerations we should add,
that during the three preceding centuries the nobility of the
Roman empire had, for the most part, fallen into decay; no
body had grown up in the state to supply the defect of the
aristocratical influence; and hence it arose that the vacant place
in the social system was occupied by the Christian hierarchy.
This order, sometimes strong from other causes, always possessed peculiar advantages for the acquisition of popular influence, through the very office which forces it into contact with

the lower classes, and through the attractive character of its duties; which are such as can never fail, when faithfully and discreetly discharged, to conciliate the affections of those for whose happiness alone they are imposed.

From the above and similar causes, the authority of the Church grew with great rapidity even during the first century after its alliance with the state; of the boldness thus communicated to its individual ministers, both in speech and action, some instances have been mentioned, and many might be added. Indeed, the mere existence of eighteen hundred magistrates (to speak of the bishops only) who held their offices for life, over whose nomination the civil power had no direct control, who were connected by intimate relations with the people, and who, for the most part, were bound together by common opinions and principles and interests, was alone sufficient to establish a counterpoise against the weight of imperial despotism. In fact, under the uncertain sceptre of the successors of Constantine, it might have been difficult to moderate the progress of ecclesiastical power, had it not been checked and dissipated by the perpetual dissensions which divided the Church itself.

Unity of the Church.

The same cause which restrained the vigour, polluted the character, of the Church; for being unable immediately to repress by its own spiritual weapons the violent animosities of its ministers, and impatient of the gradual influence of time and reason, in a dark and disastrous moment it had recourse to that temporal sword, which was not intended for its service, and which it has never yet employed without disgrace, or with impunity. Thus was it, indeed, a blind, if not suspicious affection, which led even the most orthodox emperors to labour for the "Unity of the Church;" since it was the unfailing effect of their measures to influence and nourish the intolerance of the ruling party, without entirely quenching even one among the thousand eternal fountains of dissent. We repeat that the most fatal consequence which has in any age resulted from the connexion between Church and State, is the application of the penalties of the one to the disorders of the other,—the correction of spiritual offences by temporal chastisements. But that abuse of the civil power is so far from being the necessary consequence of that connexion, that it is manifestly injurious to the interests of both; and since its wickedness and its folly have been exposed and acknowledged, there can now be no circumstance, under which a wise government would employ such interference, or an enlightened priesthood desire it.

It has been observed that in the ante-Nicene Church the power of the bishop was closely limited by that of the presbytery of his diocese, though less so in the third, as it would seem, than in the preceding century. During the three following ages that restraint was gradually loosened, though not yet entirely cast away. The affairs of the diocese were still, in name at least, conducted "with the assent of the clergy" (cum assensu clericorum); and their influence, in many places, was probably more than nominal. Still we cannot fail to observe, that a higher and more independent authority was assumed by the prelates; a broader interval was interposed between the different ranks of the hierarchy; the government lost most of the remains of its popular character, and assumed the form of an active and powerful aristocracy. Some of the causes of this change have been incidentally mentioned in the preceding pages; and among them we should particularly notice the prevalence of councils, both general and provincial, by which the public affairs of the Church were now regulated, and in which the only influential members were the bishops*. The legislative authority thus exercised by the order, added to the judicial power which was vested in the individual, raised the prelacy to a necessary and legal pre-eminence before the next inferior grade of the ministry. It would appear, moreover, especially from the records of the fifth and sixth centuries, that the greater portion of the learning of those times was in possession of the episcopal order. Such reasons are sufficient to account for the aggrandizement of that order; while, at the same time, they

margin note: Internal administration of the Church.

margin note: Aggrandizement of the hierarchy.

---

* Fifteen councils are recorded to have been held in France alone during the fourth and five-and-twenty during the fifth century. The bishops still attended as the deputies of their people, but presbyters appear now to have been never present, unless as representatives of their bishop. Many canons of the councils of the fifth century (especially of that of Orange, held in 441) declare that no council shall ever separate without appointing the time of the next meeting. The ancient canonical regulation for meeting twice a year was still in force, but in those disturbed ages it was not easily observed. See Guizot, Cours d'Histoire Moderne, leçon iii.

show us, that the steps by which it rose were neither unlawful
nor dishonourable. The change in the form of Church government naturally followed the change in other circumstances;
and it would be unjust to qualify that as usurpation, which proceeded from causes independent of private interest or professional ambition. It is not denied that such motives may frequently have stimulated many to individual encroachment;
but the elevation of the body was the natural effect of ecclesiastical, of political, and even of moral combinations.

Having observed in what respect the alteration in the general administration of the Church extended to the economy of
its several dioceses, we shall shortly retrace some of those early
vestiges of the monarchical form of administration, which were
already discernible during the rise and progress of the religious
aristocracy; or, in other words, we shall search among the
component parts of the episcopal system for some elements of
the papal government. Before the establishment of the Church,
notwithstanding one or two attempts at aggression on the part
of Rome, which were immediately repelled, the various sees
were, without any acknowledged distinction, equal and independent. Thus far, at least, the bishop of that city had no
superiority, or even claim to superiority, above his brethren;
and it was to the imperial dignity of his see that in fact* he owed
any accidental and voluntary deference which may have been
offered to him. The next circumstance, second in time and
very considerable in influence, which contributed to his exaltation, was the name (for it was little more than the name)
of patriarch. This title was conferred first upon three, subsequently upon four, of the prelates of the Eastern Church; but
in the West it was confined to the Bishop of Rome: and the
distinction was not without effect in creating, especially among
the distant and the ignorant, that sort of blind and indefinite
respect, which is so easily converted into submission.

The next event which may be mentioned, as having aug-

First ves-
tiges of the
papal go-
vernment.

---

* It is proper to cite, as we find it, the celebrated passage of Irenæus on this
subject:—" Adhanc ecclesiam (Romanum) propter potiorem principalitatem ne-
cesse est omnem convenire ecclesiam—hoc est, eos qui sunt undique fideles, in qua
semper ab his, qui sunt undique, conservata est ea, quæ est ab Apostolis traditio."
This passage only remains in the Latin translation, and is not free from obscurity.

mented the authority of the see, was the removal of the civil government from Rome to Ravenna by Honorius. The domestic importance of the bishop was essentially increased, and facilities for usurpation were created by the absence of the emperor.

That which follows, perhaps, next in time (for we are disposed to place it towards the end of the fifth century), but which yields to none in importance, was the claim to the especial protection of St. Peter, so loudly asserted by the same see. *Connexion of St. Peter with the see of Rome.* While some have invented circumstantial fables respecting the marvellous success of that apostle in Italy and at Rome, others have advanced ingenious arguments to show, that he never at all visited that city. To us, so far as any opinion can be formed on so obscure a matter, it appears probable that St. Peter died at Rome, as well as St. Paul; and during their previous residence there, it is not impossible that the one may have presided over the Jewish, while the other superintended the heathen, converts. But the question itself can now possess so little importance in the mind of any reasonable being, that we care not to leave it in uncertainty. However, it is undisputed, that in the fifth and following ages a vast accession of honour and sanctity accrued to the see of Rome from its perseverance in that claim. In times when the particular protection of Heaven was believed to attend the possession of the meanest relic of the most obscure martyr; when stupendous prodigies were performed by the fragment of the garment of some nameless saint, or the dust which had been brought from his tomb, was it strange that a peculiar impression of holiness should attach to that spot where the chief of the apostles had suffered a barbarous death, and where his bones still lay inviolate in sacred repose? But this was not all—the martyr of Christ had been at the same time the Bishop of Rome; and the *keys* which had been confided to his inspired wisdom were still preserved, through a long and uninterrupted chain, to the bishops his successors. Such assertions were first advanced about this period, or very soon afterwards; and it is one of the most certain proofs of the credit they obtained, that applications now began very commonly to be made, from many parts of Europe, for counsel or opinion, on points of discipline or faith, to the Roman see. It might, indeed, not rarely happen that its rescripts were neither obeyed nor respected; still the appeal was becoming customary, and each successive reference confirmed a practice, which could not fail in time to give some authority to the decision.

These are some of the leading circumstances, which were so far improved by the genius of two among the popes, and the perseverance of almost all, that at the death of Gregory the Great, the Bishop of Rome, though he might in vain dispute the name of universal supremacy with the Patriarch of Constantinople, was unquestionably acknowledged to be the leading member of the ecclesiastical aristocracy of Europe, the spiritual head or president of the western hierarchy. Nevertheless, his *authority* was not generally acknowledged even in the west. Fleury* fairly admits that Gregory exercised no definite jurisdiction beyond the Churches which immediately depended on the holy see, and were therefore called Suburbicarian—that is, those of the south of Italy, of Sicily, and some other islands. It is true that the Bishop of Arles was his vicar in Gaul, as that of Thessalonica was in Western Illyria; and that he exercised some inspection over the Churches of Africa for the assembling of councils and the observation of the canons; but he possessed no ordinary official authority over those Churches, nor did they yet acknowledge any direct positive dependance on Rome.

From Gregory to Charlemagne.

III. An account of the general changes which took place in the Church, during the two centuries between Gregory and Charlemagne, has been given in a preceding chapter; and in respect to particular abuses in belief or discipline, it appears not that any remarkable novelty presented itself during this period.

Distinction between the Eastern & Western Churches.

Among its leading features, we have observed, *first*, an increasing dissimilarity in character and institutions between the Eastern and Western Churches, which gradually loosened the bonds of their union, and prepared them for dissolution. The alterations which caused the distinction originated for the most part in the West, and are chiefly to be ascribed to the entire

* Liv. xxxv., s. 19. Giannone, Hor. di Napol. lib. ii., c. 8.

social revolution, which was effected by the barbarian conquests : whereas, in the East, the undisputed supremacy of the
civil power and the unvarying character of the government prevented any important innovations.   Those prevailed, indeed, to
such an extent, that even the divisions which during this period
disturbed the Oriental Communion,—those respecting the "two
wills of Christ," and the "worship of images,"—received in
both instances their first impulse from the *Throne.*   In the
West, the subdivision of the empire into numerous and variously-
constituted kingdoms, the peculiar institutions, the superstitions and the ignorance of the people, opened an extensive field
for ecclesiastical exertion.   That many among the clergy availed
themselves of these circumstances for personal or professional
aggrandizement, the voice of history is ever forward to proclaim
to us ; but the private piety of the more numerous and obscure
members of that order, who interposed, not ineffectually, their
religious offices to alleviate the wretchedness and soften the
barbarism of those dreary times, is slightly and incidentally
recorded, though better deserving of celebrity, since its claims
are on the gratitude of the latest posterity.

The *second* characteristic of this period (and we here confine Growth of
ourselves to the Western Church) was the continued and even Episcopal
authority.
inordinate growth of episcopal authority.   A great number of
causes contributed to that result, some of which had been in
continual operation since the establishment of Christianity ;
others had grown up in later ages.   The most direct and
effectual were the extensive and increasing domains of the
Bishops ; the judicial and even municipal power which they
exercised each in his metropolis ; their political influence in the
great national assemblies ; the exclusive possession of a contracted learning, which, nevertheless, was mistaken for wisdom,
in an age nearly destitute of both.   To these we may add the
removal of some legitimate restraints.   The superintendence of
the metropolitans was abolished, and it was supplied by no
other ; for the civil governments were then too weak and un-
stable to enforce a disputed authority, while that of the pope
was distant and indefinite, even where it was acknowledged to

be rightful*. On the other hand, the degraded condition of the priesthood and the independence conferred on the prelate by the disuse of popular election, placed him above any apprehension of opposition or censure from the lower ranks of the clergy. And since the Councils, to whose legislation he was liable, were entirely composed of his own order, he had little reason to expect severity from that quarter. We have observed into what great license that unbridled episcopal power was carried.

Aggrandizement of the Bishop of Rome.

Thirdly. The Bishop of Rome failed not to profit, at least in an equal degree, by the various causes which conspired to the exaltation of his brethren; and let us add to these, since we can add it with truth, that the conduct of the pope during this period was for the most part such as inspired respect, and even commanded gratitude. If they were stained with the superstitions of the day, they lost nothing in popular opinion by that failing; born at Rome and at once elevated from the native priesthood, not translated from a foreign see, they began with some claims on the attachment of their subjects, and they maintained them by the severe and uncorrupted sanctity of their morals. But besides these circumstances, we should also recollect that two events occurred in the eighth century, which exclusively promoted the advancement of that see—the political separation of Rome from the Eastern empire, and the Donation of Pepin. During the short republic which followed the former, the nations (as Gibbon has remarked) began once more " to seek, on the banks of the Tiber, the kings, the laws, and the oracles of their fate;" and the solid power conferred by the latter, and confirmed by Charlemagne, did much more than compensate for the loss of a recent and precarious independence. Once more associated as a powerful member of the Western empire, Rome re-occupied the proper field of her ambition and her

---

* It would scarcely appear, for instance, that the Pope had any official communication with the Church of Gaul between the times of Gregory I. and Gregory II., *i. e.* for about a hundred and ten years. Yet the Bishop of Arles presided over that Church in the character, or rather under the name, of his Vicar. See Guizot, Hist. de la Civil. de la France, leçon xix.

triumphs. It is true that the nature of her warfare, and the character of her weapons, were now wholly changed; nevertheless, the temporalities, so profusely conferred upon her, failed not to give great additional efficacy to her spiritual claims—claims which she had already advanced with some boldness, and which she was now qualified to press, if disposed so to press them, to the last extremity of usurpation.

Before we take leave of this period, it is proper to mention, that the first appearance of the Creed, commonly called Athanasian, is ascribed to it with great probability*. There can be no doubt that this exposition of faith was composed in the West, and in Latin; but the exact date of its composition has been the subject of much difference. The very definite terms, in which it expresses the Church doctrine of the Incarnation, are sufficient to prove it posterior to the Councils of Ephesus and Chalcedon, or later than the middle of the fifth century. Again, if we are to consider the doctrine of the *double* procession of the Holy Spirit as being expressly declared in it, since that mystery was scarcely made matter of public controversy until the eighth century, it might seem difficult to refer a creed, positively asserting the more recent doctrine, to an earlier age. But the historical monuments of the Church do not quite support this supposition; the Creed, such probably as it now exists, is mentioned by the Council of Autun† in the year 670, and its faithful repetition by the Clergy enjoined; and we find the same injunction repeated in the beginning of the ninth age.

The Athanasian Creed.

* Bishop Pearson, Archbishop Usher, Hammond, L'Estrange, Dr. Cave, Schelstrate, Pagi, and Du Pin, are all of opinion that this creed was composed, not by Athanasius, but by a later and a Latin writer. Vossius, Quesnel, and others, go so far as to ascribe it to Vigilius Tapsensis, an African Bishop, who lived at the end of the fifth century. This last position, however, is not indisputable; though Vigilius certainly published some writings under the name of Athanasius, with which this creed is frequently joined.

† " Siquis Presbyter, Diaconus, Subdiaconus, vel Clericus, Symbolum, quod inspirante S. Spiritu, Apostoli tradiderant, vel *Fidem S. Athanasii Præsulis* irreprehensibiliter non recensuerit, ab Episcopo condemnetur." Conc. Augustodun. Can. ult., as cited by Bingham. At a Council, held at Toledo in 675, an exposition of the Trinitarian doctrine was published, very nearly resembling that contained in the Athanasian Creed. (Semler, Cent. vii. cap. iii.) In 794 Theodulphus Aurelianensis again mentions the Creed as Athanasius's.

Thus it gradually gained ground; nevertheless, there seems to be great reason for the opinion, that it was not universally received even in the Western Church until nearly two centuries afterwards.

Considered as an exposition of doctrine, the Athanasian creed contains a faithful summary of the high mysteries of Christianity, as interpreted by the Church of Rome. Considered as a rule of necessary faith enforced by the penalty of eternal condemnation, the same creed again expresses one of the most rigid principles of the same Church. The Unity of the Church comprehended unity of belief: there could be no salvation out of it; nor any hope for those who deviated even from the most mysterious among its tenets. And thus, by constant familiarity with the declaration of an exclusive faith, the heart of many a Romish priest may have been closed against the sufferings of the heretic, rescued (as he might think) by the merciful chastisement of the Church from the flames which are never quenched!

It would be irrelevant in this work, and wholly unprofitable, to inquire, how far any temporary circumstances may have justified the introduction of the Athanasian Creed into the Liturgy of our own Church—constructed as that Church is on the very opposite principle of universal charity. But we cannot forbear to offer one remark, naturally suggested by the character and history of this creed, that if, at any future time, it should be judged expedient to expunge it, there is no reason, there is scarcely any prejudice, which could be offended by such erasure*. The sublime truths which it contains are not ex-

---

* The opinions of some of our own Churchmen on this subject are collected by Clarke in his Book on the Trinity. The expressions of Bishop Tomline cannot be too frequently repeated.—" We know (he says) that different persons have deduced different and even opposite doctrines from the words of Scripture, and consequently there must be many errors among Christians; but since the Gospel no where informs us what degree of error will exclude from eternal happiness, I am ready to acknowledge that, in my judgment, notwithstanding the authority of former times, our Church would have acted more wisely and more consistently with its general principles of mildness and toleration, if it had not adopted the damnatory clauses of the Athanasian Creed. Though I firmly believe that the doctrines themselves of this Creed are all founded in Scripture, I cannot but

pressed in the language of Holy Scripture; nor could they possibly have been so expressed, since the inspired writers were not studious minutely to expound inscrutable mysteries. Neither can it plead any sanctity from high antiquity or even traditional authority; since it was composed many centuries after the time of the apostles, in a very corrupt age of a corrupt Church, and composed in so much obscurity, that the very pen from which it proceeded is not certainly known to us. . . . . . . The inventions of men, when they have been associated for ages with the exercise of religion, should indeed be touched with respect and discretion: but it is a dangerous error to treat them as inviolable; and it is something worse than error to confound them in holiness and reverence with the words and things of God.

IV. There are two subjects which we have hitherto refrained from noticing, notwithstanding their great importance—the jurisdiction and judicial immunities of the clergy and the revenues of the Church. We have purposely deferred them until this occasion, because both were deeply influenced by the ecclesiastical policy of Charlemagne; and the former can scarcely be said to have assumed any definite or tangible form before his reign. United, they constituted the temporal power of the clergy; and that object will be so constantly before our eyes in the future pages of this history, that we must no longer delay to examine the materials which formed it.

The arbitrative authority of the primitive bishops was tolerated or overlooked by the Pagan emperors; if it received no direct discouragement from the civil power, it was never aided nor even recognized by it. It reached, of course, only those who voluntarily sought it, and was binding upon none, who chose to appeal from it to the secular courts. The ecclesiastical offences of bishops were subject to the decision of provincial councils; but in respect to all temporal matters, they were on the same footing with the other subjects of the empire.

The arbitration of the bishops was ratified by Constantine;

Jurisdiction and judicial immunities of the clergy.

conceive it to be both unnecessary and presumptuous to say, that 'except every one do keep them whole and undefiled, without doubt he shall perish everlastingly.'" Exposition, part iii., art. viii.

and the magistrates were instructed to execute the episcopal decrees *. At the same time, it seems certain that this power was for some time confined (1.) to spiritual differences and offences; (2.) to such questions of a temporal nature as were brought before the bishop by the joint reference of both parties; (3.) to civil suits, in which both parties were clerks. And it is even probable, that in the second of these, the decision of the bishop was then liable to an appeal to the civil tribunals. The succeeding emperors, for nearly two hundred years, were contented to publish such occasional edicts, as seem rather intended to check any encroachments by which the ecclesiastical privileges may have gained or suffered, than to alter the nature of the laws on that subject. For instance, in the year 398, Honorius proclaimed that it was permitted to those who desired it, to plead before the bishop, but in civil matters only; and in 408, he ordered the arbitrative sentence of the bishop to be executed without appeal to the civil officers. In 456, Marcian ordained that a plaintiff, who should object to bring a clerk before the archbishop, had no resource, except to summon him before the prætorian prefect, which he might do. In 452, Valentinian III. declared that the bishop had no power to judge even clerks, unless by their own consent, and in virtue of a compromise; because ecclesiastics had no tribunal established by law, nor any legal cognizance, except of religious matters. There were constitutions of Arcadius and Honorius and of Theodosius to the same effect. Thus far, then, it seems clear that the episcopal courts (if we are to give them that name) possessed no coercive authority over laymen, nor indeed any which could properly be designated jurisdiction.

Changes introduced by Justinian.
The first change was introduced by Justinian; and it is important to observe exactly to what extent it went. That legislator, willing to enlarge the privileges of the Church, enacted (1.), That in civil actions, monks and clerks should, in the first instance, go before the bishop, who should decide the dif-

---

* Gibbon (who quotes Euseb. Vit. Const. iv. 27; and Sozom. i. 9) has treated this subject in his twentieth chapter; but in the following account, we have chiefly followed Fleury, in his Seventh Discourse; and Giannone, Storia di Napoli, l. ii. c. 8; l. iii. c. 6; l. vi. c. 7.

ference without any publicity or judicial parade; still, if either party, within ten days, declared himself discontented with the decision, that the civil magistrate should take cognizance of the cause, not as a superior, in form of appeal, but as an equal, examining a new question. Their agreement was conclusive; if they differed, an appeal was open to the imperial court. (2.) In criminal causes, a clerk might be sued either before the bishop or in the ordinary court; but if the defendant should be found guilty by a lay judge, still the sentence could not be executed, nor the priest degraded, without the approbation of the bishop. In case that were refused, there was a direct appeal to the Emperor. (3.) The bishops were entirely exempted from lay jurisdiction. It may seem scarcely necessary to add, that all cognizance of spiritual matters—from the crime of heresy down to what were held the more venial offences of simony, clerical insubordination, and even the violation of the ecclesiastical discipline *by laymen*,—was confided, as it had always been, to the unrestricted authority of the Church. Still we should observe, that as temporal power was not yet entrusted to the spiritual judges for the enforcement of their sentence, the only penalties which they could immediately inflict were censure, suspension, deposition, fasting, penance, excommunication—penalties which, in those ages, not only inspired terror, but involved much positive suffering; but to touch the person or property of the culprit, the aid of the secular authority was still necessary.

After the time of Justinian, we are not informed that any material change was introduced into this department of the constitution of the Eastern Church; in fact and practice, it is not probable that the clergy then encroached with any success on the civil, which was so nearly identified with the imperial, power, and which at all times was jealously maintained. In the West, during the period of dark confusion which divided Justinian from Charlemagne, some additions were made to the immunities of the clergy in most of the provinces, and especially in Gaul; but neither were these universally acknowledged, nor securely enjoyed; and it was not till the great restorer of the Western empire had leisure to legislate for the happiness

(as he believed) of his subjects, that the character of ecclesiastical jurisdiction and immunity was wholly and permanently
By Charle- altered. Charlemagne voluntarily conceded to the Church (1.)
magne. that the jurisdiction of the bishop should extend to all causes
which either of the parties, whether clerks or not, might choose
to refer to it; and that there should be no appeal from his decision*; (2.) that the whole body of the clergy should be entirely exempt from secular jurisdiction. The enormous extent
of power † conferred by the first of these capitularies was confirmed by the right of imprisonment (the Jus Carceris), which
was also granted to the episcopal judge; so that the means
which he thus possessed of executing his own decisions rendered him, in a great degree, independent of the civil authorities. The effect of the second was to widen the distinction,
already too broad, which subsisted between clerks and laymen,
and to increase the distrust, with which the sacred orders already
began to be regarded, by entirely withdrawing their offences
from the cognizance of secular justice.

It seems, indeed, to be true that Charlemagne thus granted
to the clergy both greater power and greater immunity than the
existing state of society permitted them to exert or enjoy. Such,
nevertheless, were become their rights; and in as far as the
mere possession of them was the object of the struggles which
they maintained in after ages, we cannot justly censure them.
Neither ought we to forget that a different, and even a more
solid, groundwork of judicial authority began to fall into their
occupation during this period. Many of the sees were already
enriched with large territorial endowments, and consequently
exercised all the rights in those days annexed to them; and
not the least valuable among these was the administration of
justice. By this circumstance, the character of the ecclesiastical jurisdiction became inextricably complicated; and the

---

* The testimony of one bishop was received in every cause as conclusive.

† By the council held at Arles in 813, the edicts of which were confirmed by
Charlemagne, it was ordained, " that if judges and people in power do not pay
deference to the bishop's instructions, he shall give information thereof to the
king. All the people shall obey the bishop, even the counts and judges; and
they shall act in concert for the maintenance of peace and justice." See Fleury,
H. E., l. 46, sect. ii. Concil. tom. vii.

lines by which it was separated from the authority of the civil tribunals were rendered so indistinct, even where they really existed, that incessant and unavoidable occasions were afforded for artful encroachment on the one hand, and violent aggression on the other. But these were the evils of after ages; the design of Charlemagne was probably no more than to vest extensive judicial power in the most enlightened body in his empire; and no doubt he trusted to prevent its abuse by the vigorous exercise of his own supremacy.

In the mean time, while the episcopal order was thus generally strengthened and aggrandized, the particular interests of the bishop of Rome were especially promoted. Adrian I., a man of great talents and much influence with the French king, occupied the papal chair at this crisis; and while he profited, as he was justified in doing, by the voluntary and legitimate donations of that monarch, he also adopted (as some historians think) a less ingenuous method of exalting his own see. So much, at least, is certain, that two instruments, now denominated the " False Decretals," and the " Donation of Constantine," the two most celebrated monuments of human imposture and credulity, were put forth about the conclusion of the eighth century, and immediately and universally received as genuine. Probably they were the composition of some monk or scribe of that age*. Their direct object was the unlimited advancement of the Roman see; and for that purpose, the Decretals furnished the spiritual, the Donation the temporal, authority. The former, professing to be a compilation of the epistles and decrees of primitive popes and early emperors, derived from the first ages the ghostly omnipotence of Rome †. While

The False Decretals and the Donation of Constantine.

---

* See Mosh. Cent. viii. p. ii. chap. ii. The former of these forgeries is frequently called the " Decretals of Isidore." There was a celebrated bishop of Seville of that name in the sixth century, and it was probably thought, that it would add some authority to the *Collection*, if it could be received as his work. But, unfortunately, it contains some mention of the Sixth General Council, which was later than the death of that of Isidore. The clumsiness of the fabrication is acknowledged and exposed by Fleury, liv. xliv. sect. 22.

† The False Decretals advanced to this end, to the great detriment both of Church and State, chiefly by three methods: (1.) They diminished the frequency of provincial councils by asserting for the pope the exclusive right to summon them; and those councils contributed very usefully both to the discipline and in-

the latter proclaimed no less than that Constantine, on removing the seat of government to the East, had consigned the Western empire to the temporal as well as spiritual government of the bishop of Rome—unbounded dominion over Churches, and nations, and kings, was delegated to the successor of St. Peter and the vicar of Christ. It was asserted, that the original deed of the emperor had been recently discovered: the monstrous forgery went forth, and spread itself through the world without confutation, seemingly without suspicion; and it continued for above six hundred years to form the most prominent, and not the least solid, among the bulwarks of papacy.

If, indeed, Charlemagne shared in this matter the credulity of his subjects, we may reasonably infer the very narrow extent of his own learning, and his little familiarity with the annals of preceding ages. That he did so is not impossible; at least it appears certain, that his capitulary respecting episcopal jurisdiction was in part founded on another forgery—a constitution which was for many ages attached, under the name of Constantine, to the Theodosian Code, but which has long been condemned as a production of the eighth or preceding century. The credit of this preliminary fraud may have emboldened its patrons to make a more audacious attempt on his facility. Upon the whole, however, we are very far from attributing so decided a course of policy in so great a Prince to the success of an ecclesiastical imposture. Without any knowledge of the pretensions or existence of those fabrications, there were reasons sufficient, why Charlemagne should be willing to aggrandize a prelate, whose interests were closely connected with his own; and to propitiate an order*, of which the power was very

dependence of the Church. (2.) They gave great encouragement to episcopal license by subjecting the bishops to papal authority only, and thus offering them a fair prospect of impunity. (3.) They disturbed the course, and diverted the efficacy, of justice, by promoting the practice of appeal to the Roman see.

* The increase of papal power was very fairly balanced *within* the Church by the general augmentation of episcopal authority and influence which accompanied it. The entire ecclesiastical body was exceedingly aggrandized, but in such measure that the head did not immediately exceed the proportion of the other principal members. It is true that, by the seeds then sown, the disease of after ages was engendered; but time was required to give them vitality, and during the century which followed Charlemagne, the power of the bishops, or (as they called it) their *independence*, was boldly and commonly asserted.

considerable, and the influence still greater than the power; from which he was receiving and expecting eminent personal as well as political services; which he considered as a counterpoise to the licentiousness of his nobles, and to which he looked for the gradual improvement and civilization of his subjects. It should be remembered, too, that during the whole of his long reign, he maintained the royal authority indisputably paramount to every other, and that if his posterity, some of whom were the feeblest of the human race, had inherited any share of his talent or vigour, the subsequent usurpations of the clergy could not have been accomplished, and might not have been meditated; while the advantages, which Charlemagne reasonably anticipated for the State from their subordinate co-operation with the Prince, would have been certainly and splendidly realized.

V. During the first three centuries the clergy were supported by the voluntary oblations of the faithful; these were, in the first instance, daily or weekly: they were offered on the altar, and for the most part by communicants. This example led at an early period to the payment of monthly offerings, which were placed in the treasury of the Church. " Every one" (says Tertullian*) " brings a moderate contribution once a month, or when he chooses, and only if he chooses and is able; for there is no compulsion, but the gift is spontaneous—being, as it were, the deposit of piety." The sums which were thus presented by the generous devotion of the converts, and which, in the third century at least, were far from inconsiderable, were entrusted to the administration of the Bishop; and employed in the main-

margin notes: Revenues of the Church. Oblations of the early Church.

* Apolog. c. 29. His words are these—" Neque pretio ulla res Dei constat. Etiam siquod Arcæ genus est, non de oneraria summa quasi redemptæ religionis congregatur; modicam unusquisque *stipem* menstrua die, vel cum velit, et si modo velit et si modo possit, apponit. Nam nemo compellitur, sed sponte confert. Hæc quasi deposita pietatis sunt." The term (stipem) is borrowed from the use of the heathen in the collections made by them for religious purposes. Tertullian proceeds to enumerate several charitable objects to which the Christian offerings were applied. " Egenis alendis humandisque, et pueris ac puellis re et parentibus destitutis, ætateque domitis senibus, item naufragis et si qui in metallis et si qui in insulis vel in custodiis duntaxat ex causa Dei sectæ alumni confessionis suæ fiunt."

tenance of the clergy*, in the support of public worship, in the
relief of widows and orphans, and persons suffering persecution.
It also appears, that, before the reign of Diocletian, the Church
had become possessed of some fixed property, which that Emperor confiscated. We do not learn whether it was obtained by
purchase or donation†; in either case it must have borne a
very trifling proportion to the revenues derived from customary
oblation.

Growth of
Ecclesi-
astical
wealth.

Constantine restored and confirmed to the Church such property as it had acquired under the heathen Emperors, and then
enacted laws to permit and encourage its increase. Thus the
sources of ecclesiastical wealth were varied and multiplied, and
the work which was begun by Constantine was somewhat promoted by his immediate successors. Occasional allowances
were advanced from the exchequer; the estates of martyrs and
confessors dying without heirs were settled on the Church;
presently those of all clergymen so dying were similarly disposed of ‡; and while some Princes transferred to the Christian
establishment the temples of the Heathen and their revenues,
there were others who extended the same principle to the
Churches of the heretics. At the same time, the original oblations continued to be abundantly supplied; and a still broader
field was opened by the general and unlimited permission which
was given, to bestow real property upon the Church, both by
donation and legacy. The disposition, not uncommonly existing, to act on that permission was encouraged by the baser portion of the clergy; and their persuasions were sometimes conducted with so little decency, that it became necessary to impose a legal restraint § upon their cupidity. Nevertheless, in

* The monthly salaries given to the Ministers of the Gospel are mentioned by
Cyprian by the name of Mensurnæ Divisiones.

† Padre Paolo (Hist. Eccles. Benefices) ascribes it to donations made during
the confusion which prevailed in the empire after the imprisonment of Valerian,
when the general Roman law, which forbade the bequeathing of real estates to
any college, society, or corporation, without the approbation of the Senate or the
Prince, may have been violated with safety.

‡ The former by a law of Constantine, the latter by one of Theodosius II. and
Valentinian III. See Bingham's Antiq. book v., ch. iv.

§ There is a remarkable law of Valentinian (made in 370, and particularly ad-

spite of occasional interruption, the tide flowed onward; the
partial derelictions of the ecclesiastical body were forgotten in
their general power, their dignity, and their virtues*; and, before the close of the fifth century, the Church had very amply
profited by the pious generosity of the faithful.

The increase of the ecclesiastical revenues was further aided Exemp-
by certain exemptions, granted to the clergy by the first tions.
Christian Emperors. These, though not so general as some
have supposed, were numerous and important. It appears certain that Church lands were liable to the ordinary tax (census
agrorum) or canonical tribute †; and also, that they continued
subject after donation to all burdens which might have been

dressed to Damasus, Bishop of Rome), which forbids Churchmen to frequent
the houses of widows and ophans, or to receive any gifts, directly or indirectly,
by will or donation, from women to whom they might have attached themselves
under pretext of religion.   " Ecclesiastici, aut ex ecclesiasticis, viduarum et
pupillorum domus non adeant, sed publicis exterminentur judiciis, si eos affines
eorum vel propinqui putaverint deferendos. Censemus etiam ut memorati nihil
de ejus mulieris, cui se privatim sub pretextu religionis adjunxerint, liberalitate
quacunque vel extremo judicio possint adipisci, et omne in tantum inefficax sit
quod alicui horum ab his fuerit derelictum, ut nec per subjectam personam va-
leant aliquid vel donatione vel testamento recipere."   (Lege 20. Cod. Theod. de
Episc. et Eccles.)   This was presently (in 390) followed by another to the same
effect, but more generally expressed. The former would not seem to preclude
gifts to the Church, as a body, only to individual ministers; the latter goes so far
as to ordain " nullam Ecclesiam, nullum Clericum, nullum pauperem scribat
hæredes."   We may here also observe, that Charlemagne made a law to prevent
the Church from receiving any gifts which disinherited children and kindred. See
Padre Paolo, ch. vi.

   * The most pious among the Fathers raised their voices very early *against* the
practice of making over fixed property to the Church. St. Chrysostom (Homil. 86
in Matth.) attributes the great corruption of the Bishops and other Churchmen to
the possession of lands and fixed revenues; since they forsook their spiritual oc-
cupations to sell their corn and wine, to increase the value of their property, or to
defend it in courts of law. He looks back with admiration on the Apostolical
purity of the Church, when it was nourished only by oblation and charity. It is
likewise related of St. Augustin, that he would neither purchase land, nor even
accept inheritances which were left to the Church; also maintaining, that the
system of oblation and tithe would be better calculated to preserve the peculiar
character of the clergy. P. Simon observes that the possession of any great
wealth was for a long time confined to the Churches of the principal cities. The
opulence of the Bishop of Rome, as mentioned by Ammianus Marcellinus (lib.
xxvii.), must have been derived almost entirely from oblation; but towards the
end of the sixth century we find that Prelate in enjoyment of ample " Patrimonies,"
not in Italy only, but far beyond its limits. See Fleury, liv. xxxv. sect. 15.

   † See Bingham, book v. ch. iii.

previously charged upon them; but a law of Theodosius II. exempted them from all extraordinary impositions. Moreover, ecclesiastics were not liable, even from the time of Constantine, to the census capitum, or capitation tax; they were also excepted (by Honorius and Theodosius II.) from the payment of a number of occasional imposts, many of which are specified by Bingham; and it was not a trifling privilege, even in a pecuniary view, that they were relieved from the discharge of all the civil offices of whatsoever degree, which were attached to the possession of fixed property. So studious were those early princes to observe the distinction between the spiritual and the temporal character, and, while they prevented the encroachments of the clergy on that which did not belong to them, to give them the full benefit of that which was peculiarly their own.

The ancient manner of dispensing the revenues of the Church was for some time maintained without any remarkable alteration. All alms and incomes arising from real* estates were yet in common, under the immediate care of Deacons and Subdeacons, but under the control and at the discretion of the Bishop, who ordered all the distributions. The whole of the clergy in every Church was maintained from the general funds of that Church; and in many places we find, that great multitudes of poor were nourished by the same resources.

We are not informed that any material change in the application of its revenues at any time took place in the Eastern Church; and we may even be allowed to doubt, whether its property received any very great augmentation after the fifth or sixth century. At least such increase was incessantly watched by a powerful and jealous Sovereign†; and the political revo-

---

* See Padre Paolo, Eccles. Benef., ch. vi.

† At an early period stewards were appointed to superintend the temporalities of the Churches, and were chosen by the Bishop. But as abuses were found to proceed from this arrangement, the Council of Chalcedon decreed, that the stewards should for the future be chosen from among the clergy, and that the administration of the revenues should no longer be left in the power of the Bishop. That office became afterwards so considerable in the Church of Constantinople, that the Emperors took from the clergy the nomination of the stewards into their own hands. This practice lasted till the time of Isaac Comnenus, who remitted that right to the discretion of the Patriarch. See P. Simon's History of Ecclesiastical Revenues.

lutions, which finally raised the hierarchy of the West to such inordinate opulence, extended neither in act nor influence beyond the Adriatic. The prevalence of the monastic spirit did not fail, indeed, to create new establishments, enriched by new endowments; but even that spirit, after two or three centuries from the days of St. Basil, blazed with little comparative ardour in the East, where it was neither renovated by perpetual reformations, nor nourished and diversified by the interested patronage of Papacy.

But in the West, the confusion introduced by the invaders made it necessary, even in the fifth century, to legislate more expressly respecting the revenues of the Church. It was discovered that the confidence placed from the earliest ages in the discretion of the Bishop, was now occasionally abused, and began to require the restraint of some canonical regulations. It was, therefore, ordained, about the year 470*, that the revenue should be divided into four parts; the first for the Bishop, the second for the rest of the Clergy, the third for the fabric of the Church, the fourth for the poor. The duties of hospitality, which included the entertainment of indigent strangers, were annexed to the Episcopal office. This distribution related only to the income of the several Churches: the funds whence they proceeded, whether immoveables, oblations, or alms, continued, as heretofore, the common property of the body. In the mean time, it would be incorrect to suppose that the above division was necessarily made into four equal portions: the great variation in the number of the clergy and of the poor, in the size and splendour of the fabrics, in the extent of the diocese, must have subjected so very broad a rule to very frequent modification.

Quadripartite division of the Church revenue.

During the tumultuous ages which followed, it is asserted, without any improbability, that the bishops and clergy in many places enlarged their own portions to the neglect of the sacred buildings and the destitution of the poor; that the minister

---

* We follow the probable conclusion of Padre Paolo, without being ignorant that this division has been sometimes ascribed to Pope Sylvester (who lived one hundred and fifty years before), on the faith of some writings falsely attributed to him.

frequently converted to his own use the offerings deposited in his own church; and, in some places, that the lands themselves were divided for the usufruct of particular individuals. These innovations may have gained footing insensibly at different times, in different places; and the last was ultimately absorbed in that great change in the nature and distribution of church property, which was introduced by the system of feudalities.

The term Benefice.

Those estates, which the Franks and Lombards called Fiefs, were, by the Latins, designated *Beneficia,* as being held by the bounty of the prince. This term was originally confined to baronial or military tenures, and thence it afterwards passed into the service of the Church. To the endowments of sees or churches, in those times so commonly made by princes, the word "Benefice" was applied, perhaps without impropriety; it was easily extended to such dignities as were conferred by the bishops with the permission of the princes; and thus it became common to all the separate portions of the ecclesiastical estates. These alterations, though not completed till a much later period*, were in gradual process during the seventh and eighth centuries : in the mean time the territorial possessions of the Church were spreading widely; and they had already swelled to a considerable bulk, when Charlemagne ascended the throne of the Western empire.

Means by which the wealth of the Church was acquired.

Some portion of those possessions was unquestionably acquired by methods disgraceful to individual churchmen, or through the corruptions of the Church itself; and this was more especially the case (for reasons which we have already

---

* Some footsteps of the foundations of Benefices and the right of patronage may perhaps be discovered in the 10th Canon of the First Council of Orange, held in 441 :—" But the custom of that time (as P. Simon remarks) was far different from the present practice." Again, about the year 500, under Pope Symmachus, it appears that to some Churchmen portions of land were assigned to be enjoyed by them for life; this appears from an epistle of that pope to Cæsarius, where he prohibits the alienation of Church lands, unless it should be in favour of Clerks meriting such reward—" nisi Clericis honorem meritis, aut Monasteriis, religionis intuitu, aut certe peregrinis necessitas largiri suaserit—sic tamen ut hæc ipsa non perpetuo, sed temporaliter, donec vixerint, perfruantur." But the establishment of the modern system of Benefices is not commonly referred to an earlier period than the end of the tenth, or the beginning of the eleventh century.

given) in the Latin communion. As to the former means—
the gross ignorance of the barbarian conquerors, and their
hereditary reverence for the ministers of religion, offered irresistible temptation to the astute avarice of the French and
Italian clergy: for thus, besides that general abuse of spiritual
influence for the spoliation of weak, or superstitious, or dying persons, which was common to them with their Eastern brethren,
peculiar facilities and invitations to imposture were almost
pressed upon them by the popular credulity. The efficacy of
gifts to expiate offences was a profitable principle, for which
the minds of the converts were already prepared by their previous prejudices: the wild rapacity of the savage is usually
associated with reckless profusion; and we cannot doubt that
many individuals of the sacred order successfully availed themselves of dispositions so favourable to their own temporal interests. Respecting the corruptions of the Church, it would probably be too much to assert, that masses for the release of souls,
and the fruitful fable of purgatory, were actually *invented* for
the purpose of enriching that body; but we need not hesitate
to assign that among the leading causes of the encouragement
which was given to them. The pernicious swarm of superstitious practices, such as the worship of images, the adoration of
saints, and, above all, the demoralizing custom of pilgrimage*,
was nourished and multiplied principally with that object; and
the state of the Church at that period affords just grounds for
the melancholy reflection, that the grossest perversions of religious truth were carefully fostered, if they were not actually
produced, by the most sordid of human motives.

The monastic orders did not lag behind their secular com-

---

* Pilgrimages, chiefly to the shrines of St. Peter at Rome, and St. Martin at
Tours, were, in the eighth age, so common, that it is made a matter almost of
reproach to Charlemagne himself (by his historian Eginhart), that in the course
of his long reign he had undertaken only four. The Council of Chalons (in 813)
acknowledges the *abuses* of pilgrimage. "The clergy pretend thereby to purge
themselves from sin, and to be restored to their functions; the laity to acquire
impunity for sins past or future; the powerful convert them into a pretext of
extortion, the poor of mendicity. Still, we praise the devotion of those, who, to
accomplish the penance which their priest has imposed on them, make such pilgrimages accompanied by prayer, alms, and correction of morals." Fleury, H. E.,
l. xlvi., sect. v.

petitors in the race of avarice : it appears indeed that a great proportion of the rewards, at least during the seventh and eighth centuries, flowed into their establishments; and though their members did not possess the same facilities of private acquisition, the communities have obtained their full share of the profits of ecclesiastical corruption in all ages of the Church.

It would be unjust, however, to suppose that any very material part of the property of the Church was amassed by the shameful methods which we have mentioned. They have contributed, indeed, somewhat to swell its treasures and greatly to soil its reputation; but the most solid, and by far the largest, portion of its riches was derived from sources not only lawful but honourable. The most abundant of these was the pious, or politic, munificence of those princes, who employed the clergy as the means of improving, or of governing, their people. Such were extremely common during the sixth, seventh, and eighth centuries; and the respect and preference, which they thus exhibited for the sacred order, evince its moral as well as intellectual superiority over other classes of their subjects. Again, the voluntary donations of wealthy individuals were not always made from superstitious hope or idle persuasion; but much more frequently, because the Church was the only channel, through which the charity of the rich could effectually relieve the poor. This object was connected with many even of the earliest donations, and is conspicuous in the numerous monuments of the eighth and ninth centuries*; and the large sums which were thus entrusted to religious persons or establishments for that purpose, while they multiplied and maintained the indigent dependents of the Church, became the safest and the noblest ground of its influence and popularity. Again, a great proportion of the territorial endowments of the cathedrals and monasteries consisted of unappropriated and uncultivated lands. These were gradually brought to fertility by the superior skill and industry of their new possessors; and they thus

* See Muratori's Dissert. xxxvii., De Hospitalibus, &c.; and also his lvith, De Religione per Italiam, post ann. 500.

acquired the most substantial right of possession by labours which were beneficial to society. Lastly—the abundance of some establishments and the economy of others frequently enabled the community to amass sums which were expended from time to time in the purchase of additional estates. These were annexed to the original patrimony; and since, in the general insecurity of property prevailing in turbulent ages, there were few individuals who exercised foresight or economy, these virtues, almost peculiar to the ecclesiastical establishments, were a sure and effective instrument of their prosperity.

On the other hand, they were peculiarly exposed to the evils of that turbulence, both by their wealth and their defence-lessness. Amidst the tumults of unsettled governments and uncivilized society, what had been lavished by the bounty of one was frequently torn away by the rapacity of another; and not the nobles only, and other powerful subjects engaged in the work of spoliation, but even princes* would sometimes reward their greedy followers by grants of Church property. By such injustice its increasing dimensions were restrained; and if we have sufficient reason to lament that the means by which it was acquired were not *all* without reproach, there may at least be room for reasonable doubt, whether, upon the whole, the Church did not suffer as much by violence as it gained by fraud, in ages equally favourable to the exercise of both. *Spoliations of the Church.*

There is another source of ecclesiastical wealth which we have not yet mentioned, because it acquired no certain existence before the reign of Charlemagne—the possession of tithes; but it is here proper to employ a few sentences on that subject. It seems quite clear that no sort of tithe was paid to the ante-Nicene Church, nor imposed by any of its councils, nor even directly claimed by its leading ministers. The Levitical insti-tution is indeed mentioned both by Cyprian and Origen; by *On Tithes.* *The ex-pressions of some of the early Fa-thers.*

---

* Charles Martel, for instance, very amply compensated his military followers for their successful defence of Christianity by the monasteries and other ecclesi-astical endowments, which he distributed among them. He thus incurred the indignation of St. Boniface; but as to the celebrated vision of Pulcherius, there seems great reason to doubt whether the bishop did not *precede* the prince in the race of mortality. See Baron. apud Selden, ch. v.

the former* slightly and almost incidentally; by the latter
with rather more fulness†, in a homily respecting the first-fruits
in the law.   But even Origen goes no farther in his conclusion,
than "that the command concerning the *first fruits* of corn
and cattle should still be observed according to the letter;"
and we have no evidence to persuade us that even that limited
position was carried into general practice.

In the records of Constantine's generosity to the new establishment there is no mention made of tithes: nevertheless, the
expressions both of St. Ambrose and St. Augustine on this
subject forbid us to doubt that such payment was voluntarily,
though perhaps very partially, made, at least in the Western
Church, before the end of the fourth century.   St. Ambrose
boldly claims it as due by the law of God—"It is not enough
that we bear the name of Christians, if we do not Christian
works: the Lord exacts of us the annual tithe of all our corn,
cattle," &c. &c.   "Whosoever is conscious that he hath not
faithfully given his tithes, let him supply what is deficient; and
what *is* the faithful payment of tithes, except to offer to God
neither more nor less than that portion, whether of your corn
or your wine, or the fruit of your trees, or your cattle, or of the
produce of your garden, your business, or your hunting?   Of
all substance which God has given to man, he has reserved the
tenth part to himself, and, therefore, man may not retain that
which God has appropriated to his own use."   St. Augustine,
in a homily on that subject, presses the same right to the same
extent‡, in terms not less positive; with this difference, how-

---

* Epist. 66. De Unitat. Eccles. sec. xxiii.   In the former place he is reproach-
ing one Geminius Faustinus, a priest, for having undertaken the discharge of a
secular office—"quæ nunc ratio et forma in Clero tenetur, ut qui in Ecclesia
Domini ad ordinationem Clericalem promoventur, nullo modo ab administratione
divini avocentur, sed, in honore sportulantium fratrum, tanquam Decimas ex
fructibus accipientes ab altari et sacrificiis non recedant. . . ."   In the latter,
while deploring the lukewarm devotion of the faithful, he complains, "at nunc de
patrimonio nec decimas damus."   See Selden, chap. iv.

† This may surprise those historians who distinguish Origen from the *Church*
writers, and exalt him accordingly.   Had Cyprian published a homily to inculcate the divine obligation of paying first-fruits to the priest, he would have been
stigmatized as the most avaricious (he is already denounced as the most ambitious) among those early churchmen.

‡ "Quodcunque te pascit ingenium Dei est; et inde decimas expetit unde

ever, that he puts forward more zealously the charitable purpose of the institution. About the same time St. Chrysostom
and St. Jerome added their exhortations to the same effect,
though they did not specify so exactly the nature of the contribution, nor insist so strongly on the divine obligation. There
can be no question, that the exertions of individual ministers
effectually influenced the more devout amongst their listeners,
especially in the Western nations, and in somewhat later ages:
accordingly we find that in sundry places tithes* were paid
both to monasteries, to the poor, and to the clergy, by many
pious individuals during the four centuries which followed.
It has also been asserted (though the evidence is not sufficiently
clear) that they already engaged the attention, and even
claimed the authority, of one or two provincial† councils.
Moreover, it seems probable, that some special endowments of
them were made on particular Churches before the time of
Charlemagne, though these were few in number, and scarcely
earlier than the end of the seventh age. But, on the other
hand, it is unquestionably certain, that no canon or other law
for the purpose of compelling the payment of tithes was generally received, before the concluding part of the eighth century.
The offerings, hitherto contributed under that name, were made
in compliance with the doctrine which pleaded the divine right,
or with the precepts, or perhaps even with the practice of particular Churches, but they were not yet exacted either by civil
or ecclesiastical legislation—not even in the West; and in the
Eastern Church we have not observed that any law has at any
time been promulgated on this subject.

---

vivis; de militia, de negotio, de artificio redde decimas: aliud enim pro terra de-
pendimus, aliud pro usura vitæ pensamus." Selden appears to share in a doubt
that has been raised, whether the homily in question be really the production of
Augustine.

 * These may not have been in fact exactly tenths, but some indefinite proportion of things titheable, varying according to the abundance or devotion of
the contributor.

 † We refer particularly to Selden's 5th chap., and his remarks on the Council
of Maçon (in 586). Thomassin (Vetus et Nova Ecclesiæ Disciplina, P. III. l. i.
c. vi.) presses the authority of the Second Council of Tours. At any rate the
prelates on that occasion proceeded no farther than exhortation—" commonemus,"
—those of Maçon *decree*—" statuimus et decernimus."

Charle-
magne es-
tablished
the right to
tithe,

The first strictly legislative act, which conferred on the clergy the right to tithe, was passed by Charlemagne. In the year 778, the eleventh of his reign over France and Germany, in a general assembly of estates, both spiritual and temporal, held under him, it was ordained, " That every one should give his tenth, and that it should be disposed of according to the orders of his bishop *." Other constitutions to the same effect were afterwards published by the same prince, and repeated and confirmed by some of his descendants; they were reiterated by the canons of numerous provincial councils†, and re-echoed from the pulpits of France and Italy. Nevertheless, it was found exceedingly difficult to enforce them‡. The laity were strongly disposed to disobey such commands as went to diminish their revenues, and the violation of any law was easy in those disordered times. But the long and lawful perseverance of the clergy at length prevailed; and, during a contest of nearly four cen-

---

* " Ut unusquisque suam decimam donet; atque per jussionem Episcopi sui (or Pontificis, as some copies read) dispensetur." This must be understood with some limitation, since the triparite division of tithes seem to be properly ascribed to Charlemagne; that of one share for the bishop and clergy, a second for the poor, a third for the fabric of the Church. It seems uncertain what part of these was at first intended for the maintenance of a *resident* clergy. Parochial divisions, such as they now exist, were still not very common, though they may be traced to the endowment of churches by individuals as early as the time of Justinian. The rural churches were, in the first instance, chapels dependent on the neighbouring cathedral, and were served by itinerant ministers of the bishop's appointment. It was some time before any of them obtained the privileges of baptism and burial; but these were indeed accompanied by a fixed share of the tithes, and appear to have implied in each case the independence of the Church and the residence of a minister.

† The celebrated Council of Francfort (in 794) published a canon for the universal payment of tithes, besides the rents due to the Church for benefices. See Fleury, l. xliv., s. lx. and Thomassin, P. III. l. i., cap. vii.

‡ There is an epistle of Alcuin, in which he exhorts his master not yet to impose upon the tender faith of his new converts, the Saxons and Huns, what he calls the "yoke of tithes." The passage deserves citation—" Vestra sanctissima pietas sapienti consilio prævideat, si melius sit rudibus populis in principio fidei jugum imponere Decimarum, ut plena fiat per singulas domus exactio illarum; an apostoli quoque ab ipso Deo Christo edocti et ad prædicandum, mundo missi exactiones Decimarum exegissent, vel alicui demandassent dari, considerandum est. Scimus quia Decimatio substantiæ nostræ valdè bona est. Sed melius est illam amittere quam fidem perdere. Nos vero in fide Catholica nati, nutriti et edocti vix consentimus substantiam nostram pleniter decimari; quanto magis tenera fides et infantilis animus et avara mens illorum largitati non consentit?" The passage is quoted by Selden in ch. v.

turies, they gradually entered into the possesion of an unpopular, but unquestioned right.

We can scarcely consider the payment of tithes to have been universally enforced until the end of the twelfth century, when ecclesiastical authority had risen to a great height, through the exaltation of the See of Rome. The first of the *General* Councils which mentions them is the Ninth, that of Lateran, held under Calixtus II., in the year 1123; but even there they are spoken of only as they were received by special consecrations. Nor does it appear that the payment was expressly commanded as " a duty of common* right" before the Pontifical Council held in the year 1215. It was held under Innocent III.; and in that age, and especially during that pontificate, the canons of the Church were not lightly received, nor contemned with security.

which was made universal by Innocent III.

Such are the principal quarters from which the revenues of the Western Church were derived. They varied in fruitfulness in different times and provinces, according to the extent of ecclesiastical influence, or the degree of civil anarchy which prevailed. In the ages *immediately* following the barbarian conquests, they may have lost by the violence of the invaders more than they gained by their piety or superstition; but those losses were afterwards compensated by a liberality which was sometimes heedless, sometimes political; and, upon the whole, in spite of occasional spoliations, the funds of the Church continued to extend themselves. They did not, however, reach any unreasonable extent until the reign of Charlemagne and those of his successors; but thenceforward, as their security increased with their magnitude, they swelled to such inordinate dimensions,

---

* See Selden, chap. vi. There were various pontifical decrees respecting Tithes by Nicholas II., Alexander II., and Gregory VII. in the eleventh century. Selden mentions the direct command of Nicholas in 1059. " Præcipimus ut Decimæ et Primitiæ seu oblationes vivorum et mortuorum Ecclesiis Dei fideliter reddantur a Laicis, et ut in dispositione Episcoporum sint, quas qui retinuerint a S. Ecclesiæ Communione separentur." Ten years earlier we observe that Leo IX., in his council against Simony, *restored* Tithes to all the Churches, with the admission, " that no mention was at that time made of them in Apulia, and some other parts of the world." A double division of them is on that occasion mentioned—between the Bishop, and the Altar, or Minister of the Church. See Wibertus, ap. Pagi, Vit. Leo IX.

and assumed so substantial a shape, that they are not incredibly asserted to have comprehended, in the twelfth century, one-half of the cultivated soil of Europe. Nevertheless, it is impossible to dispute, that by far the greater proportion of that property was acquired by just and lawful means; and that we may not depart from this inquiry with the impression, that the prosperity of the Church was either universally abused, or wholly unmerited, it is proper to mention some of the blessings which it conferred upon society, during a period when the condition of man stood most in need of aid and consolation.

General benefits conferred by the Church.

We do not here propose to enumerate the beneficial effects of the religion itself, which are scarcely contested by any one; but only to mention some of the good fruits of the *Institution* called the Church—benefits produced in subservience to *Christianity,* in as far as its principles and motives were derived from that source, but in contradistinction to it, in as far as its outward form, government and discipline were of human creation. With all its earthly imperfections and impurities, the Church was still a powerful, if not necessary, instrument for the support of the religion and the diffusion of its principles; and even among those very imperfections there were some which it pleased Providence to turn to its own honour, by converting them to the service of man.

Power and dignity of the Church.

Before the end of the fifth century, the ecclesiastical body was in possession of very considerable dignity and power throughout the whole of Christendom; and in that body the episcopal order had risen into a pre-eminence, not indeed in unison with its ancient humility, but attributable to its activity and its virtues more than to its ambition, and perhaps to the circumstances of the empire even more than to either. In the enjoyment of extensive revenues, of some* municipal authority, of certain judicial privileges and immunities, of high rank and reputation, and of very powerful influence over the people, and united for all grand purposes by common principles and common interests, the hierarchy occupied the first station among

---

* See Cod. Justin. l. i., tit. iv. De Episcopali Audientia, s. 26—30. The superintendence of public works, and of the funds for defraying their expenses, was intrusted to the bishop, together with some of the leading men in the city.

the subjects of the empire. Its weight was felt and acknow-ledged by all ranks of society, from the court downwards: the more so, as it formed the only moral tie which bound them together. The Unity of the Church was not *merely* the watch-word of bigotry, the signal for injustice and oppression, but also a principle of some effect in maintaining the unity of Christen-dom. Such was the position of the Church, and such the means at its disposal, when the Western Empire was overthrown and occupied by unbelieving barbarians.

At this crisis it is not too much to assert, that the Church was the instrument of Heaven for the preservation of the Reli-gion. Christianity itself (unless miraculously sustained) would have been swept away from the surface of the West*, had it not been rescued by an established body of ministers, or had that body been less zealous or less influential. Among the con-quered, the common people were, for the most part, recent and not always very serious converts from polytheism; the higher classes were neither numerous nor powerful, nor had any inter-est in the support of Christianity. The clergy alone composed the vital and efficient portion of the aristocracy. Among the con-querors, the rudest soldier brought with him a superstitious re-verence for the office and person of a religious minister, which prepared him for adhesion to the religion itself, especially where the ministers were honoured and the ceremonies splendid; and the illiterate prince readily gave attention to the counsels of the bishops, who were the most learned and the most respected among his new subjects. Thence resulted the gradual con-version† of the invaders, by the agency of the visible Church.

* Guizot—who treats ecclesiastical matters with profoundness, ingenuity, and judgment, and has brought to that subject (a rarer merit) a mind unbiassed by the prejudices of a churchman, or the antipathies of a sectarian or an infidel, and that fearless, uncompromising candour which becomes a philosopher and a histo-rian—Guizot (Histoire Générale, &c. Leçon II.) has expressed the same opinion with the same confidence. " Je ne crois pas trop dire en affirmant qu'à la fin du quatrième et commencement du cinquième siècle, c'est l'Eglise Chrétienne qui a sauvé le Christianisme. C'est l'Eglise, avec ses institutions, ses magistrats, son pouvoir qui s'est défendue vigoureusement contre la dissolution intérieure de l'empire, contre la Barbarie; qui a conquis les barbares, qui est devenue le lien, le moyen, le principe de civilisation entre le monde Romain et le monde bar-bare," &c. &c.

† That their conversion was, in the first instance, imperfect, perhaps in many

Without those means—had Christianity then existed as a mere individual belief, or even under a less vigorous form of human government—the religious society would have possessed neither the energy nor discipline necessary for resistance to the deluge which endangered it.

Beneficial influence of the Church. Let us next inquire what influence did the Church afterwards exert on the society which it had assembled in the name of Christ? by what exertions, by what habits, did it enforce the principles of the religion which it had preserved? *First*—by the general exercise of Charity. The generosity of its benefactors had often been directed, in part at least, to that purpose. That excellent rule which had been received from the earliest ages was not discontinued ; the relief of the poor was associated with the ministry of religion ; the worldly necessities of the wretched were alleviated by their spiritual pastors, and the most excellent virtue of Christianity was inculcated by the practice of its Ministers. We intend not to exalt the merit of that body in dispensing among the indigent the funds intrusted to them for that purpose ; we only assert its great utility as a channel for the transmission of blessings, which in those ages could not otherwise have reached their object—as a sacred repository, where the treasures of the devout were stored up for the mitigation of misery which had no other resource or hope. *Secondly*—the penitential discipline of the Church was extremely efficacious in enforcing the moral precepts of the religion ; and whatsoever advantage may have been conferred on ancient Rome by the venerable office of the Censor, whatsoever restraints may have been imposed on the habits of a high-minded people by the fear of ignominious reproach ; awe more deep and lasting must have been impressed upon the superstitious crowd by the terrible denunciations of the Church, by the deep humiliation of the penitent, by his prolonged exposure to public shame, by the bitterness and intensity of his remorse. Without affecting to regret, as some have done, the present disuse of the penitential system in the present enlightened state both of

---

cases merely nominal, has been already admitted. Still, where the affair was with a *nation*, and that too a very barbarous nation, it was impossible, humanly speaking, that it could have been otherwise than imperfect.

society and religion, we cannot close our eyes against its extraordinary power, as an instrument of moral improvement, in
ages when the true spirit of religion was less felt and comprehended; when education furnished very slender means for self-
correction; and when even the secular laws were feebly or partially executed.   *Thirdly*—After the fifth century the office of
Legislation throughout the Western provinces devolved in a
great measure on the ecclesiastical body—directly, in so far as
they composed, or assisted in, public assemblies; indirectly, as
they influenced the councils of princes and their nobility. Their
power was effectually exerted for the improvement of the barbarous system of the invaders, the suppression of absurd practices, and the substitution of reasonable principles.   " I have
already spoken," says Guizot, " of the difference which may be
observed between the laws of the Visigoths, proceeding in a
great measure from the Councils of Toledo, and those of the
other barbarians. It is impossible to compare them without
being struck by the immense superiority in the ideas of the
Church in matters of legislation and justice, in all that affects
the pursuit of truth and the destiny of man. It is true that the
greater part of these ideas were borrowed from the Roman
legislation; but if the Church had not preserved and defended
them, if it had not laboured to propagate them, they would
have perished."   *Fourthly*—In furtherance of this faithful discharge of its duties to the human race, the Church unceasingly
strove to correct the vices of the social system. The worst of
these, and the principal object of her hostility, was the abomination of slavery; and if it be too much entirely to attribute its
final extirpation to the perseverance of the Church in pressing
the principles of the Faith; and if it has been speciously insinuated that her motives in the contest were not *always* disinterested, at least it is impossible to dispute either her zeal in the
righteous cause, or the power and success with which she
pleaded it*, or the great probability that, without such advo-

---

* " Il y en a une preuve irrécusable: la plupart des formules d'affranchisse-
ment, à diverses époques, se fondent sur un motif religieux ; c'est au nom des idées
religieuses, des espérances de l'avenir, de l'égalité religieuse des hommes, que l'af-
franchissement est presque toujours prononcé."—Guizot, Hist. Générale, Leçon vi.

cacy, so steadily pursued through so long and hopeless a period, the complete emancipation of the lowest classes would have been accomplished much later, perhaps not wholly accomplished even at this moment. *Fifthly*—The same spirit which was so well directed to improve the internal fabric of society turned itself also to the prevention of civil outrage and even of international warfare. In this attempt, indeed, it had not equal success, since it had to contend with the most intractable of human passions; but the pages even of profane history abound with proofs of the pacific policy and interpositions of the Church: nor were they entirely suspended even after the fatal moment, when it engaged as a party in the temporal affairs of Europe, and so frequently found its own policy and strength and triumph in the discord, devastation, and misery of its neighbours. *Lastly*—From considerations which are more immediately connected with the happiness of mankind, we may descend to mention a theme of praise which is seldom withheld from the Church by any description of historians—that of having preserved many valuable monuments of ancient genius; and also of having nourished, even in the worst times, such sort of literary instruction and acquirement as was then perhaps attainable. It is true that these advantages were not generally diffused among the people; that little desire was evinced by the Clergy to communicate such knowledge, or by the laity to share in it: still was it a possession useful, as well as honourable, to those who cherished and maintained it, and through them, in some degree, to their fellow-subjects. Some languid rays it must have reflected even at the moment upon the surface of society; at least it was preserved as a certain pledge of future improvement, as an inviolable and everlasting treasure, consecrated to the brighter destinies of ages to come.

END OF PART II.

ANALYTICAL TABLE OF CONTENTS.

VOLUME I.

INTRODUCTION.

THE Author's reasons for abandoning in this work the usual method of division by centuries.

This history is divided into five parts or periods, ending respectively at the establishment of the Church by Constantine; at the death of Charlemagne; at the death of Gregory VII.; at the secession of the Popes to Avignon; at the beginning of the Reformation

The study of ecclesiastical history teaches religious moderation

PART I.

CHAPTER I.—*The Propagation of Christianity.*

2 G 2

CHAPTER II.—*On the Numbers, Discipline, Doctrine, and Morality of
the Primitive Church.*

PART II.

CHAPTER VI.—*Constantine the Great.*

CHAPTER VII.—*On the Arian Controversy.*

Chapter VIII.—*The Decline and Fall of Paganism.*

CHAPTER IX.—*From the Fall of Paganism to the Death of Justinian.*

CHAPTER X.—*From the Death of Justinian to that of Charlemagne,*
567—814.

CHAPTER XI.—*On the Dissensions of the Church from Constantine to Charlemagne.*

* ' Quod Decimæ ante Tributa solvantur.'

A CHRONOLOGICAL TABLE OF THE PRINCIPAL EVENTS IN THE HISTORY OF THE ANTENICENE CHURCH.

It is proper to premise that several of the dates are disputed.

A.D.

32 James the Just is made Bishop of Jerusalem. Elders appointed.

37 Tiberius is succeeded by Caligula. The year of the birth of Josephus, the historian.

39 The Church of Antioch is founded by Paul and Barnabas: and the faithful first assume the name of Christian. Simon Magus is supposed to have passed from Antioch to Rome about this time.

50 Paul visits Athens and Corinth.

54 Luke writes his Gospel.

58 Peter's probable visit to Rome. Mark writes his Gospel.

60 James, Bishop of Jerusalem, is killed, and Symeon succeeds.

64 Persecution of the Christians by Nero at the burning of Rome.

65 Secession of the Christian Church to Pella.

66 Matthew writes his Gospel.

70 Ignatius succeeds Evodius as Bishop of Antioch.

72 Jerusalem destroyed by Titus.
Rise of the Ebionites.

82 Origin of the Cerinthians and Nicolaitans, heretics.

89 The trial of Apollonius Tyanæus, before Domitian, and his fabled preternatural disappearance. (Philostratus, lib. vii., and viii.)

93 Clement succeeds Anancletus as Bishop of Rome.

95 Probable date of his Letter to the Corinthians.
The grandsons of St. Jude are brought before Domitian.

96 John writes his Gospel and Epistles.

100 Evarestus succeeds Clement as Bishop of Rome.

107 Ignatius suffers martyrdom. Heros succeeds as Bishop of Antioch.
Letter addressed to Trajan by Pliny the Younger.

114 Insurrection of the Jews in Ægypt and Cyrene.
Basilides the head of the Gnostics at Alexandria, and Saturninus at Antioch.

125 Apologies presented to Hadrian by Quadratus and Aristides.

126 Hadrian writes to M. Fundanus, Proconsul of Asia, concerning the Christians, to protect them from popular fury.

129 Hadrian writes to Servianus the Consul, mentioning the Christians.

134 Foundation of Ælia Capitolina by Hadrian, after the revolt of the Jews under Barcochebas. (Semler places this event at 119.)
Testimony of Hadrian respecting the religious character of the Alexandrians. (Some place this too some years earlier.)

A.D.

135   Marcus, the first Gentile Bishop of Jerusalem.

138   Hadrian dies, and Antoninus Pius succeeds.

142   Marcion, the Gnostic, comes to Rome. Valentinus and Cerdo somewhat earlier.

     The first Apology of Justin Martyr published about this time.

151   Anicetus, Bishop of Rome.

158   Polycarp's visit to Rome.

     Hegesippus flourishes.

165   Death of Justin Martyr.

     The seven Catholic Epistles of the Bishop Dionysius.

166   Martyrdom of Polycarp under Marcus Antoninus.

166   Montanus begins his heresy,

169   The Apology of Melito.

172   Tatian, the disciple of Justin Martyr, founds the sect of Encratites.

174   Legend of the Thundering Legion.

178   On the martyrdom of Pothinus, Irenæus is made Bishop of Lyons.

180   Apology of Miltiades.

185   Pantænus enters on a mission to India, and is succeeded in the Catechetical School at Alexandria by Clemens.

189   Victor succeeds Eleutherus as Bishop of Rome.

192   Tertullian made Presbyter of the Church of Carthage.

193—6 Victor excommunicates Theodotus for denying Christ to be God; and addresses an order to the Asiatic Churches respecting the celebration of Easter, which they refuse to obey.

198   The Heresy of Praxeas.

199   Tertullian lapses into Montanism.

202   Persecution of Severus. Leonides, the father of Origen, suffers death. Origen then 17 years old.

     The Greek translation of the Old Testament, by Symmachus, is assigned to this year.

203   Origen made president of the Catechetical School.

215   A council at Carthage, concerning the Baptism administered by heretics.

228   The beginning of the war between the Romans and Persians

229   Origen is ordained at Cæsarea—visits Greece.

231   He finally leaves Alexandria and settles at Cæsarea.

     The death of Ammonius Saccas takes place about this time.

     A Council held at Iconium on the Baptism administered by Heretics.

240   Gregory Thaumaturgus, Bishop of Neocæsarea in Pontus, flourishes.

     A council of 90 Bishops at Carthage.

244   Philip, of whom it is recorded by Eusebius that he was in earlier life a Christian, succeeds Gordian in the Empire. He does not persecute.

245   Plotinus, the Platonic philosopher, settles at Rome.

246   Origen writes against Celsus.

250 (or 248) Cyprian is raised to the See of Carthage.

     Persecution of Decius.

     Origin of the Heresy of Sabellius.

A.D.

251   Cyprian holds a council at Carthage, on the subject of the lapsed.
Cornelius elected Bishop of Rome.
     Origin of the Schism of Novatian.   He is condemned by a council held at Rome.

252   Two councils held at Carthage.
A council at Antioch.
Cornelius, Bishop of Rome, is driven into exile.

253   Lucius, his successor, suffers the same fate.

253   Another council at Iconium, on the validity of the Baptism administered by Heretics.
Some place the death of Origen in this year.

255-6   Controversy between Cyprian and Stephen, Bishop of Rome, concerning the Baptism administered by Heretics.   A council of Carthage decides against its validity.
Stephen threatens the Orientals with excommunication.

257   Stephen suffers in the persecution of Valerian.

258   Cyprian suffers martyrdom.

262   Question as to the orthodoxy of Dionysius, Bishop of Alexandria.
Porphyry comes to Rome.

265   First council of Antioch against Paul of Samosata.

269   Second council deposes Paul from the See.

270   Death of Plotinus.

272   Aurelian, having defeated Zenobia, enforces the sentence of the council against Paul of Samosata.

277   Probable date of the death of Manes, or Manichæus; and of the first appearance of his sect in the West.

286   Legend of the Theban Legion.

303   Beginning of the persecution of Diocletian.
Lactantius writes in favour of Christianity.

305   Council of Cirta in Africa.
Council of Eliberis in Spain, at which Hosias was present.

306   Constantius dies at York, and Constantine assumes the title of Cæsar.

310   Arnobius writes in favour of the Christians.
Antony originates the eremitical life in Egypt.

312   Origin of the schism of the Donatists.
Constantine marches against Maxentius.   Supposed vision of the Cross. Defeat and Death of Maxentius.

313   Edict of Milan, authorizing the profession of Christianity.

END OF THE FIRST VOLUME.

LONDON: Printed by WILLIAM CLOWES and SONS, Stamford-Street.